P. 730

Literature in Canada

Volume 2

Literature in Canada

Volume 2

Edited by
DOUGLAS DAYMOND   **LESLIE MONKMAN**
Department of English   *Department of English*
University of Guelph   *University of Guelph*

Gage Educational Publishing Limited
TORONTO VANCOUVER CALGARY MONTREAL

ISBN 0-7715-1157-4

Acknowledgments for the use of copyrighted
materials appear in the Acknowledgment
pages at the end of the volume.

Design by Robert Burgess Garbutt

Printed and bound in Canada
by John Deyell Company

1 2 3 4 5 6 7 8 9 0   JD   86 85 84 83 82 81 80 79 78

Contents

Preface

The predilection of Canadians for what Northrop Frye has called "relentless cultural stock-takings and self-inventories" is nowhere more evident than in the many anthologies that serve as points of reference throughout the literary history of Canada. In the latter half of the nineteenth century, William Hartley Dewart's *Selections from Canadian Poets* (1864) and William Douw Lighthall's *Songs of the Great Dominion* (1889) reveal a concern with establishing the existence of a national literature. In the early decades of the twentieth century, *Canadian Poetry in English* (1922), edited by Bliss Carman and Lorne Pierce, and *A Book of Canadian Prose and Verse* (1923), selected by E.K. and E.H. Broadus, illustrate a developing literary tradition extending over more than one hundred years. At mid-century, the anthologies of Ralph Gustafson, A.J.M. Smith, C.F. Klinck and R.E. Watters combine modern critical standards with an enlarged historical perspective. Just as each of these anthologies illustrates a review of Canadian literature in the light of the ideas and concerns of a particular era, *Literature In Canada* reflects an examination of our literature in terms of contemporary attitudes, interests and evaluations.

Literature in Canada traces the evolution of Canadian literature from the narratives of exploration of the sixteenth century to the poetry, fiction and drama of the nineteen-seventies. It is intended for the English-speaking reader and emphasizes the development of Canadian literature in English. However, translated texts from more than two dozen authors writing in French have been included and, within the limits of translation, these selections introduce some of the major writers of French Canada. Authors whose creative imaginations have been predominant forces in shaping a Canadian literary tradition are extensively represented, but we have also included secondary figures of importance to a more complete understanding of the evolution of our literature. In addition to poetry, fiction and drama, *Literature in Canada* represents such genres as the travel book, the captivity narrative, the newspaper sketch, the missionary report and personal journal. Works originating in oral traditions have not been included since their special qualities and significance can be better examined within the larger context of folklore, a context provided by Edith Fowke's *Folklore of Canada* (1976). Critical essays have also been excluded on the grounds that the reader now has a wide choice of accessible material as indicated in the bibliography of secondary sources appended to each volume.

As very often happens with works of this kind, some readers will, no doubt, note the absence of particular works or writers who, they feel, should be included in an anthology of this scope. For the most part, these absences are the result of our own considered criteria for selection; in a very few unusual and regrettable instances it simply proved impossible to secure the rights necessary to reprint.

The two volumes are arranged in chronological order according to the birth date of each author. Volume 1 extends from Jacques Cartier in the sixteenth century to Stephen Leacock and his contemporaries in the early decades of the twentieth century. Volume 2 begins with Frederick Philip Grove, E.J. Pratt and other writers involved in the rise of modernism following World War I; it concludes with writers such as Tom Wayman and Susan Musgrave who have come into prominence in the nineteen-seventies.

The date appearing at the left margin after a selection indicates the time of first publication of that work in a volume by the author. The date at the right margin identifies the publication date of the text used by the editors. Where more than one selection by an author appears, the texts have been arranged in chronological order according to the date of first publication in a volume by the author. Archaic spelling, punctuation and abbreviations have been normalized in several cases but the language of each selection has not been altered except for the correction of obvious errors in the original text. Titles are those of the original except where printed within square brackets.

We wish to thank Conrad Wieczorek, our editor, and Laura Damania, our copy editor. We are also grateful to Grace Martin for her assistance in the compilation of the bibliography and to the secretaries of the Department of English and the library staff at the University of Guelph. Finally, we are indebted to Elizabeth Waterston for her encouragement and to our wives for their assistance and support.

DOUGLAS DAYMOND
LESLIE MONKMAN

Literature
in
Canada
Volume 2

Frederick Philip Grove
1879-1948

———◆———

FREDERICK PHILIP GROVE (Felix Paul Greve) was born in Radomno on the Polish-Prussian border in 1879 and grew up in the city of Hamburg. He attended university in Bonn and Munich and in 1902 he moved to Berlin where he published poems and novels and worked as an editor and professional translator. In 1909 he emigrated to Canada and four years later became a teacher in Manitoba. After moving to Ontario in 1929, Grove worked for the Graphic Press in Ottawa for a time and eventually settled on a farm near Simcoe, Ontario. Grove's first Canadian book, *Over Prairie Trails* (1922), was a collection of autobiographical sketches. In subsequent years he published essays, autobiographical accounts and several novels including *Settlers of the Marsh* (1925), *Fruits of the Earth* (1933) and *The Master of the Mill* (1944). Collections of his short stories and sketches include *The Turn of the Year* (1929) and *Tales from the Margin* (1971). "Snow" first appeared in *Queen's Quarterly* in 1932.

Snow

TOWARDS MORNING THE blizzard had died down, though it was still far from daylight. Stars without number blazed in the dark-blue sky which presented that brilliant and uncompromising appearance always characterizing, on the northern plains of America, those nights in the dead of winter when the thermometer dips to its lowest levels.

In the west, Orion was sinking to the horizon. It was between five and six o'clock.

In the bush-fringe of the Big Marsh, sheltered by thick but bare bluffs of aspens, stood a large house, built of logs, white-washed, solid – such as a settler who is still single would put up only when he thinks of getting married. It, too, looked ice-cold, frozen in the night. Not a breath stirred where it stood; a thin thread of whitish smoke, reaching up to the level of the tree-tops, seemed to be suspended into the chimney rather than to issue from it.

Through the deep snow of the yard, newly packed, a man was fighting his way to the door. Arrived there, he knocked and knocked, first tapping with his knuckles, then hammering with his fists.

1

Two, three minutes passed. Then a sound awoke in the house, as of somebody stirring, getting out of bed.

The figure on the door-slab — a medium-sized, slim man in sheepskin and high rubber boots into which his trousers were tucked, with the ear-flaps of his cap pulled down — stood and waited, bent over, hands thrust into the pockets of the short coat, as if he wished to shrink into the smallest possible space so as to offer the smallest possible surface to the attack of the cold. In order to get rid of the dry, powdery snow which filled every crease in his foot-gear and trousers, he stamped his feet. His chin was drawn deep into the turned-up collar on whose points his breath had settled in the form of a thick layer of hoar frost.

At last a bolt was withdrawn inside.

The face of a man peered out, just discernible in the starlight.

Then the door was opened; in ominous silence the figure from the outside entered, still stamping its feet.

Not a word was spoken till the door had been closed. Then a voice sounded through the cold and dreary darkness of the room.

"Redcliff hasn't come home. He went to town about noon and expected to get back by midnight. We're afraid he's lost."

The other man, quite invisible in the dark, had listened, his teeth chattering with the cold. "Are you sure he started out from town?"

"Well," the new-comer answered hesitatingly, "one of the horses came to the yard."

"One of his horses?"

"Yes. One of those he drove. The woman worked her way to my place to get help."

The owner of the house did not speak again. He went, in the dark, to the door in the rear and opened it. There, he groped about for matches, and, finding them, lighted a lamp. In the room stood a big stove, a coal-stove of the self-feeder type; but the fuel used was wood. He opened the drafts and shook the grate clear of ashes; there were two big blocks of spruce in the fire-box, smouldering away for the night. In less than a minute they blazed up.

The new-comer entered, blinking in the light of the lamp, and looked on. Before many minutes the heat from the stove began to tell.

"I'll call Bill," the owner of the house said. He was himself of medium height or only slightly above it, but of enormous breadth of shoulder: a figure built for lifting loads. By his side the other man looked small, weakly, dwarfed.

He left the room and, returning through the cold bare hall in front, went upstairs.

A few minutes later a tall, slender, well-built youth bolted into the room where the new-comer was waiting. Bill, Carroll's hired man, was in his underwear and carried his clothes, thrown in a heap over his arm. Without loss of time, but jumping, stamping, swinging his arms, he began at once to dress.

He greeted the visitor. "Hello, Mike! What's that Abe tells me? Redcliff got lost?"

"Seems that way," Mike said listlessly.

"By gringo," Bill went on. "I shouldn't wonder. In that storm! I'd have waited in town. Wouldn't catch me going out over the marsh in that kind of weather!"

"Didn't start till late in the afternoon," Mike Sobotski said in his shivering way.

"No. And didn't last long, either," Bill agreed while he shouldered into his overalls. "But while she lasted..."

At this moment Abe Carroll, the owner of the farm, re-entered, with sheep-skin, fur cap, and long, woollen scarf on his arm. His deeply lined, striking, square face bore a settled frown while he held the inside of his sheep-skin to the stove to warm it up. Then, without saying a word, he got deliberately into it.

Mike Sobotski still stood bent over, shivering, though he had opened his coat and, on his side of the stove, was catching all the heat it afforded.

Abe, with the least motion needed to complete dressing, made for the door. In passing Bill, he flung out an elbow which touched the young man's arm. "Come on," he said; and to the other, pointing to the stove, "Close the drafts."

A few minutes later a noise as of rearing and snorting horses in front of the house...

Mike, buttoning up his coat and pulling his mitts over his hands, went out.

They mounted three unsaddled horses. Abe leading, they dashed through the new drifts in the yard and out through the gate to the road. Here, where the shelter of the bluffs screening the house was no longer effective, a light but freshening breeze from the north-west made itself felt as if fine little knives were cutting into the flesh of their faces.

Abe dug his heels into the flank of his rearing mount. The horse was unwilling to obey his guidance, for Abe wanted to leave the road and to cut across wild land to the south-west.

The darkness was still inky-black, though here and there, where the slope of the drifts slanted in the right direction, starlight was dimly reflected from the snow. The drifts were six, eight, in places ten feet high; and the snow was once more crawling up their flanks, it was so light and fine. It would fill the tracks in half an hour. As the horses plunged through, the crystals dusted up in clouds, flying aloft over horses and riders.

In less than half an hour they came to a group of two little buildings, of logs, that seemed to squat on their haunches in the snow. Having entered the yard through a gate, they passed one of the buildings and made for the other, a little stable; their horses snorting, they stopped in its lee.

Mike dismounted, throwing the halter-shank of his horse to Bill. He went to the house, which stood a hundred feet or so away. The shack was even smaller than the stable, twelve by fifteen feet perhaps. From its flue-pipe a thick, white plume of smoke blew to the south-east.

Mike returned with a lantern; the other two sprang to the ground; and they opened the door to examine the horse which the woman had allowed to enter.

The horse was there, still excited, snorting at the leaping light and shadows from the lantern, its eyes wild, its nostrils dilated. It was covered with white frost and fully harnessed, though its traces were tied up to the back-band.

"He let him go," said Mike, taking in these signs. "Must have stopped and unhitched him."

"Must have been stuck in a drift," Bill said, assenting.

"And tried to walk it," Abe added.

For a minute or so they stood silent, each following his own gloomy thoughts. Weird, luminous little clouds issued fitfully from the nostrils of the horse inside.

"I'll get the cutter," Abe said at last.

"I'll get it," Bill volunteered. "I'll take the drivers along. We'll leave the filly here in the stable."

"All right."

Bill remounted, leading Abe's horse. He disappeared into the night.

Abe and Mike, having tied the filly and the other horse in their stalls, went out, closed the door and turned to the house.

There, by the light of a little coal-oil lamp, they saw the woman sitting at the stove, pale, shivering, her teeth a-chatter, trying to warm her hands, which were cold with fever, and looking with lack-lustre eyes at the men as they entered.

The children were sleeping; the oldest, a girl, on the floor, wrapped in a blanket and curled up like a dog; four others in one narrow bed, with hay for a mattress, two at the head, two at the foot; the baby on, rather than in, a sort of cradle made of a wide board slung by thin ropes to the pole-roof of the shack.

The other bed was empty and unmade. The air was stifling from a night of exhalations.

"We're going to hunt for him," Mike said quietly. "We've sent for a cutter. He must have tried to walk."

The woman did not answer. She sat and shivered.

"We'll take some blankets," Mike went on. "And some whisky if you've got any in the house."

He and Abe were standing by the stove, opposite the woman, and warming their hands, their mitts held under their arm-pits.

The woman pointed with a look to a home-made little cupboard nailed to the wall and apathetically turned back to the stove. Mike went, opened the door of the cupboard, took a bottle from it, and slipped it into the pocket of his sheep-skin. Then he raised the blankets from the empty bed, rolled them roughly into a bundle, dropped it, and returned to the stove where, with stiff fingers, he fell to rolling a cigarette.

Thus they stood for an hour or so.

Abe's eye was fastened on the woman. He would have liked to say a word of comfort, of hope. What was there to be said?

She was the daughter of a German settler in the bush, some six or seven miles north-east of Abe's place. Her father, an oldish, unctuous, bearded man had, some ten years ago, got tired of the hard life in the bush where work meant clearing, picking stones, and digging stumps. He had sold his homestead and bought a prairie-farm, half a section, on crop-payments, giving notes for the equipment which he needed to handle the place. He had not been able to make it 'a go'. His bush farm had fallen back on his hands; he had lost his all and returned to the place. He had been counting on the help of his two boys – big, strapping young fellows who were to clear much land and to raise crops which would lift the debt. But the boys had refused to go back to the bush; they could get easy work in town. Ready money would help. But the ready money had melted away in their hands. Redcliff, the old people's son-in-law, had been their last hope. They were on the point of losing even their bush farm. Here they might perhaps still have found a refuge for their old age – though Redcliff's homestead lay on the sand-flats bordering on the marsh where the soil was thin, dreadfully thin; it drifted when the scrub-brush was cleared off. Still, with Redcliff living, this place had been a hope. What were they to do if he was gone? And this woman, hardly more than a girl, in spite of her six children!

The two tiny, square windows of the shack began to turn grey.

At last Abe, thinking he heard a sound, went to the door and stepped out. Bill was there; the horses were shaking the snow out of their pelts; one of them was pawing the ground.

Once more Abe opened the door and gave Mike a look for a signal. Mike gathered the bundle of blankets into his arms, pulled on his mitts, and came out.

Abe reached for the lines; but Bill objected.

"No. Let me drive. I found something."

And as soon as the two older men had climbed in, squeezing into the scant space on the seat, he clicked his tongue.

"Get up there!" he shouted, hitting the horses' backs with his lines. And with a leap they darted away.

Bill turned, heading back to the Carroll farm. The horses plunged, reared, snorted, and then, throwing their heads, shot along in a gallop, scattering snow-slabs right and left and throwing wing-waves of the fresh, powdery snow, especially on the lee side. Repeatedly they tried to turn into the wind, which they were cutting at right angles. But Bill plied the whip and guided them expertly.

Nothing was visible anywhere; nothing but the snow in the first grey of dawn. Then, like enormous ghosts, or like evanescent apparitions, the trees of the bluff were adumbrated behind the lingering veils of the night.

Bill turned to the south, along the straight trail which bordered Abe Carroll's farm. He kept looking out sharply to right and left. But after a while he drew his galloping horses in.

"Whoa!" he shouted, tearing at the lines in see-saw fashion. And when the rearing horses came to a stop, excited and breathless, he added, "I've missed it". He turned.

"What is it?" Abe asked.

"The other horse," Bill answered. "It must have had the scent of our yard. It's dead...frozen stiff."

A few minutes later he pointed to a huge white mound on top of a drift to the left. "That's it," he said, turned the horses into the wind, and stopped.

To the right, the bluffs of the farm slowly outlined themselves in the morning greyness.

The two older men alighted and, with their hands, shovelled the snow away. There lay the horse, stiff and cold, frozen into a rocklike mass.

"Must have been here a long while," Abe said.

Mike nodded. "Five, six hours." Then he added, "Couldn't have had the smell of the yard. Unless the wind has turned."

"It has," Abe answered and pointed to a fold in the flank of the snow-drift which indicated that the present drift had been superimposed on a lower one whose longitudinal axis ran to the north-east.

For a moment longer they stood and pondered.

Then Abe went back to the cutter and reached for the lines. "I'll drive," he said.

Mike climbed in.

Abe took his bearings, looking for landmarks. They were only two or three hundred feet from his fence. That enabled him to estimate the exact direction of the breeze. He clicked his tongue. "Get up!"

And the horses, catching the infection of a dull excitement, shot away. They went straight into the desert of drifts to the west, plunging ahead without any trail, without any landmark in front to guide them.

They went for half an hour, an hour, and longer.

None of the three men said a word. Abe knew the sand-flats better than any other; Abe reasoned better than they. If anyone could find the missing man, it was Abe.

Abe's thought ran thus. The horse had gone against the wind. It would never have done so without good reason; that reason could have been no other than a scent to follow. If that was so, however, it would have gone in as straight a line as it could. The sand-flats stretched away to the south-west for sixteen miles with not a settlement, not a farm but Redcliff's. If Abe managed to strike that line of the scent, it must take him to the point whence the horses had started.

Clear and glaring, with an almost indifferent air, the sun rose to their left.

And suddenly they saw the wagon-box of the sleigh sticking out of the snow ahead of them.

Abe stopped, handed Bill the lines, and got out. Mike followed. Nobody said a word.

The two men dug the tongue of the vehicle out of the snow and tried it. This was part of the old, burnt-over bush land south of the sand-flats. The sleigh was tightly wedged in between several charred stumps which stuck up through the snow. That was the reason why the man had unhitched the horses and turned them loose. What else, indeed, could he have done?

The box was filled with a drift which, toward the tail-gate, was piled high, for there three bags of flour were standing on end and leaning against a barrel half-filled with small parcels the interstices between which were packed with mealy snow.

Abe waded all around the sleigh, reconnoitring; and as he did so, wading at the height of the upper edge of the wagon-box, the snow suddenly gave way beneath him; he broke in; the drift was hollow.

A suspicion took hold of him; with a few quick reaches of his arm he demolished the roof of the drift all about.

And there, in the hollow, lay the man's body as if he were sleeping, a quiet expression, as of painless rest, on his face. His eyes were closed; a couple of bags were wrapped about his shoulders. Apparently he had not even tried to walk! Already chilled to the bone, he had given in to that desire for rest, for shelter at any price, which overcomes him who is doomed to freeze.

Without a word the two men carried him to the cutter and laid him down on the snow.

Bill, meanwhile, had unhitched the horses and was hooking them to the tongue of the sleigh. The two others looked on in silence. Four times the horses sprang, excited because Bill tried to make them pull with a sudden twist. The sleigh did not stir.

"Need an axe," Mike said at last, "to cut the stumps. We'll get the sleigh later."

Mike hitched up again and turned the cutter. The broken snow-drifts through which they had come gave the direction.

Then they laid the stiff, dead body across the floor of their vehicle, leaving the side doors open, for it protruded both ways. They themselves climbed up on the seat and crouched down, so as not to put their feet on the corpse.

Thus they returned to Abe Carroll's farm where, still in silence, they deposited the body in the granary.

That done, they stood for a moment as if in doubt. Then Bill unhitched the horses and took them to the stable to feed.

"I'll tell the woman," said Mike. "Will you go tell her father?"

Abe nodded. "Wait for breakfast," he added.

It was ten o'clock; and none of them had eaten since the previous night.

On the way to Altmann's place in the bush drifts were no obstacles to driving. Drifts lay on the marsh, on the open sand-flats.

Every minute of the time Abe, as he drove along, thought of that woman in the shack: the woman, alone, with six children, and with the knowledge that her man was dead.

Altmann's place in the bush looked the picture of peace and comfort: a large log-house of two rooms. Window-frames and door were painted green. A place to stay with, not to leave....

When Abe knocked, the woman, whom he had seen but once in his life, at the sale where they had lost their possessions, opened the door — an enormously fat woman, overflowing her clothes. The man, tall, broad, with a long, rolling beard, now grey, stood behind her, peering over her shoulder. A visit is an event in the bush!

"Come in," he said cheerfully when he saw Abe. "What a storm that was!"

Abe entered the kitchen which was also dining- and living-room. He sat down on the chair which was pushed forward for him and looked at the two old people, who remained standing.

Suddenly, from the expression of his face, they anticipated something of his message. No use dissembling.

"Redcliff is dead," he said. "He was frozen to death last night on his way from town."

The two old people also sat down; it looked as if their knees had given way beneath them. They stared at him, dumbly, a sudden expression of panic fright in their eyes.

"I thought you might want to go to your daughter," Abe added sympathetically.

The man's big frame seemed to shrink as he sat there. All the unctuousness and the conceit of the handsome man dwindled out of his bearing. The woman's eyes had already filled with tears.

Thus they remained for two, three minutes.

Then the woman folded her fat, pudgy hands; her head sank low on her breast; and she sobbed, "God's will be done!"

(1971)   (1932)

E. J. Pratt
1883-1964

———◆———

BORN IN WESTERN Bay, Newfoundland, and educated at St. John's Methodist College, Edwin John Pratt taught and preached in several island outports before enrolling at Victoria College, University of Toronto, in 1907. He completed his B.A. in 1911, his B.D. in 1913, and his Ph.D. in 1917 and joined the Department of English at Victoria College in 1920. In the years following the appearance of his first volumes, *Rachel* (1917) and *Newfoundland Verse* (1923), Pratt emerged as an important figure in the development of modern English-

Canadian poetry. He published numerous collections of lyrics, and a variety of narrative poems including two major works, *Brébeuf and His Brethren* (1940) and *Towards the Last Spike* (1952).

The Toll of the Bells

I

We gave them at the harbour every token —
    The ritual of the guns, and at the mast
    The flag half-high, and as the cortege passed,
All that remained by our dumb hearts unspoken.
And what within the band's low requiem,
    In footfall or in head uncovered fails
    Of final tribute, shall at altar-rails
Around a chancel soon be offered them.

And now a throbbing organ-prelude dwells
    On the eternal story of the sea;   10
    Following in undertone, the Litany
Ends like a sobbing wave; and now begins
A tale of life's fore-shortened days; now swells
The tidal triumph of Corinthians.

II

But neither trumpet-blast, nor the hoarse din
    Of guns, nor the drooped signals from those mute
    Banners, could find a language to salute
The frozen bodies that the ship brought in.
To-day the vaunt is with the grave. Sorrow
    Has raked up faith and burned it like a pile
    Of driftwood, scattering the ashes while
Cathedral voices anthemed God's To-morrow.

Out from the belfries of the town there swung
    Great notes that held the winds and the pagan roll   20
    Of open seas within their measured toll,
Only the bells' slow ocean tones, that rose
And hushed upon the air, knew how to tongue
That Iliad of Death upon the floes.

(1923)   (1962)

The Shark

He seemed to know the harbour,
So leisurely he swam;
His fin,
Like a piece of sheet-iron,
Three-cornered,
And with knife-edge,
Stirred not a bubble
As it moved
With its base-line on the water.

His body was tubular   10
And tapered
And smoke-blue,
And as he passed the wharf
He turned,
And snapped at a flat-fish
That was dead and floating.
And I saw the flash of a white throat,
And a double row of white teeth,
And eyes of metallic grey,
Hard and narrow and slit.   20

Then out of the harbour,
With that three-cornered fin
Shearing without a bubble the water
Lithely,
Leisurely,
He swam —
That strange fish,
Tubular, tapered, smoke-blue,
Part vulture, part wolf,
Part neither — for his blood was cold.   30

(1923)   (1962)

Sea-Gulls

For one carved instant as they flew,
The language had no simile —
Silver, crystal, ivory
Were tarnished. Etched upon the horizon blue.
The frieze must go unchallenged, for the lift
And carriage of the wings would stain the drift
Of stars against a tropic indigo
Or dull the parable of snow.

Now settling one by one
Within green hollows or where curled   10
Crests caught the spectrum from the sun,
A thousand wings are furled.
No clay-born lilies of the world
Could blow as free
As those wild orchids of the sea.

(1932)   (1962)

The Sea-Cathedral

Vast and immaculate! No pilgrim bands,
In ecstasy before the Parian shrines,
Knew such a temple built by human hands,
With this transcendent rhythm in its lines;
Like an epic on the North Atlantic stream
It moved, and fairer than a Phidian dream.

Rich gifts unknown to kings were duly brought
At dawn and sunset and at cloudless noons,
Gifts from the sea-gods and the sun who wrought
Cascades and rainbows; flung them in festoons   10
Over the spires, with emerald, amethyst,
Sapphire and pearl out of their fiery mist.

And music followed when a litany,
Begun with the ring of foam bells and the purl
Of linguals as the edges cut the sea,
Crashed upon a rising storm with whirl
Of floes from far-off spaces where Death rides
The darkened belfries of his evening tides.

Within the sunlight, vast, immaculate!
Beyond all reach of earth in majesty,   20
It passed on southwards slowly to its fate —
To be drawn down by the inveterate sea
Without one chastening fire made to start
From altars built around its polar heart.

(1932)   (1962)

From Stone to Steel

From stone to bronze, from bronze to steel
Along the road-dust of the sun,
Two revolutions of the wheel
From Java to Geneva run.

The snarl Neanderthal is worn
Close to the smiling Aryan lips,
The civil polish of the horn
Gleams from our praying finger tips.

The evolution of desire
Has but matured a toxic wine,   10
Drunk long before its heady fire
Reddened Euphrates or the Rhine.

Between the temple and the cave
The boundary lies tissue-thin:
The yearlings still the altars crave
As satisfaction for a sin.

The road goes up, the road goes down —
Let Java or Geneva be —
But whether to the cross or crown,
The path lies through Gethsemane.   20

(1932)   (1962)

The Prize Cat

Pure blood domestic, guaranteed,
Soft-mannered, musical in purr,
The ribbon had declared the breed,
Gentility was in the fur.

Such feline culture in the gads
No anger ever arched her back —
What distance since those velvet pads
Departed from the leopard's track!

And when I mused how Time had thinned
The jungle strains within the cells,   10
How human hands had disciplined
Those prowling optic parallels;

I saw the generations pass
Along the reflex of a spring,
A bird had rustled in the grass,
The tab had caught it on the wing:

Behind the leap so furtive-wild
Was such ignition in the gleam,
I thought an Abyssinian child
Had cried out in the whitethroat's scream.   20

(1937)   (1962)

Come Away, Death

Willy-nilly, he comes or goes, with the clown's logic,
Comic in epitaph, tragic in epithalamium,
And unseduced by any mused rhyme.
However blow the winds over the pollen,
Whatever the course of the garden variables,
He remains the constant,
Ever flowering from the poppy seeds.

There was a time he came in formal dress,
Announced by Silence tapping at the panels
In deep apology.   10
A touch of chivalry in his approach,
He offered sacramental wine,
And with acanthus leaf
And petals of the hyacinth
He took the fever from the temples
And closed the eyelids,
Then led the way to his cool longitudes
In the dignity of the candles.

His mediaeval grace is gone —
Gone with the flame of the capitals   20
And the leisured turn of the thumb
Leafing the manuscripts,
Gone with the marbles
And the Venetian mosaics,
With the bend of the knee
Before the rose-strewn feet of the Virgin.
The *paternosters* of his priests,
Committing clay to clay,
Have rattled in their throats
Under the gride of his traction tread.   30

One night we heard his footfall — one September night —
In the outskirts of a village near the sea.
There was a moment when the storm
Delayed its fist, when the surf fell
Like velvet on the rocks — a moment only;
The strangest lull we ever knew!

A sudden truce among the oaks
Released their fratricidal arms;
The poplars straightened to attention
As the winds stopped to listen   40
To the sound of a motor drone –
And then the drone was still.
We heard the tick-tock on the shelf,
And the leak of valves in our hearts.
A calm condensed and lidded
As at the core of a cyclone ended breathing.
This was the monologue of Silence
Grave and unequivocal.

What followed was a bolt
Outside the range and target of the thunder,   50
And human speech curved back upon itself
Through Druid runways and the Piltdown scarps,
Beyond the stammers of the Java caves,
To find its origins in hieroglyphs
On mouths and eyes and cheeks
Etched by a foreign stylus never used
On the outmoded page of the Apocalypse.

(1943)   (1962)

The Truant

"What have you there?" the great Panjandrum said
To the Master of the Revels who had led
A bucking truant with a stiff backbone
Close to the foot of the Almighty's throne.

"Right Reverend, most adored,
And forcibly acknowledged Lord
By the keen logic of your two-edged sword!
This creature has presumed to classify
Himself – a biped, rational, six feet high

And two feet wide; weighs fourteen stone;   10
Is guilty of a multitude of sins.
He has abjured his choric origins,
And like an undomesticated slattern,
Walks with tangential step unknown
Within the weave of the atomic pattern.
He has developed concepts, grins
Obscenely at your Royal bulletins,
Possesses what he calls a will
Which challenges your power to kill."

"What is his pedigree?"   20

"The base is guaranteed, your Majesty —
Calcium, carbon, phosphorus, vapour
And other fundamentals spun
From the umbilicus of the sun,
And yet he says he will not caper
Around your throne, nor toe the rules
For the ballet of the fiery molecules."
"His concepts and denials — scrap them, burn them —
To the chemists with them promptly."

                              "Sire,   30
The stuff is not amenable to fire.
Nothing but their own kind can overturn them.
The chemists have sent back the same old story —
'With our extreme gelatinous apology,
We beg to inform your Imperial Majesty,
Unto whom be dominion and power and glory,
There still remains that strange precipitate
Which has the quality to resist
Our oldest and most trusted catalyst.
It is a substance we cannot cremate   40
By temperatures known to our Laboratory.' "

And the great Panjandrum's face grew dark —
"I'll put those chemists to their annual purge,
And I myself shall be the thaumaturge
To find the nature of this fellow's spark.
Come, bring him nearer by yon halter rope:
I'll analyse him with the cosmoscope."

Pulled forward with his neck awry,
The little fellow six feet short,
Aware he was about to die,
Committed grave contempt of court   50
By answering with a flinchless stare
The Awful Presence seated there.

The ALL HIGH swore until his face was black.
He called him a coprophagite,
A genus *homo*, egomaniac,
Third cousin to the family of worms,
A sporozoan from the ooze of night,
Spawn of a spavined troglodyte:
He swore by all the catalogue of terms
Known since the slang of carboniferous Time.   60
He said that he could trace him back
To pollywogs and earwigs in the slime.
And in his shrillest tenor he began
Reciting his indictment of the man,
Until he closed upon this capital crime –
"You are accused of singing out of key,
(A foul unmitigated dissonance)
Of shuffling in the measures of the dance,
Then walking out with that defiant, free
Toss of your head, banging the doors,   70
Leaving a stench upon the jacinth floors.
You have fallen like a curse
On the mechanics of my Universe.

"Herewith I measure out your penalty –
Hearken while you hear, look while you see:
I send you now upon your homeward route
Where you shall find
Humiliation for your pride of mind.
I shall make deaf the ear, and dim the eye,
Put palsy in your touch, make mute   80
Your speech, intoxicate your cells and dry
Your blood and marrow, shoot
Arthritic needles through your cartilage,
And having parched you with old age,
I'll pass you wormwise through the mire;
And when your rebel will
Is mouldered, all desire

Shrivelled, all your concepts broken,
Backward in dust I'll blow you till
You join my spiral festival of fire.   90
Go, Master of the Revels – I have spoken."

And the little genus *homo*, six feet high,
Standing erect, countered with this reply –
"You dumb insouciant invertebrate,
You rule a lower than a feudal state –
A realm of flunkey decimals that run,
Return; return and run; again return,
Each group around its little sun,
And every sun a satellite.
There they go by day and night,   100
Nothing to do but run and burn,
Taking turn and turn about,
Light-year in and light-year out,
Dancing, dancing in quadrillions,
Never leaving their pavilions.

"Your astronomical conceit
Of bulk and power is anserine.
Your ignorance so thick,
You did not know your own arithmetic.
We flung the graphs about your flying feet;   110
We measured your diameter –
Merely a line
Of zeros prefaced by an integer.
Before we came
You had no name.
You did not know direction or your pace;
We taught you all you ever knew
Of motion, time and space.
We healed you of your vertigo
And put you in our kindergarten show,   120
Perambulated you through prisms, drew
Your mileage through the Milky Way,
Lassoed your comets when they ran astray,
Yoked Leo, Taurus, and your team of Bears
To pull our kiddy cars of inverse squares.

"Boast not about your harmony,
Your perfect curves, your rings

Of *pure and endless light* — 'Twas we
Who pinned upon your Seraphim their wings,
And when your brassy heavens rang   130
With joy that morning while the planets sang
Their choruses of archangelic lore,
'Twas we who ordered the notes upon their score
Out of our winds and strings.
Yes! all your shapely forms
Are ours — parabolas of silver light,
Those blueprints of your spiral stairs
From nadir depth to zenith height,
Coronas, rainbows after storms,
Auroras on your eastern tapestries   140
And constellations over western seas.

"And when, one day, grown conscious of your age,
While pondering an eolith,
We turned a human page
And blotted out a cosmic myth
With all its baby symbols to explain
The sunlight in Apollo's eyes,
Our rising pulses and the birth of pain,
Fear, and that fern-and-fungus breath
Stalking our nostrils to our caves of death —   150
That day we learned how to anatomize
Your body, calibrate your size
And set a mirror up before your face
To show you what you really were — a rain
Of dull Lucretian atoms crowding space,
A series of concentric waves which any fool
Might make by dropping stones within a pool,
Or an exploding bomb forever in flight
Bursting like hell through Chaos and Old Night.

"You oldest of the hierarchs   160
Composed of electronic sparks,
We grant you speed,
We grant you power, and fire
That ends in ash, but we concede
To you no pain nor joy nor love nor hate,
No final tableau of desire,
No causes won or lost, no free
Adventure at the outposts — only

The degradation of your energy
When at some late   170
Slow number of your dance your sergeant-major Fate
Will catch you blind and groping and will send
You reeling on that long and lonely
Lockstep of your wave-lengths towards your end.

"We who have met
With stubborn calm the dawn's hot fusillades;
Who have seen the forehead sweat
Under the tug of pulleys on the joints,
Under the liquidating tally
Of the cat-and-truncheon bastinades;   180
Who have taught our souls to rally
To mountain horns and the sea's rockets
When the needle ran demented through the points;
We who have learned to clench
Our fists and raise our lightless sockets
To morning skies after the midnight raids,
Yet cocked our ears to bugles on the barricades,
And in cathedral rubble found a way to quench
A dying thirst within a Galilean valley –
No! by the Rood, we will not join your ballet."   190

(1943)   (1962)

Towards the Last Spike

It was the same world then as now – the same,
Except for little differences of speed
And power, and means to treat myopia
To show an axe-blade infinitely sharp
Splitting things infinitely small, or else
Provide the telescopic sight to roam
Through curved dominions never found in fables.
The same, but for new particles of speech –
Those algebraic substitutes for nouns
That sky cartographers would hang like signboards   10
Along the trespass of our thoughts to stop
The stutters of our tongues with their equations.

As now, so then, blood kept its ancient colour,
And smoothly, roughly, paced its banks; in calm
Preserving them, in riot rupturing them.
Wounds needed bandages and stomachs food:
The hands outstretched had joined the lips in prayer —
"Give us our daily bread, give us our pay."
The past flushed in the present and tomorrow
Would dawn upon today: only the rate   20
To sensitize or numb a nerve would change;
Only the quickening of a measuring skill
To gauge the onset of a birth or death
With the precision of micrometers.
Men spoke of acres then and miles and masses,
Velocity and steam, cables that moored
Not ships but continents, world granaries,
The east-west cousinship, a nation's rise,
Hail of identity, a world expanding,
If not the universe: the feel of it   30
Was in the air — *"Union required the Line."*
The theme was current at the banquet tables,
And arguments profane and sacred rent
God-fearing families into partisans.
Pulpit, platform and floor were sounding-boards;
Cushions beneath the pounding fists assumed
The hues of western sunsets; nostrils sniffed
The prairie tang; the tongue rolled over texts:
Even St. Paul was being invoked to wring
The neck of Thomas in this war of faith   40
With unbelief. Was ever an adventure
Without its cost? Analogies were found
On every page of history or science.
A nation, like the world, could not stand still.
What was the use of records but to break them?
The tougher armour followed the new shell;
The newer shell the armour; lighthouse rockets
Sprinkled their stars over the wake of wrecks.
Were not the engineers at work to close
The lag between the pressures and the valves?   50
The same world then as now thirsting for power
To crack those records open, extra pounds
Upon the inches, extra miles per hour.
The mildewed static schedules which before
Had like asbestos been immune to wood

Now curled and blackened in the furnace coal.
This power lay in the custody of men
From down-and-outers needing roofs, whose hands
Were moulded by their fists, whose skins could feel
At home incorporate with dolomite,   60
To men who with the marshal instincts in them,
Deriving their authority from wallets,
Directed their battalions from the trestles.

THE GATHERING

("Oats — a grain which in England is generally given to horses, but in Scotland supports the people." — Dr. Samuel Johnson. "True, but where will you find such horses, where such men?" — Lord Elibank's reply as recorded by Sir Walter Scott.)

Oatmeal was in their blood and in their names.
Thrift was the title of their catechism.
It governed all things but their mess of porridge
Which, when it struck the hydrochloric acid
With treacle and skim-milk, became a mash.
Entering the duodenum, it broke up
Into amino acids: then the liver   70
Took on its natural job as carpenter:
Foreheads grew into cliffs, jaws into juts.
The meal, so changed, engaged the follicles:
Eyebrows came out as gorse, the beards as thistles,
And the chest-hair the fell of Grampian rams.
It stretched and vulcanized the human span:
Nonagenarians worked and thrived upon it.
Out of such chemistry run through by genes,
The food released its fearsome racial products: —
The power to strike a bargain like a foe,   80
To win an argument upon a burr,
Invest the language with a Bannockburn,
Culloden or the warnings of Lochiel,
Weave loyalties and rivalries in tartans,
Present for the amazement of the world
Kilts and the civilized barbaric Fling,
And pipes which, when they acted on the mash,
Fermented lullabies to *Scots wha hae.*

Their names were like a battle-muster — Angus
(He of the Shops) and Fleming (of the Transit),   90
Hector (of the *Kicking Horse*), Dawson,
"Cromarty" Ross, and Beatty (Ulster Scot),
Bruce, Allan, Galt and Douglas, and the "twa" —
Stephen (Craigellachie)* and Smith (Strathcona) —
Who would one day climb from their Gaelic hide-outs,
Take off their plaids and wrap them round the mountains.
And then the everlasting tread of the Macs,
Vanguard, centre, and rear, their roving eyes
On summits, rivers, contracts, beaver, ledgers;
Their ears cocked to the skirl of Sir John A.,   100
The general of the patronymic march.

*(Sir John revolving round the Terms of Union with
British Columbia. Time, late at night.)*

Insomnia had ripped the bed-sheets from him
Night after night. How long was this to last?
Confederation had not played this kind
Of trickery on him. That was rough indeed,
So gravelled, that a man might call for rest
And take it for a life accomplishment.
It was his laurel though some of the leaves
Had dried. But this would be a longer tug
Of war which needed for his team thick wrists   110
And calloused fingers, heavy heels to dig
Into the earth and hold — men with bull's beef
Upon their ribs. Had he himself the wind,
The anchor-waist to peg at the rope's end?
'Twas hard enough to have these questions hit
The waking mind:'twas much worse when he dozed;
For goblins had a way of pinching him,
Slapping a nightmare on to dwindling snoozes.
They put him and his team into a tug
More real than life. He heard a judge call out —   120
"Teams settle on the rope and take the strain!"
And with the coaches' *heave,* the running welts
Reddened his palms, and then the gruelling *backlock*

---

* *"Stand Fast, Craigellachie,"* the war-cry of the Clan Grant, named after a rock in the Spey
Valley, and used as a cable message from Stephen in London to the Directors in Montreal
[Author's note].

Inscribed its indentations on his shoulders.
This kind of burn he knew he had to stand;
It was the game's routine; the other fire
Was what he feared the most for it could bake him —
That white dividing rag tied to the rope
Above the centre pole had with each heave
Wavered with chances equal. With the backlock,   130
Despite the legs of Tupper and Cartier,
The western anchor dragged; the other side
Remorselessly was gaining, holding, gaining.
No sleep could stand this strain and, with the nightmare
Delivered of its colt, Macdonald woke.

Tired with the midnight toss, lock-jawed with yawns,
He left the bed and, shuffling to the window,
He opened it. The air would cool him off
And soothe his shoulder burns. He felt his ribs:
Strange, nothing broken — how those crazy drowses   140
Had made the fictions tangle with the facts!
He must unscramble them with steady hands.
Those Ranges pirouetting in his dreams
Had their own knack of standing still in light,
Revealing peaks whose known triangulation
Had to be read in prose severity.
Seizing a telescope, he swept the skies,
The north-south drift, a self-illumined chart.
Under Polaris was the Arctic Sea
And the sub-Arctic gates well stocked with names: 150
Hudson, Davis, Baffin, Frobisher;
And in his own day Franklin, Ross and Parry
Of the Canadian Archipelago;
Kellett, McClure, McClintock, of *The Search*.
Those straits and bays had long been kicked by keels,
And flags had fluttered on the Capes that fired
His youth, making familiar the unknown.
What though the odds were nine to one against,
And the Dead March was undertoning trumpets,
There was enough of strychnine in the names   160
To make him flip a penny for the risk,
Though he had palmed the coin reflectively
Before he threw and watched it come down *heads*.
That stellar path looked too much like a road map

Upon his wall – the roads all led to market –
The north-south route. He lit a candle, held
It to a second map full of blank spaces
And arrows pointing west. Disturbed, he turned
The lens up to the zenith, followed the course
Tracked by a cloud of stars that would not keep   170
Their posts – Capella, Perseus, were reeling;
Low in the north-west, Cassiopeia
Was qualmish, leaning on her starboard arm-rest,
And Aries was chasing, butting Cygnus,
Just diving. Doubts and hopes struck at each other.
Why did those constellations look so much
Like blizzards? And what lay beyond the blizzards?

'Twas chilly at the window. He returned
To bed and savoured soporific terms:
Superior, the *Red River, Selkirk, Prairie,*   180
Port Moody and *Pacific.* Chewing them,
He spat out *Rocky* grit before he swallowed.
Selkirk! This had the sweetest taste. Ten years
Before, the Highland crofters had subscribed
Their names in a memorial for the Rails.
Sir John reviewed the story of the struggle,
That four months' journey from their native land –
The Atlantic through the Straits to Hudson Bay,
Then the Hayes River to Lake Winnipeg
Up to the Forks of the Assiniboine.   190

He could make use of that – just what he needed,
A Western version of the Arctic daring,
Romance and realism, double dose.
How long ago? Why, this is '71.
Those fellows came the time Napoleon
Was on the steppes. For sixty years they fought
The seasons, 'hoppers, drought, hail, wind and snow;
Survived the massacre at Seven Oaks,
The "Pemmican War" and the Red River floods.
They wanted now the Road – those pioneers   200
Who lived by spades instead of beaver traps.
Most excellent word that, pioneers! Sir John
Snuggled himself into his sheets, rolling
The word around his tongue, a theme for song,
Or for a peroration to a speech.

THE HANGOVER AT DAWN

He knew the points that had their own appeal.
These did not bother him: the patriot touch,
The Flag, the magnetism of explorers,
The national unity. These could burn up
The phlegm in most of the provincial throats.   210
But there was one tale central to his plan
(The focus of his headache at this moment),
Which would demand the limit of his art —
The ballad of his courtship in the West:
Better reveal it soon without reserve.

THE LADY OF BRITISH COLUMBIA

Port Moody and Pacific! He had pledged
His word the Line should run from sea to sea.
"From sea to sea", a hallowed phrase. Music
Was in that text if the right key were struck,
And he must strike it first, for, as he fingered   220
The clauses of the pledge, rough notes were rasping —
"No Roads, No Union", and the converse true.
East-west against the north-south run of trade,
For California like a sailor-lover
Was wooing over-time. He knew the ports.
His speech was as persuasive as his arms,
As sinuous as Spanish arias —
Tamales, Cazadero, Mendecino,
Curling their baritones around the Lady.
Then Santa Rosa, Santa Monica,   230
Held absolution in their syllables.
But when he saw her stock of British temper
Starch at ironic sainthood in the whispers —
*"Rio de nuestra señora de buena guia,"**
He had the tact to gutturalize the liquids,
Steeping the tunes to drinking songs, then take
Her on a holiday where she could watch
A roving sea-born Californian pound
A downy chest and swear by San Diego.

Sir John, wise to the tricks, was studying hard   240
A fresh proposal for a marriage contract.

* *"River of Our Lady of Safe Conduct"* [Author's note].

He knew a game was in the ceremony.
That southern fellow had a healthy bronze
Complexion, had a vast estate, was slick
Of manner. In his ardour he could tether
Sea-roses to the blossoms of his orchards,
And for his confidence he had the prime
Advantage of his rival — *he was there.*

THE LONG-DISTANCE PROPOSAL

A game it was, and the Pacific lass
Had poker wisdom on her face. Her name   250
Was rich in values — *British*; this alone
Could raise Macdonald's temperature: so could
Columbia with a different kind of fever,
And in between the two, *Victoria.*
So the *Pacific* with its wash of letters
Could push the Fahrenheit another notch.
She watched for bluff on those Disraeli features,
Impassive but for arrowy chipmunk eyes,
Engaged in fathoming a contract time.
With such a dowry she could well afford   260
To take the risk of tightening the terms —
"Begin the Road in two years, end in ten" —
Sir John, a moment letting down his guard,
Frowned at the Rocky skyline, but agreed.

*(The Terms ratified by Parliament, British
Columbia enters Confederation July, 1871, Sand-
ford Fleming being appointed engineer-in-chief
of the proposed Railway, Walter Moberly to co-
operate with him in the location of routes. "Of
course, I don't know how many millions you
have, but it is going to cost you money to get
through those canyons." — Moberly to Macdonald.)*

THE PACIFIC SCANDAL

*(Huntingdon's charges of political corruption
based on correspondence and telegrams rifled
from the offices of the solicitor of Sir Hugh Allan,*

*Head of the Canada Pacific Company; Sir John's
defence; and the appearance of the Honourable
Edward Blake who rises to reply to Sir John at
2 a.m.)*

BLAKE IN MOOD

Of all the subjects for debate here was
His element. His soul as clean as surf,
No one could equal him in probing cupboards
Or sweeping floors and dusting shelves, finding
A skeleton inside an overcoat;
Or shaking golden eagles from a pocket   270
To show the copper plugs within the coins.
Rumours he heard had gangrened into facts –
Gifts nuzzling at two-hundred-thousand dollars,
Elections on, and with a contract pending.
The odour of the bills had blown his gorge.
His appetite, edged by a moral hone,
Could surfeit only on the Verities.

November 3, 1873

A Fury rode him to the House. He took
His seat, and with a stoic gloom he heard
The Chieftain's great defence and noted well   280
The punctuation of the cheers. He needed all
The balance of his mind to counterpoise
The movements of Macdonald as he flung
Himself upon the House, upon the Country,
Upon posterity, upon his conscience.
That plunging played the devil with Blake's tiller,
Threatened the set of his sail. To save the course,
To save himself, in that five hours of gale,
He had to jettison his meditation,
His brooding on the follies of mankind,   290
Clean out the wadding from his tortured ears:
That roaring mob before him could be quelled
Only by action; so when the last round
Of the applause following the peroration
Was over, slowly, weightily, Blake rose.

A statesman-chancellor now held the Floor.
He told the sniffing Commons that a sense
Keener than smell or taste must be invoked
To get the odour. Leading them from facts
Like telegrams and stolen private letters,   300
He soared into the realm of principles
To find his scourge; and then the men involved,
Robed like the Knights of Malta, Blake undressed,
Their cloaks inverted to reveal the shoddy,
The tattered lining and bare-threaded seams.
He ripped the last stitch from them – by the time
Recess was called, he had them in the dock
As brigands in the Ministry of Smells,
Naked before the majesty of Heaven.

For Blake recesses were but sandwiches   310
Provided merely for cerebral luncheons –
No time to spread the legs under the table,
To chat and chaff a while, to let the mind
Roam, like a goblet up before the light
To bask in natural colour, or by whim
Of its own choice to sway luxuriously
In tantalizing arcs before the nostrils.
A meal was meant by Nature for nutrition –
A sorry farinaceous business scaled
Exactly to caloric grains and grams   320
Designed for intellectual combustion,
For energy directed into words
Towards proof. Abuse was overweight. He saw
No need for it; no need for caricature,
And if a villainous word had to be used,
'Twas for a villain – keen upon the target.
Irrelevance was like a moral lesion
No less within a speech than in a statute.
What mattered it who opened up the files,
Sold for a bid the damning correspondence –   330
That Montreal-Chicago understanding?
A dirty dodge, so let it be conceded.
But *here* the method was irrelevant.
Whether by legal process or by theft,
The evidence was there unalterable.
So with the House assembled, he resumed
Imperial indictment of the bandits.

The logic left no loopholes in the facts.
Figures that ran into the hundred-thousands
Were counted up in pennies, each one shown   340
To bear the superscription of debasement.

Again recess, again the sandwiches,
Again the invocation of the gods:
Each word, each phrase, each clause went to position,
Each sentence regimented like a lockstep.
The only thing that would not pace was time;
The hours dragged by until the thrushes woke –
Two days, two nights – someone opened a window,
And members of the House who still were conscious
Uncreaked their necks to note that even Sir John   350
Himself had put his fingers to his nose.

*(The appeal to the country: Macdonald defeat-
ed: Mackenzie assumes power, 1874.)*

A change of air, a drop in temperature!
The House had rarely known sobriety
Like this. No longer clanged the *"Westward Ho!"*
And quiet were the horns upon the hills.
Hard times ahead. The years were rendering up
Their fat. Measured and rationed was the language
Directed to the stringency of pockets.
The eye must be convinced before the *vision*.
"But one step at a time," exclaimed the feet.   360
It was the story of the hen or egg;
Which came before the other? *"'Twas the hen,"*
Cried one; *"undoubtedly the hen must lay
The egg, hatch it and mother it."* *"Not so,"*
Another shouted, *"'Twas the egg or whence
The hen?"* For every one who cleared his throat
And called across the House with Scriptural passion –
"The Line is meant to bring the loaves and fishes,"
A voting three had countered with the question –
"Where are the multitudes that thirst and hunger?"   370
Passion became displaced by argument.
Till now the axles justified their grease,
Taught coal a lesson in economy.
All doubts here could be blanketed with facts,
With phrases smooth as actuarial velvet.

For forty years in towns and cities men
Had watched the Lines baptized with charters, seen
Them grow, marry and bring forth children.
Parades and powder had their uses then
For gala days; and bands announced arrivals,   380
Betrothals, weddings and again arrivals.
Champagne brimmed in the font as they were named
With titles drawn from the explorers' routes,
From Saints and Governors, from space and seas
And compass-points – Saints Andrew, Lawrence, Thomas,
Louis and John; Champlain, Simcoe; Grand Trunk,
Intercolonial, the Canadian Southern,
Dominion-Atlantic, the Great Western – names
That caught a continental note and tried
To answer it. Half-gambles though they were,   390
Directors built those Roads and heard them run
To the sweet silver jingle in their minds.

The airs had long been mastered like old songs
The feet could tap to in the galleries.
But would they tap to a new rhapsody,
A harder one to learn and left unfinished?
What ear could be assured of absolute pitch
To catch this kind of music in the West?
The far West? Men had used this flattering name
For East or but encroachment on the West.   400
And was not Lake Superior still the East,
A natural highway which ice-ages left,
An unappropriated legacy?
There was no discord in the piston-throbs
Along this Road. This was old music too.
That northern spine of rock, those western mountains,
Were barriers built of God and cursed of Blake.
Mild in his oaths, Mackenzie would avoid them.
He would let contracts for the south and west,
Push out from settlement to settlement.   410
This was economy, just plain horse-sense.
The Western Lines were there – American.
He would link up with them, could reach the Coast.
The Eagle and the Lion were good friends:
At least the two could meet on sovereign terms
Without a sign of fur and feathers flying.

As yet, but who could tell? So far, so good.
Spikes had been driven at the boundary line,
From Emerson across the Red to Selkirk,
And then to Thunder Bay — to Lake Superior;   420
Across the prairies in God's own good time,
His plodding, patient, planetary time.

Five years' delay: surveys without construction;
Short lines suspended, discord in the Party.
The West defrauded of its glittering peaks,
The public blood was stirring and protesting
At this continuous dusk upon the mountains.
The old conductor off the podium,
The orchestra disbanded at the time
The daring symphony was on the score,   430
The audience cupped their ears to catch a strain:
They heard a plaintive thinning oboe-A
That kept on thinning while slow feeble steps
Approached the stand. Was this the substitute
For what the auditorium once knew —
The maestro who with tread of stallion hoofs
Came forward shaking platforms and the rafters,
And followed up the concert pitch with sound
Of drums and trumpets and the organ blasts
That had the power to toll out apathy   440
And make snow peaks ring like Cathedral steeples?
Besides, accompanying those bars of music,
There was an image men had not forgotten,
The shaggy chieftain standing at his desk,
That last-ditch fight when he was overthrown,
That desperate five hours. At least they knew
His personal pockets were not lined with pelf,
Whatever loot the others grabbed. The words
British, the West instead of South, the Nation,
The all-Canadian route — these terms were singing   450
Fresher than ever while the grating tones
Under the stress of argument had faded
Within the shroud of their monotony.

*(Sir John returns to power in 1878 with a
National Policy of Protective Tariff and the
Transcontinental.)*

Two years of tuning up: it needed that
To counterpoint Blake's eloquence or lift
Mackenzie's non-adventurous common sense
To the ignition of an enterprise.
The pace had to be slow at first, a tempo
Cautious, simple to follow. Sections strewn
Like amputated limbs along the route   460
Were sutured. This appealed to sanity.
No argument could work itself to sweat
Against a prudent case, for the terrain
Looked easy from the Lake to the Red River.
To stop with those suspensions was a waste
Of cash and time. But the huge task announced
Ten years before had now to start afresh –
The moulding of men's minds was harder far
Than moulding of the steel and prior to it.
It was the battle of ideas and words   470
And kindred images called by the same name,
Like brothers who with temperamental blood
Went to it with their fists. Canyons and cliffs
Were precipices down which men were hurled,
Or something to be bridged and sheared and scaled.
Likewise the Pass had its ambiguous meaning.
The leaders of the factions in the House
And through the country spelled the word the same:
The way they got their tongue around the word
Was different, for some could make it hiss   480
With sound of blizzards screaming over ramparts:
The Pass – the Yellowhead, the Kicking Horse –
Or jam it with *coureur-de-bois* romance,
Or join it to the empyrean. Eagles,
In flight banking their wings above a fish-stream,
Had guided the explorers to a route
And given the Pass the title of their wings.
The stories lured men's minds up to the mountains
And down along the sandbars of the rivers.
Rivalling the *"brown and barren"* on the maps,   490
Officially *"not fit for human life"*,
Were vivid yellows flashing in the news –
"Gold in the Cariboo," "Gold in the Fraser."
The swish of gravel in the placer-cradles
Would soon be followed by the spluttering fuses,
By thunder echoing thunder; for one month

After Blake's Ottawa roar would Onderdonk
Roar back from Yale by ripping canyon walls
To crash the tons by millions in the gorges.

The farther off, as by a paradox   500
Of magnets, was the golden lure the stronger:
Two thousand miles away, imagined peaks
Had the vacation pull of mountaineering,
But with the closer vision would the legs
Follow the mind? 'Twas Blake who raised the question
And answered it. Though with his natural eyes
Up to this time he had not sighted mountains,
He was an expert with the telescope.

THE ATTACK

Sir John was worried. The first hour of Blake
Was dangerous, granted the theme. Eight years   510
Before, he had the theme combined with language.
Impeachment – word with an historic ring,
Reserved for the High Courts of Parliament,
Uttered only when men were breathing hard
And when the vertebrae were musket-stiff:
High ground was that for his artillery,
And *there*, despite the hours the salvos lasted.

But *here* this was a theme less vulnerable
To fire, Macdonald thought, to Blake's gunfire,
And yet he wondered what the orator   520
Might spring in that first hour, what strategy
Was on the Bench. He did not mind the close
Mosaic of the words – too intricate,
Too massive in design. Men might admire
The speech and talk about it, then forget it.
But few possessed the patience or the mind
To tread the mazes of the labyrinth.
Once in a while, however, would Blake's logic
Stumble upon stray figures that would leap
Over the walls of other folds and catch   530
The herdsmen in their growing somnolence.
The waking sound was not – *"It can't be done"*;
That was a dogma, anyone might say it.
It was the following burning corollary:

"To build a Road over that sea of mountains."
This carried more than argument. It was
A flash of fire which might with proper kindling
Consume its way into the public mind.
The House clicked to the ready and Sir John,
Burying his finger-nails into his palms,   540
Muttered — *"God send us no more metaphors*
Like that — except from Tory factories."

Had Blake the lift of Chatham as he had
Burke's wind and almost that sierra span
Of mind, he might have carried the whole House
With him and posted it upon that sea
Of mountains with sub-zeros on their scalps,
Their glacial ribs waiting for warmth of season
To spring an avalanche. Such similes
Might easily glue the members to their seats   550
With frost in preparation for their ride.
Sir John's *"from sea to sea"* was Biblical;
It had the stamp of reverent approval;
But Blake's was pagan, frightening, congealing.
The chieftain's lips continued as in prayer,
A fiercely secular and torrid prayer —
"May Heaven intervene to stop the flow
Of such unnatural images and send
The rhetorician back to decimals,
Back to his tessellated subtleties."   560
The prayer was answered for High Heaven did it.
The second hour entered and passed by,
A third, a fourth. Sir John looked round the House,
Noticed the growing shuffle of the feet,
The agony of legs, the yawn's contagion.
Was that a snore? Who was it that went out?
He glanced at the Press Gallery. The pens
Were scratching through the languor of the ink
To match the words with shorthand and were failing.
He hoped the speech would last another hour,   570
And still another. Well within the law,
This homicidal master of the opiates
Loosened the hinges of the Opposition:
The minds went first; the bodies sagged; the necks
Curved on the benches and the legs sprawled out.
And when the Fundy Tide had ebbed, Sir John,

Smiling, watched the debris upon the banks,
For what were yesterday grey human brains
Had with decomposition taken on
The texture and complexion of red clay.   580

*(In 1880 Tupper lets contract to Onderdonk for
survey and construction through the Pacific Section of the mountains. Sir John, Tupper, Pope,
and McIntyre go to London to interest capital
but return without a penny.)*

Failing to make a dent in London dams,
Sir John set out to plumb a reservoir
Closer in reach. He knew its area,
Its ownership, the thickness of its banks,
Its conduits – if he could get his hands
Upon the local stopcocks, could he turn them?
The reservoir was deep. Two centuries
Ago it started filling when a king
Had in a furry moment scratched a quill
Across the bottom of His Royal Charter –   590
*"Granting the Governor and His Company
Of Gentlemen Adventurers the right
Exclusive to one-third a continent."*
Was it so easy then? A scratch, a seal,
A pinch of snuff tickling the sacred nostrils,
A puff of powder and the ink was dry.
Sir John twisted his lips: he thought of London.
Empire and wealth were in that signature
For royal, princely, ducal absentees,
For courtiers to whom the parallels   600
Where nothing but chalk scratches on a slate.
For them wild animals were held in game
Preserves, foxes as quarry in a chase,
And hills were hedges, river banks were fences,
And cataracts but fountains in a garden
Tumbling their bubbles into marble basins.
Where was this place called Hudson Bay? Some place
In the Antipodes? Explorers, traders,
Would bring their revenues over that signet.
Two centuries – the new empire advanced,   610
Was broken, reunited, torn again.
The *fleur-de-lis* went to half-mast, the *Jack*

To the mast-head, but fresher rivalries
Broke out — Nor'-Westers at the Hudson's throat
Over the pelts, over the pemmican;
No matter what — the dividends flowed in
As rum flowed out like the Saskatchewan.

The twist left Sir John's lips and he was smiling.
Though English in ambition and design,
This reservoir, he saw there in control   620
Upon the floodgates not a Londoner
In riding breeches but, red-flannel-shirted,
Trousered in homespun, streaked and blobbed with seal-oil,
A Scot with smoke of peat fire on his breath —
Smith? Yes: but christened Donald Alexander
And loined through issue from the Grants and Stuarts.

To smite the rock and bring forth living water,
Take lead or tin and transmute both to silver,
Copper to gold, betray a piece of glass
To diamonds, fabulize a continent,   630
Were wonders once believed, scrapped and revived;
For Moses, Marco Polo, Paracelsus,
Fell in the same retort and came out *Smith.*
A miracle on legs, the lad had left
Forres and Aberdeen, gone to Lachine —
"Tell Mr. Smith to count and sort the rat-skins."
Thence Tadoussac and Posts off Anticosti;
From there to Rigolet in Labrador,
A thousand miles by foot, snowshoe and dog-sled.
He fought the climate like a weathered yak,   640
And conquered it, ripping the stalactites
From his red beard, thawing his feet, and wringing
Salt water from his mitts; but most of all
He learned the art of making change. Blankets,
Ribbons and beads, tobacco, guns and knives,
Were swapped for muskrat, marten, fox and beaver.
And when the fur trade thinned, he trapped the salmon,
Canned it; hunted the seal, traded its oil
And fertilized the gardens with the carcass.
Even the melons grew in Labrador.   650
What could resist this touch? Water from rock!
Why not? No more a myth than pelts should be
Thus fabricated into bricks of gold.

If rat-skins, why not tweeds? If looms could take
Raw wool and twill it into selling shape,
They could under the draper's weaving mind
Be patterning gold braid:
                    So thought George Stephen.

His legs less sturdy than his cousin Donald's,
His eyes were just as furiously alert.   660
His line of vision ran from the north-west
To the Dutch-held St. Paul-Pacific Railway.
Allied with Smith, Kitson and Kennedy,
Angus, Jim Hill and Duncan McIntyre,
Could he buy up this semi-bankrupt Road
And turn the northern traffic into it?
Chief bricklayer of all the Scotian clans,
And foremost as a banking metallurgist,
He took the parchments at their lowest level
And mineralized them, roasted them to shape,   670
Then mortared them into the pyramid,
Till with the trowel-stretching exercise
He grew so Atlas-strong that he could carry
A mountain like a namesake on his shoulders.

*(The Charter granted to The Canadian Pacific
Railway, February 17, 1881, with George Stephen
as first President . . . One William Cornelius
Van Horne arrives in Winnipeg, December 31,
1881, and there late at night, forty below zero,
gives vent to a soliloquy.)*

Stephen had laid his raw hands on Van Horne,
Pulled him across the border, sent him up
To get the feel of northern temperatures.
He knew through Hill the story of his life
And found him made to order. Nothing less
Than geologic space his field of work,   680
He had in Illinois explored the creeks
And valleys, brooded on the rocks and quarries.
Using slate fragments, he became a draughtsman,
Bringing to life a landscape or a cloud,
Turning a tree into a beard, a cliff
Into a jaw, a creek into a mouth
With banks for lips. He loved to work on shadows.

Just now the man was forcing the boy's stature,
The while the youth tickled the man within.
Companioned by the shade of Agassiz,   690
He would come home, his pockets stuffed with fossils —
Crinoids and fish-teeth — and his tongue jabbering
Of the earth's crust before the birth of life,
Prophetic of the days when he would dig
Into Laurentian rock. The morse-key tick
And tape were things mesmeric — space and time
Had found a junction. Electricity
And rock, one novel to the coiling hand,
The other frozen in the lap of age,
Were playthings for the boy, work for the man.   700
As man he was the State's first operator;
As boy he played a trick upon his boss
Who, cramped with current, fired him on the instant;
As man at school, escaping Latin grammar,
He tore the fly-leaf from the text to draw
The contour of a hill; as boy he sketched
The principal, gave him flapdoodle ears,
Bristled his hair, turned eyebrows into quills,
His whiskers into flying buttresses,
His eye-tusks into rusted railroad spikes,   710
And made a truss between his nose and chin.
Expelled again, he went back to the keys,
To bush and rock and found companionship
With quarry-men, stokers and station-masters,
Switchmen and locomotive engineers.

Now he was transferred to Winnipeg.
Of all the places in an unknown land
Chosen by Stephen for Van Horne, this was
The pivot on which he could turn his mind.
Here he could clap the future on the shoulder   720
And order Fate about as his lieutenant,
For he would take no nonsense from a thing
Called Destiny — the stars had to be with him.
He spent the first night in soliloquy,
Like Sir John A. but with a difference.
Sir John wanted to sleep but couldn't do it:
Van Horne could sleep but never wanted to.
It was a waste of time, his bed a place
Only to think or dream with eyes awake.

Opening a jack-knife, he went to the window,   730
Scraped off the frost. Great treks ran through his mind,
East-west. Two centuries and a half gone by,
One trek had started from the Zuyder Zee
To the new Amsterdam. 'Twas smooth by now,
Too smooth. His line of grandsires and their cousins
Had built a city from Manhattan dirt.
Another trek to Illinois; it too
Was smooth, but this new one it was his job
To lead, then build a highway which men claimed
Could not be built. Statesmen and engineers   740
Had blown their faces blue with their denials:
The men who thought so were asylum cases
Whose monomanias harmless up to now
Had not swept into cells. His bearded chin
Pressed to the pane, his eyes roved through the west.
He saw the illusion at its worst — the frost,
The steel precision of the studded heavens,
Relentless mirror of a covered earth.
His breath froze on the scrape: he cut again
And glanced at the direction west-by-south.   750
That westward trek was the American,
Union-Pacific — easy so he thought,
Their forty million stacked against his four.
Lonely and desolate this. He stocked his mind
With items of his task: the simplest first,
Though hard enough, the Prairies, then the Shore
North of the Lake — a quantity half-guessed.
Mackenzie like a balky horse had shied
And stopped at this. Van Horne knew well the reason,
But it was vital for the all land route.   760
He peered through at the South. Down there Jim Hill
Was whipping up his horses on a road
Already paved. The stations offered rest
With food and warmth, and their well-rounded names
Were tossed like apples to the public taste.

He made a mental note of his three items.
He underlined the Prairies, double-lined
The Shore and triple-lined *Beyond the Prairies,*
Began counting the Ranges — first the Rockies;
The Kicking Horse ran through them, this he knew;   770
The Selkirks? Not so sure. Some years before

Had Moberly and Perry tagged a route
Across the lariat loop of the Columbia.
Now Rogers was traversing it on foot,
Reading an aneroid and compass, chewing
Sea-biscuit and tobacco. Would the steel
Follow this trail? Van Horne looked farther west.
There was the Gold Range, there the Coastal Mountains.
He stopped, putting a period to the note,
As rivers troubled nocturnes in his ears.   780
His plans must not seep into introspection –
Call it a night, for morning was at hand,
And every hour of daylight was for work.

*(Van Horne goes to Montreal to meet the
Directors.)*

He had agenda staggering enough
To bring the sweat even from Stephen's face.
As daring as his plans, so daring were
His promises. To build five hundred miles
Upon the prairies in one season: this
Was but a cushion for the jars ahead.
The Shore – he had to argue, stamp and fight   790
For this. The watercourses had been favoured,
The nation schooled to that economy.
He saw that Stephen, after wiping beads
From face and forehead, had put both his hands
Deep in his pockets – just a habit merely
Of fingering change – but still Van Horne went on
To clinch his case: the north shore could avoid
The over-border route – a national point
If ever there was one. He promised this
As soon as he was through with buffalo-grass.   800
And then the little matter of the Rockies:
This must be swallowed without argument,
As obvious as space, clear as a charter.
But why the change in Fleming's survey? Why
The Kicking Horse and not the Yellowhead?
The national point again. The Kicking Horse
Was shorter, closer to the boundary line;
No rival road would build between the two.
He did not dwell upon the other Passes.
He promised all with surety of schedule,   810
And with a self-imposed serenity
That dried the sweat upon the Board Room faces.

NUMBER ONE

Oak Lake to Calgary. Van Horne took off
His coat. The North must wait, for that would mean
His shirt as well. First and immediate
This prairie pledge – five hundred miles, and it
Was winter. Failure of this trial promise
Would mean – no, it must not be there for meaning.
An order from him carried no repeal:
It was as final as an execution.   820
A cable started rolling mills in Europe:
A tap of Morse sent hundreds to the bush,
Where axes swung on spruce and the saws sang,
Changing the timber into pyramids
Of poles and sleepers. Clicks, despatches, words,
Like lanterns in a night conductor's hands,
Signalled the wheels: a nod put Shaughnessy
In Montreal: supplies moved on the minute.
Thousands of men and mules and horses slipped
Into their togs and harness night and day.   830
The grass that fed the buffalo was turned over,
The black alluvial mould laid bare, the bed
Levelled and scraped. As individuals
The men lost their identity; as groups,
As gangs, they massed, divided, subdivided,
Like numerals only – sub-contractors, gangs
Of engineers, and shovel gangs for bridges,
Culverts, gangs of mechanics stringing wires,
Loading, unloading and reloading gangs,
Gangs for the fish-plates and the spiking gangs,   840
Putting a silver polish on the nails.
But neither men nor horses ganged like mules:
Wiser than both they learned to unionize.
Some instinct in their racial nether regions
Had taught them how to sniff the five-hour stretch
Down to the fine arithmetic of seconds.
They tired out their rivals and they knew it.
They'd stand for overwork, not overtime.
Faster than workmen could fling down their shovels,
They could unhinge their joints, unhitch their tendons;   850
Jumping the foreman's call, they brayed *"Unhook"*
With a defiant, corporate instancy.
The promise which looked first without redemption
Was being redeemed. From three to seven miles

A day the parallels were being laid,
Though Eastern throats were hoarse with the old question –
Where are the settlements? And whence the gift
Of tongues which could pronounce place-names that purred
Like cats in relaxation after kittens?
Was it a part of the same pledge to turn   860
A shack into a bank for notes renewed;
To call a site a city when men saw
Only a water-tank? This was an act
Of faith indeed – substance of things unseen –
Which would convert preachers to miracles,
Lure teachers into lean-to's for their classes.
And yet it happened that while labourers
Were swearing at their blisters in the evening
And straightening out their spinal kinks at dawn,
The tracks joined up Oak Lake to Calgary.   870

NUMBER TWO

On the North Shore a reptile lay asleep –
A hybrid that the myths might have conceived,
But not delivered, as progenitor
Of crawling, gliding things upon the earth.
She lay snug in the folds of a huge boa
Whose tail had covered Labrador and swished
Atlantic tides, whose body coiled itself
Around the Hudson Bay, then curled up north
Through Manitoba and Saskatchewan
To Great Slave Lake. In continental reach   880
The neck went past the Great Bear Lake until
Its head was hidden in the Arctic Seas.
This folded reptile was asleep or dead:
So motionless, she seemed stone dead – just seemed:
She was too old for death, too old for life,
For as if jealous of all living forms
She had lain there before bivalves began
To catacomb their shells on western mountains.
Somewhere within this life-death zone she sprawled,
Torpid upon a rock-and-mineral mattress.   890
Ice-ages had passed by and over her,
But these, for all their motion, had but sheared
Her spotty carboniferous hair or made

Her ridges stand out like the spikes of molochs.
Her back grown stronger every million years,
She had shed water by the longer rivers
To Hudson Bay and by the shorter streams
To the great basins to the south, had filled
Them up, would keep them filled until the end
Of Time.   900

        Was this the thing Van Horne set out
To conquer? When Superior lay there
With its inviting levels? Blake, Mackenzie,
Offered this water like a postulate.
"Why those twelve thousand men sent to the North?
Nonsense and waste with utter bankruptcy."
And the Laurentian monster at the first
Was undisturbed, presenting but her bulk
To the invasion. All she had to do
Was lie there neither yielding nor resisting.   910
Top-heavy with accumulated power
And overgrown survival without function,
She changed her spots as though brute rudiments
Of feeling foreign to her native hour
Surprised her with a sense of violation
From an existence other than her own –
Or why take notice of this unknown breed,
This horde of bipeds that could toil like ants,
Could wake her up and keep her irritated?
They tickled her with shovels, dug pickaxes   920
Into her scales and got under her skin,
And potted holes in her with drills and filled
Them up with what looked like fine grains of sand,
Black sand. It wasn't noise that bothered her,
For thunder she was used to from her cradle –
The head-push and nose-blowing of the ice,
The height and pressure of its body: these
Like winds native to clime and habitat
Had served only to lull her drowsing coils.
It was not size or numbers that concerned her.   930
It was their foreign build, their gait of movement.
They did not crawl – nor were they born with wings.
They stood upright and walked, shouted and sang;
They needed air – that much was true – their mouths
Were open but the tongue was alien.

The sounds were not the voice of winds and waters,
Nor that of any beasts upon the earth.
She took them first with lethargy, suffered
The rubbing of her back — those little jabs
Of steel were like the burrowing of ticks   940
In an elk's hide needing an antler point,
Or else left in a numb monotony.
These she could stand but when the breed
Advanced west on her higher vertebrae,
Kicking most insolently at her ribs,
Pouring black powder in her cavities,
And making not the clouds but her insides
The home of fire and thunder, then she gave
Them trial of her strength: the trestles tottered;
Abutments, bridges broke; her rivers flooded: 950
She summoned snow and ice, and then fell back
On the last weapon in her armoury —
The first and last — her passive corporal bulk,
To stay or wreck the schedule of Van Horne.

NUMBER THREE

The big one was the mountains — seas indeed!
With crests whiter than foam: they poured like seas,
Fluting the green banks of the pines and spruces.
An eagle-flight above they hid themselves
In clouds. They carried space upon their ledges.
Could these be overridden frontally,   960
Or like typhoons outsmarted on the flanks?
And what were on the flanks? The troughs and canyons,
Passes more dangerous to the navigator
Than to Magellan when he tried to read
The barbarous language of his Strait by calling
For echoes from the rocky hieroglyphs
Playing their pranks of hide-and-seek in fog:
As stubborn too as the old North-West Passage,
More difficult, for ice-packs could break up;
And as for bergs, what polar architect   970
Could stretch his compass points to draught such peaks
As kept on rising there beyond the foothills?
And should the bastions of the Rockies yield
To this new human and unnatural foe,
Would not the Selkirks stand? This was a range

That looked like some strange dread outside a door
Which gave its name but would not show its features,
Leaving them to the mind to guess at. This
Meant tunnels — would there be no end to boring?
There must be some day. Fleming and his men   980
Had nosed their paths like hounds; but paths and trails,
Measured in every inch by chain and transit,
Looked easy and seductive on a chart.
The rivers out there did not flow: they tumbled.
The cataracts were fed by glaciers;
Eddies were thought as whirlpools in the Gorges,
And gradients had paws that tore up tracks.

Terror and beauty like twin signal flags
Flew on the peaks for men to keep their distance.
The two combined as in a storm at sea —   990
"Stay on the shore and take your fill of breathing,
But come not to the decks and climb the rigging."
The Ranges could put cramps in hands and feet
Merely by the suggestion of the venture.
They needed miles to render up their beauty,
As if the gods in high aesthetic moments,
Resenting the profanity of touch,
Chiselled this sculpture for the eye alone.

(Van Horne in momentary meditation at the Foothills.)

His name was now a legend. The North Shore,
Though not yet conquered, yet had proved that he   1000
Could straighten crooked roads by pulling at them,
Shear down a hill and drain a bog or fill
A valley overnight. Fast as a bobcat,
He'd climb and run across the shakiest trestle
Or, with a locomotive short of coal,
He could supply the head of steam himself.
He breakfasted on bridges, lunched on ties;
Drinking from gallon pails, he dined on moose.
He could tire out the lumberjacks; beat hell
From workers but no more than from himself.   1010
Only the devil or Paul Bunyan shared
With him the secret of perpetual motion,
And when he moved among his men they looked
For shoulder sprouts upon the Flying Dutchman.

But would his legend crack upon the mountains?
There must be no retreat: his bugles knew
Only one call — the summons to advance
Against two fortresses: the mind, the rock.
To prove the first defence was vulnerable,
To tap the treasury at home and then   1020
Untie the purse-strings of the Londoners,
As hard to loosen as salt-water knots —
That job was Stephen's, Smith's, Tupper's, Macdonald's.
He knew its weight: had heard, as well as they,
Blake pumping at his pulmonary bellows,
And if the speeches made the House shock-proof
Before they ended, they could still peal forth
From print more durable than spoken tones.
Blake had returned to the attack and given
Sir John the ague with another phrase   1030
As round and as melodious as the first:
"The Country's wealth, its millions after millions
Squandered — LOST IN THE GORGES OF THE FRASER":
A beautiful but ruinous piece of music
That could only be drowned with drums and fifes.
Tupper, fighting with fists and nails and toes,
Had taken the word *scandal* which had cut
His master's ballots, and had turned the edge
With his word *slander,* but Blake's *sea,* how turn
That edge? Now this last devastating phrase!   1040
But let Sir John and Stephen answer this
Their way. Van Horne must answer it in his.

INTERNECINE STRIFE

The men were fighting foes which had themselves
Waged elemental civil wars and still
Were hammering one another at this moment.
The peaks and ranges flung from ocean beds
Had wakened up one geologic morning
To find their scalps raked off, their lips punched in,
The colour of their skins charged with new dyes.
Some of them did not wake or but half-woke;   1050
Prone or recumbent with the eerie shapes
Of creatures that would follow them. Weather
Had acted on their spines and frozen them

To stegosaurs or, taking longer cycles,
Divining human features, had blown back
Their hair and, pressing on their cheeks and temples,
Bestowed on them the gravity of mummies.
But there was life and power which belied
The tombs. Guerrilla evergreens were climbing
In military order: at the base   1060
The *ponderosa* pine; the fir backed up
The spruce; and it the Stoney Indian lodge-poles;
And these the white-barks; then, deciduous,
The outpost suicidal Lyell larches
Aiming at summits, digging scraggy roots
Around the boulders in the thinning soil,
Till they were stopped dead at the timber limit —
Rock *versus* forest with the rock prevailing.
Or with the summer warmth it was the ice,
In treaty with the rock to hold a line   1070
As stubborn as a Balkan boundary,
That left its caves to score the Douglases,
And smother them with half a mile of dirt,
And making snow-sheds, covering the camps,
Futile as parasols in polar storms.
One enemy alone had battled rock
And triumphed: searching levels like lost broods,
Keen on their ocean scent, the rivers cut
The quartzite, licked the slate and softened it,
Till mud solidified was mud again,   1080
And then, digesting it like earthworms, squirmed
Along the furrows with one steering urge —
To navigate the mountains in due time
Back to their home in worm-casts on the tides.

Into this scrimmage came the fighting men,
And all but rivers were their enemies.
Whether alive or dead the bush resisted:
Alive, it must be slain with axe and saw,
If dead, it was in tangle at their feet.
The ice could hit men as it hit the spruces.   1090
Even the rivers had betraying tricks,
Watched like professed allies across a border.
They smiled from fertile plains and easy runs
Of valley gradients: their eyes got narrow,
Full of suspicion at the gorges where

They leaped and put the rickets in the trestles.
Though natively in conflict with the rock,
Both leagued against invasion. At Hell's Gate
A mountain laboured and brought forth a bull
Which, stranded in mid-stream, was fighting back   1100
The river, and the fight turned on the men,
Demanding from this route their bread and steel.
And there below the Gate was the Black Canyon
With twenty-miles-an-hour burst of speed.

(ONDERDONK BUILDS THE "SKUZZY"
TO FORCE THE PASSAGE.)

'Twas more than navigation: only eagles
Might follow up this run; the spawning salmon
Gulled by the mill-race had returned to rot
Their upturned bellies in the canyon eddies.
Two engines at the stern, a forrard winch,
Steam-powered, failed to stem the cataract.   1110
The last resource was shoulders, arms and hands.
Fifteen men at the capstan, creaking hawsers,
Two hundred Chinese tugging at shore ropes
To keep her bow-on from the broadside drift,
The *Skuzzy* under steam and muscle took
The shoals and rapids, and warped through the Gate,
Until she reached the navigable water –
The adventure was not sailing: it was climbing.

As hard a challenge were the precipices
Worn water-smooth and sheer a thousand feet.   1120
Surveyors from the edges looked for footholds,
But, finding none, they tried marine manoeuvres.
Out of a hundred men they drafted sailors
Whose toes as supple as their fingers knew
The wash of reeling decks, whose knees were hardened
Through tying gaskets at the royal yards:
They lowered them with knotted ropes and drew them
Along the face until the lines were strung
Between the juts. Barefooted, dynamite
Strapped to their waists, the sappers followed, treading   1130
The spider films and chipping holes for blasts,
Until the cliffs delivered up their features
Under the civil discipline of roads.

RING, RING THE BELLS

Ring, ring the bells, but not the engine bells:
Today only the ritual of the steeple
Chanted to the dull tempo of the toll.
Sorrow is stalking through the camps, speaking
A common mother-tongue. 'Twill leave tomorrow
To turn that language on a Blackfoot tepee,
Then take its leisurely Pacific time 1140
To tap its fingers on a coolie's door.
Ring, ring the bells but not the engine bells:
Today only that universal toll,
For granite, mixing dust with human lime,
Had so compounded bodies into boulders
As to untype the blood, and, then, the Fraser,
Catching the fragments from the dynamite,
Had bleached all birthmarks from her swirling dead.

Tomorrow and the engine bells again!

THE LAKE OF MONEY

(The appeal to the Government for a loan of
twenty-two-and-a-half million, 1883.)

Sir John began to muse on his excuses. 1150
Was there no bottom to this lake? One mile
Along that northern strip had cost – how much?
Eleven dollars to the inch. The Road
In all would measure up to ninety millions,
And diverse hands were plucking at his elbow.
The Irish and the Dutch he could outface,
Outquip. He knew Van Horne and Shaughnessy
Had little time for speeches – one was busy
In grinding out two thousand miles; the other
Was working wizardry on creditors, 1160
Pulling rabbits from hats, gold coins from sleeves
In Montreal. As for his foes like Blake,
He thanked his household gods the Irishman
Could claim only a viscous brand of humour,
Heavy, impenetrable till the hour
To laugh had taken on a chestnut colour.

But Stephen was his friend, hard to resist.
And there was Smith. He knew that both had pledged
Their private fortunes as security
For the construction of the Road. But that   1170
Was not enough. Sir John had yet to dip
And scrape farther into the public pocket,
Explore its linings: his, the greater task;
His, to commit a nation to the risk.
How could he face the House with pauper hands?
He had to deal with Stephen first — a man
Laconic, nailing points and clinching them.
Oratory, the weapon of the massed assemblies
Was not the weapon here — Scot meeting Scot.
The burr was hard to take; and Stephen had   1180
A Banffshire-cradled *r*. Drilling the ear,
It paralysed the nerves, hit the red cells.
The logic in the sound, escaping print,
Would seep through channels and befog the cortex.

Sir John counted the exits of discretion:
Disguise himself? A tailor might do much;
A barber might trim down his mane, brush back
The forelock, but no artist of massage,
Kneading that face from brow to nasal tip,
Could change a chunk of granite into talc.   1190
His rheumatism? Yet he still could walk.
Neuralgia did not interfere with speech.
The bronchial tubing needed softer air?
Vacations could not cancel all appointments.
Men saw him in the flesh at Ottawa.
He had to speak this week, wheedling committees,
Much easier than to face a draper's clerk,
Tongue-trained on Aberdonian bargain-counters.
He raised his closed left hand to straighten out
His fingers one by one — four million people.   1200
He had to pull a trifle on that fourth,
Not so resilient as the other three.
Only a wrench could stir the little finger
Which answered with a vicious backward jerk.

The dollar fringes of one hundred million
Were smirching up the blackboard of his mind.
But curving round and through them was the thought

He could not sponge away. Had he not fathered
The Union? Prodigy indeed it was
From Coast to Coast. Was not the Line essential?   1210
What was this fungus sprouting from his rind
That left him at the root less clear a growth
Than this Dutch immigrant, William Van Horne?
The name suggested artificial land
Rescued from swamp by bulging dikes and ditches;
And added now to that were bogs and sloughs
And that most cursèd diabase which God
Had left from the explosions of his wrath.
And yet this man was challenging his pride.
North-Sea ancestral moisture on his beard,   1220
Van Horne was now the spokesman for the West,
The champion of an all-Canadian route,
The Yankee who had come straight over, linked
His name and life with the Canadian nation.
Besides, he had infected the whole camp.
Whether acquired or natural, the stamp
Of faith had never left his face. Was it
The artist's instinct which had made the Rockies
And thence the Selkirks, scenes of tourist lure,
As easy for the passage of an engine   1230
As for the flight of eagles? Miracles
Became his thought: the others took their cue
From him. They read the lines upon his lips.
But miracles did not spring out of air.
Under the driving will and sweltering flesh
They came from pay-cars loaded with the cash.
So that was why Stephen had called so often –
Money – that lake of money, bonds, more bonds.

(The Bill authorizing the loan stubbornly carries the House.)

DYNAMITE ON THE NORTH SHORE

The lizard was in sanguinary mood.
She had been waked again: she felt her sleep   1240
Had lasted a few seconds of her time.
The insects had come back – the ants, if ants
They were – dragging *those* trees, *those* logs athwart
Her levels, driving in *those* spikes; and how

The long grey snakes unknown within her region
Wormed from the east, unstriped, sunning themselves
Uncoiled upon the logs and then moved on,
Growing each day, ever keeping abreast!
She watched them, waiting for a bloody moment,
Until the borers halted at a spot,   1250
The most invulnerable of her whole column,
Drove in that iron, wrenched it in the holes,
Hitting, digging, twisting. Why that spot?
Not this the former itch. That sharp proboscis
Was out for more than self-sufficing blood
About the cuticle: 'twas out for business
In the deep layers and the arteries.

And this consistent punching at her belly
With fire and thunder slapped her like an insult,
As with the blasts the caches of her broods   1260
Broke – nickel, copper, silver and fool's gold,
Burst from their immemorial dormitories
To sprawl indecent in the light of day.
Another warning – this time different.

Westward above her webs she had a trap –
A thing called muskeg, easy on the eyes
Stung with the dust of gravel. Cotton grass,
Its white spires blending with the orchids,
Peeked through green table-cloths of sphagnum moss.
Carnivorous bladder-wort studded the acres,   1270
Passing the water-fleas through their digestion.
Sweet-gale and sundew edged the dwarf black spruce;
And herds of cariboo had left their hoof-marks,
Betraying visual solidity,
But like the thousands of the pitcher plants,
Their downward-pointing hairs alluring insects,
Deceptive – and the men were moving west!
Now was her time. She took three engines, sank them
With seven tracks down through the hidden lake
To the rock bed, then over them she spread   1280
A counterpane of leather-leaf and slime.
A warning, that was all for now. 'Twas sleep
She wanted, sleep, for drowsing was her pastime
And waiting through eternities of seasons.
As for intruders bred for skeletons –

Some day perhaps when ice began to move,
Or some convulsion ran fires through her tombs,
She might stir in her sleep and far below
The reach of steel and blast of dynamite,
She'd claim their bones as her possessive right   1290
And wrap them cold in her pre-Cambrian folds.

THREATS OF SECESSION

The Lady's face was flushed. Thirteen years now
Since that engagement ring adorned her finger!
Adorned? Betrayed. She often took it off
And flung it angrily upon the dresser,
Then took excursions with her sailor-lover.
Had that man with a throat like Ottawa,
That tailored suitor in a cut-away,
Presumed compliance on her part? High time
To snub him for delay – for was not time   1300
The marrow of agreement? At the mirror
She tried to cream a wrinkle from her forehead,
Toyed with the ring, replaced it and removed it.
Harder, she thought, to get it on and off –
This like the wrinkle meant but one thing, age.
So not too fast; play safe. Perhaps the man
Was not the master of his choice. Someone
Within the family group might well contest
Exotic marriage. Still, her plumes were ruffled
By Blake's two-nights' address before the Commons: 1310
Three lines inside the twenty-thousand words
Had maddened her. She searched for hidden meanings –
"Should she insist on those preposterous terms
And threaten to secede, then let her go,
Better than ruin the country." "Let her go,"
And *"ruin"* – language this to shake her bodice.
Was this indictment of her character,
Or worse, her charm? Or was it just plain dowry?
For this last one at least she had an answer.
Pay now or separation – this the threat.   1320
Dipping the ring into a soapy lather,
She pushed it to the second knuckle, twirled
It past. Although the diamond was off-colour,
She would await its partner ring of gold –
The finest carat; yes, by San Francisco!

BACK TO THE MOUNTAINS

As grim an enemy as rock was time.
The little men from five-to-six feet high,
From three-to-four score years in lease of breath,
Were flung in double-front against them both
In years a billion strong; so long was it   1330
Since brachiapods in mollusc habitats
Were clamping shells on weed in ocean mud.
Now only yesterday had Fleming's men,
Searching for toeholds on the sides of cliffs,
Five thousand feet above sea-level, set
A tripod's leg upon a trilobite.
And age meant pressure, density. Sullen
With aeons, mountains would not stand aside;
Just block the path – morose but without anger,
No feeling in the menace of their frowns,   1340
Immobile for they had no need of motion;
Their veins possessed no blood – they carried quartzite.
Frontal assault! To go through them direct
Seemed just as inconceivable as ride
Over their peaks. But go through them the men
Were ordered and their weapons were their hands
And backs, pickaxes, shovels, hammers, drills
And dynamite – against the rock and time;
For here the labour must be counted up
In months subject to clauses of a contract   1350
Distinguished from the mortgage-run an age
Conceded to the trickle of the rain
In building river-homes. The men bored in,
The mesozoic rock arguing the inches.

This was a kind of surgery unknown
To mountains or the mothers of the myths.
These had a chloroform in leisured time,
Squeezing a swollen handful of light-seconds,
When water like a wriggling casuist
Had probed and found the areas for incision.   1360
Now time was rushing labour – inches grew
To feet, to yards: the drills – the single jacks,
The double jacks – drove in and down; the holes
Gave way to excavations, these to tunnels,
Till men sodden with mud and roof-drip steamed
From sunlight through the tar-black to the sunlight.

HOLLOW ECHOES FROM THE TREASURY VAULT

Sir John was tired as to the point of death.
His chin was anchored to his chest. Was Blake
Right after all? And was Mackenzie right?
Superior could be travelled on. Besides,   1370
It had a bottom, but those northern bogs
Like quicksands could go down to the earth's core.
Compared with them, quagmires of ancient legend
Were backyard puddles for old ducks. To sink
Those added millions down that wallowing hole!
He thought now through his feet. Many a time
When argument cemented opposition,
And hopeless seemed his case, he could think up
A tale to laugh the benches to accord.
No one knew better, when a point had failed   1380
The brain, how to divert it through the ribs.
But now his stock of stories had run out.
This was exhaustion at its coma level.
Or was he sick? Never had spots like these
Assailed his eyes. He could not rub them out –
Those shifting images – was it the sunset
Refracted through the bevelled window edges?
He shambled over and drew down the blind;
Returned and slumped; it was no use; the spots
Were there. No light could ever shoot this kind   1390
Of orange through a prism, or this blue,
And what a green! The spectrum was ruled out;
Its bands were too inviolate. He rubbed
The lids again – a brilliant gold appeared
Upon a silken backdrop of pure white,
And in the centre, red – a scarlet red,
A dancing, rampant and rebellious red
That like a stain spread outward covering
The vision field. He closed his eyes and listened:
Why, what was that? 'Twas bad enough that light   1400
Should play such pranks upon him, but must sound
Crash the Satanic game, reverberate
A shot fifteen years after it was fired,
And culminate its echoes with the thud
Of marching choruses outside his window:

"We'll hang Riel up the Red River,
And he'll roast in hell forever,

We'll hang him up the River
With a yah-yah-yah."

The noose was for the shot: 'twas blood for blood;   1410
The death of Riel for the death of Scott.
What could not Blake do with that on the Floor,
Or that young, tall, bilingual advocate
Who with the carriage of his syllables
Could bid an audience like an orchestra
Answer his body swaying like a reed?
Colours and sounds made riot of his mind –
White horses in July processional prance,
The blackrobe's swish, the Métis' sullen tread,
And out there in the rear the treaty-wise   1420
Full-breeds with buffalo wallows on their foreheads.

This he could stand no longer, sick indeed:
Send for his doctor, the first thought, then No;
The doctor would advise an oculist,
The oculist return him to the doctor,
The doctor would see-saw him to another –
A specialist on tumours of the brain,
And he might recommend close-guarded rest
In some asylum – Devil take them all,
He had his work to do. He glanced about   1430
And spied his medicine upon the sideboard;
Amber it was, distilled from Highland springs,
That often had translated age to youth
And boiled his blood on a victorious rostrum.
Conviction seized him as he stood, for here
At least he was not cut for compromise,
Nor curried to his nickname Old Tomorrow.
Deliberation in his open stance,
He trenched a deep one, gurgled and sat down.
What were those paltry millions after all?   1440
They stood between completion of the Road
And bankruptcy of both Road and Nation.
Those north-shore gaps must be closed in by steel.
It did not need exhilarated judgment
To see the sense of that. To send the men
Hop-skip-and-jump upon lake ice to board
The flatcars was a revelry for imps.
And all that cutting through the mountain rock,

Four years of it and more, and all for nothing,
Unless those gaps were spanned, bedded and railed.   1450
To quit the Road, to have the Union broken
Was irredeemable. He rose, this time
Invincibility carved on his features,
Hoisted a second, then drew up the blind.
He never saw a sunset just like this.
He lingered in the posture of devotion:
That sun for sure was in the west, or was it?
Soon it would be upholstering the clouds
Upon the Prairies, Rockies and the Coast:
He turned and sailed back under double-reef,   1460
Cabined himself inside an armchair, stretched
His legs to their full length under the table.
Something miraculous had changed the air –
A chemistry that knew how to extract
The iron from the will: the spots had vanished
And in their place an unterrestrial nimbus
Circled his hair: the jerks had left his nerves:
The millions kept on shrinking or were running
From right to left: the fourth arthritic digit
Was straight, and yes, by heaven, the little fifth   1470
Which up to now was just a calcium hook
Was suppling in the Hebridean warmth.
A blessèd peace fell like a dew upon him,
And soon, in trance, drenched in conciliation,
He hiccuped gently – *"Now let S-S-Stephen come!"*

*(The Government grants the Directors the right
to issue $35,000,000, guarantees $20,000,000, the
rest to be issued by the Railway Directors.
Stephen goes to London, and Lord Revelstoke,
speaking for the House of Baring, takes over the
issue.)*

SUSPENSE IN THE MONTREAL BOARD ROOM

Evening had settled hours before its time
Within the Room and on the face of Angus.
Dejection overlaid his social fur,
Rumpled his side-burns, left moustache untrimmed.
The vision of his Bank, his future Shops,   1480

Was like his outlook for the London visit.
Van Horne was fronting him with a like visage
Except for two spots glowing on his cheeks –
Dismay and anger at those empty pay-cars.
His mutterings were indistinct but final
As though he were reciting to himself
The Athanasian damnatory clauses.
He felt the Receiver's breath upon his neck:
To come so near the end, and then this hurdle!

Only one thing could penetrate that murk –   1490
A cable pledge from London, would it come?
Till now refusal or indifference
Had met the overtures. Would Stephen turn
The trick?
           A door-knock and a telegram
With Stephen's signature! Van Horne ripped it
Apart. Articulation failed his tongue,
But Angus got the meaning from his face
And from a noisy sequence of deductions: –
An inkstand coasted through the office window,   1500
Followed by shredded maps and blotting-pads,
Fluttering like shad-flies in a summer gale;
A bookshelf smitten by a fist collapsed;
Two chairs flew to the ceiling – one retired,
The other roosted on the chandelier.
Some thirty years erased like blackboard chalk,
Van Horne was in a school at Illinois.
Triumphant over his two-hundred weight,
He leaped and turned a cartwheel on the table,
Driving heel sparables into the oak,   1510
Came down to teach his partner a Dutch dance;
And in the presence of the messenger,
Who stared immobilized at what he thought
New colours in the managerial picture,
Van Horne took hold of Angus bodily,
Tore off his tie and collar, mauled his shirt,
And stuffed a Grand Trunk folder down his breeches.

*(The last gap in the mountains – between the
Selkirks and Savona's Ferry – is closed.)*

The Road itself was like a stream that men
Had coaxed and teased or bullied out of Nature.
As if watching for weak spots in her codes,   1520
It sought for levels like the watercourses.
It sinuously took the bends, rejoiced
In plains and easy grades, found gaps, poured through them,
But hating steep descents avoided them.
Unlike the rivers which in full rebellion
Against the canyons' hydrophobic slaver
Went to the limit of their argument:
Unlike again, the stream of steel had found
A way to climb, became a mountaineer.
From the Alberta plains it reached the Summit,   1530
And where it could not climb, it cut and curved,
Till from the Rockies to the Coastal Range
It had accomplished what the Rivers had,
Making a hundred clean Caesarian cuts,
And bringing to delivery in their time
Their smoky, lusty-screaming locomotives.

THE SPIKE

Silver or gold? Van Horne had rumbled *"Iron"*.
No flags or bands announced this ceremony,
No Morse in circulation through the world,
And though the vital words like Eagle Pass,   1540
Craigellachie, were trembling in their belfries,
No hands were at the ropes. The air was taut
With silences as rigid as the spruces
Forming the background in November mist.
More casual than camera-wise, the men
Could have been properties upon a stage,
Except for road maps furrowing their faces.

Rogers, his both feet planted on a tie,
Stood motionless as ballast. In the rear,
Covering the scene with spirit-level eyes,   1550
Predestination on his chin, was Fleming.
The only one groomed for the ritual
From smooth silk hat and well-cut square-rig beard

Down through his Caledonian longitude,
He was outstanding others by a foot,
And upright as the mainmast of a brig.
Beside him, barely reaching to his waist,
A water-boy had wormed his way in front
To touch this last rail with his foot, his face
Upturned to see the cheek-bone crags of Rogers.   1560
The other side of Fleming, hands in pockets,
Eyes leaden-lidded under square-crowned hat,
And puncheon-bellied under overcoat,
Unsmiling at the focused lens – Van Horne.
Whatever ecstasy played round that rail
Did not leap to his face. Five years had passed,
Less than five years – so well within the pledge.

The job was done. Was this the slouch of rest?
Not to the men he drove through walls of granite.
The embers from the past were in his soul,   1570
Banked for the moment at the rail and smoking,
Just waiting for the future to be blown.

At last the spike and Donald with the hammer!
His hair like frozen moss from Labrador
Poked out under his hat, ran down his face
To merge with streaks of rust in a white cloud.
What made him fumble the first stroke? Not age:
The snow belied his middle sixties. Was
It lapse of caution or his sense of thrift,
That elemental stuff which through his life   1580
Never pockmarked his daring but had made
The man the canniest trader of his time,
Who never missed a rat-count, never failed
To gauge the size and texture of a pelt?
Now here he was caught by the camera,
Back bent, head bowed, and staring at a sledge,
Outwitted by an idiotic nail.
Though from the crowd no laughter, yet the spike
With its slewed neck was grinning up at Smith.
Wrenched out, it was replaced. This time the hammer   1590
Gave a first tap as with apology,
Another one, another, till the spike
Was safely stationed in the tie and then

The Scot, invoking his ancestral clan,
Using the hammer like a battle-axe,
His eyes bloodshot with memories of Flodden,
Descended on it, rammed it to its home.

*　　　*　　　*

The stroke released a trigger for a burst
Of sound that stretched the gamut of the air.
The shouts of engineers and dynamiters,   1600
Of locomotive-workers and explorers,
Flanking the rails, were but a tuning-up
For a massed continental chorus. Led
By Moberly (of the Eagles and *this* Pass)
And Rogers (of *his own*), followed by Wilson,
And Ross (charged with the Rocky Mountain Section),
By Egan (general of the Western Lines),
Cambie and Marcus Smith, Harris of Boston,
The roar was deepened by the bass of Fleming,
And heightened by the laryngeal fifes   1610
Of Dug McKenzie and John H. McTavish.
It ended when Van Horne spat out some phlegm
To ratify the tumult with *"Well Done"*
Tied in a knot of monosyllables.

Merely the tuning up! For on the morrow
The last blow on the spike would stir the mould
Under the drumming of the prairie wheels,
And make the whistles from the steam out-crow
The Fraser. Like a gavel it would close
Debate, making Macdonald's *"sea to sea"*   1620
Pour through two oceanic megaphones –
Three thousand miles of *Hail* from port to port;
And somewhere in the middle of the line
Of steel, even the lizard heard the stroke.
The breed had triumphed after all. To drown
The traffic chorus, she must blend the sound
With those inaugural, narcotic notes
Of storm and thunder which would send her back
Deeper than ever in Laurentian sleep.

(1952)   (1962)

Ethel Wilson
1890 –

———◆———

BORN IN PORT Elizabeth, South Africa, Ethel (Bryant) Wilson spent her
early childhood in England; following the death of her parents in 1898,
she came to live with relatives in Vancouver. After completing her
education in England and Vancouver she worked as an elementary
school teacher until her marriage in 1920, Wilson began publishing in
1937 and has since written several novels and short stories including
Hetty Dorval (1947), *Swamp Angel* (1954) and *Mrs. Golightly and Other
Stories* (1961). "The Window" first appeared in *Tamarack Review* in
1958.

The Window

THE GREAT BIG window must have been at least twenty-five feet wide
and ten feet high. It was constructed in sections divided by segments of
something that did not interfere with the view; in fact the eye bypassed
these divisions and looked only at the entrancing scenes beyond. The
window, together with a glass door at the western end, composed a
bland shallow curve and formed the entire transparent north-west (but
chiefly north) wall of Mr. Willy's living-room.

Upon his arrival from England Mr. Willy had surveyed the various
prospects of living in the quickly growing city of Vancouver with the
selective and discarding characteristics which had enabled him to make
a fortune and retire all of a sudden from business and his country in his
advanced middle age. He settled immediately upon the very house. It
was a small old house overlooking the sea between Spanish Banks and
English Bay. He knocked out the north wall and made the window.
There was nothing particular to commend the house except that it
faced immediately on the seashore and the view. Mr. Willy had left his
wife and her three sisters to play bridge together until death should
overtake them in England. He now paced from end to end of his
living-room, that is to say from east to west, with his hands in his
pockets, admiring the northern view. Sometimes he stood with his
hands behind him looking through the great glass window, seeing the
wrinkled or placid sea and the ships almost at his feet and beyond the
sea the mountains, and seeing sometimes his emancipation. His emancipation drove him into a dream, and sea sky mountain swam before
him, vanished, and he saw with immense release his wife in still another

more repulsive hat. He did not know, nor would he have cared, that much discussion went on in her world, chiefly in the afternoons, and that he was there alleged to have deserted her. So he had, after providing well for her physical needs which were all the needs of which she was capable. Mrs. Willy went on saying '...and he would come home my dear and never speak a word I can't tell you my dear how frightful it was night after night I might say for *years* I simply can't tell you....' No, she could not tell but she did, by day and night. Here he was at peace, seeing out of the window the crimped and wrinkled sea and the ships which passed and passed each other, the seabirds and the dream-inducing sky.

At the extreme left curve of the window an island appeared to slope into the sea. Behind this island and to the north, the mountains rose very high. In the summer time the mountains were soft, deceptive in their innocency, full of crags and crevasses and *arêtes* and danger. In the winter they lay magnificent, white and much higher, it seemed, than in the summer time. They tossed, static, in almost visible motion against the sky, inhabited only by eagles and – so a man had told Mr. Willy, but he didn't believe this man – by mountain sheep and some cougars, bears, wild cats and, certainly, on the lower slopes, deer, and now a ski camp far out of sight. Mr. Willy looked at the mountains and regretted his past youth and his present wealth. How could he endure to be old and rich and able only to look at these mountains which in his youth he had not known and did not climb. Nothing, now, no remnant of his youth would come and enable him to climb these mountains. This he found hard to believe, as old people do. He was shocked at the newly realized decline of his physical powers which had proved good enough on the whole for his years of success, and by the fact that now he had, at last, time and could not swim (heart), climb mountains (heart and legs), row a boat in a rough enticing sea (call that old age). These things have happened to other people, thought Mr. Willy, but not to us, now, who have been so young, and yet it will happen to those who now are young.

Immediately across the water were less spectacular mountains, pleasant slopes which in winter time were covered with invisible skiers. Up the dark mountain at night sprang the lights of the ski-lift, and ceased. The shores of these mountains were strung with lights, littered with lights, spangled with lights, necklaces, bracelets, constellations, far more beautiful as seen through this window looking across the dark water than if Mr. Willy had driven his car across the Lions' Gate Bridge and westwards among those constellations which would have disclosed a shopping centre, people walking in the streets, street lights, innumerable cars and car lights like anywhere else and, up the slopes, peoples' houses. Then, looking back to the south across the dark water towards his own home and the great lighted window which he could not distinguish so far away, Mr. Willy would see lights again, a carpet of glitter thrown over the slopes of the city.

Fly from one shore to the other, fly and fly back again, fly to a continent or to an island, but you are no better off than if you stayed all day at your own window (and such a window), thought Mr. Willy pacing back and forth, then into the kitchen to put the kettle on for a cup of tea which he will drink beside the window, back for a glass of whisky, returning in time to see a cormorant flying level with the water, not an inch too high not an inch too low, flying out of sight. See the small ducks lying on the water, one behind the other, like beads on a string. In the mornings Mr. Willy drove into town to see his investment broker and perhaps to the bank or round the park. He lunched, but not at a club. He then drove home. On certain days a woman called Mrs. Ogden came in to 'do' for him. This was his daily life, very simple, and a routine was formed whose pattern could at last be discerned by an interested observer outside the window.

One night Mr. Willy beheld a vast glow arise behind the mountains. The Arctic world was obviously on fire – but no, the glow was not fire glow, flame glow. The great invasion of colour that spread up and up the sky was not red, was not rose, but of a synthetic cyclamen colour. This cyclamen glow remained steady from mountain to zenith and caused Mr. Willy, who had never seen the Northern Lights, to believe that these were not Northern Lights but that something had occurred for which one must be prepared. After about an hour, flanges of green as of putrefaction, and a melodious yellow arose and spread. An hour later the Northern Lights faded , leaving Mr. Willy small and alone.

Sometimes as, sitting beside the window, he drank his tea, Mr. Willy thought that nevertheless it is given to few people to be as happy (or contented, he would say) as he was, at his age, too. In his life of decisions, men, pressures, more men, antagonisms, fusions, fissions and Mrs. Willy, in his life of hard success, that is, he had sometimes looked forward but so vaguely and rarely to a time when he would not only put this life down: he would leave it. Now he had left it and here he was by his window. As time went on, though, he had to make an effort to summon this happiness, for it seemed to elude him. Sometimes a thought or a shape (was it), gray, like wood ash that falls in pieces when it is touched, seemed to be behind his chair, and this shape teased him and communicated to him that he had left humanity behind, that a man needs humanity and that if he ceases to be in touch with man and is not in touch with God, he does not matter. You do not matter any more, said the spectre, like wood ash before it fell to pieces, because you are no longer in touch with any one and so you do not exist. You are in a vacuum and so you are nothing. Then Mr. Willy, at first uneasy, became satisfied again for a time after being made uneasy by the spectre. A storm would get up and the wind, howling well, would lash the window sometimes carrying the salt spray from a very high tide which it flung against the great panes of glass. That was a satisfaction to Mr. Willy and within him something stirred and rose and met the storm and effaced the spectre and other phantoms which were really vague regrets. But the worst that happened against the window was that from time to time a little bird, sometimes but not often a seabird, flung itself like a stone against the strong glass of the window and fell, killed by the passion of its flight. This grieved Mr. Willy, and he could not sit unmoved when the bird flew at the clear glass and was met by death. When this happened, he arose from his chair, opened the glass door at the far end of the window, descended three or four steps, and sought in the grasses for the body of the bird. But the bird was dead, or it was dying, its small bones were smashed, its head was broken, its beak split, it was killed by the rapture of its flight. Only once Mr. Willy found the bird a little stunned and picked it up. He cupped the bird's body in his hands and carried it into the house.

Looking up through the grasses at the edge of the rough terrace that descended to the beach, a man watched him return into the house, carrying the bird. Still looking obliquely through the grasses the man watched Mr. Willy enter the room and vanish from view. Then Mr. Willy came again to the door, pushed it open, and released the bird which flew away, who knows where. He closed the door, locked it, and sat down on the chair facing east beside the window and began to read his newspaper. Looking over his paper he saw, to the east, the city of Vancouver deployed over rising ground with low roofs and high buildings and at the apex the tall Electric Building which at night shone like a broad shaft of golden light.

This time, as evening drew on, the man outside went away because he had other business.

Mr. Willy's investment broker was named Gerald Wardho. After a time he said to Mr. Willy in a friendly but respectful way 'Will you have lunch with me at the Club tomorrow?' and Mr. Willy said he would. Some time later Gerald Wardho said 'Would you like me to put you up at the Club?'

Mr. Willy considered a little the life which he had left and did not want to re-enter and also the fact that he had only last year resigned his memberships in three clubs, so he said 'That's very good of you, Wardho, but I think not. I'm enjoying things as they are. It's a novelty, living in a vacuum ... I like it, for a time anyway.'

'Yes, but,' said Gerald Wardho, 'you'd be some time on the waiting list. It wouldn't hurt — '

'No,' said Mr. Willy, 'no.'

Mr. Willy had, Wardho thought, a distinguished appearance or perhaps it was an affable accustomed air, and so he had. When Mrs. Wardho said to her husband 'Gerry, there's not an extra man in this town and I need a man for Saturday,' Gerald Wardho said 'I know a man. There's Willy.'

Mrs. Wardho said doubtfully 'Willy? Willy who? Who's Willy?'

Her husband said 'He's fine, he's okay, I'll ask Willy.'

'How old is he?

'About a hundred...but he's okay.'

'Oh-h-h,' said Mrs. Wardho, 'isn't there anyone anywhere unattached young any more? Does he play bridge?'

'I'll invite him, I'll find out,' said her husband, and Mr. Willy said he'd like to come to dinner.

'Do you care for a game of bridge, Mr. Willy?' asked Gerald Wardho.

'I'm afraid not,' said Mr. Willy kindly but firmly. He played a good game of bridge but had no intention of entering servitude again just yet, losing his freedom, and being enrolled as what is called a fourth. Perhaps later; not yet. 'If you're having bridge I'll come another time. Very kind of you Wardho.'

'No no no,' said Gerald Wardho, 'there'll only be maybe a table of bridge for anyone who wants to play. My wife would be disappointed.'

'Well thank you very much. Black tie?'

'Yes, Black tie,' said Gerald Wardho.

And so, whether he would or no, Mr. Willy found himself invited to the kind of evening parties to which he had been accustomed and which he had left behind, given by people younger and more animated than himself, and he realized that he was on his way to becoming old odd man out. There was a good deal of wood ash at these parties – that is, behind him the spectre arose, falling to pieces when he looked at it, and said So this is what you came to find out on this coast, so far from home, is it, or is there something else. What else is there? The spectre was not always present at these parties but sometimes awaited him at home and said these things.

One night Mr. Willy came home from an evening spent at Gerald Wardho's brother-in-law's house, a very fine house indeed. He had left lights burning and began to turn out the lights before he went upstairs. He went into the living-room and before turning out the last light gave a glance at the window which had in the course of the evening behaved in its accustomed manner. During the day the view through the window was clear or cloudy, according to the weather or the light or absence of light in the sky; but there it was – the view – never quite the same though, and that is owing to the character of oceans or of any water, great or small, and of light. Both water and light have so great an effect on land observed on any scene, rural urban or wilderness, that one begins to think that life, that a scene, is an illusion produced by influences such as water and light. At all events, by day the window held this fine view as in a frame, and the view was enhanced by ships at sea of all kinds, but never was the sea crowded, and by birds, clouds, and even aeroplanes in the sky – no people to spoil this fine view. But as evening approached, and moonless night, all the view (illusion again) vanished slowly. The window, which was not illusion, only the purveyor of illusion, did not vanish, but became a mirror which reflected against the blackness every detail of the shallow living-room. Through this clear reflection of the whole room, distant lights from across the water intruded, and so chains of light were thrown across the reflected mantlepiece, or a picture, or a human face, enhancing it. When Mr. Willy had left his house to dine at Gerald Wardho's brother-in-law's house the view through the window was placidly clear, but when he returned at 11:30 the window was dark and the room was reflected from floor to ceiling against the blackness. Mr. Willy saw himself entering the room like a stranger, looking at first debonair with such a gleaming shirt front and then – as he approached himself – a little shabby, his hair perhaps. He advanced to the window and stood looking at himself with the room in all its detail behind him.

Mr. Willy was too often alone, and spent far too much time in that space which lies between the last page of the paper or the turning-off of the radio in surfeit, and sleep. Now as he stood at the end of the evening and the beginning of the night, looking at himself and the room behind himself, he admitted that the arid feeling which he had so often experienced lately was probably what is called loneliness. And yet he did not want another woman in his life. It was a long time since he had seen a woman whom he wanted to take home or even to see again. Too much smiling. Men were all right, you talked to them about the market, the emergence of the Liberal Party, the impossibility of arriving anywhere with those people while that fellow was in office, nuclear war (instant hells opened deep in everyone's mind and closed again), South Africa where Mr. Willy was born, the Argentine where Mr. Wardho's brother-in-law had spent many years – and then everyone went home.

Mr. Willy, as the months passed by, was dismayed to find that he had entered an area of depression unknown before, like a tundra, and he was a little frightened of this tundra. Returning from the dinner party he did not at once turn out the single last light and go upstairs. He sat down on a chair beside the window and at last bowed his head upon his hands. As he sat there, bowed, his thoughts went very stiffly (for they had not had much exercise in that direction throughout his life) to some area that was not tundra but was that area where there might be some meaning in creation which Mr. Willy supposed must be the place where some people seemed to find a God, and perhaps a personal God at that. Such theories, or ideas, or passions had never been of interest to him, and if he had thought of such theories, or ideas, or passions he would have dismissed them as invalid and having no bearing on life as it is lived, especially when one is too busy. He had formed the general opinion that people who hold such beliefs were either slaves to an inherited convention, hypocrites, or nit-wits. He regarded such people without interest, or at least he thought them negligible as he returned to the exacting life in hand. On the whole, though, he did not like them. It is not easy to say why Mr. Willy thought these people were hypocrites or nit-wits because some of them, not all, had a strong religious faith, and why he was not a hypocrite or nit-wit because he had not a strong religious faith; but there it was.

As he sat on and on looking down at the carpet with his head in his hands he did not think of these people, but he underwent a strong shock of recognition. He found himself looking this way and that way out of his aridity for some explanation or belief beyond the non-explanation and non-belief that had always been sufficient and had always been his, but in doing this he came up against a high and strong almost visible wall of concrete or granite, set up between him and a religious belief. This wall had, he thought, been built by him through the period of his long life, or perhaps he was congenitally unable to have a belief; in that case it was no fault of his and there was no religious belief possible to him. As he sat there he came to have the conviction that the absence of a belief which extended beyond the visible world had something to do with his malaise; yet the malaise might possibly be cirrhosis of the liver or a sort of delayed male menopause. He recognized calmly that death was as inevitable as tomorrow morning or even tonight and he had a rational absence of fear of death. Nevertheless his death (he knew) had begun, and had begun — what with his awareness of age and this malaise of his — to assume a certainty that it had not had before. His death did not trouble him as much as the increasing tastelessness of living in this tundra of mind into which a belief did not enter.

The man outside the window had crept up through the grasses and was now watching Mr. Willy from a point rather behind him. He was a morose man and strong. He had served two terms for robbery with violence. When he worked, he worked up the coast. Then he came to town and if he did not get into trouble it was through no fault of his own. Last summer he had lain there and, rolling over, had looked up through the grasses and into, only just into the room where this guy was who seemed to live alone. He seemed to be a rich guy because he wore good close and hadn't he got this great big window and – later, he discovered – a high price car. He had lain in the grasses and because his thoughts always turned that way, he tried to figger out how he could get in there. Money was the only thing that was any good to him and maybe the old guy didn't keep money or even carry it but he likely did. The man thought quite a bit about Mr. Willy and then went up the coast and when he came down again he remembered the great big window and one or two nights he went around and about the place and figgered how he'd work it. The doors was all locked, even that glass door. That was easy enough to break but he guessed he'd go in without warning when the old guy was there so's he'd have a better chance of getting something off of him as well. Anyways he wouldn't break in, not that night, but if nothing else offered he'd do it sometime soon.

Suddenly Mr. Willy got up, turned the light out, and went upstairs to bed. That was Wednesday.

On Sunday he had his first small party. It seemed inevitable if only for politeness. Later he would have a dinner party if he still felt sociable and inclined. He invited the Wardhos and their in-laws and some other couples. A Mrs. Lessways asked if she might bring her aunt and he said yes. Mrs. Wardho said might she bring her niece who was arriving on Saturday to meet her fiancé who was due next week from Hong Kong, and the Wardhos were going to give the two young people a quiet wedding, and Mr. Willy said Please do. Another couple asked if they could bring another couple.

Mr. Willy, surveying his table, thought that Mrs. Ogden had done well. 'Oh I'm glad you think so,' said Mrs. Ogden, pleased. People began to arrive. 'Oh!' they exclaimed without fail, as they arrived, 'what a beautiful view!' Mrs. Lessways' aunt who had blue hair fell delightedly into the room, turning this way and that way, acknowledging smiles and tripping to the window. 'Oh,' she cried turning to Mr. Willy in a fascinating manner, 'isn't that just lovely! Edna says you're quite a recluse! I'm sure I don't blame you! Don't you think that's the loveliest view Edna...oh how d'you do how d'you do, isn't that the loveliest view?...' Having paid her tribute to the view she turned away from the window and did not see it again. The Aunt twirled a little bag covered with irridescent beads on her wrist. 'Oh!' and 'Oh!' she exclaimed, turning, 'my dear how *lovely* to see you! I didn't even know you were back! Did you have a good time?' She reminded Mr. Willy uneasily of his wife. Mr. and Mrs. Wardho arrived accompanied by their niece Sylvia.

A golden girl, thought Mr. Willy taking her hand, but her young face surrounded by sunny curls was stern. She stood, looking from one to another, not speaking, for people spoke busily to each other and the young girl stood apart, smiling only when need be and wishing that she had not had to come to the party. She drifted to the window and seemed (and was) forgotten. She looked at the view as at something seen for the first and last time. She inscribed those notable hills on her mind because had she not arrived only yesterday? And in two days Ian would be here and she would not see them again.

A freighter very low laden emerged from behind a forest and moved slowly into the scene. So low it was that it lay like an elegant black line upon the water with great bulkheads below. Like an iceberg, thought Sylvia, and her mind moved along with the freighter bound for foreign parts. Someone spoke to her and she turned. 'Oh thank you!' she said for her cup of tea.

Mr. Willy opened the glass door and took with him some of the men who had expressed a desire to see how far his property ran. 'You see, just a few feet, no distance,' he said.

After a while day receded and night came imperceptibly on. There was not any violence or reflected sunset tonight and mist settled down on the view with only distant dim lights aligning the north shore. Sylvia, stopping to respond to ones and twos, went to the back of the shallow room and sat down behind the out-jut of the fireplace where a wood fire was burning. Her mind was on two levels. One was all Ian and the week coming, and one – no thicker than a crust on the surface – was this party and all these people talking, the Aunt talking so busily that one might think there was a race on, or news to tell. Sylvia, sitting in the shadow of the corner and thinking about her approaching lover, lost herself in this reverie, and her lips, which had been so stern, opened slightly in a tender smile. Mr. Willy who was serving drinks from the dining-room where Mrs. Ogden had left things ready, came upon her and, struck by her beauty, saw a different sunny girl. She looked up at him. She took her drink from him with a soft and tender smile that was grateful and happy and was only partly for him. He left her, with a feeling of beauty seen.

Sylvia held her glass and looked towards the window. She saw, to her surprise, so quickly had black night come, that the end of the room which had been a view was now a large black mirror which reflected the glowing fire, the few lights, and the people unaware of the view, its departure, and its replacement by their own reflections behaving to each other like people at a party. Sylvia watched Mr. Willy who moved amongst them, taking a glass and bringing a glass. He was removed from the necessities, now, of conversation, and looked very sad. Why does he look sad, she wondered and was young enough to think, he shouldn't look sad, he is well off. She took time off to like Mr. Willy and to feel sorry that he seemed melancholy.

People began to look at their watches and say goodbye. The Aunt redoubled her vivacity. The women all thanked Mr. Willy for his tea party and for the beautiful beautiful view. They gave glances at the window but there was no view.

When all his guests had gone, Mr. Willy, who was an orderly man, began to collect glasses and take them into the kitchen. In an armchair lay the bag covered with iridescent beads belonging to the Aunt. Mr. Willy picked it up and put it on a table, seeing the blue hair of the Aunt. He would sit down and smoke for a while. But he found that when, lately, he sat down in the evening beside the window and fixed his eyes upon the golden shaft of the Electric Building, in spite of his intention of reading or smoking his thoughts turned towards this subject of belief which now teased him, eluded, yet compelled him. He was brought up, every time, against the great stone wall, how high, how wide he knew, but not how thick. If he could, in some way, break through this wall which bounded the area of his aridity and his comprehension, he knew without question that there was a light (not darkness) beyond, and that this light could in some way come through to him and alleviate the sterility and lead him, lead him. If there were some way, even some conventional way – although he did not care for convention – he would take it in order to break the wall down and reach the light so that it would enter his life; but he did not know the way. So fixed did Mr. Willy become in contemplation that he looked as though he were graven in stone.

Throughout the darkened latter part of the tea party, the man outside had lain or crouched near the window. From the sands, earlier, he had seen Mr. Willy open the glass door and go outside, followed by two or three men. They looked down talking, and soon went inside again together. The door was closed. From anything the watcher knew, it was not likely that the old guy would turn and lock the door when he took the other guys in. He'd just close it, see?

As night came on the man watched the increased animation of the guests preparing for departure. Like departing birds they moved here and there in the room before taking flight. The man was impatient but patient because when five were left, then three, then no-one but the old guy who lived in the house, he knew his time was near. (How gay and how meaningless the scene had been, of these well-dressed persons talking and talking, like some kind of a show where nothing happened – or so it might seem, on the stage of the lighted room from the pit of the dark shore.)

The watcher saw the old guy pick up glasses and take them away. Then he came back into the room and looked around. He took something out of a chair and put it on a table. He stood still for a bit, and then he found some kind of paper and sat down in the chair facing eastward. But the paper drooped in his hand and then it dropped to the floor as the old guy bent his head and then he put his elbows on his knees and rested his head in his hands as if he was thinking, or had some kind of a headache.

The watcher, with a sort of joy and a feeling of confidence that the moment had come, moved strongly and quietly to the glass door. He turned the handle expertly, slid inside, and slowly closed the door so that no draught should warn his victim. He moved cat-like to the back of Mr. Willy's chair and quickly raised his arm. At the selfsame moment that he raised his arm with a short blunt weapon in his hand, he was aware of the swift movement of another person in the room. The man stopped still, his arm remained high, every fear was aroused. He turned instantly and saw a scene clearly enacted beside him in the dark mirror of the window. At the moment and shock of turning, he drew a sharp intake of breath and it was this that Mr. Willy heard and that caused him to look up and around and see in the dark mirror the intruder, the danger, and the victim who was himself. At that still moment, the telephone rang shrilly, twice as loud in that still moment, on a small table near him.

It was not the movement of the figure in the dark mirror, it was not the bell ringing close at hand and insistently, it was an irrational and stupid fear lest his action, reproduced visibly beside him in the mirror, was being faithfully registered in some impossible way that filled the intruder with fright. The telephone rang shrilly, Mr. Willy now facing him, the play enacted beside him, and this irrational momentary fear caused him to turn and bound towards the door, to escape into the dark, banging the glass door with a clash behind him. When he got well away from the place he was angry – everything was always against him, he never had no luck, and if he hadn'ta lost his head it was a cinch he coulda done it easy.

'Damn you!' shouted Mr. Willy in a rage, with his hand on the telephone, 'you might have broken it! Yes?' he said into the telephone, moderating the anger that possessed him and continuing within himself a conversation that said It was eighteen inches away, I was within a minute of it and I didn't know, it's no use telephoning the police but I'd better do that, it was just above me and I'd have died not knowing. 'Yes? Yes?' he said impatiently, trembling a little.

'Oh,' said a surprised voice, 'it *is* Mr. Willy, isn't it? Just for a minute it didn't sound like you Mr. Willy that was the *loveliest* party and what a *lovely* view and I'm sorry to be such a nuisance I kept on ringing and ringing because I thought you couldn't have gone out so soon' (tinkle tinkle) 'and you couldn't have gone to bed so soon but I do believe I must have left my little bead bag it's not the *value* but...' Mr. Willy found himself shaking more violently now, not only with death averted and the rage of the slammed glass door but with the powerful thoughts that had usurped him and were interrupted by the dangerous moment which was now receding, and the tinkling voice on the telephone.

'I have it here. I'll bring it tomorrow,' he said shortly. He hung up the telephone and at the other end the Aunt turned and exclaimed 'Well if he isn't the rudest man I never was treated like that in my whole life d'you know what he...'

Mr. Willy was in a state of abstraction.

He went to the glass door and examined it. It was intact. He turned the key and drew the shutter down. Then he went back to the telephone in this state of abstraction. Death or near-death was still very close, though receding. It seemed to him at that moment that a crack had been coming in the great wall that shut him off from the light but perhaps he was wrong. He dialled the police, perfunctorily not urgently. He knew that before him lay the hardest work of his life – in his life but out of his country. He must in some way and soon break the great wall that shut him off from whatever light there might be. Not for fear of death oh God not for fear of death but for fear of something else.

(1961)   (1958)

W.W.E. Ross
1894 – 1966

———◆———

WILLIAM WRIGHTSON EUSTACE ROSS was born in Peterborough, Ontario, and educated at the University of Toronto. After serving in the First World War he worked as a geophysicist in Agincourt, Ontario. One of the first Canadian poets whose work reflects the influence of the Imagist movement, Ross published his first collection of poetry, *Laconics*, in 1930. A selection of his poems, *Shapes and Sounds*, appeared in 1968.

Pine Gum

The white gum showing
in the gloom
along the massive
trunk of a great
pine-tree standing
on the hill,
with a deep bed
of needles below; –

10 scarcely a breeze
along the hill;
scarcely a current
of morning air

to make the pine's
old melody,
for it is evening;
the air has ceased

its daily stirring;
the light grows dimmer
within the shadow
of the pine,   20
but ever appears
through the darkness
the ghostly glimmering
of the gum.

(1930)   (1968)

Flowers

Flowers
revolving   in the sun
spinning   colours
                     whirling
colours   yellow
red   and blue
and yellow

Flowers spinning in the sun
make the garden make one
garden in the sun.   10

       These
upon stalks   rotating
red   brick-coloured
blood-coloured   blue
yellow and pink

Flowers rotating in the sun
make the garden make one
garden   in the sun.

(1956)   (1968)

Night Scene

The lake is mirror-like tonight.
The trees on the bank
Dark, beautiful,
Look down at their reflections.

The water is shallow by the shore.
There reeds stand dimly seen,
Among whose roots
The wary pike lurks, waiting.

Perhaps a splash at the surface,
Perhaps a swift shadow   10
Will show where he pursues his victim
That cannot escape him.

Terror below the surface.
Beauty above,
As the exquisite dark trees
Gaze endlessly at their reflections.

(1956)   (1968)

Reciprocal

The shuttle swinging
to and fro;
the piston
of the locomotive
moving smoothly,
powerfully,
into the cylinder,
out of the cylinder;

dancers swaying
in one place;   10
crows' wings
in lazy flight;
waves on the ocean
up to the shore
and back swiftly
broken and foaming.

(1956)

(1968)

Winter Scene

Black of the
branches and
white of the
snow that is
lying
upon them —

New-fallen,
light, not
heavy with
liquid to
bending —

There I see
by the street
trees with
10 snow on their
branches;

Black of the
branches but
white of the
new-fallen   20
snow.

(1956)

(1968)

Blue Flowers

Blue flowers
by the road
growing in
stateliness
many together

All erect
in the air
thrusting their
blue-bearing
stems —   10

And so we
stopped to pick
some of these
blooms by the
roadside

(1968)

Breaking off
several
then, we
collected a
handful.   20

(1968)

The Diver

I would like to dive
Down
Into this still pool
Where the rocks at the bottom are safely deep,

Into the green
Of the water seen from within,
A strange light
Streaming past my eyes —

Things hostile;
You cannot stay here, they seem to say;   10
The rocks, slime-covered, the undulating
Fronds of weeds —

And drift slowly
Among the cooler zones;
Then, upward turning,
Break from the green glimmer

Into the light,
White and ordinary of the day,
And the mild air,
With the breeze and the comfortable shore.   20

(1968)   (1968)

If Ice

If

ice shall melt

if

thinly the fresh
cold clear   water
running   shall make
grooves in the sides
of the ice;
if life return

after death   10
or depart not at death,
then shall buds
burst into   May-
leafing, the blooms of May
appear like stars
on the brown dry
                    forest-bed,

(1968)

(1968)

The Creek

The creek, shining,
out of the deep woods
comes with its rippling of
water over pebbly bottom.

Moving between
banks crowded with raspberry
bushes, the ripe red
berries in their short season

to deepen slowly
among tall pines, athletes in
10   the wind, then the swampy
ground low-lying and damp

where sunlight strikes
glints on the gliding surface
of the clear cold
creek winding towards the shore

of the lake, blue,
not far through reeds and rushes,
where with a plunge, a small
waterfall, it disappears

among the waves
hastening from far to meet
the stranger, the stream issuing
from depths of green unknown.

(1968)

(1968)

Philippe Panneton
1895 – 1960

———◆———

BORN IN TROIS-RIVIERES, Quebec, Philippe Panneton earned a degree in medicine from the University of Montreal and, after postgraduate work in Paris, practised medicine in both Trois-Rivières and Montreal. When he was appointed Canadian ambassador to Portugal in 1956 he had already become famous as the author of *Trente arpents* (1938). This realistic novel, published under the pseudonym Ringuet, traces the transformation of the agrarian culture of Quebec by industrial and social changes at the beginning of the twentieth century. Panneton's other works include a collection of stories, *L'Héritage et autres contes* (1946), and *Confidences* (1965), a volume of autobiographical sketches which was published after his death.

Vocations

THE DIRECTOR OF the college was a stout man who seemed old to us. He must have been thirty-five at least. We thought him a tyrant. Well, after all, the poor devil was in charge of discipline. And the discipline was strict. Even today I would say it was unnecessarily strict. They imposed an adult calm on boys who were nine-tenths effervescence. Fifty years later I still cannot come to understand why they forced children to troop down the corridors in single file (in "orderly fashion" is apparently what they call it in the Convent of the Sacred Heart), in a cruel, monastic silence under the scrutiny of young men designated our wardens who were supposed to have eyes in the backs of their heads to pounce on and punish the slightest irregularity or the smallest whisper. To be perfectly frank, such practices seem to me to be clearly inhuman and quite simply idiotic. Especially for children benumbed from three hours of class.

To come back to the director, he was not at all a bad man. In fact he was as quick to caress as to chastise. My hands and cheek can attest to that, for the former remember well the cut of his ash ruler, the latter the feel of his rough beard that he liked to nuzzle against our velvety young skins. Neither his justice nor his tenderness ever went farther than that. Essentially he had the soul of the father of a large family – and they managed to turn him into some kind of financial administrator!

One day when I had commited a frightful crime, such as reading a novel in chapel instead of *Religion's Little Apologist*, or perhaps passing a note to some bosom pal, I was summoned before the director. There, for the benefit of the habitual criminal that I was, I found my father who had been called from the infirmary where, with a fair degree of indulgence, he used to separate the truly ill from the chronic fakers. To leave me with the strongest possible impression, my two fathers, the fleshly and the spiritual, discussed before me the sorry future that lay before me thanks to my reluctance to mend my ways. As if, in the name of Infinite Wisdom, the future were promised to the obedient and not to the energetic! I can still hear the voice of the priest saying pompously when he had finished his sermon: "My dear Doctor, your boy will assuredly amount to something…Something very good…or something very evil!"

Such an emphatic judgment was certainly beyond his own small powers of invention. He must have stolen it from some pious saint's life and been dying to find a chance to place such a sententious trifle. Unfortunately, this time his gift of prophecy fell somewhat short of the mark. I have not become a knight of the Order of the Holy Sepulchre, and it was another native of Trois-Rivières who became Prime Minister. On the other hand, I *have* served a stretch in the penitentiary. For four years I was at Saint-Vincent de Paul's in the capacity of prison doctor. This has often given me the opportunity to say, pleasantly, to new acquaintances: "Back in my days at the pen…" That always creates a little stir.

Truth to tell, all my criminal tendencies amounted to was the petty thievery typical of young scamps my age. We would sneak out at night and steal apples in the bishop's garden – huge, inedible apples. The proof that I was not undisciplined, no matter how much my father might have thought the contrary, was that I belonged to a well-organized gang. And I was far from being its leader. I obediently followed the others who steered their course outside those virtuous paths bordered with boredom along which we were obstinately urged by our masters. To lead men has never tempted me. If on occasion I may have seemed to want to bend others to share my feelings or endorse my activities, it is simply because I naively believed that in so doing I could help them on the road to happiness.

Obviously I was that kind of child who longs to become a man as soon as possible. That meant assuming a set place in society; I needed a tag: lawyer, merchant, priest. Following my natural bent would have drawn me to the profession of a person of independent means had I not observed that this occupation required white hair and extreme old age. Soon however, by the time I was five or so, I had decided my fate. This is an age when decisions are easy, the world is so clearly divided into things that are desirable or totally uninteresting. With the added advantage that nothing in it appears entirely detestable. My first certainty was that I was in no way cut out for the priesthood. The priestly part of the family was monopolised by my brother who was destined to don the violet sash of a canon.

With that possibility excluded, the choice was easy. There are three things that fascinate children equally: water, paint and fire. Perhaps the state of deep-sea diver would have suited me. It would have allowed me to go swimming without offending anyone's sense of modesty. But I had never seen a diver dive. As for painters, house painters naturally, I had been struck by the fact that they were forbidden to paint according to their own whim and inspiration, having to cover huge surfaces with a single monotonous colour. Which explained to me the listless, grumbling nature of those I knew. Besides, those big ladders you had to climb up didn't really tempt me all that much.

There remained fire. So I decided to be a fireman. What could be finer than to tear down the Rue Royale at a triple gallop, four horses striking sparks from their sixteen iron shod hooves. Necks outstretched, chests fuming, they would come towards us growing larger by the minute like animal genii. A big red-headed man whose name I've forgotten sat enthroned on a raised seat holding the reins of the careening team in both hands. The bell rang gloriously, as loud as could be. Once they had reached the scene of the disaster, the firemen were free to shout, run about and climb up and down ladders to their hearts' content. And to shoot torrents of water on the sumptuous blaze from their well-aimed hoses. Even the scarlet colour of their equipment added to their grandeur, recalling as it did the noble and ardent element they were called upon to fight. Paint, water, fire, all three elements were there. This taste for one of the only professions where heroism is an everyday affair (don't bother speaking to me of the army where "Shoulder arms!" and the military salute are the principal signs of the trade), this taste of mine in firemen was shared by another member of my family. I remember that my younger sister for several years entertained a mute passion for a Breton fireman on the Trois-Rivières brigade. True, he was a handsome man. When he passed by astraddle the fire-reel she thought she saw Apollo on his chariot.

But I fear that my vocation as fireman lacked something in originality, and that numerous children have been seduced as I was by the water, the fire, and the crimson paint. By which sign they demonstrated that they were already men. For if a man will examine his past life carefully, every last one will be forced to admit that he was attracted and repelled less by logic than by appearances; that we direct our lives by following the flow, the colour and the warmth of our illusions; in short that our so-called reasons are nothing more than the garments with which we adorn our whims, fancies and caprices.

The incendiary phase of my existence was brief. It lasted only as long as what I knew of the world depended on what was directly revealed to me by my eyes and ears. From the day I learned to read, I entertained higher ambitions. Books suddenly opened my astonished eyes to the pages of a world that was vaster and more varied than I had ever suspected. Every horizon became an intolerable barrier. The fact that a man should be yellow or black or that a landscape should be different from the one I knew gave things and people a strange and exciting quality. It is in a child's nature, or at least in some children's natures, to be perennially dissatisfied. And in this matter as in so many others, there always remains a great part of the child in the grown man. Nor is it his least precious part. In those days I did not yet know that someone had once written: "One tires of everything except knowledge." But in some obscure way that is what I already felt.

Life in my sleepy little city was a mere pittance for my ravenous appetite. The main thing wrong with Trois-Rivières was that I had been born there, whereas other places, say Montpellier or Moscow, and above all cities of the East like Baghdad, Cairo, Singapore or Peking seemed as desirable as they were inaccessible. I have since discovered that for people in Montpellier or Cairo the distant city of Trois-Rivières in Canada is undoubtedly full of a mysterious and seductive charm.

But my imagination, which was never particularly fertile, provided me no means of escape. The only world-traveller I knew was that uncle I spoke of earlier. One day, however, a White Father, an African missionary, came to Trois-Rivières. Through him I cunningly grasped a solution. In the folds of his white cloak I saw native huts under the palm trees, black warriors brandishing their spears, women dancing naked in the dazzling sunlight. The fact that being a White Father had more to do with an apostolic vocation barely bothered me. The power of the African magic drowned every other consideration. For I was already, by nature, a stranger to many things that were perfectly normal in the world I grew up in. They simply left me cold. That's the way I was.

So, as I gradually came to some understanding of myself, I no longer felt drawn to the heroic life of a missionary. No more than to that of fireman. All that has remained of that is a taste for spectacular conflagrations, as a spectator, not as an actor. Likewise, my leanings towards white priesthood have been translated into a need to travel which, thanks to the passage of time and a generous fate, has been gratified without ever being completely satisfied.

When I grew older I discovered another pleasure: that of returning home. Then too, there is the pleasurable anticipation of departure. My older brother put it this way, "Believe me, the fun of the fisherman fishing is nothing compared to the fun of the fisherman getting fixed up to fish." It's no different with travelling. Similarly, when you reach a certain place in a book you get as much satisfaction out of going over the table of contents again as you did first reading the preface because it allows you to relive happy moments. When we come home again the house smiles at us from every one of its windows. In every traveller there lurks a stay-by-the-fire. Coming back you tell yourself, home's not so bad after all. One of the advantages of travel is that it gives you a taste for the everyday.

It's only after you've been back for a month that you begin to take an interest in leafing through travel magazines again. It's only ten months later that railway timetables and tourist folders begin stealthily to make their appearance among the papers on your desk.

I still like fires. And I will always want to travel. For I will always be a child. At least I like to think so.

(1965)   (1977)

PHILIP STRATFORD (TR.)

Raymond Knister
1899-1932

———◆———

RAYMOND KNISTER WAS born and raised on farms in southwestern Ontario. He entered the University of Toronto in 1919 but illness forced him to withdraw. During the early 1920s he lived in the American Midwest where he worked on the editorial staff of *The Midland,* a literary magazine which published some of his work. Later he became a free-lance writer in Toronto and Montreal. In addition to poems, short stories and critical articles, Knister published an anthology, *Canadian Short Stories* (1928), and a novel, *White Narcissus* (1929). A second novel, *My Star Predominant* (1934), was completed shortly before his death by drowning. His *Collected Poems* was published in 1949. "The Loading" first appeared in *The Midland* in 1924.

The Plowman

All day I follow
Watching the swift dark furrow
That curls away before me,
And care not for skies or upturned flowers,
And at the end of the field
Look backward
Ever with discontent.
A stone, a root, a strayed thought
Has warped the line of that furrow –
And urge my horses 'round again.   10

Sometimes even before the row is finished
I must look backward;
To find, when I come to the end
That there I swerved.

Unappeased I leave the field,
Expectant, return.

The horses are very patient.
When I tell myself
This time
The ultimate unflawed turning   20
Is before my share,
They must give up their rest.

Someday, someday, be sure,
I shall turn the furrow of all my hopes
But I shall not, doing it, look backward.

(1949)   (1949)

Lake Harvest

Down on the flat of the lake
Out on the slate and the green,
Spotting the border of Erie's sleeping robe of silver-blue changeable
    silk,
In sight of the shimmer of silver-blue changeable silk,
In the sun,
The men are sawing the frosted crystal.
Patient the horses look on from the sleighs,
Patient the trees, down from the bank, darkly ignoring the sun.
Each saw sings and whines in a grey-mittened hand,
And diamonds and pieces of a hundred rainbows are strown around. 10

(1949)   (1949)

The Hawk

Across the bristled and sallow fields,
The speckled stubble of cut clover,
Wades your shadow.

Or against a grimy and tattered
Sky
You plunge.

Or you shear a swath
From trembling tiny forests
With the steel of your wings –

Or make a row of waves   10
By the heat of your flight
Along the soundless horizon.

(1949)   (1949)

Autumn Clouds

Here on the quiet upland
Among the withered corn
Wondering I stand:
Beauty again is born.

The thin light melts and yields,
The torn stalks shiver;
On near and far-off fields
I see pale gold, a river

That floats the fences, trees,
Golden-rod, and tarnished grasses,   10
A lift of brown like bees, —
Submerges all, and passes

Leaving all no less unspent,
Nor more lonely. And I find,
Long lost, the trees' assent
To sunlight and to wind.

(1949)   (1949)

The Loading

I

JESSE CULWORTH'S AIR that morning announced that he did not even
wish to seem tranquil. His wife, sensitive, as always, to his temper, felt
that. So did Garland, his son. When he came in at half-past six from the
before-breakfast chores he glowered silently half-sitting, half-leaning
with folded arms against the sewing machine, toward the boy, who was
washing at the kitchen sink. "Come, Ma," he said to his wife, "dish the
porridge up! We're just ready."

When he had washed they sat down. The room was dimly lit by
vine-covered windows. Sunbeams made numerous rays through the
leaves of virginia creeper, targetting at bright spots on the fading dark
paper of the opposite wall. The table at which they sat seemed to

half-fill the kitchen. Jesse, strong-looking and unbent of shoulders at forty, ate his oatmeal with melancholy gusto, at times heavily regarding his wife at the other end of the table. He held out his cup and saucer in silence for more tea. As Nettie filled the cup he said, "Whoa!", his use of the accustomed word so abrupt and morose that, startled, his wife passed the cup back. He drank the tea slowly. On his regular thick features a slight moisture could be seen in the dim light of the warm kitchen.

"Going to take them hogs in to town this morning," he announced to his son as he leaned back in his chair after finishing the tea. "Old Gus told me last night he guessed he'd take 'em."

The good humors of Jesse rather preceded than followed his visits to town. He would see Charlie Alten, or some others of his early friends driving about the village in their motors after the closing of their stores. Always after greeting one of them he would bite his lip and mutter to himself, drawing back his shoulders, "What a fool I was, what a fool! They didn't have any more schooling than I did. To go out on that blasted unearthly farm!" His mother who was living in the village after the death of her husband persuaded him into taking a farm as soon as he had finished high-school. She was intolerably afraid that he would not "settle down", for until his death her husband had not. Jesse stuck to the farm during good years because they might continue, and he wouldn't quit in a poor year because then it and the stock could not be sold for what they were worth. Of late the years seemed mostly alike. The details of his ill-luck became to him of less and less interest except as a subject for objurgation. To heavy rains and droughts he resigned himself almost with enjoyment. If anyone's clover failed to "catch", it was his; if anyone's wheat winter-killed, his did. Hoof and mouth disease broke out miles away to head straight to his stable.

"I should guess he would take 'em, the price he's paying now!" Culworth grunted, looking to his wife for approval of the wit.

There was silence. Like most men he had made a phrase of his own, which he liked to use. His was, "the devilishness of things in general". He took pleasure in using it in the presence of his wife. Aside from her feeling of a discomfortable approach to blasphemy Nettie Culworth did not like such words to be said before her son. Now Jesse eschewed it in a feeling of deprivation. Yet he came down hard on the boy if inadvertently he used any of such gross terms as naturally he would pick up. Jesse seemed to think that no one else was justified in such behavior.

Without speaking Garland finished his glass of milk and rose. Lifting his chair back from the table he set it against the wall.

"Load 'em in the wagon, eh?" he asked.

"Yes, but the darn horses haven't come up from the bush yet. You'll have to go after them. They'll stay all day."

"It's too bad they can't learn to come up in the mornings," said Nettie, looking at her fifteen-year-old son. "It's a long walk back there."

The boy had taken his broad curling hat from the nail. "Oh, I don't mind it," he mumbled as he let the screen-door swing to behind him.

II

It was the beginning of a June day, warm yet fresh. The young boy walked down the rail-fenced lane to the back of the farm; and the surrounding grass and corn, the weeds in the fence-corners, the inadvertent sounding of insects, a bird alighting on a top rail, the mist hanging in the middle distance and opening a horizon about him as he went, made a whole which was more to him than the vague thoughts which came to his mind. He was at peace. He kept steadily on his way toward the bush, still a wide hidden shape before him in the morning.

The bush was beautiful in its attempted negation of color, its fragrance and a kind of reserve of warmth. The trees stood dozing, or whispering a little softly so as not to rouse the others. Near the front of the lot, where they were fewer, some of them had always had each a character of its own for Garland. One, he could not tell why, reminded him of an old calm church elder as he stood outside the church after service and greeted the people, his long beard moving. Another one was like a statue of a lion. It was strong-rooted and gnarled. Another was some slender fleet animal, he knew not what, and he wondered, before pausing in the wake of phantasies of his earlier childhood, why it had not sprung away and left the bush since he had been there last.

The boy began calling through the thin woods as he walked. He was at a loss in what direction to go that he might find the horses. He began to walk around the edge of the bush within a few rods of the line fence. The echo of his voice seemed muffled distantly, and to come back about him through the trees and the mist. The near trees became columns upholding clouds as he moved toward them. He had made almost a complete circuit when he decided to strike in to the centre of the wood and to finish examination of the outskirts if necessary afterward.

Now uneasiness came to him, as he thought of his father's waiting, and he walked more quickly.

III

Jesse was growing more and more impatient as the time passed. When he had fed the hogs generously he greased the wagon and put the sides on the rack which was used to haul livestock to market. He could have found plenty of odd jobs for an hour yet, but he did not think of them in his increasing disquiet. He would go to the head of the lane and look down it for the string of horses which should be coming. "Blame the boy, what's ailin' him?" he muttered. The sun was beginning to shine out warmly, and to Jesse as he came forth from pitching down hay for noon from the loft to the stable below it seemed as though the morning were half gone. His annoyance was not lessened when he considered that probably he might not with a show of justice reproach the boy.

He went to the house. After he had taken a drink of water, he breathed heavily, glanced at himself in the mirror above the sink, and stood over the bare cleared wooden table a moment, his hands on each side of yesterday's paper.

Nettie Culworth came from the pantry to look into the oven.

"I wonder what on earth can be keeping that boy! There's no get-up about him. He's been gone for hours. Lot of help he is!" The back of his hand bristled across his mouth.

"He's likely doing the best he can, Jesse," his wife replied, not pausing in her work. "Don't scold him when he comes up. It's a long way back there."

He grunted as he started up from the table and the screen-door cracked to behind him, but made no answer in words. A little relieved by this passage he strode to the corner of the barn. The horses were coming up the lane, old Dan leading them, and Garland behind. Impatiently the father waited.

"Well, you've been long enough!" he called as they came nearer. "You had to run them all over the bush before you could get hold of them, eh?" He was smiling.

"No.... I couldn't find them, father."

"Oh! — Well, round 'em up there, hurry up, don't be all day." He slid the door open and stood back at one side of it.

But the other horses were not inclined to follow old Dan into the stable. They swerved away from Jesse and around the small strawstack in the middle of the barnyard.

"Git after them!" he called to his son. "*Be* quick! Bring them around the stack and I'll watch here."

The boy was already gone, and there was a moment of rustling through the straw and a dry musty smell, then the horses came tearing and plunging from around the stack. Jesse shouted and waved his arms, but he had nothing in his hands to frighten them back. They passed him and went down the lane. Garland leaped the fence and headed them off there, while Jesse strode to the stable door. "Show 'em next time," he muttered, gripping a fork-handle firmly. His impatience, or whatever it was, was augmented by the failure to stay the horses in the presence of his son.

This time one of the horses, head and tail up, came alone from behind the stack. The man ran forward to steer it into the door, but it darted away, leaving him beside the wall when a second one came toward him. He ran swiftly to the gate, growling between his clenched teeth, "Who-oah, *you!*" He thought for an instant he had it, but it was passing him. He unconsciously swerved a little when he saw that they were going through the gate together and did not see protruding at an angle from the post a stiff wire, which grazed his cheek. He stopped and held one hand to his face intently a moment, not looking around, then with set jaw and without a word twisted the wire violently until it was broken off.

Garland looked on at this a moment, then remembered the horses, and went to drive them up a third time. The animals appeared to realize that their mischief had gone far enough for that morning, and came around quietly.

Jesse and his son entered the stable in silence. The boy was making for the box containing the curry-combs and brushes, when he saw that his father took down a collar from the peg. He also lifted down a collar and began to unbuckle its top. Jesse went to a stall.

"Get over here!" he said.

The animal seemed to hesitate, and did not move, so he quietly laid the collar down and bracing his powerful frame against the planks pushed the back part of the horse violently against the opposite wall. Then he seized and held it by the halter and began to kick its stomach. "Show – you!" he grunted between the blows. After that he put on the collar.

Garland stood looking on, pale, for a few seconds, then he entered the stall of the other horse. When he had buckled the collar about its neck his father was waiting with its harness, instead of that of the horse which he had just been abusing. The animal started, knocking its knees in a tattoo against the manger, as he flung upon it the heavy harness which hung down over it behind. Jesse lifted the harness again, and came farther forward in the stall before again flinging it on the horse's back.

"What's the matter with *you?*" he asked tensely, seizing its halter and backing it in order to get at the hames. "You won't eh?" he continued as the horse made a convulsive movement forward, and struck it on the side of the muzzle.

"Father!" cried Garland.

"What's ailin' you?" asked Jesse, looking at his son for a second.

The latter said nothing, but looked shamefacedly away toward the strong glare of sunlight on the rhomboid of dirty stained cement within the door, which made the rest of the interior of the stable still more dim. Outside the sun shone fiercely on the ragged edge of the tarnished strawstack and made each straw where a forkful had been freshly taken look like a precious bit of gold. A dry stifling smell came from the hot barnyard.

"What d'you have to start them running around the stack for then? You knew too well! Or else you'll never learn." The unshaven face was yellow-black in the dim light as the man wrenched the straps into place. "What are you standing there for?" he exclaimed, raising his voice. "Haven't you lost enough time yet, eh?"

The boy reached up to the pegs, standing on his toes, and with an effort swung a heavy harness down from them. It was dankly coated with greasy sweat. Holding the front of it in his hands he moved toward the stall. Jesse came and seizing the rear of the harness swung it to the horse's back. The animal pranced and nearly trampled the boy's feet.

"What d'you got to drag it over the floor for? If you can't pick it up, leave it alone."

They went out into the heat of the sun a short distance along the dry lane to the pig yard. The enclosure was meant for a paddock but was long since beaten to a dust by the little hoofs, and only straggling unpalatable weeds stood yet, gray with dust. It was necessary to get the hogs into the pen in order to load them. Finally after a protracted hot struggle this end was accomplished. Each one demanded individual cornering and persuasion, but the last one of all required them after a few minutes' chasing to capture him. Seizing his short hind legs they dragged him raucously complaining to the pen.

When the door was closed on him and his comrades rallying around to welcome with excited gruntings his escape, Jesse had begun to accede to a grim good-humor. He had shown them! And Garland had employed quickness and a good deal of wiry strength.

"You'll make a farmer yet," he said, as though unbendingly. He took off his hat and rubbed his brow with a colored handkerchief. Then he thought of the scratch from the wire which unaccountably he had forgotten. "I'll go put something on my face," he added, glancing at Garland. "You hitch up on the wagon and we'll go over to Crampton's for their chute." He went to the house hastily.

IV

Coming home the boy remarked, referring to the neighbor whom they had just left, "So Andrew is going to retire?" though Crampton had just been informing them of his intention.

"Yes, the old sucker. After being as stingy as sin all his life and drudging night and day all his life like a slave he can go to town now to die of bein' afraid he'll last longer than his money will, and wanting to work out on some farm, even somebody's else, since he's left his own; and being ashamed to."

Without enthusiasm the old man had made his announcement, but he had thought the consummation worthy of a pride which he did not care to show, it was clear. His son, who was to have the running of the farm thenceforth, was not so well able to conceal his feeling. Turning aside from them talking together in the stable to hide his uncontrollable grin, he had shouted gruffly at a horse, putting back into its manger some hay which it had turned out.

Garland was silent as he looked absently at the surrounding fields, ashen and green rectangles in the violent sunlight. He sat on the low rear ladder of the wagon, and the irregular cackling rattle of the wheels lulled him. A lazy bit of dust hung alongside the wagon as they drove. The long road was empty, and seemed to hold, more than the farm-yard they had just left, the hush and warmth of noon.

"Never be a farmer," said Jesse, brooding. "It's one thing or another. Either you have a heavy crop and everybody else has the same, and you take what they give you for it, or else, if the price is decent you've got but little or none. And it's always work, work, – more work than if you did have a good crop. We'll have to go into business, you and I. Hardware business out West, eh? If I'm ever able to get shut of this farm," he added with an intonation of bitterness. He brought this out as though it had long since been formed in his mind.

"Maybe we'll find a buyer," said Garland. Lolling against the rear ladder he was again in the green woods of the morning, peering through the soft air cobwebbed with mist for the shapes of the horses showing through it vaguely in the depths. His calls rang on the thick air, but farther in the wood echoes were muffled, somehow. The horses made no movement or sound in answer, but did not try to escape when he came up to them. Dan raised a sleepy eye as he heard him coming. "You old rascal!" Garland said when he had caught hold of his forelock. "You brought them here, you know you did." The wise old boy shook the end of his long nose from side to side and snored. They all blinked at him lazy-eyed, enjoying their truancy, but not then interested enough to attempt to make a get-away. Slowly they twined out of the bush and up the long lane. For a distance he held Dan by the damp forelock of his lowered head, old Mack and the others following. But when they came to the foot of the lane Garland slipped back behind them all, so that his father might not scold him for taking the risk of their getting away from him; and followed whistling in the sun and the light rolling waves of fog past large maples and oaks that overhung the lane. Broad circles of ground beneath the trees were beaten to a finer dust by the hoofs of the horses and cattle. Even then the mist was spreading and thinning. There was promise of a very warm day....

"I want you to be something better than a farmer," his father was saying impressively.

"Oh, I don't know," Garland answered uncertainly.

"Get along, Dan!" shouted Jesse, slashing with the lines.

They rattled on a few hundred yards and came to the home gate. They swung out widely to enter it. Garland suddenly cried out, and his father turning saw the heavy chute which protruded from the rack about to strike the gate-post and slide back, crushing the boy's legs. He pulled and shouted at the horses, and at that instant gate-post and chute caught, but slightly, and the structure was moved only a few inches back from its place.

The boy's face was pink and sheepish, but his father was pale. "Well, what *are* you thinking of this morning?" he shouted as the wagon went down the lane. "Will you never learn? How often have I told you to look for things like that? You could see blame well what was coming. But I've got to watch you like a baby. Ever *see* such a boy! *I* haven't enough to do, I must always be turning around and watching him. I'll have to have his mother out to help me take care of him. A great lot of good – ! Whoa!"

They drove into the bare yard and reached the pig pen. Jesse jumped down indignant. Garland continued to stand shamefaced by the back ladder of the wagon. How had he come to make such a blunder? It was true that his father had frequently warned him about such things. He must have been asleep. Still, he might have been able to jump off the back of the wagon if the chute had come any farther toward him, if the wagon were not going too rapidly. Well, another time –

He was roused by hearing his father say, "Well, are you going to help me take this thing off, or aren't you?"

At that he stepped quickly forward and began lifting the heavy bulk. Slowly it was twisted back and forth and eased to the ground. Then he jumped down and helped to drag it into place inside the door of the pen.

"Go get some chunks to block the wheels – the damn horses won't stand, I know – while I back the wagon into position."

Garland went away to a pile of rubbish outside the barnyard fence. He was in a sort of daze of which he was scarcely half aware. He kept thinking of his first morning glimpse and first whiff of the sweet and gauzy-aired day from the little open window of his bedroom; of his mother's cheerful greeting, and the strange sadness he had felt at his father's early ill-temper; again, of the beauty of the morning bush, and sense of a myriad mist-thralled birds when one of them broke silence for an instant, for a note. Inappositely he began thinking of evenings when he rode down the lane home on the disks musically tinkling, grating or clanging over the stones as the hungry and tired horses made for the barn; of the wonderful pleasure it now seemed to come in at dusk to the warm supper in the little bright-windowed house. The wind would rustle the vine dryly against the clapboards and the panes, but he would be warm and replete and in the light.... Poor Mother! Poor Dan, the old slave! Unaccountable pity for everyone and everything enwrapped him.

In that instant he was fumbling about among old sticks and rubbish and pieces of rusty fence-wire for the blocks of wood. A call from his father roused him and he started up to come bringing them. He saw over in the green wheat field a horse with its head down. "It's old Mack," he thought. "We couldn't have tied him up with the others. ...But how did he get there, how will we catch him?"

The rear of the wagon was about three feet from the building. "I haven't got it just in position," said Jesse. "I thought it was no use until you brought the blocks, they fidget so."

He went forward, and Garland, taking no account of his movements, went in behind the wagon and looked down the slope of the chute at the pigs. He leaned over the straight lip of the frame. They were peaceful about the trough eating another meal before they died. The boy considered them with a strange pain at his heart. He could not understand his sorrow, and he was turning away silently when he heard a shout.

V

His father had gone to one side to consider the way in which the wagon would have to be maneuvred in order to bring it to just the right position in relation with the chute. He saw that it must be moved forward to get it in line for backing. He stepped quickly to the heads of the horses to lead them up by the bridles. With straining eyes and forward-sloping ears they both shied back from him, their powerful braced legs pushing the wagon back with a terrible inexorable swiftness, like the piston-swing of a great engine, it seemed. Yet it was a long moment....

Jesse found himself on his knees, his arm reaching up to a horse's rein. If there had been a sound he had not heard it. In silence the sun was beating down on the dirty yard about him, on the scattered grimy weeds which had withstood the browsing hogs. A little cloud of dust lazily wandered away, twisting slowly across the ground. Then he heard the guzzling of the hogs at the feed he had given them – how long? – five minutes ago. And somewhere a bob-white was calling, portent of a day of rain.

Trying to hold his eyes shut, on his hands and knees he crept around to the back of the wagon.

(1972)   (1924)

F. R. Scott
1899-

———◆———

FRANCIS REGINALD SCOTT was born in Quebec and educated at Bishop's College, Oxford University and McGill University where he studied law. He was called to the bar in 1927 and later joined the McGill Faculty of Law. An active participant in the literary, political, economic and legal affairs of Canada, Scott was one of the organizers of the League for Social Reconstruction in 1932, and was national chairman of the Co-operative Commonwealth Federation from 1942 to 1950. In 1963 he served on the Royal Commission on Bilingualism and Biculturalism and he has translated the poetry of several French-Canadian poets. Scott's earliest poems appeared in *The McGill Fortnightly Review* (1925-1927) which he co-edited with A. J. M. Smith. Since the appearance of his first collection of poems, *Overture* (1945), Scott has published several volumes including *Events and Signals* (1954), *Signature* (1964) and *The Dance is One* (1973).

Trees in Ice

these gaunt prongs and points of trees
pierce the zero air with flame
every finger of black ice
stealing the sun's drawn fire
to make a burning of a barren bush

underneath, from still branch and arm
flakes of light fall, fall
flecking the dark white snow

this cruelty is a formal loveliness
on a tree's torn limbs   10
this glittering pain

(1945)   (1966)

The Canadian Authors Meet

Expansive puppets percolate self-unction
Beneath a portrait of the Prince of Wales.
Miss Crotchet's muse has somehow failed to function,
Yet she's a poetess.   Beaming, she sails

From group to chattering group, with such a dear
Victorian saintliness, as is her fashion,
Greeting the other unknowns with a cheer —
Virgins of sixty who still write of passion.

The air is heavy with Canadian topics,
And Carman, Lampman, Roberts, Campbell, Scott,   10
Are measured for their faith and philanthropics,
Their zeal for God and King, their earnest thought.

The cakes are sweet, but sweeter is the feeling
That one is missing with the *literati*;

messing

It warms the old, and melts the most congealing.
Really, it is a most delightful party.

Shall we go round the mulberry bush, or shall
We gather at the river, or shall we
Appoint a Poet Laureate this fall,
Or shall we have another cup of tea?   20

O Canada, O Canada, Oh can
A day go by without new authors springing
To paint the native maple, and to plan
More ways to set the selfsame welkin ringing?

(1945)   (1966)

Overture

In the dark room under a cone of light,
You precisely play the Mozart sonata.   The bright
Clear notes fly like sparks through the air
And trace a flickering pattern of music there.

Your hands dart in the light, your fingers flow.
They are ten careful operatives in a row
That pick their packets of sound from steel bars
Constructing harmonies as sharp as stars.

But how shall I hear old music?   This is an hour
Of new beginnings, concepts warring for power,   10
Decay of systems – the tissue of art is torn
With overtures of an era being born.

And this perfection which is less yourself
Than Mozart, seems a trinket on a shelf,
A pretty octave played before a window
Beyond whose curtain grows a world crescendo

(1945)   (1966)

Spain: 1937

For these our hearts are bleeding: the homes burning,
The schools broken and ended, the vision thwarted,
The youths, their backs to the wall, awaiting the volley,
The child staring at the huddled form.

And Guernica, more real than our daily bread.

For these our hurt and hate, sharp couriers,
Arouse a waking world: the black crusade,
Pious brutality, mass massacre,
Sudden cohesion of class, wealth and creed,
Behind the gilded cross, the swastika,   10
Behind neutrality, the will to kill.

And Lorca, rising godlike from fascist guns.

In the spring of ideas they were, the rare spring
That breaks historic winters. Street and field
Stirring with hope and green with new endeavour,
The cracking husks copious with sprouting seed.
Here was destruction before flowering,
Here freedom was cut in its first tendrils.

This issue is not ended with defeat.

(1945)   (1945)

North Stream

Ice mothers me
My bed is rock
Over sand I move silently.

I am crystal clear
To a sunbeam.
No grasses grow in me
My banks are clean.

Foam runs from the rapid
To rest on my dark pools.

(1945)   (1966)

Lakeshore

The lake is sharp along the shore
Trimming the bevelled edge of land
To level curves; the fretted sands
Go slanting down through liquid air
Till stones below shift here and there
Floating upon their broken sky
All netted by the prism wave
And rippled where the currents are.

I stare through windows at this cave
Where fish, like planes, slow-motioned, fly.   10
Poised in a still of gravity
The narrow minnow, flicking fin,
Hangs in a paler, ochre sun,
His doorways open everywhere.

And I am a tall frond that waves
Its head below its rooted feet
Seeking the light that draws it down
To forest floors beyond its reach
Vivid with gloom and eerie dreams.

The water's deepest colonnades   20
Contract the blood, and to this home
That stirs the dark amphibian
With me the naked swimmers come
Drawn to their prehistoric womb.

They too are liquid as they fall
Like tumbled water loosed above
Until they lie, diagonal,
Within the cool and sheltered grove
Stroked by the fingertips of love.

Silent, our sport is drowned in fact   30
Too virginal for speech or sound
And each is personal and laned
Along his private aqueduct.

Too soon the tether of the lungs
Is taut and straining, and we rise
Upon our undeveloped wings
Toward the prison of our ground
A secret anguish in our thighs
And mermaids in our memories.

This is our talent, to have grown   40
Upright in posture, false-erect,
A landed gentry, circumspect,
Tied to a horizontal soil
The floor and ceiling of the soul;
Striving, with cold and fishy care
To make an ocean of the air.

Sometimes, upon a crowded street,
I feel the sudden rain come down
And in the old, magnetic sound
I hear the opening of a gate   50
That loosens all the seven seas.
Watching the whole creation drown
I muse, alone, on Ararat.

(1954)   (1966)

W.L.M.K.

How shall we speak of Canada,
Mackenzie King dead?
The Mother's boy in the lonely room
With his dog, his medium and his ruins?

He blunted us.

We had no shape
Because he never took sides,
And no sides
Because he never allowed them to take shape.

He skilfully avoided what was wrong   10
Without saying what was right,
And never let his on the one hand
Know what his on the other hand was doing.

The height of his ambition
Was to pile a Parliamentary Committee on a Royal Commission,
To have 'conscription if necessary
But not necessarily conscription',
To let Parliament decide —
Later.

Postpone, postpone, abstain.   20

Only one thread was certain:
After World War I
Business as usual,
After World War II
Orderly decontrol.
Always he led us back to where we were before.

He seemed to be in the centre
Because we had no centre,
No vision
To pierce the smoke-screen of his politics.   30

Truly he will be remembered
Wherever men honour ingenuity,
Ambiguity, inactivity, and political longevity.

Let us raise up a temple
To the cult of mediocrity,
Do nothing by halves
Which can be done by quarters.

(1957)   (1966)

Vision

Vision in long filaments flows
Through the needles of my eyes.
I am fastened to the rose
When it takes me by surprise.

I am clothed in what eye sees.
Snail's small motion, mountain's
    height,
Dress me with their symmetries
In the robing-rooms of sight.

10 Summer's silk and winter's wool
Change my inner uniform.
Leaves and grass are cavern cool
As the felted snow is warm.

When the clear and sun-drenched
    day
Makes a mockery of dress
All the fabric falls away.
I am clothed in nakedness.

(1964)

Stars so distant, stones nearby
Wait, indifferently, in space
Till an all-perceptive eye
Gives to each its form and place.   20

Mind is a chameleon
Blending with environment;
To the colours it looks on
Is its own appearance bent.

Yet it changes what it holds
In the knowledge of its gaze
And the universe unfolds
As it multiplies its rays.

Tireless eye, so taut and long,
Touching flowers and flames with 30
    ease,
All your wires vibrate with song
When it is the heart that sees.

(1966)

Japanese Sand Garden

raked
in long lines   by bamboo prongs
the white sand
is endless   a distance
is waves
circling small rocks
islands
placed here three   here two
and faraway
three   two   and two   10

                    in rock clefts
                         moss
                    makes river deltas

                        suddenly
                    horizons vanish
            in this vast ocean
                        where the most
            is made from the least
                    and the eternal relative
                        absorbs   20
                    the ephemeral absolute

(1964)   (1964)

On the Terrace, Quebec

Northward, the ice-carved land,
les pays d'en haut.

South, the softer continent,
river-split.

By Valcartier, three Laurentian
   hills.
Many years ago, as children,
looking north from the Rectory
   window
on the longest day of each year
we saw the sun set
in the second dip.

I walk these boards under the
   citadel,
see the narrow streets below,
the basin, l'Ile d'Orléans,
the gateway.

I think of the English troops
imprisoned in the broken city
in the spring of 1760
waiting the first ship.

Whose flag would it fly?

And that other army, under de   20
   Lévis,
victorious at Ste. Foy,
still strong,
watching too.

Suddenly, round the bend,
masts and sails
begin to finger the sky.

The first question was answered.

(1973)   (1973)

Winter Sparrows

Feathered leaves
      on a leafless bush.
Dropping to feed
      they fly back to the stems.

(1973)   (1973)

From

Letters from the Mackenzie River
1956

V FORT PROVIDENCE

We came out of Beaver Lake
Into swift water,
Past the Big Snye, past Providence Island,
And nosed our barges into shore
Till they grated on stones and sand.
Gang planks, thrown to the bank
Were all we had for dock
To drop four tons of freight.

A line of men were squatting
Silently above us, straight   10
Black hair, swarthy skins,
Slavies they call them, who left
Their name on Lake and River.
None of them spoke or moved –
Just sat and watched, quietly,
While the white man heaved at his hardware.
Farther on, by themselves,
The women and girls were huddled.

Then we saw Father Denis,
Oblate from Rennes, Brittany,   20
In charge of the only mission.
Young, cheerful, crucifix stuck in his waistband,
He greeted us with friendly warmth,
Would show us the school, his pride.

We had seen the school from far off.
It stood four stories high,
Grey, square, isolated,
More fortlike than anything in Fort Providence.
In the entrance hall
Walt Disney illustrations for the Kleenex Company   30
Showed children how to avoid getting colds
By constantly using Kleenex.
The gentle sister in charge,
A Grey Nun from Montreal,
Welcomed us in French.
Priests from France, nuns from Quebec,
Taught Slavies (who still speak Indian)
Grades I to VIII, in broken English.

We walked through the crowded class-rooms.
No map of Canada or the Territories,   40
No library or workshop,
Everywhere religious scenes,
Christ and Saints, Stations of the Cross,
Beads hanging from nails, crucifixes,
And two kinds of secular art –
Silk-screen prints of the Group of Seven,
And crayon drawings and masks
Made by the younger children,
The single visible expression
Of the soul of these broken people.   50

Upstairs on the second storey
Seventy little cots
Touching end to end
In a room 30 by 40
Housed the resident boys
In this firetrap mental gaol.

(1973)   (1973)

Alain Grandbois
1900-1975

———◆———

ALAIN GRANDBOIS WAS born in Saint-Casimir de Portneuf and studied law at Laval University and the University of Paris before embarking on extensive travel throughout the world. His first book, *Né à Québec,* a fictionalized biography of the explorer, Louis Jolliet, was published in 1933 and his first major volume of poetry, *Les Îles de la nuit,* appeared in 1944. Grandbois, together with Hébert and Saint-Denys Garneau, became one of the most significant figures in the development of modern poetry in Quebec, not only because of the quality of his own verse but also because of his influence on the poets of succeeding generations.

With Your Dress...

With your dress on the rock like a white wing
With drops in your hand's hollow like a fresh wound
And you laughing   head thrown back like a child alone

With your weak naked feet on the rock's hard strength
And your arms surrounding you with nonchalant lightning
And your knee round as the island of my childhood

With your young breasts that a mute song raises for a vain joy
And your body's curves all plunging towards your frail secret
And that pure mystery that your blood watches for nights
     to come

Like as you are to a dream already lost   10
Like as you are to a betrothed already dead
Mortal instant that you are of the eternal stream

Let me only shut my eyes
Let me only place the palms of my hands on my eyelids
Let me no longer see you

So as not to see in the thickness of the shadows
Slowly come ajar and turn
The heavy gates of oblivion

(1944)   (1964)
Peter Miller (Trans.)

Is It Already the Hour...

Is it already the hour
My tender fear
Is it the hour   the hour
Of tomorrow

Earth and sea
Glide into time
The rods of the sky
Roll gently
Bathed in oblivion

Where is that brow's whiteness   10
Where, the lost house
Where, on a soil
Not stealing away
Are the footsteps of today

The conspiracy of morning
Weaves in the silence
The endless journeying

Undefinable fingers
O vertical breath
O hollow of space   20

But where is the hour   my tender fear
Where, your soft snow
Fresh sister, compeer

The tunes of childhood
— Have they ever ceased
On the other side of the world
Out there, where your shadow hides its head

(1944)   (1964)
Peter Miller (Trans.)

Let Us Close the Cupboard

Close the cupboard with its magic tricks
It is too late for all those games
My hands that are no longer quick
No longer aim directly to the heart
The world I conjured had its own
Brightness, but that sun
Has left me blind
My world and I will both go under
I will sink into the deep caves
Night will inhabit me and its tragic snares   10
No neighbouring voices will reach my ears
I will possess the impassivity of minerals
Everything will be glacial
Even my doubt

It is too late   I know
Already the hillside has engulfed the day
Already my ghost appoints its hour
But the golden twilight   once again I see
      it leaning on the delicate lilacs
I see those adorable evening sails   20
      riven with stars
I see the shoreline with its inviolable shores
I have loved the extraordinarily rapt look of love
      too much not to regret love
I have adorned my women too richly with
      unrivalled aureoles
I have cultivated for too long too fabulous gardens

But once I saw the three perfect cypress
Before the white of the white house
I saw and I was silent   30
And my distress is without equal

All that is too late
Close the cupboard with its varied poisons
Put out the lamps that burn in the void
      like dead fairies
Nothing will ever again stir in the dark
The nights will never again sweep in
      the morning bells

Immaculate hands will never again
    be lifted above the doorstep 40

But you   o you   I have seen you
    walking on the sea with your hair
    full of sparkling light
You were walking erect with your white
    face lifted
You were walking with the whole horizon
    around you like a vaulted dome
You were walking and you were slowly pushing back
    the prodigious front of the waves
With your two hands before you like the two 50
    doves from the Ark
And you were bearing us to the rendez-vous
    with the archangel
And you were pure and grave and beautiful
    with the smile of one whose heart
    has been wholly given up

And the prophets laid their deep silence
    on the jealousy of the waters
And there was then only the great fraternal calm
    of the seven seas 60
Profound as the most mortal tomb

(1944)   (1974)
D.G. Jones (Trans.)

Wedding

We are standing
Standing and naked and straight
Sinking together straight down
To the bottom of the sea
Her long hair floating
Over our heads
Like thousands of quivering snakes
We are straight and standing
Bound by our ankles and wrists
Bound by our dumbfounded lips 10

Bound by our soldered hips
Scanning each other's heartbeat

We are diving we are diving straight down
Into the chasms of the sea
Slowly passing through each sea-green
Floor with uniform precision
Some fishes already turn
In a wake of misty gold
Long seaweed bend
Under the green and invisible breath   20
Of great annunciations

We are sinking straight and pure
Into the shadow of the original darkness
Flashes spurt and die
As fast as possible
Electric communications
Crackle around us like Chinese fires
Final secrets
Penetrate us insidiously
Through these phosphorescent wounds   30
Our diving always defying
The laws of atmospheres
Our diving defying
The red blood of the living heart

We are rolling we are rolling
She and I alone
In the sea's heavy dreams
Like transparent giants
Under the eternal glow

Lunar flowers lengthen   40
Glowing all around us
We are taut and straight
Feet pointing toward the bottom
Like an inverted diver's
Tearing the spectral dawns
The absolute watches us
Like a devouring wolf

Sometimes a galley's prow
With its arms of phantom sails

Sometimes thin pale suns   50
Suddenly tear the medusas
We are diving to the bottom of the ages
We are diving to the bottom of an incalculable sea
Forging and welding
The implacable destiny of our chains

Ah more darkness
Still more darkness
There are too many purple sharks
Too many anemone too dark
Let's leave the cycle of hate   60
Let's leave the gods of sword-fish
The sails above are lost
In the wrenching of stars
With the last sands
The shores deserted
By the dead gods
Stiff and smooth like two corpses
My flesh inert in her deep side
Our eyes closed as if forever
Her arms my arms don't exist anymore   70
We sink like lead
Into the sea's many caves
Soon we'll reach
The perfect couches of shadows
Ah black and total crystal
Eternal eyes
Vain shuddering of days

Earth's sign to heaven
We are diving to the death of the world
We are diving to the birth of the world   80

(1957)   (1974)
A. Poulin Jr. (Trans.)

The Ambiguous Dawn

The slowly ebbing night
Drains light from stars,

Restores clear shape
To shoreline, meadows, lakes and wooded hills;
It is the end for sleepwalkers
Staggering round roofs of invisible skyscrapers.

The end comes too
for poets and for the dying,
last lines, last rites, last agonies
of good and evil men   10
fade with the coming dawn
the shivering dance of the sun

Dawn's paths are difficult;
exacting man
caught at the anxious crossroads
of the night
winds ropes of terror round
his own emerging throat,
seeking and shunning light.

(1957)   (1973)
G.V. Downes (Trans.)

From
Born in Quebec, Louis Jolliet

[The Discovery of the Mississippi]

THE REAL ADVENTURE was just beginning. Louis had surprised the river
at its very source. He saw it develop, grow broader and longer and trace
its vital and prodigious course through the clay, the granite and the
forest. The barriers presented by the earth, tireless and tenacious,
against which it had had to struggle for thousands of years, bent now to
the whims of the river, to the reeds; the arid beaches were bathed in
golden sand; the river took from its contact with the rocks a freshness
and limpidity that were always new. And she stretched her smooth
arms around laughing wooded islands. From the primitive disorder a
loving harmony surged forth. And Louis knew that in her fluid masses
she nourished a swarming life, secret and uncountable.

Morning after morning followed. The evenings were fiery red.
Dreams were woven in the silence and the night.

There was nothing to indicate the passing or the presence of man. Jolliet was astonished that a region of such beauty had no permanent settlers. On the seventh day the hills on the edge of the left bank of the Wiskonsing were further away, disappeared. The next day, June 17, Jolliet entered the Mississippi.

Kneeling on the sand, head high, hands together, Marquette gave thanks to the Virgin. The men's hearts were filled with a new faith. They knew that they would overcome. They intoned the "Te Deum." And in the vast silence of Heaven and earth that followed the last notes of the chant, the river alone could be heard, the obsessive music of its voice. Avidly, Jolliet took possession of the River.

Peacefully and slowly the River flowed towards the south. Vast timbered plains stretched out to the east. Undulating mountains rose towards the west. At the mouth of the Wiskonsing Jolliet had marked on his map a position of 42.5°.

Now he was descending a River whose uneven width varied between three arpents and three-quarters of a league. Soundings indicated that it was some ten fathoms deep. There were a number of islands. The region was deserted but extraordinarily fertile. Game birds and animals were plentiful. Louis set up camp in the shadow of the islands, in the shelter of the bays. He had forbidden fire, song, the use of the musket. Vainly he watched for revealing smoke. Every night one man stood guard. And each day the kingdom of France was increased by ten leagues.

Beyond the 42nd degree the appearance of the landscape changed. The western mountains bent, flowed together. Enormous plains with tall grasses waving in the wind replaced the forest. Gradually the birds disappeared. The water of the river became deeper, black. In their nets the men caught pike, sturgeon, carp and a curious fish whose jaw was decorated with a bony protuberance one foot long. Later they saw swimming on the surface a monster with a bearded head like a tiger's, its huge size reminiscent of the silenes of the lower Danube.

Then the River became sinuous, with more curves and bends. The compass showed the direction to be south south-east. Marquette shook his head; it was unlikely that they would reach the shores of California this way. Jolliet, disconcerted, remarked that not a single native had been seen since the tenth of June. He became more vigilant. Deserted land often harbours unpleasant surprises. That evening the oarsmen rubbed their callused hands and talked in low voices of evil spells and sorcery.

One incomparably clear morning they had reached the 41st degree when they heard a dull rumbling sound like distant thunder. It seemed to come from the north-east and it grew more intense every second. The hills that sealed off the west prevented them from seeing very far. Soon the noise was as loud as a charging squadron. Then suddenly they saw a maddened herd of buffalo running towards the River, invading the crest of the hills and coming down the hillside. The first animals stopped short at the sight of the canoes. Others hesitated, dancing where they stood. Currents were produced in the midst of the herd and horns shone above the tall grass like an army's lances. Then the lead animals were overcome by a sudden fright. They made a half-turn and in a single burst the entire herd roared past the canoes, charging towards the south. Their heavy galloping shook the earth. They disappeared. A rust-coloured cloud ran along the horizon for some time.

More days passed. The heat became painful. Jolliet crossed the mouth of a tributary that went out to the right of the Mississippi. It was Sunday. He took a few steps on the beach. Suddenly he saw the fresh prints of bare feet.

The trail rose up towards the plain. It was outlined by a path through the grass. Should they follow it? Jolliet hesitated. If he did follow it there might be unpleasant surprises that would compromise the success of the expedition. Marquette equivocated. Had they not decided to follow the course of the great River? Thus after succumbing to an entirely verbal caution the two men soon found that they agreed about reaching a decision that would satisfy their secret desire. And Jolliet gave his orders to the oarsmen: they must make no fire, no sound, nor must they under any pretext leave the campsite: they must be on constant guard, hide at the possible approach of any native and have the canoes ready to put into the River when the first signal was given. And the Jesuit and the Canadian buried themselves in the tall grasses.

(1933)   (1974)
Sheila Fischman (Trans.)

A.J.M. Smith
1902 –

ARTHUR JAMES MARSHALL SMITH was born in Montreal and studied at McGill University before earning a Ph.D. at the University of Edinburgh in 1931. He accepted an appointment to the Department of English at Michigan State University in 1936 and continued teaching there until 1972. *News of the Phoenix and Other Poems*, the first of four collections of Smith's poetry, appeared in 1943. He has also been extremely influential as a critic and as editor or co-editor of *The McGill Fortnightly Review* (1925–1927), *New Provinces* (1936) and *The Book of Canadian Poetry* (1943).

Like an Old Proud King in a Parable

A bitter king in anger to be gone
From fawning courtier and doting queen
Flung hollow sceptre and gilt crown away,
And breaking bound of all his counties green
He made a meadow in the northern stone
And breathed a palace of inviolable air
To cage a heart that carolled like a swan,
And slept alone, immaculate and gay,
With only his pride for a paramour.

O who is that bitter king? It is not I.   10

Let me, I beseech thee, Father, die
From this fat royal life, and lie
As naked as a bridegroom by his bride,
And let that girl be the cold goddess Pride:

And I will sing to the barren rock
Your difficult, lonely music, heart,
Like an old proud king in a parable.

(1943)   (1967)

117

To a Young Poet

FOR C.A.M.

Tread the metallic nave
Of this windless day with
A pace designed and grave:
— Iphigenia in her myth

Creating for stony eyes
An elegant, fatal dance
Was signed with no device
More alien to romance

Than I would have you find
In the stern, autumnal face   10
Of Artemis, whose kind
Cruelty makes duty grace,

Whose votary alone
Seals the affrighted air
With the worth of a hard thing done
Perfectly, as though without care.

(1943)   (1967)

The Plot Against Proteus

This is a theme for muted coronets
To dangle from debilitated heads
Of navigation, kings, or riverbeds
That rot or rise what time the seamew sets
Her course by stars among the smoky tides
Entangled. Old saltencrusted Proteus treads
Once more the watery shore that water weds
While rocking fathom bell rings round and rides.

Now when the blind king of the water thinks
The sharp hail of the salt out of his eyes   10
To abdicate, run thou, O Prince, and fall
Upon him. This cracked walrus skin that stinks
Of the rank sweat of a mermaid's thighs
Cast off, and nab him; when you have him, call.

(1943)   (1967)

Ode:
on the Death of
William Butler Yeats

An old thorn tree in a stony place
Where the mountain stream has run dry,
Torn in the black wind under the race
Of the icicle-sharp kaleidoscopic white sky,
   Bursts into sudden flower.

Under the central dome of winter and night
A wild swan spreads his fanatic wing.
Ancestralled energy of blood and power
Beats in his sinewy breast. And now the ravening
Soul, fulfilled, his first-last hour   10
   Upon him, chooses to exult.

Over the edge of shivering Europe,
Over the chalk front of Kent, over Eire,
Dwarfing the crawling waves' amoral savagery,
Daring the hiding clouds' rhetorical tumult,
   The white swan plummets the mountain top.

The stream has suddenly pushed the papery leaves!
It digs a rustling channel of clear water
On the scarred flank of Ben Bulben.
The twisted tree is incandescent with flowers.   20
The swan leaps singing into the cold air:
   This is a glory not for an hour:

   Over the Galway shore
   The white bird is flying
   Forever, and crying
   To the tumultuous throng
Of the sky his cold and passionate song.

(1943)   (1967)

Sea Cliff

Wave on wave
and green on rock
and white between
the splash and black
the crash and hiss
of the feathery fall,
the snap and shock
of the water wall
and the wall of rock:

after —   10
after the ebb-flow,
wet rock,
high —
high over the slapping green,
water sliding away
and the rock abiding,
new rock riding
out of the spray.

(1943)   (1967)

The Lonely Land

Cedar and jagged fir
uplift sharp barbs
against the gray
and cloud-piled sky;
and in the bay
blown spume and windrift
and thin, bitter spray
snap
at the whirling sky;
10   and the pine trees
lean one way.

A wild duck calls
to her mate,
and the ragged
and passionate tones
stagger and fall,
and recover,
and stagger and fall,
on these stones —
20   are lost

in the lapping of water
on smooth, flat stones.

This is a beauty
of dissonance,
this resonance
of stony strand,
this smoky cry
curled over a black pine
like a broken
and wind-battered branch   30
when the wind
bends the tops of the pines
and curdles the sky
from the north.

This is the beauty
of strength
broken by strength
and still strong.

(1943)   (1967)

News of the Phoenix

They say the Phoenix is dying, some say dead.
Dead without issue is what one message said,
But that has been suppressed, officially denied.

I think myself the man who sent it lied.
In any case, I'm told, he has been shot,
As a precautionary measure, whether he did or not.

(1943)   (1967)

To Henry Vaughan

Homesick? and yet your country Walks
Were heaven'd for you. Such bright stalks
Of grasses! such pure Green! such blue
Clear skies! such light! such silver dew! —
On each brief bud and shining twig
White pregnant jewels, each one big
With meaning, rich pearls cast before
Not swine but men, who toss or snore.
     Thou didst not so: thou wert awake;
And stirring forth before the break   10
Of day, thou wouldst enquire
If, with the Cock, no angel choir
Meant to announce th'eternal Day;
If, in the sun's first quick'ning ray
Thou might'st observe the flaming hair
Of thy wish'd Lord, thy Bridegroom dear.
     Yet when the Constellations fine
Stand where the sun before did shine,
You may not in your good-night pray'r
Ask day more holy, heav'n more near: 20
Earth's angels, these tall feathery trees,
Sang in thy loved one's praise; thy bees
Gather'd his Honey; one small bird
In three clear notes his Name preferr'd.
     Celestial strings might not surpass

Thy morning breezes in long grass;
The slow rain from the laden tree,
Dropping from heaven, brought to thee
Sounds of the purest harmony,
Setting thy caged soul free to fly,   30
Borne on the breath of fruits and flow'rs
Sweeten'd and made fresh in silver show'rs.
    And add to these thy bubbling rills;
Soft winds; the intricate rich trills
Of happy larks that climb the air
Like a broad golden winding Stair
To Heaven, singing as they climb,
Lifting the rapt soul out of Time
Into a long Eternity
Where Heaven is now, and still to be.   40
    Yet art thou Homesick! to be gone
From all this brave Distraction
Wouldst seal thine ear, nail down thine eye;
To be one perfect Member, die;
And anxious to exchange in death
Thy foul, for thy Lord's precious, breath,
Thou art content to beg a pall,
Glad to be Nothing, to be All.

(1962)   (1967)

Wild Raspberry

FOR W. W. E. ROSS

Your ragged leaves
are speckled with dust

They are frayed at the edges
and sticky with sunshine

but after the rain
gashes of red

glisten
among slipp'ry green leaves

Yellow whips
and prickly little branches   10

are pulled into curves
by the big berries

The eye feasts on them
and feels refreshed

(1962)   (1967)

My Death

'I carry my death within me.'
Who was it said that? – St-Denys-Garneau?
It's true. Everyone – free
Or enslaved, Christian or Jew,
Coloured or white, believer or
Skeptic or the indifferent worldling –
Knows death, at least as metaphor.

But this says more. My death is a thing
Physical, solid, sensuous, a seed
Lodged like Original Sin   10
In the essence of being, a need
Also, a felt want within.

It lies dormant at first,
Lazy, a little romantic
In childhood, later a thirst
For what is no longer exotic.
It lives on its own phlegm,
And grows stronger as I grow stronger,
As a flower grows with its stem.

I am the food of its hunger.   20
It enlivens my darkness,
Progressively illuminating
What I know for the first time, yes,
Is what I've been always wanting.

(1962)   (1967)

Morley Callaghan
1903 –

———◆———

BORN IN TORONTO, Morley Callaghan was educated at St. Michael's College, University of Toronto, and Osgoode Law School. In 1926 he published his first short story in *This Quarter*, a Parisian literary journal. Later, following the appearance of a novel, *Strange Fugitive* (1928), and a collection of stories, *A Native Argosy* (1929), he spent several months in Paris where he associated with many of the expatriate writers of England and America. Among his best-known works are *Such Is My Beloved* (1934), *They Shall Inherit the Earth* (1935), *More Joy in Heaven* (1937), *The Loved and the Lost* (1951), *That Summer in Paris* (1963) and *A Fine and Private Place* (1975). "Ancient Lineage" was accepted for publication in Ezra Pound's journal, *Exile*, in 1927.

Ancient Lineage

THE YOUNG MAN from the Historical Club with a green magazine under his arm got off the train at Clintonville. It was getting dark but the station lights were not lit. He hurried along the platform and jumped down on the sloping cinder path to the sidewalk.

Trees were on the lawns alongside the walk, branches drooping low, leaves scraping occasionally against the young man's straw hat. He saw a cluster of lights, bluish-white in the dusk across a river, many lights for a small town. He crossed the lift-lock bridge and turned on to the main street. A hotel was at the corner.

At the desk a bald-headed man in a blue shirt, the sleeves rolled up, looked critically at the young man while he registered. 'All right, Mr. Flaherty,' he said, inspecting the signature carefully.

'Do you know many people around here?' Mr. Flaherty asked.

'Just about everybody.'

'The Rowers?'

'The old lady?'

'Yeah, an old lady.'

'Sure, Mrs. Anna Rower. Around the corner to the left, then turn to the right out the first street, the house opposite the Presbyterian church on the hill.'

'An old family,' suggested the young man.

'An old-timer all right.' The hotel man made it clear by a twitching of his lips that he was a part of the new town, canal, water power, and factories.

Mr. Flaherty sauntered out and turned to the left. It was dark and the street had the silence of small towns in the evening. Turning a corner he heard girls giggling in a doorway. He looked at the church on the hill, the steeple dark against the sky. He had forgotten whether the man had said beside the church or across the road, but could not make up his mind to ask the fellow who was watering the wide church lawn. No lights in the shuttered windows of the rough-cast house beside the church. He came down the hill and had to yell three times at the man because the water swished strongly against the grass.

'All right, thanks. Right across the road,' Mr. Flaherty repeated.

Tall trees screened the square brick house. Looking along the hall to a lighted room, Mr. Flaherty saw an old lady standing at a sideboard. 'She's in all right,' he thought, rapping on the screen door. A large woman of about forty, dressed in blue skirt and blue waist, came down the stairs. She did not open the screen door.

'Could I speak to Mrs. Anna Rower?'

'I'm Miss Hilda Rower.'

'I'm from the University Historical Club.'

'What did you want to see Mother for?'

Mr. Flaherty did not like talking through the screen door. 'I wanted to talk to her,' he said firmly.

'Well, maybe you'd better come in.'

He stood in the hall while the large woman lit the gas in the front room. The gas flared up, popped, showing fat hips and heavy lines on her face. Mr. Flaherty, disappointed, watched her swaying down the hall to get her mother. He carefully inspected the front room, the framed photographs of dead Conservative politicians, the group of military men hanging over the old-fashioned piano, the faded greenish wallpaper and the settee in the corner.

An old woman with a knot of white hair and good eyes came into the room, walking erectly. 'This is the young man who wanted to see you, Mother,' Miss Hilda Rower said. They all sat down. Mr. Flaherty explained he wanted to get some information concerning the Rower genealogical tree for the next meeting of his society. The Rowers, he knew, were a pioneer family in the district, and descended from William the Conqueror, he had heard.

The old lady laughed thinly, swaying from side to side. 'It's true enough, but I don't know who told you. My father was Daniel Rower, who came to Ontario from Cornwall in 1830.'

Miss Hilda Rower interrupted. 'Wait, Mother, you may not want to tell about it.' Brusque and businesslike, she turned to the young man. 'You want to see the family tree, I suppose.'

'Oh, yes.'

'My father was a military settler here,' the old lady said.

'I don't know but what we might be able to give you some notes,' Miss Hilda spoke generously.

'Thanks awfully, if you will.'

'Of course you're prepared to pay something if you're going to print it,' she added, smugly adjusting her big body in the chair.

Mr. Flaherty got red in the face; of course he understood, but to tell the truth he had merely wanted to chat with Mrs. Rower. Now he knew definitely he did not like the heavy nose and unsentimental assertiveness of the lower lip of this big woman with the wide shoulders. He couldn't stop looking at her thick ankles. Rocking back and forth in the chair she was primly conscious of lineal superiority; a proud unmarried woman, surely she could handle a young man, half-closing her eyes, a young man from the University indeed. 'I don't want to talk to her about the University,' he thought.

Old Mrs. Rower went into the next room and returned with a framed genealogical tree of the house of Rower. She handed it graciously to Mr. Flaherty, who read, 'The descent of the family of Rower, from William the Conqueror, from Malcolm 1st, and from the Capets, Kings of France.' It bore the *imprimatur* of the College of Arms, 1838.

'It's wonderful to think you have this,' Mr. Flaherty said, smiling at Miss Hilda, who watched him suspiciously.

'A brother of mine had it all looked up,' old Mrs. Rower said.

'You don't want to write about that,' Miss Hilda said, crossing her ankles. The ankles looked much thicker crossed. 'You just want to have a talk with Mother.'

'That's it,' Mr. Flaherty smiled agreeably.

'We may write it up ourselves some day.' Her heavy chin dipped down and rose again.

'Sure, why not?'

'But there's no harm in you talking to Mother if you want to, I guess.'

'You could write a good story about that tree,' Mr. Flaherty said, feeling his way.

'We may do it some day but it'll take time,' she smiled complacently at her mother, who mildly agreed.

Mr. Flaherty talked pleasantly to this woman, who was so determined he would not learn anything about the family tree without paying for it. He tried talking about the city, then tactfully asked old Mrs. Rower what she remembered of the Clintonville of seventy years ago. The old lady talked willingly, excited a little. She went into the next room to get a book of clippings. 'My father, Captain Rower, got a grant of land from the Crown and cleared it,' she said, talking over her shoulder. 'A

little way up the Trent River. Clintonville was a small military settlement then...'

'Oh, Mother, he doesn't want to know all about that,' Miss Hilda said
impatiently.

'It's very interesting indeed.'

The old woman said nervously, 'My dear, what difference does it
make? You wrote it all up for the evening at the church.'

'So I did too,' she hesitated, thinking the young man ought to see how
well it was written. 'I have an extra copy.' She looked at him thoughtfully. He smiled. She got up and went upstairs.

The young man talked very rapidly to the old lady and took many
notes.

Miss Rower returned. 'Would you like to see it?' She handed Mr.
Flaherty a small gray booklet. Looking quickly through it, he saw it
contained valuable information about the district.

'The writing is simply splendid. You must have done a lot of work on
it.'

'I worked hard on it,' she said, pleased and more willing to talk.

'Is this an extra copy?'

'Yes, it's an extra copy.'

'I suppose I might keep it,' he said diffidently.

She looked at him steadily. 'Well... I'll have to charge you twenty-five
cents.'

'Sure, sure, of course, that's fine.' He blushed.

'Just what it cost to get them out,' the old lady explained apologetically.

'Can you change a dollar?' He fumbled in his pocket, pulling the
dollar out slowly.

They could not change it but Miss Rower would be pleased to go
down to the corner grocery store. Mr. Flaherty protested. No trouble,
he would go. She insisted on asking the next-door neighbour to change
it. She went across the room, the dollar in hand.

Mr. Flaherty chatted with the nice old lady and carefully examined
the family tree, and wrote quickly in a small book till the screen door
banged, the curtains parted, and Miss Hilda Rower came into the
room. He wanted to smirk, watching her walking heavily, so conscious
of her ancient lineage, a virginal mincing sway to her large hips,
seventy-five cents' change held loosely in drooping fingers.

'Thank you,' he said, pocketing the change, pretending his work was
over. Sitting back in the chair he praised the way Miss Rower had
written the history of the neighbourhood and suggested she might
write a splendid story of the family tree, if she had the material, of
course.

'I've got the material, all right,' she said, trying to get comfortable
again. How would Mr. Flaherty arrange it and where should she try to

sell it? The old lady was dozing in the rocking chair. Miss Rower began to talk rather nervously about her material. She talked of the last title in the family and the Sir Richard who had been at the court of Queen Elizabeth.

Mr. Flaherty chimed in gaily, 'I suppose you know the O'Flahertys were kings in Ireland, eh?'

She said vaguely, 'I daresay, I daresay,' conscious only of an interruption to the flow of her thoughts. She went on talking with hurried eagerness, all the fine talk about her ancestors bringing her peculiar satisfaction. A soft light came into her eyes and her lips were moist.

Mr. Flaherty started to rub his cheek, and looked at her big legs, and felt restive, and then embarrassed, watching her closely, her firm lower lip hanging loosely. She was talking slowly, lazily, relaxing in her chair, a warm fluid oozing through her veins, exhausting but satisfying her.

He was uncomfortable. She was liking it too much. He did not know what to do. There was something immodest about it. She was close to forty, her big body relaxed in the chair. He looked at his watch and suggested he would be going. She stretched her legs graciously, pouting, inviting him to stay a while longer, but he was standing up, tucking his magazine under his arm. The old lady was still dozing. 'I'm so comfortable,' Miss Rower said, 'I hate to move.'

The mother woke up and shook hands with Mr. Flaherty. Miss Rower got up to say good-bye charmingly.

Half-way down the path Mr. Flaherty turned. She was standing in the doorway, partly shadowed by the tall trees, bright moonlight filtering through leaves touching soft lines on her face and dark hair.

He went down the hill to the hotel unconsciously walking with a careless stride, wondering at the change that had come over the heavy, strong woman. He thought of taking a walk along the river in the moonlight, the river on which old Captain Rower had drilled troops on the ice in the winter of 1837 to fight the rebels. Then he thought of having a western sandwich in the café across the road from the hotel. That big woman in her own way had been hot stuff.

In the hotel he asked to be called so he could get the first train to the city. For a long time he lay awake in the fresh, cool bed, the figure of the woman whose ancient lineage had taken the place of a lover in her life, drifting into his thoughts and becoming important while he watched on the wall the pale moonlight that had softened the lines of her face, and wondered if it was still shining on her bed, and on her throat, and on her contented, lazily relaxed body.

(1929)   (1959)

Thomas Raddall
1903 –

———◆———

BORN IN HYTHE, England, Thomas Raddall emigrated to Halifax with his family in 1913. Since the appearance of his first collection of stories, *The Pied Piper of Dipper Creek* (1939), he has published five historical romances, several other collections of short stories and three novels with contemporary settings, including *The Nymph and the Lamp* (1950). His autobiography, *In My Time*, was published in 1976. "The Wedding Gift" first appeared in *The Saturday Evening Post* in 1941.

The Wedding Gift

NOVA SCOTIA, IN 1794. Winter. Snow on the ground. Two feet of it in the woods, less by the shore, except in drifts against Port Marriott's barns and fences; but enough to set sleigh bells ringing through the town, enough to require a multitude of paths and burrows from doors to streets, to carpet the wharves and the decks of the shipping, and to trim the ships' yards with tippets of ermine. Enough to require fires roaring in the town's chimneys, and blue wood smoke hanging low over the roof tops in the still December air. Enough to squeal under foot in the trodden places and to muffle the step everywhere else. Enough for the hunters, whose snowshoes now could overtake the floundering moose and caribou. Even enough for the always-complaining loggers, whose ox sleds now could haul their cut from every part of the woods. But not enough, not nearly enough snow for Miss Kezia Barnes, who was going to Bristol Creek to marry Mr. Hathaway.

Kezia did not want to marry Mr. Hathaway. Indeed she had told Mr. and Mrs. Barclay in a tearful voice that she didn't want to marry anybody. But Mr. Barclay had taken snuff and said "Ha! Humph!" in the severe tone he used when he was displeased; and Mrs. Barclay had sniffed and said it was a very good match for her, and revolved the cold blue eyes in her fat moon face, and said Kezia must not be a little fool.

There were two ways of going to Bristol Creek. One was by sea, in one of the fishing sloops. But the preacher objected to that. He was a pallid young man lately sent out from England by Lady Huntingdon's Connexion, and seasick five weeks on the way. He held Mr. Barclay in some awe, for Mr. Barclay had the best pew in the meetinghouse and was the chief pillar of godliness in Port Marriott. But young Mr. Mears was firm on this point. He would go by road, he said, or not at all. Mr. Barclay had retorted "Ha! Humph!" The road was twenty miles of horse path through the woods, now deep in snow. Also the path began at Harper's Farm on the far side of the harbour, and Harper had but one horse.

"I shall walk," declared the preacher calmly, "and the young woman can ride."

Kezia had prayed for snow, storms of snow, to bury the trail and keep anyone from crossing the cape to Bristol Creek. But now they were setting out from Harper's Farm, with Harper's big brown horse, and all Kezia's prayers had gone for naught. Like any anxious lover, busy Mr. Hathaway had sent Black Sam overland on foot to find out what delayed his wedding, and now Sam's day-old tracks marked for Kezia the road to marriage.

She was a meek little thing, as became an orphan brought up as house-help in the Barclay home; but now she looked at the preacher and saw how young and helpless he looked so far from his native Yorkshire, and how ill-clad for this bitter trans-Atlantic weather, and she spoke up.

"You'd better take my shawl, sir. I don't need it. I've got Miss Julia's old riding cloak. And we'll go ride-and-tie."

"Ride and what?" murmured Mr. Mears.

"I'll ride a mile or so, then I'll get down and tie the horse to a tree and walk on. When you come up to the horse, you mount and ride a mile or so, passing me on the way, and you tie him and walk on. Like that. Ride-and-tie, ride-and-tie. The horse gets a rest between."

Young Mr. Mears nodded and took the proffered shawl absently. It was a black thing that matched his sober broadcloth coat and smallclothes, his black woollen stockings and his round black hat. At Mr. Barclay's suggestion he had borrowed a pair of moose-hide moccasins for the journey. As he walked a prayer-book in his coat-skirts bumped the back of his legs.

At the top of the ridge above Harper's pasture, where the narrow path led off through gloomy hemlock woods, Kezia paused for a last look back across the harbour. In the morning sunlight the white roofs of the little lonely town resembled a tidal wave flung up by the sea and frozen as it broke against the dark pine forest to the west. Kezia sighed, and young Mr. Mears was surprised to see tears in her eyes.

She rode off ahead. The saddle was a man's, of course, awkward to ride modestly, woman-fashion. As soon as she was out of the preacher's sight she rucked her skirts and slid a leg over to the other stirrup. That was better. There was a pleasant sensation of freedom about it, too. For a moment she forgot that she was going to Bristol Creek, in finery second-hand from the Barclay girls, in a new linen shift and drawers that she had sewn herself in the light of the kitchen candles, in white cotton stockings and a bonnet and shoes from Mr. Barclay's store, to marry Mr. Hathaway.

The Barclays had done well for her from the time when, a skinny weeping creature of fourteen, she was taken into the Barclay household and, as Mrs. Barclay so often said, 'treated more like one of my own than a bond-girl from the poorhouse.' She had first choice of the clothing cast off by Miss Julia and Miss Clara. She was permitted to sit in the same room, and learn what she could, when the schoolmaster came to give private lessons to the Barclay girls. She waited on table, of course, and helped in the kitchen, and made beds, and dusted and scrubbed. But then she had been taught to spin and to sew and to knit. And she was permitted, indeed encouraged, to sit with the Barclays in the meetinghouse, at the convenient end of the pew, where she could worship the Barclays' God and assist with the Barclay wraps at the beginning and end of the service. And now, to complete her rewards, she had been granted the hand of a rejected Barclay suitor.

Mr. Hathaway was Barclay's agent at Bristol Creek, where he sold rum and gunpowder and corn meal and such things to the fishermen and hunters, and bought split cod – fresh, pickled or dry – and ran a small sawmill, and cut and shipped firewood by schooner to Port Marriott, and managed a farm, all for a salary of fifty pounds, Halifax currency, per year. Hathaway was a most capable fellow, Mr. Barclay often acknowledged. But when after fifteen capable years he came seeking a wife, and cast a sheep's eye first at Miss Julia, and then at Miss Clara, Mrs. Barclay observed with a sniff that Hathaway was looking a bit high.

So he was. The older daughter of Port Marriott's most prosperous merchant was even then receiving polite attentions from Mr. Gamage, the new collector of customs, and a connection of the Halifax Gamages, as Mrs. Barclay was fond of pointing out. And Miss Clara was going to Halifax in the spring to learn the gentle art of playing the pianoforte, and incidentally to display her charms to the naval and military young gentlemen who thronged the Halifax drawingrooms. The dear girls laughed behind their hands whenever long solemn Mr. Hathaway came to town aboard one of the Barclay vessels and called at the big house under the elms. Mrs. Barclay bridled at Hathaway's presumption, but shrewd Mr. Barclay narrowed his little black eyes and took snuff and said "Ha! Humph!"

It was plain to Mr. Barclay that an emergency had arisen. Hathaway was a good man – in his place; and Hathaway must be kept content there, to go on making profit for Mr. Barclay at a cost of only £50 a year. 'Twas a pity Hathaway couldn't satisfy himself with one of the fishermen's girls at the Creek, but there 'twas. If Hathaway had set his mind on a town miss, then a town miss he must have; but she must be the right kind, the sort who would content herself and Hathaway at Bristol Creek and not go nagging the man to remove and try his capabilities elsewhere. At once Mr. Barclay though of Kezia – dear little Kezzie. A colourless little creature but quiet and well-mannered and pious, and only twenty-two.

Mr. Hathaway was nearly forty and far from handsome, and he had a rather cold, seeking way about him – useful in business of course – that rubbed women the wrong way. Privately Mr. Barclay thought Hathaway lucky to get Kezia. But it was a nice match for the girl, better than anything she could have expected. He impressed that upon her and introduced the suitor from Bristol Creek. Mr. Hathaway spent two or three evenings courting Kezia in the kitchen – Kezia in a quite good gown of Miss Clara's, gazing out at the November moon on the snow, murmuring now and again in the tones of someone in a rather dismal trance, while the kitchen help listened behind one door and the Barclay girls giggled behind another.

The decision, reached mainly by the Barclays, was that Mr. Hathaway should come to Port Marriott aboard the packet schooner on December twenty-third, to be married in the Barclay parlour and then take his bride home for Christmas. But an unforeseen circumstance had changed all this. The circumstance was a ship, 'from Mogador in Barbary' as Mr. Barclay wrote afterwards in the salvage claim, driven off her course by gales and wrecked at the very entrance to Bristol Creek. She was a valuable wreck, laden with such queer things as goatskins in pickle, almonds, wormseed, pomegranate skins and gum arabic, and capable Mr. Hathaway had lost no time in salvage for the benefit of his employer.

As a result he could not come to Port Marriott for a wedding or anything else. A storm might blow up at any time and demolish this fat prize. He dispatched a note by Black Sam, urging Mr. Barclay to send Kezia and the preacher by return. It was not the orthodox note of an impatient sweetheart, but it said that he had moved into his new house by the Creek and found it 'extream empty lacking a woman', and it suggested delicately that while his days were full, the nights were dull.

Kezia was no judge of distance. She rode for what she considered a reasonable time and then slid off and tied the brown horse to a maple tree beside the path. She had brought a couple of lamp wicks to tie about her shoes, to keep them from coming off in the snow, and she set out afoot in the big splayed tracks of Black Sam. The soft snow came almost to her knees in places and she lifted her skirts high. The path was no wider than the span of a man's arms, cut out with axes years before. She stumbled over a concealed stump from time to time, and the huckleberry bushes dragged at her cloak, but the effort warmed her. It had been cold, sitting on the horse with the wind blowing up her legs.

After a time the preacher overtook her, riding awkwardly and holding the reins in a nervous grip. The stirrups were too short for his long black-stockinged legs. He called out cheerfully as he passed, "Are you all right, Miss?" She nodded, standing aside with her back to a tree. When he disappeared ahead, with a last flutter of black shawl tassels in the wind, she picked up her skirts and went on. The path climbed and dropped monotonously over a succession of wooded ridges. Here and there in a hollow she heard water running, and the creak of frosty poles underfoot, and knew she was crossing a small stream, and once the trail ran across a wide swamp on half-rotten corduroy, wind-swept and bare of snow.

She found the horse tethered clumsily not far ahead, and the tracks of the preacher going on. She had to lead the horse to a stump so she could mount, and when she passed Mr. Mears again she called out, "Please, sir, next time leave the horse by a stump or a rock so I can get on." In his quaint old-country accent he murmured, "I'm very sorry," and gazed down at the snow. She forgot she was riding astride until she had passed him, and then she flushed, and gave the indignant horse a cut of the switch. Next time she remembered and swung her right leg back where it should be, and tucked the skirts modestly about her ankles; but young Mr. Mears looked down at the snow anyway, and after that she did not trouble to shift when she overtook him.

The ridges became steeper, and the streams roared under the ice and snow in the swales. They emerged upon the high tableland between Port Marriott and Bristol Creek, a gusty wilderness of young hardwood scrub struggling up amongst the gray snags of an old forest fire, and now that they were out of the gloomy softwoods they could see a stretch of sky. It was blue-grey and forbidding, and the wind whistling up from the invisible sea felt raw on the cheek. At their next meeting Kezia said, "It's going to snow."

She had no knowledge of the trail but she guessed that they were not much more than half way across the cape. On this high barren the track was no longer straight and clear, it meandered amongst the meagre hardwood clumps where the path-makers had not bothered to cut, and only Black Sam's footprints really marked it for her unaccustomed eyes. The preacher nodded vaguely at her remark. The woods, like everything else about his chosen mission field, were new and very interesting, and he could not understand the alarm in her voice. He looked confidently at Black Sam's tracks.

Kezia tied the horse farther on and began her spell of walking. Her shoes were solid things, the kind of shoes Mr. Barclay invoiced as 'a Common Strong sort, for women, Five Shillings'; but the snow worked into them and melted and saturated the leather. Her feet were numb every time she slid down from the horse and it took several minutes of stumbling through the snow to bring back an aching warmth. Beneath her arm she clutched the small bundle which contained all she had in the world – two flannel nightgowns, a shift of linen, three pairs of stout wool stockings – and of course Mr. Barclay's wedding gift for Mr. Hathaway.

Now as she plunged along she felt the first sting of snow on her face and, looking up, saw the stuff borne on the wind in small hard pellets that fell amongst the bare hardwoods and set up a whisper everywhere. When Mr. Mears rode up to her the snow was thick in their faces, like flung salt.

"It's a nor-easter!" she cried up to him. She knew the meaning of snow from the sea. She had been born in a fishing village down the coast.

"Yes," mumbled the preacher, and drew a fold of the shawl about his face. He disappeared. She struggled on, gasping, and after what seemed a tremendous journey came upon him standing alone and bewildered, looking off somewhere to the right.

"The horse!" he shouted. "I got off him, and before I could fasten the reins some snow fell off a branch – startled him, you know – and he ran off, over that way." He gestured with a mittened hand. "I must fetch him back," he added confusedly.

"No!" Kezia cried. "Don't you try. You'd only get lost. So would I. Oh, dear! this is awful. We'll have to go on, the best we can."

He was doubtful. The horse tracks looked very plain. But Kezia was looking at Black Sam's tracks, and tugging his arm. He gave in, and they struggled along for half an hour or so. Then the last trace of the old footprints vanished.

"What shall we do now?" the preacher asked, astonished.

"I don't know," whispered Kezia, and leaned against a dead pine stub in an attitude of weariness and indifference that dismayed him.

"We must keep moving, my dear, mustn't we? I mean, we can't stay here."

"Can't stay here," she echoed.

"Down there – a hollow, I think. I see some hemlock trees, or are they pines? – I'm never quite sure. Shelter, anyway."

"Shelter," muttered Kezia.

He took her by the hand and like a pair of lost children they dragged their steps into the deep snow of the hollow. The trees were tall spruces, a thick bunch in a ravine, where they had escaped the old fire. A stream thundered amongst them somewhere. There was no wind in this place, only the fine snow whirling thickly down between the trees like a sediment from the storm overhead.

"Look!" cried Mr. Mears. A hut loomed out of the whiteness before them, a small structure of moss-chinked logs with a roof of poles and birch-bark. It had an abandoned look. Long streamers of moss hung out between the logs. On the roof shreds of birch-bark wavered gently in the drifting snow. The door stood half open and a thin drift of snow lay along the split-pole floor. Instinctively Kezia went to the stone hearth. There were old ashes sodden with rain down the chimney and now frozen to a cake.

"Have you got flint and steel?" she asked. She saw in his eyes something dazed and forlorn. He shook his head, and she was filled with a sudden anger, not so much at him as at Mr. Barclay and that — that Hathaway, and all the rest of menkind. They ruled the world and made such a sorry mess of it. In a small fury she began to rummage about the hut.

There was a crude bed of poles and brushwood by the fireplace — brushwood so old that only a few brown needles clung to the twigs. A rough bench whittled from a pine log, with round birch sticks for legs. A broken earthenware pot in a corner. In another some ash-wood frames such as trappers used for stretching skins. Nothing else. The single window was covered with a stretched moose-bladder, cracked and dry-rotten, but it still let in some daylight while keeping out the snow.

She scooped up the snow from the floor with her mittened hands, throwing it outside, and closed the door carefully, dropping the bar into place, as if she could shut out and bar the cold in such a fashion. The air inside was frigid. Their breath hung visible in the dim light from the window. Young Mr. Mears dropped on his wet knees and began to pray in a loud voice. His face was pinched with cold and his teeth rattled as he prayed. He was a pitiable object.

"Prayers won't keep you warm," said Kezia crossly.

He looked up, amazed at the change in her. She had seemed such a meek little thing. Kezia was surprised at herself, and surprisingly she went on, "You'd far better take off those wet moccasins and stockings and shake the snow out of your clothes." She set the example, vigourously shaking out her skirts and Miss Julia's cloak, and she turned her small back on him and took off her own shoes and stockings, and pulled on dry stockings from her bundle. She threw him a pair.

"Put those on."

"I'm afraid they wouldn't go on."

She tossed him one of her flannel nightgowns. "Then take off your stockings and wrap your feet and legs in that."

He obeyed, in an embarrassed silence. She rolled her eyes upward, for his modesty's sake, and saw a bundle on one of the low rafters – the late owner's bedding, stowed away from mice. She stood on the bench and pulled down three bearskins, marred with bullet holes. A rank and musty smell arose in the cold. She considered the find gravely.

"You take them," Mr. Mears said gallantly. "I shall be quite all right."

"You'll be dead by morning, and so shall I," she answered vigorously, "if you don't do what I say. We've got to roll up in these."

"Together?" he cried in horror.

"Of course! To keep each other warm. It's the only way."

She spread the skins on the floor, hair uppermost, one overlapping another, and dragged the flustered young man down beside her, clutched him in her arms, and rolled with him, over, and over again, so that they became a single shapeless heap in the corner farthest from the draft between door and chimney.

"Put your arms around me," commanded the new Kezia, and he obeyed.

"Now," she said, "you can pray. God helps those that help themselves."

He prayed aloud for a long time, and privately called upon heaven to witness the purity of his thoughts in this strange and shocking situation. He said "Amen" at last; and "Amen", echoed Kezia, piously.

They lay silent a long time, breathing on each other's necks and hearing their own hearts – poor Mr. Mears' fluttering in an agitated way, Kezia's as steady as a clock. A delicious warmth crept over them. They relaxed in each other's arms. Outside, the storm hissed in the spruce tops and set up an occasional cold moan in the cracked clay chimney. The down-swirling snow brushed softly against the bladder pane.

"I'm warm now," murmured Kezia. "Are you?"

"Yes. How long must we stay here like this?"

"Till the storm's over, of course. Tomorrow, probably. Nor'easters usually blow themselves out in a day and a night, 'specially when they come up sharp, like this one. Are you hungry?"

"No."

"Abigail – that's the black cook at Barclay's – gave me bread and cheese in a handerchief. I've got it in my bundle. Mr. Barclay thought we ought to reach Bristol Creek by supper time, but Nabby said I must have a bite to eat on the road. She's a good kind thing, old Nabby. Sure you're not hungry?"

"Quite. I feel somewhat fatigued but not hungry."

"Then we'll eat the bread and cheese for breakfast. Have you got a watch?"

"No, I'm sorry. They cost such a lot of money. In Lady Huntingdon's Connexion we – "

"Oh well, it doesn't matter. It must be about four o'clock – the light's getting dim. Of course, the dark comes very quick in a snowstorm."

"Dark," echoed young Mr. Mears drowsily. Kezia's hair, washed last night for the wedding journey, smelled pleasant so close to his face. It reminded him of something. He went to sleep dreaming of his mother, with his face snug in the curve of Kezia's neck and shoulder, and smiling, and muttering words that Kezia could not catch. After a time she kissed his cheek. It seemed a very natural thing to do.

Soon she was dozing herself, and dreaming, too; but her dreams were full of forbidding faces – Mr. Barclay's, Mrs. Barclay's, Mr. Hathaway's; especially Mr. Hathaway's. Out of a confused darkness Mr. Hathaway's hard acquisitive gaze searched her shrinking flesh like a cold wind. Then she was shuddering by the kitchen fire at Barclay's, accepting, Mr. Hathaway's courtship and wishing she was dead. In the midst of that sickening wooing she wakened sharply.

It was quite dark in the hut. Mr. Mears was breathing quietly against her throat. But there was a sound of heavy steps outside, muffled in the snow and somehow felt rather than heard. She shook the young man and he wakened with a start, clutching her convulsively.

"Sh-h-h!" she warned. "Something's moving outside." She felt him stiffen.

"Bears?" he whispered.

Silly! thought Kezia. People from the old country could think of nothing but bears in the woods. Besides, bears holed up in winter. A caribou, perhaps. More likely a moose. Caribou moved inland before this, to the wide mossy bogs up the river, away from the coastal storms. Again the sound.

"There!" hissed the preacher. Their hearts beat rapidly together.

"The door – you fastened it, didn't you?"

"Yes," she said. Suddenly she knew.

"Unroll, quick!" she cried... "No, not this way – your way."

They unrolled, ludicrously, and the girl scrambled up and ran across the floor in her stockinged feet, and fumbled with the rotten door-bar. Mr. Mears attempted to follow but he tripped over the nightgown still wound about his feet, and fell with a crash. He was up again in a moment, catching up the clumsy wooden bench for a weapon, his bare feet slapping on the icy floor. He tried to shoulder her aside, crying "Stand back! Leave it to me!" and waving the bench uncertainly in the darkness.

She laughed excitedly. "Silly!" she said. "It's the horse." She flung the door open. In the queer ghostly murk of a night filled with snow they beheld a large dark shape. The shape whinnied softly and thrust a long face into the doorway. Mr. Mears dropped the bench, astonished.

"He got over his fright and followed us here somehow," Kezia said, and laughed again. She put her arms about the snowy head and laid her face against it.

"Good horse! Oh, good, good horse!"

"What are you going to do?" the preacher murmured over her shoulder. After the warmth of their nest in the furs they were shivering in this icy atmosphere.

"Bring him in, of course. We can't leave him out in the storm." She caught the bridle and urged the horse inside with expert clucking sounds. The animal hesitated, but fear of the storm and a desire for shelter and company decided him. In he came, tramping ponderously on the split-pole floor. The preacher closed and barred the door.

"And now?" he asked.

"Back to the furs. Quick! It's awful cold."

Rolled in the furs once more, their arms went about each other instinctively, and the young man's face found the comfortable nook against Kezia's soft throat. But sleep was difficult after that. The horse whinnied gently from time to time, and stamped about the floor. The decayed poles crackled dangerously under his hoofs whenever he moved, and Kezia trembled, thinking he might break through and frighten himself, and flounder about till he tumbled the crazy hut about their heads. She called out to him "Steady, boy! Steady!"

It was a long night. The pole floor made its irregularities felt through the thickness of fur; and because there seemed nowhere to put their arms but about each other the flesh became cramped, and spread its protest along the bones. They were stiff and sore when the first light of morning stained the window. They unrolled and stood up thankfully, and tramped up and down the floor, threshing their arms in an effort to fight off the gripping cold. Kezia undid her bundle in a corner and brought forth Nabby's bread and cheese, and they ate it sitting together on the edge of the brushwood bed with the skins about their shoulders. Outside the snow had ceased.

"We must set off at once," the preacher said. "Mr. Hathaway will be anxious."

Kezia was silent. She did not move, and he looked at her curiously. She appeared very fresh, considering the hardships of the previous day and the night. He passed a hand over his cheeks and thought how unclean he must appear in her eyes, with this stubble on his pale face.

"Mr. Hathaway – " he began again.

"I'm not going to Mr. Hathaway," Kezia said quietly.

"But – the wedding!"

"There'll be no wedding. I don't want to marry Mr. Hathaway. 'Twas Mr. Hathaway's idea, and Mr. and Mrs. Barclay's. They wanted me to marry him."

"What will the Barclays say, my dear?"

She shrugged. "I've been their bond-girl ever since I was fourteen, but I'm not a slave like poor black Nabby, to be handed over, body and soul, whenever it suits."

"Your soul belongs to God," said Mr. Mears devoutly.

"And my body belongs to me."

He was a little shocked at this outspokenness but he said gently, "Of course. To give oneself in marriage without true affection would be an offense in the sight of heaven. But what will Mr. Hathaway say?"

"Well, to begin with, he'll ask where I spent the night, and I'll have to tell the truth. I'll have to say I bundled with you in a hut in the woods."

"Bundled?"

"A custom the people brought with them from Connecticut when they came to settle in Nova Scotia. Poor folk still do it. Sweethearts, I mean. It saves fire and candles when you're courting on a winter evening. It's harmless – they keep their clothes on, you see, like you and me – but Mr. Barclay and the other Methody people are terrible set against it. Mr. Barclay got old Mr. Mings – he's the Methody preacher that died last year – to make a sermon against it. Mr. Mings said bundling was an invention of the devil."

"Then if you go back to Mr. Barclay – "

"He'll ask me the same question and I'll have to give him the same answer. I couldn't tell a lie, could I?" She turned a pair of round blue eyes and met his embarrassed gaze.

"No! No, you mustn't lie. Whatever shall we do?" he murmured in a dazed voice. Again she was silent, looking modestly down her small nose.

"It's so very strange," he floundered. "This country – there are so many things I don't know, so many things to learn. You – I – we shall have to tell the truth, of course. Doubtless I can find a place in the Lord's service somewhere else, but what about you, poor girl?"

"I heard say the people at Scrod Harbour want a preacher."

"But – the tale would follow me, wouldn't it, my dear? This – er – bundling with a young woman?"

" 'Twouldn't matter if the young woman was your wife."

"Eh?" His mouth fell open. He was like an astonished child, for all his preacher's clothes and the new beard on his jaws.

"I'm a good girl," Kezia said, inspecting her foot. "I can read and write, and know all the tunes in the psalter. And – and you need someone to look after you."

He considered the truth of that. Then he murmured uncertainly,

"We'd be very poor, my dear. The Connexion gives some support, but of course – "

"I've always been poor," Kezia said. She sat very still but her cold fingers writhed in her lap.

He did something then that made her want to cry. He took hold of her hands and bowed his head and kissed them.

"It's strange – I don't even know your name, my dear."

"It's Kezia – Kezia Barnes."

He said quietly, "You're a brave girl, Kezia Barnes, and I shall try to be a good husband to you. Shall we go?"

"Hadn't you better kiss me, first?" Kezia said faintly.

He put his lips awkwardly to hers; and then, as if the taste of her clean mouth itself provided strength and purpose, he kissed her again, and firmly. She threw her arms about his neck.

"Oh, Mr. Mears!"

How little he knew about everything! He hadn't even known enough to wear two or three pairs of stockings inside those roomy moccasins, nor to carry a pair of dry ones. Yesterday's wet stockings were lying like sticks on the frosty floor. She showed him how to knead the hard-frozen moccasins into softness, and while he worked at the stiff leather she tore up one of her wedding bed-shirts and wound the flannel strips about his legs and feet. It looked very queer when she had finished, and they both laughed.

They were chilled to the bone when they set off, Kezia on the horse and the preacher walking ahead, holding the reins. When they regained the slope where they had lost the path, Kezia said, "The sun rises somewhere between east and southeast, this time of year. Keep it on your left shoulder a while. That will take us back towards Port Marriott."

When they came to the green timber she told him to shift the sun to his left eye.

"Have you changed your mind?" he asked cheerfully. The exercise had warmed him.

"No, but the sun moves across the sky."

"Ah! What a wise little head it is!"

They came over a ridge of mixed hemlock and hardwood and looked upon a long swale full of bare hackmatacks.

"Look!" the girl cried. The white slot of the axe path showed clearly in the trees at the foot of the swale, and again where it entered the dark mass of the pines beyond.

"Praise the Lord!" said Mr. Mears.

When at last they stood in the trail, Kezia slid down from the horse.

"No!" Mr. Mears protested.

"Ride-and-tie," she said firmly. "That's the way we came, and that's the way we'll go. Besides, I want to get warm."

He climbed up clumsily and smiled down at her.

"What shall we do when we get to Port Marriott, my dear?"

"Get the New Light preacher to marry us, and catch the packet for Scrod Harbour."

He nodded and gave a pull at his broad hat brim. She thought of everything. A splendid helpmeet for the world's wilderness. He saw it all very humbly now as a dispensation of Providence.

Kezia watched him out of sight. Then, swiftly, she undid her bundle and took out the thing that had lain there (and on her conscience) through the night – the tinderbox – Mr. Barclay's wedding gift to Mr. Hathaway. She flung it into the woods and walked on, skirts lifted, in the track of the horse, humming a psalm tune to the silent trees and the snow.

(1947)   (1947)

Earle Birney
1904–

———————◆———————

BORN IN CALGARY, Alberta, Earle Birney received his honours degree in English from the University of British Columbia in 1926 and his M.A. and Ph.D. from the University of Toronto. He has taught at several North American universities and was literary editor of *The Canadian Forum* from 1936 to 1940 and editor of *The Canadian Poetry Magazine* from 1946 to 1948. During the Second World War he served with the Canadian army in England and Holland and in more recent years he has travelled widely on lecture tours. Since the appearance of his first collection of poetry, *David and Other Poems* (1942), Birney has written reviews, essays, radio plays, two novels and several volumes of poetry including *Collected Poems* (1975).

Kootenay Still-Life

Columning up from crisscross rot
(palmed flat by a wind forgotten)
breathes a single bullpine, naked
for fifty cinnabar feet, then shakes
at the valley a glittering fist of needles
rivergreen. And stops, headless.

On the yellow fang of the bullpine's broken
neckbone sits, eyeing her beetle below,
a crow.

(1942)   (1975)

Vancouver Lights

About me the night   moonless   wimples the mountains
wraps ocean   land   air   and mounting
sucks at the stars   The city   throbbing below
webs the sable peninsula   The golden
strands overleap the seajet   by bridge and buoy
vault the shears of the inlet   climb the woods
toward me   falter   and halt   Across to the firefly
haze of a ship on the gulf's erased horizon
roll the lambent spokes of a lighthouse

Through the feckless years we have come to the time   10
when to look on this quilt of lamps is a troubling delight
Welling from Europe's bog   through Africa flowing
and Asia   drowning the lonely lumes on the oceans
tiding up over Halifax   now to this winking
outpost comes flooding the primal ink

On this mountain's brutish forehead with terror of space
I stir   of the changeless night and the stark ranges
of nothing   pulsing down from beyond and between

the fragile planets   We are a spark beleaguered
by darkness   this twinkle we make in a corner of emptiness   20
how shall we utter our fear that the black Experimentress
will never in the range of her microscope find it?   Our Phoebus
himself is a bubble that dries on Her slide   while the Nubian
wears for an evening's whim a necklace of nebulae

Yet we must speak   we the unique glowworms
Out of the waters and rocks of our little world
we conjured these flames   hooped these sparks
by our will   From blankness and cold we fashioned stars
to our size   and signalled Aldebaran
This must we say   whoever may be to hear us   30
if murk devour   and none weave again in gossamer:

These rays were ours
we made and unmade them   Not the shudder of continents
doused us   the moon's passion   nor crash of comets
In the fathomless heat of our dwarfdom   our dream's combustion
we contrived the power   the blast that snuffed us
No one bound Prometheus   Himself he chained
and consumed his own bright liver   O stranger
Plutonian   descendant   or beast in the stretching night —
there was light   40

(1942)   (1975)

The Road to Nijmegen

December my dear on the road to Nijmegen
between the stones and the bitten sky
was your face

Not yours at first
but only the countenance of lank canals
and gathered stares
(too rapt to note my passing)
of graves with frosted billy-tins for epitaphs

bones of tanks beside the stoven bridges
and old men in the mist   10
hacking the last chips
from a boulevard of stumps

These for miles and the fangs of homes
where women wheeled in the wind
on the tireless rims of their cycles
like tattered sailboats
tossing over the cobbles

and the children
groping in gravel for knobs of coal
or clustered like wintered flies   20
at the back of messhuts
their legs standing like dead-stems out of their clogs

Numbed on the long road to mangled Nijmegen
I thought that only the living of others assures us
the gentle and true we remember as trees walking
Their arms reach down from the light of kindness
into this Lazarus tomb

So peering through sleet as we neared Nijmegen
I glimpsed the rainbow arch of your eyes
Over the clank of the jeep   30
your quick grave laughter
outrising at last the rockets
brought me what spells I repeat
as I travel this road
that arrives at no future
and what creed I can bring
to our daily crimes
to this guilt
in the griefs of the old
and the graves of the young   40

(1945)   (1975)

Biography

At ten the years made tracks
plumped and sprung with pine-needles

Gaining height   overlooked
rocks balanced on ridges
swords of snow in cliffside

Twenty he lay by the lake
the bright unpredictable book
gracefully bound in green
and riffled its pages for rainbow

Life was a pup-tent   ptarmigan   10
chased along simmering slopes
bannocks and bacon
Only the night-mists died at dawn

By thirty he trudged above timber
peered over ice at the peaks

As they swung slowly around him
the veins of bald glaciers blackened
white pulses of waterfalls
beat in the bare rockflesh

Before him at forty   20
a nunatak stood like a sundial
swiftly marked time in the snow

Later a lancet of rime
hissed from the heave of the massif
a shrill wind shouldered him
and he turned
but tried without might
had lost the lake or his nerve
forgot all the trail-forks
knew at the end only_   30
the ice knuckling his eyes

(1952)   (1975)

Bushed

He invented a rainbow but lightning struck it
shattered it into the lake-lap of a mountain
so big his mind slowed when he looked at it

Yet he built a shack on the shore
learned to roast porcupine belly and
wore the quills on his hatband

At first he was out with the dawn
whether it yellowed bright as wood-columbine
or was only a fuzzed moth in a flannel of storm
But he found the mountain was clearly alive   10
sent messages whizzing down every hot morning
boomed proclamations at noon and spread out
a white guard of goat
before falling asleep on its feet at sundown

When he tried his eyes on the lake   ospreys
would fall like valkyries
choosing the cut-throat
He took then to waiting
till the night smoke rose from the boil of the sunset

But the moon carved unknown totems   20
out of the lakeshore
owls in the beardusky woods derided him
moosehorned cedars circled his swamps and tossed
their antlers up to the stars
then he knew   though the mountain slept   the winds
were shaping its peak to an arrowhead
poised

And now he could only
bar himself in and wait
for the great flint to come singing into his heart   30

(1952)   (1975)

Pachucan Miners

All day in a night of lurch   blast
bend   they have deepened the dark search
their precortesian priests began
into the cold peak's argent
mysteries   Only the ore has risen
into the tasselled wind and run
on singing rails beneath the ardent
sky to sorceries beyond their vision
But now another nugget sun
himself is floated out of thought   10
and   Orphic and helmeted as divers
are pressed upwards all the miners

Under thin stars by murky troughs
white-eyed they spit   wash rockscurf off
turn without rancour from the guarded gate
below the white Olympus of the gringos
Helmed still and wordless they tramp down
base-metalled roadways to the town
stop where peons by their braziers
shiver to sell them roasted maize   20
Yet like a defeated army still
descend past blackened walls above
the tree-abandoned valley till
at the lowest street the doors of light

peal out   tequila is a brightness
in the throat   bottles and faces gleam
receive them in a sensible dream
In the cantinas helmets roll
backs fling upright   O now legs are male
are braced   each knotty pair   to hold   30
up song and hurl it at the night
then step their own way down to where
deep in her torchy den
snakes Toltecan looping in her ears
her crucifix agleam above the sheet
Eurydice reclines and hears
the wild guitars   and daily waits
the nightly rescue of her silver men.

(1962)   (1975)

The Bear on the Delhi Road

Unreal   tall as a myth
by the road the Himalayan bear
is beating the brilliant air
with his crooked arms
About him two men   bare
spindly as locusts   leap

One pulls on a ring
in the great soft nose   His mate
flicks   flicks with a stick
up at the rolling eyes   10

They have not led him here
down from the fabulous hills
to this bald alien plain
and the clamorous world   to kill
but simply to teach him to dance

They are peaceful both   these spare
men of Kashmir   and the bear
alive is their living   too
If   far on the Delhi way
around him galvanic they dance   20
it is merely to wear   wear
from his shaggy body the tranced
wish forever to stay
only an ambling bear
four-footed in berries

It is no more joyous for them
in this hot dust to prance
out of reach of the praying claws
sharpened to paw for ants
in the shadows of deodars   30
It is not easy to free
myth from reality
or rear this fellow up
to lurch   lurch with them
in the tranced dancing of men

(1962)   (1975)

A Walk in Kyoto

all week the maid tells me bowing
her doll's body at my mat is Boys Day
also please Mans Day and gravely
bends deeper the magnolia sprig in my alcove
is it male the old discretions of Zen
were not shaped for my phallic western eye
there is so much discretion
in this small bowed body of an empire
(the wild hair of waterfalls combed straight
in the ricefields the inn-maid retreating   10
with the face of a shut flower) i stand hunched
and clueless like a castaway in the shoals of my room

when i slide my parchment door to stalk awkward
through lilliput gardens framed & untouchable
as watercolours the streets look much as everywhere
men are pulled past on the strings
of their engines the legs of boys
are revolved by a thousand pedals
& all the faces are taut & unfestive as Moscow's
or Toronto's or mine   20

Lord Buddha help us all there is vigour enough
in these islands & in all islands reefed & resounding
with cities but the pitch is high high as the ping
of cicadas (those small strained motors concealed
in the propped pines by the dying river) & only male
as the stretched falsetto of actors mincing the roles
of kabuki women or female only as the lost heroes
womanized in the Ladies Opera –
where in these alleys jammed with competing waves
of signs in two tongues & three scripts   30
can the simple song of a man be heard?

by the shoguns palace the Important Cultural Property
stripped for tiptoeing schoolgirls i stare
at the staring penned carp that flail
on each others backs to the shrunk pools edge
for the crumb this non-fish tossed
is this the Days one parable
or under that peeling pagoda the 500 tons
of hermaphrodite Word?

at the inn i prepare to surrender again   40
my defeated shoes to the bending maid   but suddenly
the closed lotus opens to a smile & she points
to where   over my shoulder   above the sagging tiles
tall in the bare sky & huge as Gulliver
a carp is rising   golden & fighting
thrusting its paper body up from the fist
of a small boy on an empty roof   higher
& higher   into the endless winds of the world

(1962)   (1975)

Wind-Chimes in a Temple Ruin

This is the moment
   for two glass leaves
dangling dumb
   from the temple eaves
This is the instant
   when the sly air breathes
and the tremblers touch
   where no man sees
Who is the moving
   or moved is no matter   10
but the birth of the possible
   song in the rafter
that dies as the wind goes
   nudging other
broken eaves
   for waiting lovers

(1962)   (1975)

North of Superior

Not here the ballad or the human story
the Scylding boaster or the water-troll
not here the mind   only the soundless fugues

of stone and leaf and lake   where but the brutish
ranges   big with haze   confine the keyboard

Barbaric the clangour of boulders   the rhythm of trees
wild where they clutch the pools   and flying with flame
of their yellow sap are the stretching poplars of May
running arpeggios up to the plangent hills

The horseman icecap rowelled the only runes   10
and snow-wild wind these eochromes upon
the raddled rocks that wear the tarns like eyes
within their saurian skulls   O none alive
or dead has cast Excalibur into
these depths   or if some lost Algonquin wooed
a dream that came and vanished here   the breeze
today shakes blades of light without a meaning

Unhaunted through the birches' blanching pillars
lopes the mute prospector   through the dead
and leprous-fingered birch that never led   20
to witches by an Ayrshire kirk nor wist
Of Wirral and a Green Knight's trysting

Close march the spruce   and 'fir that weepeth ever'
the wandering wood that holds no den of Error
Silently over the brush they lift their files
and spear forever together the empty sky
Not here the rooted home but only discords
the logger sounds   tarpaper shanty scored
with lath he deeds next year to squirrel and spider
and little wounds upon the rocks the miner   30
makes and leaves at last to mending snow
The wood returns into its soil   the caribou
are blurring hoofmarks in the scrub   gray wolf
and man make flickers on the long horizon

This world that is no world except to hunted
purblind moose and tonedeaf passing hunter
yet skirls unheard its vast inhuman pibroch
of green on swarthy bog   of ochre rock
and the wine that gleams through the spectral poplar's bark
Not here   with hymn and carol blessed   Titania's   40
night   nor will this neuter moon in anger
pale for vanished rites or broken bough

For nocturne   hypnosis of lynx and owl
No heart to harden or a god to lose
rain without father   unbegotten dews

See where the unexorcized dragon   Fire
has breathed unwieldy lances from the wilds
for wars already waged   and planted one
charred pine to fly a pennant still   a husk
of golden needles – yet no mute or glorious   50
Milton finds Azazel here   no Roland
comes to blow defiance by this serpent stream
No sounds of undistinguishable motion
stalk the guilty poet flying   only
silence where the banded logs lie down
to die and provender the luminous young
The swordless rock   the heavenless air   and land
that weeps unwept into an icy main
where but the waters wap and the waves wane

(1966)   (1975)

ka pass age alaska passage ALASKA PASSAGE alaska passage alas

our ship seems reefed
and only the land comes swimming past alaska pass

the first through   green cresc   to th
      trampdownwards the fog in   enD e fo
                                                  O   O
                                                       R
                                                       E/

SHore'S pIeD coMmotion of bristled
                              ROCK S

and blanching   drif
                                  t

uPfrom aspew sp & Ba   Logchute ws
         of linters RK A   A r o r

(one mark of few that men have scribbled
on this lucky palimpsest of ranges)

at times a shake-built shack exchanges
passive stares with Come & Gone
or eyeless waits with stoven side

to slide its bones in   a   gr e e n t i d e

age alaska passage alaska passage alas-ka pass

(1971)   (1975)

Fusion

no welding
of ores or floes
no liquidation
of salt pillars
no sunthaw of drift
deliquescence of hardness
is like the melting
wherever my bones
fuse and dissolve
in your soft body   10
and we sleep into one
twinned and twined till we wake

and rise
still
welded

(1976)   (1976)

Leo Kennedy
1907–

BORN IN LIVERPOOL, England, Leo Kennedy came to Montreal with his family in 1912. He was educated at the University of Montreal and participated in the establishment of *The McGill Fortnightly Review* (1925-1927) and *The Canadian Mercury* (1928-1929). Kennedy's only volume of poetry, *The Shrouding,* was published in 1933; several of the poems in the collection also appeared in *New Provinces* (1936).

Words for a Resurrection

Each pale Christ stirring underground
Splits the brown casket of its root,
Wherefrom the rousing soil upthrusts
A narrow, pointed shoot,

And bones long quiet under frost
Rejoice as bells precipitate
The loud, ecstatic sundering,
The hour inviolate.

This Man of April walks again –
Such marvel does the time allow –   10
With laughter in His blessèd bones,
And lilies on His brow.

(1933)   (1933)

154

Epithalamium Before Frost

FOR J. & E. K.

Now that leaves shudder from the hazel limb,
And poppies pod, and maples whirl their seed,
And squirrels dart from private stores to slim
The oak of acorns with excessive greed;
And now that sap withdraws, and black geese skim
In rigid phalanx over sedge and reed,
And rime surmised at morning pricks the rim
Of tawny stubble, husk and perishing weed –
Now shall I cry Epithalamium!
Over the bed which your two forms have pressed;   10
And bid Earth's fertile spirits stir and come
To winter at your hearth, and make it blessed;
Until returns the bridal trillium,
And the first crocus hoists its yellow crest!

(1933)   (1933)

Shore

Sand shifts with every tide, and gravel
    Slurs against the rock,
Weeds and a little lifted silt remain
Marking the reach of water, the long shock
Of an absent tide.
Here is no stencilled track of tern, no trace
Of the slight feet of curlews, here no lace
Of foam for the braided webs of gulls to press
Into the falling bosom of the sea.

...But silt left by the receded tide, a ravel   10
Of weeds thrown high by the wash of water, a crest
Of wave, distant, beyond the cove.

(1933)   (1933)

Prophesy for Icarus

No bird that streams its feathers back
   And plunges softly out
Through cubic densities of space
Then banks, and climbs aslant,
But will drop fluttering with woe,
And flex its wings, dismayed
To feel time-brittled tendons halt,
And know itself betrayed.

(1933)   (1933)

Exile Endured

What hand shall gather sweetbrier, and what breast
   Shall wear it proudly, does not matter here;
And where and how it withers, I protest
Is nothing to me, provokes no dread or fear;
And how the ragwurt fares, and how goes back
Into the soil's matrix, and whether grass
Shall perish by fire or frost, or from a lack
Of rain, does not disturb me – let it pass.
I am too long away from copse and hedge
To care what fate besets each twig and leaf;   10
To mourn for bindweed torn, or feel for sedge
Blistered by drought, the sudden prick of grief –
Who have grown harsh and arid under stone
That shrivels up the heart, and splits the bone.

(1933)   (1933)

Edward McCourt
1907 – 1972

———◆———

EDWARD MCCOURT WAS born in Ireland and his family came to Canada
in 1909. He graduated from the University of Alberta in 1932 and
entered Oxford University as a Rhodes Scholar. Following his return
to Canada in 1937, he joined the Department of English at the
University of Saskatchewan. His published works include novels, travel
books, short stories and a study of prairie literature, *The Canadian West
in Fiction* (1949). In *Saskatchewan* (1968), a travel book dealing with the
province in which he spent most of his life, McCourt reveals his
concern with the unique qualities of this particular region.

From
Saskatchewan

The Land and the People

THE INDIANS, AND after them the white men, came late to the great
central plains area of Canada which today forms the southern part of
the province of Saskatchewan. Their reluctance to establish a
permanent home on the naked plains will not surprise visitors to
Saskatchewan, particularly if they make their visit in the dead of
winter; indeed they may be moved to agree whole-heartedly with the
embittered early homesteader who expressed his distaste for his
surroundings in a verse-portrait of a lady neither sweet nor fair:

> Saskatchewan, you always seem to me
> A woman without favour in your face,
> Flat-breasted, angular, devoid of grace.
> Why do men woo you? naught is fair to see
> In that wide visage with thin unkempt hair,
> And form that squarely stands, feet splayed apart.

The lines express what is in fact a common misconception: the truth
is that the Saskatchewan landscape is never barren (except in times of
prolonged drought) and in few places flat. The great southern plains

are seamed deep by gullies and creek beds and frequently ridged by low hills which at a distance appear bathed in a romantic blue-green haze; two hundred miles north of the border the plains merge into pleasant, rolling parkland which in turn yields after another two hundred miles or more to a vast forest-lake-and-muskeg belt impinging on the subarctic terrain of the barren lands. And everywhere there are things to be seen and felt that exalt or soothe the sensitive spirit: crocuses spreading a mauve mist along railway embankments before the last patch of dirty grey snow has melted; wheatfields merging into a wave-surfaced green or golden ocean, unbounded save for an incredibly remote horizon rim at times indistinguishable from the sky itself; autumn days when the wind is miraculously quiet and premonitions of winter-death impel a man to look on a landscape of muted greys and browns with the passionate intensity of a lover parting from his beloved; mid-winter hoar-frost hanging on fence and telephone wires like strung popcorn; and the occasional vista – from the top of a ridge or butte or even a grain elevator – when a man sees all the kingdoms of the earth stretched out at his feet and feels himself a creature of utter insignificance in the sum of things or else the very centre of the universe.

But in spite of her very considerable scenic variety Saskatchewan is likely to impress the stranger with an awareness of encompassing natural forces more hostile than benevolent. This to a far greater degree than does either of her sister provinces. For Manitoba is only halfway plains country; great forests line her eastern flank, northward her land surface is engulfed by inland fresh-water seas; and her heart – so many truculent true-blue westerners affirm – yearns towards Ontario. West of Saskatchewan amply endowed Alberta floats on a lake of oil and snuggles comfortably into the protective embrace of the Rockies; and even her most exposed parts feel from time to time the caress of the genial chinook. But Saskatchewan stands defenceless, no forest belt or mountain range along her flanks to hold the wind at bay. Nowhere else in the west does the stranger feel himself more exposed to the wrath of the gods and the fury of the elements than in the middle of the Saskatchewan prairie.

Even though he may be sheltered behind walls. A sign in each unit of a Maple Creek motel reads thus: *When the wind blows please hang on to the door.*

The wind blows almost without intermission. The Earl of Southesk, in 1859 struggling through 'the glittering white intensity of the cold', reported gloomily that 'our fate seems to be that to which prophecy dooms a certain ancient family,

"The Tracies
Shall always have the wind in their faces."'

And a writer of more recent date, Anne Marriott, has encompassed within a poet's lines the frustration and heartbreak experienced by men and women battered by the searing winds of the dust-bowl years when the lamp at noon was the symbol of a wind-and-drought-tormented wasteland:

> *God, will it never rain again? What about*
> > *those clouds out west? No, that's just dust, as thick and stifling*
> > *now as winter underwear.*
> *No rain, no crop, no feed, no faith, only*
> > *wind.*

Any attempt to explain why the Saskatchewan man differs to a noticeable degree in personality and outlook from the Albertan or Manitoban who should logically be his counterpart must take into account the consequences, both physical and psychological, of the dust-bowl years. The world-wide economic depression that began in 1929 affected all of Canada; Saskatchewan bore an additional and dreadful burden – nine successive years of drought and crop failure. 'The people of Saskatchewan have suffered a reduction of income during the last decade which has probably been unparalleled in peacetime in any other civilized country,' the Royal Commission on Dominion-Provincial Relations reported in 1939. (Incredibly, the net agricultural incomes for 1931 and 1932 were reported in *minus* figures.) 'The land was a landscape of almost incredible desolation,' a Regina newspaper reporter wrote after driving through southern Saskatchewan in the midsummer of 1934, 'as lifeless as ashes, and for miles there was scarcely a thing growing to be seen. ... Gaunt cattle and horses with little save their skins to cover their bones stalked about the denuded acres, weakly seeking to crop the malign Frenchweed which seemed to be maintaining some sickly growth. When the miserable animals moved it seemed as if their frames rattled. The few people in evidence in the little towns appeared haggard and hopeless.'

At first Saskatchewan was an object of concern and charity to her sister provinces, most notably Ontario; but as the long years continued to weave the unvarying tragic design with no end in sight the charitable impulse weakened – as it always does over the long stretch – and government relief alone kept many Saskatchewan people alive. Captain John Palliser had been right, it seemed, when he reported in 1859 that the southern plains area of the North-west was unfit for cultivation, and there was talk in eastern Canada of moving the Saskatchewan farm population to the northern Ontario bush.

The year 1937 brought the worst disaster of all. No rain fell, the wind blew what little topsoil remained in the fields into roadside ditches;

dust-clouds – black, sinister, shot through here and there with eerie shafts of light – wavered all day and every day between earth and sky, and the heat was appalling. In Weyburn on a July day the temperature rose to 114 degrees above zero – a record which still stands. On the Moose Mountain Indian Reserve old Chief Sheepskin, nominally a Christian, summoned his braves to perform a rain dance. He died shortly afterwards, no doubt confirmed in the faith of his fathers, for the day before he died a heavy shower fell on Moose Mountain. In Regina, bathers in Wascana Lake found themselves unable to reach the bath-houses from the water without being coated with dust and in the end went home to scrape the mud off themselves in their own bath-tubs; and in a small town near by, a baseball player – now an archetypal dust-bowl figure – lost his way running round the bases and was later found three miles out on the prairie.

The wheat crop that year averaged two and one half bushels to the acre.

But there was little thought of quitting – and none at all of moving to the Ontario bush. The bewilderment and despair of the earlier years had by 1937 given way to a sterner emotion, and the people now took a kind of defiant pride in showing the world their strength to endure, without flinching, the worst that nature could do to them. 'The country is dismal, scorched, smashed,' the mayor of Assiniboia said, 'but the people are magnificent.' He was right. No one could survive nine years of hell without courage. Nor without faith – not in a benevolent god but in one's own capacity to endure.

Nor without scars. The rains fell at last and the erstwhile desert rejoiced and blossomed like the rose; but no amount of rainfall could ever wash away dreadful memories of the agonizing struggle to survive. For the people of Saskatchewan that nine years' sojourn in a dust-darkened wilderness was a genuinely traumatic experience which has left its mark not only on those who actually lived through the Dirty Thirties but to some degree on their descendants.

The Saskatchewan man has thus been shaped by a sterner physical environment than that of most Canadians. Having been compelled to adapt himself to that environment, he has made his own rules for survival and looks with suspicion on traditional values cherished in softer lands. He tends to take a less optimistic view of life than do his neighbours, particularly those who live in Alberta. He is less ebullient and more independent. To the stranger, Saskatchewan cities may appear dull and colourless, and in many respects they are, but at least what character they do possess is honestly their own. (In this they are to be distinguished from Calgary, now an outpost of Texas, and from Edmonton, striving frenetically to become a suburb of Dawson City.)

The Saskatchewan man is politically-minded but distrustful of all political parties, remembering that no government did more than keep him barely alive during his time of greatest need — hence his willingness to indulge in far-out political and social experiments and his refusal to conform to any voting pattern that makes sense to the orthodox outsider. What, after all, is one to make of an electorate which for twenty years returned a socialist government to power, supported the introduction of Medicare, replaced the socialists with a government of Liberals led by an ex-socialist, and at the same time sent a solid phalanx of Tories to Ottawa?

No doubt the political scientist and the sociologist can explain such goings-on in their own peculiar terms; but whenever any friend of mine from eastern Canada remarks on the multiplicity of political parties spawned on the prairies and the maverick tendencies of many of the party constituents, I am content to tell him the story of Mr. Portingale.

In the old homesteading days of more than half a century ago, Mr. Portingle was a near neighbour of ours. He was a scruffy little Englishman born, according to the nomenclature of his time, into the lower middle class. Mr. Portingale was a staunch imperialist and devout church-goer; he knew his place in the scheme of things and until he took to homesteading in the middle of the prairie was content to keep it. A meek little man (but with no hope of inheriting the earth or any part thereof), he never dreamt of calling into question the wisdom and rectitude of either God or the government.

Not, that is, until he had lived — but only barely — through part of a prairie winter. One day in mid January of his first year on the homestead he borrowed my father's team and sleigh and hauled a load of grain to town, thirty miles away. He spent the night in the hotel and next morning, in defiance of warnings from weather-wise old-timers, started for home. Ten miles out, a blizzard met him head on. Fortunately the horses, grizzled old veterans of many a winter storm, took charge of Mr. Portingale and dragged him several hours later into our yard. My father dug him out from under about two feet of snow, unwound him from the horse-blankets he had thoughtfully wrapped himself in, and half-dragged, half-carried him into our kitchen.

Mother superintended the thawing-out operations. She placed one end of Mr. Portingale in a tub of cold water (his feet were badly frost-bitten) and after first clearing a channel through the icicles festooning his scraggy moustache poured into the other end about a gallon of hot tea generously laced with ginger.

Within fifteen minutes Mr. Portingale was thawing out all right and suffering the tortures of the damned. His feet were immersed in a tub of flaming coals and the tea had peeled most of the skin off the roof of his mouth. In the ordinary way Mr. Portingale was the humblest, least aggressive of men, his voice an appropriate piping treble, and the strongest expletive any of us had heard him use – and then only when greatly moved – was 'Gryte Scott!' But now those of us gathered in the kitchen were seeing something vastly more significant than the mere restoration of Mr. Portingale's circulatory system to its more or less normal channels; we were awe-stricken witnesses to a striking spiritual phenomenon peculiar to the prairies. For of a sudden, Mr. Portingale was no longer a humble sheep content to follow the bell-wether of the flock – he was the Stag at Bay. He glared at us out of red-rimmed bloodshot eyes and flung bloated pin-cushion hands aloft.

'The bloodiest absolutely bloodiest climate on the fice of the bloody earth!' Mr. Portingale bawled. 'And by God something's bloody well got to be done abaat it!'

Saskatchewan teems with Mr Portingales. Men who, lapped in an enervating cloak of eastern smog or rendered soft and pliable by the eternal West Coast rain, would pass through life in meek unquestioning obedience to those placed in authority over them, develop, after a brief spell of prairie living, affinities with the Mau Mau or the I.R.A. Scorched by sun and battered by wind three months of the year and confined in a deep freeze for six, the prairie dweller is soon afflicted by a kind of nervous irritability which impels him to flail out in all directions. Being, as a rule, a religious man – intimate association with nature at its most awesome inclines to make him so – he hesitates to blame the Almighty for his miseries. The next authority – human, fallible, vulnerable – is the government. And something, by God, has got to be done about it!

It is also a matter of common observation that the man who survives the prairie weather for any length of time is likely to develop, in addition to a chronic irritability, an alarming measure of self-confidence. By the very fact of surviving he has proved himself a man fit to whip his weight in wildcats. (Mr. Portingale's battle against the elements assumed, in later years, the proportions of an epic drama in which Mr. Portingale led his floundering, bewildered horses to safety over twenty storm-battered miles of prairie.) Moreover, the Saskatchewan farmer's determination, once he takes action, to get something done in a hurry may be directly attributable to weather-conditioning. Outdoor plumbing in below-zero temperatures is conducive to hustle.

The self-confidence and energy thus created by climatic conditions do not weaken with the passing of time, for they are sustained and nurtured by the very air the prairie dweller breathes. The C.P.R. publicity pamphlets which flooded the country about the turn of the century – designed to encourage prairie settlement and by all odds the richest, purplest fiction ever written about the Canadian west – never tired of emphasizing the wine-like quality of prairie air. Its stimulative power, in certain peculiarly favoured localities, was freely compared to the best vintage champagne. No wonder Nicholas Flood Davin, editor of the old Regina *Leader* and one of the Grand Old Men of prairie journalism (who incidentally preferred to absorb his alcohol through the stomach rather than the lungs), looked into the future of Saskatchewan with the eye of a prophet and recorded his vision in the words of a poet:

> All the charms that belong to youth, hope, energy, are found in the North-West; and the bracing influence of the new free land on mind and character is very remarkable. The climate is akin to that which nurtured the warrior hordes, the Goths and the Vandals, who became the terror and ultimately the destroyers of the Roman Empire, and whose magnificent physique has been described by graphic pens made eloquent by fear.

It is a pity Mr. Davin did not live to see the fulfilment of his implied prophecy in the descent of the prairie Goths and Vandals – thinly disguised as Progressives, Independents, C.C.F.ers, Diefenbaker Tories – upon the beleaguered capital of the Dominion.

The proliferation of political parties in the Canadian west, astonishing to those who have never endured the rigours of the prairie climate – and particularly that of Saskatchewan – is thus seen to be not only logical but inevitable. The 'typical' westerner, whatever his racial origin or the social status of his forebears, is a man toughened by climate, inside and out, to the texture of old cowhide. He is proud of his strength, confident of his cunning, and drunk on air all the year round. Is it conceivable that such a man will be content to tag along meekly in the wake of a traditional political machine controlled from afar? In good years he will tolerate the machine's existence, make no overt move to throw a monkey-wrench into the works. But let the chill winds of winter blow just a little colder, let the sun scorch the earth a little browner, and the heavens are filled with denunciations, the meeting-houses with trigger-happy Jacquerie, and a new political party is born. Grass-roots movements always flourish when the grass stops growing.

The Saskatchewan farmer's down-east counterpart is, by comparison, a sedate and conservative fellow who, like the unconverted Mr. Portingale, knows his place and keeps it. Occasionally a prolonged rainy spell, a fall in market prices, or a rise in income tax may tempt him to timid protest, but the most drastic positive steps he ever takes to improve his lot are to replace the Tories with the Liberals or vice versa. In purely material terms his lot is probably worse than that of the prairie farmer, but he never experiences those alternating expansions and contractions induced by extremes of heat and cold which – because they create a kind of friction, both physical and spiritual – impel the sufferer to explosive action.

I speak of the 'typical' westerner in the present tense, but the sad truth is that he is in danger of becoming extinct. Natural-gas heating, T.V., improved road transportation, school buses, and indoor plumbing are sapping his vitality, may shrink him spiritually to the size of his eastern counterpart. Our farms, it seems, are getting bigger all the time and our farmers smaller.

The passing of the old breed must be, for those of us who knew it at its maverick best, a cause of bitter regret. The west in its Golden Age produced more than its share of stout-hearted, strong-lunged rebels – godlike Prometheans ready to challenge at the drop of a sombrero the wisdom and authority of an all-ruling Liberal or Tory Zeus. But never let us forget that behind the Prometheans, inspiring them, propping them up, stood (and let us hope still stands) that unsung Atlas of the prairies – Mr. Portingale.

(1968)   (1968)

Hugh MacLennan
1907–

———◆———

HUGH MACLENNAN WAS born in Glace Bay, Cape Breton Island, and studied at Dalhousie and Oxford Universities before obtaining his Ph.D. from Princeton University in 1935. He then began teaching at Lower Canada College and in 1951 he joined the Department of English at McGill University. Since the appearance of his first novel, *Barometer Rising* (1941), he has published several more novels including *Two Solitudes* (1945), *Each Man's Son* (1951), *The Watch That Ends The Night* (1959) and *The Return of the Sphinx* (1967). Many of the interests evident in these novels have also been examined in collections of MacLennan's essays such as *Cross Country* (1949), *Scotchman's Return and Other Essays* (1960) and *Seven Rivers of Canada* (1961).

Scotchman's Return

WHENEVER I STOP to think about it, the knowledge that I am three-quarters Scotch, and Highland at that, seems like a kind of doom from which I am too Scotch even to think of praying for deliverance. I can thank my father for this last-ditch neurosis. He was entirely Scotch; he was a living specimen of a most curious heritage. In spite of his medical knowledge, which was large; in spite of his quick nervous vitality and tireless energy, he was never able to lay to rest the beasties which went bump in his mind at three o'clock in the morning. It mattered nothing that he was a third-generation Canadian who had never seen the Highlands before he visited them on leave in the First World War. He never needed to go there to understand whence he came or what he was. He was neither a Scot nor yet was he Scottish; he never used those genteel appellations which now are supposed to be *de rigueur*. He was simply Scotch. All the perplexity and doggedness of the race was in him, its loneliness, tenderness and affection, its deceptive vitality, its quick flashes of violence, its dog-whistle sensitivity to sounds to which Anglo-Saxons are stone-deaf, its incapacity to tell its heart to foreigners save in terms foreigners do not comprehend, its resigned indifference to whether they comprehend or not. "It's not easy being Scotch," he told me more than once. To which I suppose another Scotchman might say: "It wasn't meant to be."

So far as I could tell, my father found it almost impossible to believe that anyone not Scotch is entirely real. Yet at the same time, buried in the fastnesses of his complex mind, was the contradictory notion that if a Scotchman ever amounts to anything important, he will not be any too real, either, for some beastie will come along and spoil him. As engineers keeping the ships going, as captains serving the owners of the lines, as surgeons, teachers, clergymen and the like, as loyal seconds-in-command – in these niches the Scotch might expect to fare well. But you seldom found them on the summit, and if by reason of an accident one them got there, something bad was pretty sure to happen. When Ramsay Macdonald became the first man with a Mac in his name to become a British Prime Minister, my father shook his head gloomily over Macdonald's picture on the front page of the paper, and when I asked him why, he said: "He won't do." He had an overweening admiration for the English so long as they stayed in England, and for the Royal Navy above all other English institutions. Indeed, one of his motives for becoming a doctor was an idea in the back of his youthful mind that as a surgeon he might become an R.N. officer. But he was no light Anglophile. I well remember a summer afternoon in the mid-twenties when a British squadron paid Halifax a courtesy call, and better still do I remember that the two leading ships were *H.M.S. Hood* and *H.M.S. Repulse.* As my father at that time was doing some work in the military hospital, he was called to perform an emergency operation on an officer of the *Repulse,* and the Commander of the ship later invited him to tea in the wardroom. He took me along, and as I also was brought up to love the Royal Navy, this was a great thrill to me. It turned out to be an experience almost traumatic.

No sooner had we taken our seats in the wardroom than the officer-of-the-watch entered resplendent in the dress of the day and carrying his cocked hat under his arm. He laid the hat beside him on the table, nodded to a steward for his tea, glanced at us, and when he saw we were civilians and natives, his lips parted in an expression of disdain in which, to quote a famous English author who has noted such expressions as carefully as Shelley the lips of Ozymandias, delicacy had no part. Ignoring my father, this officer inclined his eyes vaguely in my direction and said: "D'you live here?" "Yes, sir," I replied. "Beastly place," was his comment and then he fell silent. So did everyone else.

After several minutes the silence was broken by the racket of an R.C.A.F. training biplane stunting over the harbour and the arrogant disdain on the face of the former officer-of-the-watch was replaced by something very like a flush of anger. "So you have those wretched things over here, too?" he asked my father accusingly. I noted with some pride that my father did not reply to this officer, but instead turned to another man who had been embarrassed by his colleague's behaviour, and asked mildly if the development of aircraft had made it necessary for the Navy to alter its battle tactics. This officer was beginning to reply in some detail when the officer-of-the-watch interrupted: "Do you," he asked my father, "seriously believe that a wretched little gnat like that aircraft could possibly threaten a ship like this?"

No, it was not a successful tea party, nor did it last much longer. My father rose as soon as he felt it courteous to do so, we were escorted to the ladder and handed down into the launch, and as the launch drove through the fog my father was informatively silent. After a while he said, as though excusing the officer's rudeness: "Of course, the weather has been depressing here and they've come up from New York." But before the launch touched the jetty he added: "All the same, he shouldn't have said that." I understood then that my father had not felt himself snubbed, but that the Scotch in him had been gravely concerned by the officer's *hubris* concerning the air force. A beastie had been alerted to keep a special eye on that slim, powerful but extremely vulnerable battlecruiser which was the last brain-child of the ferocious Admiral Jackie Fisher, the ship which Winston Churchill later described as having the brilliance and the fragility one is apt to associate with the children of very old men. Years later in the terrible December of 1941, when the news came from Malaya, I recalled that afternoon aboard *Repulse* with a thrill of sheer horror.

My father was also the reason why I never visited the Highlands when I was a student in the Old Country. Nor did he think I should have done so. "You'll see them one of these days," he said. And he added as an afterthought: "If you're spared and well." And he added as another afterthought: "When you do see them you'll understand." Naturally he did not tell me what I would understand, assuming I would know, but this comment did nothing to foment a desire in me to travel north of the Highland Line.

But we can't escape ourselves forever, and more of ourselves than we choose to admit is the accumulated weight of our ancestors. As I grew older the thought of the Highlands began to haunt me, and in the summer of 1958, after having lived for a long time under a great strain, I decided to get a change and sail to England on a freight ship. I landed in Manchester and of course went south, but after spending a week in London, I went north on the train to Edinburgh and on a Monday morning I found myself in a car-rental agency in the Haymarket making a deal for a Vauxhall.

Ahead of me was the only American I saw in the Old Country that year who behaved as Europeans desire Americans to behave abroad. After complaining about the tastelessness of British food, the harshness and skiddiness of British toilet paper and the absurdity of driving on the left-hand side of the road, he finally came to the topic of the Edinburgh Sabbath which he had just survived.

"Do you realize," he said to the car dealer, "that in the United States there's not even a village as quiet as this town was yesterday?"

The Scotchman looked up at him, inwardly gratified but outwardly glum.

"Ay!" he said, and assumed incorrectly that the American understood that both himself and his country had been rebuked.

When he turned to me after the American had departed, and had identified my nationality by my driving licence, he allowed himself the luxury of an irrelevant comment.

"Ye appear to have deeficult neighbours," he said.

"Perhaps you have difficult neighbours, too?"

"Ay!" he said, and seemed pleased, for an instant later he said "Ay" again.

More or less secure in the Vauxhall I headed north for Stirling and the Highland Line, and after a night by Loch Katrine struck north by Balquhidder, mistook my road to Glencoe and went too far west, and soon found myself beside Loch Awe. I also found myself, with some surprise and mortification, unwilling to perceive any beauty in this region because Loch Awe is in Campbell country, and in the near past of several centuries ago, the Campbell chiefs had been an anathema to the less successful clans they pillaged.

The roads in the Highlands, as those will know who have travelled them, are not only so narrow that in most sections two baby Austins are unable to pass, they are also infested with livestock. Sheep fall asleep on their narrow shoulders and cars must stop again and again while bullocks make up their minds whether or not to move out of the way. The roads were built by some English general, I think his name was Wade, who had the eighteenth-century English notion that if he built roads the communications between the clans would improve. Only lately have General Wade's roads been hard-topped, and never have they been widened except at regular intervals where cars may turn out to allow approaching cars to pass. They are adequately marked if you are familiar with them, but I was not familiar with them and again lost my way. I went into the pub of a hamlet to ask where I was and discovered behind the bar an elderly gentleman with white hair and the demeanour of a Presbyterian elder, and beside the bar three workmen silently sipping ale.

"What's the name of this place?" I asked the publican.

"The Heather and Bull," he said.

"I meant, what's this community?"

"Mostly Protestant," he said, "but in recent years wi' a small smattering of Roman Catholics." He turned to one of the workmen: "John, how many Catholics now?"

"About eighteen percent. Going on for twenty."

"They're risin' fast," said a third man.

"Ay!" said the publican. And turning to me he asked when I had left Canada.

"How on earth did you guess I'm a Canadian?"

"You are not English, that is certain, and you are not American. You still have some of the voice." He put out his hand: "God bless you!"

We talked of Scotland, Canada and theology and I forgot what I had intended to ask him. An hour later, when I shook his hand and received my directions, his noble face was as solemn as a memory from childhood.

"You will be disappointed," he warned me. "Scotland is full of nothing but Irish now. Och, we have no dignity left."

An Anglo-Saxon or an American might assume a racial situation from this remark, but it was the sort of thing I grew up with, the sort of remark I have made myself, in different connotations, all my life. Its meaning was clear to me if to nobody else. The old gentleman was unburdening himself of a beastie which had nothing whatever to do with the Catholics, the Irish or with anything, possibly, that he himself could put into words.

The next day I was in the true north of Scotland among the sheep, the heather, the whin, the mists and the homes of the vanished races. Such sweeps of emptiness I never saw in Canada before I went to the Mackenzie River later in that same summer. But this Highland emptiness, only a few hundred miles above the massed population of England, is a far different thing from the emptiness of our own Northwest Territories. Above the sixtieth parallel in Canada you feel that nobody but God has ever been there before you, but in a deserted Highland glen you feel that everyone who ever mattered is dead and gone. Those glens are the most hauntingly lovely sights I have ever seen: they are vaster, more moving, more truly vacated than the southern abbeys ruined by Henry VIII. They are haunted by the lost loves and passions of a thousand years. Later that summer on the lower reaches of the Mackenzie, after talking to an Athabascan Indian with Celtic eyes and the name of McPherson, I remembered the wild loneliness of Lochaber and it occurred to me that only a man from a country as lonely and ghost-ridden as the Highlands could have had the insane determination to paddle a canoe through the Rocky Mountains and down La Grande Rivière-en-bas to the Beaufort Sea, and that nothing was more in the life-style of the Highlander than Alexander Mackenzie's feat in searching for the Northwest Passage in a canoe. After an achievement of incredible boldness and endurance, what, after all, did this Highlander find but nothing?

Yet, as a by-product, he and others like him surely found much of Canada, even though one of them, solitary on the Qu'Appelle or the Saskatchewan, admitting the grandeur of the woods and prairies of the New World, sang from a broken heart that he was an exile from his native land, and while making possible the existence of a country so vast that Scotland would be lost in it, regretted his inability to wield a claymore in defence of a barren glen presided over by an imbecile chief. The exiled Irish never forgave their landlords, but the exiled

Highlanders pined for the scoundrel Pretender, and even regretted the proprietors who preferred sheep to humanity, enclosed their own people and drove them starving across the western ocean with such an uncomprehended yearning in their souls that some of them ended up in log cabins along the Athabasca and on the shores of James Bay.

In the parish of Kintail, whence some of my own people were driven a century and a half ago, I was told there are now barely four hundred inhabitants. In my ancestors' days there were more than twelve thousand.

"Where are they?" the minister said when I asked him. "Where indeed but in Canada? And some in Australia and New Zealand of course, but most of them in Canada."

With them they brought – no doubt of this – that nameless haunting guilt they never understood, and the feeling of failure, and the loneliness of all the warm-hearted, not very intelligent folk so outmoded by the Anglo-Saxon success that they knew they were helpless unless they lived as the Anglo-Saxons did, failures unless they learned to feel (or not to feel at all) as the Anglo-Saxons ordained. Had my father been clairvoyant when he told me I would understand when I went to the Highlands?

I'm not sure that I do understand or ever will understand what he wanted me to know. But one evening watching a rainbow form over Loch Leven, the mists drop down the hills into rain, then watching the sky rent open and such a tumult of golden light pour forth that the mountains themselves moved and were transfigured, still moved and then were lifted up until they ceased to be mountains and turned themselves into an abstraction of sheer glory and gold – watching this I realized, or thought I did, why these desperate people had endured so long against the civilization of the south. Unlike Ulysses, they had failed to stop their ears when the sirens sang, and the sirens that sing in the Highlands, suddenly and when you least expect to hear them, have voices more dangerously beguiling than any in the Aegæan Isles. Beauty is nearly the most dangerous thing on earth, and those who love her too much, or look too deeply into her eyes, they pay the price for her, which often is an empty stomach and a life of misunderstanding.

So it was here, though an economist would point out that the land is barren and that in the early days the people lacked education and civilized techniques. But this practical attitude merely begs the question of why the people stayed so long: stayed, in fact, until they were driven out. These mountains are almost as useless to the cultivator as the upper reaches of the Laurentian Shield. The Gaelic tongue sounds soft and lovely, but compared with English and French it is a primitive means of communication. The ancestors of almost a quarter of modern Canada never did, and in their native glens they never could, develop even the rudiments of an urban culture. When they made the acquaintance of the English this must have sorely troubled their conscience, for they were religious, they were Christianized after a fashion, and the parable that meant most to them was the Parable of the Talents. Only a few of their chiefs could possibly be called intelligent, and the conduct of the chiefs of their only really successful clan (it shall be nameless here, though every Highlander knows the one I have in mind) was of the crafty peasant sort, the more base because it exploited the loyalty of a people who were already enslaved by their own conception of honour. But though these chiefs did well for themselves, they only became rich and famous after they had conspired with the English enemy. No leader, not even a genius, could have raised in the terrain of the Highlands a civilization capable of competing with England's. Yet the Highlanders held on to the glens; incredibly they held on to them until the end of the eighteenth century. Often I have said to myself that my grandfathers three times removed lived in a culture as primitive as Homer's, and last summer in the Highlands I knew that they really had.

Driving south through Glencoe where the Campbells massacred the Macdonalds, I remembered the first time I met Angus L. Macdonald, who then was Premier of Nova Scotia and previously had been Canada's Minister for the Navy. With a suddenness that would have been startling to anyone but another clansman, Mr. Macdonald turned to me in a company of people and from the depths of a mutual empathy he said: "To be a Celt is never to be far from tears."

But we Celts are withal a mercurial people also; our sorrowful moods pass like the mists on the braes and the sunlight strikes through when we least expect it. A week later I was in the most fatally civilized country in the world, Sweden, waiting for a Pan-American Clipper to take me home.

Just as I belong to the last Canadian generation raised with a Highland nostalgia, so also do I belong to the last which regards a trans-Atlantic flight as a miracle. When I was a boy I saw the first tiny plane to fly the ocean, the American seaplane N.C.4, which took a very long time moving by stages from Halifax to Sydney, to Bonavista Bay, to the Azores and finally to Lisbon. Eight years later plane after plane set out on non-stop ventures and disappeared into the sea.

Now, eating a filet mignon and sipping champagne in the supreme luxury of this Pan-American aircraft, I looked down on the waste of seas which, together with the mountains of British Columbia, had divided the clansmen from their homes over a century ago. Sitting there idle I felt an unwarranted lift of joy and omnipotent power. The plane nuzzled into the stratospheric wind, she rolled as slowly and surely as a shark speeding through the water in which it was born, she went so fast that though she left Stockholm as late as 4.30 in the afternoon it was still bright daylight when she put down in a rainstorm in Keflavik. She took on fuel and set out again, I slept for an hour or two, wakened to a change in the propeller pitch and learned we were circling Gander, which as usual was buried in fog. After an hour the pilot said over the intercom:

"The weather in Gander has deteriorated to zero-zero. We are now proceeding to New York. We will arrive in Idlewild at 7.40 Eastern Daylight Time. We will arrive on schedule."

Here, of course, was the supreme triumph of the civilization which, in wrecking the clansmen, had made it possible for me to think of Canada as home. The plane tore through the fog, the stewardess brought a delicious breakfast, and just as I was sipping my coffee the sun broke dazzlingly through the window into the cabin. I looked out and there, in a semi-circle of sunshine, the only sunshine apparently in the whole northern hemisphere at that particular moment, lay Cape Breton Island. The plane sloped down to eight thousand feet and I saw beside the Bras d'Or lake the tiny speck which was the house where my mother and sister at that very moment lay asleep. We did reach New York on schedule and that same day I ate my lunch in the Medical Arts restaurant on the corner of Sherbrooke Street and Guy. The man next to me at the counter asked where I had been and I told him I had been in the Scottish Highlands.

"It must have been nice," he said.

"It was. But it's also nice to be home."

Am I wrong, or is it true that it is only now, after so many years of not knowing who we were or wanted to be, that we Canadians of Scotch descent are truly at home in the northern half of North America?

(1960)   (1960)

Ernest Buckler
1908 –

———◆———

ERNEST BUCKLER WAS born in Dalhousie West, Nova Scotia, and received his B.A. from Dalhousie University in 1929 and his M.A. from the University of Toronto in 1930. Between 1931 and 1936 he worked for an insurance company in Toronto and then returned to rural Nova Scotia. Since 1938, when he won a writing prize in *Coronet* magazine, Buckler has published several books including *The Mountain and the Valley* (1952), *The Cruelest Month* (1963) and *Ox Bells and Fireflies* (1968). "Penny in the Dust" was first published in *Maclean's* in 1948 and reappears in a collection of Buckler's short stories, *The Rebellion of Young David and Other Stories* (1975).

Penny in the Dust

MY SISTER AND I were walking through the old sun-still fields the evening before my father's funeral, recalling this memory or that – trying, after the fashion of families who gather again in the place where they were born, to identify ourselves with the strange children we must have been.

"Do you remember the afternoon we thought you were lost?" my sister said. I did. That was as long ago as the day I was seven, but I'd had occasion to remember it only yesterday.

"We searched everywhere," she said. "Up in the meetinghouse, back in the blueberry barrens – we even looked in the well. I think it's the only time I ever saw Father really upset. He didn't even stop to take the oxen off the wagon tongue when they told him. He raced right through the chopping where Tom Reeve was burning brush, looking for you – right through the flames almost; they couldn't do a thing with him. And you up in your bed, sound asleep!"

"It was all over losing a penny or something, wasn't it?" she went on, when I didn't answer. It was. She laughed indulgently. "You were a crazy kid, weren't you?"

I was. But there was more to it than that. I had never seen a shining new penny before that day. I'd thought they were all black. This one was bright as gold. And my father had given it to me.

You would have to understand about my father, and that is the hard thing to tell. If I say that he worked all day long but never once had I seen him hurry, that would make him sound like a stupid man. If I say that he never held me on his knee when I was a child and that I never heard him laugh out loud in his life, it would make him sound humourless and severe. If I said that whenever I'd be reeling off some of my fanciful plans and he'd come into the kitchen and I'd stop short, you'd think that he was distant and that in some kind of way I was afraid of him. None of that would be true.

There's no way you can tell it to make it sound like anything more than an inarticulate man a little at sea with an imaginative child. You'll have to take my word for it that there was more to it than that. It was as if his sure-footed way in the fields forsook him the moment he came near the door of my child's world and that he could never intrude on it without feeling awkward and conscious of trespass; and that I, sensing that but not understanding it, felt at the sound of his solid step outside, the child-world's foolish fragility. He would fix the small spot where I planted beans and other quick-sprouting seeds before he prepared the big garden, even if the spring was late; but he wouldn't ask me how many rows I wanted and if he made three rows and I wanted four, I couldn't ask him to change them. If I walked behind the load of hay, longing to ride, and he walked ahead of the oxen, I couldn't ask him to put me up and he wouldn't make any move to do so until he saw me trying to grasp the binder.

He, my father, had just given me a new penny, bright as gold.

He'd taken it from his pocket several times, pretending to examine the date on it, waiting for me to notice it. He couldn't offer me *anything* until I had shown some sign that the gift would be welcome.

"You can have it if you want it, Pete," he said at last.

"Oh, thanks," I said, Nothing more. I couldn't expose any of my eagerness either.

I started with it, to the store. For a penny you could buy the magic cylinder of "Long Tom" popcorn, with Heaven knows what glittering bauble inside. But the more I thought of my bright penny disappearing forever into the black drawstring pouch the storekeeper kept his money in, the slower my steps lagged as the store came nearer and nearer. I sat down in the road.

It was that time of magic suspension in an August afternoon. The lifting smells of leaves and cut clover hung still in the sun. The sun drowsed, like a kitten curled up on my shoulder. The deep flour-fine dust in the road puffed about my bare ankles, warm and soft as sleep. The sound of the cowbells came sharp and hollow from the cool swamp.

I began to play with the penny, putting off the decision. I would close my eyes and bury it deep in the sand; and then, with my eyes still closed, get up and walk around, and then come back to search for it. Tantalizing myself, each time, with the excitement of discovering afresh its bright shining edge. I did that again and again. Alas, once too often.

It was almost dark when their excited talking in the room awakened me. It was Mother who had found me. I suppose when it came dusk she thought of me in my bed other nights, and I suppose she looked there without any reasonable hope but only as you look in every place where the thing that is lost has ever lain before. And now suddenly she was crying because when she opened the door there, miraculously, I was.

"Peter!" she cried, ignoring the obvious in her sudden relief, "*where* have you been?"

"I lost my penny," I said.

"You lost your penny ... ? But what made you come up here and hide?"

If Father hadn't been there, I might have told her the whole story. But when I looked up at Father, standing there like the shape of everything sound and straight, it was like daylight shredding the memory of a foolish dream. How could I bear the shame of repeating before him the childish visions I had built in my head in the magic August afternoon when almost anything could be made to seem real, as I buried the penny and dug it up again? How could I explain that pit-of-the-stomach sickness which struck through the whole day when I had to believe, at last, that it was really gone? How could I explain that I wasn't really hiding from *them*? How, with the words and the understanding I had then, that this was the only possible place to run from that awful feeling of loss?

"I lost my penny," I said again. I looked at Father and turned my face into the pillow. "I want to go to sleep."

"Peter," Mother said, "It's almost nine o'clock. You haven't had a bite of supper. Do you know you almost scared the *life* out of us?"

"You better get some supper," Father said. It was the only time he had spoken.

I never dreamed that he would mention the thing again. But the next morning when we had the hay forks in our hands, ready to toss out the clover, he seemed to postpone the moment of actually leaving for the field. He stuck his fork in the ground and brought in another pail of water, though the kettle was chock-full. He took out the shingle nail that held a broken yoke strap together and put it back in exactly the same hole. He went into the shed to see if the pigs had cleaned up all their breakfast.

And then he said abruptly: "Ain't you got no idea where you lost your penny?"

"Yes," I said, "I know just about."

"Let's see if we can't find it," he said.

We walked down the road together, stiff with awareness. He didn't hold my hand.

"It's right here somewhere," I said. "I was playin' with it, in the dust."

He looked at me, but he didn't ask me what game anyone could possibly play with a penny in the dust.

I might have known he would find it. He could tap the alder bark with his jackknife just exactly hard enough so it wouldn't split but so it would twist free from the notched wood, to make a whistle. His great fingers could trace loose the hopeless snarl of a fishing line that I could only succeed in tangling tighter and tighter. If I broke the handle of my wheelbarrow ragged beyond sight of any possible repair, he could take it and bring it back to me so you could hardly see the splice if you weren't looking for it.

He got down on his knees and drew his fingers carefully through the dust, like a harrow; not clawing it frantically into heaps as I had done, covering even as I uncovered. He found the penny almost at once.

He held it in his hand, as if the moment of passing it to me were a deadline for something he dreaded to say, but must. Something that could not be put off any longer, if it were to be spoken at all.

"Pete," he said, "you needn'ta hid. I wouldn'ta beat you."

"*Beat* me? Oh, Father! You didn't think that was the reason...?" I felt almost sick. I felt as if I had struck *him*.

I had to tell him the truth then. Because only the truth, no matter how ridiculous it was, would have the unmistakable sound truth has, to scatter that awful idea out of his head.

"I wasn't hidin', Father," I said, "honest. I was...I was buryin' my penny and makin' out I was diggin' up treasure. I was makin' out I was findin' gold. I didn't know what to *do* when I lost it, I just didn't know where to *go*...." His head was bent forward, like mere listening. I had to make it truer still.

"I made out it was gold," I said desperately, "and I – I was makin' out I bought you a mowin' machine so's you could get your work done early every day so's you and I could go into town in the big automobile I made out I bought you – and everyone'd turn around and look at us drivin' down the streets...." His head was perfectly still, as if he were only waiting with patience for me to finish. "*Laughin'* and *talkin'*," I said. Louder, smiling intensely, com*pell*ing him, by the absolute conviction of some true particular, to believe me.

He looked up then. It was the only time I had ever seen tears in his eyes. It was the only time in my seven years that he had ever put his arm around me.

I wondered, though, why he hesitated, and then put the penny back in his own pocket.

Yesterday I knew. I never found any fortune and we never had a car to ride in together. But I think he knew what that would be like, just the same. I found the penny again yesterday, when we were getting out his good suit – in an upper vest pocket where no one ever carries change. It was still shining. He must have kept it polished.

I left it there.

(1975)   (1975)

Sinclair Ross
1908 –

———◆———

BORN NEAR PRINCE Albert, Saskatchewan, Sinclair Ross joined the staff of the Royal Bank of Canada in 1924. With the exception of a period during the Second World War when he served with the Royal Canadian Ordnance Corps, he continued his banking career until his retirement in 1967. Since then he has lived in Greece and Spain. In addition to several novels, including *As For Me and My House* (1941), *The Well* (1958) and *Sawbones Memorial* (1974), Ross has published many short stories. A collection of these, *The Lamp at Noon and Other Stories*, appeared in 1968. "The Lamp at Noon" was first published in *Queen's Quarterly* in 1938.

The Lamp at Noon

A LITTLE BEFORE noon she lit the lamp. Demented wind fled keening past the house: a wail through the eaves that died every minute or two. Three days now without respite it had held. The dust was thickening to an impenetrable fog.

She lit the lamp, then for a long time stood at the window motionless. In dim, fitful outline the stable and oat granary still were visible;

beyond, obscuring fields and landmarks, the lower of dust clouds made the farmyard seem an isolated acre, poised aloft above a sombre void. At each blast of wind it shook, as if to topple and spin hurtling with the dust-reel into space.

From the window she went to the door, opening it a little, and peering towards the stable again. He was not coming yet. As she watched there was a sudden rift overhead, and for a moment through the tattered clouds the sun raced like a wizened orange. It shed a soft, diffused light, dim and yellow as if it were the light from the lamp reaching out through the open door.

She closed the door, and going to the stove tried the potatoes with a fork. Her eyes all the while were fixed and wide with a curious immobility. It was the window. Standing at it she had let her forehead press against the pane until the eyes were strained apart and rigid. Wide like that they had looked out to the deepening ruin of the storm. Now she could not close them.

The baby started to cry. He was lying in a home-made crib over which she had arranged a tent of muslin. Careful not to disturb the folds of it she knelt and tried to still him, whispering huskily in a sing-song voice that he must hush and go to sleep again. She would have liked to rock him, to feel the comfort of his little body in her arms, but a fear had obsessed her that in the dust-filled air he might contract pneumonia. There was dust sifting everywhere. Her own throat was parched with it. The table had been set less than ten minutes, and already a film was gathering on the dishes. The little cry continued, and with wincing, frightened lips she glanced around as if to find a corner where the air was less oppressive. But while the lips winced the eyes maintained their wide, immobile stare. "Sleep," she whispered again. "It's too soon for you to be hungry. Daddy's coming for his dinner."

He seemed a long time. Even the clock, still a few minutes off noon, could not dispel a foreboding sense that he was longer than he should be. She went to the door again – then recoiled slowly to stand white and breathless in the middle of the room. She mustn't. He would only despise her if she ran to the stable looking for him. There was too much grim endurance in his nature ever to let him understand the fear and weakness of a woman. She must stay quiet and wait. Nothing was wrong. At noon he would come – and perhaps after dinner stay with her a while.

Yesterday, and again at breakfast this morning, they had quarrelled bitterly. She wanted him now, the assurance of his strength and nearness, but he would stand aloof, wary, remembering the words she had flung at him in her anger, unable to understand it was only the dust and wind that had driven her.

Tense she fixed her eyes upon the clock, listening. There were two winds: the wind in flight, and the wind that pursued. The one sought refuge in the eaves, whimpering, in fear; the other assailed it there, and shook the eaves apart to make it flee again. Once as she listened this first wind sprang into the room, distraught like a bird that has felt the graze of talons on its wing; while furious the other wind shook the walls, and thudded tumbleweeds against the window till its quarry glanced away again in fright. But only to return – to return and quake among the feeble eaves, as if in all this dust-mad wilderness it knew no other sanctuary.

Then Paul came. At his step she hurried to the stove, intent upon the pots and frying-pan. "The worst wind yet," he ventured, hanging up his cap and smock. "I had to light the lantern in the tool shed too."

They looked at each other, then away. She wanted to go to him, to feel his arms supporting her, to cry a little just that he might soothe her, but because his presence made the menace of the wind seem less, she gripped herself and thought, "I'm in the right. I won't give in. For his sake too I won't."

He washed, hurriedly, so that a few dark welts of dust remained to indent upon his face a haggard strength. It was all she could see as she wiped the dishes and set the food before him: the strength, the grimness, the young Paul growing old and hard, buckled against a desert even grimmer than his will. "Hungry?" she asked, touched to a twinge of pity she had not intended. "There's dust in everything. It keeps coming faster than I can clean it up."

He nodded. "To-night though you'll see it go down. This is the third day." She looked at him in silence a moment, and then as if to herself muttered broodingly, "Until the next time. Until it starts again."

There was a dark timbre of resentment in her voice now that boded another quarrel. He waited, his eyes on her dubiously as she mashed a potato with her fork. The lamp between them threw strong lights and shadows on their faces. Dust and drouth, earth that betrayed alike his labor and his faith, to him the struggle had given sternness, an impassive courage. Beneath the whip of sand his youth had been effaced. Youth, zest, exuberance – there remained only a harsh and clenched virility that yet became him, that seemed at the cost of more engaging qualities to be fulfilment of his inmost and essential nature. Whereas to her the same debts and poverty had brought in a plaintive indignation, a nervous dread of what was still to come. The eyes were hollowed, the lips pinched dry and colorless. It was the face of a woman that had aged without maturing, that had loved the little vanities of life, and lost them wistfully.

"I'm afraid, Paul," she said suddenly. "I can't stand it any longer. He cries all the time. You will go Paul – say you will. We aren't living here – not really living – "

The pleading in her voice now after its shrill bitterness yesterday made him think that this was only another way to persuade him. Evenly he answered, "I told you this morning, Ellen: we keep on right where we are. At least I do. It's yourself you're thinking about, not the baby."

This morning such an accusation would have stung her to rage; now, her voice swift and panting, she pressed on, "Listen, Paul — I'm thinking of all of us — you, too. Look at the sky — and your fields. Are you blind? Thistles and tumbleweeds — it's a desert, Paul. You won't have a straw this fall. You won't be able to feed a cow or a chicken. Please, Paul — say that we'll go away — "

"No Ellen — " His voice as he answered was still remote and even, inflexibly in unison with the narrowed eyes, and the great hunch of muscle-knotted shoulder. "Even as a desert it's better than sweeping out your father's store and running his errands. That's all I've got ahead of me if I do what you want."

"And here — " she flared. "What's ahead of you here? At least we'll get enough to eat and wear when you're sweeping out his store. Look at it — look at it, you fool. Desert — the lamp lit at noon — "

"You'll see it come back," he said quietly. "There's good wheat in it yet."

"But in the meantime — year after year — can't you understand, Paul? We'll never get them back — "

He put down his knife and fork and leaned towards her across the table. "I can't go, Ellen. Living off your people — charity — stop and think of it. This is where I belong. I've no trade or education. I can't do anything else."

"Charity!" she repeated him, letting her voice rise in derision. "And this — you call this independence! Borrowed money you can't even pay the interest on — seed from the government — grocery bills — doctor bills — "

"We'll have crops again," he persisted. "Good crops — the land will come back. It's worth waiting for."

"And while we're waiting, Paul!" It was not anger now, but a kind of sob. "Think of me — and him. It's not fair. We have our lives too to live."

"And you think that going home to your family — taking your husband with you — "

"I don't care — anything would be better than this. Look at the air he's breathing. He cries all the time. For his sake, Paul. What's ahead of him here, even if you do get crops?"

He clenched his lips a minute, then with his eyes hard and contemptuous struck back, "As much as in town, growing up a pauper. You're the one who wants to go, Ellen — it's not for his sake. You think that in town you'd have a better time — not so much work — more clothes — "

"Maybe – " She dropped her head defencelessly. "I'm young still. I like pretty things."

There was silence now – a deep fastness of it enclosed by rushing wind and creaking walls. It seemed the yellow lamplight cast a hush upon them. Through the haze of dusty air the walls receded, dimmed, and came again. Listlessly at last she said, "Go on – your dinner's getting cold. Don't sit and stare at me. I've said it all."

The spent quietness in her voice was harder even than her anger to endure. It reproached him, against his will insisted that he see and understand her lot. To justify himself he tried, "I was a poor man when you married me. You said you didn't mind. Farming's never been easy, and never will be."

"I wouldn't mind the work or the scrimping if there was something to look forward to. It's the hopelessness – going on – watching the land blow away."

"The land's all right," he repeated. "The dry years won't last forever."

"But it's not just dry years, Paul!" The little sob in her voice gave way suddenly to a ring of exasperation. "Will you never see? It's the land itself – the soil. You've plowed and harrowed it until there's not a root or fibre left to hold it down. That's why the soil drifts – that's why in a year or two there'll be nothing left but the bare clay. If in the first place you farmers had taken care of your land – if you hadn't been so greedy for wheat every year – "

She had taught school before she married him, and of late in her anger there had been a kind of disdain, an attitude almost of condescension, as if she no longer looked upon the farmers as her equals. He sat still, his eyes fixed on the yellow lampflame, and seeming to know how her words had hurt him she went on softly, "I want to help you Paul. That's why I won't sit quiet while you go on wasting your life. You're only thirty – you owe it to yourself as well as me."

Still he sat with his lips drawn white and his eyes on the lampflame. It seemed indifference now, as if he were ignoring her, and stung to anger again she cried, "Do you ever think what my life is? Two rooms to live in – once a month to town, and nothing to spend when I get there. I'm still young – I wasn't brought up this way."

Stolidly he answered, "You're a farmer's wife now. It doesn't matter what you used to be, or how you were brought up. You get enough to eat and wear. Just now that's all that I can do. I'm not to blame that we've been dried out five years."

"Enough to eat!" she laughed back shrilly, her eyes all the while fixed expressionless and wide. "Enough salt pork – enough potatoes and eggs. And look – " Springing to the middle of the room she thrust out a foot for him to see the scuffed old slipper. "When they're completely gone I suppose you'll tell me I can go barefoot – that I'm a farmer's wife – that it's not your fault we're dried out – "

"And look at these – " He pushed his chair away from the table now to let her see what he was wearing. "Cowhide – hard as boards – but my feet are so calloused I don't feel them anymore."

Then hurriedly he stood up, ashamed of having tried to match her hardships with his own. But frightened now as he reached for his smock she pressed close to him. "Don't go yet. I brood and worry when I'm left alone. Please, Paul – you can't work on the land anyway."

"And keep on like this?" Grimly he buttoned his smock right up to his throat. "You start before I'm through the door. Week in and week out – I've troubles enough of my own."

"Paul – please stay – " The eyes were glazed now, distended a little as if with the intensity of her dread and pleading. "We won't quarrel any more. Hear it! I can't work – just stand still and listen – "

The eyes frightened him, but responding to a kind of instinct that he must withstand her, that it was his self-respect and manhood against the fretful weakness of a woman, he answered unfeelingly, "In here safe and quiet – you don't know how well off you are. If you were out in it – fighting it – swallowing it –"

"Sometimes, Paul, I wish I were. I'm so caged – if I could only break away and run. See – I stand like this all day. I can't relax. My throat's so tight it aches – "

Firmly he loosened his smock from the clutch of her hands. "If I stay we'll only keep on like this all afternoon. To-morrow when the wind's down we can talk things over quietly."

Then without meeting her eyes again he swung outside, and doubled low against the buffets of the wind, fought his way slowly towards the stable. There was a deep hollow calm within, a vast darkness engulfed beneath the tides of moaning wind. He stood breathless a moment, hushed almost to a stupor by the sudden extinction of the storm and the incredible stillness that enfolded him. It was a long, far-reaching stillness. The first dim stalls and rafters led the way into cavernlike obscurity, into vaults and recesses that extended far beyond the stable walls. Nor in these first quiet moments did he forbid the illusion, the sense of release from a harsh, familiar world into one of immeasurable peace and darkness. The contentious mood that his stand against Ellen had roused him to, his tenacity and clenched despair before the ravages of wind, it was ebbing now, losing itself in the cover of darkness. Ellen and the wheat seemed remote, unimportant. At a whinney from the bay mare Bess he went forward and into her stall. She seemed grateful for his presence, and thrust her nose deep between his arm and body. They stood a long time thus, comforting and assuring each other.

For soon again the first deep sense of quiet and peace was shrunken to the battered shelter of the stable. Instead of release or escape from the assaulting wind, the walls were but a feeble stand against it. They creaked and sawed as if the fingers of a giant hand were tightening to collapse them; the empty loft sustained a pipelike cry that rose and fell but never ended. He saw the dust-black sky again, and his fields blown smooth with drifted soil.

But always, even while listening to the storm outside, he could feel the tense and apprehensive stillness of the stable. There was not a hoof that clumped or shifted, not a rub of halter against manger. And yet, though it had been a strange stable, into which he had never set foot before, he would have known, despite the darkness, that every stall was filled. They too were all listening.

From Bess he went to the big grey gelding Prince. Prince was twenty years old, with rib-grooved sides, and high, protruding hipbones. Paul ran his hand over the ribs, and felt a sudden shame, a sting of fear that Ellen might be right in what she said. For wasn't it true – nine years a farmer now on his own land, and still he couldn't even feed his horses? What then could he hope to do for his wife and son?

There was much he planned. And so vivid was the future of his planning, so real and constant, that often the actual present was but half-felt, but half-endured. Its difficulties were lessened by a confidence in what lay beyond them. A new house for Ellen, new furniture, new clothes. Land for the boy – land and still more land – or education, whatever he might want.

But all the time was he only a blind and stubborn fool? Was Ellen right? Was he trampling on her life, and throwing away his own? The five years since he married her, were they to go on repeating themselves, five, ten, twenty, until all the brave future he looked forward to was but a stark and futile past?

She looked forward to no future. She had no faith or dream with which to make the dust and poverty less real. He understood suddenly. He saw her face again as only a few minutes ago it had begged him not to leave her. The darkness round him now was as a slate on which her lonely terror limned itself. He went from Prince to the other horses, combing their manes and forelocks with his fingers, but always still it was her face he saw, its staring eyes and twisted suffering. "See Paul – I stand like this all day. I just stand still – My throat's so tight it aches –"

And always the wind, the creak of walls, the wild lipless wailing through the loft. Until at last as he stood there, staring into the livid face before him, it seemed that this scream of wind was a cry from her parched and frantic lips. He knew it couldn't be, he knew that she was safe within the house, but still the wind persisted as a woman's cry. The cry of a woman with eyes like those that watched him through the dark.

Eyes that were mad now – lips that even as they cried still pleaded, "See, Paul – I stand like this all day. I just stand still – so caged! If I could only run!"

He saw her running, pulled and driven headlong by the wind, but when at last he returned to the house, compelled by his anxiety, she was walking quietly back and forwards with the baby in her arms. Careful, despite his concern, not to reveal a fear or weakness that she might think capitulation to her wishes, he watched a moment through the window, and then went off to the tool shed to mend old harness. All afternoon he stitched and rivetted. It was easier with the lantern lit and his hands occupied. There was wind whining high past the tool shed too, but it was only wind. He remembered the arguments with which Ellen had tried to persuade him away from the farm, and one by one he defeated them. There would be rain again – next year, or the next. Maybe she was right. Maybe in his ignorance he had farmed his land the wrong way, seeding wheat every year, working the soil till it was lifeless dust – but he would do better now. He would plant clover and alfalfa, breed cattle, acre by acre and year by year restore to his land its fibre and fertility. That was something to work for, a way to prove himself. It was ruthless wind, blackening the sky with his earth, screaming in derision of his labour, but it was not his master. Out of his land it had made a wilderness. He now, out of the wilderness, would make a farm and home again.

To-night he must talk with Ellen. Patiently, when the wind was down, and they were both quiet again. It was she who had told him to grow fibrous crops, who had called him an ignorant fool because he kept on with summer fallow and wheat. Now she might be gratified to find him acknowledging her wisdom. Perhaps she would begin to feel the power and steadfastness of the land, to take a pride in it, to understand that he was not a fool, but working for her future and their son's.

And already the wind was slackening. At four o'clock he could sense a lull. At five, straining his eyes from the tool shed doorway, he could make out a neighbour's buildings half a mile away. It was over – three days of blight and havoc like a scourge – three days so bitter and so long that for a moment he stood still, unseeing, his senses idle with a numbness of relief.

But only for a moment. Suddenly he emerged from the numbness; suddenly the fields before him struck his eyes to comprehension. They lay black, naked. Beaten and mounded smooth with dust as if a sea in gentle swell had turned to stone. And though he had tried to prepare himself for such a scene, though he had known since yesterday that not a blade would last the storm, still now, before the utter waste confronting him, he sickened and stood cold. Suddenly like the fields he was naked. Everything that had sheathed him a little from the realities of existence: vision and purpose, faith in the land, in the future, in himself – it was all rent now, all stripped away. "Desert," he heard her voice begin to sob. "Desert, you fool – the lamp lit at noon!"

In the stable again, measuring out their feed to the horses, he wondered what he would say to her to-night. For so deep were his instincts of loyalty to the land that still, even with the images of its betrayal stark upon his mind, his concern was how to withstand her, how to go on again and justify himself. It had not occurred to him yet that he might or should abandon the land. He had lived with it too long. Rather was his impulse to defend it still – as a man defends against the scorn of strangers even his most worthless kin.

He fed his horses, then waited. She too would be waiting, ready to cry at him, "Look now – that crop that was to feed and clothe us! And you'll still keep on! You'll still say 'Next year – there'll be rain next year'!"

But she was gone when he reached the house. The door was open, the lamp blown out, the crib empty. The dishes from their meal at noon were still on the table. She had perhaps begun to sweep, for the broom was lying in the middle of the floor. He tried to call, but a terror clamped upon his throat. In the wan, returning light it seemed that even the deserted kitchen was straining to whisper what it had seen. The tatters of the storm still whimpered through the eaves, and in their moaning told the desolation of the miles they had traversed. On tiptoe at last he crossed to the adjoining room; then at the threshold, without even a glance inside to satisfy himself that she was really gone, he wheeled again and plunged outside.

He ran a long time – distraught and headlong as a few hours ago he had seemed to watch her run – around the farmyard, a little distance into the pasture, back again blindly to the house to see whether she had returned – and then at a stumble down the road for help.

They joined him in the search, rode away for others, spread calling across the fields in the direction she might have been carried by the wind – but nearly two hours later it was himself who came upon her. Crouched down against a drift of sand as if for shelter, her hair in matted stands around her neck and face, the child clasped tightly in her arms.

The child was quite cold. It had been her arms, perhaps, too frantic to protect him, or the smother of dust upon his throat and lungs. "Hold him," she said as he knelt beside her. "So – with his face away from the wind. Hold him until I tidy my hair."

Her eyes were still wide in an immobile stare, but with her lips she smiled at him. For a long time he knelt transfixed, trying to speak to her, touching fearfully with his fingertip the dust-grimed cheeks and eyelids of the child. At last she said, "I'll take him again. Such clumsy hands – you don't know how to hold a baby yet. See how his head falls forward on your arms."

Yet it all seemed familiar – a confirmation of what he had known since noon. He gave her the child, then, gathering them both up in his arms, struggled to his feet and turned towards home.

It was evening now. Across the fields a few spent clouds of dust still shook and fled. Beyond, as if through smoke, the sunset smouldered like a distant fire.

He walked with a long dull stride, his eyes before him, heedless of her weight. Once he glanced down and with her eyes she still was smiling. "Such strong arms, Paul – and I was so tired with carrying just him..."

He tried to answer, but it seemed that now the dusk was drawn apart in breathless waiting, a finger on its lips until they passed. "You were right, Paul –" Her voice came whispering, as if she too could feel the hush. "You said to-night we'd see the storm go down. So still now, and the sky burning – it means to-morrow will be fine."

(1968)   (1938)

Gratien Gélinas
1909 –

———◆———

BORN IN SAINT-TITE, Quebec, Gratien Gélinas was educated in Montreal. In 1937 he began writing radio sketches based on a character named Fridolin; these sketches became the focus for nine theatrical revues, *Fridolinons*, produced annually from 1938 to 1946. One of these sketches, "The Conscript's Return," was subsequently expanded into *Tit-Coq*, Gélinas' first play. *Tit-Coq* was first produced in 1948 and was followed by *Bousille et les justes* (1959) and *Hier les enfants dansaient* (1967). Each of these plays has since been published in both French and English editions. A founder and first artistic director of the Comédie Canadienne (1958) and a founding member of the National Theatre School of Canada, Gélinas was appointed chairman of the Canadian Film Development Corporation in 1969.

From
The Conscript's Return

[A Conscript Goes to War]

(The curtain opens on a small cafe across from Windsor Station in Montreal: there is a restaurant counter, its back turned three-quarters towards the audience, in front of a panel vaguely representing a shop window. The waitress is wiping off the counter.)

CONSCRIPT: *(He comes in singing, his knapsack on his back. All signs suggest he is in high spirits.)*
"It's a long way to Tipperary
It's a long way to go..."
(Putting his sack on the counter) Bonjour, mam'zelle. Sorry, I don't know that song too good, but I hear they used to really belt it out in the war before this one!

WAITRESS: What'll you have?

CONSCRIPT: Me, I don't need nothing. I looked in the window before crossing to the Windsor Station, I saw you and I came in – because you look like you could cheer up a fellow.

WAITRESS: *(Chewing her gum)* Who, me?

CONSCRIPT: Not that I need cheering up. Not even one tiny bit.

WAITRESS: That's good.

CONSCRIPT: No, mam'zelle, as far as I'm concerned life's just fine tonight. Everything's in order *(He snaps his fingers)* just like that. Absolutely everything's fine and dandy – except that I leave in ten minutes.

WAITRESS: The Halifax train?

CONSCRIPT: Oui, mam'zelle.

WAITRESS: So you don't want nothing, eh?

CONSCRIPT: No. It's me that's going to give you something. Here's twenty-five cents; take it and buy yourself whatever you want – an ice cream cone, a lipstick, a three-storey house – whatever you want! Me, I don't need anything. *(He takes a small flask from his coat pocket.)*

WAITRESS: I can see that.

CONSCRIPT: *(Who has taken out a cigarette and is hunting in his pockets for a match.)* How about giving me a glass?

WAITRESS: *(handing him one)* There you go.

CONSCRIPT: Yup, mam'zelle: phttt! My furlough's over tonight. Salut!

188 / Gratien Gélinas

(He drinks.) Two weeks of perfect happiness — except for the two days I spent waiting outside the liquor store.

WAITRESS: Lucky you finally got something.

CONSCRIPT: A hell of a good furlough. I saw my girl and we played a little hide-and-seek.

WAITRESS: She must've been glad to see you.

CONSCRIPT: Yeah, but you never know with women. Besides, I went to the wrestling three times and I shot some craps. Ah! and then I went to the National to see La Poune. — I laughed, by God...she puts on one hell of a show!

WAITRESS: So you're leaving tonight?

CONSCRIPT: Yeah. Don't you think I'm a hell of a lucky guy? First I leave for Halifax and then I go on a nice boat trip. And on top of everything else, the government pays the shot! Whoopee! *(He drinks.)*

WAITRESS: So you aren't too ticked off about going?

CONSCRIPT: Me? I'd even let them take my picture for propaganda: "Another conscript leaves for the front with a smile on his lips." That wouldn't look so bad in the papers, eh?

WAITRESS: Wouldn't you look a little green around the gills?

CONSCRIPT: Bah! That wouldn't show up in a black-and-white picture: There's one little thing that's bugging me though.

WAITRESS; Yeah?

CONSCRIPT: Even if a guy seems perfectly happy, look hard enough and there's always some fly in the ointment. Take this guy, mam'zelle: I roomed with him before the war. We're around the same age. A guy that always seemed to be in perfect health, like me. But apparently there was something wrong. I don't know if it was in the cellar or up in the attic or on the mezzanine; anyway, some little thing wasn't right, so he got his discharge. He's staying in Montreal, right at home, no risks, making ten bucks a day in the munitions...and on top of it all, I bet he'll try and steal my girl. While me, with my A-1 rating, I'm shipped to the other end of the world, risking my neck for a buck thirty a day. Whoopee! *(He takes another gulp.)*

WAITRESS: I know what you mean. But it isn't your buddy's fault if he got his discharge.

CONSCRIPT: OK, you're right. He isn't fit for service. But how come they don't stick him in a uniform and send him off to make cartridges — at a buck thirty a day just like me?

WAITRESS: Well, I...

CONSCRIPT: It wouldn't be any harder than sending the rest of us overseas, would it?

WAITRESS: No, it shouldn't be. But what difference would it make to the rest of you?

CONSCRIPT: Well, it would mean that when the war's over they'd let us go just a couple of hours before the rest of them, so we'd have first crack at our old jobs, instead of finding out that somebody else has had his flat feet there for five years!

WAITRESS: That's the least you'd deserve.

CONSCRIPT: Now mind you, I haven't got anything against that other guy. I'm too well off in this whole shebang to hold a grudge against anybody. But sometimes, you know, you talk just for the sake of talking. Still, it makes me laugh when I hear all that propaganda shouting like hell that we're going off to fight for Justice!

WAITRESS: Bah! They just talk to hear themselves too.

CONSCRIPT: Yeah. And besides, if they paid a buck thirty a day for the munitions instead of ten bucks, it'd be cheaper for the population, and maybe our taxes wouldn't be so rotten.

WAITRESS: You're right. I don't know how come they didn't think about that.

CONSCRIPT: Simple: because it doesn't make sense. Me, I had a drink and that gave me some crazy ideas. But they thought about it and they realized that a buck thirty a day for munitions, that'd be a hell of a dirty trick to play on the big bugs with all the war contracts. There wouldn't be any profits, mam'zelle, and without profits, the big companies wouldn't be interested. With the sad result that we'd be left without any wars!

WAITRESS: And so much the better.

CONSCRIPT: No, you don't understand, because you haven't got an education. You see, mam'zelle, anybody will tell you this: war is progress! The guns we've got are a lot bigger than the ones our ancestors had back in 1914.

WAITRESS: Sure.

CONSCRIPT: Yeah. I'm starting to think too hard: better have a little drink. Still five minutes to go in this goddamn furlough. Got to have fun till the last drop! *(He drinks.)* Hey, there's no record-player here with a slot for a nickel.

WAITRESS: No, sorry.

CONSCRIPT: Ah, that's too bad. We could have put on some music, loud enough to break the windows, and then we could have danced ... Because I'm happy tonight, mam'zelle, disgustingly happy. Ah! the hell with it! That goddamn war's going to come to an end. One fine day there'll be an Armistice and I'll be coming back ... maybe.

WAITRESS: With a medal.

CONSCRIPT: A medal? *Medals*, mam'zelle, medals all over me – even in my pockets. And then we'll have a grand parade, all the way down Sherbrooke Street...and when we get to the corner of Atwater, dis-miss! Then we'll all stampede to get ourselves a corner where we'll sell pencils and shoelaces... Ah! I'm not worried: I already picked out a nice spot, sheltered from the wind. And if business is good I might even sell razor blades.

WAITRESS: Don't forget your train, eh?

CONSCRIPT: Yeah, you're right. Mustn't keep the conductor of my private compartment cooling his heels. He's probably waiting with a lantern and white gloves. (*He gets up reluctantly, picks up his knapsack.*)

WAITRESS: Well, goodbye...and good luck.

CONSCRIPT: Thanks a lot. Anyway, don't miss me too much. But if you're ever in the mood you could write to me. My address is number D-620283, somewhere in England...or somewhere else on the earth. Unless it's in the other world. So long!

WAITRESS: So long:

CONSCRIPT: You aren't so bad looking, you know. (*He goes out singing*):
"O Canada, our home and native land,
True patriot love, from all thy sons command."

CURTAIN

(1977)

Sheila Fischman (Trans.)

John Glassco
1909 –

———◆———

BORN IN MONTREAL, John Glassco was attending McGill University in 1928 when he decided to leave Canada in order to explore the bohemian and literary worlds of Paris. His memoirs of his experiences in Europe from 1928 to 1931, *Memoirs of Montparnasse*, although written during that time, were not published until 1970. In addition to an early collection of poetry which appeared in pamphlet form in 1928, Glassco has published three volumes of poetry including *Selected Poems* (1971) which received the Governor General's Award for poetry. He has also published several volumes of fiction and has been extremely influential as a translator and anthologist of French-Canadian poetry.

Deserted Buildings
Under Shefford Mountain

These native angles of decay
   In shed and barn whose broken wings
Lie here half fallen in the way
Of headstones amid uncut hay —
   Why do I love you, ragged things?

What grace unknown to any art,
   What beauty frailer than a mood
Awake in me their counterpart?
What correspondence of a heart
   That loves the failing attitude?   10

Here where I grasp the certain fate
   Of all man's work in wood and stone,
And con the lesson of the straight
That shall be crooked soon or late
   And crumble into forms alone,

Some troubled joy that's half despair
   Ascends within me like a breath:
I see these silent ruins wear
The speaking look, the sleeping air
   Of features newly cast in death,   20

Dead faces where we strive to see
   The signature of something tossed
Between design and destiny,
Between God and absurdity,
   Till, harrowing up a new-made ghost,

We half embrace the wavering form,
    And half conceive the wandering sense
Of some imagined part kept warm
And salvaged from the passing storm
    Of time's insulting accidents.   30

So I, assailed by the blind love
    That meets me in this silent place,
Lift open arms: Is it enough
That restless things can cease to move
    And leave a ruin wreathed in grace,

Or is this wreck of strut and span
    No more than solace for the creed
Of progress and its emmet plan,
Dark houses that are void of man,
    Dull meadows that have gone to seed?   40

(1958)   (1971)

Utrillo's World

I

He sat above it, watching it recede,
A world of love resolved to empty spaces,
Streets without figures, figures without faces,
Desolate by choice and negative from need.
But the hoardings weep, the shutters burn and bleed;
Colours of crucifixion, dying graces,
Spatter and cling upon these sorrowful places.
— Where is the loved one? Where do the streets lead?

There is no loved one. Perfect fear
Has cast out love. And the streets go on forever   10
To blest annihilation, silently ascend
To their own assumption of bright points in air.
It is the world that counts, the endless fever,
And suffering that is its own and only end.

II

Anguished these sombre houses, still, resigned.
Suffering has found no better face than wood
For its own portrait, nor are tears so good
As the last reticence of being blind.
Grief without voice, mourning without mind,
I find your silence in this neighbourhood
Whose hideous buildings ransom with their blood
The shame and the self-loathing of mankind.

They are also masks that misery has put on
Over the faces and the festivals: 10
Madness and fear must have a place to hide,
And murder a secret room to call his own.
I know they are prisons also, these thin walls
Between us and what cowers and shakes inside.

(1958)   (1971)

Quebec Farmhouse

Admire the face of plastered stone,
    The roof descending like a song
    Over the washed and anointed walls,
Over the house that hugs the earth
Like a feudal souvenir: oh see
The sweet submissive fortress of itself
    That the landscape owns!

And inside is the night, the airless dark
    Of the race so conquered it has made
    Perpetual conquest of itself,   10
Upon desertion's ruin piling
The inward desert of surrender,
Drawing in all its powers, puffing its soul,
    Raising its arms to God.

    This is the closed, enclosing house
        That set its flinty face against
        The rebel children dowered with speech
    To break it open, to make it live
    And flower in the cathedral beauty
    Of a pure heaven of Canadian blue –   20
        The larks so maimed

    They still must hark and hurry back
        To the paradisal place of gray,
        The clash of keys, the click of beads,
    The sisters walking leglessly,
    While under the wealth and weight of stone
    All the bright demons of forbidden joy
        Shriek on, year after year.

(1964)   (1971)

One Last Word

FOR M. McC.

Now that I have your hand, let me persuade you
The means are more important than the end,
Ends being only an excuse for action,
For adventures sought for their own sake alone,
Pictures along the way, feelings
Released in love: so, acting out our dreams
We justify movement by giving it a purpose
(Who can be still forever?)
This is the rationale of travel
And the formula of lovers.   10

Dearest, it is not for the amusement of certain tissues,
Nor for whatever may thread our loins like a vein of miraculous water
That now (under the music) I speak your name –
But for the journey we shall take together
Through a transfigured landscape
Of beasts and birds and people

Where everything is new.
                    Listen,
The embarkation for Cythera
Is eternal because it ends nowhere: 20
No port for those tasselled sails! And for our love
No outcome,
Only the modesty
The perfection
Of the flight or death of a bird.

(1971)   (1971)

From
Memoirs of Montparnasse

WE SAW A good deal of Morley and Loretto during the next few weeks and liked them even more. As soon as they had moved from the Hotel New York into a cheap apartment they were much more relaxed. He told me a curious story about their landlady.

'My French isn't so good, but as far as I can make out her husband sings in the Metropolitan Opera in New York,' said Morley. 'But she has this lover who comes in at two o'clock every morning. A little guy in a uniform like a postman's.'

'These Frenchwomen,' said Loretto, 'they certainly make time.'

Morley was now working on another novel, and his example drove me back to this book with such urgency that I managed to finish the third chapter by the end of June. I did not have the courage to show my work-in-progress to him, thinking of the superlative technique and polish of his own stories.

Morley did not work on Saturday nights, and on one of these he suggested we see a little Parisian night life. I at once proposed the brothel at 25 rue St. Apolline, but he was more interested in Montmartre. My knowledge of that quarter was still confined to the smart cabarets around the Place Pigalle, such as Bricktop's, Le Grand Duc, and La Boîte Blanche. I told him how expensive they were.

'Not all of them,' he said. 'There's this Le Palermo run by a guy called Joe Zelli. I hear they've got a good floor show, and if you sit at the bar it doesn't cost too much.'

'All right. But not in the *salle*. I think it's the kind of place where they have telephones at the tables so you can speak to any girl you fancy, and that means a hefty cover charge.'

'We'll sit at the bar. It's on me.'

We took the last Métro to Pigalle and walked along the boulevard de Clichy. The ambiance was better than I thought: the boulevard still had its trees, the lights danced on the leaves, and the whores were out in full strength. The girls in Montmartre are the most aggressive in Paris, and as this was a Saturday night in the height of the tourist season they were on their mettle.

'Say,' said Morley after he had been accosted and man-handled for the fourth or fifth time, 'what goes on here? Do we look as rich as all that?'

'It's just our clothes. They think we're Americans.'

'If I'd known, I'd have worn an old sweater and sneakers.'

'They'd still know the cut of your trousers. No, if you want to get by here you have to wear two-dollar French pants without cuffs, a knitted shirt and a pair of fancy pointed shoes. Also you're not supposed to pay any attention to the scenery and horse along as if you owned the whole street. And don't look at the girls. Look over their heads.'

'But then you miss everything. Heck, I want to enjoy myself!'

We went down the rue Blanche (a street I was to know all too well within a year) to the corner where Le Palermo displayed its big electric sign. Morley studied the photographs of bare-breasted women posted up outside, squared his boxer's shoulders, and led the way in. By luck we found two empty places at the bar where, by craning our necks, we had an oblique view of the chorus performing on the dance floor; the noise was so deafening that at first we could not exchange a word. Morley ordered a beer and I a brandy and water.

The girls in the chorus were young and beautiful and their costumes elaborate, but unfortunately none of them was able to dance. Moreover they all seemed dead tired, doubtless because they had to put on a five-minute show every fifteen minutes. I watched this ton of listless flesh, these fixed smiles, these snowy pink-tipped contours, with a feeling of sadness. This place was after all only a mutual concourse of wolves, in which the appetites of desire, glamour and money were opposed and never met, where each was expensively dangled before the other and where the only real gainer was Joe Zelli himself – though even this was doubtful, since he was rumoured to be going bankrupt.

Morley also was pensive. In an interval of comparative quiet he pointed to a sign above the bar that read CONSOMMATIONS, 40 FRANCS. 'What's a *consommation*?' he asked. 'Does that mean – intercourse?'

'No, it's just a drink.'

He shook his head pityingly. 'Think of the dopes who'll pay forty francs for a drink. *Consommation*! What's it made of?'

The resumed noise of the band temporarily spared him the news. But when he realized we each had one in front of us he took it very well.

'We can sit here all night on these two drinks, of course,' I said.

'Well then, why not? We'll have to take a taxi home anyway.'

'True. And it's not a bad place. The little dark girl in the chorus, the one on the end there, has some good points.'

'I'd like another beer, but not at any forty francs. I wish I'd brought along something on the hip.'

'If you want some brandy, I've got a flask. But be careful. Here, pour a shot in your beer.'

He did so with unobtrusive skill. 'Boy, this is just like the King Eddy in Toronto! You've got to drink hootch out of a teacup there.' He tested his drink with satisfaction. 'Beer and brandy – that's not a bad *consommation* at all. I'm beginning to like this place.'

His pleasure was infectious. I freshened my own drink and we sat back on our stools and watched the chorus. By now our ears had become used to the noise, and conversation was possible.

'I like you and Graeme,' he said. 'So does Loretto. But say, what's biting your friend McAlmon? I can't make him out.'

'He's always that way.'

'I admire his work – in a way. "Miss Knight" is a nice piece of writing. No one has gotten that type of fairy down on paper before. In fact McAlmon's pretty good when he's writing about fairies. How do you account for that?'

I tried to give the appearance of someone forming a considered judgement. 'He just has a natural sympathy for everthing eccentric.'

'Yes,' he said thoughtfully. 'I' d say you're right. He likes people who are pretty far out in left field, that's clear enough. But he makes no judgements, he's too uncommitted. Don't you think a writer should commit himself, some time anyway?'

'Like Dos Passos?'

'Hell no, that's just propaganda. Dos Passos will be the forgotten man of American letters in ten years. It's a shame too, becaue he's got a scope and a sweep, he knows the States up and down and inside out, he gives you the facts and the sounds and smells and talk of the whole damn country – but how come you can't remember any of his people or even what they did, their problems, their attitude?'

'Perhaps because he's so committed. Or perhaps he doesn't know anything about people. He just reduces them to stupid appetites, to organisms looking for sex or money or jobs. Like Zola, in a way.'

'Sure, Zola was over-committed, if you like.'

'And he's got a better collection of facts and sounds and smells.'

He laughed. 'Say, I'm getting a pretty fine collection myself right now. Look at those girls!'

The chorus had come out dressed as birds, with beaked and eared headdresses, trousers ruched like feathers and long pink-tipped mittens which they flapped wearily up and down.

'You were talking about commitment,' I said. 'I can think of no good writer who's committed to anything today. Except Dreiser.'

'*Dreiser?*What in hell is he committed to except telling a damn good success story?'

'I think he's committed to dishonesty in everything except art – to crime, to stealing and lying and swindling and falsehood in general. He's tapped the American dream.'

'He's got a godawful style.'

'Sure, almost as bad as McAlmon's. Because he just can't be bothered to write well, he hasn't the time, he's too busy drawing the picture and making the story move.'

'When you say he's committed to stealing and swindling and lying aren't you just thinking of those Cowperwood books? What about *Sister Carrie?*'

'She's just as bad. And everyone in the *American Tragedy.* Have you ever met such a crowd of liars anywhere in fiction? Expecially the heroines. And they lie so casually, so naturally. That's what makes Dreiser great: he's anarchic, amoral, immature, antediluvian.'

I suddenly realized I was talking like a character in a Huxley novel. This problem of commitment was Morley's, not mine. I had no commitments except, in a vague way, to remain uncommitted. I had no wife, no job, no ambition, no bank account, no use for large sums of money, no appetite for prestige, and no temptation to acquire any of them. I had at that time, I think, already unconsciously assessed them all as so many pairs of weighted diver's shoes – of no use to anyone who wanted to remain on the surface of life. If they had been wings I would have assumed them gladly; but now, vis-à-vis the deadly earnestness of Morley Callaghan, a man only ten years older than myself, I had once again the salutary sense of the abyss that yawns for everyone who has embraced the literary profession – everyone from Molière to George Gissing: literature, like every other form of gainful employment, was just another trap.

'Yeah,' said Morley, 'I guess so. But he's committed just the same. I think he's a Communist now. Oh God, here come the girls again.'

This time they were dressed as rabbits.

We watched them for a while, then simultaneously decided we had had enough of Le Palermo. We found a taxi outside and drove to Morley's apartment, splitting the fare. As it was a fine night I decided to walk the half-mile to the rue Broca when he suddenly gripped my arm.

'Look, there's our landlady's boy friend,' he whispered delightedly, drawing me into the shadows.

A small man in a baggy blue uniform was pushing the concierge's bell. As he turned, the insignia on the motorman's cap showed the intertwined initials of the Métro.'Ah, the Metropolitan,' I thought. We watched discreetly until he had gone in.

(1970)   (1970)

Ralph Gustafson
1909 –

————◆————

BORN NEAR SHERBROOKE, Quebec, Ralph Gustafson studied at Bishop's University and at Oxford. For many years he worked as a journalist in England and New York before returning to Bishop's University as a Professor of English. Since the appearance of his first book of poems, *The Golden Chalice* (1935), Gustafson has edited several anthologies of Canadian writing and published numerous volumes of his own poetry including *Selected Poems* (1972) and *Fire on Stone* (1974).

In the Yukon

In Europe, you can't move without going down into history.
Here, all is a beginning. I saw a salmon jump,
Again and again, against the current,
The timbered hills a background, wooded green
Unpushed through; the salmon jumped, silver.
This was news, was commerce, at the end of the summer
The leap for dying. Moose came down to the water edge
To drink and the salmon turned silver arcs.
At night, the northern lights played, great over country
Without tapestry and coronations, kings crowned   10
With weights of gold. They were green,

Green hangings and great grandeur, over the north
Going to what no man can hold hard in mind,
The dredge of that gravity, being without experience.

(1960)   (1972)

Armorial

I lay down with my love and there was song
Breaking, like the lilies I once saw
Lovely around King Richard, murdered
Most foully and all his grace at Pomfret,
The roses of England stolen; our love
Was like gules emblazoned at Canterbury
Most kingly in windows and leo-pards
Passant on bars of gold. This
Was our heraldry.

Our love was larks and sprang from meadows   10
Far from kingdoms, which regal grew
With rod and bloodred weed and rush
Where water ran; this was our love,
The place where she chose, I could not but come,
A field without myth or rhetoric.
She lay down with love and my hand
Was gold with dust of lily. This
Was our province.

There was song in that kingly country
But I saw there, stuck like a porcupine   20
On Bosworth Field the arrows through him,
That regal and most royal other
Richard, runt and twitch in a ditch,
His hand wristdeep in lily where
Henry Tudor rolled him, the gules
Of England draining on his shirt.
My love wept.

(1960)   (1972)

Aspects of Some Forsythia Branches

Waiting for these dry sticks in a vase –
Cut (with deliberate shears taken
From the third drawer down on the left) from the bush
In snow – complicated with leaf
And yellow in the earth elaborated, even
In the wintering sun; as the spiral of a protein
Divides and duplicates the thrust
Of love, the hereditary nose of Caesar,
Alexander's brow and Jennie's
Mole; the aggregation of a galaxy!:   10
So the April science of a bunch
Of sticks cut for an etched glass vase –
Waiting for these to flower in a March
Room – waiting for all this business –
As an act of love, a science of gravel,
A suffering, is this not done
With reliance? One way, dry sticks
Lead to buds, presumably wanted,
To yellow eventually. What trivial aspects
Can be got! We handle love   20
For small purposes. Yet they serve.
Shrubs are cut for what is believed in.
Somewhere death's in it. Dignity
Is demanded even for the dead.
So we cut branches two
Days ago. Take great precautions.
Go carefully through a door. Stand
Among deathbeds as though among heroes,
Pausing in winter along windy corridors
With the knowledge ahead of us, to wrap our throats.   30

(1966)   (1972)

The Philosophy of the Parthenon

Proportion is all things of beauty.
Dimension, go beyond dimension,
Calculation, measure nothing,
Only in relation, the cornice balanced
Against the line, the line against
The truth, not as an existence
But as a meaning, the marble line
The respect to itself, the incumbent gods.

(1969)   (1972)

On the Top of Milan Cathedral

Four thousand saints surround me.
My soul is utterly taken by the man
Selling Cokes from a red refrigerator
On the roof of Milan Cathedral.

I am unused to this commercial society
And walk the lead slope near the balustrade
With mine eyes as if they did not see
The solid wooden booth and the counter

But it is no use: the sun broils
And the cathedral is a million dollar failure.   10
The Virgin Mary and Christ holding
Open like a miraculous cardiac his bleeding

Heart, are for sale in coloured plaster.
There are assorted bottlecaps
Amongst the sleeves of straws and paper.
I have sat amid angels and pinnacles

Being hot and closed mine eyes to commerce.
The man's wife argues about money
But it is in a dialect beyond my comprehension.
I think of the indeterminate profit   20

Of martyrs and the shareholders in a better Company.
I shall unroll the end of a Verichrome
And feed it into my Kodak before
The host risen about me is substantial.

(1969)   (1972)

Hyacinths with Brevity

You will use whatever watering can
You can, what knife to plant the bulbs.
I smell leaves and crab-apples
On the ground; the crabbed progression is under
Way, blossom poured, jelly
In jars crimson in the sun along
The sill. That hardens it, you tell me.
I shall have toast in the morning.
                              But be quick.
The valves of the heart are pesky things   10
And shut down. We shall no more see
The like of these leaves again. They blow
Across the garden with this brief wind
That blows. So you will use what you can.
This trowel with last summer's caked
Dirt on the blade, and this can
And these forty bulbs which should be
Already in the ground so swift the wind
Blows and brief the constituency
Of sun. This piece of hose will do...   20
But you have the watering can....

(1974)   (1974)

Green Disposition

The world's a green world. The phlox is red:
Against the stone wall brilliant the clusters
Stand out appointing the grey and green of

Cedar hedge and wall – counterpoint
Of His brilliance, the garden in His mind
When thrown were primal suns, green
Assertions. Looked up from this vantage, the hill
And trees and hedge and lawn are green, only
Birch tree, bark white, is against
This ordering, this green world, enclosing round   10
Red rose and saffron marigold
And yellow rose arranged not by God
This time but proof of how this shambles
Of magnificence when brought to arbitration
By our love is provident enough
Of joy. In this garden-world of scraps
Of God, the world is green. The claim of snow
Is only time's matter, no dominion.
Scarlet phlox and stone affirm green.

(1974)   (1974)

A. M. Klein
1909 – 1972

———◆———

THE SON OF Russian immigrants, Abraham Moses Klein was born in Montreal, received his B.A. from McGill in 1930 and was called to the bar in 1933. In addition to practising law in Montreal, he edited *The Canadian Jewish Chronicle* from 1939 to 1955 and was a visiting lecturer in poetry at McGill University from 1945 to 1947. Illness forced him to live in seclusion after 1955. Although Klein's first collection, *Hath Not a Jew,* did not appear until 1940, he had published numerous poems in the preceding decade. Klein's subsequent work includes his best-known collection of poetry, *The Rocking Chair and Other Poems* (1948), and a novel, *The Second Scroll* (1951).

Sonnet in Time of Affliction

The word of grace is flung from foreign thrones
And strangers lord it in the ruling-hall;
The shield of David rusts upon the wall;
The lion of Judah seeks to roar, and groans...
Where are the brave, the mighty? They are bones.
Bar Cochba's star has suffered its last fall.
On holy places profane spiders crawl;
The jackal leaves foul marks on temple-stones.
Ah, woe, to us, that we, the sons of peace,
Must turn our sharpened scythes to scimitars,   10
Must lift the hammer of the Maccabees,
Blood soak the land, make mockery of stars...
And woe to me, who am not one of these,
Who languish here beneath these northern stars...

(1940)   (1940)

From
The Hitleriad

I

Heil heavenly muse, since also thou must be
Like my song's theme, a sieg-heil'd deity,
Be with me now, but not as once, for song:
Not odes do I indite, indicting Wrong!
Be with me, for I fall from grace to sin,
Spurning this day thy proffered hippocrene,
To taste the poison'd lager of Berlin!

Happier would I be with other themes –
(Who rallies nightmares when he could have dreams?)
With other themes, and subjects more august –   10
Adolf I sing but only since I must.
I must! Shall I continue the sweet words
That praise the blossoming flowers, the blossoming birds,
While, afar off, I hear the stamping herds?

Shall I, within my ivory tower, sit
And play the solitaire of rhyme and wit,
While Indignation pounds upon the door,
And Pity sobs, until she sobs no more,
And, in the woods, there yelp the hounds of war?

I am the grandson of the prophets! I   20
Shall not seal lips against iniquity.
Let anger take me in its grasp; let hate,
Hatred of evil prompt me, and dictate!
And let the world see that swastika-stain,
That heart, where no blood is, but high octane,
That little brain —
So that once seen the freak be known again!

Oh, even as his truncheon'd crimes are wrought,
And while the spilt blood is still body-hot,
And even as his doom still seems in doubt,   30
Let deeds unspeakable be spoken out.
Wherefore, O Muse, I do invoke thy aid,
Not for the light and sweetness of the trade,
But seeing I draw a true bill of the Goth,
For the full fire of thy heavenly wrath!
Aid me, and in good time, for as I talk
The knave goes one step nearer to the dock;
And even as triumphant cannon boom
He marches on his victories — to doom!

(1944)   (1944)

Psalm VI

*A psalm of Abraham, concerning that which
he beheld upon the heavenly scarp:*

I

And on that day, upon the heavenly scarp,
The hosannahs ceased, the hallelujahs died,
And music trembled on the silenced harp.

An angel, doffing his seraphic pride,
Wept; and his tears so bitter were, and sharp,
That where they fell, the blossoms shrivelled and died.

II

Another with such voice intoned the psalm
It sang forth blasphemy against the Lord.
Oh, that was a very imp in angeldom
Who, thinking evil, said no evil word –   10
But only pointed, at each *Te Deum*
Down to the earth, and its unspeakable horde.

III

The Lord looked down, and saw the cattle-cars:
Men ululating to a frozen land.
He saw a man tear at his flogged scars,
And saw a babe look for its blown-off hand.
Scholars, he saw, sniffing their bottled wars,
And doctors who had geniuses unmanned.

IV

The gentle violinist whose fingers played
Such godly music, washing a pavement, with lye,   20
He saw. He heard the priest who called His aid.
He heard the agnostic's undirected cry.
Unto Him came the odor Hunger made,
And the odor of blood before it is quite dry.

V

The angel who wept looked into the eyes of God.
The angel who sang ceased pointing to the earth.
A little cherub who'd spied the earthly sod
Went mad, and flapped his wings in crazy mirth.
And the good Lord said nothing, but with a nod
Summoned the angels of Sodom down to earth.
                                                                     30

(1944)   (1944)

Psalm XXXVI

A Psalm touching genealogy:

Not sole was I born, but entire genesis:
For to the fathers that begat me, this
Body is residence. Corpuscular,
They dwell in my veins, they eavesdrop at my ear,
They circle, as with Torahs, round my skull,
In exit and in entrance all day pull
The latches of my heart, descend, and rise —
And there look generations through my eyes.

(1944)   (1944)

Lookout: Mount Royal

Remembering boyhood, it is always here
the boy in blouse and kneepants on the road
trailing his stick over the hopscotched sun;
or here, upon the suddenly moving hill;
or at the turned tap its cold white mandarin mustaches;
or at the lookout, finally,
breathing easy, standing still

to click the eye on motion forever stopped:
the photographer's tripod and his sudden faces
buoyed up by water on his magnet caught   10
still smiling as if under water still;
the exclamatory tourists descending the caleches;
the maids in starch; the ladies in white gloves;
other kids of other slums and races;
and on the bridle-paths
the horsemen on their horses like the tops of f's:

or from the parapet make out
beneath the green marine
the discovered road, the hospital's romantic

gables and roofs, and all the civic Euclid   20
running through sunken parallels and lolling
in diamond and square, then proud-pedantical
with spire and dome
making its way to the sought point, his home.

home recognized: there: to be returned to —

lets the full birdseye circle to the river,
its singsong bridges, its mapmaker curves, its
island with the two shades of green, meadow and wood;
and circles round that water-tower'd coast;
then, to the remote rhapsodic mountains; then,   30
— and to be lost —
to clouds like white slow friendly animals
which all the afternoon across his eyes
will move their paced spaced footfalls.

(1948)   (1948)

The Rocking Chair

It seconds the crickets of the province. Heard
in the clean lamplit farmhouses of Quebec, —
wooden, — it is no less a national bird;
and rivals, in its cage, the mere stuttering clock.
To its time, the evenings are rolled away;
and in its peace the pensive mother knits
contentment to be worn by her family,
grown-up, but still cradled by the chair in which she sits.

It is also the old man's pet, pair to his pipe,
the two aids of his arithmetic and plans,   10
plans rocking and puffing into market-shape;
and it is the toddler's game and dangerous dance.
Moved to the verandah, on summer Sundays, it is,
among the hanging plants, the girls, the boy-friends,
sabbatical and clumsy, like the white haloes
dangling above the blue serge suits of the young men.

It has a personality of its own;
is a character (like that old drunk Lacoste,
exhaling amber, and toppling on his pins);
it is alive; individual; and no less   20
an identity than those about it. And
it is tradition. Centuries have been flicked
from its arcs, alternately flicked and pinned.
It rolls with the gait of St. Malo. It is act

and symbol, symbol of this static folk
which moves in segments, and returns to base, –
a sunken pendulum: *invoke, revoke;*
loosed yon, leashed hither, motion on no space.
O, like some Anjou ballad, all refrain,
which turns about its longing, and seems to move   30
to make a pleasure out of repeated pain,
its music moves, as if always back to a first love.

(1948)   (1948)

Grain Elevator

Up from the low-roofed dockyard warehouses
it rises blind and babylonian
like something out of legend. Something seen
in a children's coloured book. Leviathan
swamped on our shore? The cliffs of some other river?
The blind ark lost and petrified? A cave
built to look innocent, by pirates? Or
some eastern tomb a travelled patron here makes local?

But even when known, it's more than what it is:
for here, as in a Josephdream, bow down   10
the sheaves, the grains, the scruples of the sun
garnered for darkness; and Saskatchewan
is rolled like a rug of a thick and golden thread.
O prison of prairies, ship in whose galleys roll
sunshines like so many shaven heads,
waiting the bushel-burst out of the beached bastille!

Sometimes, it makes me think Arabian,
the grain picked up, like tic-tacs out of time:
first one; an other; singly; one by one; –
to save life. Sometimes, some other races claim 20
the twinship of my thought, – as the river stirs
restless in a white Caucasian sleep,
or, as in the steerage of the elevators,
the grains, Mongolian and crowded, dream.

A box: cement, hugeness, and rightangles –
merely the sight of it leaning in my eyes
mixes up continents and makes a montage
of inconsequent time and uncontiguous space.
It's because it's bread. It's because
bread is its theme, an absolute. Because 30
always this great box flowers over us
with all the coloured faces of mankind...

(1948)   (1948)

The Cripples

(ORATOIRE DE ST. JOSEPH)

Bundled their bones, upon the ninety-nine stairs –
St. Joseph's ladder – the knobs of penance come;
the folded cripples counting up their prayers.

How rich, how plumped with blessing is that dome!
The gourd of Brother André! His sweet days
rounded! Fulfilled! Honeyed to honeycomb!

whither the heads, upon the ninety-nine trays,
the palsied, who double their aspen selves, the lame,
the unsymmetrical, the dead-limbed, raise

their look, their hope, and the *idée fixe* of their maim, – 10
knowing the surgery's in the heart. Are not
the ransomed crutches worshippers? And the fame

of the brother sanatorial to this plot? –
God mindful of the sparrows on the stairs?
Yes, to their faith this mountain of stairs, is not!

They know, they know, that suddenly their cares
and orthopedics will fall from them, and they
stand whole again.

         Roll empty away, wheelchairs,
and crutches, without armpits, hop away!   20

And I who in my own faith once had faith like this,
but have not now, am crippled more than they.

(1948)   (1948)

Portrait of the Poet as Landscape

I

Not an editorial-writer, bereaved with bartlett,
mourns him, the shelved Lycidas.
No actress squeezes a glycerine tear for him.
The radio broadcast lets his passing pass.
And with the police, no record. Nobody, it appears,
either under his real name or his alias,
missed him enough to report.

It is possible that he is dead, and not discovered.
It is possible that he can be found some place
in a narrow closet, like the corpse in a detective story,   10
standing, his eyes staring, and ready to fall on his face.
It is also possible that he is alive
and amnesiac, or mad, or in retired disgrace,
or beyond recognition lost in love.

We are sure only that from our real society
he has disappeared; he simply does not count,
except in the pullulation of vital statistics –

somebody's vote, perhaps, an anonymous taunt
of the Gallup poll, a dot in a government table –
but not felt, and certainly far from eminent –   20
in a shouting mob, somebody's sigh.

O, he who unrolled our culture from his scroll –
the prince's quote, the rostrum-rounding roar –
who under one name made articulate
heaven, and under another the seven-circled air,
is, if he is at all, a number, an x,
a Mr. Smith in a hotel register, –
incognito, lost, lacunal.

II

The truth is he's not dead, but only ignored –
like the mirroring lenses forgotten on a brow
that shine with the guilt of their unnoticed world.
The truth is he lives among neighbours, who, though
          they will allow
him a passable fellow, think him eccentric, not solid,
a type that one can forgive, and for that matter, forego.

Himself he has his moods, just like a poet.
Sometimes, depressed to nadir, he will think all lost,
will see himself as throwback, relict, freak,
his mother's miscarriage, his great-grandfather's ghost,   10
and he will curse his quintuplet senses, and their tutors
in whom he put, as he should not have put, his trust.

Then he will remember his travels over that body –
the torso verb, the beautiful face of the noun,
and all those shaped and warm auxiliaries!
A first love it was, the recognition of his own.
Dear limbs adverbial, complexion of adjective,
dimple and dip of conjugation!

And then remember how this made a change in him
affecting for always the glow and growth of his being;   20
how suddenly was aware of the air, like shaken tinfoil,
of the patents of nature, the shock of belated seeing,
the loneliness peering from the eyes of crowds;
the integers of thought; the cube-roots of feeling.

Thus, zoomed to zenith, sometimes he hopes again,
And sees himself as a character, with a rehearsed role:
the Count of Monte Cristo, come for his revenges;
the unsuspected heir, with papers; the risen soul;
or the chloroformed prince awaking from his flowers;
or – deflated again – the convict on parole.　　　　　　　　30

III

He is alone; yet not completely alone.
Pins on a map of a colour similar to his,
each city has one, sometimes more than one;
here, caretakers of art, in colleges;
in offices, there, with arm-bands, and green-shaded;
and there, pounding their catalogued beats in libraries, –

everywhere menial, a shadow's shadow.
And always for their egos – their outmoded art.
Thus, having lost the bevel in the ear,
they know neither up nor down, mistake the part　　　　　　10
for the whole, curl themselves in a comma,
talk technics, make a colon their eyes. They distort –

such is the pain of their frustration – truth
to something convolute and cerebral.
How they do fear the slap of the flat of the platitude!
Now Pavlov's victims, their mouths water at bell,
the platter empty.
　　　　　　　　　See they set twenty-one jewels
into their watches; the time they do not tell!

Some, patagonian in their own esteem,　　　　　　　　20
and longing for the multiplying word,
join party and wear pins, now have a message,
an ear, and the convention-hall's regard.
Upon the knees of ventriloquists, they own,
of their dandled brightness, only the paint and board.

And some go mystical, and some go mad.
One stares at a mirror all day long, as if

to recognize himself; another courts
angels, — for here he does not fear rebuff;
and a third, alone, and sick with sex, and rapt,   30
doodles him symbols convex and concave.

O schizoid solitudes! O purities
curdling upon themselves! Who live for themselves,
or for each other, but for nobody else;
desire affection, private and public loves;
are friendly, and then quarrel and surmise
the secret perversions of each other's lives.

IV

He suspects that something has happened, a law
been passed, a nightmare ordered. Set apart,
he finds himself, with special haircut and dress,
as on a reservation. Introvert.
He does not understand this; sad conjecture
muscles and palls thrombotic on his heart.

He thinks an impostor, having studied his personal biography,
his gestures, his moods, now has come forward to pose
in the shivering vacuums his absence leaves.
Wigged with his laurel, that other, and faked with his face,   10
he pats the heads of his children, pecks his wife,
and is at home, and slippered, in his house.

So he guesses at the impertinent silhouette
that talks to his phone-piece and slits open his mail.
Is it the local tycoon who for a hobby
plays poet, he so epical in steel?
The orator, making a pause? Or is that man
he who blows his flash of brass in the jittering hall?

Or is he cuckolded by the troubadour
rich and successful out of celluloid?   20
Or by the don who unrhymes atoms? Or
the chemist death built up? Pride, lost impostor'd pride,
it is another, another, whoever he is,
who rides where he should ride.

V

Fame, the adrenalin: to be talked about;
to be a verb; to be introduced as *The:*
to smile with endorsement from slick paper; make
caprices anecdotal; to nod to the world; to see
one's name like a song upon the marquees played;
to be forgotten with embarrassment; to be —
to be.

It has its attractions, but is not the thing;
nor is it the ape mimesis who speaks from the tree
ancestral; nor the merkin joy...   10
Rather it is stark infelicity
which stirs him from his sleep, undressed, asleep
to walk upon roofs and window-sills and defy
the gape of gravity.

VI

Therefore he seeds illusions. Look, he is
the nth Adam taking a green inventory
in world but scarcely uttered, naming, praising,
the flowering fiats in the meadow, the
syllabled fur, stars aspirate, the pollen
whose sweet collision sounds eternally.
For to praise

the world — he, solitary man — is breath
to him. Until it has been praised, that part
has not been. Item by exciting item —   10
air to his lungs, and pressured blood to his heart. —
they are pulsated, and breathed, until they map,
not the world's, but his own body's chart!

And now in imagination he has climbed
another planet, the better to look
with single camera view upon this earth —
its total scope, and each afflated tick,
its talk, its trick, its tracklessness — and this,
this he would like to write down in a book!

To find a new function for the declassé craft   20
archaic like the fletcher's; to make a new thing;
to say the word that will become sixth sense;
perhaps by necessity and indirection bring
new forms to life, anonymously, new creeds –
O, somehow pay back the daily larcenies of the lung!

These are not mean ambitions. It is already something
merely to entertain them. Meanwhile, he
makes of his status as zero a rich garland,
a halo of his anonymity,
and lives alone, and in his secret shines   30
like phosphorus. At the bottom of the sea.

(1948)   (1948)

Autobiographical

Out of the ghetto streets where a Jewboy
Dreamed pavement into pleasant Bible-land,
Out of the Yiddish slums where childhood met
The friendly beard, the loutish Sabbath-goy,
Or followed, proud, the Torah-escorting band,
Out of the jargoning city I regret,
Rise memories, like sparrows rising from
The gutter-scattered oats,
Like sadness sweet of synagogal hum,
Like Hebrew violins   10
Sobbing delight upon their Eastern notes.

Again they ring their little bells, those doors
Deemed by the tender-year'd, magnificent:
Old Ashkenazi's cellar, sharp with spice;
The widows' double-parlored candy-stores
And nuggets sweet bought for one sweaty cent;
The warm fresh-smelling bakery, its pies,
Its cakes, its navel'd bellies of black bread;

The lintels candy-poled
Of barber-shop, bright-bottled, green, blue, red;   20
And fruit-stall piled, exotic,
And the big synagogue door, with letters of gold.

Again my kindergarten home is full —
Saturday night — with kin and compatriot:
My brothers playing Russian card-games; my
Mirroring sisters looking beautiful,
Humming the evening's imminent fox-trot;
My uncle Mayer, of blessed memory,
Still murmuring maariv, counting holy words;
And the two strangers, come   30
Fiery from Volhynia's murderous hordes —
The cards and humming stop.
And I too swear revenge for that pogrom.

Occasions dear: the four-legged aleph named
And angel pennies dropping on my book;
The rabbi patting a coming scholar-head;
My mother, blessing candles, Sabbath-flamed,
Queenly in her Warsovian perruque;
My father pickabacking me to bed
To tell tall tales about the Baal Shem Tov —   40
Letting me curl his beard.
Oh memory of unsurpassing love,
Love leading a brave child
Through childhood's ogred corridors, unfear'd!

The week in the country at my brother's — (May
he own fat cattle in the fields of heaven!)
Its picking of strawberries from grassy ditch,
Its odor of dogrose and of yellowing hay —
Dusty, adventurous, sunny days, all seven! —
Still follow me, still warm me, still are rich   50
With the cow-tinkling peace of pastureland.
The meadow'd memory
Is sodded with its clover, and is spanned
By that same pillow'd sky
A boy on his back one day watched enviously.

And paved again the street: the shouting boys,
Oblivious of mothers on the stoops,

Playing the robust robbers and police,
The corncob battle — all high-spirited noise
Competitive among the lot-drawn groups.   60
Another day, of shaken apple trees
In the rich suburbs, and a furious dog,
And guilty boys in flight;
Hazelnut games, and games in the synagogue —
The burrs, the Haman rattle,
The Torah dance on Simchas Torah night.

Immortal days of the picture calendar
Dear to me always with the virgin joy
Of the first flowering of senses five,
Discovering birds, or textures, or a star,   70
Or tastes sweet, sour, acid, those that cloy;
And perfumes. Never was I more alive.
All days thereafter are a dying off,
A wandering away
From home and the familiar. The years doff
Their innocence.
No other day is ever like that day.

I am no old man fatuously intent
On memoirs, but in memory I seek
The strength and vividness of nonage days,   80
Not tranquil recollection of event.
It is a fabled city that I seek;
It stands in Space's vapors and Time's haze;
Thence comes my sadness in remembered joy
Constrictive of the throat;
Thence do I hear, as heard by a Jewboy,
The Hebrew violins,
Delighting in the sobbed Oriental note.

(1951)   (1951)

Dorothy Livesay
1909–

BORN IN WINNIPEG, Dorothy Livesay received her B.A. from the University of Toronto in 1931. After attending graduate school at the Sorbonne she studied social science at the University of Toronto and was a social worker in Montreal and New Jersey. Following her marriage to Duncan Macnair in 1937, she lived for many years in Vancouver. In addition to writing poetry, Livesay has worked as a newspaper reporter, has edited anthologies and has held several university posts. In 1975 she became editor of *CV II*, a journal devoted to the discussion and review of Canadian poetry. Since the appearance of her first collection of poetry, *Green Pitcher* (1928), Livesay has established herself as one of the most important Canadian poets. Her *Collected Poems, The Two Seasons* was published in 1972.

Fire and Reason

I cannot shut out the night –
Nor its sharp clarity.

The many blinds we draw,
You and I,
The many fires we light
Can never quite obliterate
The irony of stars,
The deliberate moon,
The last, unsolved finality of night.

(1928)   (1972)

Green Rain

I remember long veils of green rain
Feathered like the shawl of my grandmother —
Green from the half-green of the spring trees
Waving in the valley.

I remember the road
Like the one which leads to my grandmother's house,
A warm house, with green carpets,
Geraniums, a trilling canary
And shining horse-hair chairs;
And the silence, full of the rain's falling   10
Was like my grandmother's parlour
Alive with herself and her voice, rising and falling —
Rain and wind intermingled.

I remember on that day
I was thinking only of my love
And of my love's house.
But now I remember the day
As I remember my grandmother.
I remember the rain as the feathery fringe of her shawl.

(1932)   (1972)

Day and Night

1

Dawn, red and angry, whistles loud and sends
A geysered shaft of steam searching the air.
Scream after scream announces that the churn
Of life must move, the giant arm command.
Men in a stream, a moving human belt
Move into sockets, every one a bolt.
The fun begins, a humming, whirring drum —
Men do a dance in time to the machines.

2

One step forward
Two steps back
Shove the lever,
Push it back

While Arnot whirls
A roundabout
And Geoghan shuffles
Bolts about.

One step forward
Hear it crack   10
Smashing rhythm —
Two steps back

Your heart-beat pounds
Against your throat
The roaring voices
Drown your shout

Across the way
A writhing whack
Sets you spinning
Two steps back —   20

One step forward
Two steps back.

3

Day and night are rising and falling
Night and day shift gears and slip rattling
Down the runway, shot into storerooms
Where only arms and a note-book remember
The record of evil, the sum of commitments.
We move as through sleep's revolving memories
Piling up hatred, stealing the remnants,
Doors forever folding before us —
And where is the recompense, on what agenda
Will you set love down? Who knows of peace?   10

Day and night
Night and day
Light rips into ribbons
What we say.

I called to love
Deep in dream:
Be with me in the daylight
As in gloom.

Be with me in the pounding
In the knives against my back   20
Set your voice resounding
Above the steel's whip crack.

High and sweet
Sweet and high
Hold, hold up the sunlight
In the sky!

Day and night
Night and day
Tear up all the silence
Find the words I could not say...   30

4

We were stoking coal in the furnaces; red hot
They gleamed, burning our skins away, his and mine.
We were working together, night and day, and knew
Each other's stroke; and without words, exchanged
An understanding about kids at home,
The landlord's jaw, wage-cuts and overtime.
We were like buddies, see? Until they said
That nigger is too smart the way he smiles
And sauces back the foreman; he might say
Too much one day, to others changing shifts.   10
Therefore they cut him down, who flowered at night
And raised me up, day hanging over night —
So furnaces could still consume our withered skin.

Shadrach, Meshach and Abednego
Turn in the furnace, whirling slow.
    Lord, I'm burnin' in the fire
    Lord, I'm steppin' on the coals
    Lord, I'm blacker than my brother
    Blow your breath down here.

    Boss, I'm smothered in the darkness   20
    Boss, I'm shrivellin' in the flames
    Boss, I'm blacker than my brother
    Blow your breath down here.
Shadrach, Meshach and Abednego
Burn in the furnace, whirling slow.

5

Up in the roller room, men swing steel
Swing it, zoom; and cut it, crash.
Up in the dark the welder's torch
Makes sparks fly like lightning reel.

Now I remember storm on a field
The trees bow tense before the blow
Even the jittering sparrows' talk
Ripples into the still tree shield.

We are in storm that has no cease
No lull before, no after time   10
When green with rain the grasses grow
And air is sweet with fresh increase.

We bear the burden home to bed
The furnace glows within our hearts:
Our bodies hammered through the night
Are welded into bitter bread.

Bitter, yes:
But listen, friend:
We are mightier
In the end.   20

We have ears
Alert to seize
A weakness
In the foreman's ease

We have eyes
To look across
The bosses' profit
At our loss.

Are you waiting?
Wait with us   30
After evening
There's a hush —

Use it not
For love's slow count:
Add up hate
And let it mount

Until the lifeline
Of your hand
Is calloused with
A fiery brand!   40

Add up hunger,
Labour's ache
These are figures
That will make

The page grow crazy
Wheels go still,
Silence sprawling
On the till —

Add your hunger,
Brawn and bones,   50
Take your earnings:
Bread, not stones!

6

Into thy maw I commend my body
But the soul shines without
A child's hands as a leaf are tender
And draw the poison out.

Green of new leaf shall deck my spirit
Laughter's roots will spread:
Though I am overalled and silent
Boss, I'm far from dead!

One step forward
Two steps back   10
Will soon be over:
Hear it crack!

The wheels may whirr
A roundabout
And neighbour's shuffle
Drown your shout

The wheel must limp
Till it hangs still
And crumpled men
Pour down the hill.   20

Day and night
Night and day
Till life is turned
The other way!

(1944)   (1972)

Fantasia

FOR HELENA COLEMAN, TORONTO POET

And I have learned how diving's done
How breathing air, cool wafted trees

Clouds massed above the man-made tower
How these
Can live no more in eye and ear:
And mind be dumb
To all save Undine and her comb.

Imagination's underworld: where child goes down
Light as a feather. Water pressure
Hardly holds him, diving's easy   10
As the flight of bird in air
Or bomber drumming to his lair.

Child goes down, and laughingly
(He's not wanted yet, you see)
Catches fishes in his hand
Burrows toe in sifting sand
Seizes all the weeds about
To make a small sub-rosa boat.

Then up he bobs, as easily
As any blown balloon   20
To greet the bosky, brooding sky
And hunger for the sun.

                    *   *   *   *

And child grown taller, clothed in man's
Long limbs, and shaggy hair, his chin outthrust
Searches for years the rounded world
Climbs to its peaks, falls to its valleys green
Striding the trim and trailing towns
Fingering the fond arteries
Possessing things, and casting them
Cloakwise to earth for sleeping time...   30

Sometime the lust wanderer
Will sleep, will pause; will dream of plunging deep
Below it all, where he will need
No clock companion, thorn in flesh, no contact man
To urge him from the ground.
For flying's easy, if you do it diving
And diving is the self unmoored
Ranging and roving – man alone.

                    *   *   *   *

And I have learned how diving's done
Wherefore the many, many   40
Chose the watery stair
Down, down Virginia
With your fêted hair
Following after Shelley
Or wordcarvers I knew
(Bouchette; and Raymond, you) –
Here is the fascination
Of the salty stare:
And death is here.
Death courteous and calm, glass-smooth   50
His argument so suave, so water-worn
A weighted stone.

And death's deliberation, his
Most certain waiting-room
His patience with the patient, who will be
His for infinity...

So no astounded peerers
On the surface craft
No dragging nets, no cranes
No gnarled and toughened rope   60
Not any prayer nor pulley man-devised
Will shake the undersea
Or be
More than a brief torpedo, children's arrow
More than a gaudy top outspun
Its schedule done...

*   *   *   *

Wise to have learned: how diving's done
How breathing air, cool wafted trees
Clouds massed above the man-made tower
How these   70
Can live no more in eye and ear:
And mind be dumb
To all save Undine and her comb...

(1944)   (1972)

Bartok and the Geranium

She lifts her green umbrellas
Towards the pane
Seeking her fill of sunlight
Or of rain;
Whatever falls
She has no commentary
Accepts, extends,
Blows out her furbelows,
Her bustling boughs;

And all the while he whirls   10
Explodes in space,
Never content with this small room:
Not even can he be
Confined to sky
But must speed high and higher still
From galaxy to galaxy,
Wrench from the stars their momentary notes
Steal music from the moon.

She's daylight
He is dark   20
She's heaven-held breath
He storms and crackles
Spits with hell's own spark.

Yet in this room, this moment now
These together breathe and be:
She, essence of serenity,
He in a mad intensity
Soars beyond sight
Then hurls, lost Lucifer,
From heaven's height.   30

And when he's done, he's out:
She leans a lip against the glass
And preens herself in light.

(1955)   (1972)

On Looking into Henry Moore

I

Sun, stun me, sustain me
Turn me to stone:
Stone, goad me and gall me
Urge me to run.

When I have found
Passivity in fire
And fire in stone
Female and male
I'll rise alone
10   Self-extending and self-known.

2

The message of the tree is this:
Aloneness is the only bliss

(1957)

Self-adoration is not in it
(Narcissus tried, but could not win it)

Rather, to extend the root
Tombwards, be at home with death

But in the upper branches know
A green eternity of fire and snow.

3

The fire in the farthest hills
Is where I'd burn myself to bone: 20
Clad in the armour of the sun
I'd stand anew, alone

Take off this flesh, this hasty dress
Prepare my half-self for myself:
One unit, as a tree or stone
Woman in man, and man in womb.

(1972)

Eve

Beside the highway
at the motel door
        it roots
the last survivor of a pioneer
        orchard
miraculously   still
        bearing.

A thud   another apple falls
            I stoop   and O
that scent, gnarled, ciderish   10
            with sun in it
that woody pulp
            for teeth and tongue
            to bite and curl around
that spurting juice
            earth-sweet!

In fifty seconds, fifty summers sweep
            and shake me –
I am alive!   can stand
            up still   20
hoarding this apple
            in my hand.

(1967)   (1972)

House amongst Trees

It's the stillness   no wind   or else
no excitement   a sudden ruffle
calm expression   upward   from the sea
into sun   or cloud   and tossing trees
no dismay   obeying whatever will
on a dark day   is there
no demands made   expectant   accepting
to the sky   no more demanding than
                              the day itself asks   20
it's the quiet   creeping under
10 lighting on   a dark shield of leaves.
dark branches

(1969)   (1972)

Another Journey

i

Now you have released me
from your grip
now I can slip   alone
into the forest

rest
upon stone

ii

A switchback trail
returns
        almost upon itself
10 then flicks its tail
against the flank
of yesterday

iii

I climb
        stolidly
looking neither right
        nor upward
in the dust

(1969)

I see
wing swoops
        (hawk   shadow)   20
following me

iv

A path curls
a rope loops
a cracked whip
scoops a corner

        signals
                sparkle

v

Night
spills stars
into the valley   30

I am aware
of cedars   breathing
turning
the trees   move with me
                up   the mountain

(1972)

Schizoid

As you come through the forest
wearing your mask of fox
your cloak of incognito
she crouches down amongst
        leaves
hides under mushrooms

As you strut through the
        evergreen
everglades
acting the part of hunter
she is a willow branch waving
over the water   10

O when will you cup your hands
and drink of that water?
when will you peer
into that mirror?

(1975)

So fast your changes
the air registers nothing
the water in the still pool
stares back
empty of eyes

(1975)

Unexpected Guests

Some sacrificial act was done
digging the grave up
scattering pampas grass
finding the young dogwood tree
and planting

Some ancient rite performed
the dying fire re-lighted
the supper table set
the bread and wine taken

And last, the paintings shown   10
and looked at with surprise
images of sun, moon, stars
man in a boat
rowing with all his might
towards the ICE

Some final pact was made
between the parent and the child
they travelled for an instant
towards the mine
shot on the same shaft   20
down to roots
their same breath caught
pulled upward to the sun.

(1975)   (1975)

Gabrielle Roy
1909 –

———◆———

THE DAUGHTER OF an official in the Department of Immigration, Gabrielle Roy was born in St. Boniface, Manitoba. After teaching in rural Manitoba and studying drama in Europe, Roy published her first novel, *Bonheur d'occasion,* in 1945. Marking an important stage in the emergence of urban realism in French-Canadian fiction, this work was translated into English in 1947 under the title, *The Tin Flute.* Since 1947, Roy has lived in Quebec City and has published a large number of novels and short stories including *Rue Deschambault* (1955) (translated as *Street of Riches,* 1957), a volume of stories in which she draws on her early memories and experiences in Manitoba.

By Day and by Night

MY FATHER, SO sad and withdrawn during the day, toward night began somewhat to revive. You might have thought that the sun as it set, the daylight as it faded, freed him of a dreadful verity which he ceaselessly carried before his eyes. Was it that he constantly kept seeing the day when, on his return from a trip to his settlements, he stopped in at his office in Winnipeg to pick up the mail and found this letter addressed to him: "For which reason we ask you kindly to offer your resignation ... realize the value of your services, the devotion of your life to the settlers, of whom several have spoken in your behalf.... But other circumstances...The new law regarding the retirement age..."? From its first reading, I think my father must have known this letter by heart, and perhaps he never succeeded in driving the words from his mind. He went through a few ridiculous days during which, urged on by my mother and by friends, he tried to appeal his case to the government, but he had not enough confidence in himself to undertake the visits, the pleas to which he would have had to agree. And maybe he was especially repelled by the idea – monstrous to him – of having to display his merits, his life. For with this letter, not only had he no longer confidence in what he was, in what he could do, but he even lost the feeling of ever having been useful. By this letter he was in a sense stripped of all his achievements, and he kept on living only to bear the daily weight of this defeat upon his shoulders. Happily the night was still gentle to him. When it came, so simple and sweet-smelling along our street, my father greeted it like a familiar guest. Was this a merely physical well-being? Or had this hour still sufficient empire over his soul to revive within it hope of happiness? Whatever the case, this phenomenon was so familiar to each of us that, if we wished to obtain my father's permission for something we wanted, we waited – as Maman advised – "until it is dark."

But Maman was a creature of the day. I have never seen anyone so impatient to get up in the morning to go out in summer at the sun's first rays in order to care for her flowers, which were as full of health as Maman herself. She took it very ill that we should sleep late, and if her kindliness forbade her to make noise for fear of waking us, soon her vitality overcame her caution – or perchance it was her unconscious desire to make us get up which led to her clattering the saucepans. Even in winter she arose very early to light the fires, now that my father was so ailing, and to set the porridge to boil; then, in bitter cold, and through the darkness, Maman trotted off to the earliest Mass. When we got up, the house was already warm, a going concern, its sleepiness well shaken off. Yes, Maman's activities were full to overflowing as long as they were accompanied and sustained by daylight; but the moment dusk fell, she abruptly lost all her momentum; she would yawn; never did she show her age except in the evening, under the harsh electric light. She put me in mind of those flowers, so living by day which at night so sadly hang their heads. And toward ten o'clock, if we expected no company, if there were nothing extraordinary to revive Maman in her overpowering drowsiness, she would say to us, "Well, I'm going to bed; I'm dropping on my feet." And she would beg us, "Do try not to stay up until some impossible hour."

It was one of her ideas that to be in good health you must retire early, rise early; that sitting up by electric light ruined one's eyes.

At this hour, however, Papa was just coming back to life. Yes, he greatly helped himself with coffee which he made very strong, and indeed very good, as compared to Maman's dishwater. Thus it happened that evening, while he was watching his coffee on the stove and its aroma was spreading everywhere, that Papa glanced at Maman.

"Already!"

He was always as astonished at seeing Maman go to bed come ten o'clock as she was to see him sleep almost all day.

Maman arose to leave us. And although she had lived with father for thirty-six years and must have known that her recommendations and reproaches were unavailing with him, on that evening as on every other

Maman said to my father, "Really, Edouard, I don't understand you, drinking coffee at ten o'clock! What's more, it isn't even coffee, but essence of coffee! It's no wonder that afterward you are fidgety, that you should be ill and unable to sleep! You turn night into day!"

My father made no answer to this ancient reproach. In the daytime he might have made a fairly biting rejoinder. But at this hour he grew indulgent, even though he more and more obstinately followed his own sweet will: the ease night brought him was too precious to him for him to be able to give it up. Most likely he was ready, were it necessary, to pay for it with what remained to him of health, of life. At times, watching my father, I would already say to myself, "It's not so much to life that he clings, that many others cling, maybe, as it is to certain rare and brief moments in life...."

"Well, then, go!" said he to Maman. "Seeing you can sleep with the hens. I don't know how you do it....Go sleep, poor Maman!"

For, now that he was very old, she much younger than he, like all of us he called her "Maman."

This evening, however, my mother seemed more resolved than ever to prevent my father's having his way. A terrible weariness spread over her face, as though she could truly no longer endure seeing him so little careful of his health, hastening – you might say – his end. She must have done herself a real violence not to register a final reproach, a last prayer; she began to move away, her arms hanging by her sides. Still young, I realized how desperate a business it is to be in the right concerning those one loves.

With her hand Maman made me a brief sign which meant, "Don't you be too late. You, at least, could follow my example...." And was she, by this poor little gesture, asking me to remain her ally?

I was myself hesitating as between day and night. Like Maman, I felt, when I had gone to bed early, a joyous haste to greet the dawn, to run to my open window; I inherited from her that feeling of possession for things which in so many human beings is a product of the morning: the world seemed then to me as though at its beginning. Here was a new slate on which to write my life. I got up with my head full of resolutions: to give my hair a hundred brush strokes, to put a fresh collar on my convent uniform, to go over my homework....Then, again, if I stayed up a little late, if I succeeded in repelling the first assaults of sleep, I would attain a kind of overexcitement very different from the fine calm of morning – but how wonderful! Morning seemed to me the time of logic, night of something perhaps truer than logic....In any case, I was far older than my years as far as the evening went, and possessed an understanding beyond my experience. I had noticed that the words and sentences of my compositions flowed quite easily in the morning; but thought itself – or rather that nimbus which surrounds it while it is still unshaped and precious – I experienced at night. I was divided between these two sides of my nature, which came to me from my parents, sundered by the day and the night.

I lingered on for some time that evening with Papa. To induce us to stay with him, he would practice such obvious wiles. First he would offer us some of his black coffee, as well as toast which he made with a long fork over the coals. And if, through these halting advances, we were kept from hurrying elsewhere, then – sometimes – it happened that my father began to talk – and the full effect of the coffee aroused in him a sort of sparkling lucidity, precise, vivid, and very well-chosen words. The few times when he told me of his life were on such occasions, almost in the dark, alongside the stove now barely warm.

Once he had led me into the small room that contained his old roll-top desk and his wall maps of the colonization regions. As they were very detailed and large scale, a single corner of Saskatchewan covered a wall. That particular evening he unrolled one of them and showed me where he had formerly established some tenscore Mennonites. He spoke of "my people, my settlers," and likewise, "my immigrants," stressing the possessive pronoun so that this word "immigrant," rather than signifying a stranger, took on a curious value of blood relationship. "Here," he would say, "I found them a heavy layer of black earth, true gumbo, the soil that best suits wheat, and it yielded them sixty bushels to the acre." He pulled the string on another map, and with his finger pointed out the location of a Galician hamlet founded by him. I date my passion for maps from the time when my father made me behold upon them the low-lying little houses of the plain, some new dwelling place in emptiness...perhaps even the people themselves, inside their homes, gathered around the table. At least once my father grew spirited enough to relive, in front of the map, his long voyages of other days – and perhaps it made him forget, for a few moments, *the* letter: "Have to replace you with a younger man...necessary to apply the most up-to-date methods..." – that letter which set forth so many reasons in order not to have to give the only real one, and the one which would have been the least wounding: "We must hand over your job to a man of the right political party. ...What we need is not a servant of the country, but a servant of our own...."

In this little study of my father's there was also a full-length portrait of Sir Wilfrid Laurier. It showed the statesman in an attitude that must have been habitual with him while he was speaking in public: the high forehead lifted, as though illumined by a thought that had just come into being, the right hand open to present the evidence, the long hair, white and supple, floating behind as though in a breeze. And Papa said to me of Laurier: "Whatever words may be spoken about him, remember that this man labored to unite Canadians, never to divide them — and that's the best tribute you can pay a man when he's conquered and beaten, when he's dead."

Oh, had I been better able to sit up at night, I should better have learned to know my father! But I was unaware then that a somewhat more patient attention on my part would have freed him from silence.

The last time he talked to us, it was, I believe, about Verigin. "The Dukhobors," explained my father, "thought that Verigin, their leader, was Christ reincarnate, that they could never be wrong if they heeded his words. Poor people! To such an extent bewitched by Verigin they did not see his faults; or rather, seeing him, they believed only in him; to their Little Father Verigin, all was permitted, since he was of divine essence.... For one does not impute evil to God! So Verigin could exact from them the harshest penances, abstinence, continence, whereas he himself!...I saw him occasionally: he was richly clad, well-fed, surrounded by young girls. He traveled only with an escort of young maidens dressed in white, bedecked with flowers. Oh, we were long fooled by him! He played a double game, claiming to make his people subject to the country's laws, to work with Ottawa, whereas more and more he pushed his adepts toward a crazy mysticism. I should have liked to have known him better, grasp the devil's part, maybe, in this strange nature, understand the dark satisfaction he can have felt in obtaining from others more than from himself."

Thereupon Agnès complained, "Lord, Papa! How late it is! And tomorrow I must help Maman with the house cleaning."

And yet she liked, more than anyone else, to hear Papa tell about the country, the past, and she loved to see him forget his sorrows. But with such delicate health, sitting up late wore her out, and she insisted on husbanding her strength to help Maman as much as possible. Little by little, through her own efforts and almost joyously, she had fashioned for herself at home a very useful little niche, by no means brilliant, even dull. Martha's part, if you will. That evening she must have undergone a long struggle against fatigue and the headaches so constantly hers.

"Papa, half past eleven!"

My father drew his big watch from his pocket. "Not at all, Agnès; only eleven!"

"You know very well, Papa, that we set our clock by the church, when the Angelus rang."

"Sometimes they are ahead of time, even at the church."

But it was obvious that his spirits had been quenched by all these remarks about the hour. He looked at Agnès anxiously. "True enough," said he, "you are pale and your face is drawn. You're failing...you, too, Agnès."

She went to him and kissed his forehead, then moved away, leaning against the furniture out of sheer weariness.

We remained alone, Papa and I, in the feeble glow of the stove. Even on summer nights he kept it, as he said, "just alive," for often enough was not the fire his sole companion? He offered me some of his coffee.

"Just for once!" said he. "A little cup; I don't think it will do you any harm."

And he deceived himself so skillfully, he so ably bent truth to his own purposes, that he announced, with deep seriousness, "I never found that coffee prevented me from sleeping; it merely helps you to remember better, to sort your impressions, and sometimes also to recapture flavors, names, maybe a soul that is not so old...."

I accepted a cup, which he brought me steaming to the table corner where I had rested my elbows. Despite myself, my eyes were closing. With some slight remorse I thought of my unfinished homework, of the approaching examinations. I drank a little coffee.

"I diluted it a bit for you," said my father, "which is bad, for coffee does not stand baptising. Your mother really should try it; then she could sit up a little later nights...."

"But Maman is out of bed at five in the morning, Papa!"

"Yes," said he. "That's something I've never understood, that at the very crack of dawn your mother should feel such a need of bustling about."

I had never heard Papa talk in this almost teasing, joking way. In the dark cosiness of the kitchen, with all the doors shut, he walked back and forth, his hands behind him, limber, full of plans. When he turned toward me, once, a sudden spurt of flame in the fire showed me the brilliance of his eyes; I saw them overflowing with confidence. But also I saw his bent back, the dreadful lines which life had etched into his face. And it was surely at that moment that I thought, "Why, Papa is a broken man!"

Abruptly he asked me, "Little one, what do you think of an idea I have? Your mother has no faith in my ideas. But, after all, even at seventy-two, one can still be useful...within limits...."

He sat down close to me, as though to establish that I had become an adult in his eyes; I felt as though I had a child beside me, a sad, unruly child.

"I still have a little – a very little – money," my father confided to me, "a little remainder of what I once earned. Were I to buy a business, a grocery store, don't you think it would bring in something? We should take turns at the counter; I myself would be there the most frequent of all. I think," said he, "I have a talent for dealing with people...."

It was so farfetched: Papa a shopkeeper, he who now fled people's company, he whom we had to nurse all day, who could scarcely stir after his nocturnal vigils! Only toward six in the morning, his exaltation spent, did he sleep, at times as though in an abyss, his terrible defeat written in the folds of his half-open mouth, in his ravaged features.

He continued telling me about his schemes. "If I have only six months to live, it would be better to stretch our savings as far as we can; but if I have still several years left, would it not be wise to invest the little money remaining to us? Perhaps – for instance – in a mushroom farm?..."

I could barely follow what he was saying. I was so tired that instead of stimulating me the coffee had made me drowsier.

"Papa, it's past midnight!"

"Midnight," he exclaimed, and added – he who found the years interminable – "Heavens! How time flies!..."

"Tomorrow I have a class I haven't yet prepared for...in contemporary history."

"Oh yes! Contemporary history," he repeated somberly. "Of course. You're still going to school!"

He seemed fearfully unhappy to have to cede so simple a fact, maybe to be reminded of his own age.

"One shouldn't have children when one is old," he said to me, his head bowed. "One can quit this world without knowing them, without knowing much about them, and that's a heartbreaking loss...."

Suddenly he asked me, "Could you not stay with me another hour?"

At the moment, I grasped but the bare meaning of his rather unreasonable request. Only later did the precise words recur to me.... And the exams soon to be taken, the scholastic success to be won, the good grades, my future, if you like – I had one to prepare for, as people say – yes, it must have been my future which intervened at that moment between my father and me. I told him, "Papa, it would be more sensible for you to go to bed rather than sit up all night. You can't do anything useful during the day if you've not slept well."

"You talk just like your mother," was his reply.

But he took pity on me: "Poor child! You're asleep on your feet!...Oh well, go; get your rest." Yet in the same breath he accused me with a sort of bitterness: "You're all like her, down deep. Even you. She has you all to herself...that Maman of yours!..."

Moved by loyalty to Maman, I replied, "Surely you wouldn't have us behave the way you do!"

"Oh no!" he at once agreed. "Certainly not!"

And I saw him accept, his eyes wide open, his madness of solitude.

He poured himself another cup of black coffee. Like Maman, I thought, "There's nothing for it; he's resolved to be his own undoing." I went up to bed. Perhaps he wandered about the whole night long. For thus it was when we left him; he would pace the downstairs hall, then to and fro in the kitchen. His peregrinations would even make him forget to mend the fire. Sometimes, waking in the night, I would hear that regular, monotonous tread, the tread of a man too actively engaged in his mind, perhaps launched upon one of those illusions which make men take themselves off into the desert.

The next day he was unable to quit his bed. He was completely worn out. He would not speak much of the great pain he was beginning to suffer; perhaps he had already been having these attacks a long time. Uncomplaining, but with his usual stubbornness, he would say, "It's true. I can't stand it any longer. Give me something to lessen the pain a bit. I'm too old to be able to put up with it any longer...." They had to give him morphine.

His liver was completely used up. Once or twice more he asked for coffee, at about the hour when it had been his habit to drink some, and the doctor said to Maman, "What difference can it make now?"

But in the end coffee also betrayed his faith and brought him only nausea.

At night Maman sat up with him. But she was so contrary to the hours of darkness that, despite her worry, despite her distress over my father's inert form, she would bend her head a little and, like a child, slip briefly into the haven of sleep... until pain once more claimed her.

My father died at the hour that was the most cruel for him, when the sun rises over the earth.

(1955)   (1957)

H.L. Binsse (Trans.)

Gwen Ringwood
1910 –

GWEN (PHARIS) RINGWOOD was raised in Magrath, Alberta, and studied at the University of Alberta where she became active in the development of rural community drama. From 1937 to 1939 she worked with the Carolina Playmakers at the University of North Carolina; she now lives in Williams Lake, British Columbia. Since the production of her first play, *The Dragons of Kent*, at the Banff School of Fine Arts in 1936, she has written more than twenty radio and stage plays. *Still Stands The House* was first produced by the Carolina Playmakers in 1938.

Still Stands the House

Cast of Characters

RUTH WARREN
ARTHUR MANNING
HESTER WARREN
BRUCE WARREN

SCENE: A living room.

The icy wind of a northern blizzard sweeps across the prairie, lashes about the old Warren farmhouse, and howls insistently at the door and windows. But the Warren house was built to withstand the menace of the Canadian winter and scornfully suffers the storm to shriek about the chimney corner, to knock at the door and rattle the windows in a wild attempt to force an entrance.

The living-room of this house has about it a faded austerity, a decayed elegance that is as remote and cheerless as a hearth in which no fire is ever laid. The room has made a stern and solemn pact with the past. Once it held the warm surge of life: but as the years have gone by, it has settled in a rigid pattern of neat, uncompromising severity.

As if in defiance of the room, the frost has covered the window in the rear wall with a wild and exotic design. Beside the window is an imposing leather armchair, turned toward the handsome coal stove in the Right corner. A footstool is near the chair. A door at the Center of the rear wall leads to the snow-sheeted world outside. Along the Left wall, between a closed door to a bedroom (now unused) and an open door to the kitchen, is a mahogany sideboard. Above it is a portrait of old Martin Warren, who built this house and lived in it until his death. The portrait is of a stern and handsome man in his early fifties, and in the expression of the eyes the artist has caught something of his unconquerable will.

An open staircase, winding to the bedrooms upstairs, extends into the room at Right. There is a rocking chair by the stove with a small stand-table beside it. A mahogany dining table and two matching chairs are placed at a convenient distance from the side-board and the kitchen door. The figured wall paper is cracked and faded. The dark rug, the heavy curtains, and the tablecloth show signs of much wear, but there is nothing of cheapness about them.

Two coal oil lanterns have been left beside the kitchen door. Blooming bravely on the table, in contrast to its suroundings, is a pot of lavender hyacinths.

(RUTH WARREN *is standing near the outside door, talking to* ARTHUR MANNING, *who is about to leave.* RUTH *is small, fair-haired, and pretty, twenty-five or twenty-six years of age. There is more strength in her than her rather delicate appearance would indicate. She wears a soft blue house-dress, with a light wool cardigan over it.* MANNING *is a middle-aged man of prosperous appearance. He wears a heavy overcoat over a dark business suit. His hat, gloves and scarf are on the armchair.*)

RUTH. Do you think you'd better try to go back tonight, Mr. Manning? The roads may be drifted.

MANNING. It's a bad blizzard, all right, but I don't think I'll have any trouble. There's a heater in the car, and I've just had the engine checked over.

RUTH. You'll be welcome if you care to spend the night.

MANNING. Thank you, but I'm afraid I've got to get back to town. I'd hate to try it in an old car, but this one of mine can pull through anything.

RUTH. I've never seen a storm come up so quickly.

MANNING. These prairie blizzards are no joke. One of my sheepherders got lost in one last year, just half a mile from the house. He froze to death out there trying to find his way.

244 / Gwen Ringwood

RUTH. How frightful!

MANNING. One of the ranch hands found him the next morning. Poor old fellow – he'd herded for me for twenty years. I never knew how he came to be out in a storm like that.

RUTH. They say when a person gets lost he begins to go round in a circle, although it seems straight ahead.

MANNING. Yes, I've always heard that. The winters are the one thing I've got against this country.

RUTH. (*Wistfully*) I used to like them in town. We went skating on the river and tobogganing. But out here it's different.

MANNING. If Bruce sells the farm and takes this irrigated place near town, you won't notice the winter so much, Mrs. Warren.

RUTH. No. I hope he does take your offer, Mr. Manning. I want him to.

MANNING. He'll never get a better. Five thousand dollars and an irrigated quarter is a good price for a dryland farm these days.

RUTH. If only we didn't have to decide so soon.

MANNING. I talked it all over with Bruce in town a couple of weeks ago, and I think he's pretty well made up his mind. All he needs to do is sign the papers.

RUTH. I thought he'd have until spring to decide.

MANNING. I've got orders to close the deal before I go South next week. You tell Bruce I'll come by tomorrow or the next day, and we can get it all settled.

RUTH. I'll tell him. I hope he does take it, Mr. Manning.

MANNING. I know you do and you're right. I think all he needs is a little persuading. He's had a hard time here these dry years.

RUTH. I don't know what Hester will say.

MANNING. I understand she's very much attached to the place. Is it true that she never leaves the farm?

RUTH. Not often.

MANNING. She'd be better off where she could get out more.

RUTH. I don't know.

MANNING. I suppose all those years out here, keeping house for Bruce and her father, were pretty hard on her.

RUTH. The house has come to mean so much to her. But maybe she won't mind. (*Smiling hopefully*.) We'll see.

> *The door to the bedroom, Left, is opened quietly, and* HESTER WARREN *enters the room. She closes and locks the door behind her and stands looking at the two in the room with cold surmise.* HESTER *is*

forty years old. She is tall, dark and unsmiling. The stern rigidity of her body, the bitter austerity of her mouth, and the almost arrogant dignity of her carriage seem to make her a part of the room she enters. There is bitter resentment in her dark eyes as she confronts RUTH *and* MANNING. *She holds a leather-bound Bible close to her breast.*)

RUTH.　*(Startled)* Why, Hester! I thought you never unlocked that door.

HESTER.　*(Quietly)* No. I keep Father's room as it was.

RUTH.　Then why were you —

HESTER.　I was reading in Father's room. I heard a stranger.

RUTH.　You know Mr. Manning, Hester.

MANNING.　*(With forced friendliness)* I don't suppose you remember me, Miss Warren.

HESTER.　*(Without moving)* How do you do?

MANNING.　*(Embarrassed at her coldness and anxious to get away)* Well, I'll be getting on home. I'll leave these papers for Bruce to sign, Mrs. Warren. Tell him I'll come by tomorrow. He'll find it's all there, just as we talked about it. *(He lays the document on the table.)*

RUTH.　Thank you, Mr. Manning.

MANNING.　*(Turning to go)* Take care of yourselves. Good-night. *(To* HESTER.*)* Good-night, Miss Warren.

(HESTER *barely nods.*)

RUTH.　You're sure you ought to try it in the storm?

MANNING. Sure. There's no danger if I go right away. *(He goes out.)*

RUTH.　*(Calling after him as she shuts the door)* Good-night.

(HESTER *watches* MANNING *out and, as* RUTH *returns, she looks at her suspiciously. There is a silence which* HESTER *finally breaks.*)

HESTER.　What did he want here?

RUTH.　*(Uncomfortable under* HESTER'S *scrutiny)* He just left some papers for Bruce to look over, Hester. He was in a hurry so he didn't wait to see Bruce.

HESTER. I see. What has Arthur Manning got to do with Bruce?

RUTH.　It's something to do with the farm, Hester. I'll put these away. *(She starts to take up the document on the table, but* HESTER *is before her.)*

HESTER.　*(After a long look at the document)* A deed of sale. *(Turning angrily upon* RUTH.*)* So this is what you've been hiding from me.

RUTH.　*(Quickly)* Oh, no! Nothing's settled, Hester. Mr. Manning made an offer, and Bruce wants to think it over. That's all.

HESTER. *(Her eyes betraying her intense agitation)* Bruce isn't going to sell this place!

RUTH. It just an offer. Nothing has been decided.

HESTER. Your hand's in this! You've been after him to leave here.

RUTH. *(Trying to conciliate her)* Let's not quarrel. You can talk to Bruce about it, Hester.

HESTER. You hate this house, I know that.

RUTH. No. *(Facing HESTER firmly.)* But I think Bruce ought to sell.

HESTER. You married him. You made your choice.

RUTH. *(Quietly)* I've not regretted that. It's just that we're so cut off and lonely here; and this is the best offer we could get. But let me put these away. *(Indicating the deed of sale.)* We'll talk about it later, the three of us.

HESTER. *(Allowing RUTH to take the papers)* You may as well burn them. He isn't going to sell.

RUTH. Please, Hester — we'll discuss it when Bruce comes. *(She places the document on the sideboard, then crosses to the stove.)* I'll build up the fire.

HESTER. *(Takes the Bible to the sideboard and places it under her father's portrait. She stands looking up at the portrait.)* This house will not be sold. I won't allow it.

RUTH. *(Puts some coal on the fire. Shivering)* It's so cold it almost frightens me. The thermometer has dropped ten degrees within the hour.

HESTER. I hope Bruce knows enough to get the stock in. They'll freeze where they stand if they're left out tonight. *(She moves to the window and takes her knitting from the ledge.)*

RUTH. He'll have them in. *(Crossing to the table.)* Look, Hester, how the hyacinths have bloomed. I could smell them when I came in the room just now.

HESTER. Hyacinths always seem like death to me.

RUTH. *(Her voice is young and vibrant)* Oh, no. They're birth, they're spring! They say in Greece you find them growing wild in April. *(She takes an old Wedgwood bowl from the sideboard, preparing to set the pot of hyacinths in it.)*

HESTER. *(In a dry, unfriendly tone)* I've asked you not to use that Wedgwood bowl. It was my grandmother's. I don't want it broken.

RUTH. I'm sorry. *(Replacing the bowl, she gets a plain one from inside the sideboard.)* I thought the hyacinths would look so pretty in it, but I'll use the plain one.

HESTER. You've gone to as much trouble for that plant as if it were a child. (HESTER *sits in the rocking chair by the stove.*)

RUTH. *(Placing the hyacinths in the bowl)* They're so sweet. I like to touch them.

HESTER. They'll freeze tonight, I'm thinking.

RUTH. Not in here. We'll have to keep the fire up anyway. *(Leaving the bowl of hyacinths on the table,* RUTH *returns to the sideboard, taking some bright chintz from the drawer. She holds it up for* HESTER *to see.)* I've almost finished the curtains, Hester.

HESTER. *(Tonelessly)* You have?

RUTH. Don't you think they'll make this room more cheerful?

HESTER. The ones we have seem good enough to me.

RUTH. But they're so old.

HESTER. *(Coldly)* Old things have beauty when you've eyes to see it. That velvet has a richness that you can't buy now.

RUTH. *(Moving to the window)* I want to make the room gay and happy for the spring. You'll see how much difference these will make.

HESTER. I've no doubt. (HESTER *rises and goes to the table to avoid looking at the curtains.)*

RUTH. *(Measuring the chintz with the curtains at the window)* I wonder if I have them wide enough.

(The WIND *rises.)*

(As if the sound had quelled her pleasure in the bright curtains, RUTH *turns slowly away from the window. A touch of hysteria creeps into her voice.)* The wind swirls and shrieks and raises such queer echoes in this old house! It seems to laugh at us in here, thinking we're safe, hugging the stove! As if it knew it could blow out the light and the fire and — *(Getting hold of herself.)* I've never seen a blizzard when it was as cold as this. Have you. Hester?

HESTER. *(Knitting)* Bruce was born on a night like this.

(Throughout this scene HESTER *seldom looks at* RUTH *but gives all her attention to her knitting. She seems reluctant to talk and yet impelled to do so.)*

RUTH. I didn't know.

HESTER. Father had to ride for the doctor while I stayed here with Mother.

RUTH. Alone?

HESTER. Yes. I was rubbing Father's hands with snow when we heard the baby crying. Then we helped the doctor bathe him.

RUTH. You were such a little girl to do so much.

HESTER. After Mother died I did it all.

RUTH.   I know, but it was too hard for a child. I don't see how you managed.

HESTER.   Father always helped me with the washing.

RUTH.   Not many men would stay in from the field to do that.

HESTER.   No. *(Her knitting drops to her lap, and for a moment she is lost in the past.)* "We'll have to lean on one another now, Daughter." – Those were his words. – And that's the way it was. I was beside him until – I never left him.

RUTH.   *(At HESTER's side)* You've never talked of him like this before.

HESTER.   *(Unconscious of RUTH)* He always liked the snow. *(Her eyes are on the portrait of her father.)* He called it a moving shroud, a winding-sheet that the wind lifts and raises and lets fall again.

RUTH.   It is like that.

HESTER.   He'd come in and say, "The snow lies deep on the summer fallow, Hester. That means a good crop next year."

RUTH.   I know. It's glorious in the fall with the wheat like gold on the hills. No wonder he loved it.

HESTER.   *(Called out of her dream, she abruptly resumes her knitting)* There hasn't been much wheat out there these last years.

RUTH.   That isn't Bruce's fault, Hester.

HESTER.   You have to love a place to make things grow. The land knows when you don't care about it, and Bruce doesn't care about it any more. Not like Father did.

RUTH.   *(Her hands raised to touch the portrait above the sideboard)* I wish I'd known your father.

HESTER.   *(Rising and facing RUTH with a sudden and terrible anger)* Don't touch that picture. It's mine.

RUTH.   *(Startled, she faces HESTER)* Why, Hester –

HESTER.   Can't I have anything of my own? Must you put your fingers on everything I have?

RUTH.   *(Moving to HESTER)* Hester, you know I didn't mean – What is the matter with you?

HESTER.   I won't have you touch it.

RUTH.   *(Gently)* Do you hate my being here so much?

HESTER.   *(Turning away)* You've more right here than I have now, I suppose.

RUTH.   *(Crossing over to the stove)* You make me feel that I've no right at all.

HESTER.   *(A martyr now)* I'm sorry if you don't approve my ways. I can go, if that's what you want.

RUTH. *(Pleading)* Please – I've never had a sister, and when Bruce told me he had one, I thought we'd be such friends –

HESTER. *(Sitting in the chair by the stove)* We're not a family to put words to everything we feel. *(She resumes her knitting.)*

RUTH. *(Trying to bridge the gulf between them)* I get too excited over things: I know it. Bruce tells me I sound affected when I say too much about the way I feel, the way I like people – or the sky in the evening. I –

HESTER. *(Without looking up)* Did you get the separator put up? Or shall I do it?

RUTH. *(Discouraged, RUTH turns away, and going to the table, sits down with her sewing.)* It's ready for the milk when Bruce brings it. I put it together this morning.

HESTER. The lanterns are empty.

RUTH. I'll fill them in a minute.

HESTER. When I managed this house, I always filled the lanterns right after supper. Then they were ready.

RUTH. *(Impatiently)* I said I'd fill them, Hester, and I will. They're both there in the corner. *(She indicates the lanterns at the end of the sideboard.)*

HESTER. Bruce didn't take one, then?

RUTH. No.

HESTER. You'd better put a lamp in the window.

RUTH. *(Lights a small lamp on the sideboard and takes it to the window)* I wish he'd come. It's strange how women feel safer when their men are near, close enough to touch, isn't it? No matter how strong you think you are. *(As she speaks, RUTH drapes some of the chintz over the armchair.)*

HESTER. I can't say that I need my strength from Bruce, or could get it if I needed it.

RUTH. That's because he's still a little boy to you. *(A pause. Then RUTH speaks hesitantly.)* Hester –

HESTER. Yes?

RUTH. Will you mind the baby in the house?

HESTER. *(After a silence, constrainedly)* No, I won't mind. I'll keep out of the way.

RUTH. *(Warmly, commanding a response)* I don't want you to. You'll love him, Hester.

HESTER. *(Harshly)* I loved Bruce, but I got no thanks for it. He feels I stand in his way now.

RUTH. *(Suddenly aware that HESTER has needed and wanted love)* You mustn't say that. It isn't true.

HESTER. When he was little, after Mother died, he'd come tugging at my hand – He'd get hold of my little finger and say, "Come, Hettie – come and look." Everything was "Hettie" then.

RUTH. (*Eagerly, moving to* HESTER) It will be like that again. This baby will be almost like your own.

HESTER. (*As if* RUTH's *words were an implied reproach*) I could have married, and married well if I'd had a mind to.

RUTH. I know that. I've wondered why you didn't, Hester.

HESTER. The young men used to ride over here on Sunday, but I stopped that. (*A pause.*) I never saw a man I'd let touch me. Maybe you don't mind that kind of thing. I do.

RUTH. (*Involuntarily; it is a cry*) No! (*Attempting to put her arms around* HESTER.) What hurt you?

HESTER. (*Rising*) Don't try your soft ways on me. (*She moves behind the armchair, her hand falls caressingly on the back of the chair.*) I couldn't leave Bruce and Father here alone. My duty was here in this house. So I stayed. (HESTER *notices the chintz material draped over the chair and, taking it up, turns to* RUTH *angrily.*) What do you intend to do with this?

RUTH. I thought – there's enough left to make covers for the chair to match the curtains –

HESTER. (*Throwing the chintz down*) This is Father's chair. I won't have it changed.

RUTH. I'm sorry, Hester. (*With spirit.*) Must we keep everything the same forever?

HESTER. There's nothing in this house that isn't good, that wasn't bought with care and pride by one of us who loved it. This stuff is cheap and gaudy.

RUTH. It isn't dull and falling apart with age.

HESTER. Before my father died, when he was ill, he sat here in this chair where he could see them threshing from the window. It was the first time since he came here that he'd not been in the fields at harvest. Now you come – you who never knew him, who never saw him – and you won't rest until –

RUTH. Hester!

HESTER. You've got no right to touch it! (*Her hands grip the back of the old chair as she stands rigid, her eyes blazing.*)

> (BRUCE WARREN *enters from outside, carrying a pail of milk. He is tall and dark, about thirty years old, sensitive and bitter. His vain struggle to make the farm pay since his father's death has left him with an oppressive sense of failure. He is proud and quick to resent an imagined reproach. He has dark hair, his shoulders are a little*

stooped, and he moves restlessly and abruptly. Despite his moodiness, he is extremely likeable. He is dressed warmly in dark trousers, a sweater under his heavy leather coat; he wears gloves, cap and high boots. He brushes the snow from his coat as he enters.)

BRUCE. *(Carrying the milk into the kitchen)* Is the separator up, Ruth?

RUTH. Yes, it's all ready, Bruce. Wait, I'll help you. *(She follows him into the kitchen.)*

(HESTER *stands at the chair a moment after they have gone; her eyes fall on the plant on the table. Slowly she goes towards it, as if drawn by something she hated. She looks down at the lavender blooms for a moment. Then with a quick, angry gesture, she crushes one of the stalks. She turns away and is winding up her wool when* BRUCE *and* RUTH *return.*

You must be frozen.

BRUCE. *(Taking off his coat and gloves)* I'm cold, all right. God, it's a blizzard: thirty-eight below, and a high wind. *(He throws his coat over a chair at the table.)*

RUTH. *(With pride)* Did you see the hyacinths? They've bloomed since yesterday.

BRUCE. *(Smiling)* Yes, they're pretty. *(Touching them, he notices the broken stalk.)* Looks like one of them's broken.

RUTH. Where? *(She sees it.)* Oh, it is! And that one hadn't bloomed yet! I wonder – It wasn't broken when I – (RUTH *turns accusingly to* HESTER.) Hester!

HESTER. *(Returns look calmly. Coldly)* Yes?

RUTH. Hester, did you –

BRUCE. *(Going over to the fire)* Oh, Ruth, don't make such a fuss about it. It can't be helped.

HESTER. I'll take care of the milk. *(She takes the small lamp from the window.)*

RUTH. I'll do it.

HESTER. *(Moving toward the kitchen)* You turn the separator so slow the cream's as thin as water.

RUTH. *(Stung to reply)* That's not true. You never give me a chance to –

BRUCE. *(Irritably)* For God's sake, don't quarrel about it. *(He sits in the chair by the stove.)*

HESTER. I don't intend to quarrel. *(She goes into the kitchen.)*

(RUTH *follows* HESTER *to the door. The* SOUND *of the separator comes from the kitchen.* RUTH *turns wearily, takes up the pot of hyacinths, and places them on the stand near the stove. Then sits on the footstool.)*

RUTH.   It's always that way.

BRUCE.   *(Gazing moodily at the stove)* Why don't you two try to get along?

(A silence.)

RUTH.   Did you put the stock in? *(The question is merely something to fill the empty space of silence between them.)*

BRUCE. Yes. That black mare may foal tonight. I'll have to look at her later on.

RUTH.   It's bitter weather for a little colt to be born.

BRUCE.   Yes.

(Another silence. Finally RUTH, to throw off the tension between them, gets up and moves her footstool over to his chair.)

RUTH.   I'm glad you're here. I've been lonesome for you.

BRUCE.   *(Putting his hand on hers)* I'm glad to be here.

RUTH.   I thought of you out at the barn, trying to work in this cold.

BRUCE.   I was all right. I'd hate to walk far tonight, though. You can't see your hand before your face.

RUTH.   *(After a look at the kitchen)* Hester's been so strange again these last few days, Bruce.

BRUCE.   I know it's hard, Ruth.

RUTH.   It's like it was when I first came here. At everything I touch, she cries out like I'd hurt her somehow.

BRUCE.   Hester has to do things her own way. She's always been like that.

RUTH.   If only she could like me a little. I think she almost does sometimes, but then —

BRUCE.   You think too much about her.

RUTH.   Maybe it's because we've been shut in so close. I'm almost afraid of her lately.

BRUCE.   She's not had an easy life, Ruth.

RUTH.   I know that. She's talked about your father almost constantly today.

BRUCE.   His death hit us both hard. Dad ran the farm, decided everything.

RUTH.   It's been six years, Bruce.

BRUCE.   There are things you don't count out by years.

RUTH.   He wouldn't want you to go on remembering forever.

BRUCE.   *(Looking at the floor)* No.

RUTH.   You should get free of this house. It's not good for you to stay here. It's not good for Hester. *(Getting up, she crosses to the sideboard and returns with the deed of sale, which she hands to* BRUCE.) Mr. Manning left this for you. He's coming back tomorrow for it, when you've signed it.

BRUCE. *(Takes the papers. Annoyed by her assurance)* He doesn't need to get so excited. I haven't decided to sign yet. He said he wouldn't need to know till spring. *(He goes over to the lamp at the table and studies the document.)*

RUTH. His company gave him orders to close the deal this week or let it go.

BRUCE. This week?

RUTH. That's what he said.

BRUCE. Well. I'll think about it.

RUTH. You'll have to decide tonight, Bruce. No one else will offer you as much. Five thousand dollars and an irrigated farm a mile from town seems a good price.

BRUCE. I'm not complaining about the deal. It's fair.

RUTH. *(Urgently)* You're going to take it, aren't you, Bruce?

BRUCE. I don't know. God, I don't know. *(He throws the document on the table.)* I don't want to sell, Ruth. I think I'll try it another year.

RUTH. Bruce, you've struggled here too long now. You haven't had a crop, a good crop, in five years.

BRUCE. I need to be told that!

RUTH. It's not your fault. But you've told me you ought to give it up, that it's too dry here.

BRUCE. We may get a crop this year. We're due for one.

RUTH. If you take this offer, we'll be nearer town. We'll have water on the place. We can have a garden, and trees growing.

BRUCE. That's about what those irrigated farms are – gardens.

RUTH. And, Bruce, it wouldn't be so lonely there, so cruelly lonely.

BRUCE. I told you how it was before you came.

RUTH. *(Resenting his tone)* You didn't tell me you worshipped a house. That you made a god of a house and a section of land. You didn't tell me that!

BRUCE. *(Angrily)* You didn't tell me that you'd moon at a window for your old friends, either. *(He stands up and throws the deed of sale on the table.)*

RUTH. How could I help it here?

BRUCE. And you didn't tell me you'd be afraid of having a child. What kind of a woman are you that you don't want your child?

RUTH. That's not true.

BRUCE.   No? You cried when you knew, didn't you?

RUTH.   Bruce!

BRUCE.   *(Going blindly on)* What makes you feel the way you do, then? Other women have children without so much fuss. Other women are glad.

RUTH.   *(Intensely angry)* Don't speak to me like that. Keep your land. Eat and sleep and dream land, I don't care!

BRUCE.   *(Turning to the portrait of his father)* My father came out here and took a homestead. He broke the prairie with one plough and a team of horses. He built a house to live in out of the sod. You didn't know that, did you? He and Mother lived here in a sod shanty and struggled to make things grow. Then they built a one-roomed shack: and when the good years came, they built this house. The finest in the country! I thought my son would have it.

RUTH.   *(Moving to him)* What is there left to give a son? A house that stirs with ghosts! A piece of worn-out land where the rain never comes.

BRUCE.   That's not all. I don't suppose you can understand.

RUTH.   *(Turning away from him, deeply hurt)* No. I don't suppose I can. You give me little chance to know how you feel about things.

BRUCE.   *(His anger gone)* Ruth, I didn't mean that. But you've always lived in town. *(He goes to the window and stands looking out for a moment, then turns.)* Those rocks along the fence out there, I picked up every one of them with my own hands and carried them with my own hands across the field and piled them there. I've ploughed that southern slope along the coulee every year since I was twelve. *(His voice is torn with a kind of shame for his emotion.)* I feel about the land like Hester does about the house, I guess. I don't want to leave it. I don't want to give it up.

RUTH.   *(Gently)* But it's poor land, Bruce.

(BRUCE *sits down, gazing gloomily at the fire,* HESTER *comes in from the kitchen with the small lamp and places it on the sideboard. Then she sits at the table, taking up her knitting. As* BRUCE *speaks, she watches him intently.)*

BRUCE.   Yes, it's strange that in a soil that won't grow trees a man can put roots down, but he can.

RUTH.   *(At his side)* You'd feel the same about another place, after a little while.

BRUCE.   I don't know. When I saw the wind last spring blowing the dirt away, the dirt I'd ploughed and harrowed and sowed to grain, I felt as though a part of myself was blowing away in the dust. Even now, with the land three feet under snow, I can look out and feel it waiting for the seed I've saved for it.

RUTH.   But if we go, we'll be nearer other people, not cut off from everything that lives.

BRUCE.   You need people, don't you?

HESTER.   Yes. She needs them. I've seen her at the window looking toward the town. Day after day she stands there.

(BRUCE *and* RUTH, *absorbed in the conflict between them, had forgotten* HESTER's *presence. At* HESTER's *words,* RUTH *turns on them both, flaming with anger.*)

RUTH.   You two. You're so *perfect!*

HESTER.   *(Knitting)* We could always stand alone, the three of us. We didn't need to turn to every stranger who held his hand out.

RUTH.   No! You'd sit in this husk of a house, living like shadows, until these four walls closed in on you, buried you.

HESTER.   I never stood at a window, looking down the road that leads to town.

RUTH.   *(The pent-up hysteria of the day and the longing of months breaks through, tumbling out in her words)* It's not for myself I look down that road, Hester. It's for the child I'm going to have. You're right, Bruce. I am afraid. It's not what you think, though, not for myself. You two and your father lived so long in this dark house that you forgot there's a world beating outside, forgot that people laugh and play sometimes. And you've shut me out! *(There is a catch in her voice.)* I never would have trampled on your thoughts if you'd given them to me. But as it is, I might as well not be a person. You'd like a shadow better that wouldn't touch your house. A child would die here. A child can't live with shadows.

BRUCE.   *(Much disturbed,* BRUCE *rises and goes to her.)* Ruth! I didn't know you hated it so much.

RUTH.   I thought it would change. I thought I could change it. You know now.

BRUCE.   *(Quietly)* Yes.

RUTH.   *(Pleading)* If we go, I'll *want* this child, Bruce. Don't you see? But I'm not happy here. What kind of a life will our child have? He'll be old before he's out of school. *(She looks at the hyacinth on the stand.)* He'll be like this hyacinth that's broken before it bloomed.

BRUCE.   *(Goes to the table and stands looking down at the deed of sale. His voice is tired and flat, but resolved.)* All right. I'll tell Manning I'll let him have the place.

HESTER.   *(Turning quickly to* BRUCE) What do you mean?

BRUCE.   I'm going to sell the farm to Manning. He was here today.

HESTER.   *(Standing up, her eyes blazing)* You can't sell this house.

BRUCE. *(Looking at the deed of sale)* Oh, Ruth's right. We can't make a living on the place. *(He sits down, leafing through the document.)* It's too dry. And too far from school.

HESTER. It wasn't too far for you to go, or me.

BRUCE. *(Irritably)* Do you think I want to sell?

HESTER. *She* does. But she can't do it. *(Her voice is low.)* This house belongs to me.

BRUCE. Hester, don't start that again! I wish to God the land had been divided differently, but it wasn't.

HESTER. Father meant for us to stay here and keep things as they were when he was with us.

BRUCE. The soil wasn't blowing away when he was farming it.

HESTER. He meant for me to have the house.

RUTH. You'll go with us where we go, Hester.

HESTER. *(To* RUTH*)* You came here. You plotted with him to take this house from me. But it's mine!

BRUCE. *(His voice cracks through the room)* Stop that, Hester! I love this place as much as you do, but I'm selling it. I'm selling it, I tell you. *(As he speaks, he gets up abruptly and, taking up his coat, puts it on.)*

> HESTER *sinks slowly into the chair, staring.* RUTH *tries to put her hand on* BRUCE's *arm.)*

RUTH. Bruce! Not that way! Not for me. If it's that way, I don't care enough.

BRUCE. *(Shaking himself free)* Oh, leave me alone!

RUTH. Bruce!

BRUCE. *(Going to the door)* I'll be glad when it's over, I suppose.

RUTH. Where are you going?

BRUCE. *(Taking his cap and gloves)* To look at that mare.

RUTH. Bruce!

> *(But he has gone.)*

HESTER. *(Getting up, she goes to her father's chair and stands behind it, facing* RUTH; *she moves and speaks as if she were in a dream.)* This is my house. I won't have strangers in it.

RUTH. *(At the table, without looking at* HESTER*)* Oh, Hester! I didn't want it to be this way. I tried —

HESTER. *(As if she were speaking to a stranger)* Why did you come here?

RUTH. I've hurt you. But I'm right about this. I know I'm right.

HESTER. There isn't any room for you.

RUTH. Can't you see? It's for all of us.

(HESTER *comes toward* RUTH *with a strange, blazing anger in her face.*)

HESTER. I know your kind. You tempted him with your bright hair.

RUTH. Hester!

HESTER. Your body anointed with jasmine for his pleasure.

RUTH. Hester, don't say such things!

HESTER. Oh, I know what you are! You and women like you. You put a dream around him with your arms, a sinful dream.

RUTH. (*Drawing back*) Hester!

HESTER. You lift your white face to every stranger like you offered him a cup to drink from. (*Turning from* RUTH, *as if she had forgotten her presence,* HESTER *looks fondly at the room.*) I'll never leave this house.

BRUCE. (*Opens the door and comes in quickly and stormily. He goes into the kitchen as he speaks.*) That mare's got out. She jumped the corral. I'll have to go after her.

RUTH. (*Concerned*) Bruce, where will she be?

BRUCE. (*Returning with an old blanket*) She'll be in the snowshed by the coulee. She always goes there when she's about to foal.

(HESTER *sits in the chair by the stove, her knitting in her hand. She pays no attention to the* OTHERS.)

RUTH. But you can't go after her in this storm.

BRUCE. I'll take this old blanket to cover the colt, if it's born yet. Where's the lantern? (*He sees the two lanterns by the kitchen door and, taking one of them to the table, lights it.*)

RUTH. It's three miles, Bruce. You mustn't go on foot. It's dangerous.

BRUCE. I'll have to. She'd never live through the night, or the colt either. (*He turns to go.*) You'd better go to bed. Good-night, Hester.

RUTH. Let me come with you.

BRUCE. No. (*Then, as he looks at her, all resentment leaves him. He puts down the lantern, goes to her, and takes her in his arms.*) Ruth, forget what I said. You know I didn't mean —

RUTH. (*Softly*) I said things I didn't mean, too —

BRUCE. I love you, Ruth. You know it, don't you?

RUTH. Bruce!

(*He kisses her, and for a moment their love is a flame in the room.*)

BRUCE. Don't worry. I won't be long.

RUTH. I'll wait.

(BRUCE *goes out.* RUTH *follows him to the door, and, as it closes, she stands against it for a moment. There is a silence.* HESTER *is slowly unravelling her knitting but is unaware of it. The black wool falls in spirals about her chair.*)

HESTER. *(Suddenly)* It's an old house. I was born here. *(Then in a strange, calm voice that seems to come from a long distance.)* You shouldn't let Bruce be so much alone. You lose him that way. He comes back to *us* then. He'll see you don't belong here unless you keep your hand on him all the time.

(RUTH *looks curiously at* HESTER *but does not give her all her attention.*)

(HESTER *suddenly becomes harsh.*) This is my house. You can't change it.

(RUTH *starts to say something but remains silent.*)

Father gave it to me. There isn't any room for you. *(In a high, childlike tone, like the sound of a violin string breaking.)* No room. *(She shakes her head gravely.)*

RUTH. *(Aware that something is wrong)* Hester –

HESTER. *(As if she were telling an often-recited story to a stranger)* I stayed home when Mother died and kept house for my little brother and my father. *(Her voice grows stronger.)* I was very beautiful, they said. My hair fell to my knees, and it was black as a furrow turned in spring. *(Proudly.)* I can have a husband any time I want, but my duty is here with Father. You see how it is. I can't leave him.

RUTH. *(Goes quickly to* HESTER. *With anxiety and gentleness)* Hester, what are you talking about?

HESTER. That's Father's chair. I'll put his Bible out. *(She starts from her chair.)*

RUTH. *(Preventing her)* Hester, your father's not here – not for six years. You speak of him as if you thought – Hester –

HESTER. *(Ignoring* RUTH *but remaining seated)* When I was a girl I always filled the lanterns after supper. Then I was ready for his coming.

RUTH. *(In terror)* Hester, I didn't fill them! I didn't fill the lanterns! *(She runs to the kitchen door and takes up the remaining lantern.)*

HESTER. *(Calmly)* Father called me the wise virgin then.

RUTH. Hester, Bruce took one! He thought I'd filled them. It will burn out and he'll be lost in the blizzard.

HESTER. I always filled them.

RUTH. *(Setting the lantern on the table)* I've got to go out after Bruce. If he gets down to the coulee and the lantern goes out, he'll never find the way back. I'll have to hurry! Where's the coal oil?

(RUTH *goes to the kitchen and returns with a can of coal oil and a pair of galoshes.* HESTER *watches her closely. As* RUTH *comes in with the oil,* HESTER *slowly rises and goes to her.*)

HESTER.   I'll fill the lantern for you, Ruth.

RUTH.   *(Trying to remove the top of the can)* I can't get the top off. My hands are shaking so.

HESTER.   *(Taking the oil can from* RUTH*)* I'll fill it for you.

RUTH.   Please, Hester. While I get my things on! *(Giving* HESTER *the oil can,* RUTH *runs to the footstool and hurriedly puts on her galoshes.)* I'm afraid that lantern will last just long enough to get him out there. He'll be across the field before I even get outside. *(She runs up the stairs.)*

HESTER.   *(Standing motionless, the oil can in her hand)* You're going now. That's right. I told you you should go.

(RUTH *disappears up the stairs.* HESTER *moves a step towards the lantern, taking off the top of the coal oil can. She hesitates and looks for a long moment after* RUTH. *With the strange lucidity of madness, slowly, deliberately, she places the top back again on the can and, moving behind the table, sets it on the floor without filling the lantern.* RUTH *hurries down the stairs excited and alarmed. She has on heavy clothes and is putting on her gloves.)*

RUTH.   Is it ready?
(HESTER *nods.*)
Will you light it for me, Hester? Please.
(HESTER *lights the lantern.*)
I'll put the light at the window. *(She crosses with the small lamp and places it at the window.)* Hurry, Hester! *(With a sob.)* Oh, if only I can find him!

(HESTER *crosses to* RUTH *and gives her the lantern,* RUTH *takes the lantern and goes out. A gust of* WIND *carries the snow into the room and blows shut the door after her.* HESTER *goes to the window.*)

HESTER.   *(Her voice is like an echo)* The snow lies deep on the summer fallow – The snow is a moving shroud – a winding sheet that the wind lifts and raises and lets fall again. *(Turning from the window.)* They've gone. They won't be back now. *(With an intense excitement,* HESTER *blows out the lamp at the window and pulls down the shades. Her eyes fall on the bowl of hyacinths in the corner. Slowly she goes to it, takes it up and, holding it away from her, carries it to the door. Opening the door, she sets the flowers outside. She closes the door and locks it. Her eyes blazing with excitement, she stands with her arms across the door as if shutting the world out. Then softly she moves to the door of her father's bedroom, unlocks it, and goes in, returning at once with a pair of men's bedroom slippers. Leaving the bedroom door open, she crosses to the sideboard, takes up the Bible and, going to her father's chair, places the slippers beside it. She speaks very softly.)* I put your slippers out. *(She draws the footstool up to the chair.)* Everything will be the same now, Father. *(She opens the Bible.)* I'll read to you, Father. I'll read the one you like. *(She reads with quiet contentment.)* "And the winds blew, and beat upon the house; and it fell not: for it was founded upon a rock."

(1939)   (1939)

Anne Wilkinson
1910 – 1961

————◆————

ANNE (GIBBONS) WILKINSON was born in Toronto and lived there for most of her life. A founding editor of *Tamarack Review* and the author of a volume of children's fiction and a history of the Osler family, Wilkinson is best known as a poet. Her first volume of verse *Counterpoint to Sleep* was published in 1951 and was succeeded by *The Hangman Ties the Holly* (1955). In recognition of the importance of Wilkinson's poetry, A.J.M. Smith edited her *Collected Poems* in 1968.

Lens

I

The poet's daily chore
Is my long duty;
To keep and cherish my good lens
For love and war
And wasps about the lilies
And mutiny within.

My woman's eye is weak
And veiled with milk;
My working eye is muscled
With a curious tension,   10
Stretched and open
As the eyes of children;
Trusting in its vision
Even should it see
The holy holy spirit gambol
Counterheadwise,
Lithe and warm as any animal.

My woman's iris circles
A blind pupil;
The poet's eye is crystal,   20
Polished to accept the negative,
The contradictions in a proof
And the accidental
Candour of the shadows;

The shutter, oiled and smooth
Clicks on the grace of heroes
Or on some bestial act
When lit with radiance
The afterwords the actors speak
Give depths to violence,   30

Or if the bull is great
And the matador
And the sword
Itself the metaphor.

II

In my dark room the years
Lie in solution,
Develop film by film.
Slow at first and dim
Their shadows bite
On the fine white pulp of paper.

An early snap of fire
Licking the arms of air
I hold against the light, compare
The details with a prehistoric view 10
Of land and sea
And cradles of mud that rocked
The wet and sloth of infancy.

A stripe of tiger, curled
And sleeping on the ribs of reason
Prints as clear
As Eve and Adam, pearled
With sweat, staring at an apple core;

And death, in black and white
Or politic in green and Easter film, 20
Lands on steely points, a dancer
Disciplined to the foolscap stage,
The property of poets
Who command his robes, expose
His moving likeness on the page.

(1955)   (1968)

Easter Sketches, Montreal

I

South of North
Men grow soft with summer,
Lack the winter muscle
Set to tauten at the miracle;
Boom and shrapnel,
March of Easter, loud
Where guns of ice salute
The cracking god.

Vision dims where flowers
Blur the lens   10
But here, intemperate

The ropes of air
Whip the optic nerve
Till eyes are clean with crying
For the melting hour
When flocks of snow stampede
And rocks are split by spring
And intimations of fertility
In water ring.

South of North   20
Men grow deaf with summer,
Sound is muffled by the pile of lawns,
But where the air is seeded fresh
And skies can stretch their cloudy loins
To the back of the long north wind
The ear is royal pitched
And hears the dying snows
Sing like swans.

II

Where campanile of rock steeples the town
Water bells the buoy of all our birthdays;
Rivers swell in tumbling towers of praise,
Ice in aqua risen hails
The bearing down in labour of the sun.

And after sun, guards of northern lights
Stand their swords; green fires kindled
By the green shoots in our wood
Cut the natal cord,

Freeing the animal sensual man with astral   10
Spears of grass.
Cerebral ore conceives when pollen
Falls from heaven in a buzz of stars

And time and the rolling world
Fold the birthday children in their arms.

III

North of South
Winter is Jehovah, we
The Jobs who scold the frosty Lord
Till wings of weather
Clap the air
And crows unfrock the melting God.

On our nativity
The mellowed sun is grown,
A man to kill our father,
A sun with breath so warm   10
It seeds the body of our summer.

(1955)   (1968)

Tigers Know from Birth

My bones predict the striking hour of thunder
And water as I huddle under
    The tree the lightning renders

I'm hung with seaweed, winding in its caul
The nightmare of a carp whose blood runs cold,
    A crab who apes my crawl

My lens is grafted from a jungle eye
To focus on the substance of a shadow's
    Shadow on the sky

My forest filtered drum is pitched to hear   10
The serpent split the grass before the swish
    Is feather in my ear

I've learned from land and sea of every death
Save one, the easy rest, the little catnap
    Tigers know from birth

(1955)   (1968)

South, North

Countries where the olive
And the orange ripen
Grow their men
On slopes unpuritan;
Joy a food
Deserving rites of measure.

(1955)

Where winter pulls the blind
A bliss as keen –
On native stone of sin
Cold men whet their pleasure
Cussed by the black north wind.

(1968)

Poem in Three Parts

I

Those behind me
Those about me
Millions crowding to come after me
Look over my shoulder.

Together we consider
The merit of stone
(I hold a stone in my hand for all to see)
A geologist tells the time it has endured
Endurance, a virtue in itself, we say,
Makes its own monument.   10

We pause, resent
The little span
A miser's rule
Inched out for man

But blood consoles us
Can be squeezed from us
Not from stone.

Saying this fools no one
A sudden bluster of words
Claims for human seed   20
A special dispensation

Foxes and flowers and other worthies
All excluded.

Immediately sixteen creeds
Cry out to be defended —
A state of emergency exists;

Flying buttresses
Revolving domes, a spire extended
By the spirit of
A new and startling growth of thorns   30

Skies in Asia catch
On uptilted wings of temples
In the Near East the talk is of stables.

II

Above-below the din
A few quiet men
Observe the cell's fragility

How Monday's child
Makes Tuesday's vegetable
And Wednesday petrifies
The leaf to mineral
While Friday sparks the whole in fire
And Sunday's elements disperse
And rise in air.   10

III

The stone in my hand
IS my hand
And stamped with tracings of
A once greenblooded frond,
Is here, is gone, will come,
Was fire, and green, and water,
Will be wind.

(1955)   (1968)

Nature Be Damned

I

Pray where would lamb and lion be
If they lay down in amity?
Could lamb then nibble living grass?
Lamb and lion both must starve;
Bird and flower, too, must die of love.

II

I go a new dry way, permit no weather
Here, on undertaker's false green sod
Where I sit down beneath my false tin tree.
There's too much danger in a cloud,
In wood or field, or close to moving water.
With my black blood – who can tell?
The dart of one mosquito might be fatal;

Or in the flitting dusk a bat
Might carry away my destiny.
Hang it upside down from a rafter   10
In a barn unknown to me.

I hide my skin within the barren city
Where artificial moons pull no man's tide,
And so escape my green love till the day
Vine breaks through brick and strangles me.

III

I was witch and I could be
Bird of leaf
Or branch and bark of tree.

In rain and two by two my powers left me;
Instead of curling down as root and worm
My feet walked on the surface of the earth,
And I remember a day of evil sun
When forty green leaves withered on my arm.

And so I damn the font where I was blessed,
Am unbeliever; was deluded lover; never   10
Bird or leaf or branch and bark of tree.
Each, separate as curds from whey,
Has signature to prove identity.

And yet we're kin in appetite;
Tree, bird in the tree and I.
We feed on dung, a fly, a lamb
And burst with seed
Of tree, of bird, of man,
Till tree is bare
And bird and I are bone   20
And feaster is reborn
The feast, and feasted on.

IV

Once a year in the smoking bush
A little west of where I sit
I burn my winter caul to a green ash.
This is an annual festival,
Nothing to stun or startle;
A coming together – water and sun
In summer's first communion.

Today again I burned my winter caul
Though senses nodded, dulled by ritual.

One hundred singing orioles   10
And five old angels wakened me;
Morning sky rained butterflies
And simple fish, bass and perch,
Leapt from the lake in salutation.
St. Francis, drunk among the daisies,
Opened his ecstatic eye.

Then roused from this reality I saw
Nothing, anywhere, but snow.

(1968)   (1968)

Roches Point

This land rings,
In stone of its houses,
In cedar and sod,
The myths of my kin.
The long lake knows our bones;
Skin and scar and mole, sings
Them like a lover, truly.

Here eternity lit
On sunburned shoulders
10 Till seven cat-black summers
Stalked each other and us,
And for our terror

Deadly nightshade
Flowered in our wood.

The body still goes back
For of necessity
It makes strange journeys.
I, my being,
Shut the door against return
And in the attic pack   20
One hundred summers,
Seven burning wounds,
A root of deadly nightshade
And the silky waters
Where our epochs drowned.

(1968)   (1968)

Saint-Denys Garneau
1912 – 1943

————————◆————————

HECTOR DE SAINT-DENYS GARNEAU, a great-grandson of the nineteenth-century historian François-Xavier Garneau, spent most of his childhood at his family's ancestral home near Quebec. After studying at the Collège Sainte-Marie and L'Ecole des Beaux Arts in Montreal, Garneau pursued his interests in painting and poetry until, haunted by a sense of guilt and feelings of alienation, he returned to the isolation of his family's home several years before his premature death. During his life, Garneau published only one volume of poetry, *Regards et jeux dans l'espace* (1937), but since his death his collected poems and his journal of the years between 1935 and 1939 have appeared in French, and in English translations by John Glassco.

The Game

Don't bother me I'm terribly busy

A child is starting to build a village
It's a city, a county
And who knows
        Soon the universe.

He's playing

These wooden blocks are houses he moves about
    and castles
This board is the sign of a sloping roof
                not at all bad to look at
It's no small thing to know the place where the
    road of cards
                will turn   10
This could change completely
                the course of the river
Because of the bridge which makes so beautiful a
    reflection
        on the water of the carpet
It's easy to have a tall tree
And to put a mountain underneath
            so it'll be high up

Joy of playing! Paradise of liberties!
But above all don't put your foot in the room
One never knows what might be in this corner
Or whether you are not going to crush the
    favourite
            among the invisible flowers

This is my box of toys
Full of words for weaving marvellous patterns   20
For uniting separating matching
Now the unfolding of the dance
And soon a clear burst of the laughter
That one thought had been lost

A gentle flip of the finger
And the star
Which hung carelessly
At the end of too flimsy a thread of light
Falls and makes rings in the water.

Of love and tenderness who would dare to doubt   30
But not two cents of respect for the established order
Or for politeness and this precious discipline
A levity and practices fit to scandalize grown-up
     people

He arranges words for you as if they were simple songs
And in his eyes one can read his mischievous pleasure
At knowing that under the words he moves
     everything about
And plays with the mountains
As if they were his very own.
He turns the room upside down and truly we've
     lost our way
As if it was fun just to fool people.   40

And yet in his left eye when the right is smiling
A supernatural importance is imparted to the
     leaf of a tree
As if this could be of great significance
Had as much weight in his scales
As the war of Ethiopia
In England's.

We are not book-keepers

Everyone can see a green dollar bill
But who can see through it
          except a child
Who like him can see through it with full freedom   50
Without being in the least hampered by it
          or its limitations
Or by its value of exactly one dollar

For he sees through this window thousands of
    marvellous toys
And has no wish to choose between these
    treasures
Nor desire nor necessity
Not he
 For his eyes are wide open to take everything.

(1937)   (1970)

F.R. Scott (Trans.)

Pines Against the Light

In the light their leafwork is like water
Islands of clear water
On the black of the spruce shadowed against the light

They are all flowing
Each feathery plume, and the spray
An island of bright water at the branch's tip

Each needle a lustre a thread of living water

Each plume a little gushing spring

Running away
Who knows where   10

They are flowing as I have seen in spring
The willows flowing, the whole tree
Nothing but silver all lustre all a wave
All watery foaming flight
Like the wind made visible
And seeming
A liquid thing
In a magic window.

(1937)   (1975)

John Glassco (Trans.)

A Sealed House

I think of the desolation of winter
Through the long days of solitude
In the dead house –
For a house is dead when nothing is open –
In the sealed house, ringed by the woods

The black woods filled
With bitter wind

In the house clasped by cold
In the desolation of an endless winter

Alone, tending a little fire in a great chimney   10
Feeding it with dry branches
Piece by piece
To make it last
To stave off the final death of the fire,
Alone with the sadness that can find no vent
That you shut within yourself
And that spreads into the room
Like the smoke of a poor chimney
Drawing badly
When the wind beats on the roof   20
Puffing the smoke into the room
Until you stifle in the sealed house

Alone with a sadness
Hardly disturbed by the empty fear
That suddenly comes upon you
When the frost snaps the nails in the floor
And the wind makes the woodwork crack
The long nights to keep yourself from freezing
And then with the morning comes the light
More icy than the night.   30

So, the long months of waiting
For the end of the grasping winter.

I think of the loneliness of winter
Alone
In a sealed house.

(1937)   (1975)

John Glassco (Trans.)

Autrefois

Once I made poems
That followed the whole radiant line
From centre to circumference and beyond
As if there were no circumference   only a centre
And as if I were the sun: all around me limitless space

This is to make the elemental force flash all along the radiant
To gain prodigious meteoric speed –
What central pull can then hinder our escape
What heavenly concave dome keep us from piercing it
When we have power to burst into the infinite?   10

But we learn the earth is not flat
But a sphere, and the centre's only focus
Is at the centre
And we learn the length of the radiant line, that too well-
    travelled road
And soon we know the surface of the globe
Measured inspected surveyed   an old
Well-beaten track

And then the weary task
Of pushing the perimeter to its bounds
Hoping to find a crack in the surface of the globe   20
Hoping to burst the boundaries
And find once more the liberty of light and air.

Alas soon comes despair
The strength of all that radiant line becomes
This still point on the surface

Just like a man
Who taking too short a road, dreading his destination,
Shortens his stride and so defers his goal,
I must learn subtlety
Must infinitely divide the infinitesimal distance   30
Between chord and arc
To create a space a little like what is beyond
And find in it a hiding-place
A reason for my life and art.

(1937)   (1975)
John Glassco (Trans.)

Bird Cage

I am a bird cage   It is a bird held captive
A cage of bone   It is death in my cage of bone
With a bird
                                    Would he not like to fly away
The bird in the cage of bone   Is it you who will hold him back
Is death building his nest   Is it I
                                    What is it
When nothing is happening
One can hear him ruffle his wings   He cannot fly away
                                    Until he has eaten all   20
And when one has laughed a lot   My heart
If one suddenly stops   The source of blood
10 One hears him cooing   With my life inside
Far down
Like a small bell   He will have my soul in his beak.

(1937)   (1962)
F.R. Scott (Trans.)

Another Icarus

It's out of the wind it's in the wind
It's only a hole we make in our passage through it
A knot we tie in the fleeting thread of time

And well we know that across this slender thread we've made,
Across these shaky stations built on the journey of our going,
There is only a cry toward the depths that are forever
There is only a cry
                  from a place that lasts forever
Where the stems of the fruits are already broken
And all the stalks of the flowers and petals of the flowers   10
    are devoured
Where these feather-wings of our waxen soul have already
    melted
Only feathers in the wind feathers floating on the wind
With no home port.

(1949)   (1975)
John Glassco (Trans.)

Un Bon Coup De Guillotine

One good stroke of the guillotine
To emphasize the space between

I put my head on the mantelpiece
And the rest goes about its work

My feet go where they have to go
My hands their little business do

On the slab of the mantelpiece
My head has an air of holiday

A smile is on my lips
As if I were but newly born   10
My gaze is sent forth, calm and clear
Like a soul saved and released

It is as if I'd lost my memory
And this has made my head a pretty fool's.

(1949)   (1975)
John Glassco (Trans.)

Irving Layton
1912 –

———◆———

THE SON OF Roumanian immigrants, Irving Layton attended high school
and university in Montreal. Later he taught at a parochial school and at
Sir George Williams University before accepting a position as Professor
of English at York University. One of Canada's most accomplished
writers, Layton published his first volume of poetry, *Here and Now,* in
1945 and has subsequently published more than twenty collections of
poems. Active in *First Statement,* a literary magazine of the early 1940s,
Layton was also a founding editor of Contact Press in the early 1950s.
He has edited several anthologies and in 1972 he published
Engagements, a collection of prose including prefaces, critical articles
and short stories.

The Swimmer

The afternoon foreclosing, see
The swimmer plunges from his raft,
Opening the spray corollas by his act of war –
The snake heads strike
Quickly and are silent.

Emerging see how for a moment
A brown weed with marvellous bulbs,
He lies imminent upon the water
While light and sound come with a sharp passion
From the gonad sea around the Poles   10
And break in bright cockle-shells about his ears.

He dives, floats, goes under like a thief
Where his blood sings to the tiger shadows
In the scentless greenery that leads him home,
A male salmon down fretted stairways
Through underwater slums...

Stunned by the memory of lost gills
He frames gestures of self-absorption
Upon the skull-like beach;
Observes with instigated eyes   20
The sun that empties itself upon the water,
And the last wave romping in
To throw its boyhood on the marble sand.

(1945)   (1971)

The Black Huntsmen

Before ever I knew men were hunting me
I knew delight as water in a glass in a pool;
The childish heart then
Was ears nose eyes twiceten fingers,
And the torpid slum street, in summer,
A cut vein of the sun
That shed goldmotes by the million
Against a boy's bare toe foot ankle knee.

Then when the old year fell out of the window
To break into snowflakes on the cold stones of City Hall   10
I discovered Tennyson in a secondhand bookstore;
He put his bugle for me to his bearded mouth,
And down his Aquitaine nose a diminutive King Arthur
Rode out of our grocery shop bowing to left and to right,
Bearing my mother's *sheitel* with him;
And for a whole week after that
I called my cat Launcelot.

Now I look out for the evil retinue
Making their sortie out of a forest of gold;
Afterwards their dames shall weave my *tzitzith*   20
Into a tapestry,
Though for myself I had preferred
A death by water or sky.

(1952)   (1971)

Cemetery in August

In August, white butterflies
Engage twig and rock;
Love-sheaths bloom in convenient fissures
On a desiccated stalk;
The generation of Time brings
Rind, shell, delicate wings

And mourners. Amidst this
Summer's babble of small noises
They weep, or interject
Their resentful human voices;   10
At timely intervals
I am aware of funerals.

And these iambic stones
Honouring who-knows-what bones
Seem in the amber sunlight
Patient and confounded,
Like men enduring an epoch
Or one bemused by proofs of God.

(1953)   (1971)

The Birth of Tragedy

And me happiest when I compose poems.
        Love, power, the huzza of battle
        are something, are much;
yet a poem includes them like a pool
        water and reflection.
In me, nature's divided things —
        tree, mould on tree —
        have their fruition;
I am their core. Let them swap,
bandy, like a flame swerve   10
I am their mouth; as a mouth I serve.

And I observe how the sensual moths
　　　big with odour and sunshine
　　　dart into the perilous shrubbery;
or drop their visiting shadows
　　　upon the garden I one year made
of flowering stone to be a footstool
　　　for the perfect gods:
　　　who, friends to the ascending orders,
sustain all passionate meditations　　　　　　　　　　20
and call down pardons
for the insurgent blood.

A quiet madman, never far from tears,
　　　I lie like a slain thing
　　　under the green air the trees
inhabit, or rest upon a chair
　　　towards which the inflammable air
tumbles on many robins' wings;
　　　noting how seasonably
　　　leaf and blossom uncurl　　　　　　　　　　　　30
and living things arrange their death,
while someone from afar off
blows birthday candles for the world.

(1954)　　　　　　　　　　　　　　　　　　　　　(1971)

Red Chokecherries

In the sun
The chokecherries are a deep red.
They are like clusters of red jewels.

They are like small rubies
For a young queen who is small and graceful.
When the leaves turn, I see her white shoulder.

They are too regal to eat
And reduce to moist yellow pits.
I will let the air masticate them

And the bold maggot-making sun.   10
So I shall hardly notice
How perfection of form is overthrown.

(1956)   (1971)

For Mao Tse-Tung:
A Meditation on Flies and Kings

So, circling about my head, a fly.
Haloes of frantic monotone.
Then a smudge of blood smoking
On my fingers, let Jesus and Buddha cry.

Is theirs the way? Forgiveness of hurt?
Leprosariums? Perhaps. But I
Am burning flesh and bone,
An indifferent creature between
Cloud and a stone;
Smash insects with my boot,   10
Feast on torn flowers, deride
The nonillion bushes by the road
(Their patience is very great.)
Jivatma, they endure,
Endure and proliferate.

And the meek-browed and poor
In their solid tenements
(Etiolated, they do not dance.)
Worry of priest and of commissar:
None may re-create them who are   20
Lowly and universal as the moss
Or like vegetation the winds toss
Sweeping to the open lake and sky.
I put down these words in blood
And would not be misunderstood:
They have their Christs and their legends
And out of their pocks and ailments
Weave dear enchantments —
Poet and dictator, you are as alien as I.

On this remote and classic lake 30
Only the lapsing of the water can I hear
And the cold wind through the sumac.
The moneyed and their sunburnt children
Swarm other shores. Here is ecstasy,
The sun's outline made lucid
By each lacustral cloud
And man naked with mystery.
They dance best who dance with desire,
Who lifting feet of fire from fire
Weave before they lie down 40
A red carpet for the sun.

I pity the meek in their religious cages
And flee them; and flee
The universal sodality
Of joy-haters, joy-destroyers
(O Schiller, wine-drunk and silly!)
The sufferers and their thick rages;
Enter this tragic forest where the trees
Uprear as if for the graves of men,
All function and desire to offend 50
With themselves finally done;
And mark the dark pines farther on,
The sun's fires touching them at will,
Motionless like silent khans
Mourning serene and terrible
Their Lord entombed in the blazing hill.

(1958)   (1971)

Butterfly on Rock

The large yellow wings, black-fringed,
were motionless

They say the soul of a dead person
will settle like that on the still face

But I thought: the rock has borne this;
this butterfly is the rock's grace,

its most obstinate and secret desire
to be a thing alive made manifest

Forgot were the two shattered porcupines
I had seen die in the bleak forest.   10
Pain is unreal; death, an illusion:
There is no death in all the land,
I heard my voice cry;
And brought my hand down on the butterfly
And felt the rock move beneath my hand.

(1963)   (1971)

A Tall Man Executes a Jig

I

So the man spread his blanket on the field
And watched the shafts of light between the tufts
And felt the sun push the grass towards him;
The noise he heard was that of whizzing flies,
The whistlings of some small imprudent birds,
And the ambiguous rumbles of cars
That made him look up at the sky, aware
Of the gnats that tilted against the wind
And in the sunlight turned to jigging motes.
Fruitflies he'd call them except there was no fruit   10
About, spoiling to hatch these glitterings,
These nervous dots for which the mind supplied
The closing sentences from Thucydides,
Or from Euclid having a savage nightmare.

II

Jig jig, jig jig. Like minuscule black links
Of a chain played with by some playful
Unapparent hand or the palpitant
Summer haze bored with the hour's stillness.
He felt the sting and tingle afterwards
Of those leaving their orthodox unrest,   20
Leaving their undulant excitation

To drop upon his sleeveless arm. The grass,
Even the wildflowers became black hairs
And himself a maddened speck among them.
Still the assaults of the small flies made him
Glad at last, until he saw purest joy
In their frantic jiggings under a hair,
So changed from those in the unrestraining air.

III

He stood up and felt himself enormous.
Felt as might Donatello over stone,   30
Or Plato, or as a man who has held
A loved and lovely woman in his arms
And feels his forehead touch the emptied sky
Where all antinomies flood into light.
Yet jig jig jig, the haloing black jots
Meshed with the wheeling fire of the sun:
Motion without meaning, disquietude
Without sense or purpose, ephemerides
That mottled the resting summer air till
Gusts swept them from his sight like wisps of smoke.   40
Yet they returned, bringing a bee who, seeing
But a tall man, left him for a marigold.

IV

He doffed his aureole of gnats and moved
Out of the field as the sun sank down,
A dying god upon the blood-red hills.
Ambition, pride, the ecstasy of sex,
And all circumstance of delight and grief,
That blood upon the mountain's side, that flood
Washed into a clear incredible pool
Below the ruddied peaks that pierced the sun.   50
He stood still and waited. If ever
The hour of revelation was come
It was now, here on the transfigured steep.
The sky darkened. Some birds chirped. Nothing else.
He thought the dying god had gone to sleep:
An Indian fakir on his mat of nails.

V

And on the summit of the asphalt road
Which stretched towards the fiery town, the man
Saw one hill raised like a hairy arm, dark
With pines and cedars against the stricken sun   60
— The arm of Moses or of Joshua.
He dropped his head and let fall the halo
Of mountains, purpling and silent as time,
To see temptation coiled before his feet:
A violated grass snake that lugged
Its intestine like a small red valise.
A cold-eyed skinflint it now was, and not
The manifest of that joyful wisdom,
The mirth and arrogant green flame of life;
Or earth's vivid tongue that flicked in praise of earth.   70

VI

And the man wept because pity was useless.
"Your jig's up; the flies come like kites," he said
And watched the grass snake crawl towards the hedge,
Convulsing and dragging into the dark
The satchel filled with curses for the earth,
For the odours of warm sedge, and the sun,
A blood-red organ in the dying sky.
Backwards it fell into a grassy ditch
Exposing its underside, white as milk,
And mocked by wisps of hay between its jaws;   80
And then it stiffened to its final length.
But though it opened its thin mouth to scream
A last silent scream that shook the black sky,
Adamant and fierce, the tall man did not curse.

VII

Beside the rigid snake the man stretched out
In fellowship of death; he lay silent
And stiff in the heavy grass with eyes shut,
Inhaling the moist odours of the night

Through which his mind tunnelled with flicking tongue
Backwards to caves, mounds, and sunken ledges   90
And desolate cliffs where come only kites,
And where of perished badgers and racoons
The claws alone remain, gripping the earth.
Meanwhile the green snake crept upon the sky,
Huge, his mailed coat glittering with stars that made
The night bright, and blowing thin wreaths of cloud
Athwart the moon; and as the weary man
Stood up, coiled above his head, transforming all.

(1963)   (1971)

The Haunting

Why without cease do I think of a bold youth
    national origin unimportant or racial Peruvian
Russian Irish Javanese he has fine clear eyes
honest smiling mouth a pat for a child's head
talks to old women and helps them cross the street
    is friendly with mainliners anarchs and nuns
Cote St. Luc housewives their ruined husbands and brats
optometrists sign painters lumpenproletarians dumping
their humps into coffee cups plotting revenge
and clerics who've made out of Christ a bearded faggot   10

From the rotating movement of a girl's beautiful
    buttocks he draws energy as from the sun
(O lovely revolving suns on St. Catherine Street)
and from breasts and perfumed shoulders and hair
Picadilly Wilhelmstrasse Fifth Avenue Rue St. Germain
    the suns go rolling on luminous hoops pinwheels
handsprings and somersaults of desirable flesh
the bold youth with wide-apart happy eyes
stepping lightly over blossoming asphalt graves is running
after them touching a child's head smiling to old women   20

Why don't I ever meet him face to face?
    sometimes I've seen him stepping off a bus
but when I've caught up with him he's changed
into a bourgeois giving the two-fingered peace sign

or a poet shouting love as if it were a bomb
   on damp days into an office clerk smelling of papers
is he somebody's doppelganger? an emanation or
shadow I see taking shape near a plateglass window?
who is he? he haunts me like an embodied absence
and as if I had lived all my life in arrears   30

(1971)   (1971)

Pole-Vaulter

Now that grey fluff
covers my chest
and it's the glasses on my nose
that sparkle, not my eyes
what the horny girls
          want from me
is advice on
how to allure young men;
            those
10 with ideas in their head
and pimples on their ass,
my final opinion
on the Theaetetus

They say at my age
I should be guru or sage,
not foolishly behave
like passion's slave

Ignorant trulls
in a cold land;
age will dry their flesh   20
and wrinkle it with useless folds.
Spry and drugged with love
I pole-vault
           over my grave

(1974)   (1975)

The Unwavering Eye

Before my eyes
the green heads of drowned sailors
rise up and disappear at the water's edge;
the jagged stones on the beach
lie grey and menacing;
in the distance
the hills fold silently

into each other
to encircle the sea
like a Cyclops' hairy arm.   10

Above them, above ceaseless war,
the sun's glaucomic eye
journeys towards dissolution

Once, in a smiling bay
Nietzsche, hero and martyr,
beheld the gleaming spears
and shrieked, "Superman!"
He died innocent, a gentle lunatic

The abyss belched
and pulled him downward   20
by the two ends of his drooping moustache

Now I cannot look
at a solitary sunlit stone
and not think of Nietzsche's unwavering eye

(1974)   (1975)

The Human Cry

When young
I would shape carefully
                              my grief
if a friend died
or an old bookseller
I loved and admired
                         a dear aunt or cousin

I would gather
              my tears
into an urn   10

or channel them
             with honouring decorum
into elegies and songs
for the dark majestical cypresses
to iterate
          above sunlit Mediterranean graves

Now
       myself white-haired
and walking steadily
          into the mist   20
when someone dies
whom I knew way back
      a schoolfellow from Baron Byng
or the corner groceryman
            Pentelis Trogadis
I howl like a child
whose finger
      has been jammed
in the doorway

(1976)   (1976)

O Jerusalem

Jerusalem, you will be betrayed again and again:
not by the brave young men who die for you
with military cries on their blue lips
— never by these
         And never by the scholars
who know each sunken goat-track
that winds somehow into your legend, your great name
and not by those dreamers
            who looking for the beginnings
of your strange wizardry ascend from storied darkness   10
holding dust and warped harps in their blistered hands

These will always find you and bring you
offerings of blood and bone
                              lowering their grave eyes
as to an idol made neither of wood nor stone
nor brick nor any metal
                              yet clearly visible
as though sitting on a jewelled throne
                              O Jerusalem
you are too pure and break men's hearts   20
you are a dream of prophets, not for our clay,
and drive men mad by your promised
impossible peace, your harrowing oracles of love;
and how may we walk upon this earth
                              with forceful human stir
unless we adore you and betray?

(1976)   (1976)

Robertson Davies
1913 –

———◆———

BORN IN THAMESVILLE, Ontario, Robertson Davies was educated at
Queen's University and Oxford University. After working with the Old
Vic Repertory Company in London, he returned to Canada to become
literary editor of *Saturday Night* (1940-1942) and editor of the
Peterborough *Examiner* (1942-1960). He now teaches at the University
of Toronto and is Master of Massey College. The author of more than a
dozen plays including *Overlaid* (1949) and *Question Time* (1975), Davies
has also written six novels including a trilogy comprising *Fifth Business*
(1970), *The Manticore* (1972) and *World of Wonders* (1975). A collection
of essays on the art of reading was published in 1960 as *A Voice from the
Attic*.

From
A Voice from the Attic

True Humour Uncontrollable

THE SENSE OF humor, as opposed to the mere ability to see the point of a formal joke and laugh at it, cannot be dissociated from the rest of a man's personality. The fun of a bitter man, or a mean man, or a cruel man, is his sense of humor, true enough, but it is not something which we covet; a man's sense of humor is as clearly indicative of what he is as his grief, or his capacity to love. A great sense of humor can only exist in company with other elements of greatness.

Nor is a sense of humor something which can be turned on and off at the main. Many people believe that some subjects are humorous and others not. Aristotle, in his *Rhetoric,* quotes Gorgias Leontinus, whoever he may have been, very pointedly on this subject. "Humour is the only test of gravity and gravity of humour, for a subject which will not bear raillery is suspicious, and a jest which will not bear serious examination is false wit." In short, there is a time and place for jokes on every subject. But there are so many of these supposedly forbidden themes that much public joke-making is confined to a handful of subjects which vary from age to age — cuckoldry, excrement, and Latin puns in the eighteenth century; cheese, mothers-in-law, and onions in the nineteenth; these are fixed stars in the firmament of mechanical humor. But a sense of humor is not a thing which we can control completely; many people, in painful situations, have been overcome by a sense of the ridiculous, as was Bernard Shaw at his mother's funeral; sincere grief cannot utterly quell it. A man with a sense of humor may nevertheless be deeply serious in his attitude toward life. Stephen Leacock, writing of his imminent death, was serious, yet he wrote without losing his sense of humor, which was in that instance evidence of his courage. Such a man is no mere joker; his sense of humor is a glory which he carries with him to the end.

It is this uncontrollable quality which shocks people who have very little sense of humor of their own, and as a usual thing they reserve their highest admiration for people who are demonstrably and reliably serious — which frequently means merely solemn. Perhaps this is because humor is a thing of intellect rather than emotion, and people in general are more impressed by emotion than by intellect. And can we say that they are wrong? The deepest feelings of mankind are not humorous, and although Freud has shown the Unconscious to be pranksome and witty in a manner which suggests James Joyce, it is remorselessly serious in its effects. Humor is a civilizing element in the jungle of the mind, and civilizing elements never enjoy a complete or prolonged popularity.

Humor a Dangerous Profession

It is the uncontrollable quality of humor which makes it so dangerous as a profession. Robert Graves says, very justly, that the poet who seeks to live by poetry will certainly lose his gift, and the White Goddess will cease to smile upon him because she does not permit her lovers to count on her favors; that is why Graves earns his living as a writer of novels, and takes whatever comes to him through his poetry as luck money. I like his way of expressing this belief, and believe in it myself, but if it is too rich for your taste, let it be said that poetic inspiration cannot be forced, or compelled to flow tidily in the most profitable channels. This is true of humor, also. The man who sits down at his desk, saying "I shall have been funny to the extent of 1500 words before lunchtime," will shortly find himself grasping in desperation at mothers-in-law and onions. He will become the victim of a formula. Even so original and, at his best, brilliant a wit as S. J. Perelman cannot escape this professional hazard from time to time. It is one of the most striking elements in the career of James Thurber that he has been able, so far as I know, to avoid anything mechanical or forced; it is also observable that Thurber's output has not been large, which suggests great restraint on his part, for the demand that a humorist produce funny pieces is both pressing and flattering.

Career of a Popular Humorist

It may not be out of place here to consider the career of a humorist of great gifts who yielded to this demand. The late Stephen Leacock (1869-1944) was one of the most popular humorists of his time, and an examination of his work shows that he was, at his best, worthy of the admiration which was lavished on him. His humor was plenteous and bountiful, flowing in the greatest tradition, not of wit, not of irony or sarcasm, but of true and deep humor, the full and joyous recognition of the Comic Spirit at work in life. If a name must be attached to it, we may perhaps call it nonsense, that sudden upward flight from sobriety and fact which delights and illuminates. The word which occurs over and over again in contemporary references to his work and descriptions of his public lectures is "fun." It is a word which is somewhat out of favor at present, for in our nervous age fun is not well understood or valued. But the quality with which Leacock delighted his readers and convulsed his hearers – call it nonsense or fun – resists any accurate analysis.

He knew it very well. Consider this passage:

> Once I might have taken my pen in hand to write about humour with the confident air of the acknowledged professional. But that time is past. Such claim as I had has been taken from me. In fact, I stand unmasked. An English reviewer writing in a literary journal, the very name of which is enough to put contradiction to sleep, has said of my writing, "What is there, after all, in Professor Leacock's humour but a rather ingenious mixture of hyperbole and myosis?" The man was right. How he stumbled upon this trade secret, I do not know. But I am willing to admit, since the truth is out, that it has been my custom in preparing an article of a humorous nature, to go down to the cellar and mix up half a gallon of myosis with a pint of hyperbole. If I want to give the article a decided literary flavour, I find it well to put in about half a pint of paresis. The whole thing is amazingly simple.

Thus lightly he turns aside the comment of a critical jackass. On another occasion he offered this advice on writing. "Writing is no trouble: you just jot down ideas as they occur to you. The jotting is simplicity itself – it is the occurring which is difficult."

Oh, that he had left it at that! But in one of his worst books – the one called *How To Write* – he includes two embarrassing chapters on how to write humor. He could no more tell anybody else how to write humor than Jupiter could tell them how to turn into a bull or a swan, and for the same reason – it was his special gift, his godhead, not susceptible of analysis or explanation, and not communicable to anybody who wanted to be like him.

Leacock's first humorous book was *Literary Lapses,* which was published in 1910, when he was forty; he wrote fifty-seven books altogether, and though a few of these were works on political economy (the subject of which he was professor at McGill University in Montreal from 1908 to 1936), most of them were books of what he called "funny pieces." He was proud of this huge output – proud as only a Canadian who has also been a farmer can be of antlike industry for its own sake. All his life long he got up at five o'clock in the morning, to work. He declared proudly in *Who's Who* that he published at least one book every year from 1906 to 1936. That his work became mechanical and stale and that there was sometimes an hysterically forced note in his fun were less to him than that he wrote a funny book every year. In *Arcadian*

Adventures among the Idle Rich and *Moonbeams from the Larger Lunacy* he mocked industrialists who did not know how to relax, but he was quite as much under the compulsion to work, to produce, as they. He did it because it made money, of course, but also because he had an addicted public which would buy any book which had his name on it, and which seemed never to tire of fun which was in his vein, whether of the first sprightly running, or of the mere dregs. Every popular humorist has these uncritical readers; they are attracted to a writer by the special quality of his work, and they want that special thing repeated, even when it has grown forced or stale. To such readers nothing is more baffling than a writer who insists on trying something new, who experiments or improves. Is the writer to be blamed if he obliges them?

Not by me. There are critics who sit in judgment upon a writer's life, sagely putting a finger on the point where he went wrong, was false to himself, let popularity and the flattery of publishers and public lead him from the strait path. Let such critics look to their own careers, if they have indeed careers to look to. It would certainly be better if a writer like Leacock knew always what was best to do and what would look best in the eyes of posterity, but such unnatural foresight cannot be required of any man.

(1960)   (1960)

George Johnston
1913 –

———◆———

BORN IN HAMILTON, Ontario, George Johnston was educated at the University of Toronto and served as a pilot with the RCAF in the Second World War. After the war, he taught English at Mount Allison University and subsequently joined the Department of English at Carleton University. In addition to translations of *The Saga of Gisli* (1963) and *The Greenlanders' Saga* (1976), Johnston has published three volumes of poetry: *The Cruising Auk* (1959), *Home Free* (1966) and *Happy Enough: Poems 1935-1972* (1972).

The Pool

A boy gazing in a pool
Is all profound; his eyes are cool
And he's as though unborn, he's gone;
He's the abyss he gazes on.

A man searches the pool in vain
For his profundity again;
He finds it neither there nor here
And all between is pride and fear.

His eyes are warm with love and death,
Time makes a measure of his breath;   10
The world is now profound and he
Fearful, on its periphery.

(1959)   (1972)

Ice At Last

When ice at last has come across the pond
And the old angry sun dismissed himself
In roasted lobster colour;
When trees all bare divaricate their twigs
Against the salmon sky and then go black,
This is when the accomplished Mr Murple
Splendid on skates comes forth to spin the night
Upon his arms outstretched and whirling eyeballs.

Coffee drinkers fill the hut with steam;
They warm themselves within against the cold   10
That creaks without and circumvents the light,
While Mr Murple, in a cloud of frost
Centripetal,
Turns on his pivot skates the captive sky.

(1959)   (1972)

O Earth, Turn!

The little blessed Earth that turns   I love the slightly flattened sphere,
Does so on its own concerns   Its restless, wrinkled crust's my here,
As though it weren't my home at all; Its slightly wobbling spin's my now
It turns me winter, summer, fall   But not my why and not my how:
Without a thought of me.   My why and how are me.   10

(1959)   (1972)

Old-Fashioned Chords

The rain rains in its never-ending way
And someone is playing jazz in an empty hall
    Among the trees;
Mid-afternoon of a long day
And through the leaves come the old-fashioned chords.

The music comforts itself
For some old-fashioned nagging foolishness,
Confessing what no confessor will hear one say
    Not about sin or guilt
    Existence or any of that,   10
Just some remembering of good times gone
That wont come back again ever, gone to stay.

(1966)   (1972)

Remembrance

Every November eleventh after the leaves have gone,
After the heat of summer when the heats of winter come on,
Ghosts from all over the country drift to the capital then
To see what we do to remember, we left-over Ottawa men,
We veterans and near veterans left over from obsolete wars,
Hitler's war and the Kaiser's and that ancient one with the Boers;

They haunt Confederation Square to see what we do
But it cant be very exciting, there's never anything new;
Year after year we gather and shout commands in the Square,
Wait for the Governor-General, say a few words of prayer,   10
Lay our wreaths in order, mothers and big shots first,
In memory of those who have made it to the other side of
    the worst
And left us righteous survivors in the world they thought they
    might save,
Blowing our bugles and noses and making ourselves feel brave,
And not only brave but prudent, and not only prudent but wise.
Go to sleep ghosts, we say, and wave our wise good-byes.

(1966)   (1972)

Spring Moon

Moon in a town sky,
Half shut, dark one way from the middle,
Above a creek with spring peepers.

Homeward all alone, after joy,
Hands in pockets, making a thoughtful way
Over the bridge, down the street.

No voices, no women,
Only peepers,
And a solemn unsteadiness of all things.

(1966)   (1972)

Wild Apples

Gone back to the wild   Afternoon
these apples   unhurried

that round sour-skinned   in dark heat
out of their leafage.   gnaws at them.

(1972)   (1972)

Douglas Le Pan
1914 –

BORN IN TORONTO, Douglas Le Pan received his B.A. from the University of Toronto in 1935 and continued his studies at Oxford. During World War II he served in the Canadian Army and since then he has held many university and diplomatic positions. Le Pan's first volume of poems, *The Wounded Prince and Other Poems,* appeared in 1948 and a second collection, *The Net and the Sword,* won the Governor General's Award in 1953.

One of the Regiment

In this air
Breathed once by artist and *condottier,*
Where every gesture of proud men was nourished,
Where the sun described heroic virtue and flourished
Round it trumpet-like, where the face of nature
Was chiselled by bright centuries hard as sculpture;
His face on this clear air and arrogant scene,
Decisive and impenetrable, is Florentine.

Where every hill
Is castled, he stands like a brooding tower; his will   10
An angry shadow on this cloudless sky,
Gold with the dust of many a panoply
And blazonings burnt up like glittering leaves;
His only cognizance his red-patched sleeves;
Fair hair his helmet; his glancing eye, the swagger
Of his stride are gallant's sword and dagger.

And in his mind
The sifting, timeless sunlight would not find
Memories of stylish Florence or sacked Rome,
Rather the boyhood that he left at home;   20
Skating at Scarborough, summers at the Island,

These are the dreams that float beyond his hand,
Green, but estranged across a moat of flame;
And now all bridges blown the way he came.

No past, no future
That he can imagine. The fiery fracture
Has snapped that armour off and left his bare
Inflexible, dark frown to pluck and stare
For some suspected rumour that the brightness sheds
Above the fruit-trees and the peasants' heads   30
In this serene, consuming lustrousness
Where trumpet-tongues have died, and all success.

Do not enquire
What he has seen engrained in stillest fire
Or what he purposes. It will be well.
We who have shared his exile can trumpet-tell
That underneath his wild and frowning style
Such eagerness has burned as could not smile
From coats of lilies or emblazoned roses.
No greater excellence the sun encloses.   40

(1948)   (1948)

The Wounded Prince

In the eye is the wound.

Lancings of pity, blades of sensual disappointment
Have pierced the delicate pupil.
Transfixed, the bird of heavenly airs
Is struck at sundown,
Entering the leafy wood, under the heavy lintel.

Gathered in that point all sharp humiliations;
The strokes converge.
The feathered dreams fly home from fruitless voyages.
Light needles.   10
Still to and fro they hawk their costliest plumage.

In your dear eye....

The dark scar sings from the wanton thicket
Its princely grief;
Sets up in perilous leaves the crest of bravery;
Impaled, sings on;
Will not disown its fettering crest and crown;

So that what never could be dreamt of has been made.
From target's puny eye
Such liquid compass of this wide, aerial gaze;   20
From wounds, from wounds
By love inflicted, this strict and healing blade.

(1948)   (1948)

Coureurs De Bois

Thinking of you, I think of the *coureurs de bois,*
Swarthy men grown almost to savage size
Who put their brown wrists through the arras of the woods
And were lost — sometimes for months. Word would come back:
One had been seen at Crêve-cœur, deserted and starving,
One at Sault Sainte Marie shouldering the rapids.
Giant-like, their labours stalked in the streets of Quebec
Though they themselves had dwindled in distance: names only;
Rumours; quicksilvery spies into nature's secrets;
Rivers that seldom ran in the sun.   Their resource   10
Would sparkle and then flow back under clouds of hemlock.

So you should have travelled with them.   Or with La Salle.
He could feed his heart with the heart of a continent,
Insatiate, how noble a wounded animal,
Who sought for his wounds the balsam of adventure,
The sap from some deep, secret tree.   But now
That the forests are cut down, the rivers charted,
Where can you turn, where can you travel?   Unless
Through the desperate wilderness behind your eyes,
So full of falls and glooms and desolations,   20
Disasters I have glimpsed but few would dream of,

You seek new Easts.   The coats of difficult honour,
Bright with brocaded birds and curious flowers,
Stowed so long with vile packs of pemmican,
Futile, weighing you down on slippery portages,
Would flutter at last in the courts of a clement country,
Where the air is silken, the manners easy,
Under a guiltless and reconciling sun.

You hesitate.   The trees are entangled with menace.
The voyage is perilous into the dark interior.   30
But then your hands go to the thwarts.   You smile.   And so
I watch you vanish in a wood of heroes,
Wild Hamlet with the features of Horatio.

(1948)   (1948)

A Country without a Mythology

No monuments or landmarks guide the stranger
Going among this savage people, masks
Taciturn or babbling out an alien jargon
And moody as barbaric skies are moody.

Berries must be his food.   Hurriedly
He shakes the bushes, plucks pickerel from the river,
Forgetting every grace and ceremony,
Feeds like an Indian, and is on his way.

And yet, for all his haste, time is worth nothing.
The abbey clock, the dial in the garden,   10
Fade like saints' days and festivals.
Months, years, are here unbroken virgin forests.

There is no law – even no atmosphere
To smooth the anger of the flagrant sun.
November skies sting sting like icicles.
The land is open to all violent weathers.

Passion is not more quick.   Lightnings in August
Stagger, rocks split, tongues in the forest hiss,

As fire drinks up the lovely sea-dream coolness.
This is the land the passionate man must travel.   20

Sometimes — perhaps at the tentative fall of twilight —
A belief will settle that waiting around the bend
Are sanctities of childhood, that melting birds
Will sing him into a limpid gracious Presence.

The hills will fall in folds, the wilderness
Will be a garment innocent and lustrous
To wear upon a birthday, under a light
That curls and smiles, a golden-haired Archangel.

And now the channel opens.   But nothing alters.
Mile after mile of tangled struggling roots,   30
Wild-rice, stumps, weeds, that clutch at the canoe,
Wild birds hysterical in tangled trees.

And not a sign, no emblem in the sky
Or boughs to friend him as he goes; for who
Will stop where, clumsily constructed, daubed
With war-paint, teeters some lust-red manitou?

(1948)   (1948)

The Net and the Sword

Who could dispute his choice
That in the nets and toils of violence
Strangled his leafing voice
Enforced his own compassionate heart to silence,
Hunted no more to find the untangling word
And took a short, straight sword?

In this sandy arena, littered
And looped with telephone wires, tank-traps, mine-fields,
Twining about the embittered
Debris of history, the people whom he shields   10
Would quail before a stranger if they could see
His smooth as silk ferocity.

Where billowing skies suspend
Smoke-latticed rumours, enmeshed hypotheses
And mad transmitters send
Impossible orders on crossed frequencies,
His eyes thrust concentrated and austere.
Behind his lids, the skies are clear.

Not that he ever hopes
To strike the vitals of the knotted cloud.   20
But, to the condemned, those ropes
At least let in the sun. And he, grown proud,
Among the sun's bright retinue would die,
Whose care is how they fall, not why.

(1953)   (1953)

Stragglers

Suddenly he stopped running.
The air was breathless, spiked with thorn,
oak-leaves rattling from dead branches,
the scene so ruinous
a king's crown might have been found on a bush.

All he could feel was cold and pain.
Touch he had discarded like an empty cartouche-
box. For a while he could hear the angry owl,
but now not that, nothing.
Cold had burned him down to the bone.   10

He stood stock-still, like a skeleton, waiting.
Where were all his companions?
the lovely disguises that had deserted him one by one
since the sauve-qui-peut and the terrible rout.
Could they ever rejoin him as stragglers?

They had left him — his crimson sensual coat,
his suit of leaves like a man from the woods,
even the rich filigree of nerves —
left him.... Or had he left *them*?
given them up as alms to the wolves?   20

He didn't know. He was waiting.
Then like caribou over the tundra
came shambling the rags of a former richness:
a coat that once had been sleek and scarlet
but weatherbeaten now, torn, tattered

and folding itself against the cold;
and another disguise in dull rifle green
that seemed to be full of menace,
seemed now a spirit of destruction only
shorn of its old wild ambiguity.   30

They wouldn't approach too close,
these and other familiar wraiths,
but hung in the air like gaunt ruins
of a wardrobe. And he was powerless
to call or summon.

But the air seemed suddenly milder.
If a bird should sing
or a breeze breathe lightly over his hand
a word might come that would allow them to sign
a sorrowful injured concordat.   40

(1971)

Claire Martin
1914 –

———————◆———————

BORN IN QUEBEC, Claire Martin, a pseudonym of Claire (Montreuil)
Faucher, was educated in convent schools and later began a career in
radio broadcasting. After her marriage in 1945, she lived in Ottawa
and published her first book, *Avec ou sans amour*, in 1959. Since the
appearance of this collection of short stories she has published several
novels including *Doux-amer* (1960). Two volumes of autobiography,

Dans un gant de fer (1965) and *La Joue droite* (1966), have been translated by Philip Stratford under the title *In an Iron Glove* (1968). Since 1972, Martin has made her home in France and has been active as a playwright and as a translator of Inuit narratives.

You Muffed It

BEFORE ME ON the table are those letters you wrote me. Half a dozen of them. That was pretty good going when, after all, you only say one solitary thing in them, to wit, that you only wanted to make me jealous. Only!

These six letters, my dear, especially the last, demonstrate such an ignorance in affairs of the heart that I have reversed my decision to leave them unanswered. You make me wince. If you carry on this way you will never go far in your chosen career. Unless you start specializing in boarding-school girls, in which case I wish you luck. Otherwise I think you stand in great need of a little sermon. In this you must admire my generosity, for what I am about to teach you will never get you anywhere with me. You can rest absolutely easy on that score.

When I fell in love with you (I'm ashamed to have to write that), I believed you to be one of those beings, as the saying goes, whose sandals one is unworthy to unlatch. You are intelligent, you are handsome, you are clever. You are neither irascible, grasping or moody. You seem to be, as English girls say, "eligible" in every respect. From our very first meeting you struck me as too good to be true, the kind of man one dreams of winning when one is just turning fifteen. Everyone makes mistakes.

During the first months of our great romance you were everything a woman could wish in a man: tender, attentive, faithful, indulgent. With you, love was never simply a laughing matter, nor was it a medieval dungeon, two extreme ways of treating it that are equally insufferable.

In short, it may seem that I should have been satisfied with all those perfections. Needless to say, you agree entirely. Permit me to differ. Knowing how hard any fault is to bear, I scarcely know which one I might have wished you afflicted with. But your affliction is no simple fault, it's an attitude that is made up of a whole string of them. Which ones? My God, you'll jump when you hear this, so let's just say quickly that you are sadistic, egotistical, and mediocre; that you are stony-hearted and unscrupulous.

I should have suspected something when we had that little talk about the part jealousy plays in love. You expressed ideas that displeased me greatly, yet by some curious aberration on my part I dismissed them as empty words. Sometimes even the most intelligent let themselves go so far as to champion indefensible ideas just for the sport of it. You see, I was looking for ways to excuse you, and I found them, I loved you so.

However, the evening I arrived at our friends' house to find you, flirtatious and eager-eyed, sidling up to that big half-naked brunette, I was, I admit, really shocked. And I was jealous, oh yes, never doubt it. But don't expect me to go into details, I'm not writing this for your pleasure.

Let's get back to the brunette. Looking more closely I could see she was magnificent. Perhaps you hadn't even noticed, since she was just part of your game. I told myself you had fallen into temptation, that you were just a poor weak man and that you'd be grateful to me in the end if I seemed to have noticed nothing. The heart is one thing, of course, but the body's another. I was in love with a man, I wasn't going to turn him in on an angel. Let the brunette pass, I'd close my eyes as tight as possible.

This little game would start up again every time we were invited out to the same party. You'd go directly to the most beautiful woman in the room and lay siege to her. Only in appearance, you say in your letters. You swear you never saw any of them again. Then you must have made some enemies, my friend. Men have a very colourful word for women who lure them on for nothing. Since our sex hasn't had much need of the term, women have neglected to find a male equivalent. But if you get in the habit of going on with these little exercises, they may invent one, just for you.

The morning after such performances you would telephone me, as tender and as fervent as ever. I didn't dare complain and would have been ashamed to show my jealousy. Until the day you burst out in exasperation, "But what's wrong? Don't you ever get jealous?" Would you believe it, jealousy dropped from me on the spot. And at the same instant I stopped loving you. Thereafter, cry, shout, beg as you might, it was no use. Once love has taken off, there's no sense panting after it. Poor dear thing, and to think of all that song-and-dance you got up!

You write: "I wanted to frighten you. I wanted you to suffer because of me. I wanted you to love me even more." You go on interminably, explaining your little psychology to me, your little way of looking at things, your little excuses. You tell me I should be more indulgent, more understanding. You even have the nerve to say I should be flattered. Really, that's the last straw.

I am not flattered, I am badly humiliated. You are a mediocrity, and I let myself love you. There's nothing very flattering in that, I assure you. I am humiliated to have loved a man ready to do anything to achieve his ends. And when I think that those ends were nothing more than the petty satisfaction of your vanity! You wanted to be able to think, "This very moment a woman is shedding hot tears for me." And to reach that end, it was all the same to you to sow discord in the red-head's marriage, start tongues wagging against the blonde and make the brunette fall in love with you for nothing. Did you ever think of that?

And not once, I am sure, during what you call this psychological experiment, did you ever think what I was suffering by putting yourself in my place. The only way you ever thought of that was as it excited or flattered you. And you did it all deliberately. You make me vomit. To be loved more, yet more, and still more, for one aim, for your own pleasure, your own satisfaction, your own vanity, you hadn't the slightest scruple about torturing me, and you would have gone on for years or as long as the game had gone on pleasing you. What a pretty scheme! Well, you poor thing, you muffed it.

As for your little wind-off where you claim you can't go on living without me, allow me to take it for what it's worth. Yes, and by heaven, in case you mean it seriously, just let me say it's equilaterally indifferent to me. Go right ahead. What's more, you can even muff that if you want. I don't give a sweet damn.

(1959)   (1977)

PHILIP STRATFORD (TR)

W. O. Mitchell
1914 –

———————◆———————

WILLIAM ORMOND MITCHELL was born in Weyburn, Saskatchewan, and educated at the Universities of Manitoba and Alberta. After teaching school in Alberta for several years, Mitchell began a full-time career as a writer and published his first novel, *Who Has Seen the Wind,* in 1947.

He has since published two other novels, *The Kite* (1962) and *The Vanishing Point* (1973), and a collection of stories, *Jake and the Kid* (1961), which won a Leacock Medal for Humour.

The Liar Hunter

IF THERE IS anything folks are more fussy about than their own kids, Jake says, it is the truth. They will get pretty snuffy if someone tells them they haven't got any too good a grip on the truth. Jake ought to know; sometimes he will give the truth a stretch or two, but not like Old Man Gatenby. When Jake is done with her she will snap back into place; with Old Gate she is stretched for good.

Old Man Gatenby lives on his half section down Government Road from us, him and his daughter, Molly. He is about 40% wheat farmer, Jake says, 30% plain liar, and 30% magnifying glass. Even so, folks don't call him a liar. Not with the temper he's got.

Truth is a real handy thing to have lying around, Jake says, but sometimes a little of her will go a long ways. Miss Henchbaw at Rabbit Hill says Jake makes too little go too long a ways. You would expect her to say that. She is a teacher. She wouldn't be so fussy about the truth if she had got mixed up with Mr. Godfrey last summer.

Mr. Godfrey was the fellow came out West to visit with Molly Gatenby, and it was him gave Old Gate the worst dose of the truth that he ever got. Jake and me saw him the first day he was in town, because Old Man Gatenby was busy finishing up his crop and he asked us to give Mr. Godfrey a lift out from town. We did.

Without those glasses and that pale sort of a skin he had he would have been a nice-looking fellow. His eyes put me in mind of Mr. Cameron's when he goes on about the flesh being so awful and the spirit being so dandy – dark and burny. Whenever he would say anything the words came out real far apart, like flies he was picking off fly-paper. He was all the time clearing his throat just before he said something. He could have been a consolidated school principal.

He was just the kind of fellow you would expect Molly to run with, her being so schoolteacher serious too. It is funny for Old Gate to have a daughter like Molly. Her eyes are not old-timer eyes. Her face is not all creased up like some brown paper you crumple in your hand and then try to smooth out. Her eyes will put you in mind of those violets that are tangled up in prairie grass along about the end of April.

I guess she is the violet and Old Gate is the dead grass. That's how they are.

Until we were out of Crocus, with Baldy's hind quarters tipping up and down real regular and telephone poles stretching clear to the horizon, Mr. Godfrey didn't say anything. Then he cleared his throat and said:

"The smallness of man — the prairies bring it to one with — such impact — it — is almost the catharsis of tragedy."

A jack rabbit started up to the left of the road, went over the prairie in a sailing bounce. "Huh!" Jake said.

"Catharsis — cleansing — as in the Greek tragedy — cathartic."

"Oh," Jake said, "that. Thuh alkali water sure is fear..."

"Oh, no," Mr. Godfrey said. "I mean that it — has a..."

"Prairie's scarey," I said.

"Yes." He looked down at me. "That's it — exactly it."

"I heard yuh was one of them prefessers," Jake said. He spit curvy into the breeze. "Ain't diggin' in thuh bank of thuh Brokenshell, are yuh?" He meant where they're getting those bones — the big ones that are older than anything.

"I dig," Mr. Godfrey said, "in a manner of speaking — but for folklore."

"Whut kinda ore?"

"Lore. Folklore — art — the common people..."

"That's real nice." Jake jiggled the lines at Baldy's rump. "Who the heck is Art an' what's this all about?"

"Why — I..." He cleared his throat. "I look for songs — ballads that have — that express the life of the Old West."

" 'Baggage Coach Behin' the Train'?" Jake said. " 'Where Do the Flies Go in the Wintertime?' "

"But — mostly stories," Mr. Godfrey said, "tall tales."

"Is that right?" Jake looked real pleased, and he cleared his throat the way he does before he starts to yarn.

"I'm looking for liars," Mr. Godfrey said.

Those dark, hungry eyes were staring right at Jake.

Jake swallowed. "Yuh don't hafta look at me!"

"Sorry."

"You bin talkin' to Miss Henchbaw!"

"Do you think that she might help me?..."

"Her! Truthfullest woman we got aroun' here — next tuh Molly Gatenby. Why, she..."

"Would you consider Mr. Gatenby a good source — of tall tales?"

"All depends," Jake said. "Anythin' Gate tells yuh, she's blowed up to about four times natural size. You take hailstones — "

"A chronic liar."

"Say!" Jake jumped. "Jist who do you – oh – yuh mean Gate."

"Interesting type."

"How many kindsa liars you turned up so far?"

"There's the defensive liar – and the occasional liar. I mentioned the chronic liar. The pragmatic or practical liar. I'm looking for the creative liar, of course."

"Oh – a-course," Jake said. "About Gate – I wouldn't like tuh say he lied exactly – jist sorta deckerates thuh truth a bit." He looked away from Mr. Godfrey's eyes. "That's all." He looked back to Mr. Godfrey. "Tell me somethin'. You ever run intuh any trouble with folks?"

"Not yet," said Mr. Godfrey.

"Well, young fella," Jake said, "ye're gonna."

The rest of the way home we just rolled along with the buckboard wheels sort of grinding. A gopher squeaked a couple of times. The way it is in fall, the air was just like soda pop. Every once in a while would come a tickle to your nose or your forehead, and you would brush at it, only it would keep right on tickling. You couldn't see the spider webs floating on the air, except where sunshine caught onto them and slid down. Mr. Godfrey had a lost look on his face whilst he stared off to the horizon with its straw-stacks curling their smoke into the soft blue sky.

At Gatenby's corner Mr. Godfrey said thanks very much, and Jake looked like he was going to say something, then he seemed to change his mind and clucked at Baldy instead. Just before we turned in, Jake said: "I kin har'ly wait fer Gate tuh come over fer rummy tuhmorra night."

But Old Gate didn't come till a week later, and when he got to our place he wasn't joking about how he'd nail Jake's hide to a fence post. All the time he played rummy he kept drumming his fingers on the kitchen table. I saw him miss the Queen of Hearts for a run and the ten of spades to make up three of a kind. Jake marked down 45 against Gate.

"Ain't doing so smart tuhnight, Gate."

"Deal them there cards."

"Yore deal, Gate."

Gate started in shuffling the cards, all the time chewing so his chin come up almost to his nose.

Jake picked up the first card Gate dealt. "Looks like a early winter."

"Leave them cards lie till I git 'em dealt!" Gate said it real short. Then, " 'Tain't polite."

Jake didn't say anything at all.

Gate lost the whole game. When Jake shoved him the cards to deal a new hand, he said:

"Tuh hell with her, Jake."

"Ain't yuh feelin' so good, Gate?"

"Feelin' good!" Gate's voice cracked. He leaned across the table. "Right now you are lookin' a teetotal nervous wreck right between the eyes!"

"Now – that's too –"

"My nerves – plum onstrung – hangin' lose as thuh fringe on a Indian jacket. I tripped in 'em three times yesterday between thuh hog pens an' thuh stock trough. An – "

"I wouldn't take on like that, Gate," Jake said. "Yuh gotta relax."

"Take on! Relax! 'Tain't no skin offa yore knuckles! 'Tain't you she's callin' a liar – in yer own house – in fronta yer own daughter!"

Jake's mouth dropped open. "Did he do that, Gate?"

"He might as well an' be done with her!"

"Either he did," Jake said, "er he didn't. Whatta yuh mean?"

"Look," Mr. Gatenby said, "he's got him a little black notebook – keeps her in his hip pocket – every time I open my mouth, he opens that there notebook! ' 'Member thuh winter of o' six,' I sez. Out comes thuh notebook. 'Is it a fact?' he sez. 'Certain'y is,' I sez. Bang, he snaps her shet – me too. Can't git another word outa me! Like thrashin' – ready tuh roll an' he ups an' throws a ball of binder twine intuh thuh cylinders. 'Is it a fact?' he sez. Whut's he think I'm gonna tell him thuh fat-brained, stoop-shouldered – "

"Now – ain't that cathartic."

Old Gate stared at Jake.

"New way of sayin' she's tragical," Jake said quick.

Gate grunted. "I'll tell yuh one thing fer certain – they ain't gonna be no liar hunters tied up with thuh Gatenby outfit."

He meant it.

A couple of nights later I heard Ma and my Aunt Margaret talking whilst they were giving the baby his bath. Aunt Margaret stays with us whilst her husband is in the Navy. My dad fights too; he fights for the South Saskatchewans. It is Aunt Margaret's baby.

I heard her say, "With Herbert gathering this folklore, she's ashamed of her own father."

"Ashamed of her father!" Ma said.

"I hope nothing comes of it," Aunt Margaret said. "It would – "

"You can let his head back now." Ma looked at Aunt Margaret whilst she wrung out the washcloth. "Molly's nobody's fool. Her heart isn't going to break in a hurry. In many ways she's her father's daughter."

"A liar, Ma?"

"She is not! Don't you dare use that word again! That wood box – "

"I already filled it."

"Help Jake with the cream then."

I told Jake all about it. I said, "There's a dustup coming over to Gatenby's, Jake."

"Is there, now?" Jake said.

"Molly isn't so fussy about Mr. Godfrey makin' out her father's a – a – what he's makin' him out to be."

"A tradegy," Jake said, "to give a Greek thuh heartburn."

But a week later Jake was laughing on the other side of his face, when the whole works came over to our place to visit. That was the night Mr. Godfrey said something about how hot it had been down East that summer.

"Hot here too," Jake said. For a minute he worked on his teeth with a sharpened matchstick and then he said. "Take thuh second week in July – tar paper on thuh roof of thuh chicken house – she all bubbled up."

"Did it really?" said Mr. Godfrey. On the chair beside him was Molly, sitting straight up like she expected something to happen, and she wanted to be ready to take off quick. Old Gate he'd hardly said anything since they came, just stared at the gas lamp in the centre of the kitchen table.

"Bubbled right up," Jake said. "Noon of thuh second day, wispy sorta smoke was coming off of her."

"That a fact?"

Jake gave a little start like he'd stuck himself with the point of the matchstick. "Why – certain'y," he said.

"Herbert – please!" Molly said it the way Ma talks when she's holding in before company. I took a good look at her then, and I couldn't see where she was like Old Gate. Take her hair in that lamplight, real pretty – yellow as a strawstack with the sun lying on it. Take her mouth, the way it is so red; take her all around she is pretty as a sorrel colt. Gate is enough to give a gopher the heartburn.

" – a hawin' an' a cawin' jist as I come out," Jake was saying. "That there tar paper on thuh hen house roof was so sticky thuh dumb fool crow had got himself stuck up in it. Real comical he was – liftin' one foot an' then thuh other. Course she was kinda tragical too – that there tar was hot. Musta bin kinda painful."

"Why – that's a wonderful – "

Molly cleared her throat, sort of warning; Mr. Godfrey quit reaching for his hip pocket.

"Inside of 10 minnits," Jake went on, "a whole flocka crows was circlin' over, the way they will when they hear another in trouble, an' buhfore I knew it thuh whole roof was stuck up with crows somethin' fearful."

"Herbert!" Mr. Godfrey had his notebook out and was opening it on his knee. He didn't pay any attention to Molly and the funny look she had on her face.

"Aflutterin' an' ahollerin', with their wings aslapping – our hen house sort of liftin' an' then settlin' back agin. I headed fer thuh woodpile."

"What for, Jake?" I said.

"Axe – wasn't gonna let that hen house go without a fight. I chopped thuh roof loose from thuh uprights an' away she went. Cleared thuh peak of thuh barn an' headed south."

Molly was standing up and she was looking down at Mr. Godfrey writing away like anything. Her face looked kind of white to me. "It's about time we were going," she said real soft.

"But we've just come!" Mr. Godfrey said. "This is the sort of thing I – "

"Folklore!" Molly said it like a cuss word.

Mr. Godfrey smiled and nodded his head and turned to Jake. "How long after the first crow came did – "

"Let her go fer tuhnight," Jake said.

"Don't look now," Molly said with her voice tight, "but I'm tired and sick of being Exhibit A for the common people. Any time you feel you can – "

"Oh, no, Molly," Mr. Godfrey said, "you don't und – "

"I'm afraid I do. These happen to be my people. They – "

"No call tuh fly off of thuh handle," Jake told her.

"A little more tact on your part, Jake, wouldn't have hurt at all!"

"Me – I didn't do nothin'. That there story – "

"Just a tall tale," Molly cut in on him, "like the thousands I've listened to all my life. I'm funny, but – "

"You shore are!" Jake said.

"There isn't any harm in them," Ma said.

"What makes it worse," Molly said, "is they have no – no point – useless – utterly senseless and – immoral!"

"I can explain what it is that – " Mr. Godfrey began.

"You've been our guest!" Molly turned on him. "Not for one minute have you stopped insinuating that my – "

"I haven't been making any – "

"You certainly have!"

"Will you let me explain?"

"It's a little late for that!"

"It shore is!" Jake was mad. "Standin' there on yer hind feet an' sayin' I'm senseless an' useless an – an' im – immortal!"

"Please, Jake." That was Ma.

I got a look at Gate, and he had a grin clear across his face.

"That story about them – "

"Was a lie, Jake Trumper! However you want – "

"Are you callin' me a liar?" Jake he was off of the wood box.

"I hate to do it," Molly said, "but you asked for it, Jake. You are the biggest...two-handed...clod-busting liar I have ever known!"

The kitchen clock ticked real loud against the silence. I could hear Jake's breath whistling in his nose.

"With one exception," Molly said. "My dad." She turned to Old Gate. "Take me home!"

I knew then what Ma meant; she is Gate's daughter all right. I felt kind of sorry for Mr. Godfrey.

I felt even more sorry for him the day me and Jake went into Crocus for Ma's groceries. He was standing beside some yellow suitcases inside of MacTaggart's, right by the door. Halfway down the counter was Molly; she stayed there.

"Hullo," Jake said. "You catchin' thuh four-ten?"

"Yes," Mr. Godfrey said.

"Sorry tuh see yuh go."

"You're alone in your sentiment."

"Huh?"

"I say – you're the only one who is."

"Oh – I wouldn't – "

"I would," Mr. Godfrey said. "I've made a mess of things, and there's no use pretending I haven't." He was staring at Jake that way I told you about. I sort of fiddled with a double-oh gopher trap hanging down from the counter. Mr. Godfrey looked past Jake to Molly by the canned tomatoes. She turned away. "I'd like to tell you something before I go."

"Shoot," Jake said.

"Somethin' fer yuh tuhday?" That was Mr. MacTaggart, who had come out from the back and was leaning across the counter to Molly.

"My work is important," Mr. Godfrey said. "I'm not just a – a liar hunter simply." He was real serious. He wasn't looking at Jake.

"Any apples in?" Molly said.

"Apples," Mr. MacTaggart said, and wrote it down with his stubby pencil, then looked up at Molly for what was next.

"What I do is important. Important as history is important." Mr. Godfrey wasn't dropping his words in relays now, but talking straight along, maybe because he was so darn serious.

"Gee!" I said, "you should hear how Jake wrassled Looie Riel an' – "

"Hold her, Kid!"

"Not the history of great and famous men," Mr. Godfrey explained, "but of the lumberjacks and section men, hotel-keepers and teachers and ranchers and farmers. The people that really count."

"And – a tin of blackstrap," Molly said it to Mr. MacTaggart, but she was looking at Mr. Godfrey. She didn't sound like she was so fussy about getting any molasses.

"Their history isn't to be found in records or in books."

"This here Ontario cheese is real nice."

"Their history is in the stories they tell – their tall tales. That's why I gather – "

"Good an' nippy."

"And a pound of cheese," Molly said.

"And I can tell you why they lie," Mr. Godfrey said.

"Anythin' else?" Mr. MacTaggart said.

"If you're interested," Mr. Godfrey said.

"That'll be nice," Jake said.

"Was there somethin' else?" Mr. MacTaggart asked.

"This is a hard country, I don't have to tell you that. There are – drouth, blizzards, loneliness. A man is a pretty small thing out on all this prairie. He is at the mercy of the elements. He's a lot like – like a – "

"Fly on a platter," I said.

"Was there somethin' else yuh wanted?" said Mr. MacTaggart.

"That's right," Mr. Godfrey said. "These men lie about the things that hurt them most. Their yarns are about the winters and how cold they are the summers and how dry they are. In this country you get the deepest snow, the worst dust storms, the biggest hailstones."

"Mebbe yuh didn't hear me – " Mr. MacTaggart said to Molly – "Was there somethin' more yuh wanted?"

"Rust and dust and hail and sawfly and cutworm and drouth are terrible things, but not half as frightening if they are made ridiculous. If a man can laugh at them he's won half the battle. When he exaggerates things he isn't lying really; it's a defence, the defence of exaggeration. He can either do that or squeal." Mr. Godfrey picked up his bags and started for the door.

"Whilst you stand there makin' up yer mind," Mr. MacTaggart said, "I'll get tuh Mrs. Totcoal's order."

"People in this country aren't squealers." Mr. Godfrey was standing in the doorway.

"You go ahead with the Totcoal order," Molly said to Mr. MacTaggart with her eyes on Mr. Godfrey. She walked right up to him and she looked right at him. "I think I've just made up my mind."

"Hey!" yelled Mr. MacTaggart, "not right in front of – "

"Jist a new kinda hist'ry," Jake said, "gonna tickle Old Gate right up the back."

"Oh!" Molly turned around. "I'd – what are we – what about Dad! He said if Herbert ever – "

"Mr. Godfrey better come out with us," Jake said. "Don't you tell yer paw anythin' about him still bein' here. Jist say ye're invited over to our place fer tuhnight. I got me a notion." Jake leaned down and picked up Mr. Godfrey's bags. "I got me a notion about what makes Old Gate tick."

At our barn Jake told me to beat it and I did. Him and Mr. Godfrey were in there for quite a while. Me, I was wondering what made Old Man Gateby tick. I didn't find out till that night.

Gate got quite a start when he saw Mr. Godfrey.

"Ain't you went yet?" he said.

"I – I missed the train," Mr. Godfrey said. That was his first lie, what you might call a warming-up lie. Molly's face got kind of red. Gate he settled back in his chair like he was ready for a tough evening.

"Never fergit thuh year hoppers was so bad," Jake said. "Blacked out thuh sun complete."

"This district had them terribly, I understand," Mr. Godfrey said. "Of course they weren't so big, were they?"

"Big!" Jake said. "One of 'em lit on thuh airport at Broomhead an' a RAF fella run 100 gallons a gas intuh him afore he reelized – "

"Albin!" Mr. Godfrey said – "Albin Hobblemeyer, they called that grasshopper. I have him in my files. Three years ago he – "

"Is that a fact?" Jake said.

"They named him as soon as he set foot in the district, after a man named Hobblemeyer – squashed him to death. Matter of fact he's upset a number of the investigators digging for prehistoric remains in the bank of the Brokenshell. They're not so sure that – "

"Yuh mean – mebbe them Brokenshell bones belonged to the great great gran'daddies of that there hopper?" Jake said.

"He was that big," Mr. Godfrey said. "When he leaped, the back lash from his shanks licked up the topsoil for miles behind him and the tumbleweeds – "

"Say – " Old Gate was on the edge of his chair.

"He spit tobacco juice and smeared over an entire schoolhouse just newly painted. Naturally he caused a lot of excitement. People were worried sick. They couldn't destroy him – bullets, buckshot just bounced off his chitinous hide, and people began to wonder what it would be like when he – "

"That's a pretty feeble – " Gate started in.

" – began to lay eggs. They decided the only thing they could do would be to keep it on the hop."

"Why, Mr. Godfrey?" I asked.

"A grasshopper has to dig a hole and back into it before it can lay. It was unfortunate that there was a man in the district named – uh – "

"Dewdney," Jake said. "Wasn't there a fella name of – "

Gate, he had a funny look on his face, like a fellow wanting a swim real bad but not wanting to take the jump. "Ain't no fella name a Dewdney in Broomhead. There's Dooley — got one leg shorter than thuh other — one-an'-a-half-step Dooley."

"That was the man," Mr. Godfrey said, and Old Gate looked startled. "A very close man who had wanted to dig himself a reservoir to catch the spring run-off and couldn't bring himself to laying out the money it would cost. He couldn't resist the temptation to let the grasshopper dig it for him."

Gate's mouth dropped open and stayed that way.

"Unfortunately," Mr. Godfrey said, "Albin laid an egg."

Gate swallowed. "Tell me," he said, "jist — how — how big an egg would a hopper like that lay?"

"Quite round," Mr. Godfrey said, "and about the size of the average chicken house. Mr. — uh — "

"Dooley," Gate said kind of dazed.

" — he tried to crack it with an axe, and succeeded only in throwing his right shoulder out of joint when the axe bounced off the egg."

"I'll be — "

"He decided then to pile birch chunks around it and in that way — uh — fry it — so that it couldn't hatch. As soon as he had the wood lighted he got frantic as he thought that perhaps the heat might only speed up the hatching. So he put the fire out."

"What thuh hell did he do?" Old Gate was really interested now.

"He rounded up the district's entire supply of stumping powder. The last seen of the egg, it was headed for the States."

Old Gate's breath came out of him in one long swoosh.

"Is — that — a — fact?" He said it real weak.

Mr. Godfrey was looking over at Molly, and she was smiling. Jake looked like he'd just thrashed a 60-bushel crop, too.

It was a week later, after Mr. Godfrey had gone back to stay with Gatenbys, that I asked Jake about something that had bothered me ever since that night.

"Jake," I said, "he never told what happened to that hopper."

"There," Jake said, "is thuh tragical part of it. Albin, he fell in love."

"Fell in love!"

"Yep. He was settin' in this here Dooley's back 40 one day an' he looked up an' seen one a them there four-engine bombers they're flyin' tuh Roosia. She was love at first sight. He took off, an' thuh last folks seen was two little black specks disappearin' tuh thuh North. Han' me that there manure fork will yuh, Kid?"

(1961)   (1961)

Anne Hébert
1916 –

◆

A COUSIN OF Saint-Denys Garneau, Anne Hébert was born in Sainte-Catherine de Portneuf and worked briefly for the National Film Board before moving to Paris in the early 1950s. Since the appearance of her first collection of poems, *Les Songes en équilibre* in 1942, she has published two volumes of poetry, *Le Tombeau des rois* (1953) and *Poèmes* (1960). Hébert has also published several novels and collections of short stories including *Le Torrent* (1950), *Les Chambres de bois* (1958), *Kamouraska* (1970) and *Les Enfants du sabbat* (1975). English translations of her work include *The Tomb of Kings* (1967), *The Torrent* (1973), *Kamouraska* (1973), *Poems* (1975) and *Children of the Black Sabbath* (1977).

The Tomb of the Kings

I have my heart on my fist
Like a blind falcon.

The taciturn bird gripping my fingers
A swollen lamp of wine and blood
I go down
Toward the tombs of the kings
Astonished
Scarcely born.

What Ariadne-thread leads me
Along the muted labyrinths?
The echo of my steps fades away as they fall.   10

(In what dream
Was this child tied by her ankle
Like a fascinated slave?)

The maker of the dream
Pulls on the cord
And my naked footsteps come
One by one
Like the first drops of rain
At the bottom of a well.   20

Already the odour stirs in swollen storms
Seeps under the edges of the doors
Of chambers secret and round
Where the folding beds are laid out.

The motionless desire of the recumbent dead lures me.
I behold with astonishment
Encrusted upon the black bones
The blue stones gleaming.

A few tragedies patiently wrought
Lying on the breast of kings   30
As if they were jewels
Are offered me
Without tears or regrets.

In single rank arrayed:
The smoke of incense, the cake of dried rice,
And my trembling flesh:
A ceremonial and submissive offering.

A gold mask on my absent face
Violet flowers for eyes,
The shade of love paints me in small sharp strokes,   40
And this bird I have breathes
And complains strangely.

A long tremor
Like a wind sweeping from tree to tree,
Shakes the seven tall ebony Pharaohs
In their stately and ornate cases.

It is only the profundity of death which persists,
Simulating the ultimate torment
Seeking its appeasement
And its eternity   50
In a faint tinkle of bracelets

Vain rings, alien games
Around the sacrificed flesh.

Greedy for the fraternal source of evil in me
They lay me down and drink me;
Seven times I know the tight grip of the bones
And the dry hand seeking my heart to break it.

Livid and satiated with the horrible dream
My limbs freed
And the dead thrust out of me, assassinated,   60
What glimmer of dawn strays in here?
Wherefore does this bird quiver
And turn toward morning
Its blinded eyes?

(1953)   (1962)
F.R. Scott (Trans.)

The Lean Girl

I am a lean girl
And I have beautiful bones.

I tend them with great care
And feel strange pity for them.

I continually polish them
As though they were old metal.

Now jewels and flowers
Are out of season.

One day I shall clasp my lover
10 And make of him a silver shrine.

I shall hang myself
In the place of his absent heart.

O well-filled recess,

Who is this cold guest suddenly in
          you?

You walk,
 You move;
Each one of your gestures
Adorns with fear the enclosed death.

I receive your trembling   20
As a gift.

And sometimes
Fastened in your breast,
I half open
My liquid eyes

As strange and childish dreams
Swirl
Like green water.

(1953)   (1962)
F.R. Scott (Trans.)

The Water Fishermen

The water fishermen
Have caught the bird
In their dripping nets.

The whole image reversed;
It is so calm
On this water.

The tree
In leaf
And fixed pattern of the wind
10 On the leaves
And colors of summer
On the branches.

The whole tree straight,
And the bird,
That kind of king,
Tiny and artless.

And then, also,
This woman who sews
At the foot of the tree
Under the stroke of noon.   20

This seated woman
Mends, stitch by stitch,
The world's humility,
With only the gentle patience
Of her two withered hands.

(1953)   (1967)
Peter Miller (Trans.)

The Little Towns

I shall give you the little towns
The poor sad little towns,

The little towns cupped in our palms
More exigent than toys
As easy to the hand.

I play with the little towns,
I turn them over
Never a man escapes them
No flower, no child.

The little towns are empty —   10
Given into our hands.

I listen, my ear to the doors
I lean to the doors, one by one,
With my ear...

O the houses are dumb sea-shells —
No longer in the frozen spiral
Any sound of the wind
Any sound of water.

Dead, the parks and the gardens
The games are all put to sleep   20
In a dead museum.

I cannot tell where they have put
The deathstill bodies of the birds.

The streets resound with silence
The echo of their silence is a weight of lead
More leaden
Than any words of menace or of love.

And here am I too, in my turn
Forsaking the little towns of my childhood ...
I offer them to you   30
In all the infinite depth
Of their loneliness.

Now do you grasp the dangerous gift?
I have given you the strange sad little towns
For your own imagining.

(1953)   (1970)
John Glassco (Trans.)

The Wooden Room

Honey of time
On the polished walls
Ceiling of gold
Flowers in the knots and
        fancy's heart in wood

Closed room
Windowed coffer where my childhood
Rolls like beads from a broken necklace.

I sleep on leaves that know me
The smell of pines is an old servant, blind.
The song of water beats around my temples   10
Little blue broken veins
And the whole river is my memory passing.

I go for walks
In a secret closet.
The snow – barely a handful –
Flowers in a globe of glass
Like a bride's crown and veil
Two tiny hurts
Stretch
And hide their claws.   20

I shall sew my dress with this lost thread.
I have shoes of blue
And a child's eyes
That are not mine.
I have to live in here
In this polished space.

I have food for the night
If I do not grow tired
Of this monotone, the river's song
And if the trembling servant   30
Does not let fall her whole pack of odours
All at once
Beyond recall.

There is no key here, no lock
I am encircled by this ancient wood
In love with a small green taper-stand.
Noon of the silver tiles burns on
The space of the world flames like a forge
Anguish turns me to shadow
I am naked, blackened under a bitter tree.   40

(1953)   (1975)

Alan Brown (Trans.)

Life in the Castle

It is a castle of forbears
Without fire or table
Dust or tapestry.

The perverse enchantment of the place
Is only in its polished mirrors.

Here there is nothing else to do
But see yourself, day-long, night-long,

Hurl your image at the hard fountain-pools
Your hardest image without shade or colour.

See, how these mirrors are as deep   10
As cupboards
There's always a dead one living behind the foil
Covering swiftly your reflection
Clinging to you like seaweed

Fitting itself to you, naked and thin,
Simulating love in a slow bitter shudder.

(1953)   (1975)
Alan Brown (Trans.)

Snow

Snow puts us in a dream on vast plains without track or colour

Beware, my heart, snow puts us in the saddle on steeds of foam

Proclaim the coronation of childhood, snow consecrates us on high seas,
dreams fulfilled, all sails set

Snow puts us in a trance, a widespread whiteness, flaring plumes
pierced by the red eye of this bird

My heart; a point of fire under palms of frost flows the marvelling blood.

(1960)   (1962)

Spring over the City

Day harries snows long fallen, filthied, mouldy,
ruined

Frost opens its veins, and the heart of earth
loosens among jostling springs

Winter capsizes, splits like a rotten hull,
The world is naked under bitter lichens

Under mud masses an old season old papers old
butts the old dead rush downstream

Daylight has in easy reach a thousand
open cities, each street a river, every bed a fountain,   10

The dream has lost its ensign, sweet froth, sweet
green wound washed in the running stream

The chimera is roughly torn from
the madman's breast, suddenly with his rootless heart

Man overboard, the password in a bottle
the poem will roll up for all eternity

The strange dwelling of fire in dark moist places,
sacred vases, rhythm of the world

He who is without birth has not turned in his sleep
the current drags him by his hair, will turn him to   20
seaweed

The sacrifice on the sea-rocks puffs its strong breath in smoke.
Blood of the dead joins with salt, strewn on the sea
like sword-lilies by armfuls

Now the season of waters draws back; the town dries
out like a sand-beach and licks its iodine
misfortunes

Spring burns along the grey house-fronts, and stone
lepers in the sun take on the splendid glare of   30
gods, scarred but victorious.

(1960)   (1975)
Alan Brown (Trans.)

P. K. Page
1916 –

BORN IN ENGLAND, Patricia Kathleen Page came to Canada as a child and attended school in Calgary. During the early 1940s she was one of the group of poets associated with *Preview* (1942-1945), a Montreal poetry magazine founded by Patrick Anderson. In 1944 she published a novel, *The Sun and the Moon,* under the pseudonym Judith Cape, and her first individual volume of poetry, *As Ten As Twenty,* was published in 1946. A collection of her stories, *The Sun and the Moon and Other Fictions,* appeared in 1973 and more recent collections of her poetry include *Cry Ararat! Poems New and Selected* (1967) and *Poems Selected and New* (1974).

The Bands and the Beautiful Children

Band makes a tunnel of the open street
at first, hearing it;
seeing it band becomes
high: brasses ascending on the strings of sun
build their own auditorium of light,
windows from cornets
and a dome of drums.

And always attendant on bands, the beautiful children
white with running and innocence;
and the arthritic old   10
who, patient behind their windows
are no longer split by the quick yellow of imagination
or carried beyond their angular limits of distance.

But the children move
in the trembling building of sound,
sure as a choir
until band breaks and scatters,
crumbles about them and is made of men
tired and grumbling
on the straggling grass.   20

And the children, lost, lost,
in an open space,
remember the certainty of the anchored home
and cry on the unknown edge of their own city
their lips stiff from an imaginary trumpet.

(1946)   (1974)

Stories of Snow

Those in the vegetable rain retain
an area behind their sprouting eyes
held soft and rounded with the dream of snow
precious and reminiscent as those globes —
souvenir of some never-nether land —
which hold their snow-storms circular, complete,
high in a tall and teakwood cabinet.

In countries where the leaves are large as hands
where flowers protrude their fleshy chins
and call their colours,   10
an imaginary snow-storm sometimes falls
among the lilies.
And in the early morning one will waken
to think the glowing linen of his pillow
a northern drift, will find himself mistaken
and lie back weeping.
And there the story shifts from head to head,
of how in Holland, from their feather beds
hunters arise and part the flakes and go
forth to the frozen lakes in search of swans —   20
the snow-light falling white along their guns,
their breath in plumes.
While tethered in the wind like sleeping gulls
ice-boats wait the raising of their wings
to skim the electric ice at such a speed
they leap jet strips of naked water,
and how these flying, sailing hunters feel
air in their mouths as terrible as ether.
And on the story runs that even drinks

in that white landscape dare to be no colour;   30
how flasked and water clear, the liquor slips
silver against the hunters' moving hips.
And of the swan in death these dreamers tell
of its last flight and how it falls, a plummet,
pierced by the freezing bullet
and how three feathers, loosened by the shot,
descend like snow upon it.
While hunters plunge their fingers in its down
deep as a drift, and dive their hands
up to the neck of the wrist   40
in that warm metamorphosis of snow
as gentle as the sort that woodsmen know
who, lost in the white circle, fall at last
and dream their way to death.

And stories of this kind are often told
in countries where great flowers bar the roads
with reds and blues which seal the route to snow —
as if, in telling, raconteurs unlock
the colour with its complement and go
through to the area behind the eyes   50
where silent, unrefractive whiteness lies.

(1946)   (1974)

The Metal and the Flower

Intractable between them grows
a garden of barbed wire and roses.
Burning briars like flames devour
their too innocent attire.
Dare they meet, the blackened wire
tears the intervening air.

Trespassers have wandered through
texture of flesh and petals.
Dogs like arrows moved along
pathways that their noses knew.   10
While the two who laid it out

find the metal and the flower
fatal underfoot.

Black and white at midnight glows
this garden of barbed wire and roses.
Doused with darkness roses burn
coolly as a rainy moon;
beneath a rainy moon or none
silver the sheath on barb and thorn.

Change the garden, scale and plan: 20
wall it, make it annual.
There the briary flower grew.
There the brambled wire ran.
While they sleep the garden grows,
deepest wish annuls the will:
perfect still the wire and rose.

(1954)   (1974)

T-Bar

Relentless, black on white, the cable runs
through metal arches up the mountain side.
At intervals giant pickaxes are hung
on long hydraulic springs. The skiers ride
propped by the axehead, twin automatons
supported by its handle, one each side.

In twos they move slow motion up the steep
incision in the mountain. Climb. Climb.
Somnambulists, bolt upright in their sleep
their phantom poles swung lazily behind,   10
while to the right, the empty T-bars keep
in mute descent, slow monstrous jigging time.

Captive the skiers now and innocent,
wards of eternity, each pair alone.
They mount the easy vertical ascent,
pass through successive arches, bride and groom,

as through successive naves, are newly wed
participants in some recurring dream.

So do they move forever. Clocks are broken.
In zones of silence they grow tall and slow,   20
inanimate dreamers, mild and gentle-spoken
blood-brothers of the haemophilic snow
until the summit breaks and they awaken
imagos from the stricture of the tow.

Jerked from her chrysalis the sleeping bride
suffers too sudden freedom like a pain.
The dreaming bridegroom severed from her side
singles her out, the old wound aches again.
Uncertain, lost, upon a wintry height
these two, not separate, but no longer one.   30

Now clocks begin to peck and sing. The slow
extended minute like a rubber band
contracts to catapult them through the snow
in tandem trajectory while behind
etching the sky-line, obdurate and slow
the spastic T-bars pivot and descend.

(1954)   (1974)

Photos of a Salt Mine

How innocent their lives look,
how like a child's
dream of caves and winter, both combined;
the steep descent to whiteness
and the stope
with its striated walls
their folds all leaning as if pointing to
the greater whiteness still,
that great white bank
with its decisive front,   10
that seam upon a slope,
salt's lovely ice.

And wonderful underfoot the snow of salt
the fine
particles a broom could sweep,
one thinks
muckers might make angels in its drifts
as children do in snow,
lovers in sheets,
lie down and leave imprinted where they lay   20
a feathered creature holier than they.

And in the outworked stopes
with lamps and ropes
up miniature matterhorns
the miners climb
probe with their lights
the ancient folds of rock –
syncline and anticline –
and scoop from darkness an Aladdin's cave:
rubies and opals glitter from its walls.   30

But hoses douse the brilliance of these jewels,
melt fire to brine.
Salt's bitter water trickles thin and forms,
slow fathoms down,
a lake within a cave,
lacquered with jet –
white's opposite.
There grey on black the boating miners float
to mend the stays and struts of that old stope
and deeply underground   40
their words resound,
are multiplied by echo, swell and grow
and make a climate of a miner's voice.

So all the photographs like children's wishes
are filled with caves or winter,
innocence
has acted as a filter,
selected only beauty from the mine.
Except in the last picture,
it is shot   50
from an acute high angle. In a pit
figures the size of pins are strangely lit

and might be dancing but you know they're not.
Like Dante's vision of the nether hell
men struggle with the bright cold fires of salt,
locked in the black inferno of the rock:
the filter here, not innocence but guilt.

(1954)   (1974)

Portrait of Marina

Far out the sea has never moved. It is
Prussian forever, rough as teazled wool
some antique skipper worked into a frame
to bear his lost four-master.
                              Where it hangs
now in a sunny parlour, none recalls
how all his stitches, interspersed with oaths
had made his one pale spinster daughter grow
transparent with migraines – and how his call
fretted her more than waves.   10
                              Her name
Marina, for his youthful wish –
boomed at the font of that small salty church
where sailors lurched like drunkards, would, he felt
make her a water woman, rich with bells.
To her the name Marina simply meant
he held his furious needle for her thin
fingers to thread again with more blue wool
to sew the ocean of his memory.
Now, where the picture hangs, a dimity   20
young inland housewife with inherited
clocks under bells and ostrich eggs on shelves
pours amber tea in small rice china cups
and reconstructs
how great-great-grandpapa at ninety-three
his fingers knotted with arthritis, his
old eyes grown agatey with cataracts
became as docile as a child again –
that fearful salty man –
and sat, wrapped round in faded paisley shawls   30

gently embroidering.
While Aunt Marina in grey worsted, warped
without a smack of salt, came to his call
the sole survivor of his last shipwreck.

* * * *

Slightly off shore it glints. Each wave is capped
with broken mirrors. Like Marina's head
the glinting of these waves.
She walked forever antlered with migraines
her pain forever putting forth new shoots
until her strange unlovely head became   40
a kind of candelabra — delicate —
where all her tears were perilously hung
and caught the light as waves that catch the sun.
The salt upon the panes, the grains of sand
that crunched beneath her heel
her father's voice, "Marina!" — all these broke
her trembling edifice. The needle shook
like ice between her fingers.
In her head
too many mirrors dizzied her and broke.   50

* * * *

But where the wave breaks, where it rises green
turns into gelatine, becomes a glass
simply for seeing stones through, runs across
the coloured shells and pebbles of the shore
and makes an aspic of them
then sucks back
in foam and undertow —
this aspect of the sea
Marina never knew.
For her the sea was Father's Fearful Sea   60
harsh with sea serpents
winds and drowning men.
For her it held no spiral of a shell
for her descent to dreams,
it held no bells.
And where it moved in shallows it was more
imminently a danger, more alive
than where it lay off shore full fathom five.

(1954)   (1974)

Arras

Consider a new habit — classical,
and trees espaliered on the wall like candelabra.
How still upon that lawn our sandalled feet.

But a peacock rattling his rattan tail and screaming
has found a point of entry. Through whose eye
did it insinuate in furled disguise
to shake its jewels and silk upon that grass?

The peaches hang like lanterns. No one joins
those figures on the arras.
                              Who am I   10
or who am I become that walking here
I am observer, other, Gemini,
starred for a green garden of cinema?

I ask, what did they deal me in this pack?
The cards, all suits, are royal when I look.
My fingers slipping on a monarch's face
twitch and grow slack.
I want a hand to clutch, a heart to crack.

No one is moving now, the stillness is
infinite. If I should make a break....   20
take to my springy heels....? But nothing moves.
The spinning world is stuck upon its poles,
the stillness points a bone at me. I fear
the future on this arras.
                              I confess:

It was my eye.

Voluptuous it came.
Its head the ferrule and its lovely tail
folded so sweetly; it was strangely slim
to fit the retina. And then it shook   30
and was a peacock — living patina,
eye-bright, maculate!
Does no one care?

I thought their hands might hold me if I spoke.
I dreamed the bite of fingers in my flesh,
their poke smashed by an image, but they stand
as if within a treacle, motionless,
folding slow eyes on nothing. While they stare
another line has trolled the encircling air,
another bird assumes its furled disguise.   40

(1954)   (1974)

Now This Cold Man...

Now this cold man in his garden feels the ice
thawing from branches of his lungs and brain:
the blood thins out in artery and vein,
the stiff eyes slip again.

Kneeling in welters of narcissus his
dry creaking joints bend with a dancer's ease,
the roughened skin softens beneath the rain

and all that he had clutched, held tightly locked
behind the fossil frame
dissolves, flows free   10
in saffron covering the willow tree
and coloured rivers of the rockery.

Yellow and white and purple is his breath
his hands are curved and cool for cupping petals,
the sharp green shoots emerging from the beds
all whistle for him

until he is the garden; heart, the sun
and all his body soil;
glistening jonquils blossom from his skull,
the bright expanse of lawn his stretching thighs   20
and something rare and perfect, yet unknown,
stirs like a foetus just behind his eyes.

(1967)   (1974)

Cook's Mountains

By naming them he made them.
They were there
before he came
but they were not the same.
It was his gaze
that glazed each one.
He saw
the Glass House Mountains in his glass.
They shone.

And still they shine.   10
We saw them as we drove —
sudden, surrealist, conical
they rose
out of the rain forest.
The driver said,
"Those are the Glass House Mountains up ahead."

And instantly they altered to become
the sum of shape and name.
Two strangenesses united into one
more strange than either.   20
Neither of us now
remembers how they looked before they broke
the light to fragments as the driver spoke.

Like mounds of mica,
hive-shaped hothouses,
mountains of mirror glimmering
they form
in diamond panes behind the tree ferns of
the dark imagination,
burn and shake   30
the lovely light of Queensland like a bell
reflecting Cook upon a deck
his tongue
silvered with paradox and metaphor.

(1967)   (1974)

Yves Thériault
1916 –

———◆———

BORN IN QUEBEC City, Yves Thériault is one of the most prolific and versatile writers in contemporary Quebec. He has published more than thirty volumes since the appearance of his first book, *Contes pour un homme seul,* in 1944. In addition to several novels and collections of short stories, Thériault has written biography, drama, essays and science fiction. Three of his novels have been translated into English: *Agaguk* (1958), *Ashini* (1960) and *N'Tsuk* (1968).

The Hand

AROUND THE WHOLE mountain nobody had a temper like Géron's.
    This temper arose in him and lashed out from him like an August lightning bolt, and the explosion shook up all of the hamlet. During these explosions, Géron yelled with rage and everybody trembled as long as his angry temper lasted. But this anger would melt away as suddenly as it came; the whole fit of anger only took the time of two shouts, a menacing gesture, and a vicious grin which covered his whole face.

"He'll kill one day," Mourgan used to say. "One day somebody will be within reach of that wild swing and Géron will kill him."

Géron's wife always used to disagree with such statements: "He's gentle. What if he yells sometimes and has his fits of anger? Basically, he's gentle and good. He's a loving man."

She was regarded as an expert in these love matters, because she had been pining away from the anguish of unrequited love till she married her Géron.

She was just called by the simple name, Marie, and she was as simply beautiful as her name. (What I'm telling you happened one hundred years ago when the mountain was almost uninhabited, with only three hamlets clinging to its slopes. Further down, below the mountain, there was the shore of that sea which extends all the way to Africa).

"He's a mild man," Marie used to repeat, when Géron with his temper had shaken up all of the snow-covered mountain side.

Géron used to farm a long, narrow strip of land which bordered on the Gueuse, our stream. On this strip of land he grew those things which usually grow on yellowish, undernourished soil. Higher up, above the shore, he pastured a flock of sheep whose wool he sold to the peddlers who came every spring.

"At least," said Mourgan, who liked Géron and cared about him, "nobody can deny that he holds on to his Marie like the sky holds on to her stars. Both Marie and Géron are one, until death."

This was true, and it was beautiful in its truth. Their love was an example to those other couples in the three hamlets who felt little for each other and nagged each other all day long out of frustration, regret or contempt. When Géron and Marie walked down the road, he being big and strong as an animal and she being refined and discreet, an observer could easily and truthfully have said that over their heads there was a halo of pure love.

There was nothing in their life together which could ever have come between them except for Géron's frequent outbursts of temper. Marie did her share of the common chores. She was strong under that delicate exterior, and she could even be called sturdy. She was quite skilful and had agile, lively fingers, like those of a lacework-maker.

Géron, by himself, was able to take care of all that was necessary to keep the farm going.

The daily life of Marie and Géron was thus quite simple: a property that produced a living, a healthy flock, crops which were not worse than the others in the land, a peaceful life, and each other's quiet presence. This was a poor region, at the foot of mountains which were too steep, a region under the unforgiving hot summer sun which was inevitably followed by the cold winter winds. It was almost a miracle that there could be, in such a place, two people who loved each other so much and a farm which produced the necessities of life.

If only it weren't for those outbursts of temper.... They were caused by everything and they were caused by nothing. Géron could be patient and sweet all week. However, if a rock surfaced in his field at the wrong moment, or the soup wasn't hot enough, or a lamb got lost on the heights – then the anger came roaring out. The yelling, the vicious grin and the enormous crescendo of anger – all of the frightful symptoms were suddenly and terribly present. And then...came the quiet calm.

Mourgan, who was always listening nearby, shook his head and predicted: "One day he'll commit murder."

Géron didn't kill. However, he did do something terrible which came close to murder.

It happened on a Sunday, a Sunday full of flowers. Flowers are so rare in our region that three flowers are regarded as a gift from God, and if ten flowers appear at one time, then it can only mean that spring has arrived. So it was a beautiful Sunday, full of sunlight, and Géron came to the hamlet with his Marie. They came for no special purpose, only to chat, to stroll around, and to greet the neighbors.

They both came in their usual way, walking close together, side by side, arm in arm. They belonged so much together that Marie, during a conversation with others, could complete word for word Géron's unfinished sentences, and he could do the same with her talk. It was as if their thoughts, inextricably linked, came from only one brain.

For about an hour they strolled about the central square of the hamlet, chatting at one doorway, moving towards a group under the sycamore tree, coming back to still another threshold for more conversation. It was an enjoyable day filled with good company and pleasurable words which were exchanged with smiles.

And then the dog appeared. He was hardly more than a puppy, a nameless and ownerless mongrel who sprang up suddenly from the road leading to the valley. He ran here and there, barking vigorously. He threatened Mourgan, then mother Soubert, and then many others. When he moved towards Géron, he did more than simply threaten him: he jumped on the man's leg and, with a quick stroke of his jaws, bit him. Géron gave a mighty yell. First came a cry of pain which soon turned into a roar of rage.

Why did Marie have to burst out laughing at that moment, instead of comforting her Géron? Why did her laugh have to greet him just when his uncontrollable anger welled up?

Then Géron made his move – the terrible swing which all knew so well. His large, tough hand struck out viciously, and Marie received the punch, a powerful blow which blasted her cheek and sent her sprawling on the ground.

Then came the silence. Nobody moved. An air of sudden and profound shame hung over every corner of the hamlet. After all, Géron loved his Marie so much; she was the very last person in the world who should have been the target of his temper.

They both left the hamlet together. Without a moment's delay, he took the arm of the weeping woman who couldn't understand what had happened. He was almost pulling her along as if she were one of his sheep, and they headed up the road towards their farm.

Jasmin, who met them at the half-way point to the farm, said that Marie was crying, and Géron too was crying so much that the tears were almost flooding his cheeks.

After this incident, Géron never had another explosion of his famous temper. He became known for his mild and controlled nature, just as he once had been legendary for his anger. Whenever he was provoked by some unwelcome event or unpleasant incident, he quickly lifted his arm up before his eyes, and this rapidly restored his calm and quiet self-control.

Because something had happened the very evening of that day when he had punched Marie. To tame his temper forever, Géron, alone in the sheepfold, with only one swift, clean stroke of his axe, had cut off his hand.

(1964)   (1977)

HOWARD ROITER (TR.)

Miriam Waddington
1917 –

———◆———

THE DAUGHTER OF Russian immigrants, Miriam (Dworkin) Waddington was born in Winnipeg and educated at the Universities of Toronto and Pennsylvania. In 1964 she joined the Department of English at York University, Toronto. Her first collection of poetry, *Green World* (1945), was published by John Sutherland's First Statement Press. Subsequent volumes include *The Glass Trumpet* (1966), *Driving Home* (1972) and *The Price of Gold* (1976).

Green World

When I step out and feel the green world
Its concave walls must cup my summer coming
And curving, hold me
Beyond all geography in a transparent place
Where water images cling to the inside sphere
Move and distend as rainbows in a mirror
Cast out of focus.

And this crystal chrysallis
Shapes to green rhythms to long ocean flowings
Rolls toward the sun with sure and spinning speed   10
 And under the intensely golden point
Warms, expands,
Until walls crack suddenly
Uncup me into large and windy space.

(1945)   (1945)

In the Park

The child follows the sun
dizzy, lost in the circling asters
and the criss-cross of dripping
delicious honeysuckle
all the pink and exploding delicacy.
Oh what a curtain it makes for the myth
the haunted oedipus, a modern backdrop
    a very
innocence of plants and children!

And mothers, indirect, elliptical   10
under their shady hats
nod at sailboats while their smiles
pull in stormy adventurers
and their gestures
make such graceful patterns
willy nilly on the sun dial.

But I like some great eclipse
cut off the starry light
and teach him afternoon as if it were
religion, I'm a familiar island   20
hard and rock-bitten, though where
the footprint leads he cannot guess.
Unanonymous I sit, the green park benches
make me a giant, and of course
my glance is threatening.

(1955)   (1972)

Green World Two

Locked in a glassy iceland lake
I was a child chinning myself
on reflected treetops.
Into my green world
winter shone and splashed
me fresh with light.

My summer gone
the knob of light still turns

in that locked lake;
under the seal of ice   10
the cabined light still burns
and the yellow haystacks flare
on underwater beaches.
Far above the snow
fills the falling world
to its topmost branches.

(1966)   (1972)

Looking for
Strawberries in June

I have to tell you
about the words I
used to know, such
words, so sheer, thin
transparent, so light
and quick, I had such
words for wind for
whatever grew
I knew a certain
10   leaf-language from
somewhere, but now

it is all used up
I have come to the
end of some line or
other like walking
on railroad ties in
the country looking
for strawberries in
June and suddenly
20   the ties end in the
middle of no-place

and I stop to look
around to take my
direction but I

don't recognize the
landscape. It is all
grey, feathery, the
voices of birds are
foreign, yet I used
to know such words   30
japanned, brushed and
papery, whitefolded
Russian flowerwords
cabbage roses, huge
holes in the head of
the universe pouring
out rosy revolutions:

and I used to know
swarthy eastern words
heavy with Hebrew, then   40
I was kidnapped by

gypsies, I knew the
up and down of their
dark-blue anger, the
leathery touch of
the fortune-telling
begging wandering
words, but what's
become of them?
50 I don't know, I'm

just standing here
on the threshold of
a different country,
everything is made
of plastic and silence;

(1969)

what month is it any-
way? I'm knocking at
the door but nobody
answers. I mutter *Lenin*
Karl Marx, Walt Whitman   60
Chaucer, Hopkins, even
Archibald Lampman, but
nobody comes, I don't

know the password
I only know it has
nothing to do with
being good or true
nothing to do with
being beautiful.

(1972)

The Nineteen Thirties Are Over

The nineteen thirties
are over; we survived
the depression, the Sacco-
Vanzetti of childhood
saw Tom Mooney smiling
at us from photographs,
put a rose on the grave
of Eugene Debs, listened
to our father's stories
10 of the Winnipeg strike and
joined the study groups
of the OBU always keeping
one eye on the revolution.

Later we played records
with thorn needles, Josh
White's *Talking Union* and
Prokofief's *Lieutenant Kije*,
shuddered at the sound of
bells and all those wolves

whirling past us in snow   20
on the corner of Portage
and Main, but in my mind
summer never ended on the
shores of Gimli where we
looked across to an Icelandic
paradise we could never see
the other side of; and I
dreamed of Mexico and shining
birds who beckoned to me
from the gold-braided lianas   30
of my own wonder.

These days I step out
from the frame of my wind-
battered house into Toronto
city; somewhere I still
celebrate sunlight, touch
the rose on the grave of
Eugene Debs but I walk

carefully in this land
40 of sooty snow; I pass the
rich houses and double
garages and I am not really
this middle-aged professor
but someone from

Winnipeg whose bones ache
with the broken revolutions
of Europe, and even now
I am standing on the heaving
ploughed-up field
of my father's old war.   50

(1972)

(1972)

Transformations

The blood of my ancestors
has died in me
I have forsaken the steppes
of Russia for the prairies
of Winnipeg, I have turned
my back on Minneapolis
and the Detroit lakes
I love only St. Boniface
its grey wooden churches
10 I want to spend my life
in Gimli listening to the
roar of emptiness in the

wild snow, scanning the lake
for the music of rainbow-
skinned fishes, I will compose
my songs to gold-eye tunes
send them across the land
in smoke-spaces, ice-signals
and concentrate all winter
on Henry Hudson adrift   20
in a boat, when he comes home
I will come home too and
the blood of my ancestors
will flower on Mennonite bushes

(1972)

(1972)

Grand Manan Sketches

I

The island
lies in perpetual
August you have
to expect storms
and hurricanes
also strong
sunlight slanting

across triangles
of rock glossy
and black as   10
seals

Here even
the rocks
are alive and
intelligent

II

In town
I entice monarch
and other butterflies
by planting milkweed
among the flowers

In Grand Manan
I don't need
such enticements, the
butterflies, monarch
10 and swallow-tail,
crowd in skimming
through spruces
drinking the daisies
and dipping their
wings into the
rosy flames of the
fireweed

III

Nothing
burns them
in this bright
light everything

(1976)

moves to water
except me
who am motionless
stunned to stillness
covered with
gold dust   10

IV

Look how
I am hanging
like a bird from
midsummer
golden
in sky space

V

And look
how I am
burning
burning away
the distance
of water of
sun of
island

(1976)

Margaret Avison
1918 –

MARGARET AVISON WAS born in Galt, Ontario, and received her B.A. from the University of Toronto in 1940. Since the completion of postgraduate studies at the Universities of Indiana, Chicago and Toronto, she has worked as a librarian, a research assistant and a social worker. Although her first book, *The Winter Sun,* was not published until 1960, many of her poems appeared previously in American and Canadian journals and anthologies. A second collection of her poems, *The Dumbfounding,* was published in 1966.

The Iconoclasts

The dervish dancer on the smoking steppes
Unscrolled, into the level lava-cool
Of Romish twilight, baleful hyroglyphs
That had been civic architecture,
    The sculptured utterances of the Schools.

The Vikings rode the tasseled sea:
Over their shoulders, running towards their boats,
They had seen the lurking matriarchal wolves,
Ducked their bright foreheads from the iron laurels
Of a dark Scandinavian destiny,   10
And chosen, rather, to be dwarfed to pawns
    Of the broad sulking sea.

And Lampman, when he prowled the Gatineau:
Were the white vinegar of northern rivers,
The stain of punkwood in chill evening air,
The luminous nowhere past the gloomy hills,
Were these his April cave —
    Sought as the first men, when the bright release
    Of sun filled them with sudden self-disdain
    At bone-heaps, rotting pelts, muraled adventures,   20
    Sought a more primitive nakedness?

The cave-men, Lampman, Lief, the dancing dervish,
Envied the fleering wolf his secret circuit;
    But knew their doom to propagate, create,
    Their wild salvation wrapt within that white
    Burst of pure art whose only premise was
    Ferocity in them, thudding its dense
    Distracting rhythms down their haunted years.

(1964)

Perspective

A sport, an adventitious sprout
These eyeballs, that have somehow slipped
The mesh of generations since Mantegna?

Yet I declare, your seeing is diseased
That cripples space. The fear has eaten back
Through sockets to the caverns of the brain
    And made of it a sifty habitation.

We stand beholding the one plain
And in your face I see the chastening
Of its small tapering design   10
That brings up *punkt.*
    (The Infinite, you say,
    Is an unthinkable – and pointless too –
      Extension of that *punkt.*)

But do you miss the impact of that fierce
Raw boulder five miles off? You are not pierced
By that great spear of grass on the horizon?
    You are not smitten with the shock
      Of that great thundering sky?

Your law of optics is a quarrel   20
Of chickenfeet on paper. Does a train
Run pigeon-toed?

I took a train from here to Ottawa
On tracks that did not meet. We swelled and roared
Mile upon mightier mile, and when we clanged
Into the vasty station we were indeed
Brave company for giants.

   Keep your eyes though,
You, and not I, will travel safer back
        To Union station.   30

Your fear has me infected, and my eyes
That were my sport so long, will soon be apt
Like yours to press out dwindling vistas from
The massive flux massive Mantegna knew
And all its sturdy everlasting foregrounds.

(1964)

Snow

Nobody stuffs the world in at your eyes.
The optic heart must venture: a jail-break
And re-creation. Sedges and wild rice
Chase rivery pewter. The astonished cinders quake
With rhizomes. All ways through the electric air
Trundle candy-bright disks; they are desolate
Toys if the soul's gates seal, and cannot bear,
Must shudder under, creation's unseen freight.
But soft, there is snow's legend: colour of mourning
Along the yellow Yangtze where the wheel   10
Spins an indifferent stasis that's death's warning.
Asters of tumbled quietness reveal
Their petals. Suffering this starry blur
The rest may ring your change, sad listener.

(1960)   (1960)

Butterfly Bones; or Sonnet Against Sonnets

The cyanide jar seals life, as sonnets move
towards final stiffness. Cased in a white glare
these specimens stare for peering boys, to prove
strange certainties. Plane dogsled and safari
assure continuing range. The sweep-net skill,
the patience, learning, leave all living stranger.
Insect – or poem – waits for the fix, the frill
precision can effect, brilliant with danger.
What law and wonder the museum spectres
bespeak is cryptic for the shivery wings,   10
the world cut-diamond-eyed, those eyes' reflectors,
or herbal grass, sunned motes, fierce listening.
Might sheened and rigid trophies strike men blind
like Adam's lexicon locked in the mind?

(1960)   (1960)

From a Provincial

Bent postcards come from Interlaken
In August, the tired emperor of the year;
On evening tables
Midges survey their planes of brief discovery
At a half-run. In Milton's candle's light
They so employed themselves.
Some die before the light is out.
Between darkness and darkness
Every small valley shows a familiar compass
Until like all before   10
Still most unknown, it vanishes.
In Caesar's camp was order,
The locus of their lives for some centurions
Encircled by forests of sombre France.
When day and life draw the horizons
Part of the strangeness is
Knowing the landscape.

(1960)   (1960)

Meeting Together of Poles and Latitudes (In Prospect)

Those who fling off, toss head,
    Taste the bitter morning, and have at it —
    Thresh, knead, dam, weld,
    Wave baton, force
    Marches through squirming bogs,
    Not from contempt, but
    From thrust, unslakeably thirsty,
    Amorous of every tower and twig, and
    Yet like railroad engines with
    Longings for their landscapes (pistons pounding)   10
    Rock fulminating through
    Wrecked love, unslakeably loving —
    Seldom encounter at the Judgment Seat

Those who are flung off, sit
    Dazed awhile, gather concentration,
    Follow vapour-trails with shrivelling wonder,
    Pilfer, mow, play jongleur
    With mathematic signs, or
    Tracing the forced marches make
    Peculiar cats-cradles of telephone wire,   20
    Lap absently at sundown, love
    As the stray dog on foreign hills
    A bone-myth, atavistically,
    Needing more faith, and fewer miles, but
    Slumber-troubled by it,
    Wanting for death that
    Myth-clay, though
    Scratch-happy in these (foreign) brambly wilds;

But when they approach each other
    The place is an astonishment: 30
    Runways shudder with little planes
    Practising folk-dance steps or
    Playing hornet,
    Sky makes its ample ruling
    Clear as a primary child's exercise-book
    In somebody else's language,
    And the rivers under the earth

Foam without whiteness, domed down,
As they foam indifferently every
Day and night (if you'd call that day and night) 40
Not knowing how they wait, at the node, the
Curious encounter.

(1960)   (1960)

The Swimmer's Moment

For everyone
The swimmer's moment at the whirlpool comes,
But many at that moment will not say,
"This is the whirlpool, then."
By their refusal they are saved
From the black pit, and also from contesting
The deadly rapids, and emerging in
The mysterious, and more ample, further waters.
And so their bland-blank faces turn and turn
Pale and forever on the rim of suction   10
They will not recognize.
Of those who dare the knowledge
Many are whirled into the ominous centre
That, gaping vertical, seals up
For them an eternal boon of privacy,
So that we turn away from their defeat
With a despair, not for their deaths, but for
Ourselves, who cannot penetrate their secret
Nor even guess at the anonymous breadth
Where one or two have won: 20
(The silver reaches of the estuary).

(1960)   (1966)

A Nameless One

Hot in June a narrow winged
long-elbowed-thread-legged

living insect lived
and died within
the lodgers' second-floor bathroom here.

At six A.M.
wafting ceilingward,
no breeze but what it living made there;

at noon standing
still as a constellation of spruce needles
before the moment of
making it, whirling;

10

at four a
wilted flotsam, cornsilk, on the linoleum:

now that it is
over, I
look with new eyes
upon this room
adequate for one to
be, in.

20

Its insect-day
has threaded a needle
for me for my eyes dimming
over rips and tears and
thin places.

(1966)   (1966)

The Dumbfounding

When you walked here,
took skin, muscle, hair,
eyes, larynx, we
withheld all honor: "His house is clay,
how can he tell us of his far country?"

Your not familiar pace
in flesh, across the waves,
woke only our distrust.
Twice-torn we cried "A ghost"
and only on our planks counted you fast.   10

Dust wet with your spittle
cleared mortal trouble.
We called you a blasphemer,
a devil-tamer.

The evening you spoke of going away
we could not stay.
All legions massed. You had to wash, and rise,
alone, and face
out of the light, for us.

You died.   20
We said,
"The worst is true, our bliss
has come to this."

When you were seen by men
in holy flesh again
we hoped so despairingly for such report
we closed their windpipes for it.

Now you have sought
and seek, in all our ways, all thoughts,
streets, musics — and we make of these a din   30
trying to lock you out, or in,
to be intent. And dying.

Yet you are
constant and sure
the all-lovely, all-men's-way
to that far country.

Winning one, you again
all ways would begin
life: to make new
flesh, to empower   40

the weak in nature
to restore
or stay the sufferer;

lead through the garden to
trash, rubble, hill,
where, the outcast's outcast, you
sound dark's uttermost, strangely light-brimming, until
time be full.

(1966)   (1966)

Louis Dudek
1918 –

THE SON OF Polish immigrants, Louis Dudek was born in Montreal and educated at McGill University. After studying and working in New York City for eight years, he returned to Montreal in 1951 to take up a position as Professor of English at McGill University. Active as an anthologist and editor, Dudek was a founder of Contact Press (1952-1967), editor of the poetry magazine, *Delta* (1957-1966), and founder of Delta Canada, a new press established in 1967. He was one of the poets represented in *Unit of Five* (1944) and his first independent volume, *East of the City,* appeared in 1946. Subsequent collections of his poetry include *Europe* (1954), *En México* (1958), *Atlantis* (1967) and *Collected Poetry* (1971).

From a Library Window

The scene is paper-thin, pastel pale and white,
the tennis courts are horizontally smooth
chalked with flat lines; the players strike

the ball with abstract sticks;
now the field tilts to an experimental plane,
the players' faces grow light red:
this is a platform, for the play of intellect.

A wind rises and sweeps the pale sand,
a Mongolian storm taking away the land.
It thrashes at the feet of the men;   10
yet all is simple and light-swept, the wind
sounds like the singing of humming birds,
a feeble flight we can allow or end
with a motion of the hand.

At this distance, closed in glass shelves,
leaning against each other, the realities
past and present are easy,
dispersed on a level plane, in an order of line, under the
          rule of play:
but we miss the muscle wrenched from the thigh,
the eye slit by the sun racing the pin ball,   20
and the active brain broken by fight and defeat.

(1946)   (1971)

A Street in April

Look now, at this February street in April
where not a flower blossoms, or if one broke
would be like water from a blister, a yellow poke,
new bird-lime on a rail, or jet from a yolk.

Neither the fire-escapes making musical patterns
nor the filigree of stone flowery and decorating
can now accompany young April; the iron grating
jars, someone dropped a kettle in the orchestrating.

There a pale head rising from an eyeless cavern
swivels twice above the street, and swiftly dips   10
back into the gloom of the skull, whose only lips
are the swinging tin plate and the canvas strips.

And here are infants too, in cribs, with wondrous eyes
at windows, the curtains raised upon a gasping room,
angelic in white diapers and bibs, to whom
the possibilities in wheels and weather — bloom.

But I have seen a dove gleaming and vocal with peace
fly over them, when his sudden wings stirred
and cast the trembling shadow of a metal bird;
so April's without flower, and no song heard.   20

(1946)   (1971)

On Poetry

The flame of a man's imagination should be organic with his body,
coincident with an act, like an igniting spark.
But mostly, he fails in the act
and expels his bad humour in visions. A man curses,
seeing the thing he hates in pain, cursed by his vision:
this is poetry, action unrealized:
what we want most we imagine most, like self-abusing boys.

Lately, of woman man has been deprived
– the smaller man and the greater too –
and in all the language of his verse   10
love, love, love
he cries, never having enough.

Formerly, it was different.
Hairy and sensible, he needed food
when he painted steak chops (bison meat)
in a gaping cave; a bird, or juicy calves of mammoth,
his midday meals.
He carved these also on his spears
and on the handles of knives,
handing the art down the generations.   20

But with the coming of civilization
his body desired other food at times, less personal,
but unattainable. So the poet, who had vision,

wanted to be capable of commanding God, like Jeremiah;
but denied, he ranted poetry.

The poet should have been a king,
Shakespeare should have been all his monarchs, ruling England,
Homer should have been Achilles
frowning for Briseis, or fighting for his friend.
These great ones imagined grandly,   30
the life of the body having defaulted.

So in our time the poet,
in need of quiet, order in chaos,
complete community, wants something he does not have
in all nakedness. And so he wrestles
with the maiden, his wild dream, in his sleep.

(1946)   (1971)

The Pomegranate

The jewelled mine of the pomegranate, whose hexagons of honey
The mouth would soon devour but the eyes eat like a poem,
Lay hidden long in its hide, a diamond of dark cells
Nourished by tiny streams which crystallized into gems.

The seeds, nescient of the world outside, or of passionate teeth,
Prepared their passage into light and air, while tender roots
And branches dreaming in the cell-walled hearts of plants
Made silent motions such as recreate both men and fruits.

There, in a place of no light, shone that reddest blood,
And without a word of order, marshalled those grenadiers: 10
Gleaming without a sun — what art where no eyes were! —
Till broken by my hand, this palace of unbroken tears.

To wedding bells and horns howling down an alley,
Muffled, the married pair in closed caravan ride;
And then, the woman grown in secret, shining white,
Unclothed, mouth to mouth he holds his naked bride.

And there are days, golden days, when the world starts to life,
When streets in the sun, boys, and battlefields of cars,
The colours on a bannister, the vendors' slanting stands
Send the pulse pounding on like the bursting of meteors –   20

As now, the fruit glistens with a mighty grin,
Conquers the room; and, though in ruin, to its death
Laughs at the light that wounds it, wonderfully red,
So that its awful beauty stops the greedy breath.

And can this fact be made, so big, of the body, then?
And is beauty bounded all in its impatient mesh?
The movement of the stars is that, and all their light
Secretly bathed the world, that now flows out of flesh.

(1952)   (1971)

From

En Europe

19

The commotion of these waves, however strong, cannot disturb
                    the compass-line of the horizon
nor the plumb-line of gravity, because this cross coordinates
                    the tragic pulls of necessity
that chart the ideal endings, for waves, and storms
                    and sunset winds:
the dead scattered on the stage in the fifth act
– Cordelia in Lear's arms, Ophelia, Juliet, all silent –
show nature restored to order and just measure.
                    The horizon is perfect,   10
and nothing can be stricter
than gravity; in relation to these
                    the stage is rocked and tossed,
kings fall with their crowns, poets sink with their laurels.

95

The sea retains such images
      in her ever-unchanging waves;
for all her infinite variety, and the forms,
inexhaustible, of her loves,
she is constant always in beauty,
        which to us need be nothing more
      than a harmony with the wave on which we move.
All ugliness is a distortion
of the lovely lines and curves
       which sincerity makes out of hands   10
         and bodies moving in air.
Beauty is ordered in nature
      as the wind and sea
shape each other for pleasure; as the just
know, who learn of happiness
      from the report of their own actions.

(1954)   (1971)

Coming Suddenly to the Sea

Coming suddenly to the sea in my twenty-eighth year,
to the mother of all things that breathe, of mussels and whales,
I could not see anything but sand at first
and burning bits of mother-of-pearl.
But this was the sea, terrible as a torch
which the winter sun had lit,
flaming in the blue and salt sea-air
under my twenty-eight-year infant eyes.
And then I saw the spray smashing the rocks
and the angry gulls cutting the air,   10
the heads of fish and the hands of crabs on stones:
the carnivorous sea, sower of life,
battering a granite rock to make it a pebble –
love and pity needless as the ferny froth on its long smooth waves.
The sea, with its border of crinkly weed,
the inverted Atlantic of our unstable planet,

froze me into a circle of marble, sending the icy air out in
      lukewarm waves.
And so I brought home, as an emblem of that day
ending my long blind years, a fistful of blood-red weed in   20
      my hand.

(1956)   (1971)

From
Prologue to Atlantis

Of voyages: there was Ulysses' voyage,
and Cortés, the great adventurers.

But even suburban dwellers
voyage, though they commute, eat toast, get their magazines
                                           on time
even a beggar in front of Morgan's
voyages on his worn-out magic carpet of cold.

The voyage is still the prototype –
touristic now, because we city people
                        do not slosh through blood   10
but live in glass observation cars of boredom.

One could not write a poem waiting for the train to start.
 But once in motion, well in motion
how is it possible not to begin?

Travel is the life-voyage in little,
         a poem, a fiction, a structure of illusion!
And then you ask, 'What does it mean?'

Voices, baggage, a girl's knee,
            and bells, distant, obscure
Every object a word, language, the record we make   20
a literal transcription,
                then a translation
into moral, abstract meaning.

Travel, to and from (the place does not matter)
       the Ding an sich in a mirror —
Let it speak!

Anyone who travels
       sees others at the crossroads.
There is more than one road.
Who knows where the others may lead to?   30

There are infinite worlds: green lights,
                highway lines, homes,
power stations and industrial domes.

All these things are other people's lives,
effective symbols of their discovered desires.

And what new road lies ahead? What
       out of our living centre may we not create?

(1967)   (1971)

Al Purdy
1918–

———◆———

BORN NEAR WOOLER, Ontario, Alfred Purdy published his first
collection of poetry, *The Enchanted Echo,* in 1944. He has lived and
worked in various parts of Canada and now lives on Roblin Lake near
Ameliasburg, Ontario. His later collections include *The Cariboo Horses*
(1965), *North of Summer* (1967), *Wild Grape Wine* (1968), *In Search of
Owen Roblin* (1974) and *Sundance At Dusk* (1976). A volume of *Selected
Poems* appeared in 1972.

Roblin's Mills

The mill was torn down last year
and stone's internal grey light
gives way to new green
a shading of surface colour
like the greenest apple of several —
The spate of Marthas and Tabithas
        incessant Hirams and Josephs
is stemmed in the valley graveyard
where the censored quarrels of loving
and the hatred and by golly gusto   10
of a good crop of buckwheat and turnips
end naturally as an agreement between friends
(in the sandy soil that would grow nothing
but weeds or feed a few gaunt cattle)
and the spring rain takes their bodies
a little deeper down each year
        maybe the earliest settlers
some stern Martha or speechless Joseph
perhaps meet and mingle
        1000 feet down —   20
And the story about the grist mill
rented in 1914 to a man named Taylor
by the last of the Roblin family
who demanded a share of the profits:
        the lighting alters
and you can see
        how a bald man stood
sturdily indignant
        and spat on the ground
and stamped away so hard the flour   30
dust floated out from his clothes
like a white nimbus round his body
beneath the red scorn —
        Those old ones
you can hear them on a rural party line
sometimes
        when the copper wires
sing before the number is dialed and
then your own words stall some distance
from the house you said them in   40

lost in the 4th concession
or dimension of whatever
a lump in your throat
an adam's apple
half a mile down the road
permits their voices
to float by
on the party line sometimes
and you hang up then
so long now –   50

(1965)   (1965)

Necropsy of Love

If it came about you died
it might be said I loved you:
love is an absolute as death is,
and neither bears false witness to the other –
But you remain alive.

No, I do not love you
                    hate the word,
that private tyranny inside a public sound,
your freedom's yours and not my own:
but hold my separate madness like a sword,   10
and plunge it in your body all night long.

If death shall strip our bones of all but bones,
then here's the flesh, and flesh that's drunken-sweet
as wine cups in deceptive lunar light:
reach up your hand and turn the moonlight off,
and maybe it was never there at all,
so never promise anything to me:
but reach across the darkness with your hand,
reach across the distance of tonight,
and touch the moving moment once again   20
                    before you fall asleep –

(1965)   (1970)

The Cariboo Horses

At 100 Mile House the cowboys ride in rolling
stagey cigarettes with one hand reining
half-tame bronco rebels on a morning grey as stone
— so much like riding dangerous women
      with whiskey coloured eyes —
such women as once fell dead with their lovers
with fire in their heads and slippery froth on thighs
— Beaver or Carrier women maybe or
      Blackfoot squaws far past the edge of this valley
on the other side of those two toy mountain ranges   10
      from the sunfierce plains beyond

But only horses
      waiting in stables
hitched at taverns
      standing at dawn
pastured outside the town with
jeeps and fords and chevvys and
busy muttering stake trucks rushing
importantly over roads of man's devising
over the safe known roads of the ranchers   20
families and merchants of the town
      On the high prairie
are only horse and rider
      wind in dry grass
clopping in silence under the toy mountains
dropping sometimes and
      lost in the dry grass
      golden oranges of dung

Only horses
      no stopwatch memories or palace ancestors   30
not Kiangs hauling undressed stone in the Nile Valley
and having stubborn Egyptian tantrums or
Onagers racing thru Hither Asia and
the last Quagga screaming in African highlands
      lost relatives of these
      whose hooves were thunder
the ghosts of horses battering thru the wind

whose names were the wind's common usage
whose life was the sun's
               arriving here at chilly noon   40
               in the gasoline smell of the
               dust and waiting 15 minutes
               at the grocer's

(1965)   (1972)

The Country North of Belleville

Bush land scrub land —
        Cashel Township and Wollaston
Elzevir McClure and Dungannon
green lands of Weslemkoon Lake
where a man might have some
        opinion of what beauty
is and none deny him
                for miles —

Yet this is the country of defeat
where Sisyphus rolls a big stone   10
year after year up the ancient hills
picnicking glaciers have left strewn
with centuries' rubble
                backbreaking days
                in the sun and rain
when realization seeps slow in the mind
without grandeur or self deception in
                noble struggle
of being a fool —

A country of quiescence and still distance   20
a lean land
        not like the fat south
with inches of black soil on
        earth's round belly —
And where the farms are
        it's as if a man stuck
both thumbs in the stony earth and pulled

                            it apart
                         to make room
enough between the trees   30
for a wife
            and maybe some cows and
            room for some
of the more easily kept illusions —
And where the farms have gone back
to forest
            are only soft outlines
            shadowy differences —

Old fences drift vaguely among the trees
                a pile of moss-covered stones   40
gathered for some ghost purpose
has lost meaning under the meaningless sky
            — they are like cities under water
and the undulating green waves of time
                are laid on them —

This is the country of our defeat
                and yet
during the fall plowing a man
might stop and stand in a brown valley of the furrows
                and shade his eyes to watch for the same   50
                red patch mixed with gold
                that appears on the same
                spot in the hills
                year after year
                and grow old
plowing and plowing a ten-acre field until
the convolutions run parallel with his own brain —

And this is a country where the young
                        leave quickly
unwilling to know what their fathers know   60
or think the words their mothers do not say —

Herschel Monteagle and Faraday
lakeland rockland and hill country
a little adjacent to where the world is
a little north of where the cities are and

sometime
we may go back there
                              to the country of our defeat
Wollaston Elzevir and Dungannon
and Weslemkoon lake land
where the high townships of Cashel   70
                    McClure and Marmora once were —
But it's been a long time since
and we must enquire the way
            of strangers —

(1965)   (1972)

Trees at the Arctic Circle

(SALIX CORDIFOLIA — GROUND WILLOW)

> They are 18 inches long
> or even less
> crawling under rocks
> grovelling among the lichens
> bending and curling to escape
> making themselves small
> finding new ways to hide
> Coward trees
> I am angry to see them
> like this   10
> not proud of what they are
> bowing to weather instead
> careful of themselves
> worried about the sky
> afraid of exposing their limbs
> like Victorian married couple
>
> I call to mind great Douglas firs
> I see tall maples waving green
> and oaks like gods in autumn gold
> the whole horizon jungle dark   20
> and I crouched under that continual night
> But these

even the dwarf shrubs of Ontario
mock them
Coward trees

And yet – and yet –
their seed pods glow
like delicate grey earrings
their leaves are veined and intricate
like tiny parkas   30
They have about three months
to make sure the species does not die
and that's how they spend their time
unbothered by any human opinion
just digging in here and now
sending their roots down down down
And you know it occurs to me
              about 2 feet under
those roots must touch permafrost
ice that remains forever   40
and they use it for their nourishment
they use death to remain alive

I see that I've been carried away
in my scorn of the dwarf trees
most foolish in my judgments
To take away the dignity
              of any living thing
even tho it cannot understand
              the scornful words
is to make life itself trivial   50
and yourself the Pontifex Maximus
              of nullity
I have been stupid in a poem
I will not alter the poem
but let the stupidity remain permanent
as the trees are
in a poem
the dwarf trees of Baffin Island

Pangnirtung

(1967)   (1972)

Elegy for a Grandfather

Well, he died I guess. They said he did.
His wide whalebone hips will make a prehistoric barrow
men of the future may find and perhaps may not:
where this man's relatives ducked their heads
in real and pretended sorrow
for the dearly beloved gone thank Christ to God,
after a bad century: a tough big-bellied Pharaoh,
with a deck of cards in his pocket and a Presbyterian grin —

Maybe he did die, but the boy didn't understand it,
the man knows now and the scandal never grows old   10
of a happy lumberjack who lived on rotten whiskey,
and died of sin and Quaker oats age 90 or so.
But all he was was too much for any man to be,
a life so full he couldn't include one more thing,
nor tell the same story twice if he'd wanted to,
and didn't and didn't —

Just the same he's dead. A sticky religious voice
folded his century sideways to get it out of sight,
and lowered him into the ground like someone still alive
who made other people uncomfortable: 20
barn raiser and backwoods farmer,
become an old man in a one-room apartment
over a drygoods store —
And earth takes him as it takes more beautiful things:
populations of whole countries,
museums and works of art,
and women with such a glow
it makes their background vanish
                    they vanish too,
and Lesbia's singer in her sunny islands   30
stopped when the sun went down —

No, my grandfather was decidedly unbeautiful,
250 pounds of scarred slag.
And I've somehow become his memory,
taking on flesh and blood again
the way he imagined me,

floating among the pictures in his mind
where his dead body is,
laid deep in the earth –
and such a relayed picture perhaps   40
outlives any work of art,
survives among its alternatives.

(1968)   (1968)

Wilderness Gothic

Across Roblin Lake, two shores away,
they are sheathing the church spire
with new metal. Someone hangs in the sky
over there from a piece of rope,
hammering and fitting God's belly-scratcher,
working his way up along the spire
until there's nothing left to nail on –
Perhaps the workman's faith reaches beyond:
touches intangibles, wrestles with Jacob,
replacing rotten timber with pine thews,   10
pounds hard in the blue cave of the sky,
contends heroically with difficult problems
of gravity, sky navigation and mythopeia,
his volunteer time and labour donated to God,
minus sick benefits of course on a non-union job –

Fields around are yellowing into harvest,
nestling and fingerling are sky and water borne,
death is yodelling quiet in green woodlots,
and bodies of three young birds have disappeared
in the sub-surface of the new county highway –   20

That picture is incomplete, part left out
that might alter the whole Durer landscape:
gothic ancestors peer from medieval sky,
dour faces trapped in photograph albums escaping
to clop down iron roads with matched greys:
work-sodden wives groping inside their flesh
for what keeps moving and changing and flashing

beyond and past the long frozen Victorian day.
A sign of fire and brimstone? A two-headed calf
born in the barn last night? A sharp female agony?   30
An age and a faith moving into transition,
the dinner cold and new-baked bread a failure,
deep woods shiver and water drops hang pendant,
double yolked eggs and the house creaks a little —
Something is about to happen. Leaves are still.
Two shores away, a man hammering in the sky.
Perhaps he will fall.

(1968)   (1972)

Tourist Itinerary

North of Kirkland Lake raspberries are red earrings
in heat like a tropic summer
but even in August nights are cold
trees shrink a little past the height of land
that slopes down the arctic watershed
Driving north
a bear crosses the road
at his private pedestrian crossing
the first animal we had seen
and almost asked for his autograph   10
Then Cochrane and the train to Moosonee
over the soft spongy trapper's country
crossing and re-crossing the Abitibi
until it joins the big Moose
our elderly train jogging the river valley
past rocks like the heads of queens
Indians with closed faces at Moose Factory
huge wood piles and shabby houses
selling bannock and toy boats for a living
knowing it isn't a very good one   20
know it's the best there is
I add another piece of mosaic
to the coloured memory inside
I know what the place looks like
tasted the food and touched the land

which is as much as any of us can do
following a road map in the mind
a memory of the place we came from
and the way we are always returning

(1973)   (1973)

Freydis Eriksdottir in Greenland
(– after killing the Icelanders in the New World)

Three years in that country
are a grey mist floating thru the mind:
and yet my dead men remain there
my son conceived there
so that the unreal becomes
my only reality
Greenland and the ice mountains
even Erik whose daughter I am
phantoms of old remembrance now
reminders of another country   10
we called Markland:
the sea blundering inland up wild rivers
sunlight ghostly with daylong shadows
the forest with its crowded loneliness
of death cries and the birth of life
If I am a murderess as they say
instead of executioner of traitors
warrior among Karlsefni's cowards
standing off the Skraelings
beating a sword against my breasts   20
because I feared to live
unless unafraid to die
a murderess among murderers
– then nothing has changed
a world of blood is what we live in
the land of Karlsefni and Leif Eriksson
is claimed by blood
across floating ice and long drowned seas
the jetsam of when we were children
the Norns weave treachery   30

Nothing gentle here
and love is for the strong
love that holds nothing of gentleness
my child suckled on blood
axe against the bleeding trees
swords against the Skraelings
ourselves against ourselves
as it always was
The grey mist in my mind
mingles with mist along that coast   40
I claimed by being what I am
and not denying it
then or now

(1973)   (1973)

Borderlands

No way of knowing where we went
on those long journeys
Sometimes there was a whiteness
as of snow that obscured everything
but it wasn't snow
Sometimes it seemed we left a campfire
and looking for it again
couldn't even find the burned place
blundering into trees and buildings
– but then nothing   10
has ever confused me as much as light
Sometimes we arrived back separately
but still seemed inside the borders
we crossed by accident
and want to be there if we think it real
but we do not think it real
There is one memory
of you smiling in the darkness
and the smile has shaped the air
      around your face 20
someone you met in a dream
has dreamed you waking

(1976)   (1976)

Inside the Mill

It's a building where men are still working
thru sunlight and starlight and moonlight
despite the black holes plunging down
on their way to the roots of the earth
no danger exists for them
transparent as shadows they labour
in their manufacture of light

I've gone there lonely sometimes
the way I felt as a boy
and something lightened inside me   10
— old hands sift the dust that was flour
and the lumbering wagons returning
afloat in their pillar of shadows
as the great wheel turns the world

When you cross the doorway you feel them
when you cross the places they've been
there's a flutter of time in your heartbeat
of time going backward and forward
if you feel it and perhaps you don't
but it's voyaging backward and forward   20
on a gate in the sea of your mind

When the mill was torn down I went back there
birds fumed into fire at the place
a red sun beat hot in the stillness
they moved there transparent as morning
one illusion balanced another
as the dream holds the real in proportion
and the howl in our hearts to a sigh

(1976)   (1976)

Sheila Watson
1919–

———◆———

BORN IN NEW Westminster, British Columbia, Sheila (Doherty) Watson
was educated at the Universities of British Columbia and Toronto and
now teaches at the University of Alberta. In addition to several short
stories, she has published *The Double Hook* (1959), an intricately
structured symbolic novel set in the interior of British Columbia. A
collection of her stories and critical studies was published in the journal
Open Letter (Winter, 1974-75). "Antigone" first appeared in *Tamarack
Review* in 1959.

Antigone

MY FATHER RULED a kingdom on the right bank of the river. He ruled it
with a firm hand and a stout heart though he was often more troubled
than Moses, who was simply trying to bring a stubborn and moody
people under God's yoke. My father ruled men who thought they were
gods or the instruments of gods or, at very least, god-afflicted and
god-pursued. He ruled Atlas who held up the sky, and Hermes who
went on endless messages, and Helen who'd been hatched from an egg,
and Pan the gardener, and Kallisto the bear, and too many others to
mention by name. Yet my father had no thunderbolt, no trident, no
helmet of darkness. His subjects were delivered bound into his hands.
He merely watched over them as the hundred-handed ones watched
over the dethroned Titans so that they wouldn't bother Hellas again.

Despite the care which my father took to maintain an atmosphere of
sober common sense in his whole establishment, there were occasional
outbursts of self-indulgence which he could not control. For instance, I
have seen Helen walking naked down the narrow cement path under
the chestnut trees for no better reason, I suppose, than that the day was
hot and the white flowers themselves lay naked and expectant in the
sunlight. And I have seen Atlas forget the sky while he sat eating the
dirt which held him up. These were things which I was not supposed to
see.

If my father had been as sensible through and through as he was
thought to be, he would have packed me off to boarding school when I

was old enough to be disciplined by men. Instead he kept me at home with my two cousins who, except for the accident of birth, might as well have been my sisters. Today I imagine people concerned with our welfare would take such an environment into account. At the time I speak of most people thought us fortunate – especially the girls whose father's affairs had come to an unhappy issue. I don't like to revive old scandal and I wouldn't except to deny it; but it takes only a few impertinent newcomers in any community to force open cupboards which have been decently sealed by time. However, my father was so busy setting his kingdom to rights that he let weeds grow up in his own garden.

As I said, if my father had had all his wits about him he would have sent me to boarding school – and Antigone and Ismene too. I might have fallen in love with the headmaster's daughter and Antigone might have learned that no human being can be right always. She might have found out besides that from the seeds of eternal justice grow madder flowers than any which Pan grew in the gardens of my father's kingdom.

Between the kingdom which my father ruled and the wilderness flows a river. It is this river which I am crossing now. Antigone is with me.

How often can we cross the same river, Antigone asks.

Her persistence annoys me. Besides, Heraklitos made nonsense of her question years ago. He saw a river too – the Inachos, the Kephissos, the Lethaios. The name doesn't matter. He said: See how quickly the water flows. However agile a man is, however nimbly he swims, or runs, or flies, the water slips away before him. See, even as he sets down his foot the water is displaced by the stream which crowds along in the shadow of its flight.

But after all, Antigone says, one must admit that it is the same kind of water. The oolichans run in it as they ran last year and the year before. The gulls cry above the same banks. Boats drift towards the Delta and circle back against the current to gather up the catch.

At any rate, I tell her, we're standing on a new bridge. We are standing so high that the smell of mud and river weeds passes under us out to the straits. The unbroken curve of the bridge protects the eye from details of river life. The bridge is foolproof as a clinic's passport to happiness.

The old bridge still spans the river, but the cat-walk with its cracks and knot-holes, with its gap between planking and hand-rail has been torn down. The centre arch still grinds open to let boats up and down the river, but a child can no longer be walked on it or swung out on it beyond the water-gauge at the very centre of the flood.

I've known men who scorned any kind of bridge, Antigone says. Men have walked into the water, she says, or, impatient, have jumped from the bridge into the river below.

But these, I say, didn't really want to cross the river. They went Persephone's way, cradled in the current's arms, down the long halls under the pink feet of the gulls, under the booms and tow-lines, under the soft bellies of the fish.

Antigone looks at me.

There's no coming back, she says, if one goes far enough.

I know she's going to speak of her own misery and I won't listen. Only a god has the right to say: Look what I suffer. Only a god should say: What more ought I to have done for you that I have not done?

Once in winter, she says, a man walked over the river.

Taking advantage of nature, I remind her, since the river had never frozen before.

Yet he escaped from the penitentiary, she says. He escaped from the guards walking round the walls or standing with their guns in the sentry-boxes at the four corners of the enclosure. He escaped.

Not without risk, I say. He had to test the strength of the ice himself. Yet safer perhaps than if he had crossed by the old bridge where he might have slipped through a knot-hole or tumbled out through the railing.

He did escape, she persists, and lived forever on the far side of the river in the Alaska tea and bulrushes. For where, she asks, can a man go farther than to the outermost edge of the world?

The habitable world, as I've said, is on the right bank of the river. Here is the market with its market stalls — the coops of hens, the long-tongued geese, the haltered calf, the bearded goat, the shoving pigs, and the empty bodies of cows and sheep and rabbits hanging on iron hooks. My father's kingdom provides asylum in the suburbs. Near it are the convent, the churches, and the penitentiary. Above these on the hill the cemetery looks down on the people and on the river itself.

It is a world spread flat, tipped up into the sky so that men and women bend forward, walking as men walk when they board a ship at high tide. This is the world I feel with my feet. It is the world I see with my eyes.

I remember standing once with Antigone and Ismene in the square just outside the gates of my father's kingdom. Here from a bust set high on a cairn the stone eyes of Simon Fraser look from his stone face over the river that he found.

It is the head that counts, Ismene said.

It's no better than an urn, Antigone said, one of the urns we see when we climb to the cemetery above.

And all I could think was that I didn't want an urn, only a flat green grave with a chain about it.

A chain won't keep out the dogs, Antigone said.

But his soul could swing on it, Ismene said, like a bird blown on a branch in the wind.

And I remember Antigone's saying: The cat drags its belly on the ground and the rat sharpens its tooth in the ivy.

I should have loved Ismene, but I didn't. It was Antigone I loved. I should have loved Ismene because, although she walked the flat world with us, she managed somehow to see it round.

The earth is an oblate spheroid, she'd say. And I knew that she saw it there before her comprehensible and whole like a tangerine spiked through and held in place while it rotated on the axis of one of Nurse's steel sock needles. The earth was a tangerine and she saw the skin peeled off and the world parcelled out into neat segments, each segment sweet and fragrant in its own skin.

It's the head that counts, she said.

In her own head she made diagrams to live by, cut and fashioned after the eternal patterns spied out by Plato as he rummaged about in the sewing basket of the gods.

I should have loved Ismene. She would live now in some prefabricated and perfect chrysolite by some paradigm which made love round and whole. She would simply live and leave destruction in the purgatorial ditches outside her own walled paradise.

Antigone is different. She sees the world flat as I do and feels it tip beneath her feet. She has walked in the market and seen the living animals penned and the dead hanging stiff on their hooks. Yet she defies what she sees with a defiance which is almost denial. Like Atlas she tries to keep the vaulted sky from crushing the flat earth. Like Hermes she brings a message that there is life if one can escape to it in the brush and bulrushes in some dim Hades beyond the river. It is defiance not belief and I tell her that this time we walk the bridge to a walled cave where we can deny death no longer.

Yet she asks her question still. And standing there I tell her that Heraklitos had made nonsense of her question. I should have loved Ismene for she would have taught me what Plato meant when he said in all earnest that the union of the soul with the body is in no way better than dissolution. I expect that she understood things which Antigone is too proud to see.

I turn away from her and flatten my elbows on the high wall of the bridge. I look back at my father's kingdom. I see the terraces rolling down from the red-brick buildings with their barred windows. I remember hands shaking the bars and hear fingers tearing up paper and stuffing it through the meshes. Diktynna, mother of nets and high leaping fear. O Artemis, mistress of wild beasts and wild men.

The inmates are beginning to come out on the screened verandas.

They pace up and down in straight lines or stand silent like figures which appear at the same time each day from some depths inside a clock.

On the upper terrace Pan the gardener is shifting sprinklers with a hooked stick. His face is shadowed by the brim of his hat. He moves as economically as an animal between the beds of lobelia and geranium. It is high noon.

Antigone has cut out a piece of sod and has scooped out a grave. The body lies in a coffin in the shade of the magnolia tree. Antigone and I are standing. Ismene is sitting between two low angled branches of the monkey puzzle tree. Her lap is filled with daisies. She slits the stem of one daisy and pulls the stem of another through it. She is making a chain for her neck and a crown for her hair.

Antigone reaches for a branch of the magnolia. It is almost beyond her grip. The buds flame above her. She stands on a small fire of daisies which smoulder in the roots of the grass.

I see the magnolia buds. They brood above me, whiteness feathered on whiteness. I see Antigone's face turned to the light. I hear the living birds call to the sun. I speak private poetry to myself: Between four trumpeting angels at the four corners of the earth a bride stands before the altar in a gown as white as snow.

Yet I must have been speaking aloud because Antigone challenges me: You're mistaken. It's the winds the angels hold, the four winds of the earth. After the just are taken to paradise the winds will destroy the earth. It's a funeral, she says, not a wedding.

She looks towards the building.

Someone is coming down the path from the matron's house, she says.

I notice that she has pulled one of the magnolia blossoms from the branch. I take it from her. It is streaked with brown where her hands have bruised it. The sparrow which she has decided to bury lies on its back. Its feet are clenched tight against the feathers of its breast. I put the flower in the box with it.

Someone is coming down the path. She is wearing a blue cotton dress. Her cropped head is bent. She walks slowly carrying something in a napkin.

It's Kallisto the bear, I say. Let's hurry. What will my father say if he sees us talking to one of his patients?

If we live here with him, Antigone says, what can he expect? If he spends his life trying to tame people he can't complain if you behave as if they were tame. What would your father think, she says, if he saw us digging in the Institution lawn?

Pan comes closer. I glower at him. There's no use speaking to him. He's deaf and dumb.

Listen, I say to Antigone, my father's not unreasonable. Kallisto thinks she's a bear and he thinks he's a bear tamer, that's all. As for the lawn, I say quoting my father without conviction, a man must have order among his own if he is to keep order in the state.

Kallisto has come up to us. She is smiling and laughing to herself. She gives me her bundle.

Fish, she says.

I open the napkin.

Pink fish sandwiches, I say.

For the party, she says.

But it isn't a party, Antigone says. It's a funeral.

For the funeral breakfast, I say.

Ismene is twisting two chains of daisies into a rope. Pan has stopped pulling the sprinkler about. He is standing beside Ismene resting himself on his hooked stick. Kallisto squats down beside her. Ismene turns away, preoccupied, but she can't turn far because of Pan's legs.

Father said we never should
Play with madmen in the wood.

I look at Antigone.

It's my funeral, she says.

I go over to Ismene and gather up a handful of loose daisies from her lap. The sun reaches through the shadow of the magnolia tree.

It's my funeral, Antigone says. She moves possessively toward the body.

An ant is crawling into the bundle of sandwiches which I've put on the ground. A file of ants is marching on the sparrow's box.

I go over and drop daisies on the bird's stiff body. My voice speaks ritual words: Deliver me, O Lord, from everlasting death on this dreadful day. I tremble and am afraid.

The voice of a people comforts me. I look at Antigone. I look her in the eye.

It had better be a proper funeral then, I say.

Kallisto is crouched forward on her hands. Tears are running down her cheeks and she is licking them away with her tongue.

My voice rises again: I said in the midst of my days, I shall not see —

Antigone just stands there. She looks frightened, but her eyes defy me with their assertion.

It's my funeral, she says. It's my bird. I was the one who wanted to bury it.

She is looking for a reason. She will say something which sounds eternally right.

Things have to be buried, she says. They can't be left lying around anyhow for people to see.

Birds shouldn't die, I tell her. They have wings. Cats and rats haven't wings.

Stop crying, she says to Kallisto. It's only a bird.

It has a bride's flower in its hand, Kallisto says.

We shall rise again, I mutter, but we shall not all be changed.

Antigone does not seem to hear me.

Behold, I say in a voice she must hear, in a moment, in the twinkling of an eye, the trumpet shall sound.

Ismene turns to Kallisto and throws the daisy chain about her neck.

Shall a virgin forget her adorning or a bride the ornament of her breast?

Kallisto is lifting her arms towards the tree.

The bridegroom has come, she says, white as a fall of snow. He stands above me in a great ring of fire.

Antigone looks at me now.

Let's cover the bird up, she says. Your father will punish us all for making a disturbance.

He has on his garment, Kallisto says, and on his thigh is written King of Kings.

I look at the tree. If I could see with Kallisto's eyes I wouldn't be afraid of death, or punishment, or the penitentiary guards. I wouldn't be afraid of my father's belt or his honing strap or his bedroom slipper. I wouldn't be afraid of falling into the river through a knot-hole in the bridge.

But, as I look, I see the buds falling like burning lamps and I hear the sparrow twittering in its box: Woe, woe, woe because of the three trumpets which are yet to sound.

Kallisto is on her knees. She is growling like a bear. She lumbers over to the sandwiches and mauls them with her paw.

Ismene stands alone for Pan the gardener has gone.

Antigone is fitting a turf in place above the coffin. I go over and press the edge of the turf with my feet. Ismene has caught me by the hand.

Go away, Antigone says.

I see my father coming down the path. He has an attendant with him. In front of them walks Pan holding the sprinkler hook like a spear.

What are you doing here? my father says.

Burying a bird, Antigone says.

Here? my father asks again.

Where else could I bury it? Antigone says.

My father looks at her.

This ground is public property, he says. No single person has any right to an inch of it.

I've taken six inches, Antigone says. Will you dig the bird up again?

Some of his subjects my father restrained since they were moved to throw themselves from high places or to tear one another to bits from jealousy or rage. Others who disturbed the public peace he taught to walk in the airing courts or to work in the kitchen or in the garden.

If men live at all, my father said, it is because discipline saves their life for them.

From Antigone he simply turned away.

(1959)   (1959)

Jacques Ferron
1921-

BORN IN LOUISEVILLE, Quebec, Jacques Ferron was educated at the Seminary of Trois Rivières and at Laval University. A medical doctor, he has practised in Ville Jacques-Cartier, a suburb of Montreal, since 1949. One of Quebec's most prolific writers, Ferron has published plays, novels, stories and essays. Three novels, *Cotnoir* (1962), *L'Amélanchier* (1970) and *Le Saint-Elias* (1972), have been translated into English as *Dr. Cotnoir* (1973), *The Juneberry Tree* (1975) and *The Saint Elias* (1973). A selection of stories from his first two collections was published in translation as *Tales from the Uncertain Country* in 1972.

The Bridge

THIS WAS SOME time ago. The Seaway Canal had not yet been dug. In the evenings I was in the habit of forgetting my practice and seeking out another world on the other side of the river. The bridge marked the half-way point, and was itself divided, both architecturally and according to the direction in which I was going. When I approached it from the south, crossing over to the north, no structure was visible overhead, and I hardly noticed I had left the road. I would walk under an open sky as far as the Ile Sainte-Hélène. There it seemed I was already in Montreal. I was no longer aware of the bridge, so eager was I for promising encounters. But as I returned, tired, disappointed, my eyes could not escape the compelling power of its superstructure and the magnificent tracery of its steel girders. Night enclosed it like a cathedral. I would enter it with remorse, regretting the time I had wasted and my neglected duties. The high black arch came to an end and opened out onto the lights of the lowest stars, and those along the plain which stretches from Longueuil to Chambly, from Saint Lambert to Saint-Amable, these lights variously grouped in constellations, small villages, and large suburbs. In the midst of this glimmering rose the dark shapes of the mountains — Saint-Bruno, Beloeil, and Rougemont. This sight would reconcile me to my side of the river. Each time I would vow never to leave it again.

Sometimes I would pass a horse and cart. The driver was a woman. In the cart she carried scrap-metal to Montreal, then headed back to Coteau Rouge, where she was a fellow-citizen of mine. I knew her. She was one of those English women, still marked by Europe who for some strange reason flee their race and feel happy only among French Canadians. The latter in return assimilate them. This is where we get a good many of our red-heads. One does one's best to gallicize, usually from the bottom up, while Englishness asserts itself from the top down. Nothing could have been more wretched nor at the same time more proud than this woman. The shack she lived in was divided in two by a semi-partition: on one side the horse, on the other side her family. This family: her husband, pin boy in a bowling alley, a good-for-nothing, and two rather snotty children.

There and back, her expedition took her about four hours. She left around ten o'clock in the evening. That was roughly the hour I left the south shore. And my return often coincided with hers. Now, at the time, because of a photographer friend who wanted to go into film-making, I was thinking in terms of cinema. I had thought of using this strange group. The action of the film, its climax and its dénouement, would take place within four hours. By showing from time to time the horse, the cart, the English woman, I felt I could indicate in an interesting way the precious moments allotted to the characters for their happiness or unhappiness. However the idea was not new, and I was all the less original for having seen "The Phantom Carriage"*. Besides the photographer did not go into films, and I stopped thinking about my scenario. Yet I was left with the pretext for the film — this little group, which measured the passing of time and was

*Körkarlen (1920) by Victor Sjöström, a classic of the Swedish cinema, based on the novel by Selma Lagerlöf [Translator's note].

a reminder of destiny. Today I cannot think of the bridge without remembering them. I have always had a weakness for fine words and beautiful images – even secondhand. That is probably why I write.

During the day the English woman would go along the streets of the suburb before the arrival of the garbage trucks. Old springs, the remains of washing machines and stoves, any old metal interested her. She went to a great deal of trouble and earned very little money. Perhaps it was to make use of her horse, quite a fine animal. But what do I know? What did I ever know about her? Everything was an enigma, even her age. Was she twenty-five, thirty, thirty-five? Thin, bony, red haired, and not in the least feminine, she did not arouse desire or even pity. She seemed to expect nothing from anyone and to remain, in everything she did, an outsider. Perhaps she was mad. She had fine features and her skin was extremely white. She never struck me as vulgar; on the contrary, by a strange air of authority, she commanded respect. But this authority was due perhaps to her origins and to our own feeling of inferiority. I had noticed that she was growing rather stout. One night I was called to her shack. She had given birth alone. I cut the cord and completed the delivery. She did not utter a word or make a sound. She seemed to be thinking of something else. This third child did not prevent her from going back to work. But a few months later she disappeared. I still meet her good-for-nothing husband reeling along. No one has seen her since, neither her nor her horse, the last one to cross the river regularly. The cart has become, like that carriage, a phantom one. If I see it again some night on the deserted bridge I shall know I have had an accident.

(1962)   (1972)

Betty Bednarski (Trans.)

The Flood

A HABITANT AND good farmer, who had managed to obtain from his wife thirteen children, all well-grown though of unequal size, lived with his family in a farmhouse which was a strange kind of house, for every year in winter it would float on the snow for forty days or more; yet in spring it would become a house like any other, returning to the very spot it had occupied before, in Fontarabie *rang*, Sainte-Ursule de Maskinongé. This house had two doors; the front door opened onto the King's Highway, the back door onto the habitant's land. Now one spring the eldest son went out the back door and began to help his father, whose heir he subsequently became. That door was never used again. Every spring from then on the children went out by the front door; boys and girls in the flower of youth, they set out one by one on the King's Highway to sow their seeds elsewhere. The habitant shook hands with each and every one, saying: "Bon voyage, my pigeon, bon voyage, my dove. Come and see me at Christmas; I'll be expecting you." But these children bore more resemblance to the crow: they never came back. With the exception of one. When he appeared in Fontarabie, having failed to found a family elsewhere, the old man was sitting on his front steps, his beard bristling, his stick between his knees, raising himself up from time to time to get a better look at any creature that happened by. When he saw his son he asked himself whose offspring this runt could be, for he looked familiar. He started with the most distant families, then, having no success, worked closer and with some apprehension began to go through local names and names of relatives. "You don't understand," said the runt, "I'm your son." The old man did not deny it; it was quite possible.

"Have you come to see your mother?" he asked.

"Yes," replied the son.

"Well, you're out of luck: your mother's dead and buried."

The runt took the news very well; he had been away for a long time.

"I haven't married again," added the old habitant; but so saying he raised himself up with the help of his stick, peering into the distance to see if there were not by chance a woman in sight.

"What about you, son; have you got any children?"

"No," the poor devil replied.

The old man grew thoughtful.

"And your wife, what's she like?" he asked, without getting up, but tightening his grip on the stick, his beard flashing sparks. He was thinking that his runt of a son might invite him to his house, where he would be alone all day with a young daughter-in-law. The answer shattered his hopes.

"Have you at least been to the city?"

"Yes," replied the son.

Then the old man, who knew perfectly well, having seen it in the papers, that in the city there were hundreds and hundreds of girls gathered together in an enclosure, raised himself up on his stick, filled with the greatest indignation:

"Stay here," he shouted, "I'll go in your place!"

And off he went. Winter was not far away. Soon the snow came down and the strange house broke loose from Fontarabie and began to float; it floated slowly over the lost generation, an absurd ark, raft of the helpless; it floated over the old man, who, from the depths of the flood, brandished his terrible stick.

(1964)   (1972)

Betty Bednarski (Trans.)

Raymond Souster
1921–

BORN AND EDUCATED in Toronto, Raymond Souster served in the RCAF in England during World War II. Following his discharge, he returned to Toronto where he has worked for many years in the Canadian Imperial Bank of Commerce. Since 1946, when he published his first collection of poems *When We Are Young,* Souster has published more than twenty volumes of poetry and has edited and co-edited several anthologies of Canadian verse. In addition, he founded and edited two "little magazines," *Contact* (1952-1953) and *Combustion* (1957-1960), and was a founder and editor of Contact Press.

Young Girls

With the night full of spring and stars we stand
here in this dark doorway and watch the young
girls pass, two, three together, hand in hand.
Like flowers they are whose fragrance has not sprung
or awakened, whose bodies dimly feel
the flooding upward welling of the trees;
whose senses, caressed by the wind's soft fingers, reel
with a delirium that makes them ill at ease.
They lie awake at night unable to sleep
and walk the streets kindled by strange desires;   10
they steal glances at us, unable to keep
control upon those subterranean fires.
We whistle after them, then laugh, for they
stiffen, not knowing what to do or say.

(1946)   (1964)

Lagoons, Hanlan's Point

Mornings
before the sun's liquid
spilled gradually, flooding
the island's cool cellar,
there was the boat
and the still lagoons,
with the sound of my oars
the only intrusion
over cries of birds
10 in the marshy shallows,
or the loud thrashing
of the startled crane
rushing the air.

And in one strange
dark, tree-hung entrance,
I followed the sound
of my heart all the way
to the reed-blocked ending,
with the pads of the lily

thick as green-shining film   20
covering the water.

And in another
where the sun came
to probe the depths
through a shaft of branches,
I saw the skeletons
of brown ships rotting
far below in their burial-ground,
and wondered what strange fish
with what strange colours   30
swam through these palaces
under the water....

A small boy
with a flat-bottomed punt
and an old pair of oars
moving with wonder
throught the antechamber
of a waking world.

(1952)   (1964)

Flight of the Roller-Coaster

Once more around should do it, the man confided...

and sure enough, when the roller-coaster reached the peak
of the giant curve above me, screech of its wheels
almost drowned out by the shriller cries of the riders,

instead of the dip and plunge with its landslide of screams,
it rose in the air like a movieland magic carpet,
     some wonderful bird,

and without fuss or fanfare swooped slowly across
    the amusement-park,
over Spook's Castle, ice-cream booths, shooting-gallery.   10
    and losing no height

made the last yards above the beach, where the cucumber-cool
brakeman in the last seat saluted
a lady about to change from her bathing-suit.

Then, as many witnesses reported, headed leisurely
    out over the water,
disappearing all too soon behind a low-flying flight of clouds.

(1955)   (1964)

Legende

gaston	saint-denis
miron	neon
poet	bars
unshaven	alleys
hungry	rooms 20
confused	whores
inspired	bums
homeless	addicts
loved	C
10 unloved	C
drunkenness	F
despair	poet
books	gaston
roses	miron
l'hexagone	

(1958)   (1975)

The Six-Quart Basket

The six-quart basket   sits in the centre of the lawn
one side gone   and slowly fills up
half the handle torn off   with the white fruits of the snow.

(1958)   (1964)

All This Slow Afternoon

All this slow afternoon
the May winds blowing
honey of the lilacs,
sounds of waves washing
through the highest branches
of my poplar tree.

Enough in such hours
to be simply alive;
10 I will take death tomorrow
without bitterness.

(1962)

Today all I ask
is to be left alone
in the wind
in the sunshine,
with the honey of lilacs
down the garden;

to fall asleep tired
of small birds' gossip,
of so much greenness
pushed behind my eyes.   20

(1968)

Words Before a Statue of Champlain

COUCHICHING PARK, ORILLIA

Whether or not he wore spurs
(which bothers my father
once in the cavalry)
is a moot question,
but well in keeping
with the high-flowing plume
the broad-brimmed hat
the sword in scabbard
his loose-flowing robes.

10 The sculptor, no Rodin,
has at least caught
the look of vision
in the man's eyes
the gleam of unrest
(slow flame burning
beneath the brow):

the other figures cluttering
the statue's base
garbage,

thrown in for good measure   20
to give the town
its money's worth —
the crazy-eyed Jesuit
the cowering Indians —
Samuel should run them through
two at a time right now
for defiling this moment
of history:

"Samuel de Champlain
with fifteen companions   30
arrived in these parts
Summer 1615,
and spent the winter
at Cahiagué,
chief village of the Hurons
near this place."

This Easter Sunday
the sun strong

the wind warm with spring,
but the ice core still solid
40   far as eye can see
on Lake Couchiching,
as if refusing
to believe in its death
foretold on the front page
of the local daily:

George Creagh,
Coldwater Road,
retired minister:
"I think April 24th
50   would be a good day
for the ice to go out"
(the town's favourite guessing
      game):

but standing here now
on Government Wharf,
looking down at the ice-slabs
still four feet thick,
the 24th looks
very optimistic indeed.

As for Samuel —
60   what would he say
looking at us here
in this April?

The boy and girl
strolling up the road,
arms around each other
as only lovers twine them,
the kids playing baseball
on the bumpy diamond,
one winding up to throw
70   the way you'd expect
a Canadian to do it,
much strength, no finesse;

me with my weak eyes
so slapped by the ice glare
I have to turn away,
with a small boy making mud-pies

down at the water's edge
with what must be ice-water:

otherwise the lake   80
not that much different
when he scanned it then
wondering what lay beyond.

But the rest of it,
these times, this town,
these people he never knew,
all different, changed,
torn up, confused,
turned inward, buried under.

The town of course   90
Leacock's still
(the Stephen Leacock Hotel,
TV in every room),
the many signs,
his summer house
out old Brewery Bay,

Sunshine Sketches
of a Little Town
with its old houses
on quiet tree-heavy   100
streets still beautiful
and hiding well
what twisted lives
what family skeletons,

but as solid still
as the red-grained rock
the highway going north
to Gravenhurst, Bracebridge
cuts harshly through;

yet curiously stiff,   110
out of joint,
like the top face carved
on the curious, miniature
totem-pole over yonder —
not a real totem-pole

but like so much
in this faked-over world
a joke, a caricature
(not really intended)
120 of a lost people,
Indian:

(a word people say
with the self-same love
they spit phlegm from the throat.
Indian.
Furtive, poorly dressed,
in the back-water streets
of this town,
sun-bronzed faces
130 of the past and no future)

(1962)

but once allies,
fellow warriors,
of this man cast in bronze,
man with comic-opera clothes,
sword dragging the ground,
man with vision obsolete
as these sixteen-pounders
dated 1810
they've dragged from the lake,

man with that spirit 140
of an age we deny,
still defiling the destiny
these ancestors charted

passed to barren hands.

(1975)

The Sirens

Though you may escape them,
bound tight to the mast,
ears well plugged,
sight the one betrayer –

some day, when least expected,
you'll hear that singing
(grown more compelling, you can only guess),
see every gesture eyes once telegraphed
from that throbbing shore
(now at the moment of the writhing climax), 10

and know your good captain lied,
that his ropes and wax
did you only disservice:
that all your life
you'll hear those mocking voices,
see those bodies sinuously beckoning,
insidious by day, tumultuous by night.

(1967)

(1967)

Queen Anne's Lace

It's a kind of flower
that if you didn't know it
you'd pass by the rest of your life.

But once it's pointed out
you'll look for it always,
even in places
where you know it can't possibly be.

You will never tire
of bending over to examine,
to marvel at this,   10
shyest filigree of wonder
born among grasses.

You will imagine poems
as brief, as spare,
so natural with themselves
as to take breath away.

(1972)   (1974)

First Holiday Morning

Easily morning's earliest
most beautiful, laziest thought —

you lying beside me
far away in sleep,
while all through this city
alarum clocks are piercing brains,
breakfasts are being gobbled,
sleepy faces smear on lipstick, creams,
blades nick too deeply into skins,
car exhausts roar,   10
buses pack bodies to spew them
underground into subway trains

for flashing mole-deep rides
to offices still half-asleep themselves,
to streets still yawning in the weekend dust....

There the thought ends,
returns to you
resting easily beside me,
leaves me too as I
try to hunt you out,   20
catch up to you, walk beside you
in some strange country you may be entering now.

(1974)   (1974)

These Wild Crab-Apples

No bigger than cherries,
skin-shrivelled, pulp-empty,

these wild crab-apples
nevertheless cling hard
to their wind-tortured branches,

though being dead
they need not fear death.

But looking at them
from my safe window,
this must be the thing   10
that frightens me.

(1977)   (1977)

Elizabeth Brewster
1922-

BORN IN CHIPMAN, New Brunswick, Elizabeth Brewster was educated at Radcliffe College and the Universities of New Brunswick, London, Toronto and Indiana. She has worked as a librarian and as a teacher in many Canadian universities. Since the publication of her first collection of poetry, *East Coast* (1951), she has published several volumes including *Passage of Summer* (1969), *Sunrise North* (1972), *In Search of Eros* (1974) and *Sometimes I Think of Moving* (1977).

Granite's Not Firm Enough

Granite's not firm enough
To stay my mind;
I must in harder stone
Foundation find.

Fire cannot burn enough,
Ice cannot freeze.

(1951)

Some fiercer agony
Heal my disease.

Steel cannot cut me true
To touch the bone;   10
Sharper blade must divide
To make me one.

(1969)

Valley by 'Bus: November

The familiar landscape
Appears through the mist
As foreign,
Chinese.

The river is grey silk.
The trees are picture language
Written on the sky,
A bare alphabet.

394

Rocks, barns, mail boxes
10 Are matching grey.
A watery sun reveals
Brown, curled ferns,

A spray of amber leaves,
A sudden field
Wet and green as spring
Against the brown.

(1969)

(1969)

Sunrise North

Drawing my drapes, I see
pink and purple clouds of dawn
over the white-roofed city,
smoke in rising fountains,
the lights of early risers
twinkling far off,
the new moon, hanging low,
beginning to pale in the morning sky.

The beautiful northern city
is a child's Christmas toy   10
spread out like blocks
with here and there a tree
deftly placed
discreetly frosted;
and, like a child,
I want to pick it up,
move a house here, a tree there,
put more frost on that distant dome.

The colours fade, the pale blue sky grows higher.
Now I see the sun   20
gradually rising
over the rim of water-flat plain,
bonfire bright, triumphant.
Soon I shall walk out,
through the white snow, dry as sugar,
into the real street.

(1972)

(1972)

Christmas Day: Road to Oban

Driving a snowy road towards Oban
I think of the homesick Scots of the world
and understand both why they leave home
and why they are homesick.

This landscape haunts dreams;
and the closed eye sees
rocks, hills, water, bending roads,
sheep on the roads, a flight of birds,
a few sparse trees
remote from houses   10
in a veil of snow.

Caesar did not conquer here,
nor the English really.
A stubborn, Northern land,
difficult to come by,
I can imagine it still
when H-bombs have wrecked other countries
sheltering a rugged soul or two
in its borders
and a few birds and sheep.   20

(1972)   (1972)

Mirrors

Mirrors are always magical.
So the child knows
who first sees one: the strange object
in which the other little girl appears
wearing the same dress, encircled in the same arms;
smiles, frowns, looks puzzled, cries, all the same
but somehow different.
For the other child does not have flesh, feels shiny to touch
and cold like the mirror's surface.

Mirrors are magic, and behind their surface   10
surely there is another Alice world
where you can walk and talk.

Mirrors are solid lakes,
and you could drown
beneath them if their outer layer cracked,
spin down and meet your real self far below,
a mermaid princess combing out your hair
before a magic mirror.

(1974)   (1974)

On Becoming An Ancestor

Too late in life
for children, the building
of flesh and bone
out of flesh and bone,
all that blood and guts
other women talk of.

By chance or intention
whatever touching
of body or mind
10 came too late.

Not my fault, it seems to me,
I would have liked
I think

Or maybe I was scared.
Many things scared me.

Does it matter?
Flesh becomes
the green blood of grass.
Poems disintegrate
to their original syllables.   20

There is no avoiding
the process of transformation,
of becoming
a sort of ancestor,
like the lovers in old songs
from whose buried mouths
grew briars and roses.

My fears were unnecessary
but after all did not change
the end result   30
which (whether I fear or hope)
is not an end

(1977)   (1977)

Eli Mandel
1922-

———◆———

BORN IN ESTEVAN, Saskatchewan, Eli Mandel was educated at the Universities of Saskatchewan and Toronto. After teaching at various colleges and universities, he became a Professor of English and Humanities at York University in 1967. Influential as a critic and editor, Mandel published his first independent volume, *Fuseli Poems*, in 1960. Subsequent collections include *An Idiot Joy* (1967), *Stoney Plain* (1973) and *Crusoe: Poems Selected and New* (1973).

From
Minotaur Poems

II

My father was always out in the garage
building a shining wing, a wing
that curved and flew along the edge of blue air
in that streamed and sunlit room
that smelled of oil and engines
and crankcase grease, and especially
the lemon smell of polish and cedar.
Outside there were sharp rocks, and trees,
cold air where birds fell like rocks
and screams, hawks, kites, and cranes.   10
The air was filled with buzzing and flying
and the invisible hum of a bee's wings was honey
in my father's framed and engined mind.
Last Saturday we saw him at the horizon
screaming like a hawk as he fell into the sun.

(1954)   (1973)

Children of the Sun

Light falls upon them and they see the form
That gave them birth and praise it with the names
Of northern trees, the cedar and the pine and fir,
The wood within the wood to build the form
That all may praise what the eye sees and the ear
Hears amid the rock and in the weary hills
Over the sleeping land where night falls.

I think about my past and try to change
Into a singing metaphor a silent heart,
A frail red parrot perched within its cage   10
Repeating what it hears and cackling without change
All that ear hears and tongue speaks. I form in thought
The singing form that forms the silent heart.

But parrots bring in sleep only the surly shape
Of images of men turned into beasts
Carrying their loads of shame upon their backs,
That forest where the trees are shapes of girls
And every stone an image of a face, and eyes
Are in the flowers, and I could weep for all
Those lost and stoned and silent faces.   20

Such images rise up in thought as out of dreams
Rose from the sea, still hung in weeds,
To haunt poor Shelley or to torment Yeats,
Such as, oh fury of the winged and hopeful mind,
Could wear this great world and show to naught,
One, that would drive among the children of the sun
Bearing a singing sword, and in his hands,
Held for the eyes of all to see, the head
Of that great bull and all to hear his bellowing.

(1960)   (1960)

David

.all day the gopher-killing boys
    their sling-shot arms
      their gopher-cries

the king insisting
    my poetry must stop

I have written nothing since May

instead
    walk among the boys
gopher-blood on their stretched
hands   10
    murder will end murder
the saying goes, someone must
do something about the rodents
and poems do not:
        even the doctors
admit that it's plague
ask me about my arms
    look
at my shadow hanging
    like a slingshot   20

the world turns like a murderous stone
    my forehead aching with stars

(1964)   (1973)

Marina

Because she spoke often of the sea we thought she had known
    another country, her people distant, not forgotten

We did not know then who was calling her or what songs she
    listened to or why the sea-birds came to rest
    upon her long fingers

Or why she would shudder like a sea-bird about to take flight,
    her eyes changing with the changing light

As the sea-changing opal changes, as a shell takes its
    colours from the sea as if it were the sea

As if the great sea itself were held in the palm of a hand   10

They say the daughters of the sea know the language of birds,
    that in their restless eyes the most fortunate learn
    how the moon rises and sets

We do not know who is calling her or why her eyes change
    or what shore she will set her foot upon

(1967)   (1967)

Houdini

I suspect he knew that trunks are metaphors,
could distinguish between the finest rhythms
unrolled on rope or singing in a chain
and knew the metrics of the deepest pools

I think of him listening to the words
spoken by manacles, cells, handcuffs,
chests, hampers, roll-top desks, vaults,
especially the deep words spoken by coffins

escape, escape: quaint Harry in his suit
his chains, his desk, attached to all attachments   10
how he'd sweat in that precise struggle
with those binding words, wrapped around him
like that mannered style, his formal suit

and spoken when? by whom? What thing first said
"there's no way out?"; so that he'd free himself,
leap, squirm, no matter how, to chain himself again,
once more jump out of the deep alive
with all his chains singing around his feet
like the bound crowds who sigh, who sigh.

(1967)   (1973)

At Wabamun the Calgary Power Station

leans white in the moon
light puts white slabs up
light shanty whiteness leans

as if it owned the land

daytime horses crop grass
unknowing transformers hum

transformers   at the word
it takes on fiery hair
blazing it transmits
10 messages furious and hairy
it sends and receives from stars
ancient planets   people
who speak like horses new words

then sparks perform dead
parabolas and loops die
fireplace quietens it is
morning it is light only
the power the power hums

and the lake grows green
again in sunlight   20
                        it is
morning algae and weeds
thicken
                  the green lake
wobbles
            we look at
each other   alien forms

(1973)   (1973)

Estevan, 1934

remembering the family we
called breeds   the Roques
their house smelling of urine
my mother's prayers before
the dried fish she cursed
them for their dirtiness their
women I remember too
                        how
seldom they spoke and
10 they touched one another

even when the sun killed
cattle and rabbis
                        even
in the poisoned slow air
like hunters
                        like lizards
they touched   stone
they touched
                        earth

(1973)   (1973)

Envoi

my country is not a country
                    but winter
rivers of ice
from St. Hubert terrible knives
run through the whiteness of my veins

politics pierce my heart
on a floor littered with history
I shiver while wardens shovel in
lunatic sentences, rag upon rag

it must be cold in prison, in québec   10

and your heart hurt singer
what do you see through its pane

icy slaves circle the river
montréal tense against the steel of its manacles
your words drifting like frozen wounds
                                    blessing
a sick bride
a murderous bridegroom
                    that wedding
whose children will be colder killers   20
than the words of this or any other song

(1973)   (1973)

Milton Acorn
1923–

BORN IN CHARLOTTETOWN, Milton Acorn served in the Canadian army during World War II and then worked as a carpenter until he gave up his trade and began a full-time career as a poet. Since the appearance of *In Love and Anger* (1956), his first book of poems, Acorn has published several collections including *I've Tasted My Blood* (1969) and *The Island Means Minago* (1975).

The Island

Since I'm Island-born home's as precise
as if a mumbly old carpenter,
shoulder-straps crossed wrong,
laid it out, refigured
to the last three-eighths of shingle.

Nowhere that plowcut worms
heal themselves in red loam;
spruces squat, skirts in sand
or the stones of a river rattle its dark
tunnel under the elms,   10
is there a spot not measured by hands;
no direction I couldn't walk
to the wave-lined edge of home.

Quiet shores — beaches that roar
but walk two thousand paces and the sea
becomes an odd shining
glimpse among the jeweled
zigzag low hills. Any wonder
your eyelashes are wings
to fly your look both in and out?   20
In the coves of the land all things are discussed.

In the fanged jaws of the Gulf,
a red tongue.
Indians say a musical God
took up his brush and painted it,
named it in His own language
"The Island".

(1960)   (1975)

The Trout Pond

The woods, spruce twisted
into spooky shapes,
echo the trickle of water
from raised oars.

Above pale ripples
a redwing blackbird fastens,
legs crooked and beak alert,
to a springing reed.

My father's whiteheaded now,
but oars whose tug   10
used to start my tendons
pull easily these years.

His line curls, his troutfly drops
as if on its own wings,
marks a vee on the mirrored
ragged spruceheads, and
a crane flapping past clouds.

(1960)   (1975)

I've Tasted My Blood

If this brain's over-tempered
consider that the fire was want
and the hammers were fists.
I've tasted my blood too much
to love what I was born to.

But my mother's look
was a field of brown oats, soft-bearded;
her voice rain and air rich with lilacs:

and I loved her too much to like
how she dragged her days like a sled over gravel.   10

Playmates? I remember where their skulls roll!
One died hungry, gnawing grey perch-planks;
one fell, and landed so hard he splashed;
and many and many
come up atom by atom
in the worm-casts of Europe.

My deep prayer a curse.
My deep prayer the promise that this won't be.
My deep prayer my cunning,
my love, my anger,   20
and often even my forgiveness
that this won't be and be.
I've tasted my blood too much
to abide what I was born to.

(1963)   (1969)

Pastoral

That sudden time I heard
the pulse of song in a thrush throat
my windy visions fluttered
like snow-clouds buffeting the moon.

I was born into an ambush
of preachers, propagandists, grafters,
("Fear life and death!" "Hate and pay me!")
and tho I learned to despise them all
my dreams were of rubbish and destruction.

But that song, and the drop-notes   10
of a brook truckling thru log-breaks and cedars,
I came to on numb clumsy limbs,
to find outside the beauty inside me.

(1963)   (1969)

On Saint-Urbain Street

My room's bigger than a coffin
but not so well made.
The couple on my left drink, and
at two a.m. the old man shouts
of going back to Russia.
About five he or his wrung-out
    wife
puke up their passage money.

The janitor (pay, five a week
plus a one-bed apartment
10 with furnace in kitchen) has
one laughing babe at home
and two girls, for lack of room,

in the orphanage.
 On holidays they appear
with their soul-smashed faces.

Upstairs the Negro girl
answers the phone, sings my
    name
in a voice like a bad angel's.
 Her boy-friends change
every week-end, like the movies.   20
But my room's cheap, tho
when the wind shifts north
 I wear my overcoat
to type this bitter little poem.

(1963)   (1969)

Knowing I Live in a Dark Age

Knowing I live in a dark age before history,
I watch my wallet and
am less struck by gunfights in the avenues
than by the newsie with his dirty pink chapped face
calling a shabby poet back for his change.

The crows mobbing the blinking, sun-stupid owl,
wolves eating a hamstrung calf hindend first,
keeping their meat alive and fresh...these
are marks of foresight, beginnings of wit:
but Jesus wearing thorns and sunstroke   10
beating his life and death into words
to break the rods and blunt the axes of Rome:
this and like things followed.

Knowing that in this advertising rainbow
I live like a trapeze artist with a headache,
my poems are no aspirins...they show

pale bayonets of grass waving thin on dunes;
the paralytic and his lyric secrets;
my friend Al, union builder and cynic,
hesitating to believe his own delicate poems   20
lest he believe in something better than himself:
and history, which is yet to begin,
will exceed this, exalt this
as a poem erases and rewrites its poet.

(1963)   (1969)

Offshore Breeze

The wind, heavy from the land, irons the surf
to a slosh on silver-damp sand.
The sea's grey and crocheted with ripples
but shadows, the backs of waves,
lengthen and lapse in the dim haze
hinting of farther, rougher doings.

The boats went out early, but now
come worm-slow through haze and distance;
the gunnels invisible, the men and engines
dots moving on a spit of foam.   10
They travel past my vision, past
that red jag of a headland, to harbour.

(1969)   (1975)

Whale Poem

Sunglare and sea pale as tears.
One long hour we watched the black whales
circling like dancers,
sliding dark backs out of water,
waving their heaved tails,

about an eyepupil-round spot
just a knife-edge
this side of the horizon.

Black whales, let me join in your dance
uncumbered by ego, my soul well anchored   10
in a brain bigger than I am
... multiplied tons of muscled flesh
roaring in organized tones of thunder
for kilometres. When I love
let me love gigantically; and when I dance
let the earth take note
as the sea takes note of you.

(1969)   (1975)

Margaret Laurence
1926 –

BORN IN NEEPAWA, Manitoba, Margaret (Wemys) Laurence was educated at United College, an affiliate of the University of Manitoba. After her marriage in 1948, she lived in England and in Africa for several years and her first novel, *This Side Jordan* (1960), is set in Ghana. She has also published a travel book dealing with Somaliland, translations of Somali poetry and a study of contemporary Nigerian literature. Laurence's best-known works are a series of linked stories and novels set in the mythical Manitoba town of Manawaka: *The Stone Angel* (1964), *A Jest of God* (1966), *The Fire-Dwellers* (1969), *A Bird In The House* (1970), *The Diviners* (1974). A collection of essays, *Heart of a Stranger,* was published in 1976.

To Set Our House in Order

WHEN THE BABY was almost ready to be born, something went wrong and my mother had to go into hospital two weeks before the expected time. I was wakened by her crying in the night, and then I heard my father's footsteps as he went downstairs to phone. I stood in the doorway of my room, shivering and listening, wanting to go to my mother but afraid to go lest there be some sight there more terrifying than I could bear.

"Hello — Paul?" my father said, and I knew he was talking to Dr. Cates. "It's Beth. The waters have broken, and the fetal position doesn't seem quite — well, I'm only thinking of what happened the last time, and another like that would be — I wish she were a little huskier, damn it — she's so — no, don't worry, I'm quite all right. Yes, I think that would be the best thing. Okay, make it as soon as you can, will you?"

He came back upstairs, looking bony and dishevelled in his pyjamas, and running his fingers through his sand-coloured hair. At the top of the stairs, he came face to face with Grandmother MacLeod, who was standing there in her quilted black satin dressing gown, her slight figure held straight and poised, as though she were unaware that her hair was bound grotesquely like white-feathered wings in the snare of her coarse night-time hairnet.

"What is it, Ewen?"

"It's all right, Mother. Beth's having — a little trouble. I'm going to take her into the hospital. You go back to bed."

"I told you," Grandmother MacLeod said in her clear voice, never loud, but distinct and ringing like the tap of a sterling teaspoon on a crystal goblet, "I did tell you, Ewen, did I not, that you should have got a girl in to help her with the housework? She would have rested more."

"I couldn't afford to get anyone in," my father said. "If you thought she should've rested more, why didn't you ever — oh God, I'm out of my mind tonight — just go back to bed, Mother, please. I must get back to Beth."

When my father went down to the front door to let Dr. Cates in, my need overcame my fear and I slipped into my parents' room. My mother's black hair, so neatly pinned up during the day, was startlingly spread across the white pillowcase. I stared at her, not speaking, and then she smiled and I rushed from the doorway and buried my head upon her.

It's all right, honey," she said. "Listen, Vanessa, the baby's just going to come a little early, that's all. You'll be all right. Grandmother MacLeod will be here."

"How can she get the meals?" I wailed, fixing on the first thing that came to mind. "She never cooks. She doesn't know how."

"Yes, she does," my mother said. "She can cook as well as anyone when she has to. She's just never had to very much, that's all. Don't worry – she'll keep everything in order, and then some."

My father and Dr. Cates came in, and I had to go, without ever saying anything I had wanted to say. I went back to my own room and lay with the shadows all around me. I listened to the night murmurings that always went on in that house, sounds which never had a source, rafters and beams contracting in the dry air, perhaps, or mice in the walls, or a sparrow that had flown into the attic through the broken skylight there. After a while, although I would not have believed it possible, I slept.

The next morning I questioned my father. I believed him to be not only the best doctor in Manawaka, but also the best doctor in the whole of Manitoba, if not in the entire world, and the fact that he was not the one looking after my mother seemed to have something sinister about it.

"But it's always done that way, Vanessa," he explained. "Doctors never attend members of their own family. It's because they care so much about them, you see, and –"

"And what?" I insisted, alarmed at the way he had broken off. But my father did not reply. He stood there, and then he put on that difficult smile with which adults seek to conceal pain from children. I felt terrified, and ran to him, and he held me tightly.

"She's going to be fine," he said. "Honestly she is. Nessa, don't cry –"

Grandmother MacLeod appeared beside us, steel-spined despite her apparent fragility. She was wearing a purple silk dress and her ivory pendant. She looked as though she were all ready to go out for afternoon tea.

"Ewen, you're only encouraging the child to give way," she said. "Vanessa, big girls of ten don't make such a fuss about things. Come and get your breakfast. Now, Ewen, you're not to worry. I'll see to everything."

Summer holidays were not quite over, but I did not feel like going out to play with any of the kids. I was very superstitious, and I had the feeling that if I left the house, even for a few hours, some disaster would overtake my mother. I did not, of course, mention this feeling to Grandmother MacLeod, for she did not believe in the existence of fear, or if she did, she never let on. I spent the morning morbidly, in seeking hidden places in the house. There were many of these – odd-shaped nooks under the stairs, small and loosely nailed-up doors at the back of clothes closets, leading to dusty tunnels and forgotten recesses in the heart of the house where the only things actually to be seen were drab oil paintings stacked upon the rafters, and trunks full of outmoded clothing and old photograph albums. But the unseen presences in these secret places I knew to be those of every person, young or old, who had ever belonged to the house and had died, including Uncle Roderick who got killed on the Somme, and the baby who would have been my sister if only she had managed to come to life. Grandfather MacLeod, who had died a year after I was born, was present in the house in more tangible form. At the top of the main stairs hung the mammoth picture of a darkly uniformed man riding upon a horse whose prancing stance and dilated nostrils suggested that the battle was not yet over, that it might indeed continue until Judgment Day. The stern man was actually the Duke of Wellington, but at the time I believed him to be my grandfather MacLeod, still keeping an eye on things.

We had moved in with Grandmother MacLeod when the Depression got bad and she could no longer afford a housekeeper, but the MacLeod house never seemed like home to me. Its dark red brick was grown over at the front with Virginia creeper that turned crimson in the fall, until you could hardly tell brick from leaves. It boasted a small tower in which Grandmother MacLeod kept a weedy collection of anaemic ferns. The verandah was embellished with a profusion of wrought-iron scrolls, and the circular rose-window upstairs contained glass of many colours which permitted an outlooking eye to see the world as a place of absolute sapphire or emerald, or if one wished to look with a jaundiced eye, a hateful yellow. In Grandmother MacLeod's opinion, their features gave the house style.

Inside, a multitude of doors led to rooms where my presence, if not actually forbidden, was not encouraged. One was Grandmother MacLeod's bedroom, with its stale and old-smelling air, the dim reek of medicines and lavender sachets. Here resided her monogrammed dresser silver, brush and mirror, nail-buffer and button hook and scissors, none of which must even be fingered by me now, for she meant to leave them to me in her will and intended to hand them over in the same flawless and unused condition in which they had always been kept. Here, too, were the silver-framed photographs of Uncle Roderick — as a child, as a boy, as a man in his Army uniform. The massive walnut spool bed had obviously been designed for queens or giants, and my tiny grandmother used to lie within it all day when she had migraine, contriving somehow to look like a giant queen.

The living room was another alien territory where I had to tread warily, for many valuable objects sat just-so on tables and mantelpiece, and dirt must not be tracked in upon the blue Chinese carpet with its birds in eternal motionless flight and its water-lily buds caught forever just before the point of opening. My mother was always nervous when I was in this room.

"Vanessa, honey," she would say, half apologetically, "why don't you go and play in the den, or upstairs?"

"Can't you leave her, Beth?" my father would say. "She's not doing any harm."

"I'm only thinking of the rug," my mother would say, glancing at Grandmother MacLeod, "and yesterday she nearly knocked the Dresden shepherdess off the mantel. I mean, she can't help it, Ewen, she has to run around —"

"Goddamn it, I know she can't help it," my father would growl, glaring at the smirking face of the Dresden shepherdess.

"I see no need to blaspheme, Ewen," Grandmother MacLeod would say quietly, and then my father would say he was sorry, and I would leave.

The day my mother went to the hospital, Grandmother MacLeod called me at lunch-time, and when I appeared, smudged with dust from the attic, she looked at me distastefully as though I had been a cockroach that had just crawled impertinently out of the woodwork.

"For mercy's sake, Vanessa, what have you been doing with yourself? Run and get washed this minute. Here, not that way — you use the back stairs, young lady. Get along now. Oh — your father phoned."

I swung around. "What did he say? How is she? Is the baby born?"

"Curiosity killed a cat," Grandmother MacLeod said, frowning. "I cannot understand Beth and Ewen telling you all these things at your age. What sort of vulgar person you'll grow up to be, I dare not think. No, it's not born yet. Your mother's just the same. No change."

I looked at my grandmother, not wanting to appeal to her, but unable to stop myself. "Will she — will she be all right?"

Grandmother MacLeod straightened her already-straight back. "If I said definitely yes, Vanessa, that would be a lie, and the MacLeods do not tell lies, as I have tried to impress on you before. What happens is God's will. The Lord giveth, and the Lord taketh away."

Appalled, I turned away so she would not see my face and my eyes. Surprisingly, I heard her sigh and felt her papery white and perfectly manicured hand upon my shoulder.

"When your Uncle Roderick got killed," she said, "I thought I would die. But I didn't die, Vanessa."

At lunch, she chatted animatedly, and I realised she was trying to cheer me in the only way she knew.

"When I married your Grandfather MacLeod," she related, "he said to me, 'Eleanor, don't think because we're going to the prairies that I expect you to live roughly. You're used to a proper house, and you shall have one.' He was as good as his word. Before we'd been in Manawaka three years, he'd had this place built. He earned a good deal of money in his time, your grandfather. He soon had more patients than either of the other doctors. We ordered our dinner service and all our silver from Birks' in Toronto. We had resident help in those days, of course, and never had less than twelve guests for dinner parties. When I had a tea, it would always be twenty or thirty. Never any less than half a dozen different kinds of cake were ever served in this house. Well, no one seems to bother much these days. Too lazy, I suppose."

"Too broke," I suggested. "That's what Dad says."

"I can't bear slang," Grandmother MacLeod said. "If you mean hard up, why don't you say so? It's mainly a question of management, anyway. My accounts were always in good order, and so was my house. No unexpected expenses that couldn't be met, no fruit cellar running out of preserves before the winter was over. Do you know what my father used to say to me when I was a girl?"

"No," I said. "What?"

"God loves Order," Grandmother MacLeod replied with emphasis. "You remember that, Vanessa. God loves Order – he wants each one of us to set our house in order. I've never forgotten those words of my father's. I was a MacInnes before I got married. The MacInnes is a very ancient clan, the lairds of Morven and the constables of the Castle of Kinlochaline. Did you finish that book I gave you?"

"Yes," I said. Then, feeling some additional comment to be called for, "It was a swell book, Grandmother."

This was somewhat short of the truth. I had been hoping for her cairngorm brooch on my tenth birthday, and had received instead the plaid-bound volume entitled *The Clans and Tartans of Scotland*. Most of it was too boring to read, but I had looked up the motto of my own family and those of some of my friends' families. *Be then a wall of brass. Learn to suffer. Consider the end. Go carefully.* I had not found any of these slogans reassuring. What with Mavis Duncan learning to suffer, and Laura Kennedy considering the end, and Patsy Drummond going carefully, and I spending my time in being a wall of brass, it did not seem to me that any of us were going to lead very interesting lives. I did not say this to Grandmother MacLeod.

"The MacInnes motto is *Pleasure Arises from Work*," I said.

"Yes," she agreed proudly. "And an excellent motto it is, too. One to bear in mind."

She rose from the table, rearranging on her bosom the looped ivory beads that held the pendant on which a fullblown ivory rose was stiffly carved.

"I hope Ewen will be pleased," she said.

"What at?"

"Didn't I tell you?" Grandmother MacLeod said. "I hired a girl this morning, for the housework. She's to start tomorrow."

When my father got home that evening, Grandmother MacLeod told him her good news. He ran one hand distractedly across his forehead.

"I'm sorry, Mother, but you'll just have to unhire her. I can't possibly pay anyone."

"It seems distinctly odd," Grandmother MacLeod snapped, "that you can afford to eat chicken four times a week."

"Those chickens," my father said in an exasperated voice, "are how people are paying their bills. The same with the eggs and the milk. That scrawny turkey that arrived yesterday was for Logan MacCardney's appendix, if you must know. We probably eat better than any family in Manawaka, except Niall Cameron's. People can't entirely dispense with doctors or undertakers. That doesn't mean to say I've got any cash. Look, Mother, I don't know what's happening with Beth. Paul thinks he may have to do a Caesarean. Can't we leave all this? Just leave the house alone. Don't touch it. What does it matter?"

"I have never lived in a messy house, Ewen," Grandmother MacLeod said, "and I don't intend to begin now."

"Oh Lord," my father said. "Well, I'll phone Edna, I guess, and see if she can give us a hand, although God knows she's got enough, with the Connor house and her parents to look after."

"I don't fancy having Edna Connor in to help," Grandmother MacLeod objected.

"Why not?" my father shouted. "She's Beth's sister, isn't she?"

"She speaks in such a slangy way," Grandmother MacLeod said. "I have never believed she was a good influence on Vanessa. And there is no need for you to raise your voice to me, Ewen, if you please.

I could barely control my rage. I thought my father would surely rise to Aunt Edna's defence. But he did not.

"It'll be all right," he soothed her. "She'd only be here for part of the day, Mother. You could stay in your room."

Aunt Edna strode in the next morning. The sight of her bobbed black hair and her grin made me feel better at once. She hauled out the carpet sweeper and the weighted polisher and got to work. I dusted while she polished and swept, and we got through the living room and front hall in next to no time.

"Where's her royal highness, kiddo?" she enquired.

"In her room," I said. "She's reading the catalogue from Robinson & Cleaver."

"Good Glory, not again?" Aunt Edna cried. "The last time she ordered three linen tea-clothes and two dozen serviettes. It came to fourteen dollars. Your mother was absolutely frantic. I guess I shouldn't be saying this."

"I knew anyway," I assured her. "She was at the lace handkerchiefs section when I took up her coffee."

"Let's hope she stays there. Heaven forbid she should get onto the banqueting cloths. Well, at least she believes the Irish are good for two things — manual labour and linen-making. She's never forgotten Father used to be a blacksmith, before he got the hardware store. Can you beat it? I wish it didn't bother Beth."

"Does it?" I asked, and immediately realised this was a wrong move, for Aunt Edna was suddenly scrutinising me.

"We're making you grow up before your time," she said. "Don't pay any attention to me, Nessa. I must've got up on the wrong side of the bed this morning."

But I was unwilling to leave the subject.

"All the same," I said thoughtfully, "Grandmother MacLeod's family were the lairds of Morven and the constables of the Castle of Kinlochaline. I bet you didn't know that."

Aunt Edna snorted, "Castle, my foot. She was born in Ontario, just like your Grandfather Connor, and her father was a horse doctor. Come on, kiddo, we'd better shut up and get down to business here."

We worked in silence for a while.

"Aunt Edna —" I said at last, "what about Mother? Why won't they let me go and see her?"

"Kids aren't allowed to visit maternity patients. It's tough for you, I know that. Look, Nessa, don't worry. If it doesn't start tonight, they're going to do the operation. She's getting the best of care."

I stood there, holding the feather duster like a dead bird in my hands. I was not aware that I was going to speak until the words came out.

"I'm scared," I said.

Aunt Edna put her arms around me, and her face looked all at once stricken and empty of defences.

"Oh, honey, I'm scared, too," she said.

It was this way that Grandmother MacLeod found us when she came stepping lightly down into the front hall with the order in her hand for two dozen lace-bordered handkerchiefs of pure Irish linen.

I could not sleep that night, and when I went downstairs, I found my father in the den. I sat down on the hassock beside his chair, and he told me about the operation my mother was to have the next morning. He kept on saying it was not serious nowadays.

"But you're worried," I put in, as though seeking to explain why I was.

"I should at least have been able to keep from burdening you with it," he said in a distant voice, as though to himself. "If only the baby hadn't got itself twisted around —"

"Will it be born dead, like the little girl?"

"I don't know," my father said. "I hope not."

"She'd be disappointed, wouldn't she, if it was?" I said bleakly, wondering why I was not enough for her.

"Yes, she would," my father replied. "She won't be able to have any more, after this. It's partly on your account that she wants this one, Nessa. She doesn't want you to grow up without a brother or sister."

"As far as I'm concerned, she didn't need to bother," I retorted angrily.

My father laughed. "Well, let's talk about something else, and then maybe you'll be able to sleep. How did you and Grandmother make out today?"

"Oh, fine, I guess. What was Grandfather MacLeod like, Dad?"

"What did she tell you about him?"

"She said he made a lot of money in his time."

"Well, he wasn't any millionaire," my father said, "but I suppose he did quite well. That's not what I associate with him, though."

He reached across to the bookshelf, took out a small leather-bound volume and opened it. On the pages were mysterious marks, like doodling, only much neater and more patterned.

"What is it?" I asked.

"Greek," my father explained. "This is a play called *Antigone*. See, here's the title in English. There's a whole stack of them on the shelves there. *Oedipus Rex. Electra. Medea.* They belonged to your Grandfather MacLeod. He used to read them often."

"Why?" I enquired, unable to understand why anyone would pore over those undecipherable signs.

"He was interested in them," my father said. "He must have been a lonely man, although it never struck me that way at the time. Sometimes a thing only hits you a long time afterwards."

"Why would he be lonely?" I wanted to know.

"He was the only person in Manawaka who could read these plays in the original Greek," my father said. "I don't suppose many people, if anyone, had even read them in English translations. Maybe he would have liked to be a classical scholar — I don't know. But his father was a doctor, so that's what he was. Maybe he would have liked to talk to somebody about these plays. They must have meant a lot to him."

It seemed to me that my father was talking oddly. There was a sadness in his voice that I had never heard before, and I longed to say something that would make him feel better, but I could not, because I did not know what was the matter.

"Can you read this kind of writing?" I asked hesitantly.

My father shook his head. "Nope. I was never very intellectual, I guess. Rod was always brighter than I, in school, but even he wasn't interested in learning Greek. Perhaps he would've been later, if he'd lived. As a kid, all I ever wanted to do was go into the merchant marine."

"Why didn't you, then?"

"Oh well," my father said offhandedly, "a kid who'd never seen the sea wouldn't have made much of a sailor. I might have turned out to be the seasick type."

I had lost interest now that he was speaking once more like himself.

"Grandmother MacLeod was pretty cross today about the girl," I remarked.

"I know," my father nodded. "Well, we must be as nice as we can to her, Nessa, and after a while she'll be all right."

Suddenly I did not care what I said.

"Why can't she be nice to us for a change?" I burst out. "We're always the ones who have to be nice to her."

My father put his hand down and slowly tilted my head until I was forced to look at him.

"Vanessa, he said, "she's had troubles in her life which you really don't know much about. That's why she gets migraine sometimes and has to go to bed. It's not easy for her these days, either – the house is still the same, so she thinks other things should be, too. It hurts her when she finds they aren't."

"I don't see –" I began.

"Listen," my father said, "you know we were talking about what people are interested in, like Grandfather MacLeod being interested in Greek plays? Well, your grandmother was interested in being a lady, Nessa, and for a long time it seemed to her that she was one."

I thought of the Castle of Kinlochaline, and of horse doctors in Ontario.

"I didn't know –" I stammered.

"That's usually the trouble with most of us," my father said. "You go on up to bed now. I'll phone tomorrow from the hospital as soon as the operation's over."

I did sleep at last, and in my dreams I could hear the caught sparrow fluttering in the attic, and the sound of my mother crying, and the voices of the dead children.

My father did not phone until afternoon. Grandmother MacLeod said I was being silly, for you could hear the phone ringing all over the house, but nevertheless I refused to move out of the den. I had never before examined my father's books, but now, at a loss for something to do, I took them out one by one and read snatches here and there. After I had been doing this for several hours, it dawned on me that most of the books were of the same kind. I looked again at the titles.

Seven-League Boots. Arabia Deserta. The Seven Pillars of Wisdom. Travels in Tibet. Count Lucknor the Sea Devil. And a hundred more. On a shelf by themselves were copies of the *National Geographic* magazine, which I looked at often enough, but never before with the puzzling compulsion which I felt now, as though I were on the verge of some discovery, something which I had to find out and yet did not want to know. I riffled through the picture-filled pages. Hibiscus and wild orchids grew in a soft-petalled confusion. The Himalayas stood lofty as gods, with the morning sun on their peaks of snow. Leopards snarled from the vined depths of a thousand jungles. Schooners buffetted their white sails like the wings of giant angels against the great sea winds.

"What on earth are you doing?" Grandmother MacLeod enquired waspishly from the doorway. "You've got everything scattered all over the place. Pick it all up this minute, Vanessa, do you hear?"

So I picked up the books and magazines, and put them all neatly away, as I had been told to do.

When the telephone finally rang, I was afraid to answer it. At last I picked it up. My father sounded faraway, and the relief in his voice made it unsteady.

"It's okay, honey. Everything's fine. The boy was born alive and kicking after all. Your mother's pretty weak, but she's going to be all right."

I could hardly believe it. I did not want to talk to anyone. I wanted to be by myself, to assimilate the presence of my brother, towards whom, without ever having seen him yet, I felt such tenderness and such resentment.

That evening, Grandmother MacLeod approached my father, who, still dazed with the unexpected gift of neither life now being threatened, at first did not take her seriously when she asked what they planned to call the child.

"Oh, I don't know. Hank, maybe, or Joe. Fauntleroy, perhaps."

She ignored his levity.

"Ewen," she said, "I wish you would call him Roderick."

My father's face changed. "I'd rather not."

"I think you should," Grandmother MacLeod insisted, very quietly, but in a voice as pointed and precise as her silver nail-scissors.

"Don't you think Beth ought to decide?" my father asked.

"Beth will agree if you do."

My father did not bother to deny something that even I knew to be true. He did not say anything. Then Grandmother MacLeod's voice, astonishingly, faltered a little.

"It would mean a great deal to me," she said.

I remembered what she had told me — *When your Uncle Roderick got killed, I thought I would die. But I didn't die.* All at once, her feeling for that unknown dead man became a reality for me. And yet I held it against her, as well, for I could see that it had enabled her to win now.

"All right," my father said tiredly. "We'll call him Roderick."

Then, alarmingly, he threw back his head and laughed.

"Roderick Dhu!" he cried. "That's what you'll call him, isn't it? Black Roderick. Like before. Don't you remember? As though he were a character out of Sir Walter Scott, instead of an ordinary kid who —"

He broke off, and looked at her with a kind of desolation in his face.

"God, I'm sorry, Mother," he said. "I had no right to say that."

Grandmother MacLeod did not flinch, or tremble, or indicate that she felt anything at all.

"I accept your apology, Ewen," she said.

My mother had to stay in bed for several weeks after she arrived home. The baby's cot was kept in my parents' room, and I could go in and look at the small creature who lay there with his tightly closed fists and his feathery black hair. Aunt Edna came in to help each morning, and when she had finished the housework, she would have coffee with my mother. They kept the door closed, but this did not prevent me from eavesdropping, for there was an air register in the floor of the spare room, which was linked somehow with the register in my parents' room. If you put your ear to the iron grille, it was almost like a radio.

"Did you mind very much, Beth?" Aunt Edna was saying.

"Oh, it's not the name I mind," my mother replied. "It's just the fact that Ewen felt he had to. You know that Rod had only had the sight of one eye, didn't you?"

"Sure, I knew. So what?"

"There was only a year and a half between Ewen and Rod," my mother said, "so they often went around together when they were youngsters. It was Ewen's air-rifle that did it."

"Oh Lord," Aunt Edna said heavily. "I suppose she always blamed him?"

"No, I don't think it was so much that, really. It was how he felt himself. I think he even used to wonder sometimes if – but people shouldn't let themselves think like that, or they'd go crazy. Accidents do happen, after all. When the war came, Ewen joined up first. Rod should never have been in the Army at all, but he couldn't wait to get in. He must have lied about his eyesight. It wasn't so very noticeable unless you looked at him closely, and I don't suppose the medicals were very thorough in those days. He got in as a gunner, and Ewen applied to have him in the same company. He thought he might be able to watch out for him, I guess, Rod being – at a disadvantage. They were both only kids. Ewen was nineteen and Rod was eighteen when they went to France. And then the Somme. I don't know, Edna, I think Ewen felt that if Rod had had proper sight, or if he hadn't been in the same outfit and had been sent somewhere else – you know how people always think these things afterwards, not that it's ever a bit of use. Ewen wasn't there when Rod got hit. They'd lost each other somehow, and Ewen was looking for him, not bothering about anything else, you know, just frantically looking. Then he stumbled across him quite by chance. Rod was still alive, but –"

"Stop it, Beth," Aunt Edna said. "You're only upsetting yourself."

"Ewen never spoke of it to me," my mother went on, "until once his mother showed me the letter he'd written to her at the time. It was a peculiar letter, almost formal, saying how gallantly Rod had died, and all that. I guess I shouldn't have, but I told him she'd shown it to me. He was very angry that she had. And then, as though for some reason he were terribly ashamed, he said – *I had to write something to her, but men don't really die like that, Beth. It wasn't that way at all.* It was only after the war that he decided to come back and study medicine and go into practice with his father."

"Had Rod meant to?" Aunt Edna asked.

"I don't know," my mother said slowly. "I never felt I should ask Ewen that."

Aunt Edna was gathering up the coffee things, for I could hear the clash of cups and saucers being stacked on the tray.

"You know what I heard her say to Vanessa once, Beth? *The MacLeods never tell lies.* Those were her exact words. Even then, I didn't know whether to laugh or cry."

"Please, Edna –" my mother sounded worn out now. "Don't."

"Oh Glory," Aunt Edna said remorsefully, "I've got all the delicacy of a two-ton truck. I didn't mean Ewen, for heaven's sake. That wasn't what I meant at all. Here, let me plump up your pillows for you."

Then the baby began to cry, so I could not hear anything more of interest. I took my bike and went out beyond Manawaka, riding aimlessly along the gravel highway. It was late summer, and the wheat had changed colour, but instead of being high and bronzed in the fields, it was stunted and dessicated, for there had been no rain again this year. But in the bluff where I stopped and crawled under the barbed wire fence and lay stretched out on the grass, the plentiful poplar leaves were turning to a luminous yellow and shone like church windows in the sun. I put my head down very close to the earth and looked at what was going on there. Grasshoppers with enormous eyes ticked and twitched around me, as though the dry air were perfect for their purposes. A ladybird laboured mightily to climb a blade of grass, fell off, and started all over again, seeming to be unaware that she possessed wings and could have flown up.

I thought of the accidents that might easily happen to a person – or, of course, might not happen, might happen to somebody else. I thought of the dead baby, my sister, who might as easily have been I. Would she, then, have been lying here in my place, the sharp grass making its small toothmarks on her brown arms, the sun warming her to the heart? I thought of the leather-bound volumes of Greek, and the six different kinds of iced cakes that used to be offered always in the MacLeod house, and the pictures of leopards and green seas. I thought of my brother, who had been born alive after all, and now had been given his life's name.

I could not really comprehend these things, but I sensed their strangeness, their disarray. I felt that whatever God might love in this world, it was certainly not order.

(1970)   (1970)

James Reaney
1926–

BORN NEAR STRATFORD, Ontario, James Reaney was educated at the University of Toronto and has been a Professor of English at the University of Western Ontario since 1960. He has been influential as a critic and editor through his publication of the journal *Alphabet* (1961-1971), and he has also become one of the leading dramatists in English Canada with such works as *Colours In The Dark* (1969), *Listen to the Wind* (1972) and a trilogy of plays based on the Donnelly family. Reaney's first volume of poetry, *The Red Heart*, appeared in 1949 and he has since published several collections including *A Suit of Nettles* (1958), *Twelve Letters to a Small Town* (1962) and *Poems* (1972).

Antichrist as a Child

When Antichrist was a child
He caught himself tracing
The capital letter A
On a window sill
And wondered why
Because his name contained no A.
And as he crookedly stood
In his mother's flower-garden
He wondered why she looked so sadly
Out of an upstairs window at him.   10
He wondered why his father stared so
Whenever he saw his little son
Walking in his soot-coloured suit.
He wondered why the flowers
And even the ugliest weeds
Avoided his fingers and his touch.
And when his shoes began to hurt
Because his feet were becoming hooves

He did not let on to anyone
For fear they would shoot him for a monster.   20
He wondered why he more and more
Dreamed of eclipses of the sun,
Of sunsets, ruined towns and zeppelins,
And especially inverted, upside down churches.

(1949)   (1972)

The Plum Tree

The plums are like blue pendulums
That thrum the gold-wired winds of summer.
In the opium-still noon they hang or fall,
The plump, ripe plums.
I suppose my little sister died
Dreaming of looking up at them,
Of lying beneath that crooked plum tree,
That green heaven with blue stars pied.
In this lonely haunted farmhouse
All things are voiceless save the sound   10
Of some plums falling through the summer air
Straight to the ground.
And there is no listener, no hearer
For the small thunders of their falling
(Falling as dead stars rush to a winter sea)
Save a child who, lolling
Among the trunks and old featherticks
That fill the room where he was born,
Hears them in his silent dreaming
On a dark engraving to a fairy-tale forlorn.   20
Only he hears their intermittent soft tattoo
Upon the dry, brown summer ground
At the edge of the old orchard.
Only he hears, and farther away,
Some happy animal's slow, listless moo.

(1949)   (1972)

The Red Heart

The only leaf upon its tree of blood,
My red heart hangs heavily
And will never fall loose,
But grow so heavy
After only a certain number of seasons
(Sixty winters, and fifty-nine falls,
Fifty-eight summers, and fifty-seven springs)
That it will bring bough
Tree and the fences of my bones
Down to a grave in the forest   10
Of my still upright fellows.

So does the sun hang now
From a branch of Time
In this wild fall sunset.
Who shall pick the sun
From the tree of Eternity?
Who shall thresh the ripe sun?
What midwife shall deliver
The Sun's great heir?
It seems that no one can,   20
And so the sun shall drag
Gods, goddesses and parliament buildings,
Time, Fate, gramophones and Man
To a gray grave
Where all shall be trampled
Beneath the dancing feet of crowds
Of other still-living suns and stars.

(1949)   (1972)

From
A Message to Winnipeg

SPEAKER:
I walk down the street conscious that this has
not always been like this.

I walk down the street knowing that this has not
always been so.
Once there could have been a burial mound instead
of the factory.

Winnipeg Seen as a Body of Time and Space

Winnipeg, what once were you. You were,
Your hair was grass by the river ten feet tall,
Your arms were burr oaks and ash leaf maples,
Your backbone was a crooked silver muddy river,   10
Your thoughts were ravens in flocks, your bones were
        snow,
Your legs were trails and your blood was a people
      Who did what the stars did and the sun.

Then what were you? You were cracked enamel like
Into parishes and strips that came down to the river.

Convents were built, the river lined with nuns
Praying and windmills turning and your people
Had a blood that did what a star did and a Son.

Then on top of you fell   20
A Boneyard wrecked auto gent, his hair
Made of rusted car door handles, his fingernails
Of red Snowflake Pastry signs, his belly
Of buildings downtown; his arms of sewers,
His nerves electric wires, his mouth a telephone,
His backbone — a cracked cement street. His heart
An orange pendulum bus crawling with the human fleas
Of a so-so civilization — half gadget, half flesh —
      I don't know what I would have instead —
    And they did what they did more or less.   30

SPEAKER:
In the past it was decided. While the English beat
the French at Waterloo the French Métis beat the
English at the Battle of Seven Oaks but then in the
end, dear listener, Waterloo counted for more than
Seven Oaks.

Le Tombeau de Pierre Falcon

Pierre Falcon,
You say here along with this unsingable music
That on June nineteenth these Burnt Wood people
Ah yes, the Métis were dark, so called Bois-Brûlés,
Arrived near this settlement of Lord Selkirk's   40
Fort Douglas

You say in this second verse that your Burnt Woods
Took three foreigners prisoner at Frog Plain.
These foreigners were Scotchmen from the Orkneys
Who had come, as you put it, to rob your — Pierre
   Falcon's —
Country.
Well we were just about to unhorse
When we heard two of us give, give voice.
     Two of our men cried, "Hey! Look back, look back!   50
     The Anglo-Sack
     Coming for to attack."

Right away smartly we veered about
Galloping at them with a shout!
You know we did trap all, all those Grenadiers!
     They could not move
     Those horseless cavaliers.

Now we like honourable men did act,
Sent an ambassador — yes, in fact!
"Monsieur Governor! Would you like to stay?   60
     A moment spare —
     There's something we'd like to say."

Governor, Governor, full of ire.
"Soldiers!" he cries, "Fire! Fire."
So they fire the first and their muskets roar!
     They almost kill
     Our ambassador!

Governor thought himself a king.
He wished an iron rod to swing.
Like a lofty lord he tries to act.   70
     Bad luck, old chap!
     A bit too hard you whacked!

When we went galloping, galloping by
Governor thought that he would try
For to chase and frighten us Bois-Brûlés.
 Catastrophe!
 Dead on the ground he lay.

Dead on the ground lots of grenadiers too.
Plenty of grenadiers, a whole slew.
We've almost stamped out his whole army.   80
 Of so many
 Five or four left there be.

You should have seen those Englishmen —
Bois-Brûlés chasing them, chasing them.
From bluff to bluff they stumbled that day
 While the Bois-Brûlés
 Shouted "Hurray!"

And now in this eleventh verse you ask
Who made up this song and then you tell us
That you yourself made it up — Pierre Falcon.   90
You made it up to sing the glory of the
Burnt Wood People.

Far away and dear, spunky old and early poet
I wish I could sing the praises of the Neon People
To You.

(1972)   (1961)

From
Twelve Letters to a Small Town

Letter I

To the Avon River above Stratford, Canada

What did the Indians call you!
For you do not flow
With English accents.

I hardly know
What I should call you
    Because before
I drank coffee or tea
    I drank you
    With my cupped hands
And you did not taste English to me   10
    And you do not sound
    Like Avon
    Or swans & bards
But rather like the sad wild fowl
    In prints drawn
    By Audubon
And like dear bad poets
    Who wrote
    Early in Canada
And never were of note.   20
You are the first river
    I crossed
And like the first whirlwind
    The first rainbow
    First snow, first
    Falling star I saw,
You, for other rivers are my law.
    These other rivers:
    The Red & the Thames
    Are never so sweet   30
To skate upon, swim in
    Or for baptism of sin.
    Silver and light
The sentence of your voice,
    With a soprano
Continuous cry you shall
    Always flow
    Through my heart.
The rain and the snow of my mind
Shall supply the spring of that river   40
    Forever.
Though not your name
Your coat of arms I know
    And motto:
A shield of reeds and cresses
    Sedges, crayfishes
The hermaphroditic leech

> Minnows, muskrats and farmers' geese
> And printed above this shield
> One of my earliest wishes   50
> "To flow like you."

(1962)   (1972)

LETTER XII

The Bicycle

Halfway between childhood & manhood,
  More than a hoop but never a car,
The bicycle talks gravel and rain pavement
  On the highway where the dead frogs are.

Like sharkfish the cars blur by.
  Filled with the two-backed beast
One dreams of, yet knows not the word for,
  The accumulating sexual yeast.

Past the house where the bees winter.
  I climb on the stairs of my pedals   10
To school murmuring irregular verbs
  Past the lion with legs like a table's.

Autumn blows the windfalls down
  With a twilight horn of dead leaves.
I pick them up in the fence of November
  And burs on my sweater sleeves.

Where a secret robin is wintering
  By the lake in the fir grove dark
Through the fresh new snow we stumble
  That Winter has whistled sharp.   20

The March wind blows me ruts over,
  Puddles past, under red maple buds,
Over culvert of streamling, under
  White clouds and beside bluebirds.

Fireflies tell their blinking player
    Piano hesitant tales
Down at the bridge through the swamp
    Where the ogre clips his rusty nails.

Between the highschool & the farmhouse
    In the country and the town   30
It was a world of love and of feeling
    Continually floating down

On a soul whose only knowledge
    Was that everything was something,
This was like that, that was like this –
      In short, everything was
      The bicycle of which I sing.

(1962)   (1972)

The Tall Black Hat

As a child, I dreamt of tomorrow
Of the word "tomorrow" itself.
The word was a man in a tall black hat
Who walked in black clothes through
Green fields of quiet rain that
Beneath gray cloudfields grew.

Tall as trees or Abraham Lincoln
Were that man's brothers
Who when they become To-day
Die and dissolve one by one   10
Like licorice morning shadows
When held in the mouth of the sun.

Yesterday is an old greataunt
Rocked off in her rocking chair
To cellars where old light and snow
And all yesterdays go;
To-day was a small girl bringing

China cupfuls of water and air
And cages of robins singing,
"It is positively no crime   20

To have pleasure in Present Time."
But Tomorrow is most impressive
Like the hired man back from the fair
He comes to the child still sleeping
With pockets of longer hair,
A handful of longer fingers
And the Indian I remember
At dusk, crossing Market Square.

The man in the tall black hat
Brought the gipsy who was drunk   30
And the white faced cat
Who stepped before my stepmother
The very first time she came.

He gave the child a yellow leaf,
He holds the arrow for my heart,
He dropped the playing card in the lane,
He brought the dancing weasel.
And the old man playing the jewsharp.

He brings the wind and the sun
And the stalks of dead teazle   40
Seen on a windless winter walk,
He fetches a journey's direction
From his garden of weathervanes
And mines, like diamonds, the tears
For the glittering windowpanes
Of rain and sorrow.

All the days of all the years
The dark provider hunts me
Whom I named Sir Thomas Tomorrow
After my dream of him,   50
And in the grave fields of mystery
This black man has brothers
Who have followed him and come
Ever since with all I must see,

With Earth, Heaven and the tenor drum
I played in the C.O.T.C.,
The sound of bells and stars in a tree
Are stuck to their thumb
And lie in their tall black hats and pockets
Like pictures in locked and closed lockets.   60

At midnight he knocked and arrived
As the old woman really rocked away
And he took off his tall hat which
Changed into a small white cup,
White as the new light of day.
To the girl as small as a switch,
The girl who wakes me up,
His tallness and blackness shrank
To leave behind on the floor
From his pockets of come to pass   70
Puzzles and lonely birds to see
Diamonded names upon window glass,
A whistle, a straw and a tree.

But see out where small in the dawn
Through the hanging wingflash dance
Of the little flies, the wrens and the doves
Who are the seconds and minutes and hours
Floating over the acres of distance,
See his brother with feet of slate
Begin to walk through the wet flowers   80
Towards me with his speck of Future
And a tall black hatful of Fate.

(1972)   (1972)

The Morning Dew

Shake seed of light and thunder
From where you hang,
The Word without the Flesh.

The pastures, sloughs and trees all shine
Their leaves and grasses sown
With flashing tears.

Here is Absalom's hair in crystal terms
Feverish bonfire of the sensual body,
Bloodbob.

Sharp, sharp yellow teeth, sharp sharp   10
In the dark mouth blinking of the
Fox-haired queen.

Blue as the fields of flax in the summer
That dream of retting, spreading, drying,
White linen snow.

Green as the thoughtful ancient woods
Ash contemplation of linden tree thinking,
Paththrough.

The killdeer's nest is built of gold,
Cobwebs are blessed and Eden   20
Has caught these fields within her fold.

(1972)   (1972)

Robert Kroetsch
1922–

———◆———

BORN IN HEISLER, Alberta, Robert Kroetsch attended the University of Alberta and McGill University and later joined the Department of English at the State University of New York at Binghamton. Kroetsch's first novel, *But We Are Exiles*, was published in 1965 and he has since published a travel book on Alberta, two collections of poetry and several novels including *The Words of My Roaring* (1966), *The Studhorse Man* (1969) *Gone Indian* (1973) and *Badlands* (1975). "That Yellow Prairie Sky" first appeared in *Maclean's* in 1955.

That Yellow Prairie Sky

I WAS LOOKING at the back of a new dollar bill, at that scene of somewhere on the prairies, and all of a sudden I was looking right through it and I wasn't in Toronto at all any more — I was back out west. The clouds were moving overhead as if we were traveling and I pointed to that fence that's down and I said, "Look't there, Julie, that must be Tom's place. He hasn't fixed that piece of fence these thirty years." And then I noticed the elevator wasn't getting any closer.

It never does.

My brother Tom, he was quite a guy for women. I'll bet he was the worst for twenty miles on either side of the Battle River. Or the best, whichever way you look at it. I guess I wasn't far behind. Anyway, we spent the winter courting those two girls.

The way it happened, we met them in the fall while we were out hunting. I mean, we knew them all our lives. But you know how it is, eh? You look at some girl all your life, and then one day you stop all of a sudden and take another look, and you kind of let out a low whistle.

Well, Tom was twenty-three then, with me a year younger, and we'd grown up together. He taught me how to play hockey and how to snare rabbits and anything new that came along. Out on the prairies you don't have neighbours over your head and in your back yard, and a brother really gets to be a brother.

When it rained that fall and the fields got too soft for threshing we decided to go out and take a crack at some of the ducks that were feeding on our crop. We built a big stook that would keep us out of view, facing the slough hole and the setting sun, and we crawled inside. I can still see it all in my mind....

A thousand and a thousand ducks were milling black against the yellow sky. Like autumn leaves from the tree of life they tumbled in the air; a new flock coming from the north, a flock circling down, a flock tremulous above the water, reluctant to wet a thousand feet. And silhouetted on the far horizon was a threshing machine with a blower pointed at a strawpile, and nearer was the glint of the sun on the slough, and then a rush of wings from behind, overhead, going into the sun, and with a sudden jolt the autumn-sharp smell of a smoking gun.

I let go with both barrels at a flock that was too high up, and before I could reload there was a scream that left my jaw hanging as wide open as the breech of my old 12-gauge.

"I swear," Tom said, "now ain't that the prettiest pair of mallards that ever came close to losing their pinfeathers?"

I pushed my way out of the stook, and Tom was right.

I guess they didn't see us. I mean, Kay and Julie.

They were standing back of our stook, looking scared, with their skirts tucked into — tucked up — and nobody thought of it in the excitement, or at least they didn't.

"Are you trying to kill us?" Julie asked, pushing back a blond curl and pretending she was only mad and not scared at all.

"Can't you see we're shooting ducks?" Tom said.

"I can't by the number that fell," she said.

That's when I spoke up, "They were too high and I was too anxious."

Julie looked at me and my gun and she blushed. "I didn't mean to insult your shooting. I've heard folks say you're one of the best shots around."

Funny thing. I was pretty good, but just about then I could've told a battalion of the Princess Pat's to back up and drop their guns.

It was then that the redhead, Kay, spoke up. "Really, I'm glad you missed. I hate to see things get killed."

Tom looked up at the distant ducks for a minute, and then said, "As a matter of fact, I hate it myself." It was the first time I ever heard Tom say a thing like that. Most of the time you couldn't hold him.

There was a kind of a loss for words. Then Kay explained, "We're making boxes for the box social in the church hall tonight, and we're taking the short cut over to Rittner's place to borrow four little wheels that the Rittners have left over from the little toy wagon that Halberg's new automobile ran into."

"We're in a terrible hurry," Julie said, "so instead of going around by the road we're going to wade across Rittner's slough —"

And then they noticed it too, and before Tom could say he figured as much, they were in the slough wading above their knees.

"A nice pair of shafts," Tom commented.

"A dandy pair," I said. But I soon found out I was talking about a different pair.

That night at the box social Tom paid three dollars and a half for the lunch box that looked like a pink Red River oxcart with toy wagon wheels on it. He figured it was Kay's because she had red hair, and in a pinch we could make a switch.

Some religious fellow caught on to me and ran me up to five and a quarter on the yellow one. I was a great help to the church committee, and it looked like a fair enough investment otherwise. Sure enough, I got Kay's and I wanted Julie's, so Tom and I switched and the girls never caught on; or at least they never let on that they did.

Through the rest of the fall and during the winter Dad had to do the chores quite a few times by himself. Tom and I didn't miss a dance or a hayride or a skating party within trotting range of the finest team of dapple greys in the country. We didn't have all the fancy courting facilities that folks here in the east have, but we had lots of space and lots of sky. And we didn't miss much on a frosty night, the old buffalo robe doing whatever was necessary to keep warm....

The northern lights in the winter sky were a silent symphony: flickering white, fading red and green, growing and bursting and dying in swirls and echoes of swirls, in wavering angel-shadows, in shimmering music. And on one edge of the wide white prairie shone a solitary light, and toward it moved a sleigh with the jingle of harness, the clop of hoofs, the squeak of runners on the snow; and the jingling, clopping, squeaking rose up like the horses' frozen breath to the silent music in the sky.

I guess we did pretty well. I remember the night we were driving home from a bean supper and dance, and Julie said, "You're getting pretty free with your behavior."

"Well, you're going to be my wife soon enough," I said.

"I can't be soon enough," she whispered, and she pushed my arm away. Women are always contrary that way.

Tom and Kay were curled up at the back of the sleigh and they couldn't hear us.

"Let's get out and run behind for a ways," I said. "My feet are getting cold. And I can clap my hands."

"My feet are warm," she said.

"But mine aren't."

"You're just making that up because you're mad."

"Why would I be mad?"

"You're mad because I stopped you."

"Stopped me what?"

She didn't want to say it. "Nothing," she said.

"I think I'll get out and run behind by myself," I said. "Should I?"

She reached up and kissed me right on the mouth, cold and yet warm, and that was that as far as the running behind went.

"Let's talk," she said. "We've only been engaged since midnight, and here you want to act like we're married already."

"Who, me?" I said, trying to sound like I didn't know what she was talking about.

"Let's talk," she said.

"Talk," I said. "I'm all ears."

"Don't you want to talk?"

"Sure I want to talk. If I can get a word in edgewise."

"I can't get used to being engaged," she said. "I want to talk."

"What'll we talk about?" I said. "It seems to me we've done nothing but talk since last fall."

"Let's plan," she said.

That was the end of my plans.

"We're going to get married, remember?" she went on. "You asked me and I said yes before you had hardly asked the second time."

"You weren't so sure I'd ask a third time."

She soon changed that subject. "Kay said that she and Tom are going to build a house this fall."

"It's a good idea. Living on the home place is no good for them and no good for Ma and Dad."

"Why can't we build a house?"

"We got a shack on our place."

"Shack is right. One room and a lean-to"

"It's a roof."

"Kay and Tom are going to get a new bedroom suite and a new stove, and Kay is going to start making new curtains. I could start making new curtains too if we were going to have a new house with lots of windows."

"If we get a good crop, okay. But I got enough stashed away to get married on and put a crop in, and that's it."

"I want to make a nice home for you. We'll have a family."

"We might," I said. "But things'll have to pick up."

"Promise," she said.

"Sure enough," I said.

"I mean, promise we'll have a new house."

"Don't you think it would be better to wait and see?"

She didn't answer.

"We might flood out or dry out or freeze out. How do I know?"

She still didn't answer.

"What if it's a grasshopper year? What about wireworms and wild oats and rust and buckwheat?"

"Promise me," she said. "I don't even think you love me."

That was her final word.

I talked for another ten minutes about wireworms and rust, and after that things got quiet. We sat in that sleigh for an hour, our breath freezing in our scarves (twenty-seven below, it was), wrapped in a buffalo robe and in each other's arms and never once did she speak. To a young fellow twenty-two years old it didn't make much sense. But I didn't push her away. She was soft and warm and quiet, and I thought she had fallen asleep.

"Okay," I said, finally. "Okay okay okay. I promise."

She snuggled closer.

We had a double wedding in the spring.

Tom's father-in-law fixed up two granaries near the house and we held the reception at his place. Everybody was there. My cousin had trouble with the pump, and while everybody was watching him trying to tap the keg, Tom came over to where I was watching the sky for a nice day and he shook my hand.

"We're the luckiest pair of duck hunters this side of the fourth meridian," he said. "We've each got a half section that's almost paid for, we've got a big crop to put in that'll put us on our feet, and we've each got the prettiest girl in the country. How do you like being a married man?"

"Yes sir," I said. I had one eye on a couple of my old sidekicks who were kissing the bride for the second time. "This here love business is the clear McCoy."

I remember that my cousin drew the first pitcherful just then, and it was all foam. But we were only just married....

The sky was the garment of love. It was a big sky, freckled with the stars of the universe; a happy sky, shrouding all the pain. It was the time of spring, and spring is love, and in the night sky arrow after arrow of honking geese winged across the yellow moon, driving winter from the world.

Right after the wedding we moved into the shack and really went to work. I was busy from morning till night putting in a big crop, while Julie helped with the chores and looked after her little chicks and put in a big garden. When the crop was in we started on the summer fallow, and before that was done it was haying time.

At noon she brought dinner out to me in the field out in the sun and the wind, and we sat side by side and talked and laughed, and the dust from my face got on hers sometimes, and sometimes I didn't get started quite on time. And the weather was good too....

In the evening a black cloud towered up in the west and tumbled over the land, bringing lightning and rain and hope. In the morning there was only a fragment of cloud; the dot worn on a woman's cheek beside a pair of beautiful eyes, and the beautiful sun in the fair blue sky sent warmth and growth into the earth, and the rain and the sun turned the black fields green, the green fields yellow.

I remember one Sunday we went over to Tom's for a chicken supper. Tom and Dad and I talked about the way the crops were coming along and where to get binder repairs, and we made arrangements to help each other with the cutting and stooking.

The womenfolk talked about their gardens and their chickens until Julie mentioned the drapes she was sewing.

"I'm going to have one of those living room parlours," she said, "one of those living room parlours with lots of windows, like in the magazines, and I'm making drapes for that kind of window."

"I think I will too," Kay said. "Tom cut some of the nicest plans out of last week's Free Press. I hope the fall stays nice."

"My husband is even getting enthusiastic," Julie said, giving me a teasing smile. "I caught him holding up the drapes one day and looking at them."

Ma said she was crocheting some new pillow covers for all the pillows and easy chairs that seemed to be coming up, and she thought they all better get together and do some extra canning. Entertaining takes food.

Kay said, "Ma," meaning her mother-in-law, "you'll soon have your house all to yourself again. And since Tom is afraid he'll have to help with the washing, he's going to get me a new washing machine."

"We might pick up a secondhand car," Julie said, "if the crop on our breaking doesn't go down because it's too heavy."

I had mentioned it'd be something to tinker on during the winter.

It wasn't long before Julie was talking about the washing machine and Kay was talking about a secondhand car. Wheat was a good price that year.

We menfolk laughed at the women and we found a few things in the Eaton's catalogue that we could use ourselves. It seemed that somebody was always coming up with something new that we couldn't possibly do without.

After supper we all walked out to have a look at Tom's crop. Tom could even make a gumbo patch grow wheat.

I guess it happened a week later. I mean, the storm. Julie was working on her drapes. It was a hot day, too hot and too still, and in the afternoon the clouds began to pile up in the west....

The storm came like a cloud of white dust high in the sky: not black or grey like a rain cloud, but white; and now it was rolling across the heavens with a brute unconcern for the mites below, and after awhile came the first dull roar. The hot, dead air was suddenly cool, stirring to a breeze, and then a white wall of destruction bridged earth and sky and moved across the land and crashed across the fields of ripening grain.

Old man Rittner saw it coming west of us, and he went out and drove his axe in the middle of the yard, figuring to split her. But she didn't split.

In fifteen minutes it was all over and the sun was shining as pretty as you please. Only there was no reason for the sun to shine. Our garden and our fields were flat, and the west window was broken, and half the shingles were gone from the shack. The leaves were half stripped from the trees, and the ground was more white than black and, I remember, the cat found a dead robin.

My wife didn't say a word.

I hitched up old Mag to the buggy and Julie and I drove over to Tom's place.

Tom was sitting on the porch steps with his head in his hands, and Kay was leaning on the fence, looking at her garden. It looked like they hadn't been talking much either.

I got out and walked over to Tom, and Julie stayed in the buggy.

"A hundred percent," I said.

"The works," he said. "And all I got is enough insurance to feed us this winter or to buy a ticket to hell out of here."

"The same with me," I said.

We couldn't think of much to say.

All of a sudden Tom almost shouted at Kay: "Say it and get it over with. If you want we'll go to the city and I'll get a job. I can get on a construction gang. They're paying good now. We'll get a washing machine and a secondhand car." He looked at his wheat fields, beaten flat. "We'll make a payment and get our own house."

He kicked at a hailstone.

"A house with big windows for my new drapes," Kay added.

Tom got up and he walked to the gate where Julie sat in the buggy. Kay and I, we stood there watching him, almost afraid of the storm in his eyes, and Kay looked at me as if I should stop him before he went and grabbed a pitchfork or something.

"Tom, I was joking," Kay said. "I don't need fancy curtains and a washing machine. And we never needed a car before. Did we, Tom? We got enough for us and Ma and Dad. Haven't we, Tom? And we got next year."

Tom snorted at that idea. He kicked open the gate and walked out toward the barn. There was so much helpless anger in him he couldn't talk.

Kay called after him. "We still got this, Tom." She was kind of crying. She was pointing at the black dirt that showed through the broken grass. "Look, Tom, we still got this,"

Tom, he stopped in the middle of the yard and he turned around. For a long time he was only looking at Kay's empty hand.

All of a sudden he bent down like he was going to say a prayer or something. And he scooped up a handful of hailstones, and he flung them back at the sky.

Like I say, my wife; she didn't say a word.

(1970)   (1970)

Phyllis Webb

1927 –

BORN IN VICTORIA, Phyllis Webb was educated at the University of British Columbia and at McGill University. From 1964 to 1969 she lived in Toronto and worked for the Canadian Broadcasting Corporation. Since then she has lived in Vancouver and on the islands off the west coast. A group of Webb's poems first appeared in *Trio* (1954), an anthology which also included poems by Eli Mandel and Gael Turnbull. *Even Your Right Eye,* her first individual volume, was published in 1956, and her *Selected Poems 1954-1965* appeared in 1971.

Patience

Patience is the wideness of the night
the simple pain of stars
the muffled explosion of velvet
it moves itself generally
through particulars
accepts the telling of time
without day's relativity.

But more than these accommodations
patience is love withdrawn
into the well, immersion into   10
a deep place where green begins.
It is the slow beat of slanting eyes
down the heart's years,
it is the silencer
and the loving now
involves no word.
Patience is the answer
poised in grief – the knowing –
it is the prose of tears
withheld and the aging,   20
the history in the heart
and futures where pain
is a lucid cargo.

(1954)   (1971)

Marvell's Garden

Marvell's garden, that place of solitude,
is not where I'd choose to live
yet is the fixed sundial
that turns me round
unwillingly
in a hot glade
as closer, closer I come to contradiction
to the shade green within the green shade.

The garden where Marvell scorned love's solicitude —
that dream — and played instead an arcane solitaire,   10
shuffling his thoughts like shadowy chance
across the shrubs of ecstasy,
and cast the myths away to flowering hours
as yes, his mind, that sea, caught at green
thoughts shadowing a green infinity.

And yet Marvell's garden was not Plato's
garden — and yet — he did care more for the form
of things than for the thing itself —
ideas and visions,
resemblances and echoes,   20
things seeming and being
not quite what they were.

That was his garden, a kind of attitude
struck out of an earth too carefully attended,
wanting to be left alone.
And I don't blame him for that.
God knows, too many fences fence us out
and his garden closed in on Paradise.

On Paradise! When I think of his hymning
Puritans in the Bermudas, the bright oranges   30
lighting up that night! When I recall
his rustling tinsel hopes
beneath the cold decree of steel,
Oh, I have wept for some new convulsion
to tear together this world and his.

But then I saw his luminous plumèd Wings
prepared for flight,
and then I heard him singing glory
in a green tree,
and then I caught the vest he'd laid aside   40
all blest with fire.

And I have gone walking slowly in
his garden of necessity
leaving brothers, lovers, Christ
outside my walls
where they have wept without
and I within.

(1956)   (1971)

Lament

Knowing that everything is wrong,
how can we go on giving birth
either to poems or the troublesome lie,
to children, most of all, who sense
the stress in our distracted wonder
the instant of their entry with their cry?

For every building in this world
receives our benediction of disease.
Knowing that everything is wrong
means only that we all know where we're going.   10

But I, how can I, I
craving the resolution of my earth,
take up my little gang of sweet pretence
and saunter day-dreary down the alleys, or pursue
the half-disastrous night? Where is that virtue
I would claim with tense impersonal unworth,
where does it dwell, that virtuous land
where one can die without a second birth?

It is not here, neither in the petulance
of my cries, nor in the tracers of my active fear,   20
not in my suicide of love, my dear.
That place of perfect animals and men
is simply the circle we would charm our children in
and why we frame our lonely poems in
the shape of a frugal sadness.

(1956)   (1971)

Breaking

Give us wholeness, for we are broken.
But who are we asking, and why do we ask?
Destructive element heaves close to home,
our years of work broken against a breakwater.

Shattered gods, self-iconoclasts,
it is with Lazarus unattended we belong
(the fall of the sparrow is unbroken song).
The crucifix has clattered to the ground,
the living Christ has spent a year in Paris,
travelled on the Metro, fallen in the Seine.   10
We would not raise our silly gods again.
Stigmata sting, they suddenly appear
on every blessed person everywhere.
If there is agitation there is cause.

Ophelia, Hamlet, Othello, Lear,
Kit Smart, William Blake, John Clare,
Van Gogh, Henry IV of Pirandello,
Gerard de Nerval, Antonin Artaud
bear a crown of darkness.
It is better so.   20

Responsible now each to his own attack,
we are bequeathed their ethos and our death.
Greek marble white and whiter grows
breaking into history of a west.
If we could stand so virtuously white
crumbling in the terrible Grecian light.

There is a justice in destruction.
It isn't "isn't fair".
A madhouse is designed for the insane,
a hospital for wounds that will re-open;   30
a war is architecture for aggression,
and Christ's stigmata body-minted token.
What are we whole or beautiful or good for
but to be absolutely broken?

(1962)   (1971)

Making

Quilted
patches, unlike the smooth silk loveliness
of the bought,
this made-ness out of self-madness
thrown across their bones to keep them warm.
It does.

Making
under the patches a smooth silk loveliness
of parts:
two bodies are better than one for this quilting,   10
throwing into the dark a this-ness that was not.
It does.

Fragments
of the splintered irrelevance of doubt, sharp
hopes, spear and splice into a nice consistency as once
under the pen, the brush, the sculptor's hand
music was made, arises now, blossom on fruit-tree bough.
It does.

Exercise,
exegesis of the will captures and lays   20
haloes around bright ankles of a saint.
Exemplary under the tree,
Buddha glows out now
making the intolerable, accidental sky
patch up its fugitive ecstasies.
It does.

It does,
and, all doing done, a child on the street runs
dirty from sun
to the warm infant born to soiled sheets   30
and stares at the patched external face.
It does.

From the making made and, made, now making
certain order – thus excellent despair
is laid, and in the room the patches of the quilt
seize light and throw it back upon the air.
A grace is made, a loveliness is caught
quilting a quiet blossom as a work.
It does.

And do you,   40
doubting, fractured, and untaught, St. John of the Cross,
come down and patch the particles and throw
across the mild unblessedness of day
lectures to the untranscended soul.
Then lotus-like you'll move upon the pond,
the one-in-many, the many-in-the-one,
making a numbered floral-essenced sun
resting upon the greening padded frond,
a patched, matched protection for Because.
And for our dubious value it will do.   50
It always does.

(1962)   (1971)

From
Non Linear

[a curve/broken]

a curve/broken   orange crab   pale
of green   delicates at peace
moss weed   on this sand
kelp shells pebbles   tracery of last night's
lost orange rind   tide   10

[near the white Tanabe]

near the white Tanabe
narcissus
  near Layton's *Love*
daffodils

(1965)

outside   falling on
the pavement
the plum blossoms
of Cypress Street

(1971)

Hugh Hood
1928 –

HUGH HOOD WAS born in Toronto and received his Ph.D. from the University of Toronto (1955). In 1961 he joined the Department of English at the University of Montreal, and in the following year his first collection of short stories, *Flying a Red Kite*, appeared. Hood has since published other collections of short stories and several novels including *White Figure, White Ground* (1964), *A Game of Touch* (1970), *The Fruit Man, the Meat Man and the Manager* (1971), *The Swing in the Garden* (1975) and *Dark Glasses* (1976).

The Fruit Man, the Meat Man & the Manager

A GROCER NAMED Morris Znaimer managed the Greenwood Groceteria, up on Greenwood Avenue next to the university, for over seventeen years, in partnership with Jack Genovese, fruit and vegetables, and Mendel Greenspon, an experienced butcher but not kosher.

Mister Znaimer took care of grocery inventory and the beer, and he also did the accounting and book keeping, supervised the cash desk and checkout counter with a girl named Shirley to help, and decided about charge accounts and billing; he had hardly any bad-debt items because he was a shrewd judge of credit.

Jack did the buying for fruit and vegetables, going daily to the markets before dawn, and usually getting the pick of all local crops. And Mendel Greenspon was an expert in his line, a butcher who could have worked anywhere, with a surgeon's hand with his knives and an exact honesty about weights and measures. The meat at the Greenwood was famous for blocks.

The store was half a block from Ballantyne and the competition had the better location, right on the corner of Greenwood and Ballantyne, *Marché Boisvert*, with a pharmacy and a hairdresser in the same building drawing customer traffic. Both groceries served a high-class residential quarter and a funny thing was that often the Jewish store got most of the French trade, and the French store got most of the Jewish. Why would that be?

"Boisvert, Boisvert, they stole the name from us," Mister Znaimer would often say to his partners. Both stores were precariously located because of the closeness of the university, then in a period of expansion that threatened to consume all the available frontage along Greenwood.

The Greenwood Groceteria wasn't a big store; it had a thirty-foot frontage, two show windows that weren't often re-arranged, except for the sales announcements lettered in black and red by Mister Znaimer, two main aisles and a single cash desk, no windows on either side of the interior, and usually a lot of soiled sawdust or sweeping compound on the floor, particularly in winter. At the front there was always a traffic jam of shopping carts. If the store was crowded it was hard to get your cart in and out through the people.

Mister Znaimer and Jack and Mendel kept abreast of the competition, maybe a bit ahead, by maintaining high standards of goods and services and fast free delivery — two trucks and a succession of more or less reliable drivers, a continual worry to the manager. They had a big packaged-goods inventory and a storage problem. They had very good Christmas trees, better than the competition, standing peaked with snow in a rich-smelling heap next to the delivery trucks, all through December. They made a special display of Hallowe'en pumpkins and drew kids in.

Sarah Cummings would go there for some of her groceries through the middle of the week when there was no time for a trip to the supermarket, or at the end of the month before her husband was paid. Sometimes she felt that she was taking advantage of the small tradesman, buying from him only when convenient, using credit with no carrying charge, which you couldn't get from the chains, now and then picking up two or three loss-leaders when Mister Znaimer had clearly been thinking of one to a customer. On the other hand, she paid more at the Greenwood. Meat was higher, though trimmed right down and more tasty than the artificially tenderized supermarket meat. A few prices were competitive.

She liked to take Stephen and Brent for a walk along Greenwood around ten-thirty in the morning, Tuesday or Wednesday, to get a pound of butter and two quarts of milk and cigarettes. The boys loved the store and would talk for indefinite periods to Jack Genovese, who was very fond of kids. Once when she was first going there, she caught sight of Stephen out of the corner of her eye, standing down by the fruit next to a basket of plump, succulent pears. The basket stood on a carton and Stephen's nose was flat against a pear on the top of the pile; they were wrapped in silver paper, high-quality party goods.

"Get your little nose out of there, Stevie," she said, not unkindly, while she looked in her purse to see what money she had. She saw a glance pass between Mister Znaimer and Jack, and then the fruit man said, "Naw, naw, Missus, that's fine. Here, can I give him one?"

She said, "Oh, you shouldn't. They'll both have to have one." Brent came running up.

Jack picked out two pears, peeled the silver paper, rubbed them against his sleeve, bent down and gave the boys one each. "The best," he said. "Melt in your mouth." The boys took them politely and went outside, enjoying themselves a lot.

Mrs. Cummings said, "I'll pay for that please, Mister Znaimer; would you total them in?"

"It's goodwill," he said. "We don't ask you to pay for goodwill. That'll be three dollars and seventy-nine cents, including the two cigarettes and not including the pears."

"And would you charge it, please?"

"Certainly, that's on a charge, three seventy-nine. Can I send that down for you?" Without looking he plucked her small sheaf of charge bills from the pile behind him, and added the latest.

"I don't want to trouble you."

"That's no trouble, that's what we're here for." He picked up the small bag and walked with her to the door. Stephen came over and handed him the core of the pear, and the grocer laughed and flipped it into a trash carton.

Sarah began to think of him as the fatherly type; he was stern in appearance, very erect, and he rendered his accounts very precisely at the end of each month. When she asked, as she sometimes did, if she could carry part of the balance forward, he was prompt to agree, and at no time suggested that she put a limit on her balance. The highest she ever got was once before Christmas, a bill of around two hundred dollars which her husband discharged as a Christmas present; he pinned the receipted bill to the tree and made a joke of it.

"I'm glad it's paid," she said, "I'm a little afraid of him."

"Who?"

"Mister Znaimer. He reminds me of my father. He isn't disapproving, but I think he expects good behaviour."

"So do I," said her husband defensively.

"Oh you, you're a woolly lamb."

"I see what you mean though, he's impressive."

Maybe even just, Mrs. Cummings thought, maybe a just man. She looked forward to her talks with him.

"If we didn't have the beer, we'd be out of business, Mrs. Cummings. The supermarkets aren't allowed to sell it, for that reason, to keep the small stores going."

"My husband said that was socialistic."

"It may be, it may be. Look, just give me a chance, let me handle your groceries for a month, one month, it's all I ask. What do you spend a month, a hundred and eighty? Forty, forty-five dollars a week? You spend a third of that with us."

"I know it's mean," she said.

"It's not taking advantage; it's the way things are. But you let me have all your orders for a month and I'll beat the chain stores. I deliver free — you save on gas. I don't have a service charge on accounts, and anyway you can't get one in a supermarket. I'll match their prices — if you can get it cheaper over there, come and tell me and I'll match it. I can do it. I know I can. You want pink stamps?"

"I wasn't going to say that."

"I know you weren't, you're a nice lady. Tell you what, we don't bother with stamps or booklets; you don't need to lick them or paste them. Keep your register slips. When you've got a few hundred dollars in slips, bring them in and I'll rebate two percent, same as them. Here, come and look." He led her to the show window in which a few items of soiled merchandise were carefully arranged, looking like they had been there for some time. "You want pots? A nice pot with a copper bottom, cost you seven dollars? I'll have it for you. A lamp? A little coaster wagon for your boys, red with white letters? I know what you're spending. I'll fix you up."

An old man stood next to her at the cash desk with a jar of Yuban in his hands, staring at her in mute appeal. She smiled at him and let him go through, and Mister Znaimer looked at her with approval; she felt pleased.

"Personal service, that's what we offer. Where can you find butchers like Mendel? Today we have rib steak, ask him about it, a good buy. When it comes off his block, it's clean; you aren't paying for bone and muscle, you're getting all meat. For two-fifty you can serve your family steak that you can't match anywhere, aged properly, none of this chemical tenderizer. Go and ask him about it, all red brand, the best."

"I wasn't going to buy meat, but for a treat perhaps I should see it."

"He's right there waiting, Mrs. Cummings. There's no line-up."

She went down to the meat counter and asked to see the rib steaks, watching Mendel Greenspon as he whisked a chunk of meat out of the cooler. He held it up on a sheet of bloodied brown paper and prodded it.

"Big enough? Right thickness?"

"I thought of two adult servings and another piece for the boys."

"About two and a quarter pounds is what you want." He walked into the big refrigerator and came back carrying a large beef rib. He laid it on the block and sliced, and it was wonderful how exact, how sure, his movements were; first the cleaver, just the thickness her husband loved, and then a long thin knife of extraordinary sharpness which cut like a laser beam; boned it, trimmed it, threw in a lump of suet for free. In a second he showed her two large pieces and two child-sized. They reminded her absurdly of the Cummings family walking to church.

"Just right," she said.

"It weighs a bit more, but we said two and a quarter pounds. That'll be two twenty-five," and he handed her the parcel. When they ate the steak, her husband crooned endearments at her.

"Better than filet. Boy, what a buy!"

She said, "They can't really match prices, not for long."

"We'd better keep the account paid up, if that's any help."

"I think it's only fair."

Once when she went in to pay up her account, Mister Znaimer wasn't in the store, and Jack came over and took the money.

"Morris is out with the truck," he said, "one of the drivers has been out since payday; they aren't dependable. That's Mrs. Cummings, isn't it, sure, got it right here." He fumbled through the file of accounts hanging beside the register, and a letter in a legal-sized envelope fell onto the open cash drawer from somewhere behind the accounts file. She noticed the university emblem on the envelope, the same kind of envelope her husband's salary cheques came in. Jack picked it up idly, looked at the address, stood silently for a moment and then took the letter and read it; his face changed expression, darkening. She had never seen him look so grim.

"Mendel," he called, "come and look at this. Excuse me a second, Mrs. Cummings." He strolled to the back of the store and said to the butcher, "Your hands clean?" Mendel wiped them on his apron and took the letter, and Jack came back and gave Mrs. Cummings a receipted cash slip for the balance, smiling and half bowing.

"Always a pleasure," he said. "I'll tell Morris you were in." He mentioned Mister Znaimer with a shade of embarrassment.

After that Sarah began to feel hints of impending changes; the atmosphere in the store was not as happy as before. The give and take among the partners had not the familiar ease; the drivers booked off drunk more often. Shirley the cash-girl would talk discontentedly from time to time of quitting. Always described as "the girl" by the partners, she was really a plump, tired-faced woman in her late thirties with hair that escaped from pins and straggled against her cheek. She wore a white coat that was none too clean.

"My husband wants me to retire," she would whisper to Mrs. Cummings. "He never wanted me to work."

"I didn't realize you were married."

"Oh yes, a long time. I've got a little boy, older than yours. He has eye-trouble."

Once she did quit, but it didn't take. After three or four days she was back in the store with a salary increase, but still gloomy.

"I'm glad to see you," said Mrs. Cummings.

"It won't last."

"What?"

"The store. It's folding up pretty soon now, I think."

"What's wrong?"

"The university wants the land for a new sports centre. They made a good offer and Jack and Mendel want to take it. They own two-thirds of the business, so Morris can't buck them. He can't afford to buy them out, and he can't talk them into fighting expropriation."

"But it's a good store. Wouldn't they be crazy to quit?"

"I don't know. It's a living, that's all. They might be able to fight the university for a while, but they'd lose in the end and the offer might even be reduced. Mendel and Jack are afraid, and I guess they're right; better get out while the getting's good."

"I don't understand that. I always thought they got along so well."

"It's just business, Mrs. Cummings, that's all it is."

"Well, if that's all it is...."

She felt that there should be more to it, and out of loyalty stopped dealing at supermarkets, to give the Greenwood all her business; she urged her husband's colleagues' wives to shop there, and might have been responsible for a slight up-turn in sales, nothing you'd specially notice. She felt baffled and sorry that she couldn't help to change matters. She was in and out of the store a lot, and naturally Mister Znaimer noticed it.

One October morning he mentioned it. "I appreciate it. I've been glad to have the business. I tell you what it is, Mrs. C., I like to do business with people like you, with some sense of how to behave. I could tell from the first day you came in – there's a nice lady. You can tell from the children. No complaints about substitutions on phone orders. A lot of people, to hear them talk you'd think we always sent a higher-priced item on a substitution. It isn't true. If I take a phone order I try to come as close as possible to what the customer wants, and I'll say this for Jack and Mendel, they're the same. We fill the order the way we take it."

"I've never complained."

"That's what I'm saying." He looked at her with affection. Then he had to pick up the phone and she moved to the back to negotiate a roast with the butcher. When she had made her choice, Mendel came around the corner of the meat counter and spoke to her confidentially. "I want to show you something, just so you'll know where I'll be." He handed her a business card:

HIGH QUALITY PROVISIONS

Superior Supermarkets, Corner Darlington and Soissons, are happy to announce the appointment of MENDEL GREENSPON, formerly with Greenwood Groceteria, as Manager, Meat and Poultry Department, effective November 1st, 1967. Come in and meet MENDEL. Always ready to serve friends old and new.

"You're closing so soon?" she said, feeling very sad.

"Last week in October."

"Where is Jack going?"

The butcher mentioned a well-known gourmet grocery in Westmount, and Jack came over to them and shook his head affirmatively. "I'll have to wear a clean smock every day," he said, "I'll look like a doctor. Do you ever get down there, Missus?"

"Not often. That's an expensive store."

"It is," said Jack, "but such fruit! Oh my, it's a pleasure."

"Does Mister Znaimer know about this?"

"We haven't told him officially."

"Oh, you ought to tell him."

Jack said, "It's hard to do."

"But we'll tell him," said Mendel.

Then they began to cut back on everything, the shelves showed bare in places, through the final weeks of October. When the drivers booked off drunk they didn't bother to come back, and the last week the store was open Mister Znaimer took the deliveries himself in the only remaining truck, an old Chevrolet with a ruined clutch.

The store was to close on Hallowe'en, so this year there was no festive display of pumpkins and black and orange candies, no need to attract children. What remained of the packaged goods would go back to the jobbers. Jack hadn't re-ordered on fruit for days; the meat was right down, no loss on useless inventory. It had been quite a delicate trick to cut back the stock, while retaining enough to fill orders till closing date. Mister Znaimer thought they had done a smart job of it. When he packed up the last delivery orders, he could just about fill them and that was all.

He put the truck into gear with some difficulty and drove to the corner of Ballantyne. A group of *Marché Boisvert* employees stood on their steps. He waved a hand at them and they nodded back solemnly. They'll miss us, he thought, this part of the street will be dead for retailing in another year. We drew for them; they drew for us.

He drove north, down the slope of the mountain, and made his rounds, the truck making terrible noises. Have to turn this one in, he thought, and then remembered that there was no need to replace it. It took him only an hour and a half to deliver; in the old days two drivers had been out all day. Urging the expiring truck back up the slope toward Greenwood, he noticed how bare and cold the trees looked and how the sky was steely. He was in his own place in this neighbourhood and could not bear to leave. He felt that nothing holy was left in his life.

In the store he couldn't find the partners, who were perhaps cleaning up the cellar while Shirley swept out the storage room in back. He spoke out loud: "Fools, fools to leave this, they could never have forced us out. Close one store and leave the other alone? They'd never have dared, never. Haven't you got any pride in what we have here? Seventeen years!"

Over a year later, when she had almost forgotten the three grocers, their store long since levelled, Sarah Cummings got a Christmas card from Mister Znaimer, not a business card, a personal one with a short handwritten message inside.

> Dear Mrs. Cummings: how are you and the boys? It's a long time since I've seen you. I retired, you know, when the store closed, and I'm living just a few blocks from you on Greenwood. I hope maybe I'll see you and the boys on the street sometime. I'm not sure if I'll go back into business. I might someday, if I could find a place.
> Yours sincerely, Morris J. Znaimer

Maybe other people got cards from him too.

(1971)   (1971)

Gaston Miron
1928 –

BORN IN SAINTE-AGATHE-DES-MONTS, Quebec, Gaston Miron moved to Montreal in 1947 and became one of the founders of Les Editions de l'Hexagone in 1953. In that same year he published a volume of poems, *Deux sangs,* in collaboration with Olivier Marchand. Miron has been extremely influential as poet, editor and political activist in contemporary Quebec and a collection of his poetry and prose, *L'Homme rapaillé,* published in 1970 was both a popular and a critical success. Miron's work has been translated in the journals *Ellipse* and *Contemporary Literature in Translation.*

Heritage of Sadness

Sad and confused among the fallen stars
pale, silent, nowhere and afraid, a vast phantom
here is this land alone with itself and winds and rocks
a land forever lost to the sun of its birth
a beautiful body drowned in mindless sleep
like water lost in a barren thirst of gravel

I see it bridled by chances and tomorrows
showing its face in the dreams of anguished men
whenever it burns, in wastes and undergrowth of bracken
whenever it burns, in poplars old in years and neglect,
the wasted chlorophyll of its abortive love
or whenever the will to be sleeps in the sail of its heart

10

bowed down, it awaits it knows not what redemption
among these landscapes walking through its stillness
among these rags of silence with eyes of the dying
and always this ruined smile of a poor degraded future
always the slashing of paddles in the dark
and horizons fading in a drift of promises

despoiled, its only hope is a vacant lot's
cold of cane talking with cold of bone   20
unease of the rust, the quick, the nerves, the nude
and on its livid back the blows of heated knives
it looks at you, worked out, from the depths of its quarries
and out of the tunnels of its abstraction where one day
it surrendered and lost forever the memory of man

winds that shuffle the lots of precedence by night
winds of concourse, winds with solar eyes
telluric winds, winds of the soul, universal winds
come couple, o winds, and with your river arms
embrace this face of a ruined people, give it the warmth   30
and the abundant light that rings the wake of swallows

(1970)   (1970)

Fred W. Cogswell (Trans.)

Our October

The man of our time has a face of flagellation
and you, Land of Quebec, Mother Courage,
you are big
with our sooty sorrowful dreams
and an endless drain of bodies and souls

I was born your son
in your worn-out mountains of the north
I ache and suffer

as if I were bitten by that birth
yet in my arms my youth is glowing   10

here are my knees
may our world forgive us
we have allowed our fathers to be humbled in spirit
we have allowed the light of the word to be debased
to the shame and self-contempt of our brothers
we could not bind the roots of our suffering
into the universal sorrow of every man put down

I go to join the burning company
whose struggle shares and breaks the bread of the
common lot in the quicksand of a common grief   20
we will make you, Land of Quebec,
a bed of resurrections
and in the myriad lightnings of our transformations
in this leaven of ours from which the future is rising
in our uncompromising will
men will hear your pulse beating in history
this is ourselves rippling in the autumn of October
this is the russet sound of deer in the light
the future envisioned its challenge accepted

(1970)   (1976)

Fred W. Cogswell (Trans.)

For My Repatriation

Tiller of the scorched fields of exile, governed
by your love whose hands are full of crude conquests
by your rainbow-gaze arc-ended in the winds
anticipating cities and a land that could be yours

my country
I have never travelled
towards any country but you

the day will come when I can confess my birth
I will have wheatfields in my eyes
I will go forth on a soil, impassioned and dazzled   10
by the savage innocence upheaved by the snow

a man will return
from beyond the world

(1970)   (1970)

Brenda Fleet (Trans.)

The Reign of Winter

Grey land and furious, brown and savage
split in the ghostly beauty of the cold
in tides of birch, in brotherhoods
of spruce and pine, and in your similars
of hidden rocks, of enmities

bare ancestral land, our land
over your infinite patient miles you are flowing
into a landscape maddened by loneliness
into the towns where famine chars your face
into our empty and unfurnished loves   10
and into us stiffened by restoration to your earth,
          our death

and you are helpless in this captive wealth of ours
you shiver
in this slow fire that is burning in our backs

(1970)   (1970)
John Glassco (Trans.)

Commonplaces

Nobody changes anything
neither objects nor things
nobody nobody
but one time there was a for-all-time
always this never and yet

oceanic

you were us
I was us

(1970)   (1975)

Brenda Fleet (Trans.)

Roland Giguère
1929 –

———◆———

ROLAND GIGUÈRE WAS born in Montreal and studied at l'Ecole des Arts graphiques de Montréal and at l'Ecole Estienne de Paris. After living in France from 1955 to 1963, he returned to Montreal where he has worked as a graphic designer and as director of Editions Erta. His first volume of poetry, *Faire naître* (1949), has been followed by several collections including *L'âge de la parole* (1965) and *Abécédaire* (1975).

Saisons mortes

I need a small live animal
very alive
standing in the palm of my hand
or asleep on my eyelids
or free

to get close to the seasons

(1950)   (1970)
D.G. Jones (Trans.)

Landscape Estranged

The storm raged about
and the snow blew into our breast
right in the breast

crowned with pain-sharp ice
crowned with thorns
love words driven into the brow

great storm before our eyes in a world estranged
every night tore a cry from us
and we grew up in agony
slowly we were aging   10
and the landscape aged with us-against us

the landscape was no longer the same
the landscape was sombre
the landscape no longer fitted us like a glove
no longer had the colours of our youth
the landscape the beautiful landscape was no longer beautiful
there were no more streams
no more ferns no water
there was nothing left   20

the landscape had to be remade.

(1954)   (1973)
F.R. Scott (Trans.)

Greener Than Nature

It's a time of prevailing breasts
in the fields of pleasure

the plundering hand takes its honey
from the heart of the original hive

the clover is bitter
and the sun has a face of wax

(1965)   (1977)
F.R. Scott (Trans.)

The Age of the Word

An ancient winds rips through the stage
aurochs revive upon a riven plain
the sacred is restored its ornaments of iron
its heavy sword, its golden blade
for righteous combat

flint still sleeps within the rock
and we have no more names
to constellate these bleeding suns

tomorrow we shall eat the serpent's head
swallow the venom with the forked tongue   10
what new song shall rise to charm us then?

(1965)   (1970)
D.G. Jones (Trans.)

The Song Comes from Within

snake
charmed charmer
song
spell
sound
blood
cry
melody

When music leaves many men cold
the serpent is charmed by it   10
the piercing sound — high-pitched — of a simple
little flute reaches him

The charmer is seated and lifts the flute to his mouth
he calls
calls calls
the sound rises and falls
puts forth its caress
calls the serpent

his body touching the sand for his whole length
the serpent FEELS the sound   20
and vibrates like a nerve fibre
the sand's warmth – the sound
the sand's warmth – the cry
the sound rises falls in him rises
puts forth its caress

the sound rises in the long body of the serpent
the blood rises to the charmer's head
sound and blood mingled
sound and blood melodious
the serpent rises and undulates   30
his head takes in the melody
charmed

THEN
THE SONG
TURNS AROUND

His head a space full of sound and blood
the charmer begins to quiver
the melody passes through his arteries
like a fiery tongue
his eyes in the serpent's eyes the charmer   40
is consumed
and becomes himself a serpent
proportionate to the melody thrusting through
his entrails
the melody cries out in his body
he undulates with all his limbs
as he himself becomes a long thin supple reed
unfolds on his own sward and curves around
the melody circles
the sound becomes blood   50

THEN
THE SONG – once again –
TURNS AROUND

The flute grows softer still
melts in the charmer's hands
glides between his fingers
and crawls around him
all becomes reptile now
all undulates
the serpent – the charmer charmed – the soft flute   60

all is under the charm

still the melody calls
the sound rises and falls
rises in the serpent
rises in the charmed charmer
rises from the flute
rises from the earth
rises from the sand
The muted sound rises from everywhere
like a spring of clear water   70
like the sweat that springs from all the body's pores
the melody bites
bites the flesh the body
plows
the melody runs
through maddened veins

it is venom
VENOM

the charmer yields but too late
the charm has done its work   80

all is reptile now
all undulates
all sings

(1973)   (1976)

Fred W. Cogswell (Trans.)

All My South

All my south
up there like an eagle

and my gloomy north
fled to the greatest depth
a north of iron
that attracts shields
and distracts me

all my south up there
calling me

the cry of a cardinal   10
a little shade as of a star
and a calm trajectory

(1973)   (1976)
Fred W. Cogswell (Trans.)

D. G. Jones
1929 –

BORN IN BANCROFT, Ontario, Douglas Gordon Jones was educated at McGill and Queen's Universities and now teaches in the Department of English at the University of Sherbrooke. Since the appearance of his first volume of poetry, *Frost on the Sun* (1957), he has published *The Sun Is Axeman* (1961) and *Phrases from Orpheus* (1967). In 1969 Jones was one of the founding editors of the bilingual journal of translation *Ellipse,* and in 1970 he published an influential study of English-Canadian literature, *Butterfly on Rock.*

Northern Water Thrush

The bird walks by the shore
    untouched by the falling sun
        which crashes in the alders.

Lilting on delicate feet
    among the dry reeds, the washed
        and broken skeletons of trees,

he moves through his broken world
    as one, alone surviving, moves
        through the rubble of a recent war:

a world of silence but for the sound
    of water tapping on the stones,
        a drag of wind in the pine.

Grey with his yellow, fluted breast
    he dips and halts, a string of notes
        limned on the stillness of a void:

the stillness of the early spring
    when new suns prepare
        like new buds in the leafless air

10

a pristine world, the old
    calligraphy of living things   20
        having been destroyed.

But though he walks magnificent
    upon the littered shore, holding
        the moment with his poise,

he too will whiten with the days,
    and the flawed human world
        return with his delicate bone.

(1957)   (1961)

Schoolgirls

Like juncos, or some bird by Klee,
These girls in black, with black legs,
Walk apart, as much as if
They indeed had wings.

Still what the uniform black conceals
Of flesh it does not take away
But like an art intensifies,
Reveals.

Earth's angels, not heaven's, they
Contest the hegemony of the sun   10
And, too, remark
Upon the pallid business grey.

Beneath the complex flowering stone,
The gothic Church of Our Lady, they
Inherit
Often to themselves unknown
A complex foliage and an air
Deeper, and more vast
Than our local atmosphere.

Though now they move among   20
Branches of brown leaves, or none,
The roots go down, a season
Of new leaves will yet appear.

Meanwhile they own the air,
And though their wings are black
And grave beneath the sun,
They have the seriousness of youth
And like young birds within a sky
Treeless and bare
They are profoundly gay.   30

(1957)   (1961)

Beautiful Creatures Brief as These

(For Jay Macpherson)

Like butterflies but lately come
From long cocoons of summer
These little girls start back to school
To swarm the sidewalks, playing-fields,
And litter air with colour.

So slight they look within their clothes,
Their dresses looser than the Sulphur's wings,
It seems that even if the wind alone
Were not to break them in the lofty trees,
They could not bear the weight of *things*.   10

And yet they cry into the morning air
And hang from railings upside down
And laugh, as though the world were theirs
And all its buildings, trees, and stones
Were toys, were gifts of a benignant sun.

(1961)   (1961)

Portrait of Anne Hébert

The sunlight, here and there,
Touches a table

And a draught at the window
Announces your presence,

You take your place in the room
Without fuss,

Your delicate bones,
Your frock,
Have the grace of disinterested
            passion.

10 Words are arrayed
Like surgical instruments
Neatly in trays.

Deftly, you make an incision
Probing
The obscure disease.

Your sensibility
Has the sure fingers of the blind:

Each decision
Cuts like a scalpel
Through tangled emotion.   20

You define
The morbid tissue, laying it bare

Like a tatter of lace
Dark
On the paper.

(1961)   (1961)

I Thought There Were Limits

I thought there were limits, Newtonian
Laws of emotion –

I thought there were limits to this falling away,
This emptiness. I was wrong.

The apples, falling, never hit the ground.

So much for grass, and animals –
Nothing remains,
No sure foundation on the rock. The cat

Drifts, or simply dissolves.

L'homme moyen sensuel   10
Had better look out: complete
Deprivation brings

Dreams, hallucinations which reveal
The sound and fury of machines
Working on nothing – which explains

God's creation: *ex nihilo fecit.*

Wrong again. I now suspect
The limit is the sea itself,
The limitless.

So, neither swim nor float. Relax,   20
The void is not so bleak.

Conclude: desire is but an ache,
An absence. It creates
A dream of limits

And it grows in gravity as that takes shape.

(1967)   (1967)

Winter Walk

(For Monique)

You are a figure on my horizon.   uncentered and not
            We walk   eccentric – as the immense
together the horizons   sun burns, and we wait   10
of an old discourse

                                         for the spring migration
and beyond

                                         and the loon, pale as the wind,
perhaps to discover   descends
the language of a few birds, the   shuddering
            shape   to the open river
of breath, a relation

I half fear where it may lead us
beyond
the shape of our bodies, the firm
          bone

of your arm
in the thick fur, beyond

the few days and nights of a
          village   20
scattered
gently by the steaming river

here in the hills
the frozen discourse of a lake

(1973)

Dance for One Leg

(for Avrum Malus)

Not to be driven, above all
by oneself

to improvise

as fields
forget the glacier and the driven
          plough
and move like milk.

The tall man with a cast becomes
a whitewashed wall
where flowers grow: *Pour ton
          amour*

10 *Pour te consoler.*

The one leg learns to dance.

His house has many windows.

His house is blank, a white
among the drifts of white.

How did they come here, the
          children
playing age (the one who rocks

in the rocking chair, the girl
in the diminutive long dress),
          the friend

each separate   20

the mother of the girl (her beauty
the exhausted grass)

except that deaths
like winters are occasion for a fire
a break is an occasion

to discover love.

They dance

the tall man with a cast
dances

thus, together   30

as estranged bones knit, as fields
invested in the driven snow
forget themselves

become one flesh.

(1973)

Jay Macpherson
1931–

———◆———

BORN IN ENGLAND, Jay Macpherson came to Canada at the age of nine. She attended Carleton College and in 1964 received her Ph.D. from the University of Toronto where she now teaches in the Department of English at Victoria College. After publishing two small volumes, *Nineteen Poems* (1952) and *O Earth Return* (1954), Macpherson won the Governor General's Award for *The Boatman* (1957), a collection of eighty poems arranged in six linked sections. In 1974 she published another collection of poems, *Welcoming Disaster*.

The Boatman

You might suppose it easy
For a maker not too lazy
To convert the gentle reader to an Ark:
But it takes a willing pupil
To admit both gnat and camel
– Quite an eyeful, all the crew that must embark.

After me when comes the deluge
And you're looking round for refuge
From God's anger pouring down in gush and spout,
Then you take the tender creature   10
– You remember, that's the reader –
And you pull him through his navel inside out.

That's to get his beasts outside him,
For they've got to come aboard him,
As the best directions have it, two by two.
When you've taken all their tickets
And you've marched them through his sockets,
Let the tempest bust Creation: heed not you.

For you're riding high and mighty
In a gale that's pushing ninety   20
With a solid bottom under you – that's his.

Fellow flesh affords a rampart,
And you've got along for comfort
All the world there ever shall be, was, and is.

(1957)   (1968)

The Faithful Shepherd

Cold pastoral: the shepherd under the snow
Sleeps circled with his sheep.
Above them though successive winters heap
Rigours, and wailing weathers go
Like beasts about, time only rocks their sleep,
An ark upon a deep.
And drowsy care, to keep a world from death,
Maintains his steady heartbeat and warm breath.

(1957)   (1968)

Eve in Reflection

Painful and brief the act. Eve on the barren shore
Sees every cherished feature, plumed tree, bright grass,
Fresh spring, the beasts as placid as before
Beneath the inviolable glass.

There the lost girl gone under sea
Tends her undying grove, never raising her eyes
To where on the salt shell beach in reverie
The mother of all living lies.

The beloved face is lost from sight,
Marred in a whelming tide of blood: 10
And Adam walks in the cold night
Wilderness, waste wood.

(1957)   (1968)

Of Creatures the Net

I

Of creatures the net and chain
Stretched like that great
        membrane
The soft sore ocean
Is by us not broken;

And like an eye or tongue
Is wet and sensing;
And by the ends drawn up
Will strain but not snap.

II

And in all natures we
10 The primitive he and she
Carry the child Jesus,
Those suffering senses

That in us see and taste,
With us in absence fast,
For whose scattered and bound
Sake we are joined.

(1957)

III

Of the seas the wide cup
Shrinks to a water-drop,
The creatures in its round
As in an eye contained,   20

And that eye still the globe
Wherein all natures move,
Still tough the skin
That holds their troubles in.

IV

In all the green flood
More closely binds than blood;
Though windowed like a net
Lets none forget

The forsaken brother
And elder other;   30
Divided is unbroken,
Draws with the chain of ocean.

(1968)

House Lights

Lit up, the house afloat
On the dark street
Draws us: we are a crowd,
Silent, discrete.

If you put by the blind,
Left the pane free

That holds the darkness out,
What might you see –

Strangers, or denizens,
Caught on light's hook?   10
Or would the glass give back
Your own veiled look?

(1974)

(1974)

The Well

A winter hanging over the dark well,
My back turned to the sky,
To see if in that blackness something stirs,
Or glints, or winks an eye:

Or, from the bottom looking up, I see
Sky's white, my pupil head —
Lying with all that's lost, with all that shines —
My winter with the dead:

A well of truth, of images, of words.
Low where Orion lies   10
I watch the solstice pit become a stair,
The constellations rise.

(1974)   (1974)

Lost Books & Dead Letters

Lost the books of Gad and Enoch,
Nathan's visions, Jahweh's wars,
Lost the poets' book of Jasher:
Found, though, is the book of laws.

Lost is some of God's own story,
What he did at Arnon's brook:
But my limbs, before he formed them,
And my tears, are in his book.

Muse, with thee the book of life is,
Though my Adversary doubt: 10
Let me not be put to silence,
From thy page blot me not out.

(1974)   (1974)

Alice Munro
1931 –

———◆———

ALICE (LAIDLAW) MUNRO was born in Wingham, Ontario, and studied at
the University of Western Ontario. Her first collection of short stories,
The Dance of the Happy Shades, appeared in 1968. Her subsequent
publications include a novel, *Lives of Girls and Women* (1971), and a
second collection of stories, *Something I've Been Meaning to Tell You*
(1974).

Winter Wind

FROM MY GRANDMOTHER'S bedroom window you could look across the
CPR tracks to a wide stretch of the Wawanash river, meandering in
reeds. All frozen now, all ice and untracked snow. Even on stormy days
the clouds might break before supper time, and then there was a fierce
red sunset. Like Siberia, my grandmother said, offended, you would
think we were living on the edge of the wilderness. It was all farms, of
course, and tame bush, no wilderness at all, but winter buried the fence
posts.

The storm started before noon, when we were in Chemistry, and we
watched its progress hopefully, looking forward to something disrup-
tive, to blocked roads and short supplies, and bedding down in school
corridors. I imagined myself liberated by a crisis-charged atmosphere,
aided by a power failure and candlelight and stirring songs offered
against the roar of the wind, blanketed down with Mr. Harmer, a
junior teacher whose eye I often tried to catch in Assembly, comforted
by his embrace at first merely warming and comradely, which might yet
turn, in all the darkness and confusion – candle by this time blown out
– to something more urgent and personal. Things did not get that far.
But we were dismissed early, the school buses set out with their lights
on in the middle of the afternoon. Usually I took the Whitechurch bus
to the first corner west of town, and walked from there, three-quarters
of a mile or so, to our house at the edge of the bush. This night, as two
or three times a winter, I went to stay at my grandmother's house, in
town.

The hallway of this house was all wood, polished, fragrant, smooth, cozy as the inside of a nutshell. A yellow lamp was on in the dining room. I did my homework – something I never bothered with, at home, because there was no place or time for it – on the dining room table, after Aunt Madge had spread a newspaper to protect the cloth. Aunt Madge was my great-aunt, my grandmother's sister, they were widows.

Aunt Madge was ironing (they ironed everything, down to underwear and potholders) and my grandmother was making a carrot pudding for supper. Lovely smells. Compare this to the scene at home. The only warm room there was the kitchen; we had a wood stove. My brother brought in wood, and left tracks of dirty snow on the linoleum; I swore at him. Dirt and chaos threatened all the time. My mother often had to lie down on the couch, and tell her grievances. I argued with her whenever possible, and she said my heart would be broken when I had children of my own. We were selling eggs at this time, and everywhere there were baskets of eggs with bits of straw and feathers and hen-dirt stuck to them, waiting to be cleaned. I believed that a smell of hencoops came into the house on boots and clothes and you could not get rid of it.

In the dining room I could look up at two dark oil paintings. They had been done by another sister of my grandmother's, who had died in early middle age. One showed a cottage by a stream and one a dog with a bird in its mouth. My mother had pointed out that the bird was too big, in comparison with the dog.

"Well it was not Tina's mistake, then," my grandmother said. "It was copied from a calendar."

"She was talented but she gave it up when she got married," said Aunt Madge approvingly.

There was also in the room a photograph of my grandmother and Aunt Madge, with their parents, and this sister who had died, and another sister who had married a Catholic, so that it seemed almost as bad as if she died, though peace was made later on. I did not bother to look at this photograph, except in a passing way, but after my grandmother's death and Aunt Madge's removal to a nursing-home (where she lives yet, lives on and on, unrecognizable, unrecognizing, completely divested of herself, dried up like a little monkey, past all memory and maybe past bewilderment, free), I salvaged it, and have taken it with me wherever I go.

The parents are seated. The mother firm and unsmiling, in a black silk dress, hair scanty and center-parted, eyes bulging and faded. The father handsome still, bearded, hand-on-knee, patriarchal. A bit of Irish acting here, a relishing of the part, which he might as well relish since he cannot now escape it? When young he was popular in taverns; even after his children were born he had the name of a drinker, a great celebrator. But he gave up those ways, he turned his back on his friends and brought his family here, to take up land in the newly opened Huron Tract. This photograph was the sign and record of his achievement: respectability, moderate prosperity, mollified wife in a black silk dress, the well-turned-out tall daughters.

Though as a matter of fact their dresses look frightful; flouncy and countrified. All except Aunt Madge's; a tight, simple, high-necked affair, black with some sparkle about it, perhaps of jet. She wears it with a sense of style, tilts her head a little to the side, smiles without embarrassment at the camera. She was a notable seamstress, and would have made her own dress, understanding what suited her. But it is likely she made her sisters' dresses also, and what are we to make of that? My grandmother is done up in something with floppy sleeves and a wide velvet collar, and a sort of vest with crisscrossed velvet trim; something seems askew at the waist. She wears this outfit with no authority and indeed with a shamefaced, flushed, half-grinning and half-desperate apology. She looks a great tomboy, her mop of hair rolled up but sliding forward, in danger of falling down. But she wears a wedding ring; my father had been born. She was at that time the only one married; the eldest, also the tallest of the sisters.

At supper my grandmother said, "How is your mother?" and at once my spirits dropped.

"All right."

She was not all right, she never would be. She had a slowly progressive, incurable disease.

"The poor thing," Aunt Madge said.

"I have a terrible time understanding her on the phone," my grandmother said. "It just seems the worse her voice gets, the more she wants to talk."

My mother's vocal cords were partly paralyzed. Sometimes I would have to act as her interpreter, a job that made me wild with shame.

"I wouldn't wonder she gets lonely out there," Aunt Madge said. "The poor soul."

"It would not make any difference where she was," my grandmother said, "if people cannot understand her."

My grandmother wanted then a report on our household routine. Had we got the washing done, had we got the washing dried, had we got the ironing done? The baking? My father's socks mended? She wished to be of help. She would make biscuits and muffins, a pie (did we have a pie?); bring the mending and she would do it. The ironing too. She would go out to our place for a day, to help, as soon as the roads were clear. I was embarrassed to think we needed help, and I especially tried to ward off the visits. Before my grandmother came I would be obliged to try to clean the house, reorganize the cupboards as much as possible, shove certain disgraces — a roasting-pan I had never got around to scrubbing, a basket of torn clothes I had told her were already mended — under the sink or the beds. But I never cleaned thoroughly enough, my reorganization proved to be haphazard, the disgraces came unfailingly to light, and it was clear how we failed, how disastrously we fell short of that ideal of order and cleanliness, household decency, which I as much as anybody else believed in. Believing in it was not enough. And it was not just for myself but for my mother that I had to feel shame.

"Your mother isn't well, she cannot get around to things," said my grandmother, in a voice that indicated doubt as to how much would have been gotten around to, in any case.

I tried to present good reports. In the old days, when such things were sometimes true, I would say that my mother had made some pickled beets, or that she was busy ripping worn-out sheets down the middle and sewing the outer edges together, to make them last longer. My grandmother perceived the effort, and registered the transparent falsity of this picture (false even if its details were true); she said, well, is she really?

"She's painting the kitchen cupboards," I said. It was not a lie. My mother was painting our cupboards yellow and on each of the drawers and doors she was painting some decoration: flowers or fish or a sailboat or even a flag. Although her hands and arms trembled she could control the brush sufficiently for a short time. So these designs were not so badly done. Just the same there was something crude and glaring about them, something that seemed to reflect the stiffness and intensity of the stage of the disease my mother had now got into. I did not mention them at all to my grandmother, knowing that she was going to find them extremely bizarre and upsetting. My grandmother and Aunt Madge believed, as most people do, that houses should be made to look as much as possible like other people's houses. Some of the ideas my mother had conceived and carried out could not help but make me see the sense in this conformity.

Also, the paint, the brushes, the turpentine, were left for me to clean up, since my mother always worked till she was exhausted, then stretched out groaning on the couch.

"There," said my grandmother with annoyance and satisfaction, "she will get herself involved in something like that, which she ought to know will wear her out, and she will not be able to do any of the things that have to be done. She will be painting the cupboards when she would be better off getting your father's dinner."

Truer words were never spoken.

After supper I went out, in spite of the weather. A blizzard in town hardly seemed like a blizzard to me; so much was blocked out by the

houses and the buildings. I met my friend Betty Gosley, another
country girl who was staying in town with her married sister. We were
pleased and rather excited to be in town, to be able to *go out* like this into
some kind of evening life, not just the dark and cold and rushing
storms that wrapped our houses in the country. Here were the streets
leading into one another, the lights evenly spaced, a human design that
had taken root and was working. People were curling at the curling
rink, skating at the Arena, watching the show at the Lyceum Theater,
shooting pool in the poolroom, sitting around in two cafés. From most
of these activities we were barred by age or sex or lack of money, but we
could walk around, we could drink lemon Cokes – the cheapest thing –
in the Blue Owl Café, watching who came in, talking with a girl we knew
who worked there. Betty and I were not exactly at the center of power,
and we spent a lot of time, like nonentities at court, discussing the
affairs of those more powerful and fortunate, speculating on the ups
and downs of their careers, judging harshly of their morals. We told
each other that we would not for a million dollars go out with certain
boys, the truth being that we would have dissolved in happiness if these
boys had even called us by name. We talked about which girls might be
pregnant. (The winter following this, Betty Gosley herself became
pregnant, by a neighboring farmer with a speech impediment and a
purebred dairy herd, whom she had never so much as mentioned to
me; she then withdrew, abashed and proud, into the privileged life of
married women, and could talk of nothing but kitchen showers, linens,
baby clothes, morning sickness, which made me both envious and
appalled.)

We walked past the house where Mr. Harmer lived. His were the
upstairs windows. The lights were on. What did he do in the evenings?
He did not take advantage of the entertainment offered in town, was
not to be found at the movies or the hockey games. He was not really
very popular. And this was why I had chosen him. I liked to think I had
a special taste. His pale fine hair, his soft mustache, his narrow shoulders in his worn, tweed, leather-patched jacket, the waspish words
which were his classroom substitute for physical force. Once I had
talked to him – it was the only time I had talked to him – in the town
library. He had recommended to me a novel about Welsh coal miners,
which I did not like. There was no sex in it, only strikes and unions, and
men.

Walking past his house, loitering under his windows, with Betty
Gosley, I did not show my interest in him in any straightforward way
but instead made scornful jokes about him, called him a sissy and a
hermit, accused him of shameful private practices which kept him
home evenings. Betty joined in this speculation but did not really
understand why it had to be so wild or go on so long. Then to keep her

interest up I began to tease her, I pretended to believe she was in love with him. I said I had seen him looking up her skirt going up the stairs. I said I was going to throw a snowball at the wall between his windows, call him down for her. She was entertained at first by this fantasy, but before long she grew cold and bewildered and cranky, and headed back towards the main street by herself, forcing me to follow.

And all this wildness, crudity, hilarity, was as far as possible from my private dreams, which were of most tender meetings, chaste embraces melting into holy passion, harmony shadowed by the inevitable parting, high romantic love.

Aunt Madge had been happily married. The happiness of her marriage was remembered and commented on, even in that community where it is usually thought much better to leave such things unsaid. (Even today, if you ask how somebody is, the answer will often be that they are doing well, have bought two cars, have bought a dishwasher, and this way of answering is only partly based on simple, natural, poverty-bred materialism; it comes also from a superstitious kind of delicacy, which skirts even words like *happy, frightened, sad.*)

Aunt Madge's husband had been a leisurely sort of farmer, with political interests; he was opinionated, stubborn, entertaining. There were never any children, to dilute her feelings for him. She took joy in his company. She would never refuse an invitation to go to town with him, to go for a drive with him, even though she took her life in her hands every time she got into his car. He was a terrible driver, and in his later years half-blind. She would never shame him, by learning how to drive, herself. Her support of him was perfect. She could have been held up as an example, an ideal wife, except that she gave no impression of sacrifice, of resignation, of doing one's duty, such as is looked for in ideals. She was lighthearted, impudent sometimes, so she was not particularly respected for her love, but held to be lucky, or half-dotty, whichever you liked. After his death she was not really interested in her life; she looked on it as a waiting period – she believed firmly and literally in Heaven – but she had been too well brought up to give way to moping.

My grandmother's marriage had been another matter. The story was that she had married my grandfather while still in love with, though very angry at, another man. My mother told me this. She loved stories, particularly those full of tragedy and renunciation and queer turns of fate. Aunt Madge and my grandmother, of course, never mentioned anything about it. But as I grew up I found that everybody seemed to know it. The other man remained in the district, as most people did. He farmed, and married three times. He was a cousin of both my grand-father and my grandmother, and so was often in their house, as they were in his. Before he proposed to his third wife – this was what my mother told me – he came to see my grandmother. She came out of her kitchen and rode up and down the lane in his buggy with him, for anybody to see. Did he ask her advice? Her permission? My mother strongly believed that he had asked her to run away with him. I wonder. They would both have been around fifty years old at that time. Where could they have run to? Besides, they were Presbyterians. No one ever accused them of misbehavior. Proximity, impossibility, re-nunciation. That does make for an enduring kind of love. And I believe that would be my grandmother's choice, that self-glorifying dangerous self-denying passion, never satisfied, never risked, to last a lifetime. Not admitted to, either, except perhaps that one time, one or two times, under circumstances of great stress. *We must never speak of this again.*

My grandfather was not a man to complain. He had a taste for solitude, he had married rather late, he had chosen another man's offended sweetheart, for reasons he did not divulge to anybody. In the wintertime he finished his chores early, doing everything thoroughly and efficiently. Then he read. He read books on economics and his-tory. He studied Esperanto. He read his way several times through solid shelves of Victorian novels. He did not discuss what he read. His opinions, unlike his brother-in-law's, were not made public. His de-mands on life, his expectations of other people, seemed to be so slight there was never any possibility of disappointing him. Whether my grandmother had disappointed him, privately, and so thoroughly that any offers he might have made had been withdrawn, nobody could know.

And how is anybody to know, I think as I put this down, how am I to know what I claim to know? I have used these people, not all of them, but some of them, before. I have tricked them out and altered them and shaped them any way at all, to suit my purposes. I am not doing that now, I am being as careful as I can, but I stop and wonder, I feel compunction. Though I am only doing in a large and public way what has always been done, what my mother did, and other people did, who mentioned to me my grandmother's story. Even in that close-mouthed place, stories were being made. People carried their stories around with them. My grandmother carried hers, and nobody ever spoke of it to her face.

But that only takes care of the facts. I have said other things. I have said that my grandmother would choose a certain kind of love. I have implied that she would be stubbornly, secretly, destructively romantic.

Nothing she ever said to me, or in my hearing, would bear this out. Yet I have not invented it, I really believe it. Without any proof I believe it, and so I must believe that we get messages another way, that we have connections that cannot be investigated, but have to be relied on.

This turned out to be a wild heavy storm, lasting a week. But on the third afternoon, sitting in school, I looked out and saw that the wind had apparently died, there was no snow blowing any more, there was even a break in the clouds. I thought at once, and with relief, that I would be able to go home that night. Home always looked a great deal better, after a couple of nights at my grandmother's. It was a place where I did not have to watch too closely what I said and did. My mother objected to things, but in a way I had the upper hand of her. After all, it was I who heated tubs of water on the stove and hauled the washing machine from the porch and did the washing, once a week; I who scrubbed the floor, and with an ill grace made her endless cups of tea. So I could say *shit* when I emptied the dustpan into the stove and some dirt went on the lid; I could say that I meant to have lovers and use birth control and never have any children (actually I wanted to make an enviable marriage, both safe and passionate, and I had pictured the nightgown I would wear when my lover-husband came to visit me for the first time in the maternity ward); I could say that there was nothing wrong with writing about sex in books and also that there was no such thing as a dirty word. The loud argumentative scandalous person I was at home had not much more to do with my real self than the discreet unrevealing person I was in my grandmother's house, but judging both as roles it can be seen that the first had more scope. I did not get tired of it so easily, in fact I did not get tired of it at all.

And comfort palls. The ironed sheets, the lovely eiderdown, the jasmine soap. I would give it all up for the moment in order to be able to drop my coat where I chose, leave the room without having to say where I was going, read with my feet in the oven, if I liked.

After school I went around to my grandmother's house to tell them that I was going home. By this time the wind had begun to blow again. I knew the roads would be drifted, the storm was not really over. But I wanted more than ever to go home. When I opened the door and smelled the pies baking – winter apples – and heard the two old voices greet me (Aunt Madge would always call out, "Now, whoever can *this* be?" as she had done when I was a little girl), I thought that I could not bear any more of it – the tidiness, the courtesies, the waiting. All their time was waiting time. Wait for the mail, wait for supper, wait for bed. You might imagine that my mother's time was waiting time, but it was not. Lying on the couch, sick and crippled, she was still full of outrageous plans and fantasies, demands that could not be met, fights that could be picked; she kept herself going. At home there was always confusion and necessity. Eggs to be cleaned, wood to be brought in, the fire to be kept going, food to be prepared, mess to be cleaned away. I was always hurrying and remembering and forgetting, and then I would sit down after supper in the middle of everything, waiting for the dishwater to heat on the stove, and get lost in my library book.

There was a difference too in books read at home and at my grandmother's. At my grandmother's, books could not quite get out. Some atmosphere of the place pushed them back, contained them, dimmed them. There was not room. At home, in spite of all that was going on, there was room for everything.

"I won't be here for supper," I said. "I'm going home."

I had taken off my things and sat down to have tea. My grandmother was making it.

"You can't ever set out in this," she said confidently. "Are you worrying about the work? Are you afraid they can't get on without you?"

"No, but I better get home. It's not blowing hard. The plows have been out."

"On the highway, maybe. I never heard yet of a plow getting down your road."

The place where we lived, like so much else, was a mistake.

"She's afraid of my pie crust, that's what it is," cried Aunt Madge in mock distress. "She's just plain running away from my pie."

"That may be it," I said.

"You eat a piece before you go. It won't take long to cool."

"She isn't going," my grandmother said, still lightly. "She isn't walking out into that storm."

"It isn't a *storm*," I said, looking for help towards the window, which showed solid white.

My grandmother put her cup down, rattling it on the saucer. "All right. Go then. Just go. Go if you want to. Go and get frozen to death."

I had never heard my grandmother lose control before. I had never imagined that she could. It seems strange to me now, but the fact is that I had never heard anything like plain hurt or anger in her voice, or seen it on her face. Everything had been indirect, calmly expressed. Her judgments had seemed remote, full of traditional authority, not personal. The abdication here was what amazed me. There were tears in her voice, and when I looked at her there were tears in her eyes and then pouring down her face. She was weeping, she was furious and weeping.

"Never mind then. You just go. Go and get yourself frozen to death like what happened to poor Susie Heferman."

"Oh dear," said Aunt Madge. "That's true. That's true."

"Poor Susan living all alone," my grandmother said, addressing me as if that were my fault.

"It was out on our old line, dear," said Aunt Madge comfortingly. "You wouldn't know who we mean. Susie Heferman that was married to Gershom Bell. Mrs. Gershom Bell. Susie Heferman to us. We went to school with her."

"And Gershom died last year and both her daughters are married and away," my grandmother said, wiping her eyes and her nose with a fresh handkerchief from her sleeve, composing herself somewhat, but not ceasing to look at me angrily. "Poor Susan had to go out by herself to milk the cows. She would keep on her cows and go on by herself. She went out last night and she should have tied the clothesline to the door but she didn't, and on the way back she lost her path, and they found her this noon."

"Alex Beattie phoned us," Aunt Madge said. "He was one of the ones found her. He was upset."

"Was she dead?" I said foolishly.

"They cannot thaw you back to life," my grandmother said, "after you have been lying in a snowbank overnight in this weather." She had stopped crying.

"And think of poor Susie there just trying to get from the stable to the house," Aunt Madge said. "She shouldn't have hung on to her cows. She thought she could manage. And she had the bad leg. I bet that give out on her."

"That's terrible," I said. "I won't go home."

"You go if you like," my grandmother said at once.

"No. I'll stay."

"You never know what can happen to a person," said Aunt Madge. She wept too, but more naturally than my grandmother. With her it was just a comfortable bit of leakage round the eyes, it seemed to do good. "Who would have thought that would be the end of Susie, she was more my age than your grandmother's and what a girl for dances, she used to say she'd ride twenty miles in an open cutter for a good dance. We traded dresses once, we did it for a joke. If we had ever known then what would happen now!"

"Nobody knows. What would be the use of it?" my grandmother said.

I ate a large supper. No more mention was made of Susie Heferman.

I understand various things now, though my understanding them is not of much use to anybody. I understand that Aunt Madge could feel sympathy for my mother because Aunt Madge must have seen my mother, even before her illness, as an afflicted person. Anything that was exceptional she could see, simply, as affliction. But my grandmother would have to see an example. My grandmother had schooled herself, watched herself, learned what to do and say; she had understood the importance of acceptance, had yearned for it, had achieved it, had known there was a possibility of not achieving it. Aunt Madge had never known that. My grandmother could feel endangered by my mother, could perhaps even understand — at some level she would always have to deny — those efforts of my mother's that she so successfully, and never quite openly, ridiculed and blamed.

I understand that my grandmother wept angrily for Susie Heferman and also for herself, that she knew how I longed for home, and why. She knew and did not understand how this had happened or how it could have been different or how she herself, once so baffled and struggling, had become another old woman whom people deceived and placated and were anxious to get away from.

(1974)   (1974)

Mordecai Richler
1931 –

———◆———

MORDECAI RICHLER WAS born in Montreal and attended Sir George Williams University. For many years he lived in England where he worked as a free-lance journalist and wrote scripts for radio and television. He returned to Canada in 1972 and now lives in Montreal. Since the publication of his first novel, *The Acrobats* (1954), Richler has written numerous short stories, essays, articles and several important novels including *Son of a Smaller Hero* (1955), *The Apprenticeship of Duddy Kravitz* (1959) and *St. Urbain's Horseman* (1971). "The Summer My Grandmother Was Supposed to Die" first appeared in *Ten for Wednesday Night* (1961), a collection of stories edited by Robert Weaver.

The Summer My Grandmother
Was Supposed to Die

DR. KATZMAN DISCOVERED the gangrene on one of his monthly visits. "She won't last a month," he said.

He repeated that the second month, the third, and the fourth, and now she lay dying in the heat of the back bedroom.

"If only she'd die," my mother said. "Oh, God, why doesn't she die? God in heaven, what's she holding on for?"

The summer my grandmother was supposed to die we did not chip in with the Greenbaums to take a cottage in the Laurentians. It wouldn't have been practical. The old lady couldn't be moved, the nurse came daily and the doctor twice a week, and so it seemed best to stay in the city and wait for her to die or, as my mother said, pass away. It was a hot summer, her bedroom was just behind the kitchen, and when we sat down to eat we could smell her. The dressings on my grandmother's left leg had to be changed several times a day and, according to Dr. Katzman, her condition was hopeless. "It's in the hands of the Almighty," he said.

"It won't be long now," my father said, "and she'll be better off, if you know what I mean."

"Please," my mother said.

A nurse came every day from the Royal Victorian Order. She arrived punctually at noon and at five to twelve I'd join the rest of the boys under the outside staircase to look up her dress as she climbed to our second-storey flat. Miss Monohan favoured lacy pink panties and that was better than waiting under the stairs for Cousin Bessie, for instance. She wore enormous cotton bloomers, rain or shine.

I was sent out to play as often as possible, because my mother felt it was not good for me to see somebody dying. Usually I'd just roam the scorched streets shooting the breeze. There was Arty, Gas sometimes, Hershey, Stan, and me. We talked about everything from A to Z.

"Why is it," Arty wanted to know, "that Tarzan never shits?"

"Dick Tracy too."

"Or Wonder Woman."

"She's a dame."

"*So?*"

"Jees, wouldn't it be something if Superman crapped in the sky? He could just be flying over Waverly Street when, whamo, Mr. Rabinovitch catches it right in the kisser."

Mr. Rabinovitch was our Hebrew teacher.

"But there's Tarzan," Arty insisted, "in the jungle, week in and week out, and never once does he need to go to the toilet. It's not real, that's all."

Arty told me, "Before your grandmaw dies she's going to roll her eyes and gurgle. That's what they call the death-rattle."

"Aw, you know everything. Big shot."

"I *read* it, you jerk," Arty said, whacking me one, "in Perry Mason."

Home again I'd find my mother weeping.

"She's dying by inches," she said to my father one stifling night, "and none of them even come to see her. Oh, such children! They should only rot in hell."

"They're not behaving right. It's certainly not according to Hoyle," my father said.

"When I think of all the money and effort that went into making a rabbi out of Israel — the way Mother doted on him — and for what? Oh, what's the world coming to? God."

"It's not right."

Dr. Katzman was amazed. "I never believed she'd last this long. Really, it must be will-power alone that keeps her going. And your excellent care."

"I want her to die, Doctor. That's not my mother in the back room. It's an animal. I want her to please please die."

"Hush. You don't mean it. You're tired." And Dr. Katzman gave my father some pills for my mother to take. "A remarkable woman," he said. "A born nurse."

At night in bed my brother Harvey and I used to talk about our grandmother. "After she dies," I said, "her hair will go on growing for another twenty-four hours."

"Sez who?"

"Arty. It's a scientific fact. Do you think Uncle Lou will come from New York for the funeral?"

"Sure."

"Boy, that means another fiver for me. You too."

"You shouldn't say things like that, kiddo, or *her ghost will come back to haunt you.*"

"Well," I said, "I'll be able to go to her funeral, anyway. I'm not too young any more."

I was only six years old when my grandfather died, and I wasn't allowed to go to his funeral.

I have only one memory of my grandfather. Once he called me into his study, set me down on his lap, and made a drawing of a horse for me. On the horse he drew a rider. While I watched and giggled he gave the rider a beard and the round fur-trimmed cap of a rabbi.

My grandfather was a Zaddik, one of the Righteous, and I've been told that to study Talmud with him had been a rare pleasure. I wasn't allowed to go to his funeral, but years later I was shown the telegrams of condolence that had come from Eire and Poland and Israel and even Japan. My grandfather had written many books: a translation of the Zohar into modern Hebrew — some twenty years' work — and lots of slender volumes of sermons, chassidic tales, and rabbinical commentaries. His books had been published in Warsaw and later in New York. He had been famous.

"At the funeral," my mother told me, "they had to have six motorcycle policemen to control the crowds. It was such a heat that twelve women fainted — and I'm *not* counting Mrs. Waxman from upstairs. With her, you know, *anything* to fall into a man's arms. Even Pinsky's. And did I tell you that there was even a French-Canadian priest there?"

"No kidding?"

"The priest was a real big *knacker*. A bishop maybe. He used to study with the *zeyda*. The *zeyda* was some personality, you know. Spiritual and worldly-wise at the same time. Such personalities they don't make any more. Today, rabbis and peanuts are the same size."

But, according to my father, the *zeyda* (his father-in-law) hadn't been as famous as all that. "There are things I could say," he told me. "There was another side to him."

My grandfather had come from generations and generations of rabbis, his youngest son was a rabbi, but none of his grandchildren would be one. My brother Harvey was going to be a dentist and at the time, 1937, I was interested in flying and my cousin Jerry was already a communist. I once heard Jerry say, "Our grandpappy wasn't all he was cracked up to be." When the men at the kosher bakeries went out on strike he spoke up against them on the streets where they were picketing and in the *shule*. It was of no consequence to him that they were grossly underpaid. His superstitious followers had to have bread. "Grandpappy," Jerry said, "was a prize reactionary."

A week after my grandfather died my grandmother suffered a stroke. Her right side was completely paralysed. She couldn't speak. At first, it's true, my grandmother could say a few words and move her right hand enough to write her name in Hebrew. Her name was Malka. But her condition soon began to deteriorate.

My grandmother had six children and seven step-children, for my grandfather had been married before. His first wife had died in the old country. Two years later he had married my grandmother, the only daughter of the richest man in the village, and their marriage had been a singularly happy one. My grandmother had been a beautiful girl. She had also been a wise, resourceful, and patient wife. Qualities, I fear, indispensable to life with a Zaddik. For the synagogue had paid my grandfather no stipulated salary and much of the money he had picked up here and there he had habitually distributed among rabbinical students, needy immigrants, and widows. A vice, and such it was to his hard-pressed family, which made him as unreliable a provider as a drunkard. And indeed, to carry the analogy further, my grandmother had had to make many hurried trips to the pawnbroker with her jewellery. Not all of it had been redeemed, either. But her children had been looked after. The youngest, her favourite, was a rabbi in Boston, the eldest was the actor-manager of a Yiddish theatre in New York, and another was a lawyer. One daughter lived in Toronto, two in Montreal. My mother was the youngest daughter, and when my grandmother had her stroke there was a family meeting and it was decided that my mother would take care of her. This was my father's fault. All the other husbands spoke up — they protested their wives had too much work, they could never manage it — but my father detested quarrels, and he was silent. So my grandmother came to stay with us.

Her bedroom, the back bedroom, had actually been promised to me for my seventh birthday. But all that was forgotten now, and I had to go on sharing a bedroom with my brother Harvey. So naturally I was resentful when each morning before I left for school my mother said, "Go in and kiss the *baba* good-bye."

All the same I'd go into the bedroom and kiss my grandmother hastily. She'd say, "Bouyo-bouyo," for that was the only sound she could make. And after school it was, "Go in and tell the *baba* you're home."

"I'm home, *baba*."

"Bouyo-bouyo."

During those first hopeful months — "Twenty years ago who would have thought there'd be a cure for diabetes?" my father asked, "where there's life there's hope, you know" — she'd smile at me and try to speak, her eyes charged with effort. And even later there were times when she pressed my head urgently to her bosom with her surprisingly strong left arm. But as her illness dragged on and on and she became a condition in the house, something beyond hope or reproach, like the leaky icebox, there was less recognition and more ritual in those kisses. I came to dread her room. A clutter of sticky medicine bottles and the cracked toilet chair beside the bed; glazed but imploring eyes and a feeble smile, the wet slap of her lips against my cheeks. I flinched from her touch. And after two years of it I protested to my mother. "Look, what's the use of telling her I'm going or I'm here. She doesn't even recognize me any more."

"Don't be fresh. She's your grandmother."

My uncle who was in the theatre in New York sent money regularly to help support my grandmother and, for the first few months, so did the other children. But once the initial and sustaining excitement had passed and it became likely that my grandmother might linger in her invalid condition for two or maybe even three more years, the cheques began to drop off, and the children seldom came to our house any more. Anxious weekly visits — "and how is she today, poor lamb?" — quickly dwindled to a dutiful monthly looking in, then a semi-annual visit, and these always on the way to somewhere.

"The way they act," my father said, "you'd think that if they stayed long enough to take off their coats we'd make them take the *baba* home with them."

When the children did come to visit, my mother made it difficult for them.

"It's killing me," she said. "I have to lift her on to that chair three times a day maybe. Have you any idea how heavy she is? And what makes you think I always catch her in time? Sometimes I have to change her bed twice a day. That's a job I'd like to see your wife do," she said to my uncle, the rabbi.

"We could send her to the Old People's Home," the rabbi said.

"Now there's an idea," my father said.

But my mother began to sob. "Not as long as I'm alive," she said. And she gave my father a stony look. "Say something."

"It wouldn't be according to Hoyle."

"You want to be able to complain to everybody in town about all the other children," the rabbi said. "You've got a martyr complex."

"Everybody has a point of view, you know. You know what I mean?" my father said. "So what's the use of fighting?"

Meanwhile, Dr. Katzman came once a month to examine my grandmother. "It's remarkable, astonishing," he'd say each time. "She's as strong as a horse."

"Some life for a person," my father said. "She can't speak — she doesn't recognize anybody — what is there for her?"

The doctor was a cultivated man; he spoke often for women's clubs, sometimes on Yiddish literature and other times, his rubicund face hot with impatience, the voice taking on a doomsday tone, on the cancer threat.

"Who are we to judge?" he asked.

Every evening, during the first months of my grandmother's illness, my mother read her a story by Sholem Aleichem. "Tonight she smiled," my mother would say. "She understood. I can tell." And my father, my brother, and I, would not comment. Once a week my mother used to give the old lady a manicure. Sunny afternoons she'd lift her into a wheelchair and put her out in the sun. Somebody always had to stay in the house in case my grandmother called. Often, during the night, she would begin to wail unaccountably, and my mother would get up and rock the old lady in her arms for hours. But in the fourth year of my grandmother's illness the strain and fatigue began to tell on my mother. Besides looking after my grandmother — "And believe you me," the doctor assured her with a clap on the back, "it would be a full-time job for a professional nurse" — she had to keep house for a husband and two sons. She began to quarrel with my father and she became sharp with Harvey and me. My father started to spend his evenings playing pinochle at Tansky's Cigar & Soda. Weekends he took Harvey and me to visit his brothers and sisters. And everywhere he went people had little bits of advice for him.

"Sam, you might as well be a bachelor. You're just going to have to put your foot down for once."

"Yeah, in your face maybe."

My cousin Libby, who was at McGill, said, "This could have a very damaging effect on the development of your boys. These are their formative years, Uncle Samuel, and the omnipresence of death in the house. . . ."

"What you need," my father said, "is a boy friend. *And how.*"

At Tansky's Cigar & Soda it was, "Come clean, Sam. It's no hardship. If I know you, the old lady's got a big insurance policy and when the time comes. . . ."

My mother lost lots of weight. After dinner she'd fall asleep in her chair in the middle of Lux Radio Theatre. One minute she'd be sewing a patch on my breeches or be making a list of girls to call for a bingo party (proceeds for the Talmud Torah), and the next she'd be snoring. Then, one morning, she just couldn't get out of bed, and Dr. Katzman came round a week before his regular visit. "Well, well, this won't do, will it?" He sat in the kitchen with my father and the two men drank apricot brandy out of small glasses.

"Your wife is a remarkable woman," Dr. Katzman said.

"You don't say?"

"She's got a gallstone condition."

My father shrugged. "Have another one for the road," he said.

"Thank you, but I have several more calls to make." Dr. Katzman rose, sighing. "There she lies in that back room, poor old woman," he said, "hanging desperately onto life. There's food for thought there."

My grandmother's children met again, and the five of them sat around my mother's bed embarrassed, irritated, and quick to take insult. All except my uncle who was in the theatre. He sucked a cigar and drank whiskey. He teased my mother, the rabbi, and my aunts, and if not for him I think they would have been at each other's throats. It was decided, over my mother's protests, to send my grandmother to the Old People's Home on Esplanade Street. An ambulance came to take my grandmother away and Dr. Katzman said, "It's for the best." But my father had been in the back bedroom when the old lady had held on tenaciously to the bedpost, not wanting to be moved by the two men in white — "Easy does it, granny," the younger one had said — and afterwards he could not go in to see my mother. He went out for a walk.

"She looked at me with such a funny expression," he told my brother. "Is it my fault?"

My mother stayed in bed for another two weeks. My father cooked for us and we hired a woman to do the housework. My mother put on weight quickly, her cheeks regained their normal pinkish hue and, for the first time in months, she actually joked with Harvey and me. She became increasingly curious about our schools and whether or not we shined our shoes regularly. She began to cook again, special dishes for my father, and she resumed old friendships with women on the parochial school board. The change reflected on my father. Not only did his temper improve, but he stopped going to Tansky's every other night, and began to come home early from work. Life at home had never been so rich. But my grandmother's name was never mentioned. The back bedroom remained empty and I continued to share a room with Harvey. I couldn't see the point and so one evening I said, "Look, why don't I move into the back bedroom?"

My father glared at me across the table.

"But it's empty like."

My mother left the table. And the next afternoon she put on her best dress and coat and new spring hat.

"Where are you going?" my father asked.

"To see my mother."

"Don't go looking for trouble."

"It's been a month. Maybe they're not treating her right."

"They're experts."

"Did you think I was never going to visit her? I'm not inhuman, you know."

"Alright, go," he said.

But after she'd gone my father went to the window and said, "Son-of-a-bitch."

Harvey and I sat outside on the steps watching the cars go by. My father sat on the balcony above, cracking peanuts. It was six o'clock, maybe later, when the ambulance turned the corner, slowed down, and parked right in front of the house.

"Son-of-a-bitch," my father said. "I knew it."

My mother got out first, her eyes red and swollen, and hurried upstairs to make my grandmother's bed.

"I'm sorry Sam, I had to do it."

"You'll get sick again, that's what."

"You think she doesn't recognize people. From the moment she saw me she cried and cried. Oh, it was terrible."

"They're experts there. They know how to handle her better than you do."

"Experts? Expert murderers you mean. She's got bedsores, Sam. Those dirty little Irish nurses they don't change her linen often enough, they hate her. She must have lost twenty pounds there."

"Another month and you'll be flat on your back again."

"Sam, what could I do? Please Sam."

"She'll outlive all of us. Even Muttel. I'm going out for a walk."

She was back and I was to blame.

My father became a regular at Tansky's Cigar & Soda again and every morning I had to go in and kiss my grandmother. She began to look like a man. Little hairs had sprouted on her chin, she had a spiky grey moustache and, of course, she was practically bald. This near-baldness, I guess, sprung from the fact that she had been shaving her head ever since she had married my grandfather the rabbi. My grandmother had four different wigs, but she had not worn one since the first year of her illness. She wore a little pink cap instead. And so, as before, she said, "bouyo-bouyo," to everything.

Once more uncles and aunts sent five-dollar bills, though erratically, to help pay for my grandmother's support. Elderly people, former followers of my grandfather, came to inquire after the old lady's health. They sat in the back bedroom with her for hours, leaning on their canes, talking to themselves, rocking, always rocking to and fro. "The Holy Shakers," my father called them, and Harvey and I avoided them, because they always wanted to pinch our cheeks, give us a dash of snuff and laugh when we sneezed, or offer us a sticky old candy from a little brown bag with innumerable creases in it. When the visit was done the old people would unfailingly sit in the kitchen with my mother for another hour, watching her make lockshen or bake bread. My mother always served them lemon tea and they would talk about my grandfather, recalling his books, his sayings, and his charitable deeds.

And so another two years passed, with no significant change in my grandmother's condition. But fatigue, bad temper, and even morbidity enveloped my mother again. She fought with her brothers and sisters and once, when I stepped into the living-room, I found her sitting with her head in her hands, and she looked up at me with such anguish that I was frightened.

"What did I do now?" I asked.

"If, God forbid, I had a stroke, would you send me to the Old People's Home?"

"Don't be a joke. Of course not."

"I hope that never in my life do I have to count on my children for anything."

The summer my grandmother was supposed to die, the seventh year of her illness, my brother took a job as a shipper and he kept me awake at night with stories about the factory. "What we do, see, is clear out the middle of a huge pile of lengths of material. That makes for a kind of secret cave. A hideout. Well, then you coax one of the *shiksas* inside and hi-diddle-diddle."

One night Harvey waited until I had fallen asleep and then he wrapped himself in a white sheet, crept up to my bed, and shouted, "Bouyo-bouyo."

I hit him. He shouted.

"Children. Children, please," my mother called. "I must get some rest."

As my grandmother's condition worsened – from day to day we didn't know when she'd die – I was often sent out to eat at my aunt's or at my other grandmother's house. I was hardly ever at home. On Saturday mornings I'd get together with the other guys and we'd walk all the way past the mountain to Eaton's, which was our favourite department store for riding up and down escalators and stealing.

In those days they let boys into the left-field bleachers free during the week and we spent many an afternoon at the ball park. The Montreal Royals, part of the Dodger farm system, was some ball club too. There was Jackie Robinson and Roy Campanella, Honest John Gabbard, Chuck Connors and Kermit Kitman. Kitman was our hero. It used to kill us to see that crafty little hebe running around there with all those tall dumb *goyim*. "Hey, Kitman," we'd yell. "Hey, hey, sho-head, if your father knew you played ball on *shabus* –" Kitman, unfortunately, was all field and no hit. He never made the majors. "There goes Kermit Kitman," we'd yell, after he'd gone down swinging again, "the first Jewish strike-out king of the International League." This we usually followed up by bellowing some choice imprecations in Yiddish.

It was after one of these games, on a Friday afternoon, that I came home to find a small crowd gathered in front of the house.

"That's the grandson."

"Poor kid."

Old people stood silent and expressionless across the street staring at our front door. A taxi pulled up and my aunt hurried out, hiding her face in her hands.

"After so many years," somebody said.

"And probably next year they'll discover a cure. Isn't that *always* the case?"

I took the stairs two at a time. The flat was full. Uncles and aunts from my father's side of the family, odd old people, Dr. Katzman, Harvey, neighbours, were all standing around and talking in hushed voices in the living-room. I found my father in the kitchen, getting out the apricot brandy. "Your grandmother's dead," he said.

"She didn't suffer," somebody said. "She passed away in her sleep."

"A merciful death."

"Where's Maw?"

"In the bedroom with ... you'd better not go in," my father said.

"I want to see her."

My mother's face was long with grief. She wore a black shawl, and glared down at a knot of handkerchief clutched in a fist that had been cracked by washing-soda. "Don't come in here," she said.

Several bearded, round-shouldered men in black shiny coats stood round the bed. I couldn't see my grandmother.

"Your grandmother's dead."

"Daddy told me."

"Go and wash your face and comb your hair. You'll have to get your own supper."

"O.K."

"One minute. The *baba* left some jewellery. The ring is for Harvey's wife and the necklace is for yours."

"Who's getting married?"

"Better go and wash your face. And remember behind the ears, Muttel."

Telegrams were sent, long-distance calls were made, and all through the evening relatives and neighbours came and went like swarms of fish when crumbs have been dropped into the water.

"When my father died," my mother said, "they had to have *six* motorcycle policemen to control the crowds. Twelve people fainted, such a heat. ..."

The man from the funeral parlour came.

"There goes the only Jewish businessman in town," my Uncle Harry said, "who wishes all his customers were Germans."

"This is no time for jokes."

"Listen, life goes on."

My Cousin Jerry had begun to use a cigarette holder. "Everyone's going to be sickeningly sentimental," he said. "Soon the religious mumbo-jumbo starts. I can hardly wait."

Tomorrow was the Sabbath and so, according to the law, my grandmother couldn't be buried until Sunday. She would have to lie on the floor all night. Two old grizzly women in white came to move and wash the body and a professional mourner arrived to sit up and pray for her.

"I don't trust his face," my mother said. "He'll fall asleep. You watch him, Sam."

"A fat lot of good prayers will do her now."

"Will you just watch him, please."

"I'll watch him, I'll watch him." My father was livid about my Uncle Harry. "The way he's gone after that apricot brandy you'd think that guy never saw a bottle in his life before."

Harvey and I were sent to bed, but we couldn't sleep. My aunt was sobbing over the body in the living-room — "That dirty hypocrite," my mother said — there was the old man praying, coughing, and spitting into his handkerchief each time he woke; and hushed voices and whimpering from the kitchen, where my father and mother sat. Harvey was in a good mood, he let me have a few puffs of his cigarette.

"Well, kiddo, this is our last night together. Tomorrow you can take over the back bedroom."

"Are you crazy?"

"You always wanted it for yourself."

"She died in there, but. You think I'm going to sleep in there?"

"Good night. Happy dreams, kiddo."

"Hey, let's talk some more."

Harvey told me a ghost story. "Did you know that when they hang a man," he said, "the last thing that happens is that he has an orgasm?"

"A what?"

"Forget it. I forgot you were still in kindergarten."

"I know plenty. Don't worry."

"At the funeral they're going to open her coffin to throw dirt in her face. It's supposed to be earth from Eretz. They open it and you're going to have to look." Harvey stood up on his bed, holding his hands over his head like claws. He made a hideous face. "Bouyo-bouyo. Who's that sleeping in my bed? Woo-woo."

My uncle who was in the theatre, the rabbi, and my aunt from Toronto, all came to Montreal for the funeral. Dr. Katzman came too.

"As long as she was alive," my mother said, "he couldn't even send five dollars a month. Some son! What a rabbi! I don't want him in my house, Sam. I can't bear the sight of him."

"You don't mean a word of that and you know it," Dr. Katzman said.

"Maybe you'd better give her a sedative," the rabbi said.

"Sam. Sam, will you say something, please."

My father stepped up to the rabbi, his face flushed. "I'll tell you this straight to your face, Israel," he said. "You've gone down in my estimation."

"Really," the rabbi said, smiling a little.

My father's face burned a deeper red. "Year by year," he said, "your stock has gone down with me."

And my mother began to weep bitterly, helplessly, without control. She was led unwillingly to bed. While my father tried his best to comfort her, as he said consoling things, Dr. Katzman plunged a needle into her arm. "There we are," he said.

I went to sit in the sun on the outside stairs with Arty. "I'm going to the funeral," I said.

"I couldn't go anyway."

Arty was descended from the tribe of high priests and so was not allowed to be in the presence of a dead body. I was descended from the Yisroelis.

"The lowest of the low," Arty said.

"Aw."

My uncle, the rabbi, and Dr. Katzman stepped into the sun to light cigarettes.

"It's remarkable that she held out for so long," Dr. Katzman said.

"Remarkable?" my uncle said. "It's written that if a man has been married twice he will spend as much time with his first wife in heaven as he did on earth. My father, may he rest in peace, was married to his first wife for seven years and my mother, may she rest in peace, has managed to keep alive for seven years. Today in heaven she will be able to join my father, may he rest in peace."

Dr. Katzman shook his head, he pursed his lips. "It's amazing," he said. "The mysteries of the human heart. Astonishing."

My father hurried outside. "Dr. Katzman, please. It's my wife. Maybe the injection wasn't strong enough? She just doesn't stop crying. It's like a tap. Could you come please?"

"Excuse me," Dr. Katzman said to my uncle.

"Of course."

My uncle approached Arty and me.

"Well, boys," he said, "what would you like to be when you grow up?"

(1969)   (1961)

Jane Rule
1931 –

———◆———

BORN IN PLAINFIELD, New Jersey, Jane Rule came to Canada in 1956 after studying and travelling in Europe and the United States. She taught for several years at the University of British Columbia and now lives on a small island off the coast of British Columbia. Since the appearance of her first novel, *The Desert of the Heart* (1964), she has published several other novels including *This Is Not for You* (1970), *Against The Season* (1971) and *The Young In One Another's Arms* (1977), a study of lesbian writers, *Lesbian Images* (1975), and a collection of short stories, *Themes For Diverse Instruments* (1975).

A Television Drama

AT ONE-THIRTY in the afternoon, Carolee Mitchell was running the vacuum cleaner, or she would have heard the first sirens and looked out. After the first, there weren't any others. The calling voices, even the number of dogs barking, could have been students on their way back to school, high spirited in the bright, cold earliness of the year. Thinking back on the sounds, Carolee remembered a number of car doors being slammed, that swallow of air and report which made her smooth her hair automatically even if she wasn't expecting anyone. But what caught her eye finally was what always caught her eye, the flight of a bird from a tree top in the ravine out over the fringe of trees at the bottom of her steeply sloping front lawn, nearly private in the summer, exposed now to the startling activity of the street.

Three police cars were parked in front of the house, a motorcycle like a slanted stress in the middle of the intersection, half a dozen more police cars scattered up and down the two blocks. There were men in uniform up on her neighbor's terrace with rifles and field glasses. Police with dogs were crossing the empty field at the bottom of the ravine. More cars were arriving, police and reporters with cameras and sound equipment. Mingling among the uniforms and equipment were the neighbors: Mrs. Rolston from the house across the street who had obviously not taken time to put on a coat and was rubbing her arms absent-mindedly as she stood and talked, Jane Carey from next door with a scarf tied round her head and what looked like one of her son's jackets thrown over her shoulders, old Mr. Monkson, a few small children. Cars and people kept arriving. Suddenly there was a voice magnified to reach even Carolee, surprised and unbelieving behind her picture window.

"Clear the street. All householders return to or stay in your houses. Clear the street."

Mrs. Rolston considered the idea for a moment but did not go in. The others paid no attention at all. Carolee wondered if she should go out just to find out what on earth was going on. Perhaps she should telephone someone, but everyone she might phone was already in the street. Was it a gas main? Not with all those dogs. A murder? It seemed unlikely that anyone would kill anyone else on this street, where every child had his own bedroom and most men either studies or basement workshops to retreat into. In any case, it was the middle of the afternoon. Mrs. Cole had come out on her balcony with field glasses focused on the place where the dogs and police had entered the ravine. Field glasses. Where were Pete's field glasses? Carolee thought she knew, but she did not move to get them. She would not know what she was looking for in the undergrowth or the gardens.

"Clear the street. All householders return to or stay in your houses."

Police radios were now competing with each other. "Suspect last apprehended in the alley between..." "House to house search..." "Ambulance..."

If one of those policemen standing about on the street would come to search the house, Carolee could at least find out what was going on. Was that a t.v. crew? Dogs were barking in the ravine. Did police dogs bark? Nobody on the street seemed to be doing anything, except for the motorcycle policeman who was turning away some cars. Maybe Carolee should go empty the dishwasher and then come back. It was pointless to stand here by the window. Nothing was happening, or, if something was happening, Carolee couldn't see the point of it. She went to the window in Pete's study to see if she could discover activity on the side street. There were more policemen, and far up the block an ambulance was pulling away without a siren, its red light slowly circling. Carolee watched it until it turned the corner at the top of the hill. Then she turned back toward the sound of barking dogs and radios, but paused as she turned.

There, sitting against the curve of the laurel hedge by the lily pond, was a man, quite a young man, his head down, his left hand against his right shoulder. He was sick or hurt or dead. Or not really there at all, something Carolee's imagination had put there to explain the activity in the street, part of a collage, like an unlikely photograph in the middle of a painting. But he raised his head slightly then, and Carolee saw the blood on his jacket and trousers.

"I must call the police," she said aloud, but how could she call the police when they were already there, three of them standing not seventy feet away, just below the trees on the parking strip? She must call someone, but all the neighbors were still out of doors. And what if the police did discover him? He might be shot instead of helped. Carolee wanted to help him, whoever he was. It was such an odd way he was sitting, his legs stretched out in front of him so that he couldn't possibly have moved quickly. He might not be able to move at all. But she couldn't get to him, not without being seen. Suddenly he got to his feet, his left hand still against his right shoulder and also holding the lower part of his ducked face. He walked to the end of the curve of hedge as if it was very difficult for him to move, and then he began a stumbling run across the front lawn, through the trees, and out onto the parking strip. There he turned, hesitated, and fell on his back. Carolee had heard no shot. Now her view was blocked by a gathering of police and reporters, drawn to that new center like leaves to a central drain.

"Suspect apprehended on..."

What had he done? What had that hurt and stumbling boy done? Carolee was standing with her hand on the transistor radio before it occurred to her to turn it on.

"We interrupt this program with a news bulletin. A suspect has been apprehended on..."

He had robbed a bank, run a car into a tree, shot a policeman, been shot at.

"And now, here is our reporter on the scene."

Carolee could see the reporter quite clearly, standing in the street in front of the house, but she could hear only the radio voice, explaining what had happened.

"And now the ambulance is arriving..." as indeed it was. "The suspect, suffering from at least three wounds, who seems near death, is being lifted onto a stretcher..." This she couldn't see. It seemed to take a very long time before police cleared a path for the ambulance, again silent, its red light circling to move slowly down the block and out of sight.

A newspaper reporter was walking up the front path, but Carolee didn't answer the door. She stood quietly away from the window and waited until he was gone. Then she went to the kitchen and began to empty the dishwasher. It was two-o'clock. She turned on the radio again to listen to the regular news report. The details were the same. At three o'clock the hospital had reported that the policeman was in the operating room having a bullet removed from his right lung. At four o'clock the suspect was reported in only fair condition from wounds in the shoulder, jaw, leg and hand.

At five o'clock Pete came home, the evening paper in his hand. "Well, you've had quite a day," he said. "Are you all right?"

"Yes," Carolee said, her hands against his cold jacket, her cheek against his cold face. "Yes, I'm all right. What did the paper say?"

"It's all diagrams," he said, holding out the front page to her.

There was a map of the whole neighborhood, a sketched aerial map, a view of the roof of their house Carolee had never had. She followed the dots and arrows to the hood of a car crumpled under a flower of foliage, on again across the ravine, up their side hill, and there was the laurel hedge and the jelly bean lily pond, but the dots didn't stop there, arced round rather and immediately down through the trees to a fallen doll, all alone, not a policeman or reporter in sight, lying there exposed to nothing but a God's eye view.

"You must have seen him," Pete said.

"Yes," Carolee agreed, still looking down on the roof tops of all her neighbors' houses.

"Did it frighten you?" Pete asked.

"Not exactly. It was hard to believe, and everything seemed to happen so very slowly."

"Did you get a good look at him?"

"I guess not really," Carolee said. Had he sat there by the laurel hedge at all, his long, stiff legs stretched out in front of him? The map didn't show it.

"Something has got to be done about all this violence," Pet said.

His tone and the look on his face made Carolee realize that Pete had been frightened, much more frightened than she was. Those dotted lines across his front lawn, that figure alone in the landscape – Carolee felt herself shaken by a new fear, looking at what Pete had seen.

"I'll get us a drink," Pete said.

Once they sat down, Carolee tried to tell her husband what it had been like, all those women just standing out in the street. She told him about the guns and field glasses and dogs and cameras. She did not tell him about the man, hurt, by the laurel hedge.

Pete turned on the television, and they watched three minutes of fast moving images, first the policeman lifted into an ambulance, then officers and dogs running through the field, finally glimpses of the suspect on the ground and then shifted onto a stretcher; and, while they watched, a voice told them of the robbery, the chase, the capture. Finally several people were quickly interviewed, saying such things as,

"I saw him go over the fence" or "He fell practically at my feet." That was Mrs. Rolston, still rubbing her cold arms in the winter day.

"I'm glad you had the good sense to stay inside," Pete said. He was holding her hand, beginning to relax into indignation and relief.

Carolee wasn't there, nor was the man there. If she had spoken to that reporter, if she had said then, "I saw him. He was sitting by the laurel hedge," would the dots in the paper have changed? Would the cameras have climbed into their nearly exposed winter garden? Would she believe now what she couldn't quite believe even then, that she stood at that window and saw a man dying in her garden?

Now a labor union boss was talking, explaining the unfair practices of the compensation board. Nearly at once, young marines were running, firing, falling. Planes were dropping bombs. Carolee wasn't there, but it seemed real to her, terribly real, so that for a moment she forgot Pete's hand in hers, her safe house on a safe street, and was afraid.

(1975)   (1975)

Austin Clarke
1932 –

———◆———

AUSTIN CLARKE WAS born in Barbados and immigrated to Canada in 1956. He has lectured at several universities and has written scripts for the Canadian Broadcasting Corporation. His first novel, *The Survivors of the Crossing*, was published in 1964 and subsequent novels include *Among Thistles and Thorns* (1965), *The Meeting Point* (1967) and *The Bigger Light* (1975). A collection of his short stories, *When He Was Free and Young and He Used to Wear Silks*, appeared in 1971.

They Heard a Ringing of Bells

"WHAT IS THEM I hearing?" Estelle asked, looking up at the skies.

"Them is bells, darling," Ironhorse said.

"It is a man up there playing pon them bells," Sagaboy explained. "They is bells that you and me, and Ironhorse Henry hearing play so nice."

"Bells playing hymns? God bless my eyesight! Boy, this Canada is a damn great country, in truth!" she exclaimed.

"It don't have nothing like this back in them islands, eh, old man?" Ironhorse said, really teasing Sagaboy, who was a Trinidadian.

"Well, let the three o' we sit down right here pon this piece o' grass, and listen to that man up there in the skies playing them bells." And they did what Sagaboy suggested. They sat on the grass, in front of the tower which seemed to become more powerful and mysterious with each ring of the bells that resounded in the hearts of these three West Indians. Estelle spread her dress around her like an umbrella. Sagaboy and Ironhorse Henry took off their jackets, and without offering her one of them they sat down. Estelle was sitting on the bare grass. But the grass wasn't cold.

The bells were ringing hymns. And the voice of the bells swept a tide of freshness through Estelle's heart, and washed out the heaviness of deportation that had been lingering there. The immigration department had given her one week to leave the country.

Looking up at the bells, she said, "I am too glad the Lord open up this door, boy! Imagine me, nuh, imagine me up in this big-able country. I can't imagine it is really me, Estelle, sitting down here! I sitting down here, this bright Sunday afternoon, listening to some damn man up there, saying he playing hymns on bells! Well well well, what the hell's next? Who would have think that I would ever live to see a thing so nice? I can't believe my ears at all, at all. It is the wonders o'God, boy, the wonders of the good God, cause I poor as a bird's arse and I am still up here in Canada. And I *know* that a good time can't happen to any and every man, saving that man stand in possession of money. If he have a piece of change in his pockets, he could get in a plane, God! and he could be taken to the ends of this earth, *swoosh!* in the twinkling of an eye! Man, I barely had time to swallow a mouth-ful o' hot-water tea back in Barbados, before, bram! I wasn't in a different place. And now, look me! ... I am up in this big-able Canada. From a little little village somewhere behind God back I come up here, and now enjoying a little goodness o' life. Little good living that only the white people and the rich black people back home does enjoy. And now, ha-dai! the thing turn round, boy! It turn round as good as a cent. This is what I calls *living*. This is the way *every* black person should live! Look, I putting my hand pon a blade of grass...look, Henry, look Saga, man, this blade of grass is the selfsame grass as what I left back in Barbados. The said grass that I now sitting down pon, the same grass, man; but only *different*. And it is different only becausing it situated in a different place. A different, but a more better, more advance place than where I come from; and because o' this I am telling you now, this blessed Sunday afternoon, that I glad glad as hell that life still circulating through this body o' mine."

Neither Ironhorse Henry nor Sagaboy could find words of comment for this waterfall of feeling. Ironhorse had not heard anything like it since he left Barbados, more years ago than he cared to remember. But as Estelle talked he had watched her; and, with her, he had listened to the bells singing in his heart. And there he found a deep love for her. A love so great that he could not find words to express it. But he knew he had to remain silent; that he might never get the opportunity to tell it to her. She was Sagaboy's woman. And she was going to be deported next week. There she was, so near to him now; in a few days, so far away; and he could do nothing, nothing except wish that something would happen to his good friend Sagaboy, that he would cough his guts through his mouth, that he would die from the tuberculosis that rackled in his chest like stones in a can. And Sagaboy, sitting on the other side of Estelle, remained very quiet as if he was in a dream. Then, it seemed, the bubble of his dream burst, and he tugged at a blade of grass near his feet, and exploded, "It ain't no wonders of no blasted God, woman! You have just start to live like you should have been living from the day you born. But instead, you been spending your lifetime down in Barbados, the same way as your forefathers and foremothers been spending it...in the kiss-me-arse canefield, and in slavery. Down there you didn't have food to eat, nor proper clothes to put on your back, and you didn't comprehend the piece o' histries involve in that kinda life, till one morning, bright and early, Satan get in your behind, and you look round, and bram! your eyes see that topsy-turvy world down there, and you turned round and look at yourself, and you didn't see nothing but rags and lice and filth and misery and the blasted British. And what happen? Revolutions run up inside your head, child, and you start to put two and two together. And you say, be-Christ, it ain't true, pardner, that is not true, at all! So what happen next? You pull up stakes and run abroad. You come up here in a more progressive country, but you still going exist in a worser life than what you was accustomed to back home. Look, every one o' we, you, me, Ironhorse here, we get so damn tired, we get so damn vexed...you down there in Barbados, and I in Trinidad, and brisk-brisk! it is pulling out, for so! Setting sail. Pawning things that we never own and possess, borrowing and thiefing, and we sail for Canada. It have millions o' men and women from the islands who set sail already for Britain. And that situation is a funny funny piece o'histries, too. I sits down in my bed over on Spadina Avenue, and I laugh hard hard as hell, hee-hee-hee! at all them people who say we shouldn't make Great Britain more blacker than she is or was, in the first Elizabethan era. And all the time I does be laughing, I does be thinking of long long ago when the Queen o' Britain send all them convicts and whores and swivilitic men and women overseas, to *fluck-up* and populate the islands! Well, darling, now the tables turn round, because this is the *second* Elizabethan era! And it is the islands who sending black people, *all kinds*, the good and the bad, the godly and the ungodly, and we intend to fuck-up the good old Mother Country like rass, as my Jamaican friend would say. Man, I hear if you look round in Britain this afternoon you swear to God that you ain't in Britain no longer, but that you back in the islands. Black people? Oh rass!" And straightway, he broke into the popular calypso, *Yankees Gone and Sparrow Take Over Now.*

"God, that boy does talk as if he have a mouthful o' honey inside his mouth," Ironhorse said, appreciatively.

"Sagaboy, you talking the truth. You have just talk a piece o' truth...you call it histries, but I haven't heard nobody talk it that way, yet!" Estelle said, agreeing.

And then they stopped talking, and listened. The bells were ringing. You could see how the bells changed the tense expression on Estelle's face, an expression which emigration had placed there; and how they brought fear, a fear for the wondrous works of God, in its place. And looking more closely, you could see a primitive beauty painted on the sharp cheekbones and on the large mouth which gave her the haughtiness of a black princess.

"What hymn that is, what hymn he playing there?" she asked. "Ain't that hymn name *The Day Thou Gavest Lord Is Ending*? Ain't it that said hymn? The selfsame tune, Henry, the same tune, Sagaboy. And that is the very-same song they took my father, God rest his soul, to the grave with! You should have seen him when they pull him outta the sea, drown, and with the water in his body, making him big like a whale, and still looking powerful and strong as he use to be when he was living in the flesh. Lord! and when they come and tell me that my father *dead*, oh God, Henry, Sagaboy, I cry and I cry till I couldn't find water to cry with no more. And the people in the neighbourhood come and look in at the oval hole in the top o' the mahogany coffin when the undertaker-man had bring him home. And the whole village bow down their heads in respects o' the dead, in Pappy behalfs, cause my father was a man who had lots o' respects in the whole entire village and in the districts round our village. And the old women in our village bow down their heads low low low, and say, Thank God that at least He make a good dead outta Nathan. Nathan look nice as a dead. God go with thee, son, they say. And when they say that, all the men with their big bass voices start up singing this very hymn that you and me hearing coming outta that tall tower-thing. And Lord! water come to everybody's eye. The weeping and the crying and the singing. When they was weeping all that weeping, I had a funny feeling that they wasn't weeping only for my father, but for all the fathers that was ever killed by the cruel hands of the waves in the sea. And then they start filing past the coffin, singing; and the women were wringing their hands, like they was ringing out clothes, earlier that very-same day ... God! I think I seeing it now, clear clear before my two eyes, as I listen to the magic and poetry coming outta that bell up there, this Sunday afternoon. And to think, just think that the first time I going to call back all this to mind is now that I have escape from that blasted past-tense village in Barbados to come up here, in Canada. Man, it is a long long time ago now, cause my father dead, when he dead, he left me a little girl in pigtails."

The bells were ringing still, ringing loud and clear in the quiet Toronto afternoon. Estelle's voice broke down, and she started to hum along with the carilloneur. It was a clear voice, a soft voice. A voice like a stream of crystal water fighting to reach the sea.

"A lot o' salt water separating me from the place where my father drown. And I still remember it to this day," she went on. "I even remember the dress I wear, which was the said white dress that my half-sister Bernice wore when she got baptise in the Church o' the Nazarene. A white shark skin piece o' material that Mammy had bought at a sale. And when we reach Westbury Cemetery, shadows was walking through the evergreen trees, round the graveyard. And a man come, a big, fat, ugly black man dressed down in black, come and put dirt on top o' the coffin, and then he pull off the silver things that was screwed-on to the coffin, and as quick as a fly he push them inside his pocket; and then sudden so, like how you see dusk does fall outta the skies and nobody don't know, sudden so, that same man drop my father contained in that coffin-box in the hole, and Lord! I couldn't see my father's face no more. Such a mighty screeling went up, such a terrible crying escape from the women that you would have thought the heavens was collapsing, and it weren't just a poor fisherman that was taken to his resting place under a sandbox tree. And I remember that the people in the village was so poor, most of them, that only a handful could afford to rent a motor car from Johnson's Stables to follow my father in. Most of the men had was to follow on bicycles, and some even had to carry their women and their wives on the bicycle bars." She paused for a while, it seemed, to permit the bells to return the sadness of the funeral to her mind, and stir up the memories lurking there. She went on, "I can see his face now. I can see Pappy face before my two eyes right now. And I swear then, as I take the oath now, I swear blind that he wasn't dead in truth, cause I thought I could see his lips move, or did want to move and open, and whisper something to me from the grave. And I sorry sorry that up till now I don't know, and I can't imagine what the hell it was Pappy wanted to leave with me in the way of wisdom or advice, as he parted from me in the quick. I am the onliest living soul who see the dead attempt to talk. The only one who see that happen. And because o' that, I swear blind that they put my father to rest before his time was up. You understand what I mean? What I mean to affirm and state is this: down there in that damn island, the people don't have no lot o' respect, and a undertaker-man could make a mistake like nothing and put a person in a coffin and nail up that coffin and lower him in a grave be-Christ, before that dead-man is really a dead-man, before he stop breathing. Because them undertakers is really sharks and barracudas. Once they *suspect* that you will soon be a dead-man, that you are in a poor state o' health, that you are passing away, and they know they stand to get a few coppers for burying you, well, boy, they rushes like bloody-hell and they would *kill* you and turn you into a dead person if they think you ain't deading fast enough. Some stupid old women say it is a good thing, becausing God did love Pappy, and that is why He take my only father to His grave. But I don't believe that. Even now, at my age, I still don't think that God could say He is in love with a man, and then turn round and put His hand pon that man, strangulate him, and drop him dead, and in the quick, and still say He *love* him? Standing up by that grave that evening I hold up my two hands, high high in the air, and I screamed so bloody hard that they get frightened and they had was to drag me, still screaming and twirling pon the ground, mind you, to a motor car, and administer smelling salts to my nose to revive me and pacify me. Cause, don't matter how rough and cruel a father treats you, boy, a father is a father. That happen long long ago. Long ago, the Good Lord lift up my poor father up in the heavens with Him. And that is my testimony to the two o' you, as I sitting down here betwixt the two o' you, this bright Sunday evening in Toronto Canada, hearing this hymn, this selfsame tune that carried Nathan Sobers, my father, to his grave in Westbury Cemetery. Ain't you hearing that same hymn, *The Day Thou Gavest?*"

"I hearing it, Estelle, darling, I hearing it like anything," Sagaboy said, in a whisper, as if his voice had left his body and was now distant, far off, lost in the sea of time. Estelle's words had taken him back to his family and his home, tucked away out of memory in Trinidad; and they had made him think of the recent death of his Karen, his wife from Germany.

"Ain't it strange, ain't it wondrous strange how a person remembers things that happen so long ago? And ain't it strange too, how a simple thing like a bell in a tower could cause that same person to travel miles and miles in memory..."

"Strange!" Sagaboy told her. Still, his voice was far away across the ocean, miles away from the grass and the tower and the university campus where they were sitting and from the invisible hand of the carilloneur playing hymns on his bells. And then the bells stopped ringing; and then the three of them became bored with time resting so heavily on them, for they could think of nothing to do, or say, now that the bells had stopped ringing.

All you can hear now is the heavy breathing from Sagaboy, as he chews on a match stick. Henry begins to chew a match stick too. Suddenly he stops chewing, and offers a cigarette to Sagaboy, and to Estelle.

"Back home, I won't be seen dead with one o' these in my mouth, and on a Sunday, to boot!" she said. "What is one man's medicine is a next man's poison."

"You in Canada now, darling, you not back home," Ironhorse Henry reminded her. And with that, the conversation died; and the stillness and the sterility of a Toronto Sunday returned. Estelle blew smoke through her nostrils and her mouth at the same time, looking at the cigarette as if it was a bomb, and shaking her head, and muttering again about one man's medicine being another man's poison. Sagaboy started to cough. Ironhorse Henry looked up at the tower to avoid looking into Estelle's eyes. Sagaboy got up from them, and went aside to cough freely, and to spit. He could hardly control his breathing as the coughing racked his body in two, like a hairpin. A lump came up in his throat. The lump tickled him so much that he almost laughed, that he had to shut his eyes. Water began to spring from his eyes as the lump came nearer to his mouth. Then, as if playing a game with him, it went back down deeper. Sagaboy coughed and coughed, and when he did manage to spit... "*Blood!* Is blood I see?" But he wiped his feet on it, and hid the evidence from himself, and from Ironhorse Henry and from Estelle, who did not even look behind them while he was coughing.

Estelle broke the heaviness of the evening with a rasp-like noise of her teeth, and emphasized it by shaking her head from side to side, in despair. "Ain't no fairness in this damn world, you know that?" And when Ironhorse Henry had no comment, she added, "Now, look at me. I been here now, how much weeks? Four weeks going pon five, waiting and waiting pon them bastards at the immigration office, to give me a chance so's I could make a better woman outta myself. And you think they would give me a chance?"

"Your chance going come, love," Sagaboy said, returning to join them; and knowing, of course, that her chance would never come.

"I been hearing that tune since I was a little girl in pigtails. I know a man who waited his chance cause everybody was always telling him his chance going come. And you know how old that man was when his chance come?" She paused for effect; and then she said, "On his blasted death-bed!" And they burst out laughing. It was a tense, joyless, clench-teeth laugh. "I am getting more and more older every day, sweetheart. I don't have time to wait. That is old slave talk. Wait, wait, wait. If the greedy wait, hot going cool! If you patient, God going bring you through in the name o' the Lord. If a enemy hit you in your face, on the right hand side, you must then turn round and present him with the other side o' your fisiogomy, and let him lick-in that too. Christ Almighty, I telling you now that if I could just get one *little* chance, one little opportunity to work as a domestic servant in this place, be-Jesus Christ, I not waiting. I not waiting, nor praying, nor faltering. Not Estelle."

"This is a white man country, woman," Sagaboy teased her. "You want to cause a race riot?"

"I see eye-to-eye with Estelle," Ironhorse Henry said, in a manner which he hoped Estelle would understand, and in a tone of voice which implied more than was said. "Me and you view this situation in the same fashion. It is a shame that only a certain class o' individual could get through the doors o' immigration, and a next class o' people can't even squeeze through, at all!" He cleared his throat while they pondered on his words. He spat, neatly and accurately, on a cigarette box about ten feet away. "Now, you take them Eyetalians. *Them* is people!"

"How they get into this discussion?" Sagaboy wanted to know.

"Now, take them Eyetalians," Ironhorse continued, "them Eyetalians, man, you does see them Eyetalians coming into this country be-Christ, as if Canada is in Rome and not in Northamerica, and..."

"And why the hell you don't turn into a Neyetalian, then? Why you don't learn to talk in the Eyetalian tongue, and become a Neyetalian?"

"I not arguing nor affirming that it have anything particularly wrong with not being a Neyetalian," Ironhorse Henry explained, "and I not saying that as a Westindian man, I am better off, or worse off. All I affirming is that every day you look round in this city ... now, you take the corner o' College and Spadina where you live! Man, when I first land up in Toronto, you didn't see ten Eyetalians at that corner. Now? All you seeing is Eyetalians Eyetalians and be-Christ, more Eyetalians. You in *Italy* now, old man, you aren't no longer in Toronto."

"God, but I like them Eyetalians too bad, though!" Estelle said. "I like to see them talking and holding up their two hand up in the air, and laughing and crying and shouting for blue-murder as they talks ... brabba-rabba-brabba-rabba-seenioreeta! God have given that tribe a very pretty tongue and a real sweet language. And I like to see how the women does dress-down in black, from head to toenail, and still manage to look so womanish, in a positive kind o' way, as if a woman was create to always look that way, and in that manner and fashion o' dressing, in order to be a lady. I am only a part-time citizen o' Canada, but I have never see *one* Canadian woman look as if she was glad to be a woman. She want to be a *man*! You understand what I mean? Them Canadian women, particularly the old ones, with their false hair and their false teet' and rimless glasses, Jesus Christ, they don't look as if they is really women at all. And they certainly don't behave as if they is mothers, neither! Everybody always looking as if she come outta a fashion book that gone outta print in the last century."

"Child, don't let nobody hear you say these things! Shut up your mouth tight tight, cause you not born here. Don't criticize the same people that going put bread in your mouth. Keep your tail betwixt thy legs, and live and let the blasted white people live, too. That is my philosophy of the histries o' man." It was Sagaboy cautioning her, with great excitement in his manner. And this brought out a tiny rackling in his chest. It became louder and noisier until he had to cough. But the more he coughed, the more the rackling in his chest continued. He got up from them again, and went behind the small building where he could be at ease to untie the knots in his chest, until the bulldozers there smashed up the eruption inside him. And as the cough was about to break and calm down, a lump wormed its way up to his mouth. Afraid to spit it out, he closed his eyes and swallowed hard. But the moment it hit bottom, the coughing and rackling blew up again, like a storm. The lump returned to his mouth, and he closed his eyes and spat. He moved swiftly away from the spot because he did not want to look at it. Once he did turn, and try to look down, but the memory of the previous shock made him move away fast; and he rejoined his friends. But before he could return, and while his guts were erupting, Ironhorse Henry had placed his hand on the fat of Estelle's legs, soft as a feather in a breeze; and he had looked into her eyes, and for a moment, one moment, had expressed the pain that was in his heart.

"I love you bad as arse," he told her, from the bottom of his heart.

"Look, man, behave yourself, do," she said, and then laughed away his profession of love. All this happened while Sagaboy was coughing; and all the time, Ironhorse Henry wished he would drop down dead.

"You find it getting chilly here?" Sagaboy asked them.

"You have consumption, or TB, or something?" Ironhorse asked. He glanced at Estelle to see if she was as revolted as he. And when he saw that she was not, he added, "You gotta be careful with that fresh-cold, man."

"Oh, little coughing can't harm him," she said, putting a pin in Ironhorse's balloon of love.

And then they heard the bells again, loud this time, as if the man in the tower wanted to drown out their voices. They did not recognize the tune that the bells were playing now. And for a long time they sat, silently, arguing in their minds that they did know the tune, but listening all the time to the magic in the hands that tolled the bells so beautifully. They listened, wondering how a man could receive such power of beauty, such sweetness, such purity from his hands, and put them into bells... that were made to call people to church, to toll them to the sides of graves, to drop flowers on the coffin of a friend, or a lover, or a father.

"Jesus Christ, listen. Listen to the poetry in that damn bell, though!" Ironhorse said, raising his head to catch the smallest note, the softest ting. "That man playing that bell like how great Gort used to caress his tenor pan in the steel band, back in the old days. Too blasted sweet. Man, listen to that damn bell."

"What you say this place name?" Estelle asked.

"The campus," Sagaboy told her.

"I got to come back here, again, some time soon, and hear some more o' these white people bell-music."

"You know something? I just realize that Sundy evening is the same all over the blasted world. We sitting down here in Canada, pon the grass, and it is the same thing as when we was little boys back home, sitting down in a place we used to call The Hill," Ironhorse said. Poetry also was coming with his reminiscences. "Every man should sit down on a hill at least once in his lifetime, on a Sunday afternoon or evening, preferably alone, and look at the sea, and think about the past and the present and the future, and learn how to know himself. You gotta be yourself, alone, sitting down pon that hill of time, with the sun sinking behind your back and the moon rising in your face, both at one and the same time, before you is man enough to come to me and affirm that you really know yourself."

"I remember that feeling, old man," Sagaboy said, as if he was really experiencing it again, right in their presence. "I remember that emotion. I remember, how every Sunday night back home, we used to sit down on a hill called Brittons Hill. Me and the rest o' the boys, sitting down pon that damn hill, like if we was in a upstairs house looking down in the sea. And the same feeling, like I was lost, you know, like I wasn't worth nothing like how sometimes the same feeling does over-power me in that blasted five-dollars-a-week rat-trap I lives in, on Spadina, right here in this kiss-me-arse advance country..." He took a beaten-up, half-smoked cigarette from his pocket and put a match to its black tip. "... and the birds chirping. You know something? I have never see *one* blasted bird in this place yet, and I now remember that, for the first time! Back home, the birds chirping nice songs and then they run off to sleep. And the trees, trees all round where we was sitting down, trees dress-up in a more greener coat o' green than this grass. And then a funny thing would happen. Just at that moment before shadow and darkness take them up in their hands as if they was little children put to bed, be-Christ, they would turn *more greener* still! We would be sitting down in the midst of the evening dusk and shadows, thinking bout what and what we was going to be when we grow up to be big strong men. And if on that particular Sunday we did have a nice feed, like split-pea rice and fry pork, or something nice and heavy in the bowels, well, pardner, everybody want to be something, or some-body great and powerful. Like a doctor, or a police commissioner, or even a plantation manager. And you don't know that one evening, I must have been so blasted full o' black-eye peas and rice that I say I wanted to be the *governor o' the whole blasted West Indies*. Be-Christ, if that ain't dreaming, tell me what is? But one boy, Lester Theophillis Bynoe, all he wanted to be, with a full-belly or no full-belly, was a hangman. And you know something? Be-Christ, that is what he turned out to be! He is the biggest, the blackest, and the best hangman in the whole Caribbean! But if things wasn't so great, kitchen-wise or food-wise, or if our mothers had give us a regular stiff cut-arse with a window stick or with a piece o' bamboo, well, everybody want to jump on a boat and become sailors and buccaneers. And always, after we finish wishing and dreaming, you could hear the church bells from St Barnabas Church, miles and miles of sugar canes away, over the fields, coming right up to your two earholes. Church bells, old man, *ding-dong-ding-dong!*..." His coughing aborted his reverie, and it shook him like a huckster shaking a coconut to see if there is any water inside. Ironhorse Henry rushed to him, and held him around the waist; and Estelle became very alarmed, as Ironhorse Henry beat the coughing man's chest to dislodge the thorns of pain that were inside him. And Ironhorse took out his own handkerchief, and gave it to Sagaboy to put to his mouth. "Let we go home," he said, when the heaving permitted him to form a word. "That damn bell ring till it give me a headache. And it chilly as hell here, too."

And they walked hurriedly away from the campus. Shadows were running slow races across the front lawns, and across the large circle of green grass in front of a large grey building. The bells kept ringing for a while, and then they stopped. And then Estelle pushed her arms through both their arms, through Sagaboy's, on her left, and Ironhorse Henry's, on her right, and like this they walked on in the darkness of the bells.

(1971)   (1971)

George Ryga
1932 –

BORN IN DEEP CREEK, Alberta, George Ryga worked at a variety of jobs before the production of his television drama, *Indian,* in 1962. Since then he has become well known as a dramatist with works such as *The Ecstasy of Rita Joe* (1967), *Captives of the Faceless Drummer* (1971) and *Sunrise on Sarah* (1974). Ryga has also published several novels including *Hungry Hills* (1963), *Ballad of a Stone-Picker* (1966) and *Night Desk* (1976).

Indian

Characters:

INDIAN — *transient Indian laborer. Swarthy, thin, long haired. Wears tight-fitting jeans, dirty dark shirt brightened by outlandish western designs over pockets. Also cowboy boots which are cracked and aged. A wide-brimmed black western hat.*

WATSON — *farmer and employer of Indian.*

AGENT — *comfortable civil servant. Works in the Indian Affairs Department as field worker for the service.*

Setting:

Stage should be flat, grey, stark non-country. Diametric lines (telephone poles and wire on one side, with a suggestion of two or three newly driven fence-posts on the other) could project vast empty expanse.

Set may have a few representative tufts of scraggy growth in distance — also far and faint horizon.

In front and stage left, one fence-post newly and not yet fully driven. Pile of dirt around post. Hammer, wooden box and shovel alongside.

High, fierce white light off stage left to denote sun. Harsh shadows and constant sound of low wind.

Back of stage is a pile of ashes, with a burnt axe handle and some pottery showing.

Curtain up on INDIAN *asleep, using slight hump of earth under his neck for pillow. He is facing sun, with hat over his face.* WATSON *approaches from stage right, dragging his feet and raising dust. Stops over* INDIAN's *head.*

WATSON: *(loud and angry)* Hey! What the hell! Come on... you aimin' to die like that?

INDIAN *clutches his hat and sits up. Lifts his hat and looks up, then jerks hat down over his face.*

INDIAN: Oy! Oooh! The sun she blind me, goddamn!... Boss... I am sick! Head, she gonna explode, sure as hell!

He tries to lie down again, but WATSON *grabs his arm and yanks him to his feet.*

WATSON: There's gonna be some bigger explosions if I don't get action out of you guys. What happened now? Where's the fat boy? An' the guy with the wooden leg?

INDIAN: Jus' a minute, boss. Don't shout like that. *(looks carefully around him)* They not here... Guess they run away, boss – no?... Roy, he's not got wooden leg. He got bone leg same's you an' me. Only it dried up and look like wood. Small, too... *(lifts up his own right leg)* That shoe... that was fit Roy's bad leg. The other shoe is tight. But this one, boss – she is hunder times tighter!

WATSON: *(squatting)* Is them Limpy's boots?

INDIAN: Sure, boss. I win them at poker las' night. Boss, what a time we have – everybody go haywire!

WATSON *looks around impatiently.*

WATSON: I can see. Where's your tent?

INDIAN: *(pointing to ashes)* There she is. Sonofabitch, but I never see anything burn like that before!

WATSON: The kid wasn't lying – you guys *did* burn the tent.

INDIAN: What kid?

WATSON: Your kid.

INDIAN: *(jumping to his feet)* Alphonse? Where is Alphonse? He run away when Sam and Roy start fight...

WATSON: Yeh, he run away... run all the way to the house. Told us you guys was drunk an' wild. So the missus fixed him something to eat and put him to bed.

INDIAN: He's all right? Oh, that's good, boss!

WATSON: *(smiling grimly)* Sure, he's all right. Like I said, the missus fed the kid. Then I took him and put him in the grainery, lockin' the door so he ain't gonna get out. That's for protection.

INDIAN: Protection? You don't need protection, boss. Alphonse not gonna hurt you.

WATSON: Ha! Ha! Ha! Big joke! ... Where are your pals as was gonna help you with this job? Where are they – huh?

INDIAN: I don't know. They run away when tent catch fire.

WATSON: Great! That's just great! You know what you guys done to me? Yesterday, ya nicked me for ten dollars... I'm hungry, the fat boy says to me – my stomach roar like thunder. He's gonna roar out the other end before I'm finished with you an' him! How much you figure the fence you put up is worth?

INDIAN: *(rubbing his eyes and trying to see the fence in the distance)* I dunno, boss. You say job is worth forty dollars. Five, mebbe ten dollars done...

WATSON: Five dollars! Look here, smart guy – ya've got twenty-nine posts in – I counted 'em. At ten cents apiece, you've done two dollars ninety cents worth of work! An' you got ten dollars off me yesterday!

INDIAN: *(pondering sadly)* Looks like you in the hole, boss.

WATSON: Well maybe I am ... an' maybe I ain't. I got your kid in the grainery, locked up so he'll keep. You try to run off after your pals, an' I'm gonna take my gun an' shoot a hole that big through the kid's head!

He makes a ring with his fingers to show exact size of injury he intends to make.

INDIAN: No!

WATSON: Oh, sure! So what ya say, Indian? ... You gonna work real hard and be a good boy?

INDIAN: Boss – you know me. I work! Them other guys is no good – but not Johnny. I make deal – I keep deal! You see yourself I stay when they run.

WATSON: Sure, ya stayed. You were too goddamned drunk to move, that's why you stayed! What goes on in your heads... ah, hell! You ain't worth the bother!

INDIAN: No, no, boss... You all wrong.

WATSON: Then get to work! It's half past nine, and you ain't even begun to think about the fence.

INDIAN: Boss... a little bit later. I sick man... head – she hurt to burst. An' stomach – ugh! Boss, I not eat anything since piece of baloney yesterday...

WATSON: *(turning angrily)* You go to hell – you hear me? Go to hell! I got that story yesterday. Now g'wan – I wanna see some action!

INDIAN: All right, boss. You know me. You trust me.

WATSON: Trust ya? I wouldn't trust you with the time of day, goddamn you! *(remembers something)* Hey – there's a snoop from the Indian Affairs department toolin' around today – checkin' on all you guys workin' off the reserve. I'm telling you somethin'... you're working for me, so if you got any complaints, you better tell me now. I don't want no belly-achin' to no government guys.

INDIAN: Complaints?... Me? I happy, boss. What you take me for?

WATSON: Sure, sure... Now get back to work. An' remember what I told you... you try to beat it, an' I shoot the kid. You understand?

> INDIAN *removes his hat and wipes his brow.*

INDIAN: Sure, bossman – I understand.

> INDIAN *looks towards the fence in the fields.* WATSON *stands behind him, scratching his chin and smirking insolently.* INDIAN *glances back at him, then shrugging with resignation, moves unsteadily to the unfinished fence post. He pulls the box nearer to the post, picks up hammer and is about to step on the box. Changes his mind and sits for a moment on the box, hammer across his knees. Rubs his eyes and forehead.*

WATSON: Now what the hell's the matter? Run out of gas?

INDIAN: Oh, boss ... If I be machine that need only gas, I be all right mebbe...

WATSON: So you going to sit an' let the day go by? – Indian, I've got lots of time, an' I can grind you to dirt if you're figurin' on bustin' my ass!

INDIAN: Nobody bust you, boss. I be all right right away ... Sementos! But the head she is big today. An' stomach ... she is slop-bucket full of turpentine. Boss... two dollars a quart, Sam Cardinal says to me... with four dollars we get enough bad whiskey to poison every Indian from here to Lac La Biche! Sam Cardinal tell the truth that time for sure...

WATSON: What kind of rubbish did you drink?

INDIAN: Indian whiskey, boss. You know what is Indian whiskey?

WATSON: No. You tell me, an' then you get to work!

INDIAN: Sure, boss, sure. As soon as field stop to shake. Indian whiskey ... you buy two quart. You get one quart wood alcohol... maybe half quart formalin, an' the rest is water from sick horse! That's the kind whiskey they make for Indian.

WATSON: An' it makes the field shake for you... Christ! *You* make me sick!

INDIAN: Oh, but what party it make!

WATSON: (*irritably*) Come on... come on! Get on with it.

> INDIAN *scrambles on box and starts to drive post into ground. He stops after a few seconds. He is winded.*

INDIAN: Sementos! Is hard work, boss!... I tell you, Sam Cardinal sing like sick cow ... an' Roy McIntosh dance on his bad leg. Funny! ... Alphonse an' I laugh until stomach ache. I win Roy's boots in poker, but he dance anyhow. Then Sam get mad an' he push Roy... Roy push him back... They fight... Boy, I hungry now, boss...

WATSON: Tough! I wanna see ten bucks of work done.

INDIAN: Then you feed me? Big plate potatoes an' meat?... An' mebbe big hunk of pie?

WATSON: (*laughs sarcastically*) Feed ya? Soon's I get my ten bucks squared away, you can lie down and die! But not on my field... go on the road allowance!

> INDIAN *hits the post a few more times, trying to summon up strength to get on with the work. But it is all in vain. Drops hammer heavily to the box. Rubs his stomach.*

INDIAN: You hard man, boss ... Hard like iron. Sam is bad man ... bugger up you, bugger up me. Get ten dollars for grub from you ... almost like steal ten dollars from honest man. Buy whiskey ... buy baloney an' two watermelon. He already eat most of baloney and I see him give hunk to friendly dog. I kick dog. Sam get mad ... why you do that? Dog is nothing to you? I say, he eat my grub. He can go catch cat if he hungry. I catch an' eat cat once myself, boss ... winter 1956. Not much meat an' tough like rope. I never eat cat again, that's for sure. Sementos! But the head hurt!

WATSON: One more word, Indian ... just one more word an' I'm gonna clean house on you! ... You wanna try me? Come on!

For a moment the INDIAN *teeters between two worlds, then with a violent motion he sweeps up the hammer and begins pounding the post, mechanically with an incredible rhythm of defeat.* WATSON *watches for a while his anger gone now. Scratches himself nervously, then makes a rapid exit off stage left.*
Almost immediately the hammering begins to slow, ending with one stroke when the hammer head rests on the post, and INDIAN's *head droops on his outstretched arms.*

INDIAN: Scared talk ... world is full of scared talk. I show scare an' I get a job from mister Watson. Scared Indian is a live Indian. My head don't get Alphonse free ... but hands do.

Sound of motor car approaching. INDIAN *lifts his head and peers to stage right.*

INDIAN: Hullo ... I am big man today! First mister Watson an' now car come to see me. Boy, he drive! ... If I not get out of his way he gonna hit me, sure as hell!

Jumps down from box and watches. Car squeals to stop off-stage. Puff of dust blows in from wings. Car door slams and AGENT *enters.*

AGENT: Hi there, fella, how's it going?
INDIAN: Hello, misha. Everything is going one hunder fifty percent! Yessiree ... one hunder fifty percent!

INDIAN *rises on box and lifts hammer to drive post.*

AGENT: There was talk in town your camp burned out last night ... everything okay? Nobody hurt?
INDIAN: Sure, everything okay. You want complaints?
AGENT: Well, I ... what do you mean, do I want complaints?
INDIAN: I just say if you want complaints, I give you lots. My tent, she is burn down last night. My partners ... they run away. Leave me to do big job myself. I got no money ... an' boss, he's got my Alphonse ready to shoot if I try to run. You want more complaints? *(drives down hard on hammer and groans)* Maybe you want know how my head she hurts inside?
AGENT: *(relieved)* Hey – c'mere. I'll give you a smoke to make you feel better. You're in rough shape, boy! Which would you prefer – pipe tobacco, or a cigarette? I've got both ...

INDIAN *drops hammer and comes down from box.*

INDIAN: The way I feel, misha, I could smoke old stocking full of straw. Gimme cigarette. *(examines the cigarette* AGENT *gives him)* Oh, you make lotsa money from government, boss... tobacco here... and cotton there – some cigarette! Which end you light? *(laughs)*

AGENT: Light whichever end you want. You can eat it for all I care. That's some hat you got there, sport. Where'd you get it?

INDIAN: *(accepting light* AGENT *offers him)* Win at poker, misha.

AGENT: *(examining him closely)* Aren't those boots tight? I suppose you stole them!

INDIAN: No, boss – poker.

AGENT: And that shirt – will you look at that! Have shirt, will travel.

INDIAN: I steal that from my brother, when he is sick and dying. He never catch me!

AGENT: *(laughing)* That's good ... I must tell the boys about you – what's your name?

INDIAN: You think is funny me steal shirt from my brother when he die? ... You think that funny, bossman? I think you lousy bastard! ... You think that funny, too?

AGENT: *(startled)* Now hold on – did I hear you say ...

INDIAN: You hear good what I say.

The AGENT *takes out his notebook.*

AGENT: Just give me your name, and we'll settle with you later.

INDIAN: Turn around an' walk to road. If you want to see stealer in action, I steal wheels off your car. You try catch me ...

AGENT: *(angrily)* Give me your name!

INDIAN: Mebbe I forget ... mebbe I got no name at all.

AGENT: Look here, boy ... don't give me any back-talk, or I might have to turn in a report on you, and next time Indian benefits are given out, yours might be hard to claim!

INDIAN: So – you got no name for me. How you gonna report me when you not know who I am? You want name? All right, I give you name. Write down – Joe Bush!

AGENT: I haven't got all day, fella. Are you, or are you not going to tell me your name?

INDIAN: No! I never tell you, misha! Whole world is scare. It make you scare you should know too much about me!

AGENT: *(slamming notebook shut)* That does it! You asked for it ... an' by God, if I have to go after you myself, I'm gonna find out who you are!

INDIAN: Don't get mad, misha. I sorry for what I say. I got such hurting head, I don't know what I say ...

AGENT: Been drinking again, eh?...What was it this time – homebrew? Or shaving lotion?

INDIAN: Maybe homebrew, maybe coffee. I don't know. Why you ask?

AGENT: You're no kid. You know as well as I do. Besides, bad liquor's going to kill you sooner than anything else.

INDIAN: (*excitedly*) Misha...you believe that? You really mean what you say?

AGENT: What – about bad liquor? Sure I do...

INDIAN: Then misha, please get me bottle of good, clean Canadian whiskey! I never drink clean whiskey in my life!

AGENT: Come on, now...you're as...

INDIAN: I give you twenty dollars for bottle! Is deal?

AGENT: Stop it! ... Boy, you've got a lot more than a hangover wrong in your head!

INDIAN: (*points off stage*) That car yours?

AGENT: Yes.

INDIAN: How come all that writing on door – that's not your name? Why you not tell truth?

AGENT: Well, I work for the government, and they provide us...

INDIAN: Thirty dollars?

AGENT: Look here...

INDIAN: How come you not in big city, with office job? How come you drive around an' talk to dirty, stupid Indian? You not have much school, or mebbe something else wrong with you to have such bad job.

AGENT: Shut your lousy mouth, you...

INDIAN: Thirty-five dollars? No more! ... I give you no more!

AGENT: Will you shut up?

INDIAN: (*defiantly*) No! I never shut up! You not man at all – you cheap woman who love for money! Your mother was woman pig, an' your father man dog!

AGENT: (*becoming frightened*) What ... what are you saying?

> INDIAN *comes face to face with* AGENT.

INDIAN: You wanna hit me? Come on ... hit me! You kill me easy, an' they arrest you – same people who give you car. Hit me – even little bit – come on! You coward! Just hit me like this! (*slaps his palms together*) ... Just like that – come on! You know what I do when you hit me?

AGENT: (*looks apprehensively around himself*) What?

INDIAN: I report you for beating Indian an' you lose job. Come on – show me you are man!

He dances provoçatively around AGENT. AGENT *turns in direction of his car.*

AGENT: I'm getting out of here – you're crazy!

INDIAN: *(jumps in front of* AGENT*)* No ... you not go anywhere! Maybe nobody here to see what happen, but after accident, lots of people come from everywhere. I'm gonna jump on car bumper, and when you drive, I fall off and you drive over me. How you gonna explain that, bossman?

AGENT: *(frightened now)* I got nothing against you, boy! What's the matter with you? ... What do you want with me?

INDIAN: I want nothing from you – jus' to talk to me – to know who I am. Once you go into car, I am outside again. I tell you about my brother, an' how he die ...

AGENT: Go back to your work and I'll go back to mine. I don't want to hear about your brother or anyone else. (INDIAN *walks off stage to car*) Now you get off my car!

INDIAN: *(offstage)* You gonna listen, misha. You gonna listen like I tell you. *(sounds of car being bounced)* Boy, you ride like in bed! Misha, who am I?

INDIAN *returns to stage.*

AGENT: How in the devil do I know who you are, or what you want with me. I'm just doing a job – heard your camp got burned out and ...

INDIAN: How you know who any of us are? How many of us got birth certificates to give us name an' age on reserve? ... Mebbe you think I get passport an' go to France. Or marry the way bossman get married. You think that, misha?

AGENT: I don't care who you are or what you think. Just get back to your job and leave me alone ...

INDIAN *glances admiringly off stage to car.*

INDIAN: Boy, is like pillow on wheels! If I ever have car like that, I never walk again!

AGENT: Get out of my way! I've got to get back into town.

INDIAN: No hurry. Mebbe you never go back at all.

AGENT: What ... do you mean by that?

INDIAN *turns and approaches* AGENT *until they stand face to face.*

INDIAN: You know what is like to kill someone – not with hate – not with any feelings here at all? *(places hand over heart)*

AGENT: *(stepping back)* This is ridiculous! Look, boy ... I'll give you anything I can – just get out of my hair. That whiskey you want – I'll get it for you ... won't cost you a cent, I promise!

INDIAN: Someone that mebbe you loved? Misha – I want to tell you somethin'...

AGENT: No!

INDIAN *catches hold of* AGENT's *shirt front.*

INDIAN: Listen – damn you! I kill like that once! You never know at Indian office – nobody tell you! Nobody ever tell you! ... I got to tell you about my brother ... he die three, four, maybe five years ago. My friend been collecting treaty payments on his name. He know how many years ago now...

AGENT: You couldn't ...

INDIAN: I couldn't, misha?

AGENT: There are laws in this country – nobody escapes the law!

INDIAN: What law?

AGENT: The laws of the country!

INDIAN: *(threatening)* What law?

AGENT: No man ... shall kill ... another ...

INDIAN: I tell you about my brother. I tell you everything. Then you tell me if there is law for all men.

AGENT: Leave me alone! I don't want to hear about your brother!

INDIAN: *(fiercely)* You gonna listen! Look around – what you see? Field and dust ... an' some work I do. You an' me ... you fat, me hungry. I got nothin'... and you got money, car. Maybe you are better man than I. But I am not afraid, an' I can move faster. What happen if I get mad, an' take hammer to you?

AGENT: You ... wouldn't ...

INDIAN: You wrong, misha. Nobody see us. Mebbe you lucky – get away. But who believe you? You tell one story, I tell another. I lose nothing – but you gonna listen about my brother, that's for sure!

AGENT: *(desperately)* Look boy – let's be sensible – let's behave like two grown men. I'll drive you into town – buy you a big dinner! Then we'll go and buy that whiskey I promised. You can go then – find your friends and have another party tonight ... Nobody will care, and you'll have a good time!

INDIAN: *(spitting)* You lousy dog!

AGENT: Now don't get excited! ... I'm only saying what I think is best. If you don't want to come, that's fine. Just let me go and we'll forget all about today, and that we ever even seen one another, okay?

INDIAN *releases the* AGENT.

INDIAN: You think I forget I see you? I got you here like picture in my head. I try to forget you... like I try to forget my brother, but you never leave me alone... Misha, I never forget you!

AGENT: *(struggling to compose himself)* I'm just a simple joe doing my job, boy – remember that. I know there's a lot bothers you. Same's a lot bothers me. We've all got problems... but take them where they belong.

> AGENT *pulls out cigarettes and nervously lights one for himself.*

INDIAN: Gimme that!

AGENT: This is mine – I lit it for myself! Here, I'll give you another one!

INDIAN: I want that one!

AGENT: No, damn it... have a new one!

> INDIAN *jumps behind* AGENT *and catches him with arm around throat. With other hand he reaches out and takes lit cigarette out of* AGENT's *mouth. Throws* AGENT *to the field. The* AGENT *stumbles to his knees, rubbing his eyes.*

AGENT: What's wrong with you? Why did you do that?

INDIAN: Now you know what is like to be me. Get up! Or I kick your brains in!

> AGENT *rises to his feet and sways uncertainly.*

AGENT: Dear God...

INDIAN: My brother was hungry... an' he get job on farm of white bossman to dig a well. Pay she is one dollar for every five feet down. My brother dig twenty feet – two day hard work. He call up to bossman – give me planks, for the blue clay she is getting wet! To hell with what you see – bossman shout down the hole – just dig! Pretty soon, the clay shift, an' my brother is trapped to the shoulders. He yell – pull me out! I can't move, an' the air, she is squeezed out of me! But bossman on top – he is scared to go down in hole. He leave to go to next farm, an' after that another farm, until he find another Indian to send down hole. An' all the time from down there, my brother yell at the sky. Jesus Christ – help me! White man leave me here to die! But Jesus Christ not hear my brother, an' the water she rise to his lips. Pretty soon, he put his head back until his hair an' ears in slimy blue clay an' water. He no more hear himself shout – but he shout all the same!

AGENT: I wasn't there! I couldn't help him!

INDIAN: ... He see stars in the sky – lots of stars. A man see stars even in day when he look up from hole in earth...

AGENT: I couldn't help him – I don't want to hear about him!

INDIAN: ... Then Sam Cardinal come. Sam is a coward. But when he see my brother there in well, an' the blue clay movin' around him like livin' thing, he go down. Sam dig with his hands until he get rope around my brother. Then he come up, an' he an' white bossman pull. My brother no longer remember, an' he not hear the angry crack of mud an' water when they pull him free ...

AGENT: *(with relief)* Then ... he lived? Thank God ...

INDIAN: Sure ... sure ... he live. You hunt?

AGENT: Hunt? ... You mean – shooting?

INDIAN: Yeh.

AGENT: Sure. I go out every year.

INDIAN: You ever shoot deer – not enough to kill, but enough to break one leg forever? Or maybe hit deer in eye, an' it run away, blind on one side for wolf to kill?

AGENT: I nicked a moose two years back – never did track it down. But I didn't shoot it in the eye.

INDIAN: How you know for sure?

AGENT: Well ... I just didn't. I never shoot that way!

INDIAN: You only shoot – where bullet hit you not know. Then what you do?

AGENT: I tried to track it, but there had been only a light snow ... an' I lost the tracks.

INDIAN: So you not follow?

AGENT: No. I walked back to camp... My friend an' I had supper and we drove home that night ...

INDIAN: Forget all about moose you hurt?

AGENT: No. I did worry about what happened to him!

INDIAN: You dream about him that night? ... Runnin', bawling with pain?

AGENT: What the hell ... dream about a moose? There's more important things to worry about, I'm telling you.

INDIAN: Then you not worry at all. You forget as soon as you can. Moose not run away from you – you run away from moose!

AGENT: I didn't ... hey, you're crazy! *(moves towards car off stage, but* INDIAN *jumps forward and stops him)* Here! You leave me alone, I'm telling you ... You got a lot of wild talk in your head, but you can't push your weight around with me ... I'm getting out of here ... Hey!

> INDIAN *catches him by arm and rolls him to fall face down in the dust.*
> INDIAN *pounces on him.*

INDIAN: What you call man who has lost his soul?

AGENT: I don't know. Let go of me!

INDIAN: We have name for man like that! You know the name?

AGENT: No, I don't. *You're breaking my arm!*

INDIAN: We call man like that sementos. Remember that name ... for *you* are *sementos!*

AGENT: Please, fella – leave me alone! I never hurt you that I know of...

INDIAN: Sure.

Releases AGENT, *who rises to his feet, dusty and dishevelled.*

AGENT: I want to tell you something ... I want you to get this straight, because every man has to make up his mind about some things, and I've made mine up now! This has gone far enough. If this is a joke, then you've had your laughs. One way or another, I'm going to get away from you. And when I do, I'm turning you in to the police. You belong in jail!

INDIAN: *(laughs)* Mebbe you are man. We been in jail a long time now, sementos ...

AGENT: And stop calling me that name!

INDIAN: Okay, okay ... I call you bossman. You know what bossman mean to me?

AGENT: I don't want to know.

INDIAN: *(laughs again)* You wise ... you get it. I not got much to say, then you go.

AGENT: *(bewildered)* You ... you're not going to ... bother me anymore?

INDIAN: I finish my story, an' you go ... go to town, go to hell ... go anyplace. My brother – you know what kind of life he had? He was not dead, an' he was not alive.

AGENT: You said he came out of the well safely. What are you talking about?

INDIAN: No ... He was not alive. He was too near dead to live. White bossman get rid of him quick. Here, says bossman – here is three dollars pay. I dig twenty feet – I make four dollars, my brother says. Bossman laugh. I take dollar for shovel you leave in the hole, he says. My brother come back to reserve, but he not go home. He live in my tent. At night, he wake up shouting, an' in daytime, he is like man who has no mind. He walk 'round, an' many times get lost in the bush, an' other Indian find him an' bring him back. He get very sick. For one month he lie in bed. Then he try to get up. But his legs an' arms are dried to the bone, like branches of dying tree.

AGENT: He must've had polio.

INDIAN: Is not matter... One night, he say to me: go to other side of lake tomorrow, an' take my wife an' my son, Alphonse. Take good care of them. I won't live the night... I reach out and touch him, for he talk like devil fire was on him. But his head and cheek is cold. You will live an' take care of your wife an' Alphonse yourself, I say to him. But my brother shake his head. He look at me and say – help me to die...

AGENT: Why... didn't you... take him to hospital?

INDIAN: *(laughs bitterly)* Hospital! A dollar he took from dying man for the shovel buried in blue clay... hospital? Burn in hell!

AGENT: No... no! This I don't understand at all...

INDIAN: I... kill... my... brother! In my arms I hold him. He was so light, like small boy. I hold him... rock 'im back and forward like this... like mother rock us when we tiny kids. I rock 'im an' I cry... I get my hands tight on his neck, an' I squeeze an' I squeeze. I know he dead, and I still squeeze an' cry, for everything is gone, and I am old man now ... only hunger an' hurt left now...

AGENT: My God!

INDIAN: I take off his shirt an' pants – I steal everything I can wear. Then I dig under tent, where ground is soft, and I bury my brother. After that, I go to other side of lake. When I tell my brother's wife what I done, she not say anything for long time. Then she look at me with eyes that never make tears again. Take Alphonse, she say... I go to live with every man who have me, to forget him. Then she leave her shack, an' I alone with Alphonse... I take Alphonse an' I come back. All Indians know what happen, but nobody say anything. Not to me... not to you. Some half-breed born outside reservation take my brother's name – and you, bossman, not know...

AGENT: *(quietly, as though he were the authority again)* We *have* to know, you understand, don't you? You'll have to tell me your brother's name.

INDIAN: I know... I tell you. Was Tommy Stone.

AGENT *takes out his notebook again and writes.*

AGENT: Stone – Tommy Stone ... good. You know what I have to do, you understand it's my duty, don't you? It's my job... it's the way I feel. We all have to live within the law and uphold it. Ours is a civilized country ... you understand, don't you? *(turns to car off stage)* I'm going now. Don't try to run before the police come. The circumstances were extenuating, and it may not go hard for you...

INDIAN *makes no attempt to hinder* AGENT *who walks off stage.*

INDIAN: Sure, misha ... you're right. *(hears car door open)* Wait! Misha, wait! I tell you wrong. Name is not Tommy Stone — Tommy Stone is me! Name is *Johnny* Stone!

AGENT *returns, notebook in hand.*

AGENT: Johnny Stone? Let's get this straight now ... your brother was Johnny Stone ... and you're *Tommy* Stone? (INDIAN *nods vigorously*) Okay, boy. I've got that. Now remember what I said, and just stay here and wait. *(turns to leave)*

INDIAN: No, misha ... you got whole business screwed up again! I am Johnny Stone, my brother, he is Tommy Stone.

AGENT *pockets his notebook and turns angrily to face* INDIAN.

AGENT: Look, Indian — what in hell is your name anyhow? Who are you?

INDIAN: My name? You want my name?

Suddenly catches AGENT *by arm and swings him around as in a boyish game. Places* AGENT *down on the box he used for standing on to drive posts.*

AGENT: Hey, you stop that!

INDIAN: An' yet you want my name?

AGENT: Yes, that's right ... If it's not too much trouble to give me one straight answer, what is your name?

INDIAN: Sam Cardinal is my name!

AGENT *rises with disgust and straightens out his clothes.*

AGENT: Now it's Sam Cardinal ... what do you take me for anyway? You waste my time ... you rough me up like I was one of your drunken Indian friends ... and now I can't get an answer to a simple question ... But what the hell — the police can find out who you are and what you've done.

INDIAN: No, sementos! You never find out!

INDIAN *throws legs apart and takes the stance of a man balancing on a threshold.*

INDIAN: You go to reservation with hunder policemen — you try to find Johnny Stone ... you try to find Tommy Stone ... Sam Cardinal, too. Mebbe you find everybody, mebbe you find nobody. All Indians same — nobody. Listen to me, sementos — one brother is dead — who? Tommy Stone? Johnny Stone? Joe Bush! Look — *(turns out both pockets of his pants, holding them out, showing them empty and ragged)* I got nothing ...

nothing... no wallet, no money, no name. I got no past... no future... nothing, sementos! I nobody. I not even live in this world ... I dead! You get it?...I dead! *(shrugs in one great gesture of grief)* I never been anybody. *I not just dead...I never live at all.* What is matter? ... What anything matter, sementos?

> AGENT *has the look of a medieval peasant meeting a leper – fear, pity, hatred.*

INDIAN: What matter if I choke you till you like rag in my hands?... Hit you mebbe with twenty pound hammer – break in your head like watermelon ... Leave you dry in wind an' feed ants ... What matter if police come an' take me? Misha! Listen, damn you – listen! One brother kill another brother – why? *(shakes* AGENT *furiously by the lapels)* Why? Why?... Why?

AGENT: *(clawing at* INDIAN's *hands) Let me go! LET...ME...GO!*

> AGENT *breaks free and runs off stage for car. Sounds of motor starting and fast departure. Dust.* INDIAN *stands trembling with fury.*

INDIAN: Where you go in such goddamn speed? World too small to run 'way? You hear me, sementos! Hi...*sementos*! Ugh!

> *Spits and picks up hammer. Starts to drive post vigorously. Curtain.*

(1971)   (1971)

Alden Nowlan
1933 –

———◆———

ALDEN NOWLAN WAS born near Windsor, Nova Scotia, and began a career as a journalist in 1952. Since his first collection of poetry, *The Rose and the Puritan* (1958), he has published a collection of stories, *Miracle at Indian River* (1968), and several volumes of poetry including *Bread, Wine* and *Salt* (1967), *The Mysterious Naked Man* (1969), *Playing the Jesus Game* (1970), *Between Tears and Laughter* (1971) and *I'm a Stranger Here Myself* (1974). "A Call in December" first appeared in *Queen's Quarterly* in 1961.

A Poem for Elizabeth Nancy

Emptied from Eden, I look down
into your eyes like caves behind a torrent,
into the blue-green valleys where the cattle
fatten on clover and grow drunk on apples;

into the house asleep and all the curtains
skittish and white as brides (even the wind
meeting their silence, whispers) and I come
into the house with hands that stink from milking,

into this house of candles where my feet
climbing your stairs like laughter leave me standing   10
before your door, knowing there's no one there,
knowing your room is bare and not much caring.

(1961)   (1961)

The Bull Moose

Down from the purple mist of trees on the mountain,
lurching through forests of white spruce and cedar,
stumbling through tamarack swamps,
came the bull moose
to be stopped at last by a pole-fenced pasture.

Too tired to turn or, perhaps, aware
there was no place left to go, he stood with the cattle.
They, scenting the musk of death, seeing his great head
like the ritual mask of a blood god, moved to the other end
of the field and waited.   10

The neighbours heard of it, and by afternoon
cars lined the road.   The children teased him
with alder switches and he gazed at them
like an old tolerant collie.   The women asked
if he could have escaped from a Fair.

The oldest man in the parish remembered seeing
a gelded moose yoked with an ox for plowing.
The young men snickered and tried to pour beer
down his throat, while their girl friends
took their pictures.   20

And the bull moose let them stroke his tick-ravaged flanks,
let them pry open his jaws with bottles, let a giggling girl
plant a little purple cap
of thistles on his head.

When the wardens came, everyone agreed it was a shame
to shoot anything so shaggy and cuddlesome.
He looked like the kind of pet
women put to bed with their sons.

So they held their fire.   But just as the sun dropped in the river
the bull moose gathered his strength   30
like a scaffolded king, straightened and lifted his horns
so that even the wardens backed away as they raised their rifles.
When he roared, people ran to their cars.   All the young men
leaned on their automobile horns as he toppled.

(1962)   (1970)

Dancer

The sun is horizontal, so the flesh
of the near-naked girl bouncing a ball
is netted in its light, an orange mesh
weaving between her and the shadowed wall.

Her body glistening and snake-crescendoes
electric in her lighted muscles, she

pauses before each pitch, then rears and throws
the ball against the darkness, venomously.

The interlocking stones cry out and hurl
the black globe back, all human purpose stript   10
from its wild passage, and the bounding girl
bolts in and out of darkness, after it.

Stumbling in the shadows, scalded blind
each time she whirls to face the sunlight, she
at last restores the pattern of her mind.
But every ball's more difficult to see.

(1962)   (1970)

Daughter of Zion

Seeing the bloodless lips, the ugly knot of salt-coloured hair,
the shapeless housedress with its grotesque flowers
like those printed on the wallpaper in cheap rooming houses,
sadder than if she wore black,

observing how she tries to avoid the sun,
crossing the street with eyes cast down
as though such fierce light were an indecent spectacle:
if darkness could be bought like yard goods
she would stuff her shopping bag with shadows,

noting all this and more,   10
who would look at her twice?
What stranger would suspect that only last night
in a tent by the river,
in the aisles between the rows
of rough planks laid on kitchen chairs,
before an altar of orange crates,
in the light of a kerosene lantern,
God Himself, the Old One, seized her in his arms and lifted her up
        and danced with her,
and Christ, with the sawdust clinging to his garments and   20
        the sweat of the carpenter's shop

on his body and the smell of wine and garlic on his breath,
drew her to his breast and kissed her,

and the Holy Ghost
went into her body and spoke through her mouth
the language they speak in heaven!

(1967)   (1967)

For Jean Vincent d'Abbadie,
Baron St.-Castin

Take heart, monsieur, four-fifths of this province
is still much as you left it: forest, swamp and barren.
Even now, after three hundred years, your enemies
        fear ambush, huddle by coasts and rivers,
the dark woods at their backs.

        Oh, you'd laugh to see
how old Increase Mather and his ghastly Calvinists
patrol the palisades, how they bury their money
under the floors of their hideous churches
lest you come again in the night   10
with the red ochre mark of the sun god
on your forehead, you exile from the Pyrenees,
        you baron of France and Navarre,
you squaw man, you Latin poet,
        you war chief of Penobscot
and of Kennebec and of Maliseet!

        At the winter solstice
your enemies cry out in their sleep
and the great trees throw back their heads and shout
        nabujcol!   20
Take heart, monsieur,
even the premier, even the archbishop,
even the poor gnome-like slaves
at the all-night diner and the service station
will hear you chant

The Song of Roland
as you cross yourself
and reach for your scalping knife.

(1967)   (1967)

The Fresh-Ploughed Hill

The fresh-ploughed hill slopes down to the sky.
Therefore, the sower,
broadcasting his seed, runs
faster and faster.

Bounding like a stone
the skirts of his coat
straight out behind him.

See how he falls, clawing
at the earth —
nor will let go   10
but still clutches
dirt in his fists, rolling
into the bright depths of the sun.

(1967)   (1967)

Hymn to Dionysus

The trick is to loose
        the wild bear
                but hold tight
to the chain,
        woe
                when the bear
snatches up
        the links
                and the man dances.

(1969)   (1969)

Canadian January Night

Ice storm: the hill
a pyramid of black crystal
down which the cars
slide like phosphorescent beetles
while I, walking backwards in obedience
to the wind, am possessed
of the fearful knowledge
my compatriots share
but almost never utter:
this is a country   10
where a man can die
                simply from being
caught outside.

(1971)   (1971)

Marriage

After seven years
I've almost succeeded
in freeing my wife
from her ludicrous fear
of electrical storms.

Tonight she parted
the curtains to watch
the lightning burst open
like an enormous golden
flower, consume itself, die   10
to the accompaniment
of the sound the sky might
make if it were
solid and could be
cracked open from
horizon to zenith.

And I flinched.

After seven years.

That much of her
implanted in me.   20

(1974)   (1974)

A Pinch or Two of Dust

— The dust being from Culloden, Scotland, where, in a battle fought in 1746,
the last of the great Celtic societies was extinguished.

A friend has given me
a pinch or two of dust,
an ounce at most of soil
from a field where our ancestors,
his and mine, were ploughed into
the compost bed of history, a people
who had outlived their gods,
the last of the old barbarians
destroyed by the first of the new,
magnificent fools who threw   10
stones and handfuls of earth
at the gunners until they themselves
became part of that earth and thereby
made it theirs for ever,
their blood indistinguishable now
from it, their blood contained
in this pinch or two of dust
as in my body and the body
of the friend who gave it
— this soil not only between   20
but within
my fingers, a part of
the very cells that shape this poem.

(1974)   (1974)

A Call in December

WE STOPPED AT the DeLaGarde shack. Not even tarpapered, this one: naked boards the colour of a Canadian winter, the log sills set on an island of yellowish ice.

"See that ice?" the old man asked disgustedly. "They built that shack right smack in the middle of a bog hole. Could have built it anywhere. But they built it in a bog hole. What you gonna do for that kind of people?"

At that time we were taking them Christmas gifts: twenty-four pounds of flour, a roast of beef, two packages of margarine.

The old man didn't knock. He walked into the shack and I followed him. I coughed, meeting the fumes of coal oil and the acrid smoke of green maple. Coal oil has to be poured on such wood frequently or the fire will succumb to the moisture and fizzle out.

The girl slumped on the open oven door, clutching a bundle shrouded in a dirty flannel blanket. Greasy black hair like a tangle of snarled shoe laces fell to her sloping shoulders.

She looked up at us, grinning. Her eyes narrowed suddenly, became fox-like and suspicious. The grin vanished. She bent down quickly, the hair flopping over her face, and kissed the hidden baby.

"Mummy loves you," she crooned. "Mummy won't let nobody take her baby."

The old man laid the margarine on the bed. There were neither pillows, quilts nor blankets on the bed: a pile of limp, nauseating rags, crumpled undershirts, socks, scarves, slips, shirts, sweaters, an army tunic, gathered together like a nest so that one knew without being told that something alive had slept there.

"Brought you a little somethin' from the Christmas tree in town," the old man said, shuffling in embarrassment, but also proud of what he had done and desirous of thanks.

She looked up again.

"Gee. Thanks," she giggled, her eyes soft and remote as a heifer's.

I put the flour and meat on the table, shoving aside plates which had gone unwashed so long that the scraps of food cemented to them had become unrecognizable, ceasing to be bits of bean or shreds of sardine or flecks of mustard and becoming simply dirt, obscene and anonymous.

"Billy's gone to work," she explained. "Ain't nobody here but me and the baby."

She drew the blankets back from the child's face and kissed his forehead fervently. He lay motionless, his eyes flat and unfocused, only his dull white face protruding from the stained pink flannel.

"Mummy loves you, baby. Oh yes, Mummy loves you. Yes. Mummy loves you. Mummy won't let nobody take her baby away. Mummy's gonna keep her little baby forever and ever. Yes. Mummy's gonna keep her little baby ... ain't nobody gonna take my baby."

Her voice trailed away in a wordless chant. She kissed him again and again, the moisture of her spittle glistening on his cheeks, neck and forehead, his eyes unreachable.

"Glad to hear Billy's workin'," the old man said.

He glanced down at the baby.

"Little feller looks kinda peaked," he said.

Her head jerked up, tossing the hair back.

"What you mean?" she shrilled, her voice pregnant with terror and warning, like a cornered animal's.

"Didn't mean nothin'," the old man soothed her. "Just said he looks a little peaked, that's all."

"Ain't nobody gonna take my baby."

She turned back to the child and repeated the ritual of kisses, smothering him, moaning.

"Ain't nobody gonna take my baby," she whispered. "Ain't nobody gonna take my little baby away from me."

The old man looked at me and winked and shook his head as if he were listening to a story and was not yet sure whether it was supposed to be sad or funny.

"Ain't nobody gonna take my baby," she whispered.

I looked around the room. The bed. The stove. The table. A chair without a back. Corrugated cardboard nailed to the walls to keep out the wind and prevent the snow from sifting in through the cracks. Three pictures: Jesus Christ, Queen Elizabeth II, Elizabeth Taylor. I winked back at the old man, wanting to laugh and wanting to cry and strangely ashamed that I could not choose between tears and laughter.

"Ain't nobody gonna take my baby," she reiterated with the single-mindedness found in birds, children and the insane.

"We ain't from the welfare, Rita," the old man said.

She looked up again.

"You ain't?"

"No. We just come to bring you this stuff ... just a few little things from the Christmas tree in town. Just some stuff to help you out a little bit at Christmas time."

She giggled and hid her head.

"Ain't nobody gonna take my baby."

"Hope not, Rita," the old man said. "Hope not."

I looked down at the floor. Rough boards laid on the ground, the ice visible through the cracks. Pieces of bark. Bits of something that may once have been intended for food. A crust of stale bread. A broken shoe lace. Two empty sardine cans, their tops drawn back like the open mouths of crocodiles. Beer bottle caps. Bits of tinfoil and cellophane.

"Well. Merry Christmas, Rita," the old man said, turning to the door.

"Merry Christmas," I echoed.

"Same to yourself," Rita replied, her voice muffled in the baby's blanket. Once again she was drowning the baby in kisses.

We went outside and shut the door behind us. Rita's voice rose, making certain we could hear.

"Ain't nobody gonna take my baby," she crooned.

We edged gingerly across the yellowish ice and climbed back into the stationwagon.

The old man settled back in his seat and lit his pipe.

"Why in hell does a man have to build his house in a bog hole?" he demanded angrily.

(1968)   (1968)

Joe Rosenblatt
1933 –

———◆———

JOE ROSENBLATT WAS born in Toronto where he now teaches and edits the magazine *Dialog*. His collections of poems include *The Voyage of the Mood* (1964), *The LSD Leacock* (1966), *Winter of the Luna Moth* (1968), *Vampires and Virgins* (1975) and *Top Soil* (1976) for which he received a Governor General's Award.

Heliotrope

Heliotropism: The tendency of certain
plants and other organisms to turn or
bend under the influence of sunlight.

In the hospital ward
you react to sunlight
lifting your fingers every hour
to trap the helio flies —
as they hover above
the burning oranges on the table.
And now, with each hour moving
like a slow camel
in the dryness of your bones,
you observe   10
how every object in the room
is still like clay —
only you turning
as a heliotrope
in a flower pot

(1966)   (1966)

Uncle Nathan Speaking from
Landlocked Green

Wide, wide are the margins of sleep
deep, deep, deep in the flowerbox earth
I sleep ... sleep ... sleep ...
In Carp's ethereal tabernacle
micron lips crackle
spirit embryos gestate
grow jinx wings, umbilical fins, slit gills
cold heart, lung, and lizard's spine
as from a cyanide back bone
flux of shadows strum ... spiritons   10
from Death's encrusted harp.

Nephew, in this world
no dust remains, no nickle photos of our bones.
We are beyond dust
where spiritons and atoms hum
around a perfect planetary sun.
– such is spectral sex –
from worm to fluorescent penetrant
in the grave, we all swing polar umbra.
Oye, so vengeful is Death's metamorphosis   20
that I go reincarnated in a minnow's whisper
who once dwelt as a barbaric fishmonger;
and now who can measure my sad physique?

or catch my whisper on a spectrograph.
Yet more soul pinching than worm's acetylene:
There is no commerce in the Netherworld.
Earth Momma, forgive me
for every fish I disembowelled was a child;
there is no Kaddish for aborted caviar.

Earth! Earth! is the bitch still green   30
liced with people and Aardvark powers?
And my shop on Baldwin street
does it stand? ... damp and sacred as the Wailing Wall
under the caterpillar'd canopy of God?
or has my neighbour swallowed up my Carp shrined enterprise
where I cradled images from Lake Genneserat
to fish fertiled ladies with halvah tongues
who shred my serpents into shrimp bread,
for fish food oscillates an old maid's chromosomes!
Carp, pickerel, transmogrified   40
where swimmers have been tranquilized
stomach's the body's palpitating madrigal.
God bless the primate's primeval stretch
but O to touch ... touch ...
a moon's vibration of a silver dollar
to see the fish scales rise and fall
before Lent's locust of Friday's carnivores.
Nephew, heaven is on Earth; above me
the sky is smiling like a White fish.
Its eyes are the moon and the sun.   50

(1968)   (1976)

Balloon Flowers

In the greenhouse
I'm staring down at pregnancies; tiny zeppelins –
skins: leopard
      clotted
          – soul's orgasm – bal
                loon flowers

                I reach out to touch
                I tickle their ear lobes
                rub the triggers
                of each   10
                    balloon flower, they
                    don't complain, but
                    blush out
                    at my fingers, o
                    what distilled
                    manures & minerals
                    nourished
                    these
                    air
                    brothels   20
                    I'm staring at bellies
                    clotted with leopard:
                    zeppelins swelling out
                    happy
                    pregnancies.   ALIEN
                    GLANDS,
                    they are not of this planet
                    these pregnancies: I touch
                    touch
                    fungus dreams, touch
                    passions of leopard   30
                    painted
                    on
                    blood
                    blood

                    blood

                                        (1976)

(1972)

Extraterrestrial Bumblebee

i wish i were a bumblebee
i wish i were
an
extra
terrestrial
bumblebee
building flowers, or
locked in th' greenhouse
of my senses...
leaden eyes   10
heavy, heavy heavy heavy
o the body sings
vvvvvvvvvvvvvvvv
zzzzzzzzzzzzzzzz
th' soul weaves in, & out
th' soul weaves in, & out
th' bumblebee pays th' Passion Lily a visit
every moment is an afternoon
every moment is an afternoon
th' soul is in a full eclipse   20
th' soul is in a full eclipse, th' bumblebee is dark, is dark
o th' soul is in a full eclipse, th' bumblebee is dark, is dark
is dark, oooooooooooooooo

        th' bumblebee is dark
        th' bumblebee is dark
        th' sun is melted in th' wings
        th' bumblebee
        th' sun is melted in th' wings
        th' bumblebee
        is dark, is dark, is dark, is dark   30
        hummmmmmmmmmm
        th' sun is in th' lunchpails
        th' sun is in th' lunchpails
        of th' bumblebee
        of th' bumblebee
        th' sun is in th' lunchpails, o
        praise th' pollen
        in th' lunchpails
        of th' bumblebee
        he grabs th' pollen of th' sun   40

                    th' sun is in th' lunchpails
                    praise th' pollen in th' lunchpails, vvvvv
                    th' lovely bumblebee, th' lovely bumblebee
shifts his gears, hums, & drives
in th' ocean highways of th' sun, th' breezes
th' breezes carry him
with his lunchpails
lift th' animal up
with lunchpails
into suburbia   50
th' animal hum
th' bumblebee hum
th' bumblebee hummmmmmmm
th' bumblebee hum
th' bumblebee hum
th' bumblebee hum
hummmmmmmmmm
th' bumblebee wears a pilot helmet
his vision is blurred
th' pressure of compound eyes   60
th' pressure
26,000 eyes, 26,000 eyes
in each eyeball
his vision is blurred
hexagons, hexagons, o th' pressure, th' pressure
th' bumblebee, th' bumblebee drives
in th' ocean highways of th' sun
with his pollen lunchpails
& th' Passion Lilies cry out to him
'HURRY   70
            HURRY
        WE'RE CHOKING WITH POLLEN'

wet fingers hold th' pollen up to him
'O WE'RE SO DAMNED FERTILE', cry th' Passion Lilies
            'GET RID OF TH' LOADS,
            YOU DUMB BUZZ ANIMAL'

Bzzzzzzzzzzzzzzzzzzzzzzzzzzzzzzzzzzzz
sing th' bumblebee
        shifting his gears
        moving forward   80
                    forward

over th' grieving
passion lilies
fertile
fertile
knocked up
passion lilies
th' bumblebee brushes away th' pollen
brushes away th' pollen
into th' lunchpails   90
into th' lunchpails
lunchpails
into th' lunchpails
religious
golden
pollen
th' Midas
bread
O th' bumblebee's th' soul
of a mole   100
burrows into th' throat
into Mother Nature's tenement
& th' Passion Lilies cry
'HE'S COME TO COLLECT
TH' RENT'

th' animal is seduced
all that colour, all that texture
physical animal
taste th' Passion Lily
lick th' Passion Lily   110
draw th' tongue in
draw th' tongue out
& th' Passion Lily
taste th' bumblebee
draw th' tongues in
draw th' tongues out
taste, taste
'here's th' fertile powder,' cry the white
flower
'here's th' burden
here's th' rent ...'   120

(1972)   (1976)

Of Dandelions & Tourists

Dandelions purr in their sleep.
The hillside is dotted with yellow cubs:
compromises of cat & gladiola.
They sway adagio; juices in the tubes
catch tigers & spiders; ghosts go into analysis
& meow of surplus love
to the earth alive with blissful fur.

(1972)   (1976)

The Bird of the Highest Place

That myth is made of birds, giants
above the clouds, above ledges of the mind
is the core of the senses, the travelogue

where we desire to be placed inside a landscape
creeping with warm oblivion, birds in their obscure eggs
on time-worn nests crouched in branches, dead leaves —

black supernatural birds with steely eyes
the wing span over the acres of our fear

the supremacy of bird. The suzerain terror
lording it over the intellect of man   10
because the bird is rare, uncommon, & clever.

It will breakfast under the skull of simple intruders
those who dare wander into the immensity of its domicile
the mental arboretum of presentiment, our failures.

If we desire, then the creature is a carnivorous lover
of humankind, the sensitive devourer who cares
about the meat it plucks from the frame of imagination.

Invention will build bigger & better birds
more mechanized with cruelty, to strike a deeper chord
into the imbeciles of the robot armies moving into the swamp.   20

The health is with the giant bird, ageless, virile
in its destructive beauty, the whirr of wings, the claws
cutting cleanly the mortal coils of mortal fools.

(1975)   (1975)

Tragedy

Dressed in a tiny
unconventional
dinner jacket
of yellow and black
a bee is drawn to a magnetic blossom

and drowns in the nectar.

Yet more tragic is the case
of the silent butterfly
who left an imprint
of a sun-spot with wings   10
on a page

when I closed the book.

(1976)   (1976)

Leonard Cohen
1934 –

———◆———

BORN IN MONTREAL, Leonard Cohen studied at McGill and Columbia Universities. Since the appearance of his first volume of poetry, *Let Us Compare Mythologies* (1956), he has published several collections including *The Spice Box of Earth* (1961), *Flowers for Hitler* (1964) and *The Energy of Slaves* (1972). During the 1960s, Cohen published two novels, *The Favourite Game* (1963) and *Beautiful Losers* (1966), and began a successful career as a popular composer and singer.

The Sparrows

Catching winter in their carved nostrils
the traitor birds have deserted us,
leaving only the dullest brown sparrows
for spring negotiations.

I told you we were fools
to have them in our games,
but you replied:
    They are only wind-up birds
who strut on scarlet feet
so hopelessly far
from our curled fingers.

I had moved to warn you,
but you only adjusted your hair
and ventured:
    Their wings are made of glass and gold
and we are fortunate
not to hear them splintering
against the sun.

10

Now the hollow nests
sit like tumors or petrified blossoms   20
between the wire branches
and you, an innocent scientist,
question me on these brown sparrows:
whether we should plant our yards with breadcrumbs
or mark them with the black, persistent crows
whom we hate and stone.

But what shall I tell you of migrations
when in this empty sky
the precise ghosts of departed summer birds
still trace old signs;   30
or of desperate flights
when the dimmest flutter of a coloured wing
excites all our favourite streets
to delight in imaginary spring.

(1956)   (1968)

Prayer for Sunset

The sun is tangled
        in black branches,
raving like Absolom
        between sky and water,
struggling through the dark terebinth
to commit its daily suicide.

Now, slowly, the sea consumes it,
leaving a glistening wound
        on the water,
        a red scar on the horizon;   10
In darkness
        I set out for home,
terrified by the clash of wind on grass,
and the victory cry of weeds and water.

Is there no Joab for tomorrow night,
    with three darts
    and a great heap of stones?

(1956)   (1968)

Beneath My Hands

Beneath my hands
your small breasts
are the upturned bellies
of breathing fallen sparrows.

Wherever you move
I hear the sounds of closing wings
of falling wings.

I am speechless
because you have fallen beside me
because your eyelashes   10
are the spines of tiny fragile animals.

I dread the time
when your mouth
begins to call me hunter.

When you call me close
to tell me
your body is not beautiful
I want to summon
the eyes and hidden mouths
of stone and light and water   20
to testify against you.

I want them
to surrender before you
the trembling rhyme of your face
from their deep caskets.

When you call me close
to tell me
your body is not beautiful
I want my body and my hands
to be pools   30
for your looking and laughing.

(1961)   (1968)

As the Mist Leaves No Scar

As the mist leaves no scar
On the dark green hill,
So my body leaves no scar
On you, nor ever will.

When wind and hawk encounter,
What remains to keep?
So you and I encounter,
Then turn, then fall to sleep.

As many nights endure
Without a moon or star,   10
So will we endure
When one is gone and far.

(1961)   (1968)

For Anne

With Annie gone,
Whose eyes to compare
With the morning sun?

Not that I did compare,
But I do compare
Now that she's gone.

(1961)   (1968)

For E.J.P.

I once believed a single line
        in a Chinese poem could change
            forever how blossoms fell
and that the moon itself climbed on
        the grief of concise weeping men
            to journey over cups of wine
I thought invasions were begun for crows
        to pick at a skeleton
            dynasties sown and spent
to serve the language of a fine lament
        I thought governors ended their lives
            as sweetly drunken monks
telling time by rain and candles
        instructed by an insect's pilgrimage

10

across the page — all this
so one might send an exile's perfect letter
to an ancient home-town friend

I chose a lonely country
    broke from love
        scorned the fraternity of war   20
I polished my tongue against the pumice moon
    floated my soul in cherry wine
        a perfumed barge for Lords of Memory
to languish on to drink to whisper out
    their store of strength
        as if beyond the mist along the shore
their girls their power still obeyed
    like clocks wound for a thousand years
I waited until my tongue was sore

Brown petals wind like fire around my poems   30
    I aimed them at the stars but
        like rainbows they were bent
before they sawed the world in half
    Who can trace the canyoned paths
        cattle have carved out of time
wandering from meadowlands to feasts
    Layer after layer of autumn leaves
        are swept away
Something forgets us perfectly

(1964)   (1968)

Another Night with Telescope

Come back to me
            brutal empty room
Thin Byzantine face
        preside over this new fast
I am broken with easy grace
Let me be neither
            father nor child
but one who spins
on an eternal unimportant loom
        patterns of wars and grass   10
which do not last the night
            I know the stars
are wild as dust
and wait for no man's discipline
            but as they wheel
from sky to sky they rake
        our lives with pins of light

(1964)   (1968)

From
The Energy of Slaves

[I am invisible to night]

I am invisible to night
Only certain shy women see me
All my hideous days of visibility
I longed for their smiles
Now they lean out of their shabby
plans-for-the-evening
so we may salute one another
Sisters of mine
of my own shattered people

going after third-choice lovers   10
they smile at me to indicate
that we can never meet
as long as we permit
this order of things to persist
in which we are the wretched ones

[I walk through the old yellow sunlight]

I walk through the old yellow sunlight
to get to my kitchen table
the poem about me
lying there with the books
in which I am listed
among the dead and future Dylans

You can understand
I am in no hurry to make the passage
The sunlight is old and yellow
a flood of what I laboured   10
to distill a tiny drop of
in that shabby little laboratory
called my talent

I stand here dreaming in my sweat
(you would fall in love with me again)
dreaming of a tie a shirt
a white suit a life
a new life in a warm city
far from the envious practice
of written speech   20

O look what the summer
has done to the daisies in my yard
Their skeletons must look like scrap and junk
to many lovers of the cabbage
(and to be perfectly fair
even to many lovers of the daisy)

Overheard on Every Corner

Sometimes I remember
that I have been chosen
to perfect all men
       the fireflies remind me
the stream beside my shack
If I was meant to be a poet
       I would not be able to blow
the actual flawless smokerings
for which I am renowned
       I would be distracted   10
by the possible beauty of my pen
but I am not
       I would lose myself
I would have lost myself
with the women
I so relentlessly pursued
but I did not
       I was meant to be
the seed of your new society
       I was meant to be   20
the courtless invisible king
I am that
the clearest example of royalty
who serves you tonight
       as he makes a bed for the dog
and the fireflies burn
at their different heights

(1972)   (1972)

Rudy Wiebe
1934 –

BORN NEAR FAIRHOLME, Saskatchewan, Rudy Wiebe was raised in a
Mennonite community in Alberta. He was educated at Mennonite
schools and colleges and earned an M.A. at the University of Alberta
where he now teaches. Since the appearance of his first novel, *Peace
Shall Destroy Many* (1964), he has published several novels and short
stories including *First and Vital Candle* (1966), *The Blue Mountains of
China* (1970), *The Temptations of Big Bear* (1973) and *Where Is the Voice
Coming From?* (1974). "Where Is the Voice Coming From" first ap-
peared in *The Narrative Voice* (1972), a collection of stories edited by
John Metcalf.

Where Is the Voice
Coming From?

THE PROBLEM IS to make the story.

One difficulty of this making may have been excellently stated by
Teilhard de Chardin: "We are continually inclined to isolate ourselves
from the things and events which surround us ... as though we were
spectators, not elements, in what goes on." Arnold Toynbee does
venture, "For all that we know, Reality is the undifferentiated unity of
the mystical experience," but that need not here be considered. This
story ended long ago; it is one of finite acts, of orders, of elemental
feelings and reactions, of obvious legal restrictions and requirements.

Presumably all the parts of the story are themselves available. A
difficulty is that they are, as always, available only in bits and pieces.
Though the acts themselves seem quite clear, some written reports of
the acts contradict each other. As if these acts were, at one time, too well
known; as if the original nodule of each particular fact had from

somewhere received non-factual accretions; or even more, as if, since the basic facts were so clear perhaps there were a larger number of facts than any one reporter, or several, or even any reporter had ever attempted to record. About facts that are still simply told by this mouth to that ear, of course, even less can be expected.

An affair seventy-five years old should acquire some of the shiny transparency of an old man's skin. It should.

Sometimes it would seem that it would be enough – perhaps more than enough – to hear the names only. The grandfather One Arrow; the mother Spotted Calf; the father Sounding Sky; the wife (wives rather, but only one of them seems to have a name, though their fathers are Napaise, Kapahoo, Old Dust, The Rump) – the one wife named, of all things, Pale Face; the cousin Going-Up-To-Sky; the brother-in-law (again, of all things) Dublin. The names of the police sound very much alike; they all begin with Constable or Corporal or Sergeant, but here and there an Inspector, then a Superintendent and eventually all the resonance of an Assistant Commissioner echoes down. More. Herself: Victoria, by the Grace of God etc., etc., QUEEN, defender of the Faith, etc., etc.; and witness "Our Right Trusty and Right Well-beloved Cousin and Councillor the Right Honorable Sir John Campbell Hamilton-Gordon, Earl of Aberdeen; Viscount Formartine, Baron Haddo, Methlic, Tarves and Kellie, in the Peerage of Scotland; Viscount Gordon of Aberdeen, County of Aberdeen, in the Peerage of the United Kingdom; Baronet of Nova Scotia, Knight Grand Cross of Our Most Distinguished Order of Saint Michael and Saint George, etc., Governor General of Canada". And of course himself: in the award proclamation named "Jean-Baptiste" but otherwise known only as Almighty Voice.

But hearing cannot be enough; not even hearing all the thunder of A Proclamation: "Now Hear Ye that a reward of FIVE HUNDRED DOLLARS will be paid to any person or persons who will give such information as will lead ... (etc., etc.) this Twentieth day of April, in the year of Our Lord one thousand eight hundred and ninety-six, and the Fifty-ninth year of Our Reign..." etc. and etc.

Such hearing cannot be enough. The first item to be seen is the piece of white bone. It is almost triangular, slightly convex – concave actually as it is positioned at this moment with its corners slightly raised – graduating from perhaps a strong eighth to a weak quarter of an inch in thickness, its scattered pore structure varying between larger and smaller on its perhaps polished, certainly shiny surface. Precision is difficult since the glass showcase is at least thirteen inches deep and therefore an eye cannot be brought as close as the minute inspection of such a small, though certainly quite adequate, sample of skull would normally require. Also, because of the position it cannot be determined whether the several hairs, well over a foot long, are still in some manner attached or not.

The seven-pounder cannon can be seen standing almost shyly between the showcase and the interior wall. Officially it is known as a gun, not a cannon, and clearly its bore is not large enough to admit a large man's fist. Even if it can be believed that this gun was used in the 1885 Rebellion and that on the evening of Saturday, May 29, 1897 (while the nine-pounder, now unidentified, was in the process of arriving with the police on the special train from Regina), seven shells (all that were available in PrinceAlbert at that time) from it were sent shrieking into the poplar bluffs as night fell, clearly such shelling could not and would not disembowel the whole earth. Its carriage is now nicely lacquered, the perhaps oak spokes of its petite wheels (little higher than a knee) have been recently scraped, puttied and varnished; the brilliant burnish of its brass breeching testifies with what meticulous care charmen and women have used nationally-advertised cleaners and restorers.

Though it can also be seen, even a careless glance reveals that the same concern has not been expended on the one (of two) .44 calibre 1866 model Winchesters apparently found at the last in the pit with Almighty Voice. It also is preserved in a glass case; the number 1536735 is still, though barely, distinguishable on the brass cartridge section just below the brass saddle ring. However, perhaps because the case was imperfectly sealed at one time (though sealed enough not to warrant disturbance now), or because of simple neglect, the rifle is obviously spotted here and there with blotches of rust and the brass itself reveals discolorations almost like mildew. The rifle bore, the three long strands of hair themselves, actually bristle with clots of dust. It may be that this museum cannot afford to be as concerned as the other; conversely, the disfiguration may be something inherent in the items themselves.

The small building which was the police guardroom at Duck Lake, Saskatchewan Territory, in 1895 may also be seen. It had subsequently been moved from its original place and used to house small animals, chickens perhaps, or pigs – such as a woman might be expected to have under her responsibility. It is, of course, now perfectly empty, and clean so that the public may enter with no more discomfort than a bend under the doorway and a heavy encounter with disinfectant. The door-jamb has obviously been replaced; the bar network at one window is, however, said to be original; smooth still, very smooth. The logs inside have been smeared again and again with whitewash, perhaps paint, to an insistent point of identity-defying characterlessness. Within the small rectangular box of these logs not a sound can be heard from the streets of the, probably dead, town.

Hey Injun you'll get hung for stealing that steer
Hey Injun for killing that government cow you'll get three weeks on the
woodpile Hey Injun

The place named Kinistino seems to have disappeared from the map but the Minnechinass Hills have not. Whether they have ever been on a map is doubtful but they will, of course, not disappear from the landscape as long as the grass grows and the rivers run. Contrary to general report and belief, the Canadian prairies are rarely, if ever, flat and the Minnechinass (spelled five different ways and translated some-times as "The Outside Hill", sometimes as "Beautiful Bare Hills") are dissimilar from any other of the numberless hills that everywhere block out the prairie horizon. They are bare; poplars lie tattered along their tops, almost black against the straw-pale grass and sharp green against the grey soil of the plowing laid in half-mile rectangular blocks upon their western slopes. Poles holding various wires stick out of the fields, back down the bend of the valley; what was once a farmhouse is weathering into the cultivated earth. The poplar bluff where Almighty Voice made his stand has, of course, disappeared.

The policeman he shot and killed (not the ones he wounded, of course) are easily located. Six miles east, thirty-nine miles north in Prince Albert, the English Cemetery. Sergeant Colin Campbell Cole-brook, North West Mounted Police Registration Number 605, lies pre-sumably under a gravestone there. His name is seventeenth in a very long "list of non-commissioned officers and men who have died in the service since the inception of the force." The date is October 29, 1895, and the cause of death is anonymous: "Shot by escaping Indian pris-oner near Prince Albert." At the foot of this grave are two others: Constable John R. Kerr, No. 3040, and Corporal C. H. S. Hockin, No. 3106. Their cause of death on May 28, 1897 is even more anonymous, but the place is relatively precise: "Shot by Indians at Min-etch-inass Hills, Prince Albert District."

The gravestone, if he has one, of the fourth man Almighty Voice killed is more difficult to locate. Mr. Ernest Grundy, postmaster of Duck Lake in 1897, apparently shut his window the afternoon of Friday, May 28, armed himself, rode east twenty miles, participated in the second charge into the bluff at about 6:30 p.m., and on the third sweep of that charge was shot dead at the edge of the pit. It would seem that he thereby contributed substantially not only to the Indians' bullet supply, but his clothing warmed them as well.

The burial place of Dublin and Going-Up-To-Sky is unknown, as is the grave of Almighty Voice. It is said that a Métis named Henry Smith lifted the latter's body from the pit in the bluff and gave it to Spotted Calf. The place of burial is not, of course, of ultimate significance. A gravestone is always less evidence than a triangular piece of skull, provided it is large enough.

Whatever further evidence there is to be gathered may rest on pictures. There are, presumably, almost numberless pictures of the policemen in the case, but the only one with direct bearing is one of Sergeant Colebrook who apparently insisted on advancing to complete an arrest after being warned three times that if he took another step he would be shot. The picture must have been taken before he joined the force; it reveals him a large-eared young man, hair brush-cut and ascot tie, his eyelids slightly drooping, almost hooded under thick brows. Unfortunately a picture of Constable R. C. Dickson, into whose charge Almighty Voice was apparently committed in that guardroom and who after Colebrook's death was convicted of negligence, sentenced to two months hard labour and discharged, does not seem to be available.

There are no pictures to be found of either Dublin (killed early by rifle fire) or Going-Up-To-Sky (killed in the pit), the two teen-age boys who gave their ultimate fealty to Almighty Voice. There is, however, one said to be of Almighty Voice, Junior. He may have been born to Pale Face during the year, two hundred and twenty-one days that his father was a fugitive. In the picture he is kneeling before what could be a tent, he wears striped denim overalls and displays twin babies whose sex cannot be determined from the double-laced dark bonnets they wear. In the supposed picture of Spotted Calf and Sounding Sky, Sounding Sky stands slightly before his wife; he wears a white shirt and a striped blanket folded over his left shoulder in such a manner that the arm in which he cradles a long rifle cannot be seen. His head is thrown back; the rim of his hat appears as a black half-moon above eyes that are pressed shut in, as it were, profound concentration; above a mouth clenched thin in a downward curve. Spotted Calf wears a long dress, a sweater which could also be a man's dress coat, and a large fringed and embroidered shawl which would appear distinctly Dukhobour in origin if the scroll patterns on it were more irregular. Her head is small and turned slightly towards her husband so as to reveal her right ear. There is what can only be called a quizzical expression on her crumpled face; it may be she does not understand what is happening and that she would have asked a question, perhaps of her husband, perhaps of the photographers, perhaps even of anyone, anywhere in the world if such questioning were possible for an Indian lady.

There is one final picture. That is one of Almighty Voice himself. At least it is purported to be of Almighty Voice himself. In the Royal Canadian Mounted Police Museum on the Barracks Grounds just off Dewdney Avenue in Regina, Saskatchewan, it lies in the same showcase, as a matter of fact immediately beside, that triangular piece of skull. Both are unequivocally labelled, and it must be assumed that a police force with a world-wide reputation would not label *such* evidence incorrectly. But here emerges an ultimate problem in making the story.

There are two official descriptions of Almighty Voice. The first reads: "Height about five feet, ten inches, slight build, rather good looking, a sharp hooked nose with a remarkably flat point. Has a bullet scar on the left side of his face about 1 1/2 inches long running from near corner of mouth towards ear. The scar cannot be noticed when his face is painted but otherwise is plain. Skin fair for an Indian." The second description is on the Award Proclamation: "About twenty-two years old, five feet ten inches in height, weight about eleven stone, slightly erect, neat small feet and hands; complexion inclined to be fair, wavy dark hair to shoulders, large dark eyes, broad forehead, sharp features and parrot nose with flat tip, scar on left cheek running from mouth towards ear, feminine appearance."

So run the descriptions that were, presumably, to identify a well-known fugitive in so precise a manner that an informant could collect five hundred dollars — a considerable sum when a police constable earned between one and two dollars a day. The nexus of the problems appears when these supposed official descriptions are compared to the supposed official picture. The man in the picture is standing on a small rug. The fingers of his left hand touch a curved Victorian settee, behind him a photographer's backdrop of scrolled patterns merges to vaguely paradisiacal trees and perhaps a sky. The moccasins he wears make it impossible to deduce whether his feet are "neat small". He may be five feet, ten inches tall, may weigh eleven stone, he certainly is "rather good looking" and, though it is a frontal view, it may be that the point of his long and flaring nose could be "remarkably flat". The photograph is slightly over-illuminated and so the unpainted complexion could be "inclined to be fair"; however, nothing can be seen of a scar, the hair is not wavy and shoulder-length but hangs almost to the waist in two thick straight braids worked through with beads, fur, ribbons and cords. The right hand that holds the corner of the blanket-like coat in position is large and, even in the high illumination, heavily veined. The neck is concealed under coiled beads and the forehead seems more low than "broad".

Perhaps, somehow, these picture details could be reconciled with the official description if the face as a whole were not so devastating.

On a cloth-backed sheet two feet by two and one-half feet in size, under the Great Seal of the Lion and the Unicorn, dignified by the names of the Deputy of the Minister of Justice, the Secretary of State, the Queen herself and all the heaped detail of her "Right Trusty and Right Well Beloved Cousin", this description concludes: "feminine appearance". But the pictures: any face of history, any believed face that the world acknowledges as *man* — Socrates, Jesus, Attila, Genghis Khan, Mahatma Gandhi, Joseph Stalin — no believed face is more *man* than this face. The mouth, the nose, the clenched brows, the eyes — the eyes are large, yes, and dark, but even in this watered-down reproduction of unending reproductions of that original, a steady look into those eyes cannot be endured. It is a face like an axe.

It is now evident that the de Chardin statement quoted at the beginning has relevance only as it proves itself inadequate to explain what has happened. At the same time, the inadequacy of Aristotle's much more famous statement becomes evident: "The true difference [between the historian and the poet] is that one relates what *has* happened, the other what *may* happen." These statements cannot explain the storyteller's activity since, despite the most rigid application of impersonal investigation, the elements of the story have now run me aground. If ever I could, I can no longer pretend to objective, omnipotent disinterestedness. I am no longer *spectator* of what *has* happened or what *may* happen: I am become *element* in what is happening at this very moment.

For it is, of course, I myself who cannot endure the shadows on that paper which are those eyes. It is I who stand beside this broken veranda post where two corner shingles have been torn away, where barbed wire tangles the dead weeds on the edge of this field. The bluff that sheltered Almighty Voice and his two friends has not disappeared from the slope of the Minnechinass, no more than the sound of Constable Dickson's voice in that guardhouse is silent. The sound of his speaking is there even if it has never been recorded in an official report:

> *hey injun you'll get*
> *hung*
> *for stealing that steer*
> *hey injun for killing that government*
> *cow you'll get three*
> *weeks on the woodpile hey injun*

The unknown contradictory words about an unprovable act that move a boy to defiance, an implacable Cree warrior long after the three-hundred-and-fifty-year war is ended, a war already lost the day the Cree watch Cartier hoist his gun ashore at Hochelaga and they begin the long retreat west; these words of incomprehension, of threatened incomprehensible law are there to be heard just as the unmoving tableau of the three-day siege is there to be seen on the slopes of the Minnechinass. Sounding Sky is somewhere not there, under arrest, but Spotted Calf stands on a shoulder of the Hills a little to the left, her arms upraised to the setting sun. Her mouth is open. A horse rears, riderless, above the scrub willow at the edge of the bluff, smoke puffs, screams tangle in rifle barrage, there are wounds, somewhere. The bluff is so green this spring, it will not burn and the ragged line of seven police and two civilians is staggering through, faces twisted in rage, terror, and rifles sputter. Nothing moves. There is no sound of frogs in the night; twenty-seven policemen and five civilians stand in cordon at thirty-yard intervals and a body also lies in the shelter of a gully. Only a voice rises from the bluff:

> *We have fought well*
> *You have died like braves*
> *I have worked hard and am hungry*
> *Give me food*

but nothing moves. The bluff lies, a bright green island on the grassy slope surrounded by men hunched forward rigid over their long rifles, men clumped out of rifle-range, thirty-five men dressed as for fall hunting on a sharp spring day, a small gun positioned on a ridge above. A crow is falling out of the sky into the bluff, its feathers sprayed as by an explosion. The first gun and the second gun are in position, the beginning and end of the bristling surround of thirty-five Prince Albert Volunteers, thirteen civilians and fifty-six policemen in position relative to the bluff and relative to the unnumbered whites astride their horses, standing up in their carts, staring and pointing across the valley, in position relative to the bluff and the unnumbered Indians squatting silent along the higher ridges of the Hills, motionless mounds, faceless against the Sunday morning sunlight edging between and over them down along the tree tips, down into the shadows of the bluff. Nothing moves. Beside the second gun the red-coated officer has flung a handful of grass into the motionless air, almost to the rim of the red sun.

And there is a voice. It is an incredible voice that rises from among the young poplars ripped of their spring bark, from among the dead somewhere lying there, out of the arm-deep pit shorter than a man; a voice rises over the exploding smoke and thunder of guns that reel back in their positions, worked over, serviced by the grimed motionless men in bright coats and glinting buttons, a voice so high and clear, so unbelievably high and strong in its unending wordless cry.

The voice of "Gitchie-Manitou Wayo" – interpreted as "voice of the Great Spirit" – that is, The Almighty Voice. His death chant no less incredible in its beauty than in its incomprehensible happiness.

I say "wordless cry" because that is the way it sounds to me. I could be more accurate if I had a reliable interpreter who would make a reliable interpretation. For I do not, of course, understand the Cree myself.

(1974)   (1974)

George Bowering
1935 –

———◆———

BORN IN PENTICTON, British Columbia, George Bowering attended the
University of British Columbia where he was an editor of *Tish* (1961-
1969), one of the most important literary journals of the 1960s. He has
since taught at Sir George Williams University and Simon Fraser University. He has published short stories, a novel, a study of the poetry of
Al Purdy and many volumes of poetry including *Baseball* (1967), *Rocky
Mountain Foot* (1968), *The Gangs of Kosmos* (1969), *Touch: Selected Poems
1960 – 1970* (1971) and *The Catch* (1976).

Wattle

sticks & stones

you begin to build

       from moments
       of strictest energy
       upwards

   block on block
   letting your work in solid
   harden in the sun

begun you have passed the hardest part

       you now work   10
       knowing each block
             moves you

   more room under your feet
   closer
             moves you up

and you squeeze the thing together
from the half way point
to the end
building blocks

(sticks   wattle)   to meet each other   20

at the end

(1963)   (1963)

Grandfather

Grandfather
          Jabez Harry Bowering
strode across the Canadian prairie
hacking down trees
               & building churches
delivering personal baptist sermons in them
leading Holy holy holy lord god almighty songs in them
red haired man squared off in the pulpit
reading Saul on the road to Damascus at them

Left home   10
          big walled Bristol town
at age eight
          to make a living
buried his stubby fingers in root snarled earth
for a suit of clothes & seven hundred gruelly meals a year
taking an anabaptist cane across the back every day
for four years till he was whipt out of England

Twelve years old
               & across the ocean alone
to apocalyptic Canada   20
               Ontario of bone bending labor
six years on the road to Damascus till his eyes were blinded
with the blast of Christ & he wandered west
to Brandon among wheat kings & heathen Saturday nights
young red haired Bristol boy shoveling coal
in the basement of Brandon college five in the morning

Then built his first wooden church & married
a sick girl who bore two live children & died
leaving several pitiful letters & the Manitoba night

He moved west with another wife & built children & churches   30
Saskatchewan Alberta British Columbia Holy holy holy
lord god almighty
                struck his labored bones with pain
& left him a postmaster prodding grandchildren with crutches
another dead wife & a glass bowl of photographs
& holy books unopened save the bible by the bed

Till he died the day before his eighty fifth birthday
in a Catholic hospital of sheets white as his hair

(1964)   (1971)

Family

Was there power where I sprang from?
I wonder
       over the pondering of my past,
It must have begun with
              hairpants prowlers of an earlier
Angle Land.   Picts, Jutes, Scots, carrying my seeds over a foggy
Island.   Families of Og, joining me to the Dukes of
Happy Land.

          Rich man
          poor man   10
          beggar man

          thief

In the descent and climbing, a tangled rime of time.

I know there was a singer of hymns in the centuries
And a peerage visited upon us.
                And kings related and stories
Told by idiots in stone houses.
                Under thatched roofs, others——

Sibilant growing of the Church and Nation
                                        and the Clan.   20

To where we are, now.
                        No power but the delta of time.
No past unfogged on the Island.
                                No family but me.

(1964)   (1964)

For WCW

Language lifted
            out of the ordinary
                        into the illumination
of poetry.
                    Objects: sticks & stones
                            coming together
you place before
            our eyes
                        exposed bare to the weather
rained on &   10
            crackt dry in the sun

A stick a stone
            a river cutting thru clay
a white barn in a field
            a cat coiled
                on a box

Words
            coming together
                    moving at one another
traction for the tongue   20

                    Look at that!   American
language shouting
            across the Potomac

       ring coins over the river
open out western states
      — anywhere a man can
        hear his voice

     In the machines of Paterson
rattling ten million words a day
       a voice moves   30
           physical — not understood
    as lit-er-ary, but moving

       as a machine, with traction
    fitting itself against resistance

— Song understood by
       the banging ear

           II

A sparrow
balances in the wind

voicing song
into the shifting air

It is a small thing
but big as all creation

to its mate beside it
on the wire, balancing

The wind blows
the wire snaps underfoot   10

the feet hold
the feathers have no time

to compose themselves

It is
as it should be or
as it is

III

I heard he askt the excavators
             for a boulder
dumpt in his
             front yard

They must have thought
             he was some old nut

I mean you dig a boulder
             out of the ground you dont
leave it in your front yard

I mean what good is a big rock?
             all you can do
             is look at it
             or lean on it   10

I mean if you've got a lawn
             youve got to mow around
             the damn thing
             & clip the bloody grass

I mean I hear he used to be
             a doctor, what'd he do
with the gallstones he cut out
             put them on the bloody mantel?   20

IV

The descent beckons
             as the ascent beckoned
             I understand that

till the point of
             What now?
             He is dead gone forever

& to where
             Into that black which is
             blacker than the memory
of black?   10

It is as it should be
　　or as it is.

He is a part of the history
　　he brought poems together
　　　　clutcht out of chaos

he will be the reason
　　behid a language where
　　　　epics can be clutcht

he will be sticks & stones
　　hewer of wood   20
　　　　drawer of water

　　William
　　　　Carlos
　　　　　Williams

(1965)   (1971)

The Swing

Renoir's people
　　seem to stand
　　　　on a forest floor
of blossoms.

　　　　　The girl on the swing
could be fifteen, her dress
　　of new flowers.

　　　　　She leans coyly
or thoughtfully away
　　from the two men   10
　　　　with straw hats.

They are artists
　　on a Sunday afternoon
　　　　warm in loose clothing,

> some kind of wonder
>> for the child who
>>> makes the fourth figure.

> She is clasping her empty hands
>> in front of her, her head up,
>>> her eyes the only ones   20
>>> looking outward.

(1965)   (1965)

East to West

> Ho Lem
>> again alderman in Calgary,
> smiling celestial of ward action,
> a good deal
>> fatter than
> Ho Ling,
>> 1883,
>>> bent-legged pioneer,
>> Yang Tse muscles bent
> in slave labour to the   10
>> master steel

> CPR — binding East to West
>> slab after slab laid down
>> thru Rocky Mountains
>> steel bent by will
>> and bending

> till Vancouver
>> & steel-pushers left
>> along the track

>>> Ho Ling in Calgary,   20
>>> houseboy, kitchen help,

>>> instant adaptability
>>> of coolee brain

saving Kanadian nickels
buying pioneer shack
            later dusty Calgary's
            first laundry

beside Chang
            Kanadian Restaurant
            :specialty bacon 'n' eggs   30
            served by fifteen Chinese waiters

one of which died,
            Old Chang

            leaving savings, $100
            to Presbyterian hospital with no beds
                for old Chinamen.

Ho Chin,
            1931,
                    removed long queue,
entered Presbyterian church,   40
wheeled Christian punctual
                    vegetable wagon
behind aged Indian horse

exploded venerable imported fireworks
along Bow River
on his father's New Year

            entered Chinese Masonic Lodge,
            Chinese Nationalist League,
                weekend ski club.

Ho Lem,   50
            1963,
                    pronounces "Calgary"
        with no trouble,
    wears white ten gallon hat
a $100 suit
            of political advantage,

            votes for relocation
            of city railroad tracks.

(1968)   (1968)

The Egg

The egg sat on the workbench
for weeks, me passing it every day
in my search for tools, cobwebs,
five years old, looking for

the machines of life. The source
of life, I knew, as mysterious as
my mother's bedroom. I didn't touch
the egg for weeks, my brain resembling

its contours. Till the day came
I gave up waiting for the news, I   10
contrived to make it roll & fall
to the floor beside a rusted shovel.

Bending over, I knew first the
terrible stink, & then the quills
of light, bone, or fiber, it was
a wing never to be used. It's guilt

I carried for a year & then carried
lighter for more years, as if I
myself smelled, as if I had brought
those tender stinking wings to earth.   20

(1969)   (1971)

Weight

The voice comes from
cold prairie parades
& deaths
            over the wire
over the land, it is an old friend.

Twice I have shaken the flatland from my heels, that posture

sure to make me fall,
                the same care
& disorder in the poems   10
about the cold land
& the lump of ice
now only a bit
smaller in my chest.

That cage holds more than the soil
ingested those two times.
There are deep membranes have
suffered indelible change
not to be eliminated
in any sure-heel crouch.   20

I said an old friend
for no known reason.
              Maybe
we know friends in us not
out of liking, but
rather from carrying accretion,
weight,
         to be forgotten most
of the time, remembered with any
moment of exertion, a stitch   30
in the side, a voice
over the wire.

(1974)   (1974)

Pat Lowther
1935 – 1975

BORN IN VANCOUVER, Pat (Tinmuth) Lowther was co-chairman of the League of Canadian Poets when she was murdered in 1975. Three volumes of her poetry, *This Difficult Flowering* (1968), *The Age of the Bird* (1972) and *Milk Stone* (1974), were published before her death; a fourth collection, *A Stone Diary*, was published in 1977.

A Stone Diary

At the beginning I noticed
the huge stones on my path
I knew instinctively
why they were there
breathing as naturally
as animals
I moved them to ritual patterns
I abraded my hands
and made blood prints

Last week I became   10
aware of details
cubes of fool's gold
green and blue copper
crystal formations
fossils   shell casts
iron roses   candied gems

I thought of
the Empress Josephine,
the Burning of Troy

between her breasts,   20
of Ivan the Terrible lecturing
on the virtues of rubies.
They were dilettantes.

By the turn of the week
I was madly in love
with stone. Do you know
how beautiful it is
to embrace stone
to curve all your body
against its surfaces?   30

Yesterday I began
seeing you as
desirable as a stone
I imagined you coming
onto the path with me
even your mouth
a carved stone

Today for the first time
I noticed how coarse
my skin has grown   40
but the stones shine
with their own light,
they grow smoother
and smoother

(1977)   (1977)

Rumours of War

In my very early years
I must have heard
ominous news broadcasts
on the radio;
they must have mentioned
the Black Forest

for I dreamed a black forest
moving across a map,
I and my rag doll
caught on the coast edge   10
of the country
I was too young
even to name

Austria Poland Hungary
would have meant nothing
to me
but the Black Forest
came right up our ravine
down over the mountains

and Raggedy Ann   20
and I woke screaming
out of the clutch of
evil trees

(1977)   (1977)

Last Letter to Pablo

Under the hills and veins water
comes out like stars;
your spirit
fleshy palpable
mines in the earth
dung and debris of generations;
curled shells
rags of leaves
impress your palms

I imagine you   10
a plateau city
spangled with frost,

a blue electric wind
before nightfall
that touches and takes
the breath away

How many making love
in the narrow darkness
between labours
how many bodies laid   20
stone upon stone
generations of fire and dirt
before you broke from us
a whole branch flowering

Cancer the newscast said,
and coma, but
what of the sea
also full of bones
and miracles
they said was your   30
last prison?
What of your starward-riding
cities creaking again
with steel? How long
is death?

We are weary of atrocities;
the manure of blood
you said grows
something so frightful
only you could look: 40
you smoothing wounds
we shudder from –
bloody leather
face forming in mud

Always earth was
your substance:
grain, ores and bones
elements folded in power
humans patient as time
and weather;   50
now you too lie with skeletons

heaped about you;
our small crooked hands
touch you for comfort

From the deep hollows
water comes out like stars;
you are changing, Pablo,
becoming an element
a closed throat of quartz
a calyx   60
imperishable in earth

As our species bears
the minute electric
sting, possibility,
our planet carries Neruda
bloodstone
dark jewel of history
the planet carries you
a seed patient as time.

(1977)   (1977)

Reflecting Sunglasses

Circles of sky
and storefronts in my face –
look through me:
lattice of moving air
chrome   sunburst   faces –
I'm a see-through woman
proof enough of
the proposition that we're all
mostly

empty space.   10
I swing along carrying
tunnels of vision
through the imaginary fabric
of my brain.
Lean closer and you'll see
you looking out
from me.

(1977)   (1977)

In the Silence Between

In the silence between the
notes of music
something is moving:
an animal
with the eyes of a man
multitudes
clothed in leaves

It is as if huge
migrations take place
between the steps   10
of music
like round
stones in water:
what flows between is
motion so constant
it seems still

Is it only the heart
beat
suspended

like a planet   20
in the hollow body
messages of blood
or the sensed arrival
of photons
from the outer
galaxies?

A journey that far
we begin also
advancing
between   30
progressions of music
the notes make
neuron
paths where we move
between earths
our heads full of leaves
our eyes like
the eyes of humans

(1977)   (1977)

Daryl Hine
1936 –

———————◆———————

DARYL HINE WAS born in Burnaby, British Columbia, studied classics
and philosophy at McGill University and completed his Ph.D. at the
University of Chicago in 1967. From 1958 to 1962 he travelled in
Europe and since 1969 he has edited the Chicago journal *Poetry*. His
collections of poetry include *Five Poems* (1954), *The Carnal and the Crane*
(1957), *The Devil's Picture Book* (1960), *The Wooden Horse* (1965), *Minutes*
(1968) and *Resident Alien* (1975).

In Praise of Music in Time of Pestilence

The fall which twisted love to lust,
unfranchising the physical,
and made pleasure barren, lost
innocent magnificence, and all
things change, man and animal,
air and countryside, and temporal
forms change and are lost in flux.

Yet music, which is the musician's nightmare, can
to this dreamless body give relief,
charm the labyrinthine hearts of beasts,   10
melt marmoreal cruelty, and give
safe conduct to every Lazarus from the grave.

For time's bewitched, and all
her retainers sleep in attitudes
at once antique and baronial;
but this music is, alas, too valuable,
tempting the wounded spirit with green air,
green towers gleaming beyond compare;
there in vain the prince intrudes
and seeks the secret stairway to her room.   20
Most intricate music ends, while thorns again
imprison Eden and the pilgrim.

Or time is lost, and Venus comes
with empty hands and simple beauty there,
timeless lineaments shaped from the sea's foam,
and through the senses leads the sensualist home.
Where? In the hospital of the particular thing
eternal principles sicken and expire,
and under the deceitful lure of skin
the rebellious angels play with fire.   30

(1957)   (1957)

Patroclus Putting on the Armour of Achilles

How clumsy he is putting on the armour of another,
His friend's, perhaps remembering how they used to arm each other
Fitting the metal tunics to one another's breast
And setting on each other's head the helmet's bristling crest.
Now for himself illicitly he foolishly performs
Secret ceremonial with that other's arms,
Borrowed, I say stolen, for they are not his own,
On the afternoon of battle, late, trembling, and alone.

Night terminal to fighting falls on the playing field
As to his arm he fastens the giant daedal shield.   10
A while the game continues, a little while the host
Lost on the obscure litoral, scattered and almost
Invisible pursue the endless war with words
Jarring in the darkening air impassable to swords.

But when he steps forth from the tent where Achilles broods
Patroclus finds no foe at hand, surrounded by no gods,
Only the chill of evening strikes him to the bone
Like an arrow piercing where the armour fails to join,
And weakens his knees under the highly polished greaves.
Evening gentle elsewhere is loud on the shore, it grieves   20
It would seem for the deaths of heroes, their disobedient graves.

(1960)   (1965)

Point Grey

Brought up as I was to ask of the weather
Whether it was fair or overcast,
Here, at least, it is a pretty morning,
The first fine day as I am told in months.
I took a path that led down to the beach,
Reflecting as I went on landscape, sex and weather.

I met a welcome wonderful enough
To exorcise the educated ghost
Within me. No, this country is not haunted,
Only the rain makes spectres of the mountains.   10

There they are, and there somehow is the problem
Not exactly of freedom or of generation
But just of living and the pain it causes.
Sometimes I think the air we breathe is mortal
And dies, trapped, in our unfeeling lungs.

Not too distant the mountains and the morning
Dropped their dim approval on the gesture
With which enthralled I greeted all this grandeur.
Beside the path, half buried in the bracken,
Stood a long-abandoned concrete bunker,   20
A little temple of lust, its rough walls covered
With religious frieze and votary inscription.

Personally I know no one who doesn't suffer
Some sore of guilt, and mostly bedsores, too,
Those that come from itching where it scratches
And that dangerous sympathy called prurience.
But all about release and absolution
Lie, in the waves that lap the dirty shingle
And the mountains that rise at hand above the rain.
Though I had forgotten that it could be so simple,   30
A beauty of sorts is nearly always within reach.

(1968)   (1968)

Lovers of the River

Hell's Gate is hot, a hundred degrees at Hope.
Then as we descend the infernal canyon
The cleft between its walls grows smaller,
The blank or smiling faces near the top
Indistinct, the hot rocks are dotted here and there
With pine trees like a growth of private

Hair, while curling at the bottom
The patient and inconsequential river
Flows as it will flow forever
Approximately   10
Always a deeper pathway to the sea.

This chasm is important to the eye
But tricky, a place of fissures
And lapses fatal in the winter.
At all times of the year it is better to go slowly
And keep together, for fear of rattlesnakes,
Getting lost, sunstroke and tedium,
Wahlverwandschaften,
For far away the furthest trading post.

These traditionally are the lovers of the river,   20
Bearded men, uxorious fur trappers,
Voyageurs and wicked red skin guides,
Children who lost their childhood to the river,
Unfrocked priests and frivolous runaways
Who love without responsibility,
Men with nothing but their proper
Masculinity,
In theory the half of human kind.

Where at nightfall do they make their camp?
Where are the drunken springs of inspiration?   30
Leafless groves of fir and spruce and cedar?
In glacial streams and lakes they bathe their bodies'
Hardihood,
In sunstruck meadows rest.

And live and die in spite of one another.
The myth is not unnatural to them
How one descending from the precipice,
A rope about his waist, discovered
His comrade dead and rescue come too late.
Unnatural are the newly rich motels   40
Superb highways and the love of women
That always go with easy money,
Meretriciousness
Afflicting every scenic calendar.

They love the river not in its beginnings
Nor its anticlimax in the sea,
They love it in the middle of its journey,
The difficult stretches after it emerges
From underground caverns that are none of their business,
And watch its abrupt waterfalls and rapids   50
And care as guardians should impartially
For all the tributaries that supply it, the
Distillation
Of glacier and spring.

Only they and we lose interest
When certain sandbars past it spreads and coarsens,
Matures in fact to feed a growing valley
Offering its banks to trees and cattle
And eventually to wharfs and mills and learns
To bear the busy burdens of the world.   60
They do not care as we have come to care for harbours.
They love the river as an adolescent
And remember, growing old in estuaries,
Fondly,
How rough and clear and small and cold it was.

(1968)   (1968)

On This Rock

Mountains rise above us like ideas
Vague in their superior extent,
Part of the range of disillusionment
Whose arresting outline disappears
Into the circumstantial clouds that look
Like footnotes from above. What wisdom said
The mind has mountains? Imagination read
The history of the world there like a book.

Playing peek-a-boo with famous peaks
Afflicted with the vapours leaves a sense,   10
Frowned down upon by all that bleak immense
City of rock and ice, that men are freaks,
In the original program of creation,
Afterthoughts. Each jack pine seems a brother;
Even in lichens we perceive another
Example of our own organization,

Tenacious, patient, in a century
Growing perhaps a quarter-of-an-inch:
Glaciers do more daily, an avalanche
In minutes. The eroded immobility   20
Attributed to mountains is a fable,
Like the Great Divide. They move when you're not looking,
Like stars and stocks, distinctly better looking
From a distance, and chronically unstable.

(1975)   (1975)

Tacitus Loquitur
On the Death of a Parrot

Fledged amid other scenes at other times,
From branch to branch, from tree to tree I flew,
Fed by such rare or common fruits as grew
Not in your inhospitable climes.

My plumage was more brilliant than the limes
I feasted on; my beak was coral; blue
Was my breast; my eye was bright betimes;
My species, now diminished, always few.

My only natural enemy I knew
At last, his territory time's   10
Fascinated and apterous crew,
The emperor of all that creeps and climbs.

Tacit I lived, and dying tacit too,
Innocent unless of petty crimes,
I find in these inimitable rhymes
The human tongue with which to talk to you.

(1975)   (1975)

Roch Carrier
1937 –

BORN IN SAINTE-JUSTINE-DE-DORCHESTER, a small village in the Beauce region of Quebec, Roch Carrier studied at the University of Montreal and at the Sorbonne. His first published volume was a collection of short stories, *Jolis deuils* (1964), but he gained wide recognition in both Quebec and English Canada after the publication of his first novel, *La Guerre, Yes Sir* (1968). This first volume of a trilogy was published in an English translation in 1970; the subsequent volumes, *Floralie, où es-tu?* (1969) and *Il est par là, le soleil* (1970) have also been translated as *Floralie, Where Are You?* (1971) and *Is It the Sun, Philibert?* (1972). Carrier's more recent work includes several short stories and two novels, *Le Deux-millième étage* (1973), translated as *They Won't Demolish Me* (1974), and *Le Jardin des délices* (1975).

Steps

ONE EVENING A man returned to his house. In the place where he had left his family in the morning he saw nothing but snow, mute and without memory. He was sure, however, that he had not lost his way. The man knew of a neighbouring village too. He did not find it. It was covered by a snow that seemed eternal.

The sun did not set that day and it would never set again. How long had the man been wandering in the snow? Because of the endless day he did not know. He could not even judge the time by his fatigue because fatigue did not overcome him. He was not hungry; his breathing alone nourished him.

The snow was flat, rough, lifeless. He advanced on an even plaster sea. The white surface on which he walked was an immense shell that contained the universe. Man had been rejected from it.

He had never lived in another land. He recognized neither path nor animals nor houses. Everything had crumbled into a white dust that could not be distinguished from the snow. Around him, nothing moved, nothing stirred or breathed or bloomed or died.

Sometimes the man turned around. The snow was invariable.

Then, suddenly, footprints appeared. Was he crossing his own tracks? He approached them, comparing the print with his own feet. The print was very tiny. Then there must be a woman alive too. He uttered a great cry of joy that fell like a pebble in the sea.

The man followed the tracks. His eyes never left them. He clung to the woman's little footprints as to a tight cord. He walked for days, going faster and faster. His steps became more and more impatient. He hurried towards the woman at the end of the footprints in the snow.

Farther away the woman's prints were more shallow. Her step was lighter. The traces were less precise. The man slowed down. He was afraid of confusing the tracks. Soon the woman barely marked the snow, like a bird. And then there was nothing. The snow was implacably virgin.

Then the man turned around. He noticed that the snow resisted the mark of his steps. He pressed his foot down hard. The snow had become white rock.

He refused to venture further.

Was it not his village over there? He ran. He wished for the legs of legendary giants.

His village was perfumed with flowers, musical with birdsong and children's cries. Arms embraced him, lovingly. He was invited to eat. The bread was hot, the soup was steaming.

The man refused. He left.

Since his return he has been wandering in the village and the neighbouring fields, his eyes riveted to the ground as though he were trying to read a precious sign.

(1964)   (1970)

Sheila Fischman (Trans.)

The Wedding

MARTINE WOULD HAVE scorned a thousand castles, and all the balls that might be held there, for a single little daisy from Didier. She never looked out her window without wishing to see him and her wish often came true: a great part of Didier's life was spent trying to be as close as possible to Martine. No one in the village was as happy as they were and no one envied them.

How many farmers went through their fields in search of a lost cow, how many fishermen fell asleep listening to the song of the river without knowing that close by, behind a curtain of rushes, there was being performed the simple liturgy of two people who refuse to be two!

It was astonishing, then, when the word spread that Martine was expecting a child. Martine was dumbfounded, Didier was confused. He went away, going off towards the city in search of money. Obviously, he did not return.

The child was born. Waiting for the child and waiting for Didier were mixed up together to a certain extent. The birth of the child was a little like Didier's return.

Although she grew accustomed to the child's presence Martine began once again to hope for her lover's arrival. She knew that he would consent to return only when he had made his fortune. Then he would shelter his family in a house that Martine would decorate with little daisies to prolong their youth.

Alas! she had to become reconciled not to wait any longer for Didier.

A very large stone building stood nearby, inhabited by women whose faces disappeared beneath intricate white head-dresses. Martine entrusted her child to them.

The old nun who received her took the child and clasped it tightly to her bosom, which was not completely flattened by the black fabric. Then she opened a screened door and disappeared. Martine could hear nothing but the sound of doors that creaked, one after the other and each one farther away. Finally everything was quiet except for several muffled steps that slid along the length of the corridor, silent as a viper. Martine suddenly had the impression that she had not experienced her love or her long wait or her heavy months of solitude. That road – painful, but happy as well – was erased like a chalk mark.

Martine left the building light-hearted, as though she were going to meet Didier under some musical tree, in a field where their love would add its light to the wheat. Had Didier really left her? Had he not arranged a rendezvous in one of their usual retreats? No. Martine was dreaming. An old, bent nun, the eldest of the community, approached silently and asked, "Are you ready?"

Martine was ready for anything. She followed the nun. Behind them other nuns in their complicated black robes formed a cortege. Martine, infinitely sad, listened to their hymns. The old nun walked rapidly. Martine could hear her panting. The cortege followed the road for a long way, then turned off towards a flat grey field at the end of which the sky was slanting. Now Martine saw nothing but the grass bending evenly beneath the wind that had risen with a voice like that of the nuns. She would have sworn that heaven was covered with the same grass. The wind twisted the robes and made them blacker. This atmosphere was prolonged for several minutes, several hours perhaps. As the cortege advanced the grass became higher. It reached the nuns' knees, then their thighs; it came up to their waists, touched their faces and finally covered them entirely. Then the leader made a gesture indicating that they were to stop.

They had arrived at a river of black water. The nuns, who had walked in two parallel rows, separated and lined up along the river, thereby giving Martine two great black wings. On the order of the eldest, the women in black brought their left hands to their belts and with their right, in a single gesture, they broke their rosaries. The old nun gathered them up and tied them, and then Martine let them bind her arms, hands, legs and feet.

During all this time the nuns had been singing their hymns. The eldest ordered them to be silent and said, "Look carefully at this water which has cast a veil over the truth."

The sibylline phrase appeared very simple to Martine and it did not cause her any anguish. She merely looked at the place the old nun was indicating. She was not astonished to see Didier in a black suit, rising to the surface, his limbs tied like her own. He smiled at her. The old nun gave Martine a motherly push and the current carried her gently along. One by one the nuns let themselves fall into the river after her. Their gowns were indistinguishable from the black water. They were smiling. The cortege formed perfectly parallel lines. Carried along the water and the silence they passed through the shadow without disturbing it, slid beneath the leafy arches without frightening the birds and went towards — what?

The ceremony had taken place far away, very far. However, the child of Martine and Didier had followed it with a troubled eye. She saw her mother pass below her window and she recognized her even though the water had brought her hair down over her face. She recognized her father whom she had never seen. She remembered kisses she had never received from him and rides on his back that she had never taken. She repeated words he had never taught her. Her father and mother smiled at her, she answered them and they were illuminated by an extraordinary happiness. She watched them go farther away with the water, followed by eighty old women who reflected an identical happiness.

When she could no longer see them, a key turned in her door.

"My daughter," said a soft voice, "life is waiting for you."

The child of Martine and Didier left her dungeon. She was a young girl, pretty, and her body had borrowed its movements from a flame. She wanted to smile. But her lips were dead.

Sheila Fischman (Trans.)   (1970)

Dave Godfrey
1938 –

———◆———

DAVE GODFREY WAS born in Winnipeg and educated at several univer-
sities including the Universities of Toronto and Iowa and at Stanford
University. An exponent of literary and economic nationalism, God-
frey has been involved in the founding of the House of Anansi Press,
New Press and Press Porcépic. A collection of his short stories, *Death
Goes Better with Coca Cola,* was published in 1967 and his novel, *The New
Ancestors,* won a Governor General's Award in 1970.

On the River

"WHAT IS IT? Really."

"There's nothing. It's nothing. Or you know what it is. The country's
lovely. You'd better watch for the sign."

"Christ, you know I'm watching for the sign. But I need it like these
crops need rain, not at all. Some of the most miserable moments of my
youth were spent here. Summers. Even after ten years you don't forget
roads."

"It's more like a trail."

"I'm going as slow as I can. You can't really expect gravel to stay long
on top of straight granite."

"I'm sorry. I know you're taking it easy."

"It's the odds isn't it. The fifty-fifty."

"No."

They parked the car by the barn. He knocked on the door of the house
but nobody answered. He went out into the thin wedge of soil that
made the vegetable garden and dug some worms. He felt the poverty
of the land in the thinness of the mossy soil. The meadow was gone to
weeds and he had to remember where the path had been. Age had
worn it into the ground though, and once he could feel its pattern, he
could not stray no matter how thick the weeds were. They were both
damp almost to their knees by the time they reached the dock.

The boat was half-full of water and green with thin slime even after
he had tipped all the water out by hauling the boat partially up on the

dock. The near part of the bay was full of stumps and shore birds, but beyond that the river was clear and fresh looking.

"Let's just forget about it all, babe," he said. "Here I can promise you fish for sure."

Her face was beautiful and yet when he had turned from it for a minute its outlines and clarity blurred and he couldn't bring even a photograph of it back into his mind. It started to rain and she pulled a rain hat out of her pocket and adjusted it to cover as much of her hair as possible. Her gestures were still shy and cautious as though she were yet a girl. He pulled on the oars and took careful glances at her, measuring the angle of her cheekbones and the grace of her lips. Her eyes followed carefully the bobber as it danced on the water. If you took fine green glass, and filled it full of paraffin and a wick, and lit a flame that jogged and flickered as wind blew over the lip of the glass, that would be somewhat like her eyes. Her body was only beginning to bulge with this troublesome child and he realized that she was more appropriately dressed than he. The entire shore was totally familiar except where the brush had been cleared from what were hopefully cottage lots. It wasn't likely that people would come this far, he thought. Yet here was he with his city man's raincoat rowing in an almost water-logged boat. The oars dipped into the spools of fallen rain and he moved the boat farther from the shore.

They fished and let the boat drift. She used only a child's line with the worms he had dug from near the old farm house, and she caught, as he knew she would here at this time of year, whether it rained or not, innumerable small sunfish. She hooked a small bass from time to time and he carefully released those. He cast his own plugs farther and farther out, looking for something larger. They moved across the river and tried the deeper shore and then moved farther up to where a rocky point jutted out and where he remembered there would be bass and there were and she caught some more sunfish while he boated several bass – large enough to keep, if the season were open.

"You're getting cold," he said.

"No, I'm fine. I'm really fine."

"We're just compounding our illegalities, we'd better go in."

"If you insist."

He felt he should return the fish to their own cold depths, but he saw her face glisten with rain and a smile and he realized he wouldn't forget the way she looked there, so determined to keep herself under control despite everything and to enjoy their time on the water. It was a long row back to the dock, but the movement warmed him and the rain didn't get any worse and he was glad they hadn't drowned in the leaky, decrepit boat.

They carried their catch in the bailing bucket up the path to the barn. It had stopped raining and they began to feel the cold. He said that they ought to make a fire and she asked if she had not always been his furnace and pulled him towards her to kiss her, and their bodies, draped in clothes still wet from the river, met. He set down the bait bucket. They climbed into the loft which was full of dusty straw and they made love pleasantly and he could feel the fires within him and stronger within her and nothing was imperfect about it, except that he could not lose himself in his desire as he had once been able, he couldn't somehow get beyond the world and he felt that they were not as close as they had once been.

He told her he was going to clean the fish and bake them on sticks against a fire and she said that was fine. He could tell that her anguish had caught her again and he did not mention what he had felt after the lovemaking nor ask her about that which she was choosing to hide from him. Her body was half hidden by the dusty straw and the lack of light from the rainy day. The first time she had been pregnant she had been awed by the changes in her body and had done a long series of sketches as her breasts slowly swelled and her hips widened and the child pushed her belly forward. She had made no sketches this time. He envied her ability to draw and kept his eyes upon the shapes of her body as long as he could without letting her know he was observing her.

He started a fire outside with dry straw from the barn and pieces of an old wagon seat which was rotting near the door. He cleaned the fish and set them on sticks in the ground so that they leaned near the fire and the fillets began to twist and curl about the sticks.

He didn't hear his uncle come up behind him.

"You the fellows that were out in my boat?"

"George. Hey, I thought you were the warden there for a minute. How've you been?"

"It's a dollar an hour for the boat and fifty cents for the worms. I seen you digging through the window."

He stood up and looked at the old man. His eyes were still clear, his skin was dark, yet faded from the bright red of old sun-burning, haying days.

"There's better boats, but it's a dollar an hour."

He argued with this suddenly strange old man for four or five minutes, reminding him of family ties, asking after his wife Martha, even telling him the name of the horse that had once pulled the mowing machine that sat rusting in the barn. The old man blinked his eyes unnaturally, but did not seem to be listening at all.

"Martha left of cancer some time back," the old man said. "It's a dollar an hour for the boats."

"I'm your nephew, uncle George. For God's sake, I used to come here every summer for four or five years. I know you. You should know me. You must know me. I helped you caulk that very boat once. I've been to America and I've come home. I remember you. I remember you used to laugh at old Jenkins down the road who'd only been here twenty years and got taken for his suspenders and his drawers when he bought a piece of land down near the locks. Once I came up in the winter and helped you fill the ice-house. I've looked up the family records. I know which regiment your grandfather was disbanded from when he settled here and how all the men felt cheated when they saw how much rock there was in the land and demanded larger allotments. Remember that? You may not know me, but I know who you used to be. I know where you came from. I know who you are now."

But the old man only looked at him somewhat queerly as if he couldn't understand why anyone would raise his voice at an old man. He realized that he had been shouting and he pulled out his wallet quickly and paid this old man three dollars for the time they had been out on the river and fifty cents for the worms. Because he didn't want his wife any more worried than she was now. The old man walked back up to the house and tried to lock the gate behind him, but it swung open and blew in the wind which was coming up after the storm.

She had come out to the door of the barn and was standing there with her eyes full of sorrow for him, that sorrow which he had always searched for when he was a young man and for which he had fallen so deeply in love with her, but he was sure of himself now, he didn't need that anymore, and he wanted suddenly to hurt her, or to make her at least present her weakest side in acknowledgement of submission.

"It's not the same," he said. "Nothing's the same." He glared at her for a moment but he couldn't sustain that confrontation. "Let's get the hell home. The fish is so charred nobody'll be able to tell what kind it is. I don't know why you keep bashing away at me. My whole life is flowing away looking after you."

She held herself stiffly and distant from him, as though she were willing the body which was softening for the child to a new hardness. The heater dried their clothes but she was careful to keep them neat about her as though she were a young virgin afraid of exposing herself.

When they got back to the city there was no bread in the house so he went around the corner to the College Bakery to get some challah.

He took number 66, although he saw 65 had already been replaced, but there was a blond man in front of the cash register who seemed to be taking all of Mrs. Mier's time. He was obviously begging from her and she was shrugging her shoulders at him as though he were one of thousands she turned away every day. The two of them argued in a language he didn't try to listen to, and then Mrs. Mier took a loaf of bread from the counter and gave it to the blond man. Then she took ten dollars from the cash register and gave that to him also. The blond man walked out. He had been quite handsome obviously, but his face was flushed red with years of wine and his eyes looked as though they were looking away from the objects in the store, away from the ice cream freezer, the wedding cakes, the spiced meats, the displays of small delicacies.

"Ah, Mrs. Mier sighed. "What can I do for you?"

He ordered a loaf each of challah, rye and whole wheat.

"You've been away," she said. "I don't see your wife so much anymore. To the country? All the English go up north for the summer. My husband he was always going to buy a little cottage, but the store took all the money and then he was gone."

"I'm not English."

"You're not Jewish?"

"I'm not Jewish."

"So what are you?"

"I'm an Indian" he said. She looked very unhappy and he wanted to joke with her and cheer her up.

"Sure, sure. You're dark, you wife's dark, and your little boy's got blond hair. Indians. You can never tell what's happening. You saw that man who was just in? John? He frightened your wife last time. His hair is not really blond. What can you do? He's from the same city in Europe as my husband, my own city. So we keep together here you know. And my husband always took care of him. At first we just gave him money; and when we had none we gave too. But then, you know, he was drinking; the world knew he was drinking. It was like pouring silver into a well. But my husband he never quit. He would just pay John's rent for him direct to the landlord, and take groceries over and try to get him jobs. But you just look at him now, he's not like ordinary. He would always quarrel, and fight even. Who fights? What's to do? My husband would be feeding and sheltering him, and he would take the welfare money or from the United and spend that on wine. Sweet wine. Ah, then he was sick. And now vodka. He would argue even with my husband. What's your reason? my husband would shout at him. We knew that, we knew that. He saw the Germans kill his whole family. You can't deny him reasons for being like that. But we all did – see horror. It gets too much for me sometimes and I just go up to my bedroom and cry for four or five hours. I can't do anything except that and each time I feel that it won't work, that I'm going to fall apart from sorrow this time. But after four or five hours my children bring me a little something to eat and I go on. It's hard for them to understand and we drive them so and give them too much. They can't understand why we give them so much and take so little ourselves, but then sometimes later they do, they find out that we don't believe in all the things we collect about ourselves. And now it's worse for the ones up in the high part of the city. If the children understand that, sometimes they're all right; otherwise they go bad and we get drugs and disrespect for our troubles. Who can understand drugs? My son he says John would be better off with marijuana. Can you believe that? But I think he's getting worse. I just give him money now. I don't know what to do. 'Mrs. Mier, you're rich,' he says, 'Look at all this about you; and three women in the back doing the baking. You're rich Mrs. Mier. I have nothing.' And ah, he frightened your wife. I can't understand that. She is so beautiful, and with the small boy. *Ich bin Yetzer Hara,* he said to her. I didn't want to give him anything, it seemed so useless, and then she came in and he said that to her and laughed at her. *Ich bin Yetzer Hara.* I thought that's why you were going to Dominion for your bread."

"My wife is pregnant," he said as he paid. "She's been having a bad time and the doctors say there's a good chance she'll lose the child."

"Ah, I didn't know. Why shouldn't she tell me? But if she's not sure. Ah, that John. Did he know? He is getting worse. It cannot be denied. How do you think he escaped? That is what he torments himself with. How do you think I escaped? Because I gave them up? Some did that, you know. Just to save their own skins. Ah, he is worse. Here, take. Take for the child. All will be well. Ah, I'm sorry for John. Tell that to your wife. That a man from my own city should say such a thing."

She gave him an extra loaf of challah and he took it and left the clean store.

When he got home he put one of the loaves in the freezer compartment.

His son was kicking a many-coloured ball between the two brick walls which surrounded their garden. Though the boy was young, he could kick it hard enough so that it bounced from wall to wall and he could lose himself following it, turning and spinning and chasing after its flight. He wanted to go out and comfort his wife and have her drive out of him the fear that Mrs. Mier's story had brought, but the telephone rang. It was his broker and he stood there in the kitchen, staring through the windows at his wife and son, while this man who dealt in shares of other men's business and distant mines spoke to him about rising inflation and defending one's position. He listened to him, but he watched his own son, and he thought of his uncle George, and he remembered himself when he was not much older than his own son, skipping stones from the point where today he had caught the fish. Three of his friends had been caught in a sudden storm and drowned and he had developed a game where he skipped stones at death.

The waves were paperchases in furrows of blue questionings. The stones skipped between them.

Hello death, are you a porcupine?

Three skips.

Are you a Lancaster bomber carved of balsa?

Seven skips. Flat.

Are you the spring where deer come, half a mile beyond the CNR station, where the water has made the ground all mushy and you have to walk on a board path to get to the place where it fountains among the rocks?

One skip. Overconfidence. Beware.

Are you the men who hung Mussolini by his heels?

Four skips. Caught in a crest.

Do you like blueberries?

Three skips. First repeater. He is not a porcupine.

Hello death. Do you have trouble getting through the locks that join this lake to the next? Do you know what it means to portage? Is it you who turns the lightning to thunder? Does 7-up like you? May I cross the river?

Ten skips. Second time. The answer to the tenth question is no. Come back again tomorrow. Try me tomorrow.

Goodbye child.

Goodbye death.

He went outside into the garden they had built in the midst of the city. There was only twenty-two feet between the wall of the funeral chapel and the wall of the coach house that had been turned from an artist's studio into two apartments, but they had filled the small space with grass and marigolds and odd pieces of stone work, angels and ornate stone flowers, which the mason who had built the house in the previous century had been unwilling to sell.

"The doctor phoned while you were out."

"Good news?"

"He said it was sixty-forty now."

"Well, that's better."

"I guess so."

"I shouldn't have been so sharp at the barn."

"I hope you're going to do something about your uncle."

"God, I don't know. I really don't know. He's my great-uncle really. There's nobody left of his generation, but that's not an excuse at all."

"I don't understand your family."

"They're solitary, that's true. The only thing that held them together was the queen I used to think, and of course that's absurd now. Now nothing holds them together. The land still frightens them. And poverty. I think everybody who came here was poor and is still afraid of it."

He lay down on the sheet in the late sun beside her, filled with an overwhelming love of her endurance.

"I don't understand you," she said, her anger breaking out. "I used to think I did, but I don't. Sometimes I think you want not to see me. Or to see me only as I used to be four or five years ago, when we were first together. When we used to spend all that time outdoors, running away from things. I get sick of it. I don't see why I should be afraid of saying it; I get sick of it."

He wanted to tell her that everything had been changed. That she was right. That he was sorry for how the blond man had frightened her. That he loved her for her courage of endurance, but he couldn't get those words to come out.

"I bought you some fresh challah – so your traditions don't die out in a new land. That was my broker on the phone. I'm even changing my opinions about them, the older ones. Somebody sent me some information about Levy Industries – which will double for sure – and I asked him about it. He told me I wouldn't want to get rich out of the war. Surprised the hell out of me. He said the money was really coming from war contracts, helicopter gears or something. You just can't escape it, I guess. Anyhow, I put the challah in the freezer. Mrs. Mier says hello and hopes you'll stop going to the Dominion."

"I'm not the same to you as I used to be. That's it, isn't it? That's what you said to me by the barn?"

"Look," he said, "you're right. I'm not arguing with you. Let's put the kid to bed and then we'll come back out here and lie on the sheet and watch the stars and ignore the bloody soot."

She agreed, her body loosening, and he realized that he had given in and by doing so had won a small victory. He knew he could never talk to her of the blond man, but he would be able to talk to her of how his gnawing desire for her had lessened as his fear of life had disappeared, as his acceptance of change and imperfection had increased almost miraculously, so that he no longer constantly desired to escape somewhere but was willing to accept everything, Mrs. Mier, the blond man from her city, his uncle George, the doctor's fluctuating odds, Levy Industries, everything, and still allow desire to overtake his body, and he realized somehow that what he had always desired had happened and that he had got, somehow, beyond certain desires which had blinded his early life.

In the evening, once the child was asleep, they would come out and lie on the sheet on the grass and be protected by the ugly brick walls which rose on all four sides of the small garden and he would be able to talk to her and reassure her. In the winter the new child would come, safely.

"Did the doctor say why the odds were better?"

"No. I don't know how he can tell without seeing me. He just said that if time goes by and nothing happens that even that is an improvement."

"Okay. Okay."

(1967)   (1967)

David Helwig
1938 –

———◆———

DAVID HELWIG WAS born in Toronto and received his B.A. from the University of Toronto and his M.A. from the University of Liverpool. For several years he has taught in the Department of English at Queen's University. Since the appearance of his first book, *Figures in a Landscape* (1967), Helwig has published a collection of short stories, several novels and further volumes of poetry including *The Best Name of Silence* (1972) and *Atlantic Crossings* (1974).

Lion in Macdonald Park

WINTER

Black, patched, cast bronze, proud
and still, the lion stares across the park
to the empty lake where a hundred waves knock
together their insistent rolling. Bowed

branches spring back at each weakness of the wind.
The park and beach are empty. No quick child
climbs the lion's back to stroke the wild
immovable waves of his mane with a tentative hand.

The wind blows bits of grey lake into the sky,
and throughout the city, children feel the sting   10
of age blown into the eyes and across the wings
of the swift brain, while in the cold day

outside forever the lion endures each wave
of the wind that rattles branches till they crack,
and maintains defiance in stillness facing the lake,
in cold bronze eyes that have never seen love.

SUMMER

The dry grass crunches beneath the bare
feet of the swimmers who go walking past
the lion to their blankets, or bare-legged, race
through the park, boy chasing girl, breasts   20

bouncing and legs flying, playing the game
of summer and youth, to wrestle in the sun
until the evening brings the slim
arms and legs to softness. One

girl and mother, half naked on the sand,
tans and watches her sleeping baby, wife
to the man beside her, mistress to the whole band
of boys who watch her as if she were life

itself, or sun, and they planets spinning,
or worshippers of her as mistress and mother,   30
a double deity. All around, the children
leap and splash in the bright water.

The lion stands here in the park
unmoved by this, all dignity,
all bronze his mane, eyes and bag
of seed, dead to the sun's folly.

(1967)   (1969)

One Step from an Old Dance

Will the weasel lie down with the snowshoe hare
In the calm and peaceable kingdom?
Will the wolverine cease to rend and tear
In the calm and peaceable kingdom?
Will the beasts of burden not have to bear?
Will the weasel lie down with the snowshoe hare?
Will the children feed grass to the grizzly bear
In the calm and peaceable kingdom?

Oh the wolverine will cease to tear
In the calm and peaceable kingdom,   10
The rattlesnake rattle praise and prayer
In the calm and peaceable kingdom.
Oh the wolves will wear smiles like children wear,
The wolverine will cease to tear
While the hawk and the squirrel are dancing there
In the calm and peaceable kingdom.

(1967)   (1969)

Figures in a Landscape

I

Hunting vixen, red as the sun,
lithe as a black cat, hunting
a soft doe rabbit mild as moonlight,
vixen black in the moonlight hunting,
hunting the soft black blood of the rabbit,
daring rabbit dancing in flight,
mad rabbit dancing by moon and sun,
dancing fear of the sun's vixen,
dainty feet of the hunting vixen,
tail of fire of the copper vixen.   10

Noon of the sun, still, hard fire.
Turn, turn and see them stand,
red sun, black rabbit, and black vixen.

2

Still on the thin crust of the snow,
white as bone in a light that blinds the eyes,
she stands, taken in her suddenness,
solid against the flatness of the snow.
No tracks show how she came here as the sun
dances on icicles, while all around
the blue jays hurtle on their noisy wings.
And in the pallor of the winter day
flames the black fire of her belly's hair.

(1967)   (1969)

Images of the Sun

The sun is never satisfied. Its fire
always burns hotly outward from the centre
to the circumference, into the long night.
Its time burns only forward to its end.
The cycle of its turning is the wheel
of a chariot whose driver looks ahead
into a dark space that never ends.

Because our clocks are small, it seems to us
eternal as the circle of its path.
With years the chariot wheel goes round and round,   10
it seems forever, round and round, the One,
like Egypt frozen in Nefertiti's smile
or like Versailles where the rococo king
moved through a zodiac of adulteries
and a small world spun round him, all in gold.

But time's fire burns away all unities.
Grass grows on gods and queens and courtesans.
The sun burns always forward, and his fire,
the interchange of motions with the dark,
nourishes empty night for numbered years.   20

(1967)   (1969)

The Death of Harlequin

I cannot say
why he should look
so like a broken bird
except that a pile of sticks
and a gaiety of rags
are his grave
and that his laughter
ran into the sky
and that his tears
flew upward   10
and that at his death
he dropped slowly
with a fine grace
in dying
and that his falling
brought distances into our eyes.

(1969)   (1969)

From
Barn Poems

I

The window is a hole
in the flat
wall of the old
barn. A little light
shines in.

The barn is dark. Inside
the walls around the hole
are dark with age and dirt.

Looking outside, the eye
10 moves past branch behind
          branch
leaf behind leaf to the narrow
holes into the sky.

The eye moves outward
to the narrow vents
of sky, the sun
moves down between the ranks
of branches and the leaves
move in the wind changing
the shape of sky and
of sun.   20

Across the hole
hanging on a piece of web
drops a spider
eight-legged dancer
suspended
where the wall is not.

And there
where the wall is not
between the dark inside
30 and the ranks of leaves,

(1972)

moves, extruding
the thin web that he spreads
across the hole where the eye
meets the light.

(1972)

From

The Vinland Saga

> Each of us must endure the ending of life
> in this world. Let those who can there-
> fore achieve glory before the coming of
> death.
> — *Beowulf*

Distance was a white fire, and the sea
sent men to hell or far islands.
Thorstein my husband must go
to find his brother's body.

The weeks of summer passed in flight
from storms. Clouds gathered and fell.
We turned west, and the wind turned,
and we ran before it and again
turned west. But came nowhere.
Passed weeks in a wet boat, baling,   10
food near gone. Huddled in rain,
shivering in our wet clothes,
eating dried fish, we waited.

A week before winter we made land
back in Greenland, found shelter
in the house of Thorstein the Black.

Then the disease began. Took many.
Took that huge strong woman Grimhald.
Took Thorstein my husband.

The corpse of Thorstein sat up   20
and said, Where is Gudrid?

The body stiff, emptied of life
except that on the pale skin
of his chest the small brown hairs
curled as if I might rub my face
against them and feel heat.

Eyes like wet stones.
Mouth strangely open, empty.
The beard, the curling body hair
seemed still alive. I reached out
to touch his arm. Like touching water.

30

I must tell Gudrid her destiny.

The lips, the soft curved lips
did not move. The hands that once
held my body lay still as islands
of earth and stone.

Let her accept my death.
I have come to a happy place
of rest, Gudrid.

When he spoke my name I turned
but he was not there in his dead flesh.

40

You will marry, live long,
your sons will be bright and excellent
sweet and fragrant.

The body fell back and was silent.
Beyond mourning or comfort I began
to prepare my husband for burial.

The ships came loaded with grain,
lengths of timber, iron and cloth
woven with scarlet stallions.

50

Karlsefni, the merchant captain,
offered Eirik choice of the goods,
and Eirik to match him offered
to have the men guests of his house.

Karlsefni's tall body stood near me
all that winter.
     I remember once
the wings of a raven caught
the blue of sky and held it
as the sea catches and holds   60
the darkness of black clouds.

After food and drink the men sat
by the long fire telling stories.
Karlsefni listened in silence.

Leif said, We went ashore.
There was dew on the grass.
We put it to our lips, and it
was the sweetest thing
we had ever tasted.

One morning Eirik came   70
and said Karlsefni wished to marry me.
He praised the man, and I agreed,
and we began to plan the voyage west.

     * * *

As the sun rose, Karlsefni saw
the long white beach and called out.
His arms reached up in joy,
his voice sang through me
as I lay in the boat curled round
a belly filled with his child.

All through the morning the land   80
came closer, the pine forests
holding their last snow.

I breathed deep and smelled the land
and hugged my belly.

At twilight we came ashore
at Leif's houses. The water
was the colour of light.

In the large house we lit
a driftwood fire. Listened
to the voices of the place. 90

Day after day we learned to know
the shape of the days here.

Our cattle grew happy and restless
in the meadows of long grass.

The men cut timber and left it
on the rocks to season. The air
was sweet with the smell of wood.

Clouds moving over the mountains
would suddenly open into sunlight.

The land was rich with fruit 100
and tall deer, the rivers with fish.

Each night I buried
the living fire under ashes
and slept hearing the sound
of the wind and the river.

(1975) (1975)

John Newlove
1938 –

———◆———

BORN IN REGINA, John Newlove grew up in Verigen, Saskatchewan, and attended the University of Saskatchewan. He has travelled extensively in Canada and has been a Writer-in-Residence at several universities. Since the appearance of his first book, *Grave Sirs*, in 1962, Newlove has published several collections of poetry, including *Moving In Alone* (1965), *Black Night Window* (1968), *The Cave* (1970) and *Lies* (1972).

Good Company, Fine Houses

Good company, fine houses
and consequential people,
you will not turn me
into a tin factory.

I know where the lean and half
starved gods are hiding,
I have slept in their mountains.

I have slept among them,
in their mountains turning
10 nightmarishly between the rocks
and the reaching plants,

I have seen red eyes
on my throat from behind
every bush and waterfall,
greedy for blood.

Good company, fine people,
except for the shooting,
how much will your funerals cost

in your consequential houses?
I know where the god is   20
hiding, starved. I have slept
in the turning mountain.

(1965)   (1965)

The Double-Headed Snake

Not to lose the feel of the mountains
while still retaining the prairies
is a difficult thing. What's lovely
is whatever makes the adrenalin run;
therefore I count terror and fear among
the greatest beauty. The greatest
beauty is to be alive, forgetting nothing,
although remembrance hurts
like a foolish act, is a foolish act.

Beauty's whatever   10
makes the adrenalin run. Fear
in the mountains at night-time's
not tenuous, it is not the cold
that makes me shiver, civilized man,

white, I remember
the stories of the Indians,
Sis-i-utl, the double-headed snake.

Beauty's what makes
the adrenalin run. Fear at night
on the level plains, with no horizon   20
and the stars too bright, wind bitter
even in June, in winter
the snow harsh and blowing,
is what makes me
shiver, not the cold air alone.

And one beauty cancels another. The plains
seem secure and comfortable
at Crow's Nest Pass; in Saskatchewan
the mountains are comforting
to think of; among   30
the eastwardly diminishing hills
both the flatland and the ridge
seem easy to endure.

As one beauty
cancels another, remembrance
is a foolish act, a double-headed snake
striking in both directions, but I
remember plains and mountains, places
I come from, places I adhere and live in.

(1968)   (1968)

Everyone

Everyone is so   no goose stepping
lonely in this   pompously along,
country that
it's necessary   but a crow,   10
to be fantastic –   black as life,
                                  raucously calling
a crow flew over   to no one –
my grave today,

struggling image:
necessary
to be fantastic,
almost to lie,

but incorrect,
not cautious enough,
20   though not evil
actively: it does not

have the diminishing
virtue of evilness
(a locked sea-monster
with half the

dangerous coils
waving above
the grey water),
for the tourists,
glistening crows.   30

(1968)   (1968)

Samuel Hearne in Wintertime

I

In this cold room
I remember the smell of manure
on men's heavy clothes as good,
the smell of horses.

It is a romantic world
to readers of journeys
to the Northern Ocean –

especially if their houses are heated
to some degree, Samuel.

Hearne, your camp must have smelled   10
like hell whenever you settled down
for a few days of rest and journal-work:

hell smeared with human manure,
hell half-full of raw hides,
hell of sweat, Indians, stale fat,
meat-hell, fear-hell, hell of cold.

2

One child is back from the doctor's while
the other one wanders about in dirty pants
and I think of Samuel Hearne and the land –

puffy children coughing as I think,   20
crying, sick-faced,
vomit stirring in grey blankets
from room to room.

It is Christmastime —
the cold flesh shines.
No praise in merely enduring.

3

Samuel Hearne did more
in the land (like all the rest

full of rocks and hilly country,
many very extensive tracts of land,   30
tittimeg, pike and barble,

and the islands:
the islands, many
of them abound

as well as the main
land does
with dwarf woods,

chiefly pine
in some parts intermixed
with larch and birch) than endure.   40

The Indians killed twelve deer.
It was impossible to describe
the intenseness of the cold.

4

And, Samuel Hearne,
I have almost begun to talk

as if you wanted to be
gallant, as if you went
through that land for a book —

as if you were not SAM, wanting
to know, to do a job.   50

5

There was that Eskimo girl
at Bloody Falls, at your feet

Samuel Hearne, with two spears in her,
you helpless before your helpers,

and she twisted about them like
an eel, dying, never to know.

(1968)   (1968)

The Pride

I

The image   /   the pawnees
in their earth-lodge villages,
the clear image
of teton sioux, wild
fickle people the chronicler says,

the crazy dogs, men
tethered with leather dog-thongs
to a stake, fighting until dead,

image: arikaras
with traded spanish sabre blades   10
mounted on the long
heavy buffalo lances,
riding the sioux
down, the centaurs, the horsemen
scouring the level plains
in war or hunt
until smallpox got them,
4,000 warriors,

image – of a desolate country,
a long way between fires,   2(
unfound lakes, mirages, cold rocks,
and lone men going through it,
cree with good guns
creating terror in athabaska
among the inhabitants, frightened
stone-age people, "so that
they fled at the mere sight
of a strange smoke miles away."

II

This western country crammed
with the ghosts of indians,
haunting the coastal stones and shores,
the forested pacific islands,
mountains, hills and plains:

beside the ocean ethlinga,
man in the moon, empties
his bucket, on
a sign from Spirit
of the Wind ethlinga   10
empties his bucket, refreshing
the earth, and it rains
on the white cities;

that black joker, broken-
jawed raven, most prominent
among haida and tsimshyan tribes,
is in the kwakiutl
dance masks too –
it was he who brought fire,
food and water to man,   20
the trickster;

and thunderbird hilunga,
little thought of
by haida for lack of thunderstorms
in their district, goes
by many names, exquisite disguises
carved in the painted wood,

he is nootka tootooch, the wings
causing thunder and the tongue
or flashing eyes engendering   30
rabid white lightning,
whose food was whales,

called kwunusela by the kwakiutl,
it was he who laid down the house-logs
for the people at Place
Where Kwunusela Alighted;

in full force and virtue
and terror of the law, eagle —
he is authority, the sun
assumed his form once,   40
the sun which used to be
a flicker's egg, success-
fully transformed;

and malevolence comes to the land,
the wild woman of the woods;
grinning, she wears
a hummingbird in her hair,
d'sonoqua, the furious one —

they are all ready
to be found, the legends   50
and the people, or
all their ghosts and memories,
whatever is strong enough
to be remembered.

III

But what image, bewildered
son of all men
under the hot sun,
do you worship,
what completeness
do you hope to have
from these tales,
a half-understood massiveness, mirage,
in men's minds — what
is your purpose;   10

with what force
will you proceed
along a line
neither straight nor short,
whose future
you cannot know
or result foretell,
whose meaning is still
obscured as the incidents
occur and accumulate?   20

IV

The country moves on;
there are orchards in the interior,
the mountain passes
are broken, the foothills
covered with cattle and fences,
and the fading hills covered;

but the plains are bare,
not barren, easy
for me to love their people,
for me to love their people   10
without selection.

V

In 1787, the old cree saukamappee,
aged 75 or thereabout, speaking then
of things that had happened when he was 16,
just a man, told david thompson,
of the raids the shoshonis,
the snakes, had made on the westward-
reaching peigan, of their war-parties
sometimes sent 10 days journey to enemy camps,
the men all afoot in battle array for
the encounter, crouching   10
behind their giant shields;

the peigan armed with guns
drove these snakes out of the plains,

the plains where their strength had been,
where they had been settled since living
memory (though nothing is remembered
beyond a grandfather's time),
to the west of the rockies;

these people moved without rest,
backward and forward with the wind,   20
the seasons, the game, great herds,
in hunger and abundance –

in summer and in the bloody fall
they gathered on the killing grounds,
fat and shining with fat, amused
with the luxuries of war and death,

relieved from the steam of knowledge,
consoled by the stream of blood
and steam rising from the fresh hides
and tired horses, wheeling in their pride   30
on the sweating horses, their pride.

VI

Those are all stories;
the pride, the grand poem
of our land, of the earth itself,
will come, welcome, and
sought for, and found,
in a line of running verse,
sweating, our pride;

we seize on
what has happened before,
one line only   10
will be enough,

a single line and
then the sunlit brilliant image suddenly floods us
with understanding, shocks our
attentions, and all desire
stops, stands alone;

we stand alone,
we are no longer lonely

but have roots,
and the rooted words   20
recur in the mind, mirror, so that
we dwell on nothing else, in nothing else,
touched, repeating them,
at home freely
at last, in amazement;

"the unyielding phrase
in tune with the epoch,"
the thing made up
of our desires,
not of its words, not only   30
of them, but of something else,
as well, that which we desire
so ardently, that which
will not come when
it is summoned alone,
but grows in us
and idles about and hides
until the moment is due –

the knowledge of
our origins, and where   40
we are in truth,
whose land this is
and is to be.

VII

The unyielding phrase:
when the moment is due, then
it springs upon us
out of our own mouths,
unconsidered, overwhelming
in its knowledge, complete –

not this handful
of fragments, as the indians
are not composed of
the romantic stories
about them, or of the stories   10

they tell only, but
still ride the soil
in us, dry bones a part
of the dust in our eyes,
needed and troubling
in the glare, in
our breath, in our
ears, in our mouths,
in our bodies entire, in our minds, until at   20
last we become them

in our desires, our desires,
mirages, mirrors, that are theirs, hard-
riding desires, and they
become our true forbears, moulded
by the same wind or rain,
and in this land we
are their people, come
back to life.

(1968)   (1968)

If You Would Walk

One long look down the undulating line of prairie
leads to the horizon; no mountains stop the vision;
the gold fields sway easily.

If you would walk through them,
black clattering birds rising up,
the stiff grain rasping as you pass,

if you would walk,
your body floating like a ghost,
the smallest swirl behind it,

if you would walk that undulation,   10
seeking the horizon, you would never find it,
even for one long look.

You would return through the swaying fields and rattling birds
to your own known house, of which you are the core,
more easy as you close the rasping door.

(1972)   (1972)

The Stone for His Grave

The sensible man has no dessert
except for a peeled apple.
Nor does he pray to God, though he believes in God.

He is not absurd, a hermit
in the sand among the basilisks,
grooming his hair with urine.

When everyone wears lovelocks and jeans
he looks like a banker, manager,
alive from a previous era.

He does not expect to live forever   10
or ever to be remembered. His children
are accidents, caused only
because it was Sunday and the drugstores closed.

He chooses the stone for his grave
at an early age, but does not publish it.

He is not me. A browned apple core
rolled like an empty spool along the sidewalk
is all that shows his life now,
but God believes in him.

(1972)   (1972)

Margaret Atwood
1939 –

———◆———

MARGARET ATWOOD WAS born in Ottawa and graduated from the University of Toronto in 1961 and from Radcliffe College in 1962. She has worked as an editor with the House of Anansi Press and has taught at several Canadian universities. Since the appearance of her first book of poems, *Double Persephone* (1961), Atwood has published three novels, a thematic study of Canadian writing, and several volumes of poetry including *The Circle Game* (1966), *The Journals of Susanna Moodie* (1970), *Power Politics* (1971), *You Are Happy* (1974) and *Selected Poems* (1976).

A Place: Fragments

I

Here on the rim, cringing
under the cracked whip of winter
we live
in houses of ice,

but not because we want to:
in order to survive
we make what we can and have to
with what we have.

II

Old woman I visited once
out of my way
in a little-visited province:

she had a neat
house, a clean parlour
though obsolete and poor:

a cushion with a fringe;
glass animals arranged

across the mantlepiece (a swan,
a horse,
a bull); a mirror;
a teacup sent from Scotland;
several heraldic spoons;
a lamp; and in the center
of the table, a paperweight:
hollow glass globe
filled with water, and
a house, a man, a snowstorm.

10

625

The room was as
dustless as possible
20 and free of spiders.

           I

stood in the door-
way, at the fulcrum where

this trivial but

stringent inner order
held its delicate balance
with the random scattering or
clogged merging of
things: ditch by the road; dried
reeds in the wind; flat   30
wet bush, grey sky
sweeping away outside.

III

The cities are only outposts.

Watch that man
walking on cement as though on
          snowshoes:
senses the road
a muskeg, loose mat of roots
          and brown
vegetable decay
or crust of ice that

easily might break and
slush or water under
suck him down   10

The land flows like a
sluggish current.

The mountains eddy slowly
          towards the sea.

IV

The people who come here also
flow: their bodies becoming
nebulous, diffused, quietly

spreading out into the air across
these interstellar sidewalks

V

This is what it must be
like in outer space
where the stars are pasted flat
against the total

black of the expanding
eye, fly-
specks of burning dust

VI

There is no center;
the centers
travel with us unseen
like our shadows
on a day when there is no sun.

We must move back:
there are too many foregrounds.

Now, clutter of twigs
across our eyes, tatter

10 of birds at the eye's edge; the
straggle
of dead treetrunks; patch
of lichen

and in love, tangle
of limbs and fingers, the texture
of pores and lines on the skin.

VII

An other sense tugs at us:
we have lost something,
some key to these things
which must be writings
and are locked against us
or perhaps (like a potential
mine, unknown vein
of metal in the rock)
something not lost or hidden
10 but just not found yet

that informs, holds together
this confusion, this largeness
and dissolving:

not above or behind
or within it, but one
with it: an

identity:
something too huge and simple
for us to see.

(1966)

(1966)

The Animals in That Country

In that country the animals
have the faces of people:

the ceremonial
cats possessing the streets

the fox run
politely to earth, the huntsmen
standing around him, fixed
in their tapestry of manners

the bull, embroidered
with blood and given
an elegant death, trumpets, his name
stamped on him, heraldic brand
because

10

(when he rolled
on the sand, sword in his heart, the teeth
in his blue mouth were human)

he is really a man

even the wolves, holding resonant
conversations in their
forests thickened with legend.   20

In this country the animals
have the faces of
animals.

Their eyes
flash once in car headlights
and are gone.

Their deaths are not elegant.

They have the faces of
no-one.

(1968)   (1968)

At the Tourist Centre in Boston

There is my country under glass,
a white relief-
map with red dots for the cities,
reduced to the size of a wall

and beside it 10 blownup snapshots
one for each province,
in purple-browns and odd reds,
the green of the trees dulled;
all blues however
of an assertive purity.   10

Mountains and lakes and more lakes
(though Quebec is a restaurant and Ontario the empty
interior of the parliament buildings),
with nobody climbing the trails and hauling out
the fish and splashing in the water

but arrangements of grinning tourists –
look here, Saskatchewan
is a flat lake, some convenient rocks
where two children pose with a father
and the mother is cooking something   20
in immaculate slacks by a smokeless fire,
her teeth white as detergent.

Whose dream is this, I would like to know:
is this a manufactured
hallucination, a cynical fiction, a lure
for export only?
I seem to remember people,
at least in the cities, also slush,
machines and assorted garbage. Perhaps
that was my private mirage   30

which will just evaporate
when I go back. Or the citizens will be gone,
run off to the peculiarly-
green forests
to wait among the brownish mountains
for the platoons of tourists
and plan their odd red massacres.

Unsuspecting
window lady, I ask you:

Do you see nothing   40
watching you from under the water?

Was the sky ever that blue?

Who really lives there?

(1968)   (1968)

Backdrop Addresses Cowboy

Starspangled cowboy
sauntering out of the almost-
silly West, on your face
a porcelain grin,
tugging a papier-mâché cactus
on wheels behind you with a string,

you are innocent as a bathtub
full of bullets.

Your righteous eyes, your laconic
trigger-fingers   10
people the streets with villains:
as you move, the air in front of you
blossoms with targets

and you leave behind you a heroic
trail of desolation:
beer bottles
slaughtered by the side
of the road, bird-
skulls bleaching in the sunset.

I ought to be watching   20
from behind a cliff or a cardboard storefront
when the shooting starts, hands clasped
in admiration,

but I am elsewhere.

Then what about me

what about the I
confronting you on that border
you are always trying to cross?

I am the horizon
you ride towards, the thing you can never lasso   30

I am also what surrounds you:
my brain
scattered with your
tincans, bones, empty shells,
the litter of your invasions.

I am the space you desecrate
as you pass through.

(1968)   (1968)

Further Arrivals

After we had crossed the long illness
that was the ocean, we sailed up-river

On the first island
the immigrants threw off their clothes
and danced like sandflies

We left behind one by one
the cities rotting with cholera,
one by one our civilized
distinctions

and entered a large darkness.   10

It was our own
ignorance we entered.

I have not come out yet

My brain gropes nervous
tentacles in the night, sends out
fears hairy as bears,
demands lamps; or waiting

for my shadowy husband, hears
malice in the trees' whispers.

I need wolf's eyes to see   20
the truth.

I refuse to look in a mirror.

Whether the wilderness is
real or not
depends on who lives there.

(1970)   (1970)

Disembarking at Quebec

Is it my clothes, my way of walking,
the things I carry in my hand
— a book, a bag with knitting —
the incongruous pink of my shawl

this space cannot hear

or is it my own lack
of conviction which makes
these vistas of desolation,
long hills, the swamps, the barren sand, the glare
of sun on the bone-white   10
driftlogs, omens of winter,
the moon alien in day-
time a thin refusal

The other leap, shout

       Freedom!

The moving water will not show me
my reflection.

The rocks ignore.

I am a word
in a foreign language.   20

(1970)   (1970)

Departure From the Bush

I, who had been erased
by fire, was crept in
upon by green
           (how
lucid a season)

        In time the animals
arrived to inhabit me,

first one
  by one, stealthily
(their habitual traces   10
burnt); then
having marked new boundaries
returning, more
confident, year
by year, two
by two

but restless: I was not ready
altogether to be moved into

They could tell I was
too heavy: I might   20
capsize;

I was frightened
by their eyes (green or
amber) glowing out from inside me

I was not completed; at night
I could not see without lanterns.

He wrote, We are leaving. I said
I have no clothes
left I can wear

The snow came. The sleigh was a relief;   30
its track lengthened behind,
pushing me towards the city

and rounding the first hill, I was
(instantaneous)
unlived in: they had gone.

There was something they almost taught me
I came away not having learned.

(1970)   (1970)

Procedures for Underground

(Northwest Coast)

The country beneath
the earth has a green sun
and the rivers flow backwards;

the trees and rocks are the same
as they are here, but shifted.
Those who live there are always hungry;

from them you can learn
wisdom and great power,
if you can descend and return safely.

You must look for tunnels, animal   10
burrows or the cave in the sea
guarded by the stone man;

when you are down you will find
those who were once your friends
but they will be changed and dangerous.

Resist them, be careful
never to eat their food.
Afterwards, if you live, you will be able

to see them when they prowl as winds,
as thin sounds in our village.   You will   20
tell us their names, what they want, who

has made them angry by forgetting them.
For this gift, as for all gifts, you must
suffer: those from the underland

will be always with you, whispering their
complaints, beckoning you
back down; while among us here

you will walk wrapped in an invisible
cloak.   Few will seek your help
with love, none without fear.   30

(1970)   (1970)

For Archeologists

Deep under, far back
the early horses run
on rock / the buffalo, the deer
the other animals (extinct)
run with spears in their backs

Made with blood, with coloured
dirt, with smoke, not meant
to be seen but to remain
there hidden, potent
in the dark, the link between   10
the buried will and the upper
world of sun and green feeding,
chase and the hungry kill

drawn by a hand hard
even to imagine

but passed on
in us, part of us now
part of the structure of the bones

existing still in us
as fossil skulls   20

of the bear, spearheads, bowls and
folded skeletons arranged
in ritual patterns, waiting
for the patient searcher to find them

exist in caves of the earth.

(1970)   (1970)

From
Power Politics

[you fit into me]

you fit into me   a fish hook
like a hook into an eye   an open eye

(1971)   (1971)

Tricks with Mirrors

I

It's no coincidence
this is a used
furniture warehouse.

I enter with you
and become a mirror.

Mirrors
are the perfect lovers,

that's it, carry me up the stairs
by the edges, don't drop me,

that would be bad luck,   10
throw me on the bed

reflecting side up,
fall into me,

it will be your own
mouth you hit, firm and glassy,

your own eyes you find you
are up against   closed   closed

II

There is more to a mirror
than you looking at

your full-length body
flawless but reversed,

there is more than this dead blue
oblong eye turned outwards to you.

Think about the frame.
The frame is carved, it is important,

it exists, it does not reflect you,
it does not recede and recede, it has limits   10

and reflections of its own.
There's a nail in the back

to hang it with; there are several nails,
think about the nails,

pay attention to the nail
marks in the wood,

they are important too.

III

Don't assume it is passive
or easy, this clarity

with which I give you yourself.
Consider what restraint it

takes: breath withheld, no anger
or joy disturbing the surface

of the ice.
You are suspended in me

beautiful and frozen, I
preserve you, in me you are safe.   10

It is not a trick either,
it is a craft:

mirrors are crafty.

IV

I wanted to stop this,
this life flattened against the wall,

mute and devoid of colour,
built of pure light,

this life of vision only, split
and remote, a lucid impasse.

I confess: this is not a mirror,
it is a door

I am trapped behind.
I wanted you to see me here,   10

say the releasing word, whatever
that may be, open the wall.

Instead you stand in front of me
combing your hair.

V

You don't like these metaphors.
All right:

Perhaps I am not a mirror.
Perhaps I am a pool.

Think about pools.

(1974)   (1974)

I Made No Choice

I made no choice
I decided nothing

One day you simply appeared in your stupid boat,
your killer's hands, your disjointed body, jagged
        as a shipwreck,
skinny-ribbed, blue-eyed, scorched, thirsty, the usual,
pretending to be – what? a survivor?

Those who say they want nothing
want everything.
It was not this greed   10
that offended me, it was the lies.

Nevertheless I gave you
the food you demanded for the journey
you said you planned; but you planned no journey
and we both knew it.

You've forgotten that,
you made the right decision.
The trees bend in the wind, you eat, you rest,
you think of nothing,
your mind, you say,   20
is like your hands, vacant:

vacant is not innocent.

(1974)   (1974)

There Is Only One of Everything

Not a tree but the tree
we saw, it will never exist, split by the wind
                    and bending down
like that again. What will push out of the earth

later, making it summer, will not be
grass, leaves, repetition, there will
have to be other words. When my

eyes close language vanishes. The cat
with the divided face, half black half orange
nests in my scruffy fur coat, I drink tea,   10

fingers curved around the cup, impossible
to duplicate these flavours. The table
and freak plates glow softly, consuming themselves,

I look out at you and you occur
in this winter kitchen, random as trees or sentences,
entering me, fading like them, in time you will disappear

but the way you dance by yourself
on the tile floor to a worn song, flat and mournful,
so delighted, spoon waved in one hand, wisps of
                    roughened hair   20

sticking up from your head, it's your surprised
body, pleasure I like. I can even say it,
though only once and it won't

last: I want this. I want
this.

(1974)   (1974)

Marie-Claire Blais
1939 –

———◆———

BORN IN QUEBEC, Marie-Claire Blais left school at the age of fifteen but subsequently studied briefly at Laval University. The author of several plays and two collections of poetry, Blais is best known as a novelist. After the publication of *La Belle bête* (1959) and *Tête blanche* (1960), she was awarded a Guggenheim Fellowship in 1962 and three years later published her most widely read work, *Une Saison dans la vie d'Emmanuel* (1965). Works which have been translated into English include *David Sterne* (1967), *Manuscrits de Pauline Archange* (1968), and *Le Loup* (1972). "An Act of Pity" first appeared in *liberté* in 1969.

An Act of Pity

THE CURÉ OF Vallée d'Or increasingly felt a kind of self-satisfaction born of sustained ambition, a vanity piously upheld. He would tremble with secret delight when his inflexible compassion spread around him and he felt the humble gratitude of the poor of his parish being transformed into murmurs of praise. "Ah, *M'sieur le curé,* he's the finest man on earth. We'll never get another *curé* like him in a hundred years." And yet one morning as he was walking to the shack where the Sansfaçon family lived, he knew that death was waiting on the hill, that he was going to Maria now not to entertain her or tell her stories that would make her laugh in her bed of fever, but to bless her for the last time as he closed her eyes. The thought filled him with weariness, as though he realized that even his air of holiness – the dazzling reputation he enjoyed in the village – was nothing, for he was unworthy of it, and because never in the five years of his ministry had pity truly entered his heart. Oh yes, he had loved God, with a fervour that was pleasant to his brand-new priest's vanity, but he had never been able to come close to people simply and without disgust. He thought of Maria's bleak life, soon to be extinguished in a soiled bed, carried off by consumption like so many other young people in the village, and the old feeling of disgust made him shudder. "But it's too late," he thought, "I've become too attached to their false image of me." How often had he feigned charity, compassion, even love, renouncing the deeply felt and horrifying nausea he experienced when confronted with another's frailty, his heart hardened by a princely disdain, but doing good so that later he could be intoxicated by their words: "He's Christ on earth, our *curé*." But that ideal of sweet superiority had required its share of sacrifices. He didn't live in splendid comfort like some of his colleagues in neighbouring parishes. Now he had only a roof to shelter him, but he sensed that his destitution was accompanied by too much self-esteem, that austerity and abstinence gave him a kind of pleasure he should have disapproved but – but he thirsted for it. He could fast with his flock at their empty tables – but thinking of the light meal that would be waiting for him at home that evening; and though he shared the silence of their hunger he was thinking especially of himself, of his sanctified image in other people's eyes, without allowing himself to be moved by the destitution of the hovels that he visited.

Barren fields, a drought-stricken village beneath a blazing sky, children who begged like dogs as soon as he appeared: was this the fragile empire he had dreamed of? But the only mendicity that offended him was for the one thing he could not give: pity, which he always refused. "Is it my fault if there's a wall of ice between them and me? If we're always separated by the distance of privilege? No," he thought, "there's more than that; more than that distance of concern disgusts me. I despise them." Submissive women, ageless men, resigned to the premature death of their sons as they were to the ravages of the seasons, evoked no compassion from him.

"Ah, *M'sieur le curé*, we haven't had much luck this year." But he knew that he was ruling over defeated men. "Yes, those who are already killed have no need to struggle," he thought as he walked along, despondent. "But they've never felt pity for me either, they've overwhelmed me with their confidence, their ignorance most of all, they've shown me their misery but they don't even want to be cured of it."

"Good day, *M'sieur le curé*, you going to see the little Sansfaçon girl? They're dying off fast on that side of the village. It's catching."

"*M'sieur le curé*, I hear the Létourneau baby's dying too."

Tournemule started to laugh. "Ah, *M'sieur le curé*, they're no sooner born than they're dead; come and see us; my old mother wants your blessing before she goes to Heaven."

"I'll come tomorrow," said the *curé*, controlling his anger by contemplating the beautiful landscape, created by God (he was looking at the sea outlined in the distance, on the other side of the burned-out fields, the barren trees), a landscape promising serenity and good fortune that contained only despondency and decay.

"Go on home, Tournemule, your mother's all alone. Tell her I'll come tomorrow."

But Tournemule's grey hands clutched the priest's soutane.

"What is it now?" he asked.

Tournemule didn't know. A paltry caress, a look? The *curé* nodded slightly towards the blind man, but carefully avoided touching him or meeting the ravaged eyes under the heavy, distraught lids.

"You aren't a child now, Tournemule; off with you, go home."

He spoke firmly, but in a voice vibrant with a simulated charity that reassured Tournemule, meek in his cage of night and shadow, where he could still hear his mother's sickly cries.

"Tournemule, where is he? He leaves me all alone, Tournemule does! Tournemule!"

"You hear that, *M'sieur le curé,* she calls me night and day. I don't get a minute's peace, *M'sieur le curé,* she keeps calling my name, poor mother."

"Have pity on her," said the *curé* in a chilly voice in which he could also detect disdain, and he moved away as Tournemule blocked out the strange murmurs with his hands.

He stood on the doorstep for a moment before knocking at the Sansfaçons' door. He shuddered with anguish at the prospect of the intimacy of pain and mourning that these houses in Vallée d'Or revealed to him. A distant cloud was motionless in the dark blue sky; the air was so hot that one could hardly breathe. Swarms of flies were buzzing on a pile of garbage in the garden. "Not a single flower, not a bird, everywhere there is drought and death."

"What're you doing out in that heat, *M'sieur le curé*?" a woman's voice called out. "Hurry, you have to give her the last rites. She's lost a lot of blood, *M'sieur le curé.*"

He couldn't run away now. The woman was dragging him into the house. He walked towards Maria's bed without looking up, pushing shrill children out of his path, breathing in the odour of submissive, abandoned humanity.

"Did the doctor come?" the priest asked.

"We don't need the doctor," the mother replied, "the girl's going to die."

"They die like flies," said the husband, who was rocking one of the smaller children on his knees. "I can't understand what happens to them in the summer; it's like they smother."

"It's the sun," said the mother sadly.

She sat on the edge of her child's bed and stroked her hair, waving the flies away.

"Maria, here's your friend *M'sieur le curé;* cheer up now, come on, open your eyes."

The mother's voice was soon tired and impatient again.

"She used to be an angel, *M'sieur le curé,* now all of a sudden she's a bad girl, so pig-headed she'd make a saint swear. Maria, do you hear what I'm saying?"

"You hear your mother?" the husband repeated, with a certain painful tenderness that surprised the priest. "You hear your mother, Maria?"

The priest gestured, beseeching silence around the child. He approached Maria and wanted to touch her hand, but immediately withdrew. "She doesn't like me any more," he thought. "She knows all about my struggle, she knows my hard-heartedness as well as God does." Frightened by Maria's silence and by the sudden wild look she gave him, he uttered a few words and immediately regretted his awkwardness.

"Are you suffering very much, Maria?"

She bit her lips and didn't answer. For a moment, she even seemed to forget the priest's presence as she watched the motion of some futile rays of light on her bed.

"Remember when we used to be friends?" he asked.

No, she did not remember. How could he let her die if he was her friend? How could he give his blessing to the tortures she was enduring?

"Maybe she's afraid of Hell," said the mother.

"May God protect her," said the priest, stingy with his words of consolation, for he knew that all that remained was to commend Maria to God. It was too late. Or perhaps it was too early, not yet time for pity. "How many children's ghosts are in the limbo of humiliation? They haunt me and yet I've never loved them." He gazed at Maria, lost in dreamy obstinacy as he stared at her, unaware that the sick girl's life had ended several minutes ago, lost in his own oblivion, in the bitter indifference where an appeal from a stifled body, gasping beneath the blows of an invisible hangman, could no longer reach him.

"Maria, Maria," said her mother in a low voice.

"Can't you hear your mother?" the father asked from the back of the room.

The child on his knees began to cry, its voice loud and imploring; the father slapped the baby and it was silent. But another yellow-haired child began to cry. The father looked at it wearily, but said nothing.

"Dead," said the mother.

The children came over to the bed. The familiar sight didn't frighten them. They all looked at the blood trickling from Maria's silent mouth. "These men are degenerate from the cradle," the priest thought sadly, "carriers of vermin, disease, corruption ..." But they were crowding around him, pleading with their begging eyes.

"Ah, M'sieur le curé, don't go!"

He suddenly remembered a bad dream. It was Sunday morning, at the moment of Communion. Many of the faithful were kneeling before him, waiting for the sacred host; their mouths were opened too wide, in a way he considered indecent, for as he bent towards their miserably offered faces he could see right to the backs of their throats, which were infested with sores. Scarcely had he placed the Host on the tongue of an old woman from Vallée d'Or than she showed her teeth like some enraged beast. "They're devouring me," he thought, "they're eating me up." He awoke from his dream chilled with anguish and fear. He recognized in it all the signs of his weakness. It was not with God that he should nourish them, but with himself. And he was not giving of himself, but still they devoured him as he slept. He must consent to lose himself, one day, in the affliction of his people ("My people," he thought. "Why? They're more foreign to me than I am myself."), disappear completely into their misery so that he no longer existed. ("But that kind of compassion would be suicide, and I want to live.")

As he left Maria's house he could still hear the mother sobbing discreetly behind him. Ah! to be back in the coolness of his church, abandon himself to solitude. It was too hot to pray, even to live. He was thirsty again, parched, but water was scarce in this charred land. It occurred to him then that he was living in a drought greater than his refusal to suffer. For had he not been abandoned by all, even by God? He lived like his church, uninhabited, in an austere detachment that nothing could disturb. The dying Christ on his cross represented nothing more than an image of suffering unjustly shared. He stared at the cross as he had looked at Maria's face a few hours before, thinking: "When will this anguish be over?"

In the intense time of his youth, when he had sacrificed his love of happiness and joy, he wanted to remove himself forever from all the wretched people he had seen and never been able to help. His failure at saintliness had marked his failure at happiness as well. He no longer liked the man he had been, clothed in such apparent goodness, fed by so many illusions, and he had ultimately been more mistaken about himself than about others. "If only the children of Vallée d'Or were truly children of God, not the children of my own shame and humiliation."

Closing his eyes he had a vision of Maria running towards him. "Why are your knees bleeding again, Maria?"

"Mama says I'm so weak I can't run without falling down. Don't walk so fast, *M'sieur le curé.*"

She called to him, but he refused to listen. "I've never been able to see the stigmata of the children of Vallée d'Or without considering running away. But is it my fault if you can't caress a child in this village without wanting to vomit?" The stamp of its misery clung to you, its odour and hunger penetrated you. "Lord, how can I love them, whom you have created so humble and bereft?" Perhaps, in a burst of vanity, he would once again find the courage to lie. So that he could hear the words "Our curé's a saint." He could assume a martyr's role. But since Maria's death a strange weariness had invaded him.

How many times had he rejected Maria when she was waiting for him on the church steps in the evening? "Go on, Maria, I want to be alone and you chatter away like a little bird."

"I've got things to tell you."

"You can tell me tomorrow."

But he knew that she wouldn't be there tomorrow. He had already noticed Maria's pale face during her catechism lessons, that she spat blood. But so many children coughed and spat blood in Vallée d'Or! The ravaged sound of all their coughing disturbed his sleep, broke the silence of his dreams.

"You mustn't spit on the floor, Maria; here, take my handkerchief." And he had wanted to add:

"That's the only thing I'll give you during your short life."

In Vallée d'Or people died on their feet. It was only with her first dying breath that Maria was entitled to a place in her mother's bed.

"Maria used to talk to me at night, but what did she say? I didn't listen to her, I only remember that the sound of her voice hurt me and I couldn't look at her without feeling guilty."

"M'sieur le curé, M'sieur le curé..."

Other children called to him that evening, but Maria was no longer among them. He had let her die through absentmindedness, through oversight.

In his room, the priest was stifling. The day was too long, the sun was sinking slowly over the sterile fields. Standing motionless at his window, he forgot to eat the meager meal of vegetables and bread that was waiting on the table. For several days now he had felt such disgust that the bread on his table had suddenly taken on the appearance of the rotting flesh of Vallée d'Or. The bareness and drought around him reflected his internal disarray. "Lord, may I possess nothing but the ardour of my soul; spare me all satisfaction," had been the prayer of his mortified youth. He looked at his iron bed against the white wall, the crucifix, the shabby table, and he understood that he had not lived a life of simplicity, but of avarice. "Yes, I lived that way because I was afraid of the looks of things that one possesses. Or rather, I was afraid of being possessed by them." He had scoffed at poverty, but liked the privileges and honours it bestowed. "Those pious words that flow so readily from the lips of the dying..."

"M'sieur le curé, our saviour!"

"M'sieur le curé, it's me, Tournemule!"

"What do you want now," the priest asked, opening the door to the blind man who was skipping as he laughed.

"My poor mother's asking for you, *M'sieur le curé,* she's afraid she won't last the night."

"She's always afraid of death when the sun sets. Tell her I'll come tomorrow."

"But *M'sieur le curé,* the more scared she gets the more she curses; she's a real demon. Look at how I'm shaking."

"You're the one who's scared, Tournemule; why do you always lie?" Then, looking at the chunk of bread, barely nibbled at, on the table:

"Take this bread, Tournemule, I'm not hungry tonight."

A few minutes later he went onto the dusty road ahead of Tournemule. The heat still lingered, but soon night would come.

"My child, my child," he repeated to the delirious old woman in her gloomy bed. "It's late, you must think of repentance." But Tournemule's mother was screaming with rage:

"I'm thirsty, I don't want to die." And suddenly her delirium burst into a strange gaiety, a savage joy that was almost criminal.

"You're raving; be quiet," said the priest.

But she continued her wild monologue:

"Tournemule there, he tried to kill me, yes, he tried to kill me with a pick one day, and another day he used an axe; tell him the truth, Tournemule. Ah, I don't like Tournemule, I wanted to put out his eyes like a kitten!"

"She's thirsty," said the priest. "Give her something to drink."

Tournemule, his hand trembling, gave his mother some water, then dipped his hand into the bucket and stroked the old woman's cheeks, her forehead.

"Poor mother, don't be afraid, this will cool you."

And she, remembering an old habit, perhaps, touched his eyes as though he were a small child.

"I'm telling you *M'sieur le curé,* this bad boy he wanted to kill me; yes, he wanted to slit my throat; tell *M'sieur le curé* the truth, Tournemule!"

"It's too late for hatred," said the priest, "you've been united by great misfortunes, by great privations, and who knows, perhaps some old affection is still there under the ashes. That's what you must think about, only that."

"Hypocrite," he thought, "I say words that I don't feel, that I may never have felt except today perhaps, when I had to confront Maria's cruel dignity."

The old woman died at dawn, accusing her son joyously, indecently. Then at last she let herself be carried off in a whirlwind of calm madness, melancholy, overwhelmed.

That night he had a dream. He was purifying himself of his faults by setting fire to his church. But God wanted more from him. He must be like "the smallest child of Vallée d'Or," forsaking his priestly vestments, removing himself from the world of religious appearances in which he had lived, and go onto the road naked, like a beggar in his rags, sick, exhausted, go out and beg not for bread which henceforth would no longer sustain his soul, but the freshness, the truth of a single act of pity.

"Tournemule, where are you going now? I need you, any of you, to teach me poverty." But Tournemule was pushing a black wheelbarrow. You couldn't see his face, only two thin shoulders quivering nervously.

"Tournemule, look at me."

"It's too late, *M'sieur le curé,* night's coming and I have to bury my poor mother."

Like a drunken man he sang:

> *Mother was merry*
> *Tomorrow we bury*
> *Mother was merry*
> *With an axe, Tournemule, Tournemule*
> *My old dream...*

But the words to his song were lost in the hot air. Soon Tournemule's entire silhouette disappeared into the bushes. The priest knelt to pray but no word of thanks to God came to his lips. He saw Maria walking towards him as she had in the past. This time, though, it was she who offered him bread. He wanted to speak to her, keep her near him for a few moments, for he had never felt so abandoned, so lonely; but Maria had already fled. He bit into the leaden, tasteless bread, and as he ate it icy blood poured between his fingers.

When he awoke he was weeping, and he kept saying that at last the timid tears of indifference were bursting from him. It was good to be delivered of his shame. For a moment he thought that soon he would be cured of his lack of pity, that he might accomplish great things in Vallée d'Or. "Oh yes, they'll be so proud of their *curé,* the people in Vallée d'Or." This arrogant thought plunged him again into sadness. Weeping with sincere remorse he thought: so this image of himself was what he liked, this nothingness. Did he care for nothing but that?

"Eat, eat this bread," the inner voice had said in his dream.

But this food, rather than giving him life, would bring his death. Recognizing his own weakness, of course, was already a miraculous awakening of his conscience, but it didn't prevent him from lying, from deceiving others about the hardness of his heart.

"Yes, I know what else I'll say to Tournemule tomorrow; I'll ask him for the truth, demand virtues I don't possess myself. I'll go to Maria's mother and console her without love. I..."

But did God have pity? What was known of that invisible pity so rarely expressed, so remote from humanity? "I know God's pity is a symbol, but if it were there, alive, before my eyes, as a fervent example, I wouldn't commit the sin of injustice a hundred times a day."

Sitting on his bed he looked at his clean white hands. "My hands will never be wasted and grey like Tournemule's, I'll never spit blood like Maria. God gives me too much protection!" Slowly he grew indifferent to his own tears. It was hot in his room. Flies were sticking to the window. Dawn was coming, suffocating, like yesterday. And if the priest suddenly felt some hesitant pity it was, perhaps, too late. For no one was there to receive it.

(1969)   (1977)

Sheila Fischman (Trans.)

Paul Chamberland
1939 –

BORN IN LONGUEUIL, Quebec, Paul Chamberland studied at the University of Montreal and at the Sorbonne. In 1963, he co-founded *parti pris*, a Marxist-oriented political and cultural review which, together with an affiliated publishing house Les Editions parti-pris, became an important influence in the artistic and literary development of Quebec in the 1960s. Chamberland's first collection, *Genèse* (1963), was followed in 1964 by *Terre-Québec* and in 1965 by his best-known collection, *L'Afficheur hurle*. Most of the last-named volume has been translated in Malcolm Reid's *The Shouting Signpainters: A Literary and Political Account of Quebec Revolutionary Nationalism* (1972). More recent volumes of Chamberland's work include *L'Inavouable* (1968) and *Eclats de la pierre noire d'où rejaillit ma vie* (1972).

Pre-Revolution Poem: 1

TO YVES PRÉFONTAINE

I will see the flaming face growing in the great
burgeoning of streets in the cracked shell of my own time
    and gnawing until it bursts the moorings of cold
Indifference imprisoned us, a church-ridden people,
for high treason in its dull slow midnight-masses
    the bloody wheel of revolution has turned and
returned from one age to another
    but we know only a capstan of litanies
    a poor little pendant-flame that English and Roman
angels exorcised and placed on Mary's blue robe   10
a puny star smothered in an incense box   our own
heart bleeding drop by drop that we discovered beating
in unison with our speech-dazzled eyes

    a look held secret too long in fear's empty recesses
a look that brings us back to the deep love of being born
    our land was so vast between Baffin Bay and the
Great Lakes between Hudson Bay and the Notre Dame
Mountains all that deaf-and-dumb living flesh of a fat
and feeble fowl crucified in the Yank's own America

I will see an angry look born on the soil of our curses   20
break through the barricaded doors of our darkness
    I will see it suddenly beating against our faces and
thoroughly searching our veins in order to preserve our
bodies from the twin furies of the river and the mine
    in order to restore us innocent to the elements
    we shall find our way out of mud and desire
    by our campaigns by this time of red Christs who
harvest kings and free nations from prison
emblazoned in anvil hues

O look of anger coming from where proud and open   30
nations imagine justice a land with a single cry born of
broken chains from Africa to the barracoons of Latin
America to set fire to the tropics from one sea to the other
    to draw us at last out of the polar jaws and to light
in our mole-slumbering bodies the flame of being free
and to wed the length of her thousand wounds Quebec
our soil

(1964)   (1976)

Fred W. Cogswell (Trans.)

Lament for the
Fourth of June 1963

FOR OUR COMRADES OF THE FLQ BETRAYED BY
INFORMERS THIS FUTILE KNELL

the blazoned year goes down
over dishonoured love
prison for our comrades
a curfew on our hearts

the old cow hope drools on the cobbles
in the dawn a glitter of sour spit
but our slashed fists are raised
for their blood to blacken a coarse sky
a crackling flag of rage
we remain comrades we remain   10
your cause is our own and so what
if today on the English gibbet
you swing and so what
if it's our turn tomorrow

the forge is set up in our veins
the veins of a people
the enormous land takes breath and shapes in her flesh
anvil and beetle cordite and gun
her face takes form in the bomb's opening light
with a tremor of recognition her voice fails   20
already a militant speech

thundering at her brow
she hears the shadows crackle with blood
thunder and steel the drums of revolt
welling up clear in her limbs hears the insistent sun
turn winter out and strike our gaolers through
the blazoned year goes down
over dishonoured love
prison for our comrades
a curfew on our hearts
a gag on the fires of life   30

(1964)

(1971)

Francis Sparshott (Trans.)

Open Shutters

I would live for a moment in this music
like a child I would lick the windowpane
whence the sun leads his gardens out to pasture
and the night her gardens into sleep

                      on the way
I would pass through the season the fruit
the lucky sentinel and the bread
my steps barely heard
in the burning meadow of your laughter
like stars quivering above your sleep   10

I would return without memory
to the black bellies of the fountains
where night sleeps in the womb of day
and would be a god against my will

in the climate of your summer

in the ring-star soft on your finger
I see the season   the city   the season turning
time lowering its eyelid over your eye
and the flower's violet heart reddening your flesh
    setting your mouth ablaze
where I drink the wounded healed world   20

I love you and the earth is silent at your feet like
    a ewe asleep
I love you and the sky reflects its mirrors in your
    cloudy smile
comes the rain   and your body a sun through the
    rain
the world a flower which quivers at your breasts

the things which are born in the pathway of your
    fingers   30
never will I remake their design
save in the splendour of the lamps paired
above your sleep beneath my kiss

my cupped hands framing the light of your face
I a hunter on the trail of the nights turned pale
reforging on our lips the ring of our seasons

(1964)   (1970)
John Glassco (Trans.)

From
L'Afficheur hurle

I write the circumstance of my life and yours and yours my wife my
    comrades
I write the poem of circumstance deadly and inescapable
pardon my familiar tone bear with me through my swamps of silence
I can't talk any more
I don't know what to say
poetry does not exist
except in old illuminated books sweet voices of orchid smell from the
    vaults where gods are born
I'm poor in name and poor in life
I don't know what I'm doing here
how could I speak in the right forms   with the right intonations with 10
    the rhymes with the conjuring rhythms of things and peoples

I have nothing to say but myself
a truth without poetry myself

this fate I allot myself this death I deal myself
because I will not half-live in this half-land
in this world half-caught in the boneyard of dead worlds
>   (and the idea that comes to me here the image in which I'm
>   burned "in the corrida of the stars" the beautiful image that
>   restores the poem —
out with it I won't have it it's not mine)
and too bad if I assassinate poetry
what you would call poetry
what for me is a rattle   20
for I want no more lies
in this present without poetry

for this truth without poetry myself

* * *

I am a man ashamed to be a man
I am a man from whom manhood is kept
I am a man attacked through his compatriots and who will never
>   perform for other men an act with any sense until he has effaced
>   at last the infamy it is to be a French-Canadian
no the finest sophistry will never unknot the ancestral fault
for I am like a jaundiced regret a diseased shame breaking out on the
>   leg of the day a boil on the body of God
I hear the rumble rising daily from Quebec and it's a bad novel a stupid
>   movie continuous showing in the movie-house America with
>   nobody watching nobody interested any more in comprehending
the torment of my land   30
its anguished face iced-in with inhibitions slashed with darkness
>   drugged with incense

my country with your drunkard's face your sick man's face your
>   haggard sluggard nigger face your New York pressing girl's wet
>   face
my love for you my small white sin
my quiet desperation   it's triviality doesn't matter
will a million horizons gleam for us a million auroras lick the belly of the
>   blast furnaces

are we simply the fuel of progress the surplus value chomped without
>   attention by Texaco and General Motors

strange earth which mourns softly beneath my feet distant earth
strange earth lost to its expropriated inhabitants
      expropriated of the world and of its joy
      expropriated of their present and of their future   40
      expropriated of their living and of their dying
      expropriated of anger and of love

strange earth O tenacious prowlers around the ancient domain O my
      brothers O blind creatures humiliated in your thirst and in your
      growth
(ah why was there anything but the long night scream of blood amid the
      saxophonic neon)
strange mornings world strangely removed from the carnal urges that
      pointlessly flow from my arms and legs

      gray world
      blackened world
      locked-up world
      land barely out of vague prehistory
      land captive by blood and by bone   50
      in blood and in bone
      land to my mouth like an unsaid word
      trapped beast in the underbrush of morning
      sister of shame O like to my body stopped servant
      land knotted in roots and instinct
      out of the prenatal blackness out of the savage stupor
      O land to be said   O land to be lived

in this strange lost land I beat my feet on the deserted morning ground
      the October plowing the ancestral haze
I walk toward you   I brush aside the ripplings of the world for one day
      to seize your stranger's face which nevertheless resembles mine
      and brands mine with the brand of existence
in a past beyond childhood you were given to me like bread like blood 60
      like name   and I shall release you from the icebergs of
      nonexistence from the dungeons of glaciation I shall take you like
      a woman who gives herself in giving life
mistress land
matrix land
silent and magnetic
strange land lost beneath the maze of tracks traced on the crazy dial of
      exile and unreason

bit by bit the world is crumbling horizons clash and landscapes die
    revealing through their blood the bare bone of malediction
and it has always been and it has always been
order abundance calm and lies lies
for hate and theft are all that's true
and all that's true is my love for a people ill-loved.

* * *

is it my fault that I suffer from a land aborning   70
from a land occupied
from a pain which is the sweetness of others
from a death that nourishes the life of others
yes I know   *real* wounds have the noble extravagances of bad wine
    they are beautiful they rend the heart and our wounds are gray
    mute they ring false
is it my fault that we die of half-living that our morosity is the
    half-truth of our comfort
we are denied even the epitaph of the beheaded the starved the
    massacred we leave a blank page in history
even to sing our misfortune is false   where could I find it a name a
    music
who will hear our footfalls smothered in the rut of America where we
    are preceded and already surpassed by the terrible striped death
    of red-skinned men
in the ruelle Sainte-Christophe dies a people never born their history a
    fairy-tale that ends at the beginning
once upon a time . . . and all there is is the stutter of a tramp who   80
    cannot identify his ailment
and who leaves by the rear after a bad joke ashamed of his suffering as
    of a lie

in the ruelle Saint-Christophe
in the ruelle vérité
is it death that clacks his foot
in the shadows sound of madness

(1965)   (1972)
Malcolm Reid (Trans.)

Patrick Lane
1939 –

PATRICK LANE WAS born in Nelson, British Columbia, and worked at a variety of jobs before he moved to Vancouver where he became involved in the founding of Very Stone House Press. Since then he has lived and worked in various parts of Canada. His first volume of poetry, *Letters From the Savage Mind*, was published in 1966; his best known collections of verse are *Beware the Months of Fire* (1974) and *Unborn Things: South American Poems* (1976).

Treaty-trip from Shulus Reservation

He leaned against
the dusty wall
with open pants
struggling
with drunken buttons
of his fly.

His raven woman
knelt in the dirt
like some aged black
10 supplicant bird.
Hunched forward
she puked thin gruel
on his feet
and he raised his knee
struck her in the face.

Beneath the dull lamp-yellow
outlined in counter-play

an Indian child
bounced her ball
against the flat red wall;   20
her fluttering shadow
in wild macabre dance
a part of the tableau.

I hung there
in the sightless night
like a hooded
jesse-bound hawk
my quiet hammered breath
held in rhythmic beat
with the bouncing ball   30

that neatly caught
flew out
from the child's small hand
to thump on the flat red wall.

(1966)

(1974)

Hastings Street Rooms

A wall is two sides. Here
on the inside there is nothing
to hang and I sit looking
at bare spaces around me.

On the outside is another
man. He has painted his walls
in many colours, hung pictures
of his loved ones.

Their screams come through
the plaster like shredded fingers.   10

A wall is two sides.
I would cut a window
but all that I would add
would be four more walls
and silence
like a painting of tomorrow.

(1970)

(1974)

The Bird

The bird you captured is dead.
I told you it would die
but you would not learn
from my telling. You wanted
to cage a bird in your hands
and learn to fly.

Listen again.
You must not handle birds.
They cannot fly through your fingers.
You are not a nest   10
and a feather is
not made of blood and bone.

Only words
can fly for you like birds
on the wall of the sun.
A bird is a poem
that talks of the end of cages.

(1971)

(1974)

The Sun Has Begun
To Eat The Mountain

Pines eat mist out of the sky
in the village the old
man with yellow eyes
lies stretched out on the mat
he is dying

Stones change shape as they
        breathe
in the bush the shaman
scrapes the green bark
from the devil's club
10   she will purge death
again this spring

Birds are silent when day ends
in my silence
I wonder again at the far cities

(1971)

tell me again
the story of the beginning

You who are near enough to death
please tell me
where the beginning is
look   20
the sky weeps
the woman comes

Tell me where the sun goes
when the mountains are all eaten
and the world is only a flatness
where eagles fly
cutting the sky to ribbons
with their great wings

(1974)

The Hustler

In a rainbow bus we begin to descend
a gorge that gapes open like a wound.
The women, who chattered like black beans
in a dry gourd, cover their faces and moan
while the men, not wanting to admit the fear
that turns their knuckles white,
light cigarettes and squint their eyes.

The air fills with hands making crosses.
I make the sign of the cross
with a small grey woman   10
but she doesn't see me. She has no time

for a gringo when the manifold sins
of a lifetime must be confessed.
Her eyes are buried in the hole
three thousand feet below.

The driver stops the bus, adjusts
the plastic Jesus that obscures
half of his windshield and his eyes,
gets out and stands beside each tire
shaking his head. His face is a scowl   20
of despair. He kicks each tire in turn,
opens the hood and pounds the carburetor.
Then he gets back on the bus
and crosses himself slowly as the women
begin to weep and children scream.

He mutters two Pater Nosters
and a dozen Ave Marias as he walks
through the bus with hat extended
to the people who fill it with coins.
He smiles then, bravely, as if the world   30
had been lifted from his shoulders
and like the thief that Christ forgave
walks out the broken doors to a roadside shrine
and empties his hat into the hands of a Mary
whose expression of humility
hasn't changed in a hundred years.

The people sigh and consign their souls to God
and I relax because I saw him as he knelt there
cross his hands on his crotch as if
he were imploring the Mother of God's help   40
in preserving his manhood on the road to Hell
and pour the collected sucres in his pocket
the price of safety embodied in the vulture
who lifted off her beatific head,
the men shushing their children grandly
and me, peeling a banana and eating,
gazing into the endless abyss.

Ecuador

(1975)   (1975)

Pissaro's Tomb

On the broad hills, the broken backs of mountains
and the cracks where earth has split from earth
high walls and viaducts, canals and temples
stand rooted in grey stone. But do not speak.
Only the living eye breeds language
where no language is. The words conjured
are only images. The memory of something
in the race that is unknown.

Pissaro stood by these walls
who now lies dried and shrunken   10
in his tomb beside the sea.
The great cathedral shelters him
where priests walk hooded
beside God. And Pissaro died
who broke an empire into dust.
So it is told in our histories.
And so it was. But the dead do not speak.
Only the living eye breeds language
out of dust. It is what holds this empire
still. This lust for history.   20

On broken hills the monolithic stones
that once were mountains stand.
Men move upon the land. Pissaro's
body lies in the capital he built.
The men who were his enemies are gone,
their history unknown, their language lost
as ancient times are lost
though they come and go in me
and will until what now I speak
men know as silence.   30

Lima, Peru

(1975)   (1975)

Dennis Lee
1939 –

———◆———

BORN IN TORONTO, Dennis Lee studied at the University of Toronto and has taught there and at York University. He was a co-founder and editor of the House of Anansi Press and played an important role in the development of new interest in Canadian writing during the 1960s. Since the appearance of his early collections of poetry, *Kingdom of Absence* (1967) and *Civil Elegies* (1968), Lee has expanded and republished the latter volume as *Civil Elegies and Other Poems* (1972). More recently he has published several collections of poems for children including *Alligator Pie* (1974) and *Nicholas Knock and Other People* (1974).

From
Civil Elegies

3

The light rides easy on people dozing at noon in Toronto, or
here it does, in the square, with the white spray hanging
upward in plumes on the face of the pool, and the kids, and the thrum
    of the traffic,
and the people come and they feel no consternation, dozing at
lunchtime; even the towers comply.
And they prevail in their placid continuance, idly unwrapping their
    food
day after day on the slabs by the pool, warm in the summer sun.
Day after day the light rides easy.
Nothing is important. 10
But once at noon I felt my body's pulse contract and
balk in the space of the square, it puckered and jammed till nothing
worked, and casting back and forth
the only resonance that held was in the Archer.
Great bronze simplicity, that muscled form
was adequate in the aimless expanse – it held, and tense and

662

waiting to the south I stood until the
clangor in my forearms found its outlet.
And when it came I knew that stark heraldic form is not
great art; for it is real, great art is less than its necessity.   20
But it held, when the monumental space of the square
went slack, it moved in sterner space.
Was shaped by earlier space and it ripples with
wrenched stress, the bronze is flexed by
blind aeonic throes
that bred and met in slow enormous impact,
and they are still at large for the force in the bronze churns
through it, and lunges beyond and also the Archer declares
that space is primal, raw, beyond control and drives toward a
living stillness, its own.   30
But if some man by the pool, doing his workaday
job in the city, tangled in other men's
futures with ticker-tape, hammering
type for credits or bread, or in for the day, wiped out in Long Branch
by the indelible sting of household acts of war,
or whatever; if a man strays into that
vast barbaric space it happens that he enters into
void and will go
under, or he must himself become void.

We live on occupied soil.   40
Across the barren Shield, immortal scrubland and our own,
where near the beginning the spasms of lava
settled to bedrock schist,
barbaric land, initial, our
own, scoured bare under
crush of the glacial recessions
and later it broke the settlers, towing them
deeper and deeper each year beneath the
gritty sprinkle of soil, till men who had worked their farms for a
          lifetime
could snap in a month from simple cessation of will,   50
though the brute surroundings went on — the flagrant changes
of maple and sumach, the water in ripples of light,
the faces of outcrop, the stillness, and up the slopes
a vast incessant green that drew the mind
beyond its tether, north, to muskeg and
stunted hackmatack, and then the whine of icy tundra north to the
          pole —
despotic land, inhuman yet

our *own*, where else on earth? and reaping stone
from the bush their fathers cleared, the sons gave
way and they drank all year, or went strange, or they sat and stared   60
        outside
as their cars settled back to slag and now what
races toward us on asphalt across the Shield –
by truck, by TV minds and the ore-bearing flatcars –
is torn from the land and the mute oblivion of
all those fruitless lives, it no longer
stays for us, immemorial adversary, but is shipped and
divvied abroad though wrested whole from the Shield.

Take Tom Thomson, painter; he
did his work in the Shield.
Could guide with a blindfold on. Was part of the bush. Often when   70
        night
came down in a subtle rush and the scorched scrub still
ached for miles from the fires he paddled direct through
the palpable dark, hearing only the push and
drip of the blade for hours and then very suddenly the radiance of the
renewed land broke over his canvas. So. It was his
job. But no two moments land with the same sideswipe
and Thomson, for all his savvy, is very damp and
trundled by submarine currents, pecked by the fish out
somewhere cold in the Shield and the far loons percolate
high in November and he is not painting their cry.   80

Small things ignite us, and the quirky particulars
flare on all sides.
A cluster of birches, in moonlight;
a jack pine, gnarled and
focussing heaven and earth –
these might fend off void.
Or under the poolside arches the sunlight, skidding on paper
        destroyers,
kindles a dazzle, skewing the sense. Like that. Any
combination of men and time can start the momentary
ignition. If only it were enough.   90
But it is two thousand years since Christ's carcass rose in a glory,
and now the shiny ascent is not for us, Thomson is
done and we cannot
malinger among the bygone acts of grace. For
many are called but none are chosen now, we are the evidence

for downward momentum, although despite our longing still
     restrained
within the real, as Thomson's body really did
decay and vying to praise him we
bicker about which grave the carcass fills.

New silences occur in the drone of the square's great spaces.   100
The light overbalances, shadows
appear, the people walk away.
But massy and knotted and still the Archer continues its space,
which violates our lives, and reminds us, and has no mercy upon us.
For a people which lays its whiskey and violent machines
on a land that is primal, and native, which takes that land in greedy
innocence but will not live it, which is not claimed by its own
and sells that land off even before it has owned it,
traducing the immemorial pacts of men and earth, free and
beyond them, exempt by miracle from the fate of the race –   110
that people will botch its cities, its greatest squares
will scoff at its money and stature, and prising wide
a civil space to live in, by the grace of its own invention it will
fill that space with the artifacts of death.

On Queen Street, therefore, in Long Branch, wherever the
people have come upon it, say that the
news is as bad as we thought:
we have spent the bankroll; here, in this place,
it is time to honour the void.

(1968)   (1972)

6

I am one for whom the world is constantly proving too much –
not this nor that, but the continental drift to barbarian
normalcy frightens me, I am constantly
stiffening before my other foot touches the ground and numb in my
stance I hear the country pouring on past me gladly on all sides,
towed and protesting but pelting very fast downhill,
and though I do not decry technopolis I can see only the bread and
     circuses to come,
and no man will use a mirror to shave, in case he

glimpse himself and abroad there will come obscenity, a senseless   10
    procession of holy wars
and we will carry the napalm for our side, proud of our clean hands.
I can't converse with friends without discussing Rome, this is
bad news and though the upshot is not that I am constantly
riddled with agonies my thing is often worse for I cannot get purchase
    on life.

(1968)   (1972)

Clark Blaise
1941 –

———◆———

THE SON OF Canadian parents, Clark Blaise was born in Fargo, North
Dakota, and grew up in the American Middle West and Florida. After
graduating from Dennison University, Ohio, he took a Master of Fine
Arts degree at the University of Iowa (1964). In 1966 he moved to
Montreal and began teaching at Sir George Williams University. He
has published two collections of short fiction, *A North American Educa-
tion* (1973) and *Tribal Justice* (1974) and a travel book, *Days and Nights in
Calcutta* (1977), in collaboration with Bharati Mukherjee.

A Class of New Canadians

NORMAN DYER HURRIED down Sherbrooke Street, collar turned against
the snow. "Superb!" he muttered, passing a basement gallery next to
a French bookstore. Bleached and tanned women in furs dashed from
hotel lobbies into waiting cabs. Even the neon clutter of the side streets
and the honks of slithering taxis seemed remote tonight through the
peaceful snow. *Superb*, he thought again, waiting for a light and backing from a slushy curb: a word reserved for wines, cigars, and delicate

sauces; he was feeling superb this evening. After eighteen months in Montreal, he still found himself freshly impressed by everything he saw. He was proud of himself for having steered his life north, even for jobs that were menial by standards he could have demanded. Great just being here no matter what they paid, looking at these buildings, these faces, and hearing all the languages. He was learning to be insulted by simple bad taste, wherever he encountered it.

Since leaving graduate school and coming to Montreal, he had sampled every ethnic restaurant downtown and in the old city, plus a few Levantine places out in Outremont. He had worked on conversational French and mastered much of the local dialect, done reviews for local papers, translated French-Canadian poets for Toronto quarterlies, and tweaked his colleagues for not sympathizing enough with Quebec separatism. He attended French performances of plays he had ignored in English, and kept a small but elegant apartment near a colony of *émigré* Russians just off Park Avenue. Since coming to Montreal he'd witnessed a hold-up, watched a murder, and seen several riots. When stopped on the street for directions, he would answer in French or accented English. To live this well and travel each long academic summer, he held two jobs. He had no intention of returning to the States. In fact, he had begun to think of himself as a semi-permanent, semi-political exile.

Now, stopped again a few blocks farther, he studied the window of Holt-Renfrew's exclusive men's shop. Incredible, he thought, the authority of simple good taste. Double-breasted chalk-striped suits he would never dare to buy. Knitted sweaters, and fifty-dollar shoes. One tanned mannequin was decked out in a brash checkered sportscoat with a burgundy vest and dashing ascot. Not a price tag under three hundred dollars. Unlike food, drink, cinema, and literature, clothing had never really involved him. Someday, he now realized, it would. Dyer's clothes, thus far, had all been bought in a chain department store. He was a walking violation of American law, clad shoes to scarf in Egyptian cottons, Polish leathers, and woolens from the People's Republic of China.

He had no time for dinner tonight; this was Wednesday, a day of lectures at one university, and then an evening course in English as a Foreign Language at McGill, beginning at six. He would eat afterwards.

Besides the money, he had kept this second job because it flattered him. There was to Dyer something fiercely elemental, almost existential, about teaching both his language and his literature in a foreign country — like Joyce in Trieste, Isherwood and Nabokov in Berlin, Beckett in Paris. Also it was necessary for his students. It was the first time in his life that he had done something socially useful. What difference did it make that the job was beneath him, a recent Ph.D., while most of his colleagues in the evening school at McGill were idle housewives and bachelor civil servants? It didn't matter, even, that this job was a perversion of all the sentiments he held as a progressive young teacher. He was a god two evenings a week, sometimes suffering and fatigued, but nevertheless an omniscient, benevolent god. His students were silent, ignorant, and dedicated to learning English. No discussions, no demonstrations, no dialogue.

I love them, he thought. They need me.

He entered the room, pocketed his cap and ear muffs, and dropped his briefcase on the podium. Two girls smiled good evening.

They love me, he thought, taking off his boots and hanging up his coat; I'm not like their English-speaking bosses.

I love myself, he thought with amazement even while conducting a drill on word order. I love myself for tramping down Sherbrooke Street in zero weather just to help them with noun clauses. I love myself standing behind this podium and showing Gilles Carrier and Claude Veilleux the difference between the past continuous and the simple past; or the sultry Armenian girl with the bewitching half-glasses that "put on" is not the same as "take on"; or telling the dashing Mr. Miguel Mayor, late of Madrid, that simple futurity can be expressed in four different ways, at least.

This is what mastery is like, he thought. Being superb in one's chosen field, not merely in one's mother tongue. A respected performer in the lecture halls of the major universities, equipped by twenty years' research in the remotest libraries, and slowly giving it back to those who must have it. Dishing it out suavely, even wittily. Being a legend. Being loved and a little feared.

"Yes, Mrs. David?"

A *sabra*: freckled, reddish hair, looking like a British model, speaks with a nifty British accent, and loves me.

"No," he smiled, "*I were* is not correct except in the present subjunctive, which you haven't studied yet."

The first hour's bell rang. The students closed their books for the intermission. Dyer put his away, then noticed a page of his Faulkner lecture from the afternoon class. *Absalom, Absalom!* his favorite.

"Can anyone here tell me what the *impregnable citadel of his passive rectitude* means?"

"What, sir?" asked Mr. Vassilopoulos, ready to copy.

"What about *the presbyterian and lugubrious effluvium of his passive vindictiveness?*" A few girls giggled. "O.K.," said Dyer, "take your break."

In the halls of McGill they broke into the usual groups. French-Canadians and South Americans into two large circles, then the Greeks, Germans, Spanish, and French into smaller groups. The patterns interested Dyer. Madrid Spaniards and Parisian French always spoke English with their New World co-linguals. The Middle Europeans spoke German together, not Russian, preferring one occupier to the other. Two Israeli men went off alone. Dyer decided to join them for the break.

Not *sabras*, Dyer concluded, not like Mrs. David. The shorter one, dark and wavy-haired, held his cigarette like a violin bow. The other, Mr. Weinrot, was tall and pot-bellied, with a ruddy face and thick stubby fingers. Something about him suggested truck-driving, perhaps of beer, maybe in Germany. Neither one, he decided, could supply the name of a good Israeli restaurant.

"This is really hard, you know?" said Weinrot.

"Why?"

"I think it's because I'm not speaking much of English at my job."

"French?" asked Dyer.

"French? Pah! All the time Hebrew, sometimes German, sometimes little Polish. Crazy thing, eh? How long you think they let me speak Hebrew if I'm working in America?"

"Depends on where you're working," he said.

"Hell, I'm working for the Canadian government, what you think? Plant I work in — I'm engineer, see — makes boilers for the turbines going up North. Look. When I'm leaving Israel I go first to Italy. Right away-bamm I'm working in Italy I'm speaking Italian like a native. Passing for a native."

"A native Jew," said his dark-haired friend.

"Listen to him. So in Rome they think I'm from Tyrol — that's still native, eh? So I speak Russian and German and Italian like a Jew. My Hebrew is bad, I admit it, but it's a lousy language anyway. Nobody likes it. French I understand but English I'm talking like a bum. Arabic I know five dialects. Danish fluent. So what's the matter I can't learn English?"

"It'll come, don't worry," Dyer smiled. *Don't worry, my son;* he wanted to pat him on the arm. "Anyway, that's what makes Canada so appealing. Here they don't force you."

"What's this *appealing*? Means nice? Look, my friend, keep it, eh? Two years in a country I don't learn the language means it isn't a country."

"Come on," said Dyer. "Neither does forcing you."

"Let me tell you a story why I come to Canada. Then you tell me if I was wrong, O.K.?"

"Certainly," said Dyer, flattered.

In Italy, Weinrot told him, he had lost his job to a Communist union. He left Italy for Denmark and opened up an Israeli restaurant with five other friends. Then the six Israelis decided to rent a bigger apartment downtown near the restaurant. They found a perfect nine-room place for two thousand kroner a month, not bad shared six ways. Next day the landlord told them the deal was off. "You tell me why," Weinrot demanded.

No Jews? Dyer wondered. "He wanted more rent," he finally said.

"More — you kidding? More we expected. *Less* we didn't expect. A couple with eight kids is showing up after we're gone and the law in Denmark says a man has a right to a room for each kid plus a hundred kroner knocked off the rent for each kid. What you think of that? So a guy who comes in *after* us gets a nine-room place for a thousand kroner *less*. Law says no way a bachelor can get a place ahead of a family, and bachelors pay twice as much."

Dyer waited, then asked, "So?"

"So, I make up my mind the world is full of communismus, just like Israel. So I take out applications next day for Australia, South Africa, U.S.A., and Canada. Canada says come right away, so I go. Should have waited for South Africa."

"How could you?" Dyer cried. "What's wrong with you anyway? South Africa is fascist. Australia is racist."

The bell rang, and the Israelis, with Dyer, began walking to the room.

"What I was wondering, then," said Mr. Weinrot, ignoring Dyer's outburst, "was if my English is good enough to be working in the United States. You're American, aren't you?"

It was a question Dyer had often avoided in Europe, but had rarely been asked in Montreal. "Yes," he admitted, "your English is probably good enough for the States or South Africa, whichever one wants you first."

He hurried ahead to the room, feeling that he had let Montreal down. He wanted to turn and shout to Weinrot and to all the others that Montreal was the greatest city on the continent, if only they knew it as well as he did. If they'd just break out of their little ghettos.

At the door, the Armenian girl with the half-glasses caught his arm. She was standing with Mrs. David and Miss Parizeau, a jolly French-Canadian girl that Dyer had been thinking of asking out.

"Please, sir," she said, looking at him over the tops of her tiny glasses, "what I was asking earlier — *put on* — I heard on the television. A man said *You are putting me on* and everybody laughed. I think it was supposed to be funny but *put on* we learned means get dressed, no?"

"Ah — *don't put me on*," Dyer laughed.

"I yaven't erd it neither," said Miss Parizeau.

"To put some*body* on means to make a fool of him. To put some*thing* on is to wear it. O.K.?" He gave examples.

"Ah, now I know," said Miss Parizeau. "Like bullshitting somebody. Is it the same?"

"Ah, yes," he said, smiling. French-Canadians were like children learning the language. "Your example isn't considered polite. 'Put on' is very common now in the States."

"Then maybe," said Miss Parizeau, "we'll ave it ere in twenty years." The Armenian giggled.

"No — I've heard it here just as often," Dyer protested, but the girls had already entered the room.

He began the second hour with a smile which slowly soured as he thought of the Israelis. America's anti-communism was bad enough, but it was worse hearing it echoed by immigrants, by Jews, here in Montreal. Wasn't there a psychological type who chose Canada over South Africa? Or was it just a matter of visas and slow adjustment? Did Johannesburg lose its Greeks, and Melbourne its Italians, the way Dyer's students were always leaving Montreal?

And after class when Dyer was again feeling content and thinking of approaching one of the Israelis for a restaurant tip, there came the flood of small requests: should Mrs. Papadopoulos go into a more advanced course; could Mr. Perez miss a week for an interview in Toronto; could Mr. Giguère, who spoke English perfectly, have a harder book; Mr. Coté an easier one?

Then as he packed his briefcase in the empty room, Miguel Mayor, the vain and impeccable Spaniard, came forward from the hallway.

"Sir," he began, walking stiffly, ready to bow or salute. He wore a loud gray checkered sportscoat this evening, blue shirt, and matching ascot-handkerchief, slightly mauve. He must have shaved just before class, Dyer noticed, for two fresh daubs of antiseptic cream stood out on his jaw, just under his earlobe.

"I have been wanting to ask *you* something, as a matter of fact," said Dyer. "Do you know any good Spanish restaurants I might try to-night?"

"There are not any good Spanish restaurants in Montreal," he said. He stepped closer. "Sir?"

"What's on your mind, then?"

"Please — have you the time to look on a letter for me?"

He laid the letter on the podium.

"Look *over* a letter," said Dyer. "What is it for?"

"I have applied," he began, stopping to emphasize the present perfect construction, "for a job in Cleveland, Ohio, and I want to know if my letter will be good. Will an American, I mean —"

"Why are you going there?"

"It is a good job."

"But Cleveland —"

"They have a blackman mayor, I have read. But the job is not in Cleveland."

"Let me see it."

Most honourable Sir: I humbly beg consideration for a position in your grand company ...

"Who are you writing this to?"

"The president," said Miguel Mayor.

I am once a student of Dr. Ramiro Gutierrez of the Hydraulic Institute of Sevilla, Spain ...

"Does the president know this Ramiro Gutierrez?"

"Oh, everybody is knowing him," Miguel Mayor assured, "he is the most famous expert in all Spain."

"Did he recommend this company to you?"

"No — I have said in my letter, if you look —"

An ancient student of Dr. Gutierrez, Salvador del Este, is actually a boiler expert who is being employed like supervisor is formerly a friend of mine ...

"Is he still your friend?"

Whenever you say come to my city Miguel Mayor for talking I will be coming. I am working in Montreal since two years and am now wanting more money than I am getting here now ...

"Well ..." Dyer sighed.

"Sir — what I want from you is knowing in good English how to interview me by this man. The letters in Spanish are not the same to English ones, you know?"

I remain humbly at your orders ...

"Why do you want to leave Montreal?"

"It's time for a change."

"Have you ever been to Cleveland?"

"I am one summer in California. Very beautiful there and hot like my country. Montreal is big port like Barcelona. Everybody mixed together and having no money. It is just a place to land, no?"

"Montreal? Don't be silly."

"I thought I come here and learn good English but where I work I get by in Spanish and French. It's hard, you know?" he smiled. Then he took a few steps back and gave his cuffs a gentle tug, exposing a set of jade cufflinks.

Dyer looked at the letter again and calculated how long he would be correcting it, then up at his student. How old is he? My age? Thirty? Is he married? Where do the Spanish live in Montreal? He looks so prosperous, so confident, like a male model off a page of *Playboy*. For an instant Dyer felt that his student was mocking him, somehow pitting his astounding confidence and wardrobe, sharp chin and matador's bearing against Dyer's command of English and mastery of the side streets, bistros, and ethnic restaurants. Mayor's letter was painful, yet he remained somehow competent. He would pass his interview, if he got one. What would he care about America, and the odiousness he'd soon be supporting? It was as though a superstructure of exploitation had been revealed, and Dyer felt himself abused by the very people he wanted so much to help. It had to end someplace.

He scratched out the second "humbly" from the letter, then folded the sheet of foolscap. "Get it typed right away," he said. "Good luck."

"Thank you, sir," said his student with a bow. Dyer watched the letter disappear in the inner pocket of the checkered sportscoat. Then the folding of the cashmere scarf, the draping of the camel's hair coat about the shoulders, the easing of the fur hat down to the rims of his ears. The meticulous filling of the pigskin gloves. Mayor's patent leather galoshes glistened.

"Good evening, sir," he said.

"Buenas noches," Dyer replied.

He hurried now, back down Sherbrooke Street to his daytime office where he could deposit his books. Montreal on a winter night was still mysterious, still magical. Snow blurred the arc lights. The wind was dying. Every second car was now a taxi, crowned with an orange crescent. Slushy curbs had hardened. The window of Holt-Renfrew's was still attractive. The legless dummies invited a final stare. He stood longer than he had earlier, in front of the sporty mannequin with a burgundy waistcoat, the mauve and blue ensemble, the jade cufflinks.

Good evening, sir, he could almost hear. The ascot, the shirt, the complete outfit, had leaped off the back of Miguel Mayor. He pictured how he must have entered the store with three hundred dollars and a prepared speech, and walked out again with everything off the torso's back.

I want that.

What, sir?

That.

The coat, sir?

Yes.

Very well, sir.

And *that.*

Which, sir?

All that.

"Absurd man!" Dyer whispered. There had been a moment of fear, as though the naked body would leap from the window, and legless, chase him down Sherbrooke Street. But the moment was passing. Dyer realized now that it was comic, even touching. Miguel Mayor had simply tried too hard, too fast, and it would be good for him to stay in Montreal until he deserved those clothes, that touching vanity and confidence. With one last look at the window, he turned sharply, before the clothes could speak again.

(1973)   (1973)

Gwendolyn MacEwen
1941 –

<hr/>

GWENDOLYN MACEWEN WAS born in Toronto and published her first work in *Canadian Forum* when she was fifteen. Three years later she left school to begin a full-time career as a writer. Since the appearance of two small collections of her verse, *Selah* (1961) and *The Drunken Clock* (1961), MacEwen has published a collection of short stories, *Noman* (1972), two novels, *Julian, the Magician* (1963) and *King of Egypt, King of Dreams* (1971), and several volumes of poetry: *The Rising Fire* (1963), *A Breakfast for Barbarians* (1966), *The Shadow-Maker* (1969), *The Armies of the Moon* (1972) and *The Fire Eaters* (1976).

Eden, Eden

the thunder is
a vocal monument
to the dying rain
or an obelisk in a granite sky
which roars an epitaph
through cut clouds.

in the morning
thunder is a reared stone elephant,
          a grown element of grey;
its trunk is vertical and thick as — thunder;   10
it roars down the wrenched lightning
coughing out a verse
for the suicidal rain
in the morning.

the stormed man is heavy with rain
and mumbles beneath the elephant's gargle
and his jaws lock human in the rain,
and under the unlocked jaws of the split sky
and under the bullets of the elephant's trunk

he is thinking of a thunder garden.   20

behind sense he is thinking of a warped tree
with heavy fruit falling,
peaked rock fighting the ragged fern
in *another* storm-centre —
a monolithic thunder tree
and a man and woman naked and green with rain
above its carved roots, genesis

(1961)   (1974)

Universe And

something we know of mountains
and craters within craters —
big braille under a blind God's hands

    space. our timorous temples turn
    inward, our introverted temples
    turn, as the flyer hoists our vision
    higher

on earth, the machines of our myth
grind down, grind slowly now, rusting
the wheels of human sense   10

we drink white milk while
high galactic fields open
their floodgates   open

and the terrible laughter of our children
is heard in that pocket, that
high white place above our thunder

(1963)   (1974)

A Breakfast for Barbarians

my friends, my sweet barbarians,
there is that hunger which is not for food —
but an eye at the navel turns the appetite
round
with visions of some fabulous sandwich,
the brain's golden breakfast
                          eaten with beasts
                          with books on plates

let us make an anthology of recipes,
let us edit for breakfast   10
our most unspeakable appetites —
let us pool spoons, knives
and all cutlery in a cosmic cuisine,
let us answer hunger
with boiled chimera
and apocalyptic tea,
an arcane salad of spiced bibles,
tossed dictionaries —
                     (O my barbarians
                     we will consume our mysteries)   20

and can we, can we slake the gaping eye of our desires?
we will sit around our hewn wood table
until our hair is long and our eyes are feeble,
eating, my people, O my insatiates,
eating until we are no more able
to jack up the jaws any longer —

to no more complain of the soul's vulgar cavities,
to gaze at each other over the rust-heap of cutlery,
drinking a coffee that takes an eternity —
till, bursting, bleary,   30
we laugh, barbarians, and rock the universe —
and exclaim to each other over the table
over the table of bones and scrap metal
over the gigantic junk-heaped table:

by God that was a meal

(1966)   (1974)

Poems in Braille

1

all your hands are verbs,
now you touch worlds and feel their names —
thru the thing to the name
not the other way thru (in winter
I am Midas, I name gold)

the chair and table and book
extend from your fingers;
all your movements
command these things back to their
places; a fight against familiarity   10
makes me resume my distance

2

they knew what it meant,
those egyptian scribes who drew
eyes right into their hieroglyphs,
you read them dispassionate until

the eye stumbles upon itself
blinking back from the papyrus

outside, the articulate wind
annotates this; I read carefully
lest I go blind in both eyes, reading with   20
that other eye the final hieroglyph

3

the shortest distance between 2 points
on a revolving circumference
is a curved line; O let me follow you,
Wenceslas

4

with legs and arms I make alphabets
like in those children's books
where people bend into letters and signs,
yet I do not read the long cabbala of my bones
truthfully; I need only to move   30
to alter the design

5

I name all things in my room
and they rehearse their names,
gather in groups, form tesseracts,
discussing their names among themselves

I will not say the cast is less than the print
I will not say the curve is longer than the line,
I should read all things like braille in this season
with my fingers I should read them
lest I go blind in both eyes reading with   40
that other eye the final hieroglyph

(1966)   (1974)

Inside the Great Pyramid

all day the narrow shaft
received us; everyone
came out sweating and
gasping for air, and one
old man collapsed
upon a stair;
            I thought:
the fact that it has stood
so long
is no guarantee
it will stand today,
but went in anyway
and heard when I was
halfway up a long

low rumbling like
the echo of ancient stones
first straining to their place;
            I thought:
we have made this, we
have made *this*.
I scrambled out into
the scandalous sun and saw
the desert was an hourglass
we had forgotten to invert,
a tasselled camel falling
to his knees, the River
filling the great waterclock
of earth.

(1969)

(1974)

The Heel

In the organing dark I bless those who came from the waters
scaleless and shrewd, and walked with unwebbed feet
to create memory, when every movement invented their end,
who stood beside the holy waters with upright spines
to destroy themselves, to inherit themselves, to stand
while the fish fell back and the waves erased their birth.

They were terrible with sense and torn at the tongue
and in the foreign hours when fog enveloped them
they thrashed like swimmers down the rivers of their sleep;
the sunken cities within them rose and towered high
over the bright groin of their pain, and elsewhere
they were lovers and their knees were pyramids of fire.

I bless those who turned the double face of memory around,
who turned on their naked green heels and had great dreams
and in the queer hour when they are struck at the eyes
and the last sunrise claims and cripples them, I stand
and remark that on the edge of this strand I also feel
the holy waters lapping just behind my heel.

(1969)

(1974)

Dark Pines Under Water

This land like a mirror turns you inward
And you become a forest in a furtive lake;
The dark pines of your mind reach downward,
You dream in the green of your time,
Your memory is a row of sinking pines.

Explorer, you tell yourself this is not what you came for
Although it is good here, and green;
You had meant to move with a kind of largeness,
You had planned a heavy grace, an anguished dream.

But the dark pines of your mind dip deeper   10
And you are sinking, sinking, sleeper
In an elementary world;
There is something down there and you want it told.

(1969)   (1974)

The Shadow-Maker

I have come to possess your darkness, only this.

My legs surround your black, wrestle it
As the flames of day wrestle night
And everywhere you paint the necessary shadows
On my flesh and darken the fibres of my nerve;
Without these shadows I would be
In air one wave of ruinous light
And night with many mouths would close
Around my infinite and sterile curve.

Shadow-maker create me everywhere   10
Dark spaces (your face is my chosen abyss),
For I said I have come to possess your darkness,
Only this.

(1969)   (1974)

The Armies of the Moon

now they begin to gather their forces
in the Marsh of Decay and the Sea of Crises;
their leaders stand motionless
on the rims of the craters
invisible and silver as swords turned sideways
waiting for earthrise and the coming of man.

they have always been there increasing their numbers
at the foot of dim rills, all around and under
the ghostly edges where moonmaps surrender
and hold out white flags to the night.   10

when the earthmen came hunting with wagons and golfballs
they were so eager for white rocks and sand
that they did not see them, invisible and silver
as swords turned sideways on the edge of the craters —
so the leaders assumed they were blind.

in the Lake of Death there will be a showdown;
men will be powder, they will go down under
the swords of the unseen silver armies,
become one with the gorgeous anonymous moon.

none of us will know what caused the crisis   20
as the lunar soldiers reluctantly disband
and return to their homes in the Lake of Dreams
weeping quicksilver tears for the blindness of man.

(1972)   (1974)

The Demon of Thursday

Thursdays I reserve for going mad
and wondering how the trees grow
(kiss, perhaps, of the living God?)

Thursdays I reserve for being sane
and wondering why some people do not know me
although we have been introduced in dreams

Thursdays, I presume, are for the birds
who pick around for bits of thoughts and grain
inside the garden of my head

Thursdays I reserve for whales   10
with huge mouths full of plankton
and words I understand too well

Thursdays I reserve for the animals
the angelic and demonic animals
the magic animals more real than real

(1974)   (1974)

Second-degree Burns

My friend at the party said:
You'll get second-degree burns
If you keep sneaking through the fire

I wasn't sneaking
I was hovering with my hand
And anyway
It wasn't fire
But a candle

A candle involves fire, but
So does a hand   10

Trees involve fire
Streetcars involve fire

We all have second-degree burns
And they hurt but the hurt doesn't matter

The living flame of the world is what matters
The fire is edible, and now

(1976)   (1976)

Everyone Knows

That which we took so much for granted
—Holy poetry of water and of fire—
Is suddenly debatable.

Everyone knows where the universe ends
—Where the fire begins—
Insatiable.

What you watch with me now, my friend,
Is neither birth nor end
Nor anything tenable.

Sit with me, though, at this table!   10
Eat dreams and planets, all
Are edible.

Fire invites fire.

(1976)   (1976)

Matt Cohen
1942 -

———————◆———————

BORN IN KINGSTON, Ontario, Matt Cohen was educated at the University
of Toronto. Since the appearance of his first novel *Korsoniloff* in 1969,
Cohen has published a collection of stories, *Columbus and the Fat Lady*
(1972), and several other novels including *Johnny Crackle Sings* (1971),
The Disinherited (1974) and *Wooden Hunters* (1975).

After Dinner Butterflies

THEY WERE SITTING in the library, drinking coffee. She noticed that he had a hand in one of his pockets, he seemed to be fiddling with something.

George?

What?

What have you got there?

Nothing, he said.

Show it to me immediately.

It's nothing, he said. He took his hand out of his pocket and puffed elaborately on his cigar. Good cigar, he said.

No cigar, she said. Take that thing out of your pocket.

George stood up and learned against the mantle, still puffing on his cigar. He pulled a rabbit out of a vase. Look at the nice rabbit, he said.

Put it away.

He stuck the rabbit out the window and returned to his chair. He picked up an old newspaper and started reading it. When he was sure she wasn't looking he put his hand back into his pocket.

George!

What?

Let me see it.

There's nothing here.

Oh yes there is. I saw you fiddling with it. Now let me see it.

Alright, he said. He reached into his pocket. Then he changed his mind. No, you have to guess.

I'm not playing one of your stupid games.

Okay, George said. Let's forget it then. He re-lit his cigar and stuck his hand back in his pocket. Time passed. His cigar went out. Mary got another cup of coffee. The fire was going. George kept his hand in his pocket. He got tired of the newspaper. He went over to the library table and sat down to work on the jig-saw puzzle. He was so absorbed in a little bit of orange and green that he didn't hear Mary sneak up on him.

There, she exclaimed. I've got it. Her hand was in his pocket. Then she withdrew it, puzzled. There's nothing there, she said.

They sat back down. A few moments later she noticed that George was working his hand in his pocket. When he looked up he saw her watching him. Do you want to see what's in my pocket?

You don't have anything in your pocket.

Yes I do.

Prove it.

Okay, George said. He reached into his pocket and pulled out a shiny bit of metal. It appeared to be some sort of complicated miniature. He brought it over to her, holding it cupped in the palm of his hand. But when she reached for it, he drew back. Don't touch, he said. You'll break it. He held it out to her again so she could look at it. It was a metal sphere with little red things sticking out of its silver surface.

What is it? she asked.

It's a space ship.

That's nice.

Watch this. He walked to the side of the room farthest from the fire. Come here, he said. She stood beside him. He threw his metal gizmo into the fire. There was a clicking sound, metal against brickwork.

Well, she said, you could have done that with a firecracker.

Right, George said. They sat back down. After a while Mary noticed that she had, in a very faint way, the same sort of feeling in her stomach that she sometimes got in an elevator.

George, she said.

Yes?

I feel funny. I feel like we're in an elevator.

Or in a spaceship, George said. He walked over to the sideboard and poured himself a glass of sherry. Cheers, he said.

Don't think you can upset me with your silly games.

Oh no, George said.

I was once married to a Hungarian Count.

Were there bagpipes at your wedding? Yes there were. I was there. I remember them clearly: they were off key.

Mary crossed her legs and tried to pull her skirt down over her knees. They felt strange, as if something was about to land on them. George, she said, prove to me that we are on a spaceship.

Alright, George said. He snapped his fingers. Nothing happened. Then a delicate golden butterfly landed on Mary's right knee. Isn't that beautiful?

Isn't what beautiful? Mary said. She could have sworn that a golden butterfly had landed on her knee.

The music, George said. He turned up the radio so that the library was filled with sounds. A second golden butterfly landed on Mary's knee.

I don't like it, she said. She got up and turned the radio off. The butterflies followed her, circling her head like a halo. Go on, she said when she sat down, flicking at her shoulders, go sit on someone else. But they just came back.

You'd better leave them alone, George said.

Why? I don't like them.

But they like you.

I don't like the feeling of them sitting on my shoulders, watching me.

They're very pretty.

I can't even see them without straining my neck.

I'll get you a mirror, George said.

I don't want a mirror. Let's just forget them and see if they go away.

Alright, George said. He lit a new cigar and sipped at his sherry. After a while Mary noticed that he had a hand in his pocket again and seemed to be fiddling with something.

George.

What?

What are you doing now?

Nothing, George said. He took his hand out of his pocket. I'm just trying to get this damned thing turned around.

What thing?

The spaceship.

The butterflies were still perched on Mary's shoulders, waiting patiently. George snapped his fingers again. A white wolf appeared in the middle of the room. Its eyes were as golden as butterflies. It walked over to George's chair, climbed up into it, and licked its paws. Go on, George said. Sit on the floor. The wolf looked up at him and then returned to its paws.

You see? You don't know how to do anything right.

I'm sorry, George said.

What a lovely wolf. Look at its eyes.

I wish it would get off my chair.

It likes you, Mary said. That's why it wants to sit on your chair.

If it really liked me it would get off of my chair and fetch a stick or something. He took a cigar from the mantle and waved it in the air. Fetch, doggie, he said. He threw the cigar across the room. The wolf looked at him, looked over at the cigar, raised its eyebrows, and went back to sleep.

That reminds me, Mary said. Did I ever tell you that I was once married to a Hungarian Count?

Yes, George said. You just told me five minutes ago. Do you mind if I sit on the arm of your chair? The butterflies were still perched on her shoulders, waiting patiently.

Yes, she said. I do mind. Why don't you stand at the mantle and try to look unconcerned?

There was a knock at the door. Come in, George shouted. A man wearing grey coveralls and carrying a toolbox entered the room.

Is this the place with the television?

Yes, George said, it's there in the corner. I don't know what's wrong with it.

Probably blew a tube, the repairman said. It often happens. Nice dog.

Yes.

The repairman pushed the television out from the wall and began poking at its innards.

Do you want a glass of sherry?

No thanks, the man said. He reached into the television and pulled out three stuffed camels. Here's your problem, he said. There were three stuffed camels in the back of your television set.

Oh, George said. I was hiding them there for my wife's birthday.

You should've told me. He turned on the set. Works fine now. He pushed the television back against the wall and packed up his tools. I'll send you a bill, he said, and left the room.

The repairman made two more housecalls and then went home. His wife was sitting up, waiting for him. He changed out of his coveralls, washed up, and then got his dinner out of the oven and a beer from the refrigerator.

How did it go tonight?

The usual. Is Jimmy asleep?

Yes, he went to bed hours ago.

What else did you do?

Nothing much, she said. She crossed her legs and tried to pull her skirt down over her knees. I watched TV for a while and read Jimmy a story.

Is there anything for dessert?

There's some pie. He went into the kitchen and found a coconut cream pie in the refrigerator. He brought it back into the living room.

Have you ever wanted to throw a pie in my face?

Once, she said. Remember that dance we went to just after we started going out? You put an ice cube down my dress? Well, when you took me home my parents were still up and we had strawberry pie with whipped cream. You were all sitting at the table and I was getting the pie. I could feel the ice water trickling down my skin and the inside of my dress was wet. I almost dumped the pie right on your head.

He leaned back and lit a cigarette. God, he said, that must have been ten years ago.

Eleven, she said. Eleven years and two months. I remember standing there. I was just about to turn the pie onto your head when I decided to marry you. She crossed the room and sat down beside him on the couch. I don't know why I never told you, she said. I always meant to.

What else didn't you ever tell me?

Did I ever tell you that I was once married to a Hungarian Count?

No, he said. And I wouldn't believe you if you did. He was leaning back with his eyes closed. She dipped her hand into the pie and spread it gently over his face. She formed little ridges at the eyebrows, being careful not to get any into his eyes. She spread it on his cheeks with the palms of her hands and then swirled it with her index finger so that his cheeks stood out in spiral puffs. She gave him a moustache and a beard – a nice pointed van dyke beard that reminded her of a picture. When the beard started to drip she pushed it back up onto his chin and drew a picture of a rose in it. All the whipped cream was gone. She took a fork and fed him some of the coconut filling.

How does it taste?

Good, he said.

I should have saved you some of the whipped cream.

That's alright. He stuck out his tongue and licked a path along his right cheek. Tonight I saw a woman with two golden butterflies perched on her shoulders.

That's nice dear.

(1972)   (1972)

André Major
1942 –

———————◆———————

BORN IN MONTREAL, André Major was an early contributor to the journal *parti pris* but severed his association with the magazine in 1965. His initial collections of poetry, *Le Froid se meurt* and *Holocauste à 2 voix* appeared in 1961. His subsequent publications include a volume of selected poems, *Poèmes pour durer* (1969), a collection of stories *La Chair de poule* (1965), several novels, a biography of Félix-Antoine Savard (1968) and a number of plays including *Une Soirée en octobre* (1975).

Words

When we lie together as leaves enfolded
our words are sharply beautiful,
wounding as memory,
holding us, shaken,
in an amazing dream

no longer together
our words
lie like tears

and your hand
passes like a comet   10
touching my dark with its radiance

Such leafing space between your eye and mine!

(1969)   (1970)

G.V. Downes (Trans.)

After Nightfall

leafy hands
hands   her heart's wealth
the woman shares
in her island's overthrow
when I fall like a storm
like a bird of prey

and the snow coming upon us
limb to limb
and the cold sheltering us
each in the other   10
like grass in the dew
fire in the log

such am I
o idolized world of your arms

of your lap
such am I
in the halcyon
of a perfect night
the sorrow of being man
is dust blown away in the burning   20
of my breath
my boundless desire
swelling to a single touch of yours

your island is my lair
what joy to return
after the fall of night
when midnight howls
in my veins

you know that nothing is as true
as pleasure   30
as the bird quivering
in the sullen country of your island

so by our own magic
we escape from winter
and its terrible loneliness
to dwell within this night
this shell of tawny summer

    I am lulled upon your thigh
and your tender wrist beats like a heart
against my throat   40

(1969)   (1970)

John Glassco (Trans.)

My Word is Green

in our sickness we would say
it is the sea which moulds the profile of the
    shore
and if winter comes we'll live in its season
    quietly

— like slaves we would not see our chains —

this country's sickness wrenched the greenness
    out of me
(I speak of a land so cold it feeds the frosts
I speak for the poor who curse her   10
I speak for the simple who pass through the
    machine and are squeezed dry)

without pride or fear
the blood freed of its solitude
fears not the failure of all the winds

my country lonelier than our pangs
ravaged by cold by cross by silence
we have outlived the retreat of the ice
we have outlived death

(I delight in greenery again   20
in the winds on beaches
in kisses)

I am the song and the broken sweep of the week
the egg in the morning and the coffee

I rejoice only in the pleasure of being loved by the
    sun
this is the kind of man I am
when not knocked down by my brothers'
    breathing

I am as open as a tornado   30
as a wounded bird
at the same time I am a bull among the bugs
when free as fire I love the passer-by
— my eyes dimmed with dreams
I break my heart in a kiss —

you my dear who live in the meek laugh of the
    maple tree
    my hands give you more light than daybreak
    summer the vigour of fir-trees the perfume of
        your smile   40

>   you commit my love to the noon's heat and I am
>   renewed
> this is the weather of breasts
> froth to suckle our kisses
> this is the weather of places where murmurs of
>   caresses burn
>
> the cruel landscape lives within me
> and green is my word green
> – a wound I give my country –

(1969)   (1970)

John Robert Columbo (Trans.)

Letter To a Very Dear Old Man

> and you, lost, abandoned, road brother of mine,
> base-born, full of hot air, have I ever stopped
> you from speaking with the warm glow of conviction
> speak so that I may shake your grief
> as one shakes a hand hungry for caresses
>
> the mountains where you wander are so old
> that they turn grey in the twilight
> you, a man of snows and of thoughts
> that freeze in your mouth, listen at last
> on this young March morning   10
> in the light's glaze
> to that flock of birds heralding
> the rebirth of everything
>
> soon tomorrow new blood,
> warm blood, good blood will rise to the heart
> thrilling and leaping,
> and it will be new life, young life
> reddening our cheeks
> the brightness of bursting buds
> the nuptials of soil and sun   20
>
> you have had a long dream of snow
> from which you have now withdrawn with me

your distant companion, the image of your son,
while silence has hardened your ears and the cold
listen to the tune of my lips, it tells you
that the country grows green and stretches itself
in the lazy air as clear as water

(1969)   (1976)

Fred W. Cogswell (Trans.)

Without Status

You speak to me of rain
I speak to you of good weather
and the sky turns a fine winter blue
clear as a fresh complexion
that will melt in the hands

(1969)   (1976)

Fred W. Cogswell (Trans.)

The Bugbear

Yes I truly am a man of protest
a wolf howling among a people of sheep
but if I speak again it will be for
adjusting against what is to come
the bugbear of liberty
for what will come will not be
as white and pure as you tell it
on the overleaf of your warrior hymns

a small crowd armed with insults
that loves the world only the wrong way round   10
inverted by your captious and enormous hate
an oil stain on a scattered town
hunting for the waters of the Great Lakes
those beautiful dreams on postal cards

listen a moment to the husky voice
of only one of your brothers
what he says is not told
it is heard an ear out of the heart

I was among you a young animal shaking
with red thoughts I remember more than   20
you who speak a foreign language to me and I
tell you that your words are corrupting us

(1969)   (1976)

Fred W. Cogswell (Trans.)

Michael Ondaatje
1943 –

MICHAEL ONDAATJE WAS born in Colombo, Ceylon (Sri Lanka), and lived
in England for a time before coming to Canada in 1962. He has been a
lecturer in English at several Canadian universities and has written a
critical study of Leonard Cohen (1970). His published works include
four volumes of poetry, *The Dainty Monsters* (1967), *The Man with Seven
Toes* (1969), *The Collected Works of Billy the Kid* (1970), and *Rat Jelly*
(1973), and a full-length prose work, *Coming Through Slaughter* (1976).

Biography

The dog scatters her body in sleep,
paws, finding no ground, whip at air,
the unseen eyeballs reel deep, within.
And waking – crouches,
tacked to humility all day,

children ride her, stretch,
display the black purple lips,
pull hind legs to dance;
unaware that she
tore bulls apart, loosed   10
heads of partridges,
dreamt blood.

(1967)   (1967)

Henri Rousseau and Friends

FOR BILL MUYSSON

In his clean vegetation
the parrot, judicious,
poses on a branch.
The narrator of the scene,
aware of the perfect fruits,
the white and blue flowers,
the snake with an ear for music;
he presides.

The apes
hold their oranges like skulls,   10
like chalices.
They are below the parrot
above the oranges –
a jungle serfdom which
with this order
reposes.

They are the ideals of dreams.
Among the exactness,
the symmetrical petals,
the efficiently flying angels,   20
there is complete liberation.
The parrot is interchangeable;
tomorrow in its place
a waltzing man and tiger,
brash legs of a bird.

Greatness achieved
they loll among textbook flowers

and in this pose hang
scattered like pearls
in just as intense a society.   30
On Miss Adelaide Milton de Groot's walls,
with Lillie P. Bliss in New York.

And there too
in spangled wrists and elbows
and grand façades of cocktails
are vulgarly beautiful parrots, appalled lions,
the beautiful and the forceful locked in suns,
and the slight, careful stepping birds.

(1967)   (1967)

Pyramid

For days they had toiled
sun baked, naked,
raging in the sun
their yells muted in the vast afternoons.
In rhythm they swung like leaves
and broke the horizon
nails
joining the starched blue to sand.

And while it grew
I watched them heave   10
trailing their boulders to the moon
and at dusk saw the shadows run.

Timeless here
they perfected degrees
allowing for heat and burn
and to pulsed commands
jack-knifed like chimes.
Those were their minutes,

distant I saw them mime pains
and saw their bodies churn,   20
pivot, sweat leaving them oiled.

And finishing they circled and prayed
and led me deep into the ground,
positioned me by a mirror
and sealed the form they made.

I watch
and in our conversations
grow profound.

(1967)   (1967)

From
The Collected Works Of Billy The Kid

[After shooting Gregory]

After shooting Gregory
this is what happened

I'd shot him well and careful
made it explode under his heart
so it wouldnt last long and
was about to walk away
when this chicken paddles out to him
and as he was falling hops on his neck
digs the beak into his throat
straightens legs and heaves   10
a red and blue vein out

Meanwhile he fell
and the chicken walked away

still tugging at the vein
till it was 12 yards long
as if it held that body like a kite
Gregory's last words being

get away from me yer stupid chicken

[She leans against the door]

She leans against the door, holds
her left hand at the elbow
with her right, looks at the bed

on my sheets – oranges
peeled half peeled
bright as hidden coins against the pillow

she walks slow to the window
lifts the sackcloth
and jams it horizontal on a nail
so the bent oblong of sun   10
hoists itself across the room
framing the bed the white flesh
of my arm

she is crossing the sun
sits on her leg here
sweeping off the peels

traces the thin bones on me
turns toppling slow back to the pillow
Bonney Bonney

I am very still   20
I take in all the angles of the room

[The street of the slow moving animals]

The street of the slow moving animals
while the sun drops in perfect verticals
no wider than boots
The dogs sleep their dreams off
they are everywhere
so that horses on the crowded weekend
will step back and snap a leg

/ while I've been going on
the blood from my wrist
has travelled to my heart

and my fingers touch
this soft blue paper notebook
control a pencil that shifts up and sideways
mapping my thinking going its own way
like light wet glasses drifting on polished wood.

The acute nerves spark
on the periphery of our bodies
while the block trunk of us
blunders as if we were
those sun drugged horses   20

I am here with the range for everything
corpuscle muscle hair
hands that need the rub of metal
those senses that
that want to crash things with an axe
that listen to deep buried veins in our palms
those who move in dreams over your women night
near you, every paw, the invisible hooves
the mind's invisible blackout   the intricate never
the body's waiting rut.   30

(1970)   (1970)

Dates

It becomes apparent that I miss great occasions.
My birth was heralded by nothing
but the anniversary of Winston Churchill's marriage.
No monuments bled, no instruments
agreed on a specific weather.
It was a seasonal insignificance.

I console myself with my mother's eighth month.
While she sweated out her pregnancy in Ceylon
a servant ambling over the lawn
with a tray of iced drinks,   10
a few friends visiting her
to placate her shape, and I

drinking the life lines,
Wallace Stevens sat down in Connecticut
a glass of orange juice at his table
so hot he wore only shorts
and on the back of a letter
began to write 'The Well Dressed Man with a Beard'.

That night while my mother slept
her significant belly cooled   20
by the bedroom fan
Stevens put words together
that grew to sentences
and shaved them clean and
shaped them, the page suddenly
becoming thought where nothing had been,
his head making his hand
move where he wanted
and he saw his hand was saying
the mind is never finished, no, never   30
and I in my mother's stomach was growing
as were the flowers outside the Connecticut windows.

(1973)   (1973)

Heron Rex

Mad kings
blood lines introverted, strained pure
so the brain runs in the wrong direction

they are proud of their heritage of suicides
— not the ones who went mad
balancing on that goddamn leg, but those

whose eyes turned off
the sun and imagined it
those who looked north, those who
forced their feathers to grow in   10
those who couldn't find the muscles in their arms
who drilled their beaks into the skin

those who could speak
and lost themselves in the foul connections
who crashed against black bars in a dream of escape
those who moved round the dials of imaginary clocks
those who fell asleep and never woke
who never slept and so dropped dead
those who attacked the casual eyes of children and were led away
and those who faced corners forever   20
those who exposed themselves and were led away
those who pretended broken limbs, epilepsy,
who managed to electrocute themselves on wire
those who felt their skin was on fire and screamed
                                and were led away

There are ways of going
physically mad, physically
mad when you perfect the mind
where you sacrifice yourself for the race
when you are the representative when you allow   30
yourself to be paraded in the cages
celebrity a razor in the body

These small birds so precise
frail as morning neon
they are royalty melted down
they are the glass core at the heart of kings
yet 15 year old boys could enter the cage
and break them in minutes
as easily as a long fingernail

(1973)   (1973)

bp Nichol
1944 –

BARRY PHILIP NICHOL was born in Vancouver and attended the University of British Columbia. One of Canada's leading experimental poets, he has co-edited *Ganglia* and *Gronk,* small mimeographed magazines concerned with concrete poetry, and edited *The Cosmic Chief: An Evening of Concrete* (1970), the first anthology of Canadian concrete poetry. Among Nichol's best-known books are *ABC: The Aleph Beth Book* (1971), *Monotones* (1971), *Journeying and the Returns* (1967), *Still Water* (1970) and *The Martyrology* (1972).

Blues

(1967)   (1974)

[*eeeee*]

e e e e e e e e e e e e e e e e e e e e e e e e e
EEEEEEEEEEEEEEEEEEEEEEEEE
e e e e e e e e e e e e e e e e e e e e e e e e e

EEEEEEEEEEEEEEEEEEEEEEEEE
e e e e e e e e e e e e e e e e e e e e e e e e e
EEEEEEEEEEEEEEEEEEEEEEEEE

e e e e e e e e e e e e e e e e e e e e e e e e e
EEEEEEEEEEEEEEEEEEEEEEEEE
e e e e e e e e e e e e e e e e e e e e e e e e e

oudoo doan doanna   10
tinna limn limn
la leen
untloo lima
limna doo doo

dee du deena
deena dee du
deena deena
dee du deena

ah-ooo runtroo
lintle leave lipf   20
lat lina tanta
tlalum cheena
ran tron tra troo

deena dee du
deena deena
dee du deena
deena dee du

da dee di do du
deena
deena   30

(1968)   (1968)

From
Monotones

XI

all that summer   hot
driving back   up   past
the headwaters of
               the humber
broken mills & dams
the country actual
the time confused
               spring or
summer
         driving thru   10
into
     the hills of mono

mona

moaning a name from another time
not mine   no part of
my world

mona's hills   the miller's hills
hills the water came from
turned his wheels

                       his world   20

stone fences & bent boards piled up against the mind

my time &
my world
flowing over
            into
the broken grass

"it is as if my grandfather's house were turning over with me.
   where is the person that will save me?"

"it is only crying about myself
   that comes to me in song."   30

(1971)   (1971)

Postcard Between

FOR MARGARET AVISON

looked up & saw
the winter sun

        clouds
half covering it

somewhere near
washington street
it came

into my ear
this morning

        again   10

a woman or
the sea
moved over me

like the clouds
till

     no focus

grown used to
by degrees

      and i thot

        "i have done with it"   20

vague

      like the clouds
      my language was

sun
disappearing from view

this poem for you

(1971)   (1971)

1970-71

as there are words i haven't written
things i haven't seen
so this poem continues
a kind of despair takes over
the poem is written in spite of

all the words i once believed were saints
language the holy place of consecration
gradually took flesh
becoming real

scraptures behind me   10
i am written free
so many people saying to me they do not understand
the poem they can't get into
i misplace it three times

this is not a spell
it is an act of desperation
the poem dictated to me by another will
a kind of being writing is
opposite myself i recognize these hands
smash the keys in   20
the necessary assertion of reality

ah reason there is only feeling
knowing the words are
                              i am
this moment is
everything present & tense
i write despite my own misgivings
say things as they do occur
the mind moves truly
is it free   30

nothing's free of presence
others pressing in
your friends assert themselves as loving you are
        tortured with
gradually you learn to enjoy

thus you write a history
use words you've used before
your own voice speaking in the morning whispering
holy god i do love you then praise you
take up this gift of joy
not to judge or be judged by   40
you who have given me lips   a tongue
the song sings because of you
all theory denies you
that struggle's truly won
once what's begun is done

(1972)   (1972)

From
parallel lines

a final
movement

to speak

language
is merely
memory

mere
memos re

language

(1975)   (1975)

Tom Wayman
1945 –

———◆———

TOM WAYMAN WAS born in Hawkesbury, Ontario, and moved with his parents to Prince Rupert, British Columbia, in 1952. He graduated from the University of British Columbia in 1966 and completed a Master of Fine Arts degree at the University of California in 1968. His collections of poetry include *Waiting for Wayman* (1973), *For And Against the Moon: Blues, Yells and Chuckles* (1974), and *Money and Rain: Tom Wayman Live* (1975).

Unemployment

The chrome lid of the coffee pot
twists off, and the glass knob rinsed.
Lift out the assembly, dump
the grounds out. Wash the pot and
fill with water, put everything back with
fresh grounds and snap the top down.
Plug in again and wait.

Unemployment is also
a great snow deep around the house
choking the street, and the City.   10
Nothing moves. Newspaper photographs
show the traffic backed up for miles.
Going out to shovel the walk
I think how in a few days the sun will clear this.
No one will know I worked here.

This is like whatever I do.
How strange that so magnificent a thing as a body
with its twinges, its aches
should have all that chemistry, that bulk
the intricate electrical brain   20

708

subjected to something as tiny
as buying a postage stamp.
Or selling it.

Or waiting.

(1973)

(1973)

The Ecology of Place

FOR PAUL BRYANT AND BENTON MACKAYE

The place begins with water.
Lake, inlet or river
eddies into a clearing, turns
to planks and houses, businesses.
The forests go elsewhere.

The water moves the earth: supply
for the Interior and wealth
from the bush country.
There is a read-out of names.
Distant law begins to stop   10
the geography. A mountain is cut
by a noun.

But the place is a stone.
Magnet City. Farmboy and woman arrive,
immigrant. Mills, mines, speculations
become power somewhere as the Magnet turns.

There is a startup of railroad, and thruway.
The air fills; the harbour is
crushed rock; the creek solidifies
below the foodboard plant.   20
Oolichan, the candle fish,
go nowhere to breed.
But the nights are bright. California arrives.

Then the City alone
without the forest
flows back looking for the child,
free of beginning things, of logic.
It wants to create again
wilderness, but the trails are marked
for power toboggans, no hunting.   30
It desires a countryside
but the cows stand in feedlots of
urine and dung, eating grain.
Hens turn endlessly in the tiers
rotating like huge trademarks of the corporations.

The City dreams of a balance.
Of finding land under its feet.
Of exchanging commodities that are not on fire.
But it is the dollar and oil who stay awake all night
to draw up the Plan. Fish offshore   40
begin to cough.

I walk into the street.

(1973)   (1973)

The Chilean Elegies: 1. Salvador Allende

The wood comes from a living tree
brought down, ripsawed into rough boards
and nailed together into parts-boxes and forklift pallets.

Dust has settled onto the battered wood:
a heavy dust, from metal that is drilled and pounded,
from fibreglass that is cut and shaped, and from the weariness
of the hands and legs that have done this day after day.
Eyes have looked at this dust every lunch break
and at our ten minutes mid-morning and mid-afternoon.
Dust from overtime, and carried in   10
on the wind from this factory's City.

Allende is dead. I have not followed the newspaper
for three years: the news is what happens to me.
Now he is dead another layer of dust,
black grains, has sifted in among the stacks of truck parts.
The dust makes a faint sound as it settles
like a man who sighs, far away. I believe Allende's dust
is falling into every factory in the world.

It says that whatever you might want
there is no reason to vote. Men are alive who are killers   20
and not a word or a vote anywhere can stop them.
If you love your life there will never be change.
This is one more thing the poor know
in every factory. And now Allende is with us
in the dust on the concrete floor.

(1975)   (1975)

Toronto Streetcars

FOR CHARLES PACHTER

Like blunt fish, swaying purposefully through the city's water
the maroon and faded yellow trams rattle out of the past
on their endless daily journeys. I almost expect them
to appear around a streetcorner
in black and white, from old film footage taken
in St. Petersburg during the 1905 Revolution, or the jerky
blinking frames of an uprising in Berlin.
No wonder the Toronto left has such troubles. Each day
the faces peering out of the trams' windows
merge into the faces in the stills from Barcelona, industrial   10
Hankow, or the streets of Winnipeg. Not that it's hard
to think of being taken to an electronics plant
every day in one of these – a factory
remains a factory after all – but so often in dreams

comes the documentary's image of the streetcar slowly toppling
onto its side, pushed by a thousand hands,
crashing onto the cobbled street to form the first
of the historic barricades.

The wheeled blunt boxes of the streetcars pass
clicking out *nothing changes, nothing changes*   20
like a mimeograph producing another leaflet on
What Toronto Needs Now.

(1977)   (1977)

Industrial Music

FOR MICHAEL MILLAR, MICHAEL TAYLOR, GARY WALSH

After a hundred years they paused
and they heard
music; other things were on the wind
but they heard a music filling in the continent behind them:
their own music, which grew slowly,
starting at the quietest moments
like a flower, or at prayer, and at
work, and then beginning to be pumped through
cash registers, radios, and finally even leaked in
through small grilles in elevators.   10

But as fast as the melodies get smoothed
into a dollar, a man stands up in a noisy bar and
begins to sing, and another man joins him and
another, until the air is filled again with music,
human voices. And twenty thousand of us
are put in a single vast room
to hear one famous voice with a song rise through amplifiers
and the songs also come from just Bob Garrison
driving his '55 Willys up the Canyon from Siska
on a rainy Saturday and only me and one other   20
jammed into his front seat listen.

And I remember in the truck factory Boris Hukaluk drumming
everywhere, standing in Cab Electrical
tapping out the intricate rhythms with his wire stripper
and a screwdriver, but Boris also
knows everything about Folding Hoods after years
working at that before, so he gets assigned back on the days
Hoskins doesn't show. And I asked him there
why he didn't ever become a professional musician and he said
I *didn't like the life; too many late nights all the time*   30
so he drums weekends in a cabaret, in the house band
without even a name, and does special jobs at New Year's and
drums through his days and years at the factory
his fingers and pencils falling on the metal. One day
we are up at Test fitting a hood and one of the mechanics
picks up Boris' rhythm and sends it back to him
with his wrenches, as best he can, and Boris
grins and stops what he's doing and gives out
another short riff, and this time
a couple of guys try to match him, and Boris laughs   40
and taps out another complicated run
and this time maybe half a dozen guys start
clumsily pounding away after his lead. And this
        makes so much noise
(since somebody is banging on a waste can) that the foreman
comes out of his office to find out what's up
but sees Boris and shakes his head and goes back.

Then it's lunch and someone turns a truck radio on, and the music,
rock now, pours into the echoing Test bays
like the wind when somebody rolls aside one of the huge doors
on a cold wet February morning the wind   50
flowing in off the river among the parked tires and motors,
the tool boxes, air hoses and containers of oil,
a wind that carries with it all the sounds of the City at work
this day: grudgingly, but alive, and moving.

(1977)   (1977)

Susan Musgrave
1951 –

BORN IN CALIFORNIA, Susan Musgrave lived for several years in the Queen Charlotte Islands and now resides on Vancouver Island. Her first collection of poems, *Songs of the Sea-Witch,* was published in 1970; subsequent volumes include *Entrance of the Celebrant* (1972), *Grave-Dirt and Selected Strawberries* (1973) and *The Impstone* (1976).

At Nootka Sound

Along the river
trees are stranded
bare as witches
and dark as the woman
who never learned to love one man.

(In the north
a woman can learn
to live with too much sadness.
Finding *anything* could be hard.)

The river is haunted
with the slippery black eyes
of drowned pika –
you fish for something quite improbable
expecting those thin dead eyes
to begin to see.

10

Sometimes along the way
the water cracks
and Indians must mend the river
after every other net –
men with fat dog's eyes   20
and humps
who cast themselves
toward fish in stone.

What could only be one lifetime
(who can go on pretending forever?)
is when the ground turns cold
and the night is so still
you can't remember having anything to hear.
You lose yourself
and off into the distance   30
the last birds are throbbing
black and enormous
down towards the sea.

(1970)   (1970)

Mackenzie River, North

Filled with darkness
we are already late for this river.
Shadows file behind us
seeping into the light of our eyes.
The river is blind
and refuses to stay.
We move past in our silence,
a long black mile,
cast into some huge emptiness
like continents of tooth and stone.   10

The river is not our only hunter.
White against the road
the slow rain drives us back
against the ground.
Wolves smell us out of our bones,
fish grow bored and swim away.
There is nothing about for us
but fear

And moving,
always moving,   20
out of the night
it comes.

(1970)

(1970)

Entrance of the Celebrant

If you could see me,
where I am and where
the forest grows thick and into me;
if you could reach
the darkest centre of myself
and still know the sign of the animal
where it lies apart inside your skin —

then I would say,
that kiss is *my* kiss;
where our lips have touched   10
were others, and mine are still.

No one forgets
the music of the animal. I've heard
the sound of the old skin cracking
where this heart has become
the heart of something new.
                              If he could see me,
know me, and not forget it was
he who saw me

and that circles tighten and everything   20
narrows

but that even I am nearing completion,
that everything I have become is something
already gone —

then the dark trees, the sounds
of water across water, of blood
drying still over water —

then his music is the sound of
nobody listening; the animal I carve out
is the shape of darkness, a sound   30
that nowhere would dare to form.

Animal! Animal!
You are nobody! You cannot be
anyone.

But I had known that
long before your birth.

So you died then? Only the dead
can know. My lips revealed you
and my heart has eaten the hole.
Black fingers pulled a small black night   40
from between us. Animal, animal
so small are we

that no one wanting
deserved death more.

(1972)   (1972)

Witchery Way

Sometimes an old man
crouches at the river —
sometimes he is someone
whose bones are not formed.

Sometimes an old woman
with fisher-skin quiver,
sometimes on the low bank
is hungry after blood.

First Man wrenched a
forked tree, spit   10
the bone, First Woman
was a warm pelt
to carry him into the ground.

"People don't tell out
about these things;
they keep them
down here in the body."
Be careful
of the wolf's cry – he knows
those ways well. Open   20
the toad's belly and you will
find him there.

"The bone at the back
of the head is best,
a tongue black and swollen
from skin whorls picked
at night." First Woman
was a night cat
prowling the red ant hills.
First Man was   30
victim, sometimes
a grey fox.

Sometimes an old man
whispers down the smoke hole,
sometimes an old woman
furrows in the wind.
My skin is thick
with the dark seed
of their coming –
the blade of a fine axe   40
wedged between my eyes.

(1973)   (1973)

Equinox

Sometimes under the night
I hear whales
trapped at the
sand edges
breathing their
dead sound.

I go out into the rain
and see,
my face
wrinkled like   10
moonlight
and long nights
hard under the wind's eye.

The stones lie
closer than water,
floating from darkness
like separate tides
to the same sea.

I watch you
with your shadow   20
come down over the sand:
your knife is
glutted, your cold hand
has drawn blood out of
fire.
I hear whales
pressing the blind
shore, netted
till I wake binding
weed with water –   30

How long were you
pinned down
unable to reach
or split the sound?

I hear whales ringing bells
invisible as silence

I hear whales with birds' tongues
and slippery arctic eyes.

How long
did you look   40

Before their eyes knew you?

Do you remember
the colour of their blood?

(1973)   (1973)

Anima

You smell of
the woods
you smell of
lonely places.

You smell of
death
of dreams I am
afraid of.

I reach out
to touch you   10
but you
aren't there.

You have gone
into the only darkness
animals come from.

(1976)   (1976)

Invocation

Listen.
It is too late
for sleep;
nothing escapes
the conscience of the
damned. Listen.
There is no reason

for pain – Pain began
when life
ceased.   10

I draw you in.
I wait.

One by one
the animals are
leaving.
When they go
it is something I see:
there are no
choices.

20 The animals have slept
too long, have
listened
too closely. They
creep away,
their wounds like
bridges from one past
over another.

The animals know
safety is a
30 fool's heaven,
forests
are for dying in.

My grey ones,
my broken ones,

(1976)

stealth is no
virtue when it comes to
being lost.

I know you are
happy
I know your bones are   40
sacred.

Listen.
It is too late for
anything;
I cannot provide for
more.

I wait.
I wonder.

What secrets do you have
to surrender;   50
where do you go
that it is
for ever?

(1976)

Lure

Raven
in the rain binds
silence and
cedar

one part
feather
four parts
bone.

In the wind
he weaves   10
cedar-bark,
swallows
the sun

he asks words
to feather the
dry throat

a song to spin
silence into
blood.

20 In the rain
he carves the
bone hollow
to help blow sickness
out.

Raven
hears the moon,
the tired heart
of cedar

he follows the

(1976)

frog-echo   30
under a low bank.

Raven beats
his spirit-drum,
taps for his
spirit-helper.

Salmon rises
to cedar
on wind
under dark water

river rises   40
to roots
and the echo of rain.

(1976)

Bibliography

In compiling this bibliography we have listed principal reference works for the study of Canadian literature and a selection of works by each author represented in this volume. Entries in Parts I, II, and III are presented in alphabetical order; in Part IV the books of each author are arranged in chronological order. We would like to acknowledge our indebtedness to the bibliographical studies of Michael Gnarowski, R.G. Moyles, Gérard Tougas, and especially to R.E. Watters for *A Checklist of Canadian Literature and Background Materials 1628-1960*.

I BIBLIOGRAPHIES AND GENERAL REFERENCES

BARBEAU, VICTOR and ANDRÉ FORTIER, *Dictionnaire bibliographique du Canada français* (Montreal, Académie canadienne-français, 1974) 246p.

The Brock Bibliography of Published Canadian Stage Plays in English 1900-1972 (St. Catharines, Brock University, 1972) vi + 35p. [*First supplement* (St. Catharines, Brock University, 1973) 47p.]

"Canadian Literature; An Annotated Bibliography." [Published annually in *Journal of Canadian Fiction* from 1973.]

"Canadian Literature; a Checklist." [Published annually in *Canadian Literature* from 1960 to 1971.]

Canadian Periodical Index [A continuing serial.]

COLOMBO, JOHN ROBERT, *Colombo's Canadian Quotations* (Edmonton, Hurtig, 1974) x + 735p.

———, *Colombo's Canadian References* (Toronto, Oxford University Press, 1976) viii + 576p.

FEE, MARGERY and RUTH CAWKER, *Canadian Fiction. An Annotated Bibliography* (Toronto, Peter Martin Associates, 1976) xiii + 170p.

GNAROWSKI, MICHAEL, *A Concise Bibliography of English-Canadian Literature* (Toronto, McClelland and Stewart, 1973) 125p.

HAYNE, DAVID M. and MARCEL TIROL, *Bibliographie critique du roman canadien-française 1837-1900* (Toronto, University of Toronto Press, 1968) viii + 144p.

"Letters in Canada." [Published annually in *University of Toronto Quarterly* from 1935.]

. *Livres et auteurs canadiens* (Montreal, Editions Jumonville, 1962.) [Published annually from 1962 to 1969.]

Livres et auteurs québécois (Montreal, Editions Jumonville, 1970.) [Published annually from 1970.]

LOCHHEAD, DOUGLAS, *Bibliography of Canadian Bibliographies/Bibliographie des bibliographies canadiennes* (Toronto, University of Toronto Press, 1972) xiv + 312p.

MOYLES, R.G., *English-Canadian Literature to 1900*. A Guide to Information Sources (Detroit, Gale Research Company, 1976) xi + 346p.

MOYLES, R.G. and CATHERINE SIEMENS, *English-Canadian Literature: A Student Guide and Annotated Bibliography* (Edmonton, Athabascan Publishing Company, 1972) 44p.

NEW, WILLIAM, *Critical Writing on Commonwealth Literature* (University Park, Pennsylvania, Pennsylvania State University Press, 1975) 333p.

NEWMAN, MAUREEN and PHILIP STRATFORD, *Bibliography of Canadian Books in Translation: French to English and English to French/Bibliographie de livres canadiens traduits de l'anglais au français et du français à l'anglais* (Ottawa, Humanities Research Council of Canada, 1975) vi + 57p.

TOUGAS, GERARD, *A Checklist of Printed Materials Relating to French-Canadian Literature 1763-1968./Liste de référence 1763-1968.* [Revised edition (Vancouver, University of British Columbia Press, 1973) xvi + 174p.]

TREMBLAY, JEAN PIERRE, *Bibliographie québécoise (Quebec, Educo Media, 1973) 252p.*

WATTERS, REGINALD, *A Checklist of Canadian Literature and Background Materials, 1628-1960.* [Revised edition (Toronto, University of Toronto Press, 1972) xxiv + 1085p.]

—— and Inglis Bell, *On Canadian Literature 1806-1960* (Toronto, University of Toronto Press, 1966) ix + 165p.

WOODCOCK, GEORGE, *Canadian Poets, 1960-1973* (Ottawa, Golden Dog Press, 1976) x + 69p.

II LITERARY HISTORY AND BIOGRAPHY

BAILLARGEON, SAMUEL, *Littérature canadienne-français.* Revised edition (Montreal, Fides, 1965) 525p.

BAKER, RAY P., *A History of English-Canadian Literature to the Confederation* (Cambridge, Massachusetts, Harvard University Press, 1920) xi + 200p.

BEAULIEU, VICTOR-LEVY, *Manuel de la petite littérature du Québec* (Montreal, L'Aurore, 1974) 268p.

BESSETTE, GERARD et al, *Histoire de la littérature canadienne-française par les textes* (Montreal, Centre Educatif et Culturel, 1968) 704p.

Dictionary of Canadian Biography (Toronto, University of Toronto Press, 1966)

DUHAMEL, ROGER, *Manuel de littérature canadienne-française* (Ottawa, Editions de Renouveau Pédagogique, 1967) 161p.

EDWARDS, MURRAY, *A Stage in Our Past: English-Language Theatre in Eastern Canada from the 1790's to 1914* (Toronto, University of Toronto Press, 1968) xii + 211p.

GAY, PAUL, *Notre littérature. Guide littéraire du Canada Français* (Montreal, Editions H.M.H., 1969) xvi + 214p.

GRANDPRE, PIERRE DE et al, *Histoire de la littérature française du Québec* (Montreal, Beauchemin, 1967-1969) 4 vols.

KLINCK, CARL F. (ed.), *Literary History of Canada: Canadian Literature in English* [Revised edition (Toronto, University of Toronto Press, 1976) 3 vols.]

PACEY, DESMOND, *Creative Writing in Canada: A Short History of English-Canadian Literature.* [Revised edition (Toronto, Ryerson, 1961) ix + 314p.]

——, *Ten Canadian Poets* (Toronto, Ryerson, 1958) ix + 350p.

STORY, NORAH, *Oxford Companion to Canadian History and Literature* (Toronto, Oxford University Press, 1967) xi + 935p. [*Supplement* edited by William Toye (Toronto, Oxford University Press, 1973) v + 318p.]

SYLVESTRE, GUY et al, *Canadian Writers/Ecrivains Canadiens* (Toronto, University of Toronto Press, 1966) xviii + 186p.

THOMAS, CLARA, *Our Nature, Our Voices* (Toronto, New Press, 1973) 1 7p.

TOUGAS, GERARD, *Histoire de la littérature canadienne-française.* Second edition (Paris, Presses universitaires de France, 1964) xii + 312p. Also published as *La littérature canadienne-française* (Paris, Presses Universitaires de France, 1974) 270p. [Second edition translated into English by A.L. Cook (Toronto, Ryerson, 1966) ix + 301p.]

WALLACE, W. STEWART, *The Macmillan Dictionary of Canadian Biography* (Toronto, Macmillan, 1963) 822p.

III CRITICAL STUDIES

ATWOOD, MARGARET, *Survival* (Toronto, Anansi, 1972) 287p.

BALLSTADT, CARL, *The Search for English-Canadian Literature* (Toronto, University of Toronto Press, 1975) L + 214p.

BESSETTE, GERARD, *Une littérature en ébullition* (Montreal, Editions du Jour, 1968) 315p.

BRAZEAU, J. RAYMOND, *An Outline of Contemporary French-Canadian Literature* (Toronto, Forum House, 1972) xii + 126p.

BROWN, E.K., *On Canadian Poetry* [Revised edition (Toronto, Ryerson, 1944) xi + 312p.]

——, *Responses and Evaluations. Essays on Canada.* Edited with an Introduction by David Staines (Toronto, McClelland and Stewart, 1977) xviii + 314p.

CAMERON, DONALD, *Conversations with Canadian Novelists* (Toronto, Macmillan, 1973) 2 vols.

COLLIN, W.E., *The White Savannahs* (Toronto, Macmillan, 1936) 288p.

DAVEY, FRANK, *From There to Here* (Erin, Ontario, Press Porcépic, 1974) 288p.

DORSONVILLE, MAX, *Caliban Without Prospero: Essay on Quebec and Black Literature* (Erin, Ontario, Press Porcépic, 1974) 227p.

DUDEK, LOUIS and MICHAEL GNAROWSKI, *The Making of Modern Poetry in Canada* (Toronto, Ryerson, 1967) 303p.

EGGLESTON, WILFRED, *The Frontier and Canadian Letters* (Toronto, Ryerson, 1957) ix + 164p.

EGOFF, SHIELA, *The Republic of Childhood* [Revised edition (Toronto, Oxford University Press, 1975) vii + 335p.]

FARLEY, T.E., *Exiles and Pioneers* (Ottawa, Borealis Press, 1976) xvii + 302p.

FRYE, NORTHROP, *The Bush Garden: Essays on the Canadian Imagination* (Toronto, Anansi, 1971) x + 256p.

GARNET, ELDON, *Where? The Other Canadian Poetry* (Erin, Press Porcépic, 1974) ii + 188p.

GIBSON, GRAEME, *Eleven Canadian Novelists* (Toronto, Anansi, 1973) 324p.

JONES, DOUGLAS, *Butterfly on Rock. A Study of Themes and Images in Canadian Literature* (Toronto, University of Toronto Press, 1970) + 197p.

LE MOYNE, JEAN, *Convergences* (Montreal, Editions H.M.H., 1961) 342p. [Translated by Philip Stratford (Toronto, Ryerson, 1966) xii + 256p.]

MCCOURT, EDWARD, *The Canadian West in Fiction* [Revised edition (Toronto, Ryerson, 1970) 128p.]

MCMULLEN, LORRAINE (ed.), *Twentieth Century Essays on Confederation Literature* (Ottawa, The Tecumseh Press, 1976) 151p.

MANDEL, ELI (ed.), *Contexts of Canadian Criticism* (Chicago, University of Chicago Press, 1971) vii + 304p.

MARCOTTE, GILLES, *Une littérature qui se fait* [Revised edition (Montreal, Editions H.M.H., 1968) 307p.]

MATTHEWS, JOHN, *Tradition in Exile* (Toronto, University of Toronto Press, 1962) viii + 197p.

NEW, WILLIAM, *Among Worlds* (Erin, Ontario, Press Porcépic, 1975) 287p.

——, *Articulating West* (Toronto, New Press, 1972) xxvi + 282p.

NORTHEY, MARGOT, *The Haunted Wilderness* (Toronto, University of Toronto Press, 1976) 131p.

PACEY, DESMOND, *Essays in Canadian Criticism, 1938-1968* (Toronto, Ryerson, 1969) 294p.

RASHLEY, R.E., *Poetry in Canada. The First Three Steps* (Toronto, Ryerson, 1958) xvii + 166p.

SHEK, BEN-ZION, *Social Realism in the French-Canadian Novel* (Montreal, Harvest House, 1977) 326p.

SMITH, A.J.M., *Masks of Fiction* (Toronto, McClelland and Stewart, 1961) 176p.

——, *Masks of Poetry* (Toronto, McClelland and Stewart, 1962) 144p.

——, *Towards a View of Canadian Letters* (Vancouver, University of British Columbia Press, 1973) xi + 230p.

——, *On Poetry and Poets* (Toronto, McClelland and Stewart, 1977) viii + 122p.

SUTHERLAND, RONALD, *Second Image* (Toronto, New Press, 1971) 189p.

URBAS, JEANETTE, *From Thirty Acres to Modern Times* (Toronto, McGraw-Hill Ryerson, 1976) xiv + 158p.

WARWICK, JACK, *The Long Journey* (Toronto, University of Toronto Press, 1968) x + 172p.

WATERSTON, ELIZABETH, *Survey* (Toronto, Methuen, 1973) 215p.

WILSON, EDMUND, *O Canada: An American's Notes on Canadian Culture* (New York, Farrar Strauss, 1964) 245p.

WOODCOCK, GEORGE (ed.), *The Canadian Novel in the Twentieth Century* (Toronto, McClelland and Stewart, 1975) xi + 337p.

———, (ed.), *A Choice of Critics* (Toronto, Oxford, 1966) xxi + 247p.

———, (ed.), *Colony and Confederation* (Vancouver, University of British Columbia Press, 1974) vii + 218p.

———, *Odysseus Ever Returning* (Toronto, McClelland and Stewart, 1970) xv + 158p.

———, (ed.), *Poets and Critics* (Toronto, Oxford, 1974) x + 246p.

IV INDIVIDUAL AUTHORS

MILTON ACORN (1923-)

In Love and Anger (Montreal, Author, 1957) 20p.

The Brain's the Target (Toronto, Ryerson, 1960) 16p.

Against a League of Liars (Toronto, Hawkshead Press, 1961)

Jawbreakers (Toronto, Contact Press, 1963) 54p.

I've Tasted My Blood (Toronto, Ryerson, 1969) 136p.

I Shout Love, and On Shaving Off His Beard (Toronto, Village Book Store Press, 1971)

More Poems for People (Toronto, NC Press, 1972) 112p.

This Island Means Minago (Toronto, NC Press, 1975) 122p.

Jackpine Sonnets (Toronto, Steel Rail Educational Publishing, 1977) 109p.

MARGARET ATWOOD (1939-)

Double Persephone (Toronto, Hawkshead Press, 1961) 16p.

The Circle Game (Toronto, Contact Press, 1966) 80p.

The Animals in that Country (Toronto, Oxford University Press, 1968) 80p.

The Edible Woman (Toronto, McClelland and Stewart, 1969) 281p.

The Journals of Susanna Moodie (Toronto, Oxford University Press, 1970) 64p.

Procedures for Underground (Toronto, Oxford University Press, 1970) 80p.

Power Politics (Toronto, Anansi, 1971) 58p.

Surfacing. (Toronto, McClelland and Stewart, 1972) 192p.

Survival. A Thematic Guide to Canadian Literature (Toronto, Anansi, 1972) 287p.

You Are Happy (Toronto, Oxford University Press, 1974) 96p.

Selected Poems (Toronto, Oxford University Press, 1976) 240p.

Lady Oracle (Toronto, McClelland and Stewart 1976) 345p.

Dancing Girls and Other Stories (Toronto, McClelland and Stewart, 1977) 256p.

MARGARET AVISON (1918-)

History of Ontario (Toronto, Gage, 1951) 138p.

Winter Sun and Other Poems (Toronto, University of Toronto Press, 1960) 89p.

The Dumbfounding (New York, Norton, 1966) 99p.

EARLE BIRNEY (1904-)

David and Other Poems (Toronto, Ryerson, 1942) 40p.

Now Is Time (Toronto, Ryerson, 1945) 56p.

The Strait of Anian (Toronto, Ryerson, 1948) 84p.

Turvey: A Military Picaresque (Toronto, McClelland and Stewart, 1949) 288p. [Also published as *The Kootenay Highlander* (London, Landsborough Publications, 1960) 253p.]

Trial of a City, and Other Verse (Toronto, Ryerson, 1952) 71p.

Twentieth Century Canadian Poetry. Edited with an Introduction by Earle Birney (Toronto, Ryerson, 1953) xvii + 169p.

Down the Long Table (Toronto, McClelland and Stewart, 1955) 298p.

Ice Cod Bell or Stone. A Collection of New Poems (Toronto, McClelland and Stewart, 1962) 62p.

Near False Creek Mouth. New Poems (Toronto, McClelland and Stewart, 1964) 35p.

The Creative Writer (Toronto, CBC Publications, 1966) 85p.

Selected Poems, 1940-1966 (Toronto, McClelland and Stewart, 1966) 222p.

Memory No Servant (Trumansburg, New York, New Books, 1968) 52p.

Pnomes Jukollages & other Stunzas (Toronto, Ganglia Press, 1969)

The Poems of Earle Birney (Toronto, McClelland and Stewart, 1969) 64p.

Rag and Bone Shop (Toronto, McClelland and Stewart, 1971) 64p.

The Cow Jumped Over the Moon. The Writing and Reading of Poetry (Toronto, Holt, Rinehart, 1972) 111p.

Four Parts Sand. With Bill Bissett, Judith Copithorne and Andrew Suknaski (Ottawa, Oberon, 1972) 54p.

The Bear on the Delhi Road. Selected Poems (London, Chatto and Windus, 1973)

What's So Big About Green (Toronto, McClelland and Stewart, 1973)

The Collected Poems of Earle Birney (Toronto, McClelland and Stewart, 1975) 2 vols.

The Rugging and the Moving Times. Poems New and Uncollected (Coatsworth, Ontario, Black Moss Press, 1976) 42p.

The Damnation of Vancouver (Toronto, McClelland and Stewart, 1977) 79p. [First published in *Trial of a City and Other Verse,* 1952]

Ghost in the Wheels. Selected Poems 1920– 1976 (Toronto, McClelland and Stewart, 1977) 160p.

MARIE-CLAIRE BLAIS (1939-   )

La Belle bête (Quebec, Institut littéraire de Québec, 1959) 214p. [Translated as *Mad Shadows* by Merloyd Lawrence (Toronto, McClelland and Stewart, 1961) 125p.]

Tête blanche (Quebec, Institut littéraire de Québec, 1960) 205p. [Translated as *Tête Blanche* by Charles Fullman (Toronto, McClelland and Stewart, 1961) 136p.]

Le Jour est noir (Montreal, Editions du Jour, 1962) 121p. [Translated with *Les Voyageurs sacrés* as *The Day Is Dark and Three Travellers* by Derek Coltman (New York, Farrar, Straus, 1967) 183p.]

Pays voilés: Poèmes (Quebec, Editions Garneau, 1963) 46p.

Existences: Poèmes (Quebec, Editions Garneau, 1964) 52p.

Une Saison dans la vie d'Emmanuel (Montreal, Editions du Jour, 1965) 128p. [Translated as *A Season in the Life of Emmanuel* by Derek Coltman (New York, Farrar, Straus, 1966) ix + 145p.]

L'Insoumise (Montreal, Editions du Jour, 1966) 120p.

David Sterne (Montreal, Editions du Jour, 1967) 128p. [Translated as *David Sterne* by David Lobdell (Toronto, McClelland and Stewart, 1973) 96p.]

Pays voilés, existences (Montreal, Editions de l'Homme, 1967) 90p.

L'Execution (pièce en 2 actes) (Montreal, Editions du Jour, 1968) 118p. [Translated as *The Execution* by David Lobdell (Vancouver, Talonbooks, 1976) 104p.]

Manuscrits de Pauline Archange (Montreal, Editions du Jour, 1968) 128p. [Translated with *Vivre! Vivre!* as *The Manuscripts of Pauline Archange* by Derek Coltman (New York, Farrar, Straus, 1970) 217p.]

Vivre! Vivre! La suite des manuscrits de Pauline Archange (Montreal, Editions du Jour, 1969) 170p. [Translated with *Manuscrits de Pauline Archange* as *The Manuscripts of Pauline Archange* by Derek Coltman (New York, Farrar, Straus, 1970) 217p.]

Les Voyageurs sacrés (Montreal, Editions H.M.H., 1969) 114p. [First published in *Ecrits du Canada Français,* XIV (1962)]

Les Apparences (Montreal, Editions du Jour, 1970) 203p. [Translated as *Durer's Angel* by David Lobdell (Vancouver, Talonbooks, 1976) 105p.]

Le Loup (Montreal, Editions du Jour, 1972) 243p. [Translated as *The Wolf* by Sheila Fischman (Toronto, McClelland and Stewart, 1974) 142p.]

Un Joualonais, sa joualonie (Montreal, Editions du Jour, 1973) 300p. [Translated as *St. Lawrence Blues* by Ralph Mannheim (New York, Doubleday, 1974) 229p.]

Fièvre et autres textes dramatiques (Montreal, Editions du Jour, 1974) 229p.

Une liaison parisienne (Montreal, Editions A/S et Quinze, 1975) 175p.

CLARK BLAISE (1941-   )

A North American Education (Toronto, Doubleday, 1973) 230p.

Tribal Justice (Toronto, Doubleday, 1974) 224p.

Days and Nights in Calcutta. With Bharati Mukherjee (Toronto, Doubleday, 1977) 300p.

Here And Now. Edited by Clark Blaise and John Metcalf (Ottawa, Oberon, 1977) 216p.

GEORGE BOWERING (1935-   )

Sticks and Stones (Vancouver, Tishbooks, 1963) 41p.

Points on the Grid (Toronto, Contact Press, 1964) 67p.

The Man in Yellow Boots (Mexico, El Corno
Emplumado, 1965) 112p.
The Silver Wire (Kingston, Quarry Press,
1966) 72p.
Baseball. A Poem in the Magic Number 9
(Toronto, Coach House Press, 1967)
21p.
Mirror on the Floor (Toronto, McClelland
and Stewart, 1967) 160p.
Rocky Mountain Foot. A Lyric, A Memoir
(Toronto, McClelland and Stewart,
1968) 126p.
Solitary Walk. A Book of Longer Poems by
George Bowering and Others (Toronto,
Ryerson, 1968) 75p.
The Gangs of Kosmos (Toronto, Anansi,
1969) 64p.
How I Hear "Howl" (Montreal, Beaver
Kosmos Folio, 1969) 19p.
Two Police Poems (Vancouver, Talonbooks,
1969) 23p.
Al Purdy (Toronto, Copp Clark, 1970)
117p.
George Vancouver. A Discovery Poem (To-
ronto, Weed/Flower Press, 1970) 39p.
Sitting in Mexico (Montreal, Imago, 1970).
Genève (Toronto, Coach House Press,
1971) 45p.
Touch. Selected Poems. 1960-1970 (To-
ronto, McClelland and Stewart, 1971)
128p.
The Sensible (Toronto, Massasauga Edi-
tions, 1972) 23p.
Curious (Toronto, Coach House Press,
1973)
At War With the U.S. (Vancouver, Talon-
books, 1974) 34p.
Flycatcher (Ottawa, Oberon, 1974) 114p.
In the Flesh (Toronto, McClelland and
Stewart, 1974) 112p.
Allophanes (Toronto, Coach House Press,
1976) 50p.
The Catch (Toronto, McClelland and
Stewart, 1976) 128p.
Poem and Other Baseballs (Coatsworth, On-
tario, Black Moss Press, 1976) 44p.
*The Concrete Island: Montreal Poems 1967-
71* (Montreal, Vehicule Press, 1977)

ELIZABETH BREWSTER (1922-   )

East Coast (Toronto, Ryerson, 1951) 8p.
Lillooet (Toronto, Ryerson, 1954) 28p.
Roads and Other Poems (Toronto, Ryerson,
1957) 12p.
Passage of Summer. Selected Poems (To-
ronto, Ryerson, 1969) 129p.
Sunrise North (Toronto, Clarke, Irwin,
1972) 87p.
In Search of Eros (Toronto, Clarke, Irwin,
1974) 88p.

The Sisters. A Novel (Ottawa, Oberon,
1974) 175p.
Sometimes I Think of Moving (Ottawa, Oberon, 1977) 123p.
It's Easy To Fall on the Ice (Ottawa, Oberon,
1977) 128p.

ERNEST BUCKLER (1908-   )

The Mountain and the Valley (New York,
Holt, Rinehart, 1952) 373p.
The Cruelest Month (Toronto, McClelland
and Stewart, 1963) 298p.
Ox Bells and Fireflies. A Memoir (Toronto,
McClelland and Stewart, 1968) 302p.
Nova Scotia: Window on the Sea. Photo-
graphs by Hans Weber (Toronto,
McClelland and Stewart, 1973) 127p.
*The Rebellion of Young David and Other
Stories.* Selected and arranged by Robert
D. Chambers (Toronto, McClelland and
Stewart, 1975) 138p.
Whirligig. Selected Prose and Poetry (To-
ronto, McClelland and Stewart, 1977)
144p.

MORLEY CALLAGHAN (1903-   )

Strange Fugitive (New York, Scribner,
1928) 264p.
A Native Argosy (New York, Scribner, 1929)
371p.
It's Never Over (New York, Scribner, 1930)
225p.
No Man's Meat (Paris, Black Manikin Press,
1931) 42p.
A Broken Journey (New York, Scribner,
1932) 270p.
Such is My Beloved (New York, Scribner,
1934) 288p.
They Shall Inherit the Earth (Toronto, Mac-
millan, 1935) 337p.
Now That April's Here and Other Stories (New
York, Random House, 1936) 316p.
More Joy in Heaven (New York, Random
House, 1937) 278p.
Luke Baldwin's Vow (Philadelphia,
Winston, 1948) 187p.
The Varsity Story (Toronto, Macmillan,
1948) 172p.
The Loved and the Lost (Toronto, Macmil-
lan, 1951) 234p.
Morley Callaghan's Stories (Toronto, Mac-
millan, 1959) 364p.
The Many Colored Coat (Toronto, Macmil-
lan, 1960) 318p.
A Passion in Rome (Toronto, Macmillan,
1961) 352p.
That Summer in Paris (Toronto, Macmillan,
1963) 255p.

An Autumn Penitent (Toronto, Macmillan, 1973) 171p. [Includes two novellas first published in *A Native Argosy* (1929)]
Winter. Photographs by John de Visser (Toronto, McClelland and Stewart, 1974) 150p.
A Fine and Private Place (Toronto, Macmillan, 1975) 213p.
Close to the Sun Again (Toronto, Macmillan, 1977) 192p.

ROCH CARRIER (1937-   )

Les Jeux incompris (Montreal, Editions Nocturne, 1956) 22p.
Cherche tes mots, cherche tes pas (Montreal, Editions Nocturne, 1958)
Jolis deuils (Montreal, Editions du Jour, 1964) 157p.
La Guerre, Yes Sir! (Montreal, Editions du Jour, 1968) 124p. [Translated as *La Guerre, Yes Sir!* by Sheila Fischman (Toronto, Anansi, 1970) 113p.
Floralie, où est-tu? (Montreal, Editions du Jour, 1969) 170p. [Translated as *Floralie, Where Are You?* by Sheila Fischman (Toronto, Anansi, 1971) 108p.]
Il est par là le soleil (Montreal, Editions du Jour, 1970) 142p. [Translated as *Is It the Sun, Philibert?* by Sheila Fischman (Toronto, Anansi, 1972) 100p.]
La Guerre, Yes Sir! (pièce en quatre parties) (Montreal, Editions du Jour, [1970] 139p.)
Le Deux-millième étage (Montreal, Editions du Jour, 1973) 169p. [Translated as *They Won't Demolish Me* by Sheila Fischman (Toronto, Anansi, 1974) 134p.]
Le Jardin des délices (Montreal, Editions La Presse, 1975) 215p.

PAUL CHAMBERLAND (1939-   )

Genèses (Montreal, A.G.E.U.M. 1962) 94p.
Terre Québec (Montreal, Déom, 1964) 78p.
L'Afficheur hurle (Montreal, Parti Pris, 1965) 80p.
L'Inavouable (Montreal, Parti Pris, 1968) 118p.
Eclats de la pierre noir d'où rejaillit ma vie (Montreal, Editions D. Laliberte [1972]) 108p.
Demain les dieux naîtront (Montreal, Editions de l'Hexagone, 1975) 300p.

AUSTIN CLARKE (1932-   )

The Survivors of the Crossing (Toronto, McClelland and Stewart, 1964) 202p.
Amongst Thistles and Thorns (Toronto, McClelland and Stewart, 1965) 183p.

The Meeting Point (Toronto, Macmillan, 1967) 249p.
When He Was Free and Young and He Used to Wear Silks (Toronto, Anansi, 1971) 151p.
Storm of Fortune (Boston, Little, Brown, 1973) 312p.
The Bigger Light (Boston, Little, Brown, 1975) 288p.
The Prime Minister (Toronto, General Publishing, 1977) 192p.

LEONARD COHEN (1934-   )

Let Us Compare Mythologies (Toronto, Contact Press, 1956) 79p.
The Spice-Box of Earth (Toronto, McClelland and Stewart, 1961) 99p.
The Favourite Game (London, Secker and Warburg, 1963) 223p.
Flowers for Hitler (Toronto, McClelland and Stewart, 1964) 128p.
Beautiful Losers (Toronto, McClelland and Stewart, 1966) 243p.
Parasites of Heaven (Toronto, McClelland and Stewart, 1966) 80p.
Selected Poems, 1956-1968 (Toronto, McClelland and Stewart, 1968) 245p.
Songs of Leonard Cohen (New York, Amsco Music Publishing Company, 1969) 96p.
The Energy of Slaves (Toronto, McClelland and Stewart, 1972) 127p.

MATT COHEN (1942-   )

Johnny Crackle Sings (Toronto, McClelland and Stewart, 1971)
Too Bad Galahad (Toronto, Coach House Press, 1972)
The Disinherited (Toronto, McClelland and Stewart, 1975) 240p.
Wooden Hunters (Toronto, McClelland and Stewart, 1975) 219p.
Peach Melba ([Toronto], [Coach House Press], [1974])
The Colours of War (Toronto, McClelland and Stewart, 1977) 234p.

ROBERTSON DAVIES (1913-   )

Shakespeare's Boy Actors (London, Dent, 1939) 208p.
Shakespeare for Young Players (Toronto, Clarke, Irwin, 1942) 255p.
The Diary of Samuel Marchbanks (Toronto, Clarke, Irwin, 1947) 204p. [Revised edition (Toronto, Clarke, Irwin, 1966)]
Overlaid. A Comedy (Toronto, French, 1948) 24p.
Eros at Breakfast and Other Plays (Toronto, Clarke, Irwin, 1949) 129p.
Fortune, My Foe (Toronto, Clarke, Irwin, 1949) 99p.

The Table Talk of Samuel Marchbanks (Toronto, Clarke, Irwin, 1949) 248p.
At My Heart's Core (Toronto, Clarke, Irwin, 1950) 91p.
Tempest-Tost (Toronto, Clarke, Irwin, 1951) 376p.
A Masque of Aesop (Toronto, Clarke, Irwin, 1952) 47p.
Renown at Stratford. [With Tyrone Guthrie and Grant Macdonald] (Toronto, Clarke, Irwin, 1953) 127p.
A Jig for the Gypsy (Toronto, Clarke, Irwin, 1954) 98p.
Leaven of Malice (Toronto, Clarke, Irwin, 1954) 312p.
Thrice the Brinded Cat Hath Mew'd. [With Tyrone Guthrie and Grant Macdonald] (Toronto, Clarke, Irwin, 1954) 192p.
Thrice the Brinded Cat Hath Mew'd. [With Tyrone Guthrie and Boyd Neel and Tanya Moiseiwitsch] (Toronto, Clarke, Irwin, 1955) 178p.
A Mixture of Frailties (Toronto, Macmillan, 1958) 379p.
A Voice from the Attic (Toronto, McClelland and Stewart, 1960) 360p. [Also published as *The Personal Art: Reading to Good Purpose* (London, Secker, 1961) 268p.]
A Masque of Mr. Punch (Toronto, Oxford University Press, 1963) 58p.
At My Heart's Core and Overlaid. Two Plays (Toronto, Clarke, Irwin, 1966) 124p.
Marchbank's Almanack (Toronto, McClelland and Stewart, 1967) 207p.
Four Favourite Plays (Toronto, Clarke, Irwin, 1968) 157p.
Feast of Stephen. An anthology of the less familiar writings of Stephen Leacock, with a critical introduction by Robertson Davies (Toronto, McClelland and Stewart, 1970) 154p.
Fifth Business (Toronto, Macmillan, 1970) 314p.
Stephen Leacock (Toronto, McClelland and Stewart, 1970) 63p.
Hunting Stuart and Other Plays (Toronto, New Press, 1972) 274p.
The Manticore (Toronto, Macmillan, 1972) 288p.
Question Time. A Play (Toronto, Macmillan, 1975) xv + 70p.
World of Wonders (Toronto, Macmillan, 1975) 358p.
One Half of Robertson Davies. Provocative Pronouncements on a Wide Range of Topics (Toronto, Macmillan, 1977) 256p.

LOUIS DUDEK (1918-   )

Unit of Five. Poems by Louis Dudek, Ronald Hambleton, P.K. Page, Raymond Souster, James Wreford. Edited by Ronald Hambleton (Toronto, Ryerson, 1944)
East of the City (Toronto, Ryerson, 1946) 51p.
Cerberus. Poems by Louis Dudek, Irving Layton, Raymond Souster (Toronto, Contact Press, 1952) 98p.
The Searching Image (Toronto, Ryerson, 1952) 12p.
Twenty-Four Poems (Toronto, Contact Press, 1952) 24p.
Europe (Toronto, Laocoön [Contact] Press, 1954) 139p.
The Transparent Sea (Toronto, Contact Press, 1956) 114p.
En México (Toronto, Contact Press, 1958) 78p.
Laughing Stalks (Toronto, Contact Press, 1958) 113p.
Literature and the Press. A History of Printing, Printed Media, and Their Relation to Literature (Toronto, Ryerson, 1960) 238p.
Atlantis (Montreal, Delta Canada, 1967) 151p.
The First Person in Literature (Toronto, CBC Publications, 1967) 69p.
Collected Poetry (Montreal, Delta Canada, 1971) 327p.
All Kinds of Everything. Edited by Louis Dudek (Toronto, Clarke, Irwin, 1973) 150p.

JACQUES FERRON (1921-   )

L'Ogre (Montreal, Les cahiers de la file indienne, [1949])
La Barbe de François Hertel (Montreal, Editions d'Orphée, 1951)
Le Dodu (Montreal, Editions d'Orphée, 1956) 91p.
Tante Elise (Montreal, Editions d'Orphée, 1956) 102p.
Le Cheval de Don Juan (Montreal, Editions d'Orphée, 1957) 223p.
Les Grands soleils (Montreal, Editions d'Orphée, 1958) 180p.
Le Licou (Montreal, Editions d'Orphée, 1958) 103p.
Cotnoir (Montreal, Editions d'Orphée, 1962) 99p. [Translated as *Dr. Cotnoir* by Pierre Cloutier (Montreal, Harvest House, 1973) 86p.]
Contes du pays incertain (Montreal, Editions d'Orphée, 1962) 200p.

Gazou; ou, Le prix de la virginité (Montreal, Editions d'Orphée, 1963) 86p.

La Tête du roi (Montreal, A.G.E.U.M., 1963) 93p.

Contes anglais et autres (Montreal, Editions d'Orphée, 1964) 153p.

La Nuit (Montreal, Editions Parti Pris, 1965) 134p.

Papa Boss (Montreal, Editions Parti Pris, 1966) 142p.

La Charrette (Montreal, Editions H.M.H., 1968) 207p.

Contes, édition integrale: Contes anglais, Contes du pays incertain, Contes inédits (Montreal, Editions H.M.H., 1968) 210p. [Eighteen of these translated by Betty Bednarski as *Tales from the Uncertain Country* (Toronto, Anansi, 1972) 101p.]

Théâtre 1 Les Grands Soleils, Tante Elise, Le Don Juan chrétien. (comédie en 2 actes) (Montreal, Librairie Déom, 1968) 230p.

Le Ciel de Québec (Montreal, Editions du Jour, 1969) 404p.

Historiettes (Montreal, Editions du Jour, 1969) 182p.

La Salut de l'Irlande (Montreal, Editions du Jour, 1970) 222p.

L'Amélanchier (Montreal, Editions du Jour, 1970) 164p. [Translated as *The Juneberry Tree* by Raymond Chamberlain (Montreal, Harvest House, 1975) 157p.]

Les Roses sauvages (Montreal, Editions du Jour, 1971) 177p. [Translated as *Wild Roses* by Betty Bednarski (Toronto, McClelland and Stewart, 1976) 123p.]

Le Saint-Elias (Montreal, Editions du Jour, 1972) 186p.[Translated as *The Saint Elias* by Pierre Cloutier (Montreal, Harvest House, 1975) 145p.]

La Chaise du maréchal ferrant (Montreal, Editions du Jour, 1972) 224p.

Les Confitures de coing (anciennement La Nuit) et autres textes (Montreal, Editions Parti Pris, 1972) 326p.

Du Fond de mon arrière-cuisine (Montreal, Editions du Jour, 1973) 290p.

Théâtre 2: La tête du Roi, Le dodu ou le prix du bonheur, La Mort de monsieur Borudas, Le Permis de dramaturge, L'Impromptu des deux chiens (Montreal, Librairie Déom, 1975) 192p.

Escarmouches. 2 vols. (Montreal, Editions Leméac, 1975)

SAINT-DENYS GARNEAU (1912-1943)

Regards et jeux dans l'espace (Montreal, n.p., 1937) 73p.

Journal (Montreal, Beauchemin, 1954) 270p. [Translated as *The Journal of*
Saint-Denys Garneau by John Glassco (Toronto, McClelland and Stewart, 1962) 139p.]

Poésies complètes: Regards et jeux dans l'espace, Les Solitudes (Montreal, Fides, 1949) 227p. [Translated as *The Complete Poems of Saint-Denys Garneau* by John Glassco (Ottawa, Oberon, 1975) 172p.]

Lettres à ses amis (Montreal, Editions H.M.H., 1967) 489p.

GRATIEN GÉLINAS (1909-   )

Tit-Coq. Pièce en trois actes (Montreal, Beauchemin, 1950) 196p. [Translated as *Tit-Coq* by Kenneth Johnson (Toronto, Clarke, Irwin, 1967) 84p.]

Bousille et les justes (Quebec, I.L.Q., 1960) 206p. [Translated as *Bousille and the Just* by Kenneth Johnson (Toronto, Clarke, Irwin, 1961) 104p.

Hier, les enfants dansaient (Montreal, Editions Leméac, [1968]). [Translated as *Yesterday the Children Were Dancing* by Mavor Moore (Toronto, Clarke, Irwin, 1967) 76p.]

ROLAND GIGUÈRE (1929-   )

Faire naître (Montreal, Editions Erta, 1949)

Yeux fixes (Montreal, Editions Erta, 1951) 18p.

Images apprivoisées (Montreal, Editions Erta, 1953) [35] p.

Les Armes blanches (Montreal, Editions Erta, 1954) [25] p. [A selection of eight poems translated as *Eight Poems* by Jean Beaupré and Gael Turnbull (Iroquois Falls, Ontario, Contact Press, 1955)]

Le Défaut des ruines est d'avoir des habitants (Montreal, Editions Erta, 1957) 107p.

Adorable femme des neiges (Montreal, Editions Erta, 1959)

L'Age de la parole. Poèmes, 1949-1960 (Montreal, Editions de l'Hexagone, 1965) 172p.

Naturellement; poèmes et sérigraphies de Roland Giguère (Montreal, Editions Erta, 1968) [8] p.

La Main au feu, 1949-1968 (Montreal, Editions de l'Hexagone 1973) 145p.

La Sérigraphie à la colle (Montreal, Editions Formart, 1974)

Abécédaire (Montreal, Editions Erta, 1975)

JOHN GLASSCO (1909-   )

The Deficit Made Flesh (Toronto, McClelland and Stewart, 1958) 64p.

Under the Hill. By Aubrey Beardsley and John Glassco (Paris, Olympia Press, 1959) 123p.

The English Governess. By Miles Underwood [pseud] (Paris, Olympia Press, 1960) [Also published as *Under the Birch.* The Story of an English Governess (Paris, Ophelia Press, 1965) 187p. and as *Harriet Marwood, Governess* (New York, Grove Press, 1967)]

A Point of Sky (Toronto, Oxford, 1964) 78p.

English Poetry in Quebec. Edited by John Glassco (Montreal, McGill University Press, 1965) 142p.

Memoirs of Montparnasse. With an Introduction by Leon Edel (Toronto, Oxford, 1970) 254p.

The Poetry of French Canada in Translation. Edited by John Glassco (Toronto, Oxford University Press, 1970) 260p.

Selected Poems (Toronto, Oxford University Press, 1971) 96p.

The Fatal Woman. Three Tales (Toronto, Anansi, 1974) 172p.

DAVE GODFREY (1938-)

Death Goes Better with Coca-Cola (Toronto, Anansi, 1967) 115p.

Gordon to Watkins to You. A Documentary: The Battle for Control of our Economy. Edited by Dave Godfrey and Mel Watkins (Toronto, New Press, 1970) 261p.

The New Ancestors (Toronto, New Press, 1970) 392p.

I Ching Kanada (Erin, Ontario, Press Porcépic, 1976)

ALAIN GRANDBOIS (1900-1975)

Né à Québec... Louis Jolliet (Paris, Messein, 1933) [Translated as *Born in Quebec: A Tale of Louis Jolliet* by Evelyn M. Brown (Montreal, Palm, 1964) 198p.]

Poèmes (Hangchow, China, 1934)

Les Voyages de Marco Polo (Montreal, Valiquette, [1942]) 229p.

Les Îles de la nuit (Montreal, Parizeau, 1944) 135p.

Avant le chaos (Montreal, Editions Modernes, 1945) 203p.

Rivages de l'homme (Quebec, n.p., 1948) 96p.

L'Etoile pourpre (Montreal, Editions de l'Hexagone, 1957) 79p.

Poèmes (Montreal, Editions de l'Hexagone, 1963) 250p.

Avant le chaos; suivi de quatre nouvelles inédités (Montreal, Editions H.M.H., 1964) 276p.

Selected Poems [Translated by Peter Miller (Toronto, Contact Press, 1964) xi + 101p.]

Visages du monde (Montreal, Editions H.M.H., 1971) 378p.

FREDERICK PHILIP GROVE (1879-1948)

Over Prairie Trails (Toronto, McClelland and Stewart, 1922) 231p.

The Turn of the Year (Toronto, McClelland and Stewart, 1923) 237p.

Settlers of the Marsh (New York, Doran, 1925) 341p.

A Search for America (Ottawa, Graphic, 1927) 448p.

Our Daily Bread (New York, Macmillan, 1928) 390p.

It Needs To Be Said (Toronto, Macmillan, 1929) 163p.

The Yoke of Life (New York, Smith, 1930) 355p.

Fruits of the Earth (Toronto, Dent, 1933) 335p.

Two Generations. A Story of Present Day Ontario (Toronto, Ryerson, 1939) 261p.

The Master of the Mill (Toronto, Macmillan, 1944) 393p.

In Search of Myself (Toronto, Macmillan, 1946) 457p.

Consider Her Ways (Toronto, Macmillan, 1947) 298p.

Tales from the Margin. The Selected Short Stories of Frederick Philip Grove. Edited with an Introduction and Notes by Desmond Pacey (Toronto, Ryerson, 1971) 319p.

The Master Mason's House [Translated by Paul Gubbins, with an Introduction by Douglas O. Spettigue and A.W. Riley (Ottawa, Oberon, 1976) 252 p. Originally published as *Maurermeister Ihles Haus* (Berlin, Karl Schnabel, 1906) 247p.]

The Letters of Frederick Philip Grove. Edited with an Introduction by Desmond Pacey (Toronto, University of Toronto Press, 1976) 626p.

RALPH GUSTAFSON (1909-)

The Golden Chalice (London, Nicholson & Watson, 1935) 106p.

Alfred the Great (London, Joseph, 1937) 119p.

Epithalamium in Time of War (New York, Author, 1941) 11p.

Anthology of Canadian Poetry (English). Compiled by Ralph Gustafson (Harmondsworth, England, Penguin Books, 1942) 123p.

Lyrics Unromantic (New York, Author, 1942) 19p.

A Little Anthology of Canadian Poets. Edited by Ralph Gustafson (Norfolk, Connecticut, New Directions, 1943) 26p.

Canadian Accent. A Collection of Stories and Poems. Edited by Ralph Gustafson (Harmondsworth, England, Penguin Books, 1944) 144p.

Flight Into Darkness (New York, Pantheon, 1946) 96p.

The Penguin Book of Canadian Verse. Edited with an Introduction and Notes by Ralph Gustafson (Harmondsworth, England, Penguin Books, 1958) 225p. [Revised edition, 1975. 344p.]

Rivers Among Rocks (Toronto, McClelland and Stewart, 1960) [68p.]

Rocky Mountain Poems (Vancouver, Klanak Press, 1960) 36p.

Sift in an Hour Glass (Toronto, McClelland and Stewart, 1966) 96p.

Ixion's Wheel (Toronto, McClelland and Stewart, 1969) 128p.

Selected Poems (Toronto, McClelland and Stewart, 1972) 128p.

Theme and Variations for Sounding Brass (Sherbrooke, Quebec, Progressive Publications, 1972) 24p.

Fire on Stone (Toronto, McClelland and Stewart, 1974) 89p.

Corners in the Glass (Toronto, McClelland and Stewart, 1977) 96p.

ANNE HÉBERT (1916-   )

Les Songes en équilibre (Montreal, Editions de l'Arbre, 1942) 160p.

Le Torrent (Montreal, Beauchemin, 1950) 171p. [Translated as *The Torrent* by Gwendolyn Moore (Montreal, Harvest House, 1973) 141p.]

Le Tombeau des rois (Quebec, Institut littéraire du Québec, 1953) 78p.

Les Chambres de bois (Paris, Editions du Seuil, 1958) 190p. [Translated as *The Silent Rooms* by Katherine Mezei (Don Mills, Ontario, Musson, 1974) 167p.]

Poèmes (Paris, Editions du Seuil, 1960) 110p. [Translated as *Poems* by Alan Brown (Don Mills, Ontario, Musson, 1975) 76p.]

Le Torrent. Suivi de deux nouvelles inédites (Montreal, Editions H.M.H., 1963) 256p. [Translated as *The Torrent: Novellas and short stories,* by Gwendolyn Moore (Montreal, Harvest House, 1973) 141p.]

Le Temps sauvage, La Mercière assassinée, Les Invités au procès (Montreal, Editions H.M.H., 1967) 188p.

Dialogue sur la traduction (à propos du

Tombeau des rois). [With F.R. Scott] (Montreal, Editions H.M.H., 1970) 109p.

Kamouraska (Paris, Editions du Seuil, 1970) 250p. [Translated as *Kamouraska* by Norman Shapiro (Toronto, Musson, 1973) 250p.]

Les enfants du sabbat: (Paris, Editions du Seuil, 1975) 186p. [Translated as *Children of the Black Sabbath* by Carol Dunlop-Hebert (Don Mills, Ontario, Musson, 1977)]

DAVID HELWIG (1938-   )

Figures in a Landscape (Ottawa, Oberon, 1967) 217p.

The Sign of the Gunman (Ottawa, Oberon, 1969) 151p.

The Streets of Summer (Ottawa, Oberon, 1969) 188p.

The Day Before Tomorrow (Ottawa, Oberon, 1971) 183p.

The Best Name of Silence (Ottawa, Oberon, 1972) 140p.

A Book About Billie (Ottawa, Oberon, 1972) [Also published as *Inside and Out,* 1974]

Atlantic Crossings (Ottawa, Oberon, 1974)

The Glass Knight (Ottawa, Oberon, 1976) 190p.

DARYL HINE (1936-   )

Five Poems (Toronto, Emblem Press, 1955) 13p.

The Carnal and the Crane (Montreal, McGill Poetry Series, 1957) 50p.

The Devil's Picture Book (Toronto, Abelard-Schuman, 1960) 32p.

The Prince of Darkness & Co. (Toronto, Abelard-Schuman, 1961) 190p.

Polish Subtitles: Impressions from a Journey (Toronto, Abelard-Schuman, 1963) 160p.

The Wooden Horse (New York, Atheneum, 1965) 58p.

Minutes (New York, Atheneum, 1968) 53p.

In & Out: A Confessional Poem (Chicago, n.p., 1975) 211p.

Resident Alien (New York, Atheneum, 1975)

HUGH HOOD (1928-   )

Flying a Red Kite (Toronto, Ryerson, 1962) 240p.

White Figure, White Ground (Toronto, Ryerson, 1964) 251p.

Around the Mountain. Scenes from Montreal Life (Toronto, Peter Martin, 1967) 175p.

The Camera Always Lies (New York, Harcourt, 1967) 246p.
The Game of Touch (Toronto, Longmans, 1970) 192p.
Strength Down Centre. The Jean Beliveau Story (Scarborough, Prentice-Hall, 1970) 192p.
The Fruit Man, the Meat Man & the Manager (Ottawa, Oberon Press, 1971) 207p.
You Can't Get There from Here (Ottawa, Oberon, 1972) 202p.
The Governor's Bridge Is Closed (Ottawa, Oberon, 1973) 144p.
The Swing in the Garden (Ottawa, Oberon, 1975) 210p.
Dark Glasses (Ottawa,Oberon, 1976) 143p.
A New Athens (Ottawa, Oberon, 1977) 226p.

GEORGE JOHNSTON (1913-   )

The Cruising Auk (Toronto, Oxford University Press, 1959) 72p.
The Saga of Gisli the Outlaw. Translated from the Icelandic by George Johnston (Toronto, University of Toronto Press, 1963) xiii + 146p.
Home Free (Toronto, Oxford University Press, 1966) 64p.
Happy Enough. Poems, 1935-1972 (Toronto, Oxford University Press, 1972) 154p.
The Faroe Islanders' Saga. Translated by George Johnston (Ottawa, Oberon, 1975) 144p.
The Greenlanders' Saga. Translated by George Johnston (Ottawa, Oberon, 1976) 48p.

D.G. JONES (1929-   )

Frost on the Sun (Toronto, Contact Press, 1957) 46p.
The Sun is Axeman (Toronto, University of Toronto Press, 1961) 70p.
Phrases from Orpheus (Toronto, Oxford University Press, 1967) 88p.
Butterfly on Rock. A Study of Themes and Images in Canadian Literature (Toronto, University of Toronto Press, 1970) 197p.

LEO KENNEDY (1907-   )

The Shrouding. Poems (Toronto, Macmillan, 1933) 59p.
New Provinces. Poems of Several Authors. [Edited by F.R. Scott] (Toronto, Macmillan, 1936)

A.M. KLEIN (1909-1972)

New Provinces. Poems of Several Authors [Edited by F. R. Scott] (Toronto, Macmillan, 1936)
Hath Not a Jew (New York, Behrman's Jewish Book House, 1940) 116p.
The Hitleriad (New York, New Directions, 1944) 30p.
Poems (Philadelphia, Jewish Publishing Society, 1944) 82p.
The Rocking Chair and Other Poems (Toronto, Ryerson, 1948) 56p.
The Second Scroll (New York, Knopf, 1951) 198p.
The Collected Poems of A.M. Klein. Compiled and with an Introduction by Miriam Waddington (Toronto, McGraw-Hill Ryerson, 1974) x + 373p.

RAYMOND KNISTER (1899-1932)

Canadian Short Stories. Edited by Raymond Knister (Toronto, Macmillan, 1928) xix + 340p.
White Narcissus. A Novel (New York, Harcourt, 1929) 250p.
My Star Predominant (Toronto, Ryerson, 1934) 319p.
The Collected Poems of Raymond Knister. Edited with a Memoir by Dorothy Livesay (Toronto, Ryerson, 1949) 45p.
Selected Stories of Raymond Knister. Edited with an Introduction by Michael Gnarowski (Ottawa, University of Ottawa Press, 1972) 119p.
The First Day of Spring: Stories and Other Prose. Selected and with an Introduction by Peter Stevens (Toronto, University of Toronto Press, 1976) xxx + 469p.

ROBERT KROETSCH (1927-   )

But We Are Exiles (Toronto, Macmillan, 1965) 145p.
The Words of My Roaring (Toronto, Macmillan, 1966) 211p.
Alberta (Toronto, Macmillan, 1968) 231p.
The Studhorse Man (Toronto, Macmillan, 1969) 168p.
Creation. Edited by Robert Kroetsch, James Bacque and Pierre Gravel (Toronto, New Press, 1970) 231p.
Gone Indian (Toronto, New Press, 1973) 212p.
Badlands (Toronto, New Press, 1975) 270p.
The Ledger (London, Ontario, Applegarth Follies, 1975)

The Stone Hammer Poems (Nanaimo, British Columbia, Oolichan Books, 1975) 63p.

Seed Catalogue (n.p., Turnstone Press, 1977)

PATRICK LANE (1939-   )

Letters From the Savage Mind (Vancouver, Very Stone House, 1966)

Calgary City Jail (Vancouver, Very Stone House, 1969)

For Rita – In Asylum (Vancouver, Very Stone House, 1969)

Newspaper Wall (Trumansburg, New York, New Books, 1969)

Separations (Trumansburg, New York, New Books, 1969)

Mountain Oysters (Vancouver, Very Stone House, 1971) 23p.

Hiway 401 Rhapsody ([Vancouver] Very Stone House, 1971) 11p.

The Sun Has Begun to Eat the Mountain (Montreal, Ingluvin Publications, 1972) 142p.

Passing Into Storm (Vernon, British Columbia, Traumerei Communications, 1973) [26]p.

Beware the Months of Fire (Toronto, Anansi, 1974) 100p.

Certs (Prince George, British Columbia [College of New Caledonia], 1974) [4]p.

Unborn Things: South American Poems (Madeira Park, British Columbia, Harbour Publishing, 1975) 38p.

MARGARET LAURENCE (1926-   )

A Tree of Poverty. Somali Poetry and Prose (Somaliland, Government of Somaliland, 1954) 146p.

This Side Jordan (Toronto, McClelland and Stewart, 1960) 281p.

The Prophet's Camel Bell (Toronto, McClelland and Stewart, 1963) 241p. [Also published as *New Wind in a Dry Land* (New York, Knopf, 1964)]

The Tomorrow-Tamer (Toronto, McClelland and Stewart, 1963) 244p.

The Stone Angel (Toronto, McClelland and Stewart, 1964) 308p.

A Jest of God (Toronto, McClelland and Stewart, 1966) 202p. [Also published as *Rachel, Rachel* (New York, Popular Library, 1966) 175p.]

Long Drums and Cannons. Nigerian Dramatists and Novelists 1952-1966 (Toronto, Macmillan, 1968) 209p.

The Fire Dwellers (Toronto, McClelland and Stewart, 1969) 308p.

A Bird in the House (Toronto, McClelland and Stewart, 1970) 207p.

Jason's Quest (Toronto, McClelland and Stewart, 1970) 224p.

The Diviners (Toronto, McClelland and Stewart, 1974) 383p.

Heart of a Stranger (Toronto, McClelland and Stewart, 1976) 221p.

IRVING LAYTON (1912-   )

Here and Now (Montreal, First Statement Press, 1945) 45p.

Now Is the Place. Stories and Poems (Montreal, First Statement Press, 1948) 57p.

The Black Huntsmen (Toronto, Contact Press, 1952) 56p.

Cerberus. Poems by Louis Dudek, Irving Layton, Raymond Souster (Toronto, Contact Press, 1952) 98p.

Love the Conqueror Worm (Toronto, Contact Press, 1953) 49p.

In the Midst of My Fever ([Palma de Mallorca, Spain], Divers Press, 1954) 39p.

The Long Pea-Shooter (Montreal, Laocoön Press, 1954) 68p.

The Blue Propeller (Montreal, Contact Press, 1955) 50p.

The Cold Green Element (Toronto, Contact Press, 1955) 56p.

The Bull Calf and Other Poems (Toronto, Contact Press, 1956) 49p.

The Improved Binoculars. Selected Poems, with an Introduction by William Carlos Williams (Highlands, N.C., Jonathan Williams, 1956) 106p. [Second edition, with thirty additional poems, 1957] 139p.]

Music on a Kazoo (Toronto, Contact Press, 1956) 59p.

A Laughter in the Mind (Highland, N.C., Jonathan Williams, 1958) 54p. [Second printing with twenty additional poems (Montreal, Editions d'Orphée, 1959) 97p.]

A Red Carpet for the Sun (Toronto, McClelland and Stewart, 1959) 240p.

The Swinging Flesh (Toronto, McClelland and Stewart, 1961) 189p.

Love Where the Nights Are Long. Canadian Love Poems. Selected by Irving Layton with drawings by Harold Town (Toronto, McClelland and Stewart, 1962) 78p.

Balls for a One-Armed Juggler (Toronto, McClelland and Stewart, 1963) 121p.

The Laughing Rooster (Toronto, McClelland and Stewart, 1964) 112p.

Collected Poems (Toronto, McClelland and Stewart, 1965) 353p.

Periods of the Moon (Toronto, McClelland and Stewart, 1967) 127p.

The Shattered Plinths (Toronto, McClelland and Stewart, 1968) 95p.

Selected Poems. Edited by Wynne Francis (Toronto, McClelland and Stewart, 1969) 139p.

The Whole Bloody Bird. Obs, aphs and Pomes (Toronto, McClelland and Stewart, 1969) 155p.

The Collected Poems of Irving Layton (Toronto, McClelland and Stewart, 1971) 589p.

Nail Polish (Toronto, McClelland and Stewart, 1971) 87p.

Engagements: The Prose of Irving Layton. Edited by Seymour Mayne (Toronto, McClelland and Stewart, 1972) xvi + 336p.

Lovers and Lesser Men (Toronto, McClelland and Stewart, 1973) 109p.

The Pole-Vaulter (Toronto, McClelland and Stewart, 1974) 94p.

Seventy-five Greek Poems, 1951-1974 (Athens, Hermias Publications, 1974) [68]p.

The Darkening Fire: Selected Poems, 1945-1968 (Toronto, McClelland and Stewart, 1975) xvi + 176p.

The Unwavering Eye: Selected Poems, 1969-1975 (Toronto, McClelland and Stewart, 1975) 161p.

For My Brother Jesus (Toronto, McClelland and Stewart, 1976) 128p.

The Poems of Irving Layton. Edited with an Introduction by Eli Mandel (Toronto, McClelland and Stewart, 1977) 63p.

The Uncollected Poems: 1936-1959 (Oakville, Ontario, Valley Editions/Mosaic Press, 1977) 160p.

The Covenant (Toronto, McClelland and Stewart, 1977) 112p.

Right Hand Left Hand. Edited by David Arnason and Kim Todd (Erin, Porcépic, 1977).

DENNIS LEE (1939-   )

Kingdom of Absence (Toronto, Anansi, 1967) 60p.

Civil Elegies (Toronto, Anansi, 1968) [Revised edition, Toronto, 1972]

Alligator Pie (Toronto, Macmillan, 1974) 64p.

Nicholas Knock and Other People (Toronto, Macmillan, 1974) 64p.

Garbage Delight (Toronto, Macmillan, 1977) 64p.

Savage Fields: An Essay in Literature and Cosmology (Toronto, Anansi, 1977) 200p.

DOUGLAS LE PAN (1914-   )

The Wounded Prince and Other Poems (London, Chatto and Windus, 1948) 39p.

The Net and the Sword (London, Chatto and Windus, 1953) 56p.

The Deserter (Toronto, McClelland and Stewart, 1964) 298p.

DOROTHY LIVESAY (1909-   )

Green Pitcher (Toronto, Macmillan, 1928) 16p.

Signpost (Toronto, Macmillan, 1932) 61p.

Day and Night. Poems (Toronto, Ryerson, 1944) 48p.

Poems for People (Toronto, Ryerson, 1947) 40p.

Call My People Home (Toronto, Ryerson, 1950) 24p.

New Poems (Toronto, Emblem Books, 1955) 15p.

Selected Poems 1926-1956. With an Introduction by Desmond Pacey (Toronto, Ryerson, 1957) 82p.

The Colour of God's Face. ([Vancouver], [Author], [1965?]) [11p.]

The Unquiet Bed (Toronto, Ryerson, 1967) 65p.

The Documentaries (Toronto, Ryerson, 1968) 56p.

Plainsongs (Fredericton, Fiddlehead, 1969) 32p. [Enlarged and revised edition, 1971, 48p.]

Disasters of the Sun (Burnaby, British Columbia, Blackfish, 1971) 8p.

Forty Women Poets of Canada. Edited by Dorothy Livesay with the assistance of Seymour Mayne (Montreal, Ingluvin Publications, 1971) 141p.

Collected Poems: The Two Seasons (Toronto, McGraw-Hill Ryerson, 1972) 368p.

A Winnipeg Childhood (Winnipeg, Peguis Publishers, 1973) 105p.

Ice Age (Erin, Ontario, Press Porcépic, 1975) 75p.

Woman's Eye: Twelve B.C. Poets. Edited by Dorothy Livesay (Vancouver, Air Press, 1975) xi + 101p.

The Woman I Am (Erin, Ontario, Press Porcépic, 1977) 96p.

PAT LOWTHER (1935-1975)

This Difficult Flowering (Vancouver, Very Stone House, 1968)

The Age of the Bird (Burnaby, British Columbia, Blackfish, 1972) 7p.

Milk Stone (Ottawa, Borealis Press, 1974) 95p.

A Stone Diary (Toronto, Oxford University Press, 1977) 96p.

EDWARD MCCOURT (1907-1972)

The Flaming Hour (Toronto, Ryerson, 1947) 170p.

Music at the Close (Toronto, Ryerson, 1947) 228p.

The Canadian West in Fiction (Toronto, Ryerson, 1949) [Revised edition, 1970]

Home is the Stranger (Toronto, Macmillan, 1950) 288p.

Buckskin Brigadier (Toronto, Macmillan, 1955) 157p.

The Wooden Sword (Toronto, McClelland and Stewart, 1956) 255p.

Revolt in the West (Toronto, Macmillan, 1958) 159p.

Walk Through the Valley (Toronto, McClelland and Stewart, 1958) 222p.

Fasting Friar (Toronto, McClelland and Stewart, 1963) 222p.

The Road Across Canada (London, Murray, 1965) 199p.

Remember Butler, the Story of Sir Willam Butler (Toronto, McClelland and Stewart, 1967) 276p.

Saskatchewan (Toronto, Macmillan, 1968) 238p.

The Yukon and Northwest Territories (Toronto, Macmillan, 1969) 236p.

GWENDOLYN MACEWEN (1941-   )

The Drunken Clock (Toronto, Aleph Press, 1961) 15p.

Selah (Toronto, Aleph Press, 1961) 12p.

Julian, the Magician. A Novel (Toronto, Macmillan, 1963) 151p.

The Rising Fire (Toronto, Contact Press, 1963) 82p.

A Breakfast for Barbarians (Toronto, Ryerson, 1966) 53p.

The Shadow-Maker (Toronto, Macmillan, 1969) 93p.

King of Egypt, King of Dreams. A Novel (Toronto, Macmillan, 1971) 287p.

The Armies of the Moon (Toronto, Macmillan, 1972) 75p.

Noman (Ottawa, Oberon, 1972) 121p.

Magic Animals. Selected Poems Old and New (Toronto, Macmillan, 1974) 154p.

The Fire-Eaters (Ottawa, Oberon, 1976) 63p.

HUGH MACLENNAN (1907-   )

Oxyrhynchus, An Economic and Social Study (Princeton, Princeton University Press, 1935) 93p.

Barometer Rising (Toronto, Collins, 1941) 326p.

Canadian Unity and Quebec. By Emile Vaillancourt, J.P. Humphrey and Hugh MacLennan (Montreal, n.p., 1942) 16p.

Two Solitudes (Toronto, Collins, 1945) 370p.

The Precipice (Toronto, Collins, 1948) 372p.

Cross Country (Toronto, Collins, 1949) 172p. [Also with a new Introduction by the Author (Edmonton, Hurtig, 1972) xxiii + 172p.]

Each Man's Son (Toronto, Macmillan, 1951) 244p.

The Present World as Seen in Its Literature (Fredericton, University of New Brunswick, 1952) 12p.

Thirty and Three. Edited by Dorothy Duncan (Toronto, Macmillan, 1954) 261p.

The Future of the Novel as an Art Form (Toronto, University of Toronto Press, [1959?]) 11p.

The Watch That Ends the Night (Toronto, Macmillan, 1959) 373p.

Scotchman's Return, and Other Essays (Toronto, Macmillan, 1960) 279p.

Seven Rivers of Canada (Toronto, Macmillan, 1961) 170p.

An Orange from Portugal (Thornhill, Ontario, Village Press, 1964) 13p.

The Colour of Canada (Toronto, McClelland and Stewart, 1967) 126p. [Revised edition, 1972]

Return of the Sphinx (Toronto, Macmillan, 1967) 303p.

Rivers of Canada (Toronto, Macmillan, 1974) 272p.

JAY MACPHERSON (1931-   )

Nineteen Poems (Deya, Mallorca, Seizin Press, 1952) 9p.

O Earth Return (Toronto, Emblem Books, 1954) 9p.

The Boatman (Toronto, Oxford University Press, 1957) 70p.

A Dry Light & The Dark Air (Toronto, Hawkshead Press, 1959) 4p.

The Four Ages of Man. The Classical Myths (Toronto, Macmillan, 1962) 188p.

The Boatman and Other Poems (Toronto, Oxford University Press, 1968) 86p.

Welcoming Disaster (Toronto, Saannes Publications, 1974) 63p.

ANDRÉ MAJOR (1942-   )

Le Froid se meurt (Montreal, Editions Atys, 1961) 17p.

Holocauste à 2 voix (Montreal, Editions Atys, 1962) 51p.

Nouvelles [with Jacques Brault and André Brochu] (Montreal, A.G.E.U.M., 1963) 139p.

Le Cabochon (Montreal, Editions Parti Pris, 1964) 195p.

La Chair de poule (Montreal, Editions Parti Pris, 1965) 185p.

Le Vent du diable (Montreal, Editions du Jour, 1968) 143p.

Félix-Antoine Savard (Montreal, Fides, 1968) 190p.

Poèmes pour durer (Montreal, Editions du Songe, 1969) 94p.

Le Désir, suivi de *Le Perdant* (Montreal, Editions Leméac, 1973) 70p.

L'Épouvantail (Montreal, Editions du Jour, 1974) 229p.

Une Soirée en octobre. Présentation de Martial Dassylva (Montreal, Editions Leméac, 1975) 90p.

L'épidémie (Montreal, Editions du Jour, 1975) 218p.

Les Rescapés (Montreal, Editions Quinze, 1976) 146p. [Translated as *The Scarecrows of Saint-Emmanuel* by Sheila Fischman (Toronto, McClelland and Stewart, 1977)]

ELI MANDEL (1922-   )

Trio. First Poems by Gael Turnbull, Phyllis Webb, Eli Mandel (Toronto, Contact Press, 1954) 89p.

Fuseli Poems (Toronto, Contact Press, 1960) 66p.

Poetry 62. Edited by Eli Mandel and Jean-Guy Pilon (Toronto, Ryerson, 1961) 116p.

Black and Secret Man (Toronto, Ryerson, 1964) 33p.

Criticism: The Silent-Speaking Words (Toronto, CBC Publications, 1966) 73p.

An Idiot Joy (Edmonton, Hurtig, 1967) 85p.

Irving Layton (Toronto, Forum House, 1969) 82p.

Five Modern Canadian Poets. Edited by Eli Mandel with Ray Bentley (Toronto, Holt, Rinehart, 1970) 88p.

Contexts of Canadian Criticism. Edited with an Introduction by Eli Mandel (Chicago, University of Chicago Press, 1971) vii + 304p.

English Poems of the Twentieth Century. Selected by Eli Mandel and Desmond Maxwell (Toronto, Macmillan, 1971) 221p.

Eight More Canadian Poets. Edited by Eli Mandel with Ann Mandel (Toronto, Holt, Rinehart, 1972) 88p.

Poets of Contemporary Canada 1960-1970. Edited with an Introduction by Eli Mandel (Toronto, McClelland and Stewart, 1972).

Crusoe. Poems Selected and New (Toronto, Anansi, 1973) 108p.

Stony Plain (Erin, Ontario, Press Porcépic, 1973) 96p.

Another Time (Erin, Ontario, Press Porcépic, 1977) 160p.

Out of Place (Erin, Ontario, Press Porcépic, 1977) 80p.

CLAIRE MARTIN (1914-   )

Avec ou sans amour (Montreal, Cercle du Livre de France, 1958) 185p.

Doux-Amer (Montreal, Cercle du Livre de France, 1960) 192p.

Quand j'aurai payé ton visage (Montreal, Cercle du Livre de France, 1962) 187p.

Dans un gant de fer (Montreal, Cercle du Livre de France, 1965) 235p. [Translated with *La Joue droite* as *In an Iron Glove* by Philip Stratford (Toronto, Ryerson, 1968) ix + 327p.]

La Joue droite, mémoires (Montreal, Cercle du Livre de France, 1966) 210p. [Translated with *Dans un gant de fer* as *In an Iron Glove* by Philip Stratford (Toronto, Ryerson, 1968) ix + 327p.]

Les Morts (Montreal, Cercle du Livre de France, 1970) 150p.

Moi, je n'étais qu'espoir (Montreal, Cercle du Livre de France, 1972) 54p.

La Petite fille lit (Ottawa, Editions de l'Université d'Ottawa, 1973) 18p.

GASTON MIRON (1928-   )

Deux sangs. With Olivier Marchand (Montreal, Editions de l'Hexagone, 1953) 67p.

L'homme rapaillé (Montreal, Les Presses de l'Université de Montréal, 1970) 171p.

Courtepointes (Ottawa, Editions de l'Université d'Ottawa, 1975) 51p.

W.O. MITCHELL (1914-   )

Who Has Seen the Wind (Toronto, Macmillan, 1947) 344p.
Jake and the Kid (Toronto, Macmillan, 1961) 184p.
The Kite (Toronto, Macmillan, 1962) 210p.
The Black Bonspiel of Willie MacCrimmon ([Calgary], [Frontiers Unlimited], [1964]) 55p.
The Vanishing Point (Toronto, Macmillan, 1973) 393p.
The Devil's Instrument (Toronto, Simon and Pierre [1973]) 31p.

ALICE MUNRO (1931-   )

Dance of the Happy Shades (Toronto, Ryerson, 1968) 224p.
Lives of Girls & Women (Toronto, McGraw-Hill Ryerson, 1971) 254p.
Something I've Been Meaning To Tell You (Toronto, McGraw-Hill Ryerson, 1974) 246p.

SUSAN MUSGRAVE (1951-   )

Songs of the Sea-Witch (Victoria, Sono Nis Press, 1970) 69p.
Entrance of the Celebrant (Toronto, Macmillan, 1972) 49p.
Grave-Dirt and Selected Strawberries (Toronto, Macmillan, 1973) 115p.
Gullband (Vancouver, J.J. Douglas Publishing Company, 1974) 49p.
The Impstone (Toronto, McClelland and Stewart, 1976) 112p.
Selected Strawberries and Other Poems (Vancouver, Sono Nis Press, 1977) 160p.

JOHN NEWLOVE (1938-   )

Grave Sirs (Vancouver, Reid and Tanabe, 1962) 34p.
Elephants, Mothers, and Others (Vancouver, Periwinkle Press, 1963) 31p.
Moving In Alone (Toronto, Contact Press, 1965) 83p.
Notebook Pages (Toronto, Charles Pachter, 1966)
What They Say (Kitchener; Weed/Flower Press, 1967) 23p.
Black Night Window (Toronto, McClelland and Stewart, 1968) 112p.
The Cave (Toronto, McClelland and Stewart, 1970) 85p.
Lies (Toronto, McClelland and Stewart, 1972) 96p.

Canadian Poetry: The Modern Era. Edited by John Newlove (Toronto, McClelland and Stewart, 1977) 270p.
The Fat Man. Selected Poems, 1962-1972 (Toronto, McClelland and Stewart, 1977) 127p.

bp NICHOL (1944-   )

Scrapture, second sequence (Toronto, Ganglia Press, 1965)
Calendar (Woodchester, England, Openings Press, 1966)
Scraptures, 3rd sequence (Toronto, Ganglia Press, 1966)
Scraptures, 4th sequence (Niagara Falls, New York, Press Today Niagara, 1966)
Strange Grey Town. With David Aylward (Toronto, Ganglia Press, 1966)
Scraptures, 11th sequence (Toronto, Fleye Press and Ganglia Press, 1967)
Kon 66 & 67 (Toronto, Ganglia Press, 1967)
Konfessions of an Elizabethan Fan Dancer (London, Writer's Forum Books, 1967) [Revised edition (Weed/Flower Press, 1973)]
Journeying and the Returns (Toronto, Coach House Press, 1967)
Ruth (Toronto, Fleye Press, 1967)
The Year of the Frog (Toronto, Ganglia Press, 1967)
Ballads of the Restless Are (Sacramento, California, Runcible Spoon, 1968)
Dada Lama (London, Tlaloc, 1968)
D. A. Dead (Toronto, Ganglia Press, 1968)
Lament (Toronto, Ganglia Press, 1969)
Nights on Prose Mountain (Toronto, Ganglia Press, 1969)
Two Novels: Andy and For Jesus Lunatick (Toronto, Coach House Press, 1969)
Beach Head (Sacramento, California, Runcible Spoon, 1970)
The Captain Poetry Poems (Vancouver, Blewointment Press, 1970)
Still Water (Vancouver, Talonbooks, 1970)
The True Eventual Story of Billy the Kid (Toronto, Weed/Flower Press, 1970)
ABC: the Aleph Beth Book (Ottawa, Oberon, 1971)
Beach Head (Sacramento, California, Runcible Spoon, 1971)
Monotones (Vancouver, Talonbooks, 1971)
The Other Side of the Room (Toronto, Weed/Flower Press, 1971) 58p.
Adventures of Milt the Morph in Colour. With Barbara Caruso (Toronto, Seripress, 1972)

Collbrations. With Steve McCaffery (Toronto, Ganglia Press, 1972)

The Martyrology. Books I and II (Toronto, Coach House Press, 1972)

Aleph Unit (Toronto, Seripress, 1973)

Unit of Four (Toronto, Seripress, 1973)

Love: A Book of Remembrances (Vancouver, Talonbooks, 1974)

Scraptures: basic sequences (Toronto, Massassauga Editions, 1974)

Aygal (Toronto, Coach House Press, 1974)

Horse D'Oeuvres. With The Four Horsemen (Toronto, General Publishing, 1975) 121p.

The Martyrology, Books III & IV (Toronto: Coach House Press, 1976) 116p.

Journal (Toronto, Coach House Press, 1977)

ALDEN NOWLAN (1933-)

The Rose and the Puritan (Fredericton, University of New Brunswick, 1952) 16p.

A Darkness in the Earth (Eureka, California, Hearse Press, [1959]) 16p.

Under the Ice (Toronto, Ryerson, 1960) 44p.

Wind in a Rocky Country (Toronto, Emblem Books, 1960) 16p.

The Things Which Are (Toronto, Contact Press, 1962) 71p.

Bread, Wine and Salt (Toronto, Clarke, Irwin, 1967) 74p.

A Black Plastic Button and a Yellow Yo-Yo (Toronto, Charles Pachter, 1968) 14p.

Miracle at Indian River (Toronto, Clarke, Irwin, 1968) 132p.

The Mysterious Naked Man (Toronto, Clarke, Irwin, 1969) 93p.

Playing the Jesus Game. Selected Poems (Trumansburg, New York, New/Books, 1970) 105p.

Between Tears and Laughter (Toronto, Clarke, Irwin, 1971) 119p.

Various Persons Named Kevin O'Brien. A Fictional Memoir (Toronto, Clarke, Irwin, 1973) 143p.

I'm a Stranger Here Myself (Toronto, Clarke, Irwin, 1974) 87p.

Campobello, The Outer Island (Toronto, Clarke, Irwin, 1975) 132p.

Frankenstein: the play. By Alden Nowlan and Walter Learning. *Frankenstein: the novel.* By Mary Shelley. Edited and abridged by Alden Nowlan and Walter Learning (Toronto, Clarke, Irwin, 1976) 181p.

Smoked Glass (Toronto, Clarke, Irwin, 1977) 75p.

MICHAEL ONDAATJE (1943-)

The Dainty Monsters (Toronto, Coach House Press, 1967) 77p.

The Man With Seven Toes (Toronto, Coach House Press, 1969) 41p.

The Collected Works of Billy the Kid. Left Handed Poems (Toronto, Anansi, 1970) 105p.

Leonard Cohen (Toronto, McClelland and Stewart, 1970) 64p.

The Broken Ark. A Book of Beasts. Poems chosen by Michael Ondaatje with Drawings by Tony Urqhart (Ottawa, Oberon Press, 1971) 48p.

Rat Jelly (Toronto, Coach House Press, 1973) 71p.

Coming Through Slaughter (Toronto, Anansi, 1976) 156p.

P.K. PAGE (1916-)

The Sun and the Moon. By Judith Cape [pseud] (Toronto, Macmillan, 1944) 200p.

Unit of Five. Poems by Louis Dudek, Ronald Hambleton, P.K. Page, Raymond Souster, James Wreford. Edited by Ronald Hambleton (Toronto, Ryerson, 1944)

As Ten As Twenty (Toronto, Ryerson, 1946) 43p.

The Metal and the Flower (Toronto, McClelland and Stewart, 1954) 64p.

Cry Ararat! Poems New and Selected (Toronto, McClelland and Stewart, 1967) 111p.

The Sun and the Moon and Other Fictions (Toronto, Anansi, 1973) 204p.

Poems Selected and New (Toronto, Anansi, 1974) 150p.

Leviathan in a Pool (Vancouver, Blackfish, 1974)]

PHILIPPE PANNETON (1895-1943)

30 arpents (Paris: Flammarion, [1938]) 292p. [Translated as *Thirty Acres* by Felix and Dorothea Walter (Toronto, Macmillan, 1940) 324p.]

Un Monde était leur empire (Montreal, Editions Variétés, 1943)

L'Héritage et autres contes (Montreal, Editions Variétés, 1946) 180p.

Fausse monnaie (Montreal, Editions Variétés, 1947) 236p.

Les Poids du jour (Montreal, Editions Variétés, 1949) 411p.

L'Amiral et le facteur ou Comment l'Amérique ne fut pas découverte (Montreal, Dussault, 1954) 206p.

Confidences (Montreal, Fides, 1965) 198p.

E.J. PRATT (1883-1964)

Rachel. A Story of the Sea in Verse (New York, Privately Printed, 1915) 15p.
Studies in Pauline Eschatology, and Its Background (Toronto, Briggs, 1917) 203p.
Newfoundland Verse (Toronto, Ryerson, 1923) 140p.
The Witches' Brew (London, Selwyn & Blount, 1925) 32p.
Titans (London, Macmillan, 1926) 67p.
The Iron Door. An Ode (Toronto, Macmillan, 1927) 30p.
The Roosevelt and the Antinoe (New York, Macmillan, 1930) 44p.
Verses of the Sea. With an Introduction by Charles G.D. Roberts (Toronto, Macmillan, 1930) 97p.
Many Moods (Toronto, Macmillan, 1932) 53p.
The Titanic (Toronto, Macmillan, 1935) 42p.
New Provinces. Poems of Several Authors. [Edited by F.R. Scott] (Toronto, Macmillan, 1936)
The Fable of the Goats and Other Poems (Toronto, Macmillan, 1937) 47p.
Brébeuf and His Brethren (Toronto, Macmillan, 1940) 65p.
Dunkirk (Toronto, Macmillan, 1941) 13p.
Still Life and Other Verse (Toronto, Macmillan, 1943) 40p.
Collected Poems (Toronto, Macmillan, 1944) 314 p. [Second edition with an Introduction by Northrop Frye published in 1958]
They Are Returning (Toronto, Macmillan, 1945) 15p.
Behind the Log (Toronto, Macmillan, 1947) 47p.
Ten Selected Poems. With Notes (Toronto, Macmillan, 1947) 149p.
Towards the Last Spike. A Verse Panorama of... the First Canadian Transcontinental (Toronto, Macmillan, 1952) 53p.
Magic in Everything (Toronto, Macmillan, 1955) 6p.
Here the Tides Flow. With an Introduction, Notes, and Questions by D.G. Pitt (Toronto, Macmillan, 1962) 169p.
Selected Poems. Edited by Peter Buitenhuis (Toronto, Macmillan, 1968) 221p.

AL PURDY (1918-   )

The Enchanted Echo (Vancouver, Clarke and Stuart, 1944) 62p.
Pressed on Sand (Toronto, Ryerson, 1955) 16p.
Emu, Remember! (Fredericton, Fiddlehead Books, 1956) 16p.

The Crafte so Longe to Lerne (Toronto, Ryerson, 1959) 23p.
The Blur in Between (Toronto, Emblem Books, 1962) 21p.
Poems for All the Annettes (Toronto, Contact Press, 1962) 64p.
The Cariboo Horses (Toronto, McClelland and Stewart, 1965) 112p.
North of Summer. Poems from Baffin Island (Toronto, McClelland and Stewart, 1967) 87p.
Wild Grape Wine (Toronto, McClelland and Stewart, 1968) 128p.
Fifteen Winds. A Selection of Modern Canadian Poems. Edited by Al Purdy (Toronto, Ryerson, 1969) xvi + 157p.
Love in a Burning Building (Toronto, McClelland and Stewart, 1970) 128p.
The Quest for Ouzo (Trenton, Author, 1970)
Storm Warning. The New Canadian Poets. Edited by Al Purdy (Toronto, McClelland and Stewart, 1971) 152p.
Hiroshima Poems (Trumansburg, New York, Crossing Press, 1972) 12p.
Selected Poems. With an Introduction by George Woodcock (Toronto, McClelland and Stewart, 1972) 126p.
On the Bearpaw Sea (Vancouver, Blackfish Press, 1973) [34] p.
Sex and Death (Toronto, McClelland and Stewart, 1973) 128p.
In Search of Owen Roblin (Toronto, McClelland and Stewart, 1974) [112] p.
The Poems of Al Purdy (Toronto, McClelland and Stewart, 1976) 61p.
Storm Warning 2. Selected by Al Purdy (Toronto, McClelland and Stewart, 1976) 159p.
Sundance at Dusk (Toronto, McClelland and Stewart, 1976) 112p.
No Other Country (Toronto, McClelland and Stewart, 1977) 187p.

THOMAS RADDALL (1903-   )

The Markland Sagas. With a Discussion of their Relation to Nova Scotia. With C.H.L. Jones (Montreal, Gazette, 1934) 118p.
The Pied Piper of Dipper Creek and Other Tales (Edinburgh, Blackwood, 1938) 318p.
His Majesty's Yankees (Garden City, New York, Doubleday, 1942) 409p.
Roger Sudden (Toronto, McClelland and Stewart, 1944) 358p.
Tambour and Other Stories (Toronto, McClelland and Stewart, 1945) 388p.

Pride's Fancy (Toronto, McClelland and Stewart, 1946) 308p.

The Wedding Gift and Other Stories (Toronto, McClelland and Stewart, 1947)

Halifax, Warden of the North (Toronto, McClelland and Stewart, 1948) 348p. [Revised edition, 1971]

The Nymph and the Lamp. A Novel (Boston, Little, Brown, 1950) 376p.

Sons of the Hawk (Toronto, Doubleday [c. 1950]) vii + 247p.

Tidefall (Toronto, McClelland and Stewart, 1953) 309p.

A Muster of Arms and Other Stories (Toronto, McClelland and Stewart, 1954) 236p.

The Wings of Night (New York, Doubleday, 1956) 319p.

The Path of Destiny. Canada from the British Conquest to Home Rule: 1763-1850 (Toronto, Doubleday, 1957) 468p.

The Rover. The Story of a Canadian Privateer (Toronto, Macmillan, 1958) 156p.

At the Tide's Turn, and Other Stories. With an Introduction by Allan Bevan (Toronto, McClelland and Stewart, 1959) 178p.

The Governor's Lady (Garden City, New York, Doubleday, 1960) 474p.

The Literary Art (Charlottetown, Prince of Wales College, 1954) 8p.

Hangman's Beach (Garden City, New York, Doubleday, 1966) vi + 421p.

Footsteps on Old Floors. True tales of mystery (Garden City, New York, Doubleday, 1968) 239p.

A Pictorial Guide to Historic Nova Scotia, featuring Louisburg, Peggy's Cove [and] Sable Island ([Halifax], [Book Room], [1970]) 31p.

In My Time: A Memoir (Toronto, McClelland and Stewart, 1976) 365p.

JAMES REANEY (1926-   )

The Red Heart (Toronto, McClelland and Stewart, 1949) 73p.

A Suit of Nettles (Toronto, Macmillan, 1958) 54p.

The Killdeer and Other Plays (Toronto, Macmillan, 1962) 224p.

Twelve Letters to a Small Town (Toronto, Ryerson, 1962) 32p.

The Dance of Death at London, Ontario. Poems (London, Alphabet Press, 1963) 32p.

The Boy with an R in his Hand. A Tale of the Type-Riot at Willam Lyon MacKenzie's Printing Office in 1826, (Toronto, Macmillan, 1965) 107p.

Colours in the Dark (Vancouver/Toronto, Talonplays/Macmillan, 1969) 90p. [Revised edition, 1971. 92p.]

Listen to the Wind (Vancouver, Talonbooks, 1972) 119p.

Masks of Childhood. Edited with an Afterword by Brian Parker (Toronto, New Press, 1972) ix + 292p.

Names & Nicknames & Other Plays for Young People (Vancouver, Talonplays/Macmillan, 1972)

Poems. Edited by Germaine Warkentin (Toronto, New Press, 1972) xviii + 283p.

James Reaney's Apple Butter & other plays for children (Vancouver, Talonbooks, 1973) 193p.

Selected Shorter Poems. Edited by Germaine Warkentin (Erin, Ontario, Press Porcépic, 1975) 96p.

Sticks & Stones: the Donnellys, part I (Erin, Ontario, Press Porcépic, 1975) 51p. [Revised edition, 1976]

Handcuffs: the Donnellys, part III (Erin, Ontario, Press Porcépic, 1976)

Selected Longer Poems. Edited by Germaine Warkentin (Erin, Ontario, Press Porcépic, 1976) 95p.

The St. Nicholas Hotel, Wm. Donnelly prop.: the Donnellys, part II (Erin, Ontario, Press Porcépic, 1976) 159p.

Baldoon. With C. H. Gervais (Erin, Ontario, The Porcupine's Quill, 1977) 120p.

Fourteen Barrels from Sea to Sea (Erin, Ontario, Press Porcépic, 1977)

MORDECAI RICHLER (1931-   )

The Acrobats (London, Deutsch, 1954) 204p.

Son of a Smaller Hero (London, Deutsch, 1955) 232p.

A Choice of Enemies (London, Deutsch, 1957) 256p.

The Apprenticeship of Duddy Kravitz (London, Deutsch, 1959) 319p.

The Incomparable Atuk (Toronto, McClelland and Stewart, 1963) 192p.

Cocksure (Toronto, McClelland and Stewart, 1968) 250p.

Hunting Tigers under Glass (Toronto, McClelland and Stewart, 1968) 160p.

The Street (Toronto, McClelland and Stewart, 1969) 128p.

St. Urbain's Horseman. A Novel (Toronto, McClelland and Stewart, 1971) 467p.

Shovelling Trouble (Toronto, McClelland and Stewart, 1972) 158p.
Jacob Two-two Meets the Hooded Fang (Toronto, McClelland and Stewart, 1975) 83p.

GWENDOLYN RINGWOOD (1910-   )

Still Stands the House. A Drama in One Act (Toronto, French, 1939) 28p.
The Jack and the Joker. One Act (Edmonton, University of Alberta, n.d.) First performed Banff School of Fine Arts, Summer, 1944.
Stampede. Three Acts (Edmonton, University of Alberta, n.d.) First performed University Drama Society, March, 1946.
Dark Harvest. A Tragedy of the Canadian Prairies. With notes, acting suggestions, and questions by G.L. Broderson (Toronto, Nelson, 1945) 143p.
Hatfield, the Rainmaker. One Act. (Edmonton, University of Alberta, 1946) [Also published as *The Rainmaker* (Toronto, Playwrights Co-op, n.d.) 36p.]
The Courting of Marie Jenvrin. A Comedy of the Far North (Toronto, French, 1951) 35p.
Younger Brother (Toronto, Longmans, 1959) 213p.
Lament for Harmonica. (Ottawa, Ottawa Little Theatre, [1960]) 20p.
Widger's Way (Toronto, Playwrights Co-op, n.d.) First performed University of Alberta Studio Theatre, 1952.

JOE ROSENBLATT (1933-   )

The Voyage of the Mood (Toronto, Heinrich Heine Press, 1963)
The LSD Leacock (Toronto, Coach House Press, 1966) 49p.
Winter of the Luna Moth (Toronto, Anansi, 1968) 78p.
Greenbaum (Toronto, Coach House Press, 1970)
Bumblebee Dithyramb (Erin, Ontario, Press Porcépic, 1972) 125p.
Blind Photographer (Erin, Ontario, Press Porcépic, 1973) 56p.
Dream Craters (Erin, Ontario, Press Porcépic, 1974) 80p.
Virgins and Vampires (Toronto, McClelland and Stewart, 1975) 112p.
Top Soil (Erin, Ontario, Press Porcépic, 1976) 272p.

SINCLAIR ROSS (1908-   )

As For Me and My House (New York, Reynal, 1941) 296p.
The Well (Toronto, Macmillan, 1958) 256p.
The Lamp at Noon and Other Stories. With an Introduction by Margaret Laurence (Toronto, McClelland and Stewart, 1968) 134p.
A Whir of Gold (Toronto, McClelland and Stewart, 1970) 215p.
Sawbones Memorial (Toronto, McClelland and Stewart, 1974) 140p.

W.W.E. ROSS (1894-1966)

Laconics. By E.R. [pseud] (Ottawa, Overbrook Press, 1930) 92p.
Sonnets. By E.R. [pseud] (Toronto, [Author], 1932) 72p.
Experiment 1923-1929. Poems by W.W.E. Ross (Toronto, Contact Press [1956]) 23p.
Shapes & Sounds. Poems of W.W.E. Ross. With a Memoir by Barry Callaghan, and a Note by Raymond Souster and John Robert Colombo (Toronto, Longmans, 1968) 145p.

GABRIELLE ROY (1909-   )

Bonheur d'occasion (Montreal, Editions Pascal, 1945) 2 vols. [Translated as *The Tin Flute* by Hannah Josephson (Toronto, McClelland and Stewart, 1947) 315p.]
La Petite Poule d'Eau (Montreal, Beauchemin, 1950) 272p. [Translated as *Where Nests the Water Hen* by Harry L. Binsse (New York, Harcourt, Brace, 1951) 251p.]
Alexandre Chenevert (Montreal, Beauchemin, 1954) 373p. [Translated as *The Cashier* by Harry L. Binsse (New York, Harcourt, Brace, 1955) 251p.]
Rue Deschambault (Montreal, Beauchemin, 1955) 260p. [Translated as *Street of Riches* by Harry L. Binsse (Toronto, McClelland and Stewart, 1957) 246p.]
La Montagne Secrète (Montreal, Beauchemin, 1961) 222p. [Translated as *The Hidden Mountain* by Harry L. Binsse (Toronto, McClelland and Stewart, 1962) 186p.]
La Route d'Altamont (Montreal, Editions H.M.H., 1966) 261p. [Translated as *The Road Past Altamont* by Joyce Marshall (Toronto, McClelland and Stewart, 1966) 146p.]

La Rivière sans Repos (Montreal, Beauchemin, 1970) 315p. [Translated as *Windflower* by Joyce Marshall (Toronto, McClelland and Stewart, 1970) 152p.]

Cet été qui chantait (Montreal, Editions françaises, 1972) 207p. [Translated as *Enchanted Summer* by Joyce Marshall (Toronto, McClelland and Stewart, 1976) 125p.]

Un jardin au bout du monde (Montreal, Beauchemin, 1975) 217p. [Translated as *Garden in the Wind* by Alan Brown (Toronto, McClelland and Stewart, 1977) 175p.]

JANE RULE (1931-   )

The Desert of the Heart (Toronto, Macmillan, 1964) 224p.

This Is Not for You (Toronto, Doubleday, 1970) 284p.

Against the Season (Toronto, Doubleday, 1971) 218p.

Theme for Diverse Instruments (Vancouver, Talonbooks, 1975) 185p.

Lesbian Images (Toronto, Doubleday, 1975) vi + 246p.

The Young in One Another's Arms (Toronto, Doubleday, 1977) 216p.

GEORGE RYGA (1932-   )

Hungry Hills (Toronto, Longmans, 1963) 180p.

Ballad of a Stone Picker (Toronto, Macmillan, 1966) 159p.

The Ecstasy of Rita Joe (Vancouver, Talonplays, [1970]) 90p.

The Ecstasy of Rita Joe and Other Plays. Edited with an Introduction by Brian Parker (Toronto, New Press, 1971) xxiii + 236p.

Captives of the Faceless Drummer (Vancouver, Talonbooks, [1971]) 78p.

Sunrise on Sarah (Vancouver, Talonbooks, 1974) 80p.

Night Desk (Vancouver, Talonbooks, 1976) 128p.

Country Western (Vancouver, Talonbooks, 1977) 196p.

F.R. SCOTT (1899-   )

New Provinces. Poems of Several Authors. [Edited by F.R. Scott] (Toronto, Macmillan, 1936)

Canada Today: A Study of Her National Interests and National Policy (Toronto, Oxford University Press, 1938) 163p.

Make This Your Canada. A Review of C.C.F. History and Policy. By D. Lewis and F.

Scott (Toronto, Central Canada Publishing Co., 1943) 223p.

Overture. Poems (Toronto, Ryerson, 1945) 79p.

Events and Signals (Toronto, Ryerson, 1954) 58p.

The Blasted Pine: An Anthology of Satire, Invective, and Disrespectful Verse, Chiefly by Canadian Writers. Selected and Arranged by A.J.M. Smith and F.R. Scott (Toronto, Macmillan, 1957) 138p. [Revised and enlarged edition (Toronto, Macmillan 1967) 192p.]

The Eye of the Needle. Satires, Sorties, Sundries (Montreal, Contact Press, 1957) 71p.

St.-Denys Garneau and Anne Hébert. Translations... by F.R. Scott (Vancouver, Klanak Press, 1962) 49p.

Signature (Vancouver, Klanak Press, 1964) 56p.

Selected Poems (Toronto, Oxford University Press, 1966) 176p.

Trouvailles. Poems from Prose (Montreal, Delta Canada, 1967) 43p.

The Dance Is One (Toronto, McClelland and Stewart, 1973) 95p.

Poems of French Canada. Translations by F.R. Scott (Burnaby, British Columbia, Blackfish, 1977) vi + 59p.

A.J.M. SMITH (1902-   )

New Provinces. Poems of Several Authors. [Edited by F.R. Scott] (Toronto, Macmillan, 1936)

The Book of Canadian Poetry. A Critical and Historical Anthology. Edited with an Introduction and Notes by A.J.M. Smith (Chicago, University of Chicago Press, 1943) 452p. [Revised and enlarged edition (Toronto, Gage, 1948) 487p. Third Edition, revised and enlarged (Toronto, Gage, 1957) 532p.]

News of the Phoenix and Other Poems (Toronto, Ryerson, 1943) 42p.

University of New Brunswick, Founders Day Address (Fredericton, University of New Brunswick, 1946) 19p.

The Worldly Muse. An Anthology of Serious Light Verse (New York, Abelard Press, 1951) 388p.

A Sort of Ecstasy. Poems New and Selected (Toronto, Ryerson, 1954) 55p.

The Blasted Pine. An Anthology of Satire, Invective, and Disrespectful Verse, Chiefly by Canadian Writers. Selected and Arranged by A.J.M. Smith and F.R. Scott (Toronto, Macmillan, 1957) 138p.

[Revised and enlarged edition (Toronto, Macmillan, 1967) 192p.]

The Oxford Book of Canadian Verse. Edited with an Introduction by A.J.M. Smith (Toronto, Oxford University Press, 1960) vi + 445p. [Revised edition, 1968]

Masks of Fiction: Canadian Critics on Canadian Prose. Edited with an Introduction by A.J.M. Smith (Toronto, McClelland and Stewart, 1961) 176p.

Collected Poems (Toronto, Oxford University Press, 1962) 124p.

Masks of Poetry: Canadian Critics on Canadian Verse. Edited with an Introduction by A.J.M. Smith (Toronto, McClelland and Stewart, 1962) 144p.

The Book of Canadian Prose, Vol. I: Early Beginnings to Confederation. Edited with an Introduction by A.J.M. Smith (Toronto, Gage, 1965) 261p. [Also published as *The Colonial Century* (Toronto, Gage, 1973) 261p.]

The Canadian Century: English-Canadian Writing Since Confederation. Edited with an Introduction by A.J.M. Smith (Toronto, Gage, 1973) xx + 652p. [Vol. II, The Book of Canadian Prose]

Modern Canadian Verse in English and French. Edited by A.J.M. Smith (Toronto, Oxford University Press, 1967) 426p.

Poems, New and Collected (Toronto, Oxford University Press, 1967) 160p.

Towards a View of Canadian Letters. Selected Critical Essays, 1928-1971 (Vancouver, University of British Columbia Press, 1973) 230p.

On Poetry and Poets (Toronto, McClelland and Stewart, 1977) viii + 122p.

RAYMOND SOUSTER (1921-   )

Unit of Five. Poems by Louis Dudek, Ronald Hambleton, P.K. Page, Raymond Souster, James Wreford. Edited by Ronald Hambleton (Toronto, Ryerson, 1944)

When We Are Young (Montreal, First Statement Press, 1946) 28p.

Go To Sleep, World (Toronto, Ryerson, 1947) 59p.

The Winter of Time. By Raymond Holmes [pseud] (New Toronto, Export Publishing Enterprises, 1949) 160p.

Cerberus. Poems by Louis Dudek, Irving Layton, Raymond Souster (Toronto, Contact Press, [c. 1952]) 98p.

Shake Hands with the Hangman. Poems 1940-1952 (Toronto, Contact Press, 1953) 24p.

Walking Death: Poems (Toronto, Contact Press, 1954) 24p.

A Dream That Is Dying. Poems (Toronto, Contact Press, 1955) 27p.

For What Time Slays. Poems (Toronto, Author, 1955) 24p.

Selected Poems. Chosen by Louis Dudek (Toronto, Contact Press, 1956) 135p.

Crepe-Hangers Carnival. Selected Poems. 1955-1958 (Toronto, Contact Press, 1958) 65p.

A Local Pride. Poems (Toronto, Contact Press, 1962) 131p.

A Place of Meeting. Poems 1958-60 (Toronto, Gallery Editions, 1962) 67p.

At Split Rock Falls (Norwich, Vermont, American Letter Press, 1963) 2p.

The Colour of the Times. The Collected Poems (Toronto, Ryerson, 1964) 121p.

12 New Poems ([Lanham, Maryland], [Goosetree Press], [1964)]) 5p.

Ten Elephants on Yonge Street: Poems (Toronto, Ryerson, 1965) 84p.

New Wave Canada: The New Explosion in Canadian Poetry ... with an Introduction and Working Magazine Bibliography. Edited by Raymond Souster (Toronto, Contact Press, 1966) 167p.

As Is (Toronto, Oxford University Press, 1967) 102p.

Lost and Found. Uncollected Poems, 1945-65 (Toronto, Clarke, Irwin, 1968) 113p.

So Far So Good. Poems 1938-1968 (Ottawa, Oberon, 1969) 100p.

Made in Canada. New Poems of the Seventies. Edited by Douglas Lochhead and Raymond Souster (Ottawa, Oberon, 1970) 192p.

The Years. Poems (Ottawa, Oberon, 1971) 164p.

On Target. By John Holmes [pseud] (Toronto, Village Book Store Press, 1972) 248p.

Selected Poems. Edited by Michael Macklem (Ottawa, Oberon, 1972) 127p.

Sights and Sounds. Compiled by Richard Woollatt and Raymond Souster (Toronto, Macmillan, 1973) 216p.

Change-up: new poems (Ottawa, Oberon Press, 1974) 100p.

One Hundred Poems of Nineteenth Century Canada. Selected by Douglas Lochhead and Raymond Souster (Toronto, Macmillan, 1974) ix + 218p.

These Loved, These Hated Lands. Compiled by Raymond Souster and Richard Woollatt (Toronto, Doubleday, 1975) 258p.

Double-header (Ottawa, Oberon Press, 1975) 250p.

Rain-check (Ottawa, Oberon Press, 1975)
150p.
Extra Innings (Ottawa, Oberon Press,
1977) 176p.

YVES THÉRIAULT (1916-   )

Contes pour un homme seul (Montreal, Edi-
tions de l'Arbre, 1944) 195p.
La Fille laide (Montreal, Beauchemin,
1950) 223p.
Le Dompteur d'ours (Montreal, Cercle du
Livre de France, 1951) 188p.
Les Vendeurs du temple (Quebec, L'institut
littéraire du Québec, 1951) 263p.
Aaron (Quebec, L'institut littéraire du
Québec, 1954) 163p.
Agaguk (Quebec, L'Institut littéraire du
Québec, 1958) 298p. [Translated as
Agaguk by Miriam Chapin (Toronto,
Ryerson, 1963) 229p.]
Roi de la Côte Nord, La Vie extraordinaire de
Napoléon-Alexandre Comeau (Montreal,
Editions de l'Homme, 1960) 123p.
Amour au goût de mer (Montreal, Beau-
chemin, 1961) 132p.
Ashini (Montreal, Fides, 1960) 173p.
[Translated as Ashini by Gwendolyn
Moore (Montreal, Harvest House,
1972) 134p.]
Les Commettants de Caridad (Quebec, In-
stitut Littéraire de Québec, 1961) 300p.
Cul de sac (Quebec, Institut Littéraire du
Québec, 1961) 223p.
Séjour à Moscou (Montreal, Fides, 1961)
191p.
Le Vendeur d'étoiles (Montreal, Fides, 1961)
124p.
Si la bombe m'était contée (Montreal, Editions
du Jour, 1962) 124p.
La Montagne sacrée; Le Rapt du Lac Caché
(Montreal, Beauchemin, 1962)
Le Grand roman d'un petit homme (Montreal,
Editions du Jour, 1963) 143p.
Le Ru d'Ikoué (Montreal, Fides, 1963) 96p.
La Rose de Pierre (Montreal, Editions du
Jour, 1964) 135p.
Les Temps du Carcajou (Quebec, Institut
littéraire du Québec, 1966) 244p.
L'Appelante (Montreal, Editions du Jour,
1967) 126p.
Le Marcheur (pièce en 3 actes) (Montreal,
Editions Leméac, 1968) 110p.
Kesten (Montreal, Editions du Jour, 1968)
123p.
La Mort d'eau (Montreal, Editions de
l'Homme, 1968) 118p.

N'tsuk (Montreal, Editions de l'Homme,
1968) 108p. [Translated as N'Tsuk by
Gwendolyn Moore (Montreal, Harvest
House, 1971) 110p.]
L'Ile introuvable (Montreal, Editions du
Jour, 1968) 176p.
Mahigan (Montreal, Editions Leméac,
1968) 107p.
L'Orde la felouque (Quebec, Editions
Jeunesse, 1969) 138p.
Valérie (Montreal, Editions de l'Homme,
1969) 124p.
Antoine et sa montagne (Montreal, Editions
du Jour, 1969) 172p.
Tayaout, fils d'Agaguk (Montreal, Editions
de l'Homme, 1969) 160p.
Textes et documents (Montreal, Editions
Leméac, 1969) 134p.
Fredange (pièce en deux actes) suivi de Les
Terres neuves (pièce en deux actes)
(Montreal, Editions Leméac, 1970)
147p.
Le Dernier havre (Montreal, L'Actuelle,
1970) 143p.
La passe-au-crachin (Montreal, Ferron
Editeurs, 1972) 156p.
Le Haut pays (Montreal, Ferron Editeurs,
1973) 108p.
Agoak (Montreal, Editions Internationales
et Editions Quinze, 1975)
Oeuvre de chair (Montreal, Stanké, 1975)
170p. [Translated as Ways of the Flesh by
David Ellis (Toronto, Gage, 1977)
176p.]
Moi, Pierre Huneau (Montreal, Editions
H.M.H., 1976) 135p.

MIRIAM WADDINGTON (1917-   )

Green World (Montreal, First Statement
Press, 1945) 30p.
The Second Silence (Toronto, Ryerson,
1955) 57p.
The Season's Lovers (Toronto, Ryerson,
1958) 56p.
The Glass Trumpet (Toronto, Oxford Uni-
versity Press, 1966) 96p.
Call Them Canadians (Ottawa, National
Film Board, 1968) 245p.
Say Yes (Toronto, Oxford University Press,
1969) 96p.
A.M. Klein (Toronto, Copp Clark, 1970)
145p.
Dream Telescope (London, Anvil Press,
1972) 24p.
Driving Home. Poems New and Selected
(Toronto, Oxford University Press,
1972) 176p.

John Sutherland: Essays, Controversies, Poems. Edited with an Introduction by Miriam Waddington (Toronto, McClelland and Stewart, 1973) 206p.
The Price of Gold (Toronto, Oxford University Press, 1976) 112p.

SHEILA WATSON (1919-   )

The Double Hook (Toronto, McClelland and Stewart, 1959) 127p.

TOM WAYMAN (1945-   )

Waiting for Wayman (Toronto, McClelland and Stewart, 1973)
For And Against the Moon: Blues, Yells and Chuckles (Toronto, Macmillan, 1974) 157p.
Money and Rain: Tom Wayman Live (Toronto, Macmillan, 1975) 150p.

PHYLLIS WEBB (1927-   )

Trio. First Poems by Gael Turnbull, Phyllis Webb, Eli Mandel (Toronto, Contact Press, 1954) 89p.
Even Your Right Eye (Toronto, McClelland and Stewart, 1956) 64p.
The Sea Is Also a Garden (Toronto, Ryerson, 1962) [54]p.
Naked Poems (Vancouver, Periwinkle Press, 1965) [52]p.
Selected Poems 1954-1965. Edited with an Introduction by John Hulcoop (Vancouver, Talonbooks, 1971) 166p.

RUDY WIEBE (1934-   )

Peace Shall Destroy Many (Toronto, McClelland and Stewart, 1962) 239p.
First and Vital Candle (Toronto, McClelland and Stewart, 1966) 354p.
The Blue Mountains of China (Toronto, McClelland and Stewart, 1970) 240p.
The Story-Makers. Edited with an Introduction by Rudy Wiebe (Toronto, Macmillan, 1970) xxx + 354p.

Stories From Western Canada. Edited with an Introduction by Rudy Wiebe (Toronto, Macmillan, 1972) xiv + 274p.
The Temptations of Big Bear (Toronto, McClelland and Stewart, 1973) 415p.
Stories from Pacific and Arctic Canada. Selected by Andreas Schroeder and Rudy Wiebe (Toronto, Macmillan, 1974) 284p.
Where Is the Voice Coming From? (Toronto, McClelland and Stewart, 1974) 157p.
The Scorched-Wood People (Toronto, McClelland and Stewart, 1977) 351p.

ANNE WILKINSON (1910-1961)

Counterpoint to Sleep (Montreal, First Statement Press, 1951) 36p.
The Hangman Ties the Holly (Toronto, Macmillan, 1955) 57p.
Lions in the Way: A Discursive History of the Oslers (Toronto, Macmillan, 1956) 274p.
Swann and Daphne (Toronto, Oxford University Press, 1960) 48p.
The Collected Poems of Anne Wilkinson and a Prose Memoir. Edited with an Introduction by A.J.M. Smith (Toronto, Macmillan, 1968) 212p.

ETHEL WILSON (1890-   )

Hetty Dorval (Toronto, Macmillan, 1947) 116p.
The Innocent Traveller (Toronto, Macmillan, 1949) 276p.
The Equations of Love: Tuesday and Wednesday and Lilly's Story (Toronto, Macmillan, 1952) 280p.
Lilly's Story (New York, Harper, 1953) 208p.
Swamp Angel (Toronto, Macmillan, 1954) 215p.
Love and Salt Water (Toronto, Macmillan, 1956) 202p.
Mrs. Golightly and Other Stories (Toronto, Macmillan, 1961) 209p.

Index

749

Acknowledgments*

MILTON ACORN: "The Island," "The Trout Pond," "Offshore Breeze," "Whale Poem," from *This Island Means Minago* © 1975, by permission of NC Press; "I've Tasted My Blood," "Pastoral," "On Saint-Urbain Street," "Knowing I Live in a Dark Age" from *I've Tasted My Blood* by courtesy of the author.

MARGARET ATWOOD: "A Place: Fragments" from *The Circle Game,* "You Fit into Me" from *Power Politics* by permission of House of Anansi Press Limited. "Tricks With Mirrors," "There Is Only One of Everything," "I Made No Choice" from *You Are Happy* (Toronto, Oxford, 1974) by permission of the Author. "The Animals in that Country," "At the Tourist Centre in Boston," "Backdrop Addresses Cowboy," "Further Arrivals," "Disembarking at Quebec," "Departure from the Bush," "Procedures for Underground," "For Archaeologists" from *Selected Poems* by permission of Oxford University Press.

MARGARET AVISON: "The Iconoclasts," "Perspective" from *Poets of Mid-Century,* "Snow," "Butterfly Bones; or Sonnet Against Sonnets," "From a Provincial," "Meeting Together of Poles and Latitudes" from *Winter Sun and Other Poems* by permission of the author. "The Swimmer's Moment," "A Nameless One," "The Dumbfounding" reprinted from *The Dumbfounding,* Poems, by Margaret Avison. By permission of W.W. Norton & Company, Inc. © 1966 by Margaret Avison.

EARLE BIRNEY: "Fusion" from *The Rugging and the Moving Times* (Coatsworth, Black Moss Press, 1976) © 1976 Earle Birney, by permission of the author. "Kootenay Still-Life," "Vancouver Lights," "The Road to Nijmegen," "Biography," "Bushed," "Pachucan Miners," "The Bear on the Delhi Road," "A Walk in Kyoto," "Wind-Chimes in a Temple Ruin," "North of Superior," "ka pass age alaska passage ALASKA PASSAGE alaska passage alas," from *The Collected Poems of Earle Birney* by Earle Birney reprinted by permission of The Canadian Publishers, McClelland and Stewart Limited, Toronto.

MARIE-CLAIRE BLAIS: "An Act of Pity" translated by Sheila Fischman from "Un acte de pitié" in *Liberté.* XI, 2 (mars-avril, 1969) by permission of the author and the translator.

CLARK BLAISE: "A Class of New Canadians" from *A North American Education* by Clark Blaise. Copyright © 1973 by Clark Blaise. Reprinted by permission of Doubleday & Company, Inc.

GEORGE BOWERING: "Wattle" from *Sticks & Stones* (Vancouver, Tishbooks, 1963) by permission of the author. "The Swing" from *The Man in the Yellow Boots* by per-

*We wish to acknowledge the support of The Canada Council for new translations of works by Gratien Gélinas, Claire Martin, Phillipe Panneton, and Yves Thériault.

mission of the author. "Weight" from *In the Flesh* by George Bowering, "Grandfather," "For W. C. W.," "The Egg" from *Touch* by George Bowering, "Family" from *Points on the Grid* by George Bowering, and "East to West" from *Rocky Mountain Foot* by George Bowering reprinted by permission of The Canadian Publishers, McClelland and Stewart Limited, Toronto.

ELIZABETH BREWSTER: "Granite's Not Firm Enough," "Valley by Bus: November" from *Passage of Summer* by Elizabeth Brewster. Copyright © Elizabeth Brewster, 1969. Reprinted by permission of McGraw-Hill Ryerson Limited. "Sunrise North," "Christmas Day: Road to Oban" from *Sunrise North* and "Mirrors" from *In Search of Eros* by Elizabeth Brewster used by permission of Clarke, Irwin and Company Limited. "On Becoming an Ancestor" from *Sometimes I Think of Moving* by Elizabeth Brewster is reprinted by permission of Oberon Press.

ERNEST BUCKLER: "Penny in the Dust" from *The Rebellion of Young David and Other Stories* by Ernest Buckler reprinted by permission of The Canadian Publishers, McClelland & Stewart Limited, Toronto.

MORLEY CALLAGHAN: "Ancient Lineage" from *A Native Argosy* by Morley Callaghan, copyright 1929, 1957 by Morley Callaghan, reprinted by permission of Harold Matson Co. Inc.

ROCH CARRIER: "The Wedding," Trans. Sheila Fischman, reprinted by permission of Roch Carrier and Sheila Fischman. "Steps," Trans. Sheila Fischman, reprinted by permission of Editions du Jour Inc., Montreal and Sheila Fischman.

PAUL CHAMBERLAND: "Lament for the Fourth of June," Trans. Francis Sparshott (from *Terre Québec*; Montreal, Déom 1964) reprinted by permission of Librairie Déom Ltée and Francis Sparshott. "Pre-Revolution Poem: 1," from *The Poetry of Modern Quebec* Trans. Fred W. Cogswell (from *Terre Québec*; Montreal, Déom, 1964) reprinted by permission of Librairie Déom Ltée and Fred W. Cogswell. "Open Shutters," Trans. John Glassco from *The Poetry of*

French Canada in Translation (from *Terre Québec*; Montreal, Déom 1964) reprinted by permission of Librairie Déom Ltée and John Glassco. "The Signpainter Screams" from *The Shouting Signpainters* by Paul Chamberland reprinted by permission of The Canadian Publishers, McClelland and Stewart Limited, Toronto.

AUSTIN CLARKE: "They Heard a Ringing of Bells" from *When He Was Free & Young & He Used to Wear Silks* by Austin Clarke reprinted by permission of House of Anansi Press Limited.

LEONARD COHEN: "The Sparrows," "Prayer for Sunset," "Beneath My Hands," "As the Mist Leaves No Scar," "For Anne," "For E. J. P.," "Another Night With Telescope," "I am invisible to night," "I walk through the old yellow sunlight," "Overheard On Every Corner," all copyright © Leonard Cohen; all used by permission of Leonard Cohen; all rights reserved.

MATT COHEN: "After Dinner Butterflies" from *Columbus and the Fat Lady and Other Stories* (Toronto, Anansi, 1972) by permission of Matt Cohen.

ROBERTSON DAVIES: "True Humor Uncontrollable," "Humor a Dangerous Profession," "Career of a Popular Humorist" from *A Voice from the Attic* by Robertson Davies reprinted by permission of The Canadian Publishers, McClelland and Stewart Limited, Toronto.

LOUIS DUDEK: "From a Library Window," "A Street in April," "On Poetry," "The Pomegranate," "En Europe: 19, The Commotion of these waves; 95, The sea retains such images," "Coming Suddenly to the Sea," Prologue to *Atlantis* from *Collected Poetry* by Louis Dudek (Montreal, Delta, 1971) reprinted by permission of Louis Dudek.

JACQUES FERRON: "The Bridge," "The Flood," from *Tales from the Uncertain Country*, Trans. Betty Bednarski, reprinted by permission of House of Anansi Press Limited.

SAINT-DENYS GARNEAU: "The Game," Trans. F.R. Scott from *The Poetry of French Canada in Translation* (from *Poésies complètes*, Montreal, Fides, 1949) reprinted by permission of Les Editions Fides and F.R. Scott. "The Bird Cage,"

Trans. F.R. Scott from *Saint-Denys Garneau and Anne Hébert* (from *Poésies complètes,* Montreal, Fides, 1949) reprinted by permission of Les Editions Fides and F.R. Scott. "Pines Against the Light," "A Sealed House," "Autrefois," "Another Icarus," "Un Bon Coup de Guillotine" from *Complete Poems of Saint-Denys Garneau,* Trans. John Glassco reprinted by permission of Oberon Press.

GRATIEN GÉLINAS: Excerpt from "The Conscript's Return" Trans. Sheila Fischman used by permission of Gratien Gélinas and Sheila Fischman.

ROLAND GIGUÈRE: "All My South" from *The Poetry of Modern Quebec,* Trans. Fred W. Cogswell (from *La main au feu*; Montreal, Hexagone, 1973) by permission of Les Editions de l'Hexagone and Fred W. Cogswell. "Greener Than Nature" from *Poems of French Canada,* Trans. F.R. Scott (from *L'Age de la parole*; Montreal Hexagone, 1965) by permission of Les Editions de L'Hexagone and F.R. Scott. "Saisons Mortes," "The Age of the Word" Trans. D.G. Jones in *Ellipse II,* Winter, 1970 (from *Les nuits abat jour*; Montreal, 1950, and *L'Age de la parole*; Montreal, Hexagone, 1965) by permission of Les Editions de l'Hexagone and D.G. Jones. "Landscape Estranged," Trans. F.R. Scott from *The Dance is One* (from *Les armes blanches,* Montreal, 1954) by permission of Les Editions de l'Hexagone and F.R. Scott. "The Song Comes from Within" from *The Poetry of Modern Quebec*; Trans. Fred W. Cogswell (from *La main au feu*; Montreal, Hexagone, 1973) by permission of Les Editions de l'Hexagone and Fred W. Cogswell.

JOHN GLASSCO: "Deserted Buildings Under Shefford Mountain," "One Last Word," "Quebec Farmhouse," "Utrillo's World" from *Selected Poems* by John Glassco, excerpt from *Memoirs of Montparnasse* by John Glassco reprinted by permission of Oxford University Press (Canadian Branch).

DAVE GODFREY: "On the River" from *Death Goes Better With Coca Cola* © 1967 is used by permission of Press Porcepic Ltd.

ALAIN GRANDBOIS: "With Your Dress," "Is it Already the Hour" from *Selected Poems* Trans. Peter Miller (from *Les îles de la nuit*; Montreal, 1944) by permission of Les Editions de l'Hexagone and Peter Miller. "Let Us Close the Cupboard" Trans. D.G. Jones in *Ellipse* 14/15, 1974 (from *Les îles de la nuit,* Montreal, 1944) by permission of Les Editions de l'Hexagone and D.G. Jones. "Wedding" Trans. A. Poulin Jr. in *Ellipse* 14/15, 1974 (from *L'Etoile pourpre,* Montreal, Hexagone, 1957) by permission of Les Editions de l'Hexagone and A. Poulin Jr. "The Discovery of the Mississippi" from *Born in Quebec* Trans. Sheila Fischman in *Ellipse* 14/15, 1974 (from *Né à Québec,* Montreal, 1948) by permission of Les Editions de l'Hexagone and Sheila Fischman. "The Ambiguous Dawn" from *"When We Lie Together,* Trans. G.V. Downes (from *L'Etoile pourpre,* Montreal, Hexagone, 1957) by permission of Les Editions de l'Hexagone and G.V. Downes.

FREDERICK PHILIP GROVE: "Snow" used by permission of A. Leonard Grove, Toronto.

RALPH GUSTAFSON: "In the Yukon," "Armorial," "Aspects of Some Forsythia Branches," "The Philosophy of the Parthenon," "On Top of Milan Cathedral" from *Selected Poems* by Ralph Gustafson; "Hyacinths With Brevity," "Green Disposition" from *Fire and Stone* by Ralph Gustafson reprinted by permission of The Canadian Publishers McClelland and Stewart Limited, Toronto.

ANNE HÉBERT: "The Wooden Room," "Life in the Castle," "Spring Over the City" from *Poems* by Anne Hébert, Trans. Alan Brown, used by permission of Musson Book Company, Don Mills, Ontario. "The Lean Girl," "Tomb of the Kings," "Snow" from *Saint-Denys Garneau and Anne Hébert,* Trans. F.R. Scott (from *Poèmes*; Paris, Editions du Seuil, 1960) by permission of Editions du Seuil and F.R. Scott. "The Water Fisherman" from *The Tomb of Kings,* Trans. Peter Miller (from *Poèmes*; Paris, Editions du Seuil, 1960) by permission of Editions du Seuil and Peter Miller. "The Little Towns" Trans. John Glassco, from *The Poetry of French Canada in Translation* (from *Poèmes*; Paris, Editions du Seuil, 1960) by permission of Editions du Seuil and John Glassco.

DAVID HELWIG: "The Vinland Saga" from *Atlantic Crossings* by David Helwig; "Lion in Macdonald Park," "One Step from an Old Dance," "Figures in a Landscape," "Images of the Sun," "The Death of Harlequin" from *The Sign of the Gunman* by David Helwig; "Barn Poems, I" from *The Best Name of Silence* by David Helwig, reprinted by permission of Oberon Press.

HUGH HOOD: "The Fruit Man, the Meat Man & the Manager" from *The Fruit Man, the Meat Man & the Manager* by Hugh Hood is reprinted by permission of Oberon Press.

DARYL HINE: "Point Grey" and "Lovers of the River" are from *Minutes* by Daryl Hine. Copyright © 1965, 1966, 1967, 1968 by Daryl Hine. "On This Rock" and "Tacitus Loquitur" are from *Resident Alien* by Daryl Hine. Copyright © 1975 by Daryl Hine. "Patroclus Putting on the Armour of Achilles" is from *The Wooden Horse* by Daryl Hine. Copyright © 1960, 1965 by Daryl Hine. Reprinted by permission of Atheneum Publishers. "In Praise of Music in Time of Pestilence" from *The Carnal and the Crane* reprinted by permission of Daryl Hine.

GEORGE JOHNSTON: "The Pool," "Ice at Last," "O Earth, Turn," "Old-Fashioned Chords," "Remembrance," "Spring Moon," "Wild Apples" from *Happy Enough: Poems 1935-1972* reprinted by permission of Oxford University Press (Canadian Branch).

D.G. JONES: "Northern Water Thrush," "Schoolgirls," "Beautiful Creatures Brief as These," "Portrait of Anne Hébert," reprinted from *The Sun is Axeman* by D.G. Jones, by permission of University of Toronto Press. © University of Toronto Press 1961. "I Thought There Were Limits" from *Phrases From Orpheus*; "Winter Walk," and "Dance for One Leg," reprinted by permission of D.G. Jones.

LEO KENNEDY: "Words for a Resurrection," "Epithalamium Before a Frost," "Shore," "Prophesy for Icarus," "Exile Endured" from *The Shrouding* by Leo Kennedy reprinted by permission of The Macmillan Company of Canada Limited.

A.M. KLEIN: "Autobiographical," "The Cripples," "Grain Elevator," "Lookout: Mount Royal," "Portrait of the Poet as Landscape," "The Rocking Chair" from *The Collected Poems of A.M. Klein* edited by Miriam Waddington. Copyright © McGraw-Hill Ryerson Limited 1974. Reprinted by permission. "The Hitleriad – Part 1" from A.M. Klein, *The Hitleriad*. Copyright 1944 by New Directions. Reprinted by permission of New Directions Publishing Corporation. "Sonnet in Time of Affliction" from *Hath Not a Jew* reprinted by permission of Behrman House Inc. "Psalm VI," "Psalm XXXVI" from *Poems* © 1944 used through the courtesy of The Jewish Publication Society of America.

RAYMOND KNISTER. "The Loading" reprinted by permission of Imogen Givens. "Autumn Clouds," "The Hawk," "Lake Harvest," "The Plowman" from *The Collected Poems of Raymond Knister*. Copyright 1949. Reprinted by permission of McGraw-Hill Ryerson Limited.

ROBERT KROETSCH: "That Yellow Prairie Sky" from *Creation* reprinted by permission of Robert Kroetsch.

PATRICK LANE: "Treaty Trip from Shulus Reservation," "Hastings Street Rooms," "The Bird," "The Sun Has Begun to Eat the Mountain" from *Beware the Months of Fire*; "The Hustler," "Pissaro's Tomb" from *Unborn Things: South American Poems*, reprinted by permission of Patrick Lane.

MARGARET LAURENCE: "To Set Our House in Order" from *A Bird in the House* by Margaret Laurence reprinted by permission of The Canadian Publishers, McClelland and Stewart Limited, Toronto.

IRVING LAYTON: "The Birth of Tragedy," "The Black Huntsmen," "Butterfly on Rock," "Cemetery in August," "For Mao Tse-Tung," "The Haunting," "Red Chokecherries," "The Swimmer," "A Tall Man Executes a Jig" from *The Collected Poems of Irving Layton*; "The Unwavering Eye," "Pole Vaulter" from *The Unwavering Eye: Selected Poems 1969-1975* by Irving Layton; "The Human Cry," "O Jerusalem" from *For My Brother Jesus* by Irving Layton reprinted by permission of The Canadian Publishers, McClelland and Stewart Limited, Toronto.

DENNIS LEE: Elegies 3 and 6 from *Civil Elegies and Other Poems*, House of Anansi, 1972, reprinted by permission of House of Anansi Press Limited.

DOUGLAS LE PAN: "One of the Regiment," "The Wounded Prince," "Coureurs de Bois," "A Country Without a Mythology" from *The Wounded Prince* reprinted by permission of Chatto and Windus Ltd. "The Net and the Sword" from *The Net and the Sword* by Douglas Le Pan. Copyright 1953, reprinted by permission of Clarke, Irwin & Company Limited. "Stragglers" first published in *Poetry*, © 1971 by The Modern Poetry Association, reprinted by permission of the Editor of *Poetry* and Douglas Le Pan.

DOROTHY LIVESAY: "Fire and Reason," from *Green Pitcher*; "Green Rain" from *Signpost*; "Another Journey," "House Amongst Trees" from *Plainsongs* reprinted by permission of Dorothy Livesay. "Bartok and the Geranium," "Day and Night," "Eve," "Fantasia," "On Looking into Henry Moore" from *Collected Poems: Two Seasons* by Dorothy Livesay. Copyright © Dorothy Livesay 1972. Reprinted by permission of McGraw-Hill Ryerson Limited. "Schizoid," "Unexpected Guests" from *Ice Age* © 1975 are used by permission of Press Porcepic Ltd.

PAT LOWTHER: "A Stone Diary," "Rumours of War," "Last Letter to Pablo," "Reflecting Sunglasses," "In the Silence Between" from *A Stone Diary* reprinted by permission of Oxford University Press (Canadian Branch).

GWENDOLYN MACEWAN: "Inside the Great Pyramid," "The Heel," "Dark Pines Under Water," "The Shadow-Maker" from *The Shadow-Maker* by Gwendolyn MacEwan; "The Armies of the Moon" from *The Armies of the Moon* by Gwendolyn MacEwan; "The Demon of Thursday," "Eden, Eden," "Universe And," "A Breakfast for Barbarians," "Poems in Braille" from *Magic Animals* by Gwendolyn MacEwan reprinted by permission of The Macmillan Company of Canada Limited. "Second Degree Burns," "Everyone Knows" from *The Fire-Eaters* by Gwendolyn MacEwan, reprinted by permission of Oberon Press.

HUGH MACLENNAN: "Scotchman's Return" from *Scotchman's Return and Other Essays* by Hugh MacLennan, reprinted by permission of Macmillan Company of Canada Limited.

JAY MACPHERSON: "House Lights," "The Well," "Lost Books and Dead Letters" from *Welcoming Disaster* reprinted by permission of Jay Macpherson. "The Boatman," "The Faithful Shepherd," "Eve in Reflection," "Of Creatures the Net" from *The Boatman and Other Poems* reprinted by permission of Oxford University Press (Canadian Branch).

ANDRÉ MAJOR: "Words" Trans. G.V. Downes from *When We Lie Together*; "After Nightfall," Trans. John Glassco from *The Poetry of French Canada in Translation*; "My Word is Green," Trans. John Robert Columbo from *The Poetry of French Canada in Translation*; "Letter to a Very Dear Old Man," "Without Status," "The Bugbear" from *The Poetry of Modern Quebec* Trans. Fred W. Cogswell; (all from *Poèmes Pour Durer*; Montreal, Editions du Songe, 1970) reprinted by permission of André Major and G.V. Downes, John Glassco, John Robert Columbo and Fred W. Cogswell.

ELI MANDEL: "At Wabamum the Calgary Power Station," "Estevan, 1934," "Envoi" from *Stony Plain* © 1973 are used by permission of Press Porcepic Ltd. "David" from *Black and Secret Man* by Eli Mandel. Copyright 1964. Reprinted by permission of McGraw-Hill Ryerson Limited. "Minotaur Poems II" from *Trio*; "Children of the Sun," "Acis" from *Fuseli Poems*; "Marina," "Houdini" from *An Idiot Joy* reprinted by permission of Eli Mandel.

CLAIRE MARTIN: "You Muffed It (C'est Raté) Trans. Philip Stratford (from *Avec ou Sans Amour*; Paris, Laffont, 1959) used by permission of Le Cercle du Livre de France and Philip Stratford.

EDWARD MCCOURT: "The Land and the People" from *Saskatchewan* by Edward McCourt, reprinted by permission of The Macmillan Company of Canada Limited.

GASTON MIRON: "The Reign of Winter," Trans. John Glassco from *The Poetry of French Canada in Translation*; "For My Repatriation," Trans. Brenda Fleet (Ellipse, V, 1975), "Commonplaces," Trans. Brenda Fleet (*Contemporary Liter-*

ature in Translation, XXI, 1975); "Heritage of Sadness," "October" Trans. Fred. W. Cogswell from *One Hundred Poems of Modern Quebec* (all from *L'Homme Rapaillé*; Montreal, Les Presses de l'Université de Montréal, 1970) reprinted by permission of Les Presses de l'Université de Montréal and John Glassco, Brenda Fleet and Fred W. Cogswell.

W.O. MITCHELL: "The Liar Hunter" from *Jake and the Kid* by W.O. Mitchell, reprinted by permission of The Macmillan Company of Canada Limited.

ALICE MUNRO: "Winter Wind" from *Something I've Been Meaning to Tell You.* Copyright © Alice Munro 1974. Reprinted by permission of McGraw-Hill Ryerson Limited.

SUSAN MUSGRAVE: "At Nootka Sound," "Mackenzie River, North" from *Songs of the Sea-Witch* © 1970 reprinted by permission of Sono Nis Press Ltd. "Lure," "Invocation," "Anima" from *The Impstone* by Susan Musgrave reprinted by permission of The Canadian Publishers, McClelland and Stewart Limited, Toronto. "Equinox," "Witchery Way" from *Grave-Dirt and Selected Strawberries*; "Entrance of the Celebrant" from *Entrance of the Celebrant* reprinted by permission of Susan Musgrave.

JOHN NEWLOVE: "Good Company, Fine Houses" from *Moving in Alone*; "If You Would Walk," "The Stone for His Grave" from *Lies*; "The Pride," "Samuel Hearne in Wintertime," "Everyone," "The Double-Headed Snake" from *Black Night Window* by John Newlove, reprinted by permission of The Canadian Publishers, McClelland and Stewart Limited, Toronto.

bp NICHOL: "Blues" from *Love: A Book of Remembrances*; "eeeeee" from *Dada Lama*; "M" from *Monotones*; "Postcard Between" from *The Other Side of the Room*; "1970-1971" from *The Martyrology* by bp Nichol reprinted by permission of B.P. Nichol. "from parallel lines" by bp Nichol from *Horse d'Oeuvres* © 1975 by Four Horsemen, published by Paperjacks and used by permission of General Publishing Co. Limited, Don Mills, Ontario.

ALDEN NOWLAN: "A Poem for Elizabeth Nancy" from *Under the Ice*; "Dancer," "The Bull Moose" from *Playing the Jesus Game*, reprinted by permission of Alden Nowlan. "Daughters of Zion," "For Jean Vincent D'Abbadie," "The Fresh-Ploughed Hill" from *Bread, Wine and Salt*; "Hymn to Dionysius" from *The Mysterious Naked Man*; "Canadian January Night" from *Between Tears and Laughter*; "A Pinch or Two of Dust," "Marriage" from *I'm a Stranger Here Myself*; "A Call in December" from *Miracle at Indian River*, by Alden Nowlan, used by permission of Clarke, Irwin and Company Limited.

MICHAEL ONDAATJE: "After Shooting Gregory," "She Leans Against the Door," "The Street of the Slow Moving Animals" from *The Collected Works of Billy the Kid*, reprinted by permission of House of Anansi Press Limited. "Henry Rousseau and Friends," "Pyramid," "Biography" first appeared in *The Dainty Monsters* (Coach House Press, Toronto, 1967) copyright Michael Ondaatje. "Dates" and "Heron Rex" first appeared in *Rat Jelly* (Coach House Press, Toronto, 1973) copyright Michael Ondaatje. Reprinted with permission of the author.

P.K. PAGE: "The Bands and the Beautiful Children," "Stories of Snow," "The Metal and the Flower," "T-Bar," "Photos of a Salt Mine," "Portrait of Marina," "Arras," "Now this Cold Man," "Cook's Mountains" from *Poems Selected and New* reprinted by permission of House of Anansi Press Limited.

PHILIPPE PANNETON (RINGUET): "Vocations" Trans. Philip Stratford (from *Confidences*; Montreal, Fides, 1965) used by permission of Les Editions Fides and Philip Stratford.

E.J. PRATT: "The Toll of the Bells," "The Shark," "Sea Gulls," "The Sea Cathedral," "From Stone to Steel," "The Prize Cat," "Come Away Death," "The Truant," "Towards the Last Spike" from *The Collected Works of E.J. Pratt*, reprinted by permission of the Estate of E.J. Pratt and The Macmillan Company of Canada Limited.

AL PURDY: "Roblins Mills" from *The Cariboo Horses*; "Necropsy of Love" from *Love in a Burning Building*; "The Cariboo Horses," "The Country North of Belleville," "Trees at the Arctic Circle," "Wilderness Gothic" from *Selected Poems*; Elegy for a Grandfather" from *Wild Grape Wine*; "Tourist Itinerary,"

"Freydis Eriksdottir in Greenland" from *Sex and Death*; "Inside the Mill" from *Sundance at Dusk* by Al Purdy, reprinted by permission of The Canadian Publishers, McClelland and Stewart Limited, Toronto.

THOMAS RADDALL: "The Wedding Gift" from *The Wedding Gift and Other Stories* by Thomas Raddall reprinted by permission of The Canadian Publishers, McClelland and Stewart Limited, Toronto.

JAMES REANEY: For the inclusion of the following poems from *Poems,* James Reaney copyright Canada 1972, and edited by Germaine Warkentin, thanks are due to the Author and New Press: "Antichrist as a Child," "The Plum Tree," "The Red Heart," "Winnipeg Seen as a Body of Time and Space" (from "A Message to Winnipeg"), "I–To the Avon River Above Stratford, Canada," "XII–The Bicycle" (from "Twelve Letters to a Small Town"), "The Tall Black Hat," "The Morning Dew."

MORDECAI RICHLER: "The Summer My Grandmother Was Supposed to Die" from *The Street* by Mordecai Richler reprinted by permission of The Canadian Publishers, McClelland and Stewart Limited, Toronto.

GWEN PHARIS RINGWOOD: *Still Stands The House* reprinted by permission of Samuel French, Inc. All Rights Reserved. Copyright 1939, in *American Folk Plays* by D. Appleton–Century Co. Inc. Caution: Professionals and amateurs are hereby warned that *Still Stands the House,* being fully protected under the copyright laws of the United States of America, the British Empire, including the Dominion of Canada, and all other countries of the Copyright Union, is subject to a royalty. All rights, including professional, amateur, motion pictures, recitation, public reading, radio and television broadcasting and the rights of translation into foreign languages are strictly reserved. Amateurs may produce this play upon payment of a royalty of five dollars for each performance, payable one week before the play is to be given to Samuel French (Canada) Ltd., at 80 Richmond Street East, Toronto, Ontario. M5C 1P1.

JOE ROSENBLATT: "Uncle Nathan Speaking from Landlocked Green," "Balloon Flowers," "Extraterrestrial Bumblebee," "Of Dandelions and Tourists," "Tragedy" from *Top Soil* by Joe Rosenblatt are used by permission of Press Porcepic Ltd. "Heliotrope" from *The LSD Leacock* used by permission of Joe Rosenblatt. "The Bird of the Highest Place" from *Virgins and Vampires* by Joe Rosenblatt reprinted by permission of The Canadian Publishers, McClelland and Stewart Limited, Toronto.

SINCLAIR ROSS: "The Lamp at Noon" from *The Lamp at Noon and Other Stories* by Sinclair Ross reprinted by permission of The Canadian Publishers, McClelland and Stewart Limited, Toronto.

W.W.E. ROSS: "Pine Gum," "Flowers," "Night Scene," "Reciprocal," "Winter Scene," "Blue Flowers," "The Diver," "If Ice," "The Creek" from *Shapes and Sounds* by W.W.E. Ross reprinted by permission of Longman Canada Limited.

GABRIELLE ROY: "By Day and By Night" Trans. H.L. Binse from *Street of Riches* by Gabrielle Roy reprinted by permission of The Canadian Publishers, McClelland and Stewart Limited, Toronto.

GEORGE RYGA: "Indian" from *The Ecstasy of Rita Joe and Other Plays,* by George Ryga. Used by permission of the author and New Press, 30 Lesmill Road, Don Mills, Ontario. Rights to produce "Indian" are retained by the author. Interested persons are requested to apply for terms to Ryga & Associates, P.O. Box 430, Summerland, B.C. V0H 1Z0.

JANE RULE: "A Television Drama" from *Themes for Diverse Instruments,* reprinted by permission of Jane Rule. Copyright © 1975 by Jane Rule.

F.R. SCOTT: "Japanese Sand Garden" from *Signature*; "Trees in Ice," "The Canadian Authors Meet," "Overture," "North Stream," "Lakeshore," "W.L.M.K.," "Vision," "Mount Royal" from *Selected Poems*; "Spain: 1937" from *Vision*; "On the Terrace: Quebec," "V–Fort Providence" (from "Letters from the Mackenzie River") "Winter Sparrows" from *The Dance is One,* reprinted by permission of F.R. Scott.

A.J.M. SMITH: "To Henry Vaughan," "Wild Raspberry," "My Death" from *Collected Poems*; "Like an Old Proud King in a Parable," "The Lonely Land," "News of the Phoenix," "Ode: On the Death of William Butler Yeats," "The Plot Against Proteus," "Sea Cliff," "To a Young Poet" from *News of the Phoenix and Other Poems*, reprinted by permission of A.J.M. Smith.

RAYMOND SOUSTER: "The Sirens" from *As Is*; "First Holiday Morning" from *Change-Up*; "Queen Anne's Lace" from *Selected Poems*; "Words Before a Statue of Champlain" from *Rain Cheque*; "These Wild Crabapples" from *Extra Innings*; "All This Slow Afternoon" from *Lost and Found* by Raymond Souster are reprinted by permission of Oberon Press. "Flight of the Roller Coaster," "Lagoons, Hanlan's Point," "The Six-Quart Basket," "Young Girls" from *The Colour of the Times/Ten Elephants on Yonge Street* by Raymond Souster. Reprinted by permission of McGraw-Hill Ryerson Limited.

YVES THERIAULT: "The Hand" Trans. Howard Roiter (from *La Rose de Pierre*; Montreal, Editions du Jour, 1964) used by permission of Editions du Jour Inc. and Howard Roiter.

MIRIAM WADDINGTON: "Green World One," "The Nineteen Thirties Are Over," "Transformations," "Looking for Strawberries in June," "Green World Two" from *Driving Home: Poems New and Selected*, reprinted by permission of Oxford University Press (Canadian Branch). "Grand Manan Sketches," "The Price of Gold" from *The Price of Gold*; "In the Park" from *The Second Silence* reprinted by permission of Miriam Waddington.

SHEILA WATSON: "Antigone" © 1959 by Sheila Watson, reprinted by permission of Sheila Watson.

TOM WAYMAN: "Industrial Music," "Toronto Streetcars" from *Free Time* by Tom Wayman; "The Chilean Elegies: 1 Salvador Allende" from *Money and Rain* by Tom Wayman reprinted by permission of The Macmillan Company of Canada Limited. "Unemployment," "The Ecology of Place" from *Waiting for Wayman* by Tom Wayman, reprinted by permission of The Canadian Publishers, McClelland and Stewart Limited, Toronto.

PHYLLIS WEBB: "Patience" from *Trio*; "Marvell's Garden," "Lament" from *Even Your Right Eye*; "Making," "Breaking," "Non Linear" from *Selected Poems, 1954-1965* by Phyllis Webb, reprinted by permission of Phyllis Webb.

RUDY WIEBE: "Where is the Voice Coming From?" from *Where is the Voice Coming From* by Rudy Wiebe reprinted by permission of The Canadian Publishers, McClelland and Stewart Limited, Toronto.

ANNE WILKINSON: "Lens," "Easter Sketches, Montreal," "Tigers Know From Birth," "South, North," "Poem in Three Parts," "Nature Be Damned," "Roche's Point" from *The Collected Poems of Anne Wilkinson* ed. A.J.M. Smith reprinted by permission of the Estate of Anne Wilkinson and The Macmillan Company of Canada Limited.

ETHEL WILSON: "The Window" from *Mrs. Golightly and Other Stories* by Ethel Wilson reprinted by permission of The Macmillan Company of Canada Limited.